Fish and Game Patrol officer, ca. 1935. The officer, stationed aboard the patrol vessel *Albacore*, is shown here boarding a crab boat to inspect the fisher's catch. Photo courtesy of National Maritime Museum, San Francisco.

THE FISHERMAN'S PROBLEM

STUDIES IN ENVIRONMENT AND HISTORY

THE FISHERMAN'S PROBLEM

ECOLOGY AND LAW IN THE
CALIFORNIA FISHERIES,
1850–1980

ARTHUR F. McEVOY

Department of History
and
Center for Urban Affairs and Policy Research
Northwestern University

CAMBRIDGE
UNIVERSITY PRESS

PUBLISHED BY THE PRESS SYNDICATE OF THE UNIVERSITY OF CAMBRIDGE
The Pitt Building, Trumpington Street, Cambridge CB2 1RP, United Kingdom

CAMBRIDGE UNIVERSITY PRESS
The Edinburgh Building, Cambridge CB2 2RU, UK   http: //www.cup.cam.ac.uk
40 West 20th Street, New York, NY 10011-4211, USA   http: //www.cup.org
10 Stamford Road, Oakleigh, Melbourne 3166, Australia

First published 1986
First paperback edition 1990
Reprinted 1993, 1995
Transferred to digital printing 1998

Printed in the United States of America

Typeset in Caledonia

A catalogue record for this book is available from the British Library

Library of Congress Cataloguing-in-Publication Data is available

ISBN 0-521-32427-0 hardback
ISBN 0-521-38586-5 paperback

In honor of the memory

Arthur F. McEvoy, Jr.
Helen Mayes McEvoy
Sr. Regina McEvoy, M. M.

. . . And some certain significance lurks in all things, else all things are little worth, and the round world itself but an empty cipher, except to sell by the cartload, as they do hills about Boston, to fill up some morass in the Milky Way.

– Herman Melville, *Moby-Dick: or, The Whale* (1851)

Contents

Figures

Tables

Preface

This book is a history of the living communities – plant, animal, and human – that have cohabited the rivers and offshore waters of California. It is not an altogether happy story. It features prominently the wanton destruction of some of the most valuable fisheries in the world and the immense human losses that attended it. It is a history of bitter and sometimes violent conflict among the many and diverse groups that have built livelihoods on the region's fisheries. It chronicles the repeated failure of public agencies to take effective action against the depletion of resources that, given a modicum of care, might have remained productive indefinitely. The story has value, nonetheless, for the picture it offers of the remarkable ways in which ecology, economic enterprise, and legal processes interacted to shape the course of change in an important extractive industry. The interaction among the three is the key concern of this book. Like the pieces of a watch, the elements of the story evince their full significance only in working relationship to each other.

My interest in the fisheries began during my years in graduate school at the University of California at San Diego, when for a seminar led by Professor Earl Pomeroy I studied a local community of Chinese immigrants who by chance happened to be abalone hunters. I was struck by the way in which non-Chinese fishers used what ostensibly were conservationist concerns, that is, that the immigrants' fishing methods depleted stocks on which others depended, for what clearly was the racist purpose of driving the Chinese themselves out of business by any means necessary. I then began to wonder what it was that actually drove the development of public policy for natural resources and environment and pursued this line of inquiry in seminar and in reading with my mentor, Professor Harry N. Scheiber (now of the University of California, Berkeley, School of Law). Some years later, this book is the result.

This book does not pretend to be encyclopedic. Rather than attempt to detail every fisheries controversy that emerged over California's 135 years of statehood, it intends only to analyze those that have been most important to the development of public policy and to point out the ecological, historical, and theoretical links between them. Likewise, the book makes no specific recommendation for policymaking in the future, only pointing out how policy

developed in the past and what may be an alternative approach to environmental and resource issues emerging in the public activity of the past decade
or so. This book is multidisciplinary and its language, under Robert Wiebe's
valuable injunction always to write in English, so cast as to be accessible to
readers in any of the fields for which fisheries pose interesting problems.

There are individual actors in this book, as sometimes there are not in
studies of environmental issues, but I have tried to refrain from naming
heroes or villains. Some of the characters fare badly in the story, whereas
others seem blind to the human and ecological destruction in which they
take part. The critical point about "the fisherman's problem," however, is
that it is by nature a *social* problem and thus beyond the control of individuals
qua individuals. I am thus interested in how environmental problems come
to the attention of social groups and how they try to deal with them. Communities of American Indian or immigrant fishers did this in ways different
from that of modern U.S. society, but to say that these groups were badly
treated is to sanctify neither them nor their methods. It is only to say that
their mistreatment was entwined with that of the natural environment. On
the latter, it seems to me, the record speaks vehemently for itself. What
follows is an effort to understand what it says to us.

Evanston, Illinois   Arthur F. McEvoy

Acknowledgments

Earlier versions of parts of the book appeared in article form, as "In Places Men Reject: The Chinese Fishermen at San Diego 1870–1893," *Journal of San Diego History*, 23:4 (Fall 1977): 12–24; "Scientific Research and the Twentieth-Century Fishing Industry," *California Cooperative Oceanic Fisheries Investigations Reports*, 23 (1982): 48–55; "Law, Public Policy, and Industrialization in the California Fisheries, 1900–1925," *Business History Review*, 57 (1983): 494–521; and "Scientists, Entrepreneurs, and the Policy Process: A Study of the Post–1945 California Sardine Depletion" (with Harry N. Scheiber), *Journal of Economic History*, 44 (1984): 393–406. I am grateful to those journals for permission to rely on parts of those articles for use in this publication.

Parts of Chapters 7–10 are the result of research sponsored in part by NOAA, National Sea Grant College Program, Department of Commerce, under grant number NA80AA-D–00120, through the California Sea Grant College Program, and in part by the California State Resources Agency, project number R/MA–13, Earl Warren Legal Institute, School of Law, University of California, Berkeley. The U.S. government is authorized to reproduce and distribute for government purposes. The Sea Grant Project provided me with funds and office space (through the Warren Institute at Berkeley) in 1982 and 1983 to undertake research on the fisheries and other resource issues in collaboration with Harry Scheiber and Berta Schweinberger. I am grateful to those people for sharing their research and writing with me, especially on the use of the initiative process in resource management and on the immediate aftermath of the post–World War II sardine failure.

A number of other agencies provided valuable support for my research. The Law and Society Center of the University of California, Berkeley, School of Law provided office space and clerical help during the summer of 1981. The National Endowment for the Humanities provided funds to attend a summer workshop on "Law, Lawyers, and Regulation" at the University of Wisconsin, Madison, School of Law during the summer of 1983. The Center for Urban Affairs and Policy Research and the Department of History at Northwestern University provided precious time released from teaching to enable me to pursue the writing of the project, and Northwestern's Office of Research and Sponsored Projects supplied funds for travel to California, for typing the manuscript for submission, and for illustrations.

The interdisciplinary character of this project has made it a singularly cooperative enterprise; I have incurred more personal debts over the course of researching and writing it than I can mention here. Chief among these is to my mentor, Professor Harry N. Scheiber of the Jurisprudence and Social Policy Program at the University of California, Berkeley, School of Law. I owe a good share of my professional development to him alone. Berta Schweinberger, a graduate student in the JSP program, provided invaluable research assistance and found, to the delight of both of us, that sardines were interesting creatures after all. I also wish to thank Rod Watanabe at the Law and Society Center, Cathy Hill at the Warren Institute, Deborah Cozort Day at the Scripps Institution of Oceanography Archives, Renee Jusserand at the National Archives in Washington, Sylvia Arden at the San Diego Historical Society Library, Karyl Winn and Janet Ness at the Manuscripts Division of the University of Washington Library at Seattle, Paul Gregory at the California Department of Fish and Game library at Long Beach, and not least Katie Melody of the Department of History at Northwestern University. Joan Stahl and I cooperated in typing the manuscript for submission; the maps are the work of Ann Bartz and Cece Martin.

My colleagues at Northwestern University remained patient with me and interested in my work throughout its gestation, even though it fell outside the areas in which they normally work. Henry Binford, George Fredrickson, Robert Finlay, Paul Friesema, Karen Halttunen, J. R. T. Hughes, Carol Rose, Michael Sherry, and Robert Wiebe criticized drafts and/or discussed with me issues with which I had problems from time to time. I am especially grateful to Betty Jo Teeter Dobbs, Margaret A. Gordon, and Joel Mokyr for nurturing the scholar as well as the scholarship.

Completing this work would have been impossible without the help and encouragement of specialists in other fields. At the National Marine Fisheries Service, Southwest Fisheries Center at La Jolla Roger Hewitt, Dan Huppert, Reuben Lasker, Alec MacCall, and Valerie Loeb all shared ideas and information with me and welcomed me into a field with which I was unfamiliar. Paul E. Smith of NMFS sustained interest and priceless support over the many years I worked on the fisheries. I took lessons in anthropology from Arnold Pilling, Olivia Ruiz, and Priscilla Russo. Huey Johnson, formerly California Secretary for Resources, encouraged me by taking an interest in the work and by providing an example of a public official who was eager to consider new ideas. During my summer at the National Endowment for the Humanities Legal History Workshop at Madison, Fred Carstensen, Dirk Hartog, Willard Hurst, Ellen Jordan, Stanley Kutler, Chuck McCurdy, and Rayman Solomon all honed my interest in legal studies and helped give purpose and direction to the work. Frank Smith, my editor at Cambridge

Acknowledgments XV

University Press, and Donald Worster, one of the editors of the series in which this book appears, had the last shot at the manuscript and offered important suggestions for its polishing and clarification.

It was my great fortune, finally, to work closely with a number of students at Northwestern University, Caryl Athanasiades, Andrew Hurley, Linda Przybyszewski, Tom Russell, and especially Barbara Leibhardt, all of whose interests bordered on my own and whose intelligence and spirit did much to shape the ideas that went into this book. Perhaps most important of all, Andrew Baldwin, Ann Bartz, and Lucy Salyer remained steadfast friends and staunch allies throughout a long and sometimes painful struggle with this project.

A. F. M.

Abbreviations

AR-CIA	Annual Report, Commissioner of Indian Affairs
AR-DOI	Annual Report, Secretary of the Interior
BIA	U.S. Department of the Interior, Bureau of Indian Affairs
BuREC	U.S. Department of the Interior, Bureau of Reclamation
CalCOFI	California Cooperative Oceanic Fisheries Investigations
CCF	California Commissioners of Fisheries (1871–86)
CDFG	California Department of Natural Resources, Division of Fish and Game (1926–51)
CFGC	California Fish and Game Commission (1910–)
CLHP	Carl Leavitt Hubbs Papers, Scripps Institution of Oceanography Archives, La Jolla, California
CMC	California Advisory Commission on Coastal and Marine Resources (1968–73)
CPUE	Catch per unit of fishing effort
CSFC	California State Board of Fish Commissioners (1887–1910)
Ct. Cl.	United States Court of Claims
DFG	California Department of Fish and Game (1951–)
FAO	United Nations Food and Agriculture Organization
FCMA	Fishery Conservation and Management Act of 1976
GACOR	California Governor's Advisory Commission on Ocean Resources (1964–7)
IATTC	Inter-American Tropical Tuna Commission
ICOR	California Interagency Council on Ocean Resources (1967–9)
IMARPE	Instituto Del Mar del Peru
IMR	University of California Institute of Marine Resources
LD	Decisions of the General Land Office, U.S. Department of the Interior
MLRP	Scripps Institution of Oceanography, Marine Life Research Program
MMPA	Marine Mammals Protection Act of 1972
mmt	Million metric tons (all other tonnages in short tons)
MRC	California Marine Research Committee
MSY	Maximum substainable yield
NARS-DC	National Archives and Records Service, Washington, D.C.
NARS-LA	National Archives and Records Service, Los Angeles Federal Records Center, Laguna Niguel, California
NEPA	National Environmental Policy Act of 1969

Abbreviations xvii

NMFS	U.S. Department of Commerce, National Oceanic and Atmospheric Administration, National Marine Fisheries Service (1970–)
NOAA	U.S. Department of Commerce, National Oceanic and Atmospheric Administration
PFMC	Pacific Fishery Management Council
PMFC	Pacific Marine Fisheries Commission
POFI	U.S. Fish and Wildlife Service, Pacific Oceanic Fisheries Investigations
SIO	University of California, Scripps Institution of Oceanography
UC	University of California
UCAR	University of California Anthropological Records
UC-ASR	University of California Archaeological Survey Records
UC-PAAE	University of California Publications in American Archaeology and Ethnology
USBCF	U.S. Department of the Interior, Bureau of Commercial Fisheries (1956–70)
USBF	U.S. Bureau of Fisheries (1903–40)
USCA	U.S. Code, Annotated (1985)
USDA	U.S. Department of Agriculture
USDI	U.S. Department of the Interior
USFC	U.S. Fish Commission (1870–1902)
USFWS	U.S. Department of the Interior, Fish and Wildlife Service (1940–)
WMCP	Wilbert McLeod Chapman Papers, University of Washington Library Manuscripts Division, Seattle (box/file)

Introduction

1

The problem of environment

> With every day that passes we are acquiring a better
> understanding of these laws and getting to perceive both
> the more immediate and the more remote consequences
> of our interference with the traditional course of nature
> ... the more this progresses the more will men not only
> feel but also know their oneness with nature, and the
> more impossible will become the senseless and unnatural
> idea of a contrast between mind and matter, man and
> nature, soul and body. ...   – Frederick Engels (1876)[1]

The pelagic, or open-sea, fisheries of California owe their productivity to
the California Current, a stream of water roughly 350 miles wide that flows
slowly along the coast from north to south. Off the central California coast
and in the Southern California Bight, winds and currents interact seasonally
to generate upwellings of deep, cold, nutrient-rich water to the lighted
surface of the ocean. Blooms of plankton fertilized by this upwelled water
feed the coastal pelagic schooling fishes – sardine, anchovy, and the like –
which in turn provide fodder for still other fish and mammals higher on the
food chain. What portion of this great, complex aggregation of living matter,
or biomass, that does not leave the system in the bellies of migratory animals
or fishing boats dies and drifts slowly to the ocean floor, only to be upwelled
later to enter the cycle again. As coastal upwelling areas go, that off California
is moderately productive; combined, all such areas account for about one-
half of humanity's total fishery harvest.[2]

Life in California waters is as diverse as it is productive. The rocks and
canyons that extend from the land down into the seafloor mix nearshore
currents into complex patterns and provide homes for a great many different
plants and animals. A sharp temperature gradient off Point Conception,
roughly two-thirds of the way down the state's 1,100-mile coast, divides the
nearshore zone into subtropical and subarctic regions (see Figure 1.1). To
the south live tuna and other warm-water species, while to the north are
salmon and other animals that prefer colder temperatures. The great forests
of kelp that line the coast just offshore enhance the system's fertility and
diversity still further as they provide food and shelter for a great many
nearshore and intertidal species.

3

Figure 1.1. California, showing major waterways and fishing ports. Map drawn by Ann Bartz and C. M. Martin.

1. *The problem of environment*   5

Estuaries, among the most fertile environments on the planet, are few and far between in this geologically youthful and restless region. Those that have formed, however, are vitally important to the ecology of nearby waters, providing food for animals living in them as well as nursery for many that spend most of their lives in the open ocean. Premier among California estuaries is the outflow of the Sacramento–San Joaquin river system, which includes Suisun, San Pablo, and San Francisco Bays. Before 1850, the salt marshes and mudflats that ringed the three bays may have held, at high water, as much as two-thirds of all the water flowing in and out of the Golden Gate with each tide. Twice daily, immense quantities of water washed over these tidelands and retreated, by turns fertilizing them and carrying off algae and detritus to supply an important share of the food consumed by animals both inside and outside the Gate.[3]

Inshore, the rivers that drain the Coast Range and the Sierra Nevada are home to a wide variety of freshwater fishes, as well as to salmon and other anadromous species that spend most of their lives in the ocean but return inland to spawn. The largest of these is the Sacramento–San Joaquin system, which reaches back into the great Central Valley of California and beyond into the Sierra Nevada, and the Klamath–Trinity system in the northwestern corner of the state. Each of these river systems lies at the ecological heart of its watershed. Fish in them feel the pulse of every significant change in the ecology of the surrounding lands. Together, these two watersheds encompass most of the land area of California. The changing fortunes of their fish, then, provide an index to the ecological history of much of the state.

The Sacramento–San Joaquin drainage is second in size only to the Columbia among western U.S. watersheds. The Sacramento, largest of the two rivers, arises from a vast network of tributaries in the Sierra Nevada, each of which is home to its own genetically unique population of salmon. Downstream, before the Central Valley was reclaimed for agriculture, the Sacramento flowed through a finely adjusted system of natural sloughs and levees that allowed the river to overflow during the heaviest winter floods, thereby inundating a broad plain that extended as far north as present-day Chico. Partly covered with swamps and marshes, the floodplain stored overflow water for a time and then gradually released it back into the river's main channel, while settling debris and sediment carried down from the mountains. The visible product was some of the finest grassland that early explorers had ever seen.[4]

In its lower reaches, the Sacramento merged with the Cosumnes, the Mokelumne, and the San Joaquin Rivers in a huge expanse of freshwater marsh, dotted with islands and laced with endless winding sloughs and channels, all teeming with life. Tides extended as far upstream as the mouth of the Feather River, north of Sacramento City. In 1850, delta lands may have encompassed some 533 square miles and contained perhaps two-thirds of all marshland in the entire watershed. The delta further regulated and filtered the flow of water through it as well as providing homes for infinite indigenous and migratory birds, mammals, and fish.

The commercial development of California's lush and varied fisheries has followed a repetitive pattern of boom and bust, one typical of fisheries the world over. Usually, after a few pioneers demonstrate a fishery's profitability, capital and labor rush into it, and the harvest increases exponentially for a time. At some point, unable to bear the strain of exploitation indefinitely without sacrificing its ability to replenish itself, the resource begins to yield less and less to economic effort. As depletion erodes its productivity, a fishing industry may even improve its technical ability to find and catch fish, thereby sustaining profits for a time but drawing ever more effort into the harvest and ever more life out of the stock of fish. Ultimately, harvesting so depletes the resource as to cripple it.[5]

A stock of fish is a renewable resource: It sustains itself by breeding or "recruiting" enough new adults to balance its losses to predators and other causes from year to year. A fishing industry is simply another predator added to the environment. According to the so-called sustained yield theory, the amount of fish that any given level of harvesting effort will yield over the long term is a function of both the intensity of fishing and the capacity of the stock to reproduce. At some maximum sustainable yield (MSY), fishers take exactly as many fish as the stock recruits in a season and so do not impair the resource's long-term productivity. Less fishing, of course, will produce fewer fish. A higher level of effort, however, will also produce fewer fish in the long run by leaving fewer adults to breed. The task of fishery management under this rudimentary model, then, is to calculate each stock's MSY and limit the take to that point.[6]

Developed gradually over the first half of the twentieth century, the sustained-yield model guided most scientific thinking about fisheries, game animals, timber, and other living resources until the 1960s. It represented a considerable improvement over earlier thinking, which held that oceanic fisheries at least were so vast in relation to the harvest as to be practically inexhaustible. If certain grounds lost productivity from time to time, fishers would simply move to new ones and give them time to replenish. Regulating the harvest in that case simply made no sense.[7] This idea, perfectly in keeping with late nineteenth-century laissez-faire ideology, made the very important assumption that there existed a radical dichotomy between the fishing industry and the ecology of its resources: Nature, in the form of the stock of fish, was a passive object to be exploited at will and without significant consequences either for the resource or for the industry itself.[8]

For its part, the sustained-yield theory rested on the important postulate that the stock of fish existed in isolation from its environment; that is, that the only influence on its productivity was the number of breeding adults left after harvest. Most fisheries, however, do not behave as neatly as the theory suggested because, like any other biological resource, fish live in a complex and constantly changing environment. Thus, for a given level of fishing effort, any stock's sustainable yield shifts constantly and for all practical purposes at random in response to conditions in its habitat. Targeting a conservative yield from a real fishery is thus a problem in stochastic, or random-variable, analysis – more like predicting the weather or the outcome of an election than, say, the sustainable yield of guppies from a well-maintained aquarium.

Some species reproduce less efficiently at lower levels of population, so that recruitment is not a simple algebraic function of breeding stock. It only takes two whales of the appropriate sex, for example, to make more whales, but if there were only two in an entire ocean they might not be able to find each other. Similarly, a schooling fish like the sardine must spread its spawn over a large expanse of ocean to ensure that enough offspring find conditions favorable to their survival. A fishery under intensive harvesting pressure may thus be more brittle and vulnerable to collapse than an unexploited one.[9]

Some environmental changes that impinge on the productivity of fisheries occur in nature without reference to human activity, as when currents shift or the weather changes. Fish are much more sensitive to such changes than are organisms that live in the air. Scientists now believe, for example, that environmental conditions during the first year of life have a larger role in the recruitment of sardine and other herring-like fishes than does the size of the parent stock, although, again, environmentally induced recruitment failure will have a much more catastrophic effect on a heavily fished stock than on an abundant one.[10] A sudden drop in temperature can blanket a coast with tides of dead sardines or anchovies. The Spanish explorer Vizcaino observed this phenomenon at the southern end of Baja California in 1602; Monterey newspapers reported another such incident the last week of May 1858.[11] More subtle shifts in climate may drastically influence the migration and survival of larger fish such as albacore or salmon as well.

In general, the effects of climatic or other ecological change will be more pronounced if a fishery is under stress and more so at the margins of the stock's range than near its center. California fisheries are the more responsive to ecological change, then, because many species taken on either side of the climatic boundary at Point Conception live near the limits of their tolerance for heat or cold. Very slight shifts in conditions will cause wide fluctuations in the behavior of many of California's fishes, with dramatic economic consequences for the industries that harvest them. Such remote events as the El Niño–Southern Oscillation, a complex oceanic–atmospheric interaction that takes place in the equatorial Pacific every six years or so, can have a significant impact on fisheries in California waters.[12]

Introduction

.....ay and Weather Service records of temperature and precipitation for many parts of California date back to the 1840s. Records for two representative locations, Sacramento in the Central Valley and San Diego on the Southern California Bight, are reproduced in Appendix A. The influence of weather on riverine ecology, hence on inland fisheries, is quite direct. Because coastal air temperatures correlate closely with those of adjoining seas, the atmospheric data give evidence of changes in the ocean environment as well.[13] Shifts between warm and cool periods correspond with historical records of shifts in the range of northern and southern species as much as several hundred miles up and down the coast. Shifts between "marine" climates, characterized by high rainfall, cool summers, and moderate winters, and "continental" climates marked by drier weather and greater seasonal variation in temperature, correspond roughly to periods of high and low productivity, respectively, in the salmon fishery. All of these changes, both in the long and short term, have had a discernible impact on the development of California fisheries and on political controversies over their use.

Some of the most fascinating evidence in the ecological history of California waters derives from the geology of the ocean floor. Where upwelling occurs, as it does off Baja California and in the Southern California Bight, water at the seafloor contains very little oxygen and consequently very few creatures to disturb the orderly accumulation of sediment on the bottom. Winter deposits, augmented by runoff from the coast, are darker and thicker than summer ones. Cylindrical cores extracted from the seafloor thus provide an annulated record, in the fashion of tree rings, of plankton, fish scales, and other detritus deposited by the California Current ecosystem over the centuries. By counting the scales from different kinds of fish in each cross section and calibrating the counts to modern estimates of their populations, scientists at the Scripps Institution of Oceanography at La Jolla, California, have compiled a census of sardines, anchovies, and other coastal schooling species that reaches back some two millenia. Because these fishes are fodder for most of the larger animals in the system, the record provides a rough index of the productivity of the system as a whole. That productivity has fluctuated widely for as long as the record exists.[14]

Biomasses of sardine and anchovy, moreover, fluctuate with respect to each other. The two species are ecologically quite similar, except that the anchovy has a shorter life and breeds at a higher rate than does the sardine. In any ecological system, unsettled conditions tend to favor species such as the anchovy, which turn their population over more rapidly. A relatively high ratio of sardine to anchovy thus indicates stable environmental conditions, whereas a low ratio evinces environmental instability and consequently a more volatile fishing industry. Data for the nineteenth and twentieth centuries appear in Appendix B. Over the long term, as one biologist put it, "if ecological theory concerning high reproductive rate holds, this means that the California Current area is one of almost continual environmental disturbance favouring the anchovy."[15] Changes in the stability and overall productivity of the system clarify otherwise opaque historical data on the fisheries, including newspaper accounts, contemporary scientific observations, fishers' testimony about their luck and, most importantly, records of political conflict in the industry.

Human activity can also alter the productivity of fisheries in ways other than by harvesting them. All fish occupy places in a food chain, so that human impact on a stock's prey, its predators, or its competitors for food and space can increase or decrease its potential yield. Some such impacts, moreover, stem from human activities only remotely related to the fisheries themselves. Any economic activity that uses water – which includes most of them – or that alters the character of the seabeds, tidal areas, or rivers in which fish live will have some impact on the ecology, hence on the productivity of a resource. Mining, agriculture, and urban development have all had a major impact on the development of California fisheries and on controversies over their use and management.

Nature is a very careful accountant. Because evolution has built such a complex pathway for energy and materials to follow on their way through the food chain, every change in one part of an ecosystem sooner or later has some effect, however minute, on every other part. Human beings and their industries are no less part of the ecosystems in which they work than are the plants and animals they harvest. Human economies, however, account for the costs and benefits of their activities through the market mechanism, which unfortunately is much less efficient a transmitting medium than an ecosystem is. The injuries that fishers impose on each other by overharvesting, for example, or that water polluters inflict on the fishing industry as a whole, do not normally come to account because the market diffuses them too broadly – too many victims each suffering a little bit – for any one person or coherent group to demand compensation for them in the marketplace or in the courts. They are what the economist R. H. Coase called "social costs," that is, costs that fall to society at large because the expense of making and enforcing contracts to pay them is too great to make the effort worth anyone's while.[16] Fish are remarkably efficient builders of protein, fat, and other good things for people but are themselves unable to bid the price of their services up to their comparable value in the market. They are free for the taking because they neither strike, nor sue, nor vote.

A self-preserving fishing industry would respect the biological limits of its resource's productivity, limiting its seasonal take to some safe minimum so as to guarantee future harvests. Fishing industries, however, do not generally manage their affairs in such a rational way. This is primarily because fishery stocks are "common property" resources; that is, although many different individuals or firms may compete with each other for fish, no one of them owns the resource so as to keep others away from it. As a result, everyone has an incentive to keep fishing so long as there is any money to be made in the effort, whereas no one has an individual incentive to refrain from fishing so as to conserve the stock. Every harvester knows that if he or she leaves a fish in the water someone else will get it, and the profit, instead. This is what economists call "the fisherman's problem": In a competitive economy, no market mechanism ordinarily exists to reward individual forbearance in the use of shared resources.

It falls to government to consider the interrelated environmental effects of economic activity, to set safe standards for resource use, and to regulate the behavior of resource users so as to protect the community's long-term interest in its natural endowment.[17] One of the first scholars to point out the importance of legal and institutional arrangements for fishery conservation was an economist, H. Scott Gordon. In a 1954 article criticizing the sustained-yield theory of fishery management, Gordon analyzed fishery problems as the inevitable result of the industry's legal and economic organization rather than in terms of biology or population dynamics. The sustained-yield theory, he wrote, "overlooked essential elements of the problem" by neglecting the powerful incentives to overfish that operated in a common-property regime.[18]

Gordon proposed maximizing the economic return from fishing rather than the raw yield of fish, demonstrating in theory that a fishery would always produce its highest financial yield at a lower, hence safer, level of fishing effort than that required to produce its MSY. This was because the cost of fishing rises proportionally with the amount of effort expended, but sustainable yield reaches a maximum at some point and then begins to decline. The *marginal* return from fishing at MSY, then, is zero. A good businessperson tries to maximize revenues over costs and will cease fishing at precisely the point at which the price of one extra fish exactly balances the cost of catching it, well before the total yield reaches MSY and the marginal yield reaches zero. Fishing at the sustainable maximum produces more fish but costs disproportionately more money and so produces less profit. An unlimited fishery typically produces no income over costs at all, Gordon wrote, because as long as anyone who wants to can enter the fishery, new effort will go into the business until total costs equal total yields and the *average* return from fishing equals zero, at some point beyond and below the sustainable maximum. This, as economists are fond of pointing out, is why fishers are in financial trouble most of the time.[19]

In Gordon's model, if the industry lowers its cost of fishing by developing more efficient gear, it produces more income for a time but only draws more effort into the harvest until total yields again equal total costs. By fishing the stock harder, it also produces fewer and fewer fish in the long run. Such economic irrationalities as subsidies designed to keep fishers solvent or hungry people fed and the traditional reluctance of fishers to leave their chosen line of work can push a fishery well past the point at which earnings no longer cover costs and on toward commercial or even biological extinction. Gordon's idea was that market forces, properly channeled under a limited-entry rather than a common-property regime, would tend to reward ecologically prudent behavior and thus work automatically to conserve the resource. He concluded that imposing such a regime on a fishery would require making it "private property or public (government) property, in either case subject to a unified directing power" able to exclude outsiders and adjust harvesting effort to maximum advantage.[20]

Although he used the fisheries as a model, Gordon thought his conclusions "applicable generally to all cases where natural resources are owned in common but exploited under conditions of individualistic competition."[21] In 1968 the biologist Garrett Hardin fit the theory to a wide range of environmental issues in a popular article whose title, "The Tragedy of the Commons," subsequently became an inclusive symbol of environmental problems generally.[22] Hardin cast the fisherman's problem in terms of a group of farmers grazing cows on a common pasture. Because no one farmer owns the pasture, each finds it more profitable to graze one more cow than the pasture can feed in the long run because all the profit from the extra cow goes to the individual farmer, while each bears only an average share of the cost of ruining the pasture. Eventually, everyone goes broke. Collectively and inevitably – tragically, to Hardin's mind – industry degrades and eventually destroys resources owned in common but used competitively. The model, Hardin believed, applied not only to rangeland and to fish and other wildlife. It also applied to national parks and the air and water that citizens "own" in common but pollute as competitors, to underground aquifers, which collapse because competing users draw out more water than natural flow can replenish, and even to the planet's ultimate capacity to support the ever-increasing numbers of new people that individual families produce.

Hardin asserted that the fisherman's problem had "no technical solution." He observed that throughout history, as human population had increased and environmental degradation proceeded apace, some form of private property had supplanted "the commons" in one resource area after another. By itself, however, privatization was no answer: Pointing to Coase's "social cost" problem, Hardin allowed that the Anglo-American concept of private property actually encouraged people to pollute their neighbors' air and water. Concluding his article, Hardin could only point to what he called "mutual coercion mutually agreed upon" to restrain people from destroying the planet. Nature ran a closed economy, he reasoned, so that the utilitarian notion of providing "the greatest good for the greatest number" was ecologically absurd. It was simply not possible to maximize both environmental values and the satisfaction of human wants. In order to save the future of the species, the wants of many people in the here and now would have to be denied. Hardin admitted that the kinds of coercion that his "lifeboat ethics" would require might be Draconian and at times unjust, as the privatization of property in land had been in the early days of capitalism. The alternative, however, was "too horrifying to contemplate." "Injustice," he wrote, "is preferable to total ruin."[23]

During the 1960s and 1970s, Hardin's formulation of the problem defined the terms in which most scientists, environmentalists, and policymakers understood environmental issues, of which, again, the fisheries offered the laboratory case. The great contribution made by the Gordon–Hardin analysis was to emphasize that environmental problems arose from the interaction between human activity and a responsive Nature. The sustained-yield theory had posited an abstract mathematical model of the resource, in isolation from its environment. Likewise, "the ecosystem of the fisheries biologist," Gordon observed, was one in which "man is regarded as an exogenous factor," and not as a variable element, along with the fish, in "a system of mutual interdependence."[24] Property rights and market structure, as Gordon showed, had much to do with the ways in which people behaved.

Yet there were those who believed that even the Gordon–Hardin line of thinking failed to integrate environment and society sufficiently in addressing the fisherman's problem. Some economists pointed to situations in which, given a high enough interest rate, even a private owner might find it economically rational to turn all her fish into cash at once and invest the proceeds in a bank: "to clean up now and let future generations eat soybeans," as one put it.[25] S. V. Ciriacy-Wantrup, a noted California agricultural economist, criticized Hardin's characterization of private-property and common-property regimes, pointing to traditional societies that had managed commonly owned resources successfully and to privatized economies that had utterly wasted theirs.[26]

Taking a fresh look at precapitalist societies during the 1960s and 1970s, anthropologists drew attention to the "unified directing power" side of Gordon's equation; they suggested that the competitive individualism that Hardin believed inevitably led to "the tragedy of the commons" might not be a generic failing of the human species but rather the specific historical consequence of the social changes that followed the advent of modern capitalist modes of production and social organization. "Indeed," wrote one anthropologist, it signified a breakdown of "one of the most important ecological functions of human social systems," that of integrating individuals' perception of their short-term personal advantage with that of the community as a whole over the long run.[27] Ciriacy-Wantrup agreed. Hardin's analysis, he argued, treated the institutions of private property and commons as exogenous factors in the economy–environment interaction, in much the same way that Gordon had criticized the fishery biologists' earlier treatment of economic forces and the biologists, in turn, had criticized the laissez-faire theory's treatment of Nature itself.[28]

Forms of property and other legal and social institutions, too, are not immutable; rather, they are creatures of history, evolving in response to their social and natural environments even as they mediate the interaction between the two. Confronting the problem of environment, then, requires analysis of the interaction among three elements – ecology, production, and legal process – each of which changes on its own while interacting with the other two.

In several decades of work, the most prominent product of which was a legal history of the lumber industry in Wisconsin, J. Willard Hurst has directed attention to the historical contingency of law, criticizing the older idea that legal forms and doctrines evolve solely in response to their own internal logic with as little reference to social context as, say, the laws of physics. The legal system – judges, legislators, and administrators, as well as the rules they produce – evolves together with the rest of society, at times giving conscious direction to the course of social change and at others simply responding passively to events. "Law" and "the market," Hurst showed, do not exist independently of one another but rather create each other: The law develops in response to challenges posed by the material conditions of life but at the same time, by defining the nature of such institutions as property and contract, creates and sustains the life of the market economy.[29]

Hardin assumed that the farmers in his model behaved in characteristically "human" ways. *Homo sapiens* was *Homo economicus*, a rational, individual, and wealth-maximizing creature. Yet here, too, may be another dynamic element in an interdependent system. Anthropologists have suggested that there is no such thing as a "human nature" independent of time, place, and culture. According to one anthropologist, "what man is may be so entangled with where he is, who he is, and what he believes that it is inseparable from them."[30] It is through culture – "organized systems of significant symbols" – that people "orient themselves in a world otherwise opaque" and give coherence to their responses to it.[31] People not only exist as part of their natural environment but also comprehend that environment in socially and historically contingent ways. In turn, by acting on the basis of that comprehension in a responsive environment, they help create the world in their own image.[32]

Modern U.S. culture is preeminently a legal one: U.S. society as a whole relies on legal forms and legal processes to order its social and natural environments, to bring problems to its corporate attention, and to make choices among alternative means of addressing them.[33] Other cultures in other places and times have relied on tradition or charismatic authority to bring meaning and order to their social lives. That U.S. culture is what

Weber termed a "legal–rational" one does not mean that the symbols and ideologies that knit it together are any less historically contingent than legal or economic institutions themselves.[34] In particular, people's perceptions of what is "fair" or "just," on the one hand, and what is necessary evil, part of the "natural" order of things, or "tragic," on the other, change over time in tandem with the social and material conditions of life.[35] What was done to Chinese and Indian fishers during the late nineteenth century, for example, or indeed even to whales or salmon, would be unconscionable a century later. The farmers on Hardin's common pasture, then, are not tragic in the sense that their undoing flows from some flaw in their inherent nature; rather, they are products of a particular culture with a particular history and a particular view of the world.

As important to resource ecology as are market forces and the legal rules that guide them are the social and cultural factors that lead people to use resources, to perceive resource problems, and to respond to those problems in the ways that they do.[36] All three processes, ecological, economic, and cultural, are dynamic in themselves. Yet they are holocoenotic, that is, interdependent parts of a coherent, indivisible whole. The product of their interaction over time is the history of human industry in relation to the "natural" world. When policymaking proceeds on an ideological or theoretical foundation that posits fundamental dichotomies among any of the three, as it has in the California fisheries for most of the state's history, it ignores the fundamentally ecological character of human experience. From the gap between policy and reality, in this case, springs what we perceive as "the tragedy of the commons."

Again, although Hardin wrote primarily with regard to the problem of overpopulation, he based his thinking on economic models of the fishing industry propounded by Gordon and others. Fisheries simply provide a laboratory example of the problem of environment because they are ecologically volatile and because in most cases it is impossible to consign their husbandry to private owners as if they were cropland or stands of timber. "The fisheries," wrote one economist, "present in one form or another all of the major causes of market-mechanism failure that call for public intervention."[37] A detailed contextual analysis of one region's fisheries, therefore, taking into account the complex interaction among resource ecology, production, and social or legal regulation of the harvest, might suggest conclusions not only about fishery management per se but about modern industrial society's difficulties in sustaining its natural environment generally.

What follows in this volume is a history of the interaction between ecology and human affairs in the fisheries of California's rivers and coastal waters. It differs from some other treatments of resource issues in demonstrating that environment not only provided the stage on which history took place but took an active part in it as well. Environment influenced the course of events by means of both its own independent dynamism and its characteristic responses to human impact across a range of activities far broader than the fisheries alone. The study analyzes the different ways in which different groups of people at different times understood the problems before them and the ways in which they tried to respond to them. It falls into four parts, each corresponding to one of four overlapping, but nonetheless coherent, cultural regimes under which human beings have taken fish from California waters.

Part I concerns the original inhabitants whose methods of production and whose ways of organizing their use of the fisheries differed radically from those that followed but whose success in meeting the challenge of environment easily matched that of their successors. Although peoples of European stock forcibly divested the American Indians of their rights to the land and its resources in most parts of California, Indian fishing and Indian culture remain an important part of the story to its end.

Part II deals with the second half of the nineteenth century, when people from many widely scattered parts of the world came to California and began to fish. The immigrants' efforts to adapt familiar methods of using and husbanding fisheries to the California environment and the competition between them provide an illuminating perspective on fisheries problems as formally constituted government began to exert control over the resources at the end of the century.

Part III begins with the early years of the twentieth century, when new ways of using energy transformed the nature of resource use and resource problems across the entire breadth of the California economy and drew more tightly the ecological links between different water-using industries. It ends with the collapse of the California sardine fishery, which at the time was probably the most intensive fishery the world had ever seen and the loss of which ranks as one of the most egregious failures in the history of U.S. wildlife management. Regulatory strategies that had apparently served public officials well under late nineteenth-century conditions proved poorly adapted to an industrial economy.

Part IV, finally, concerns the period after World War II. Legal and economic changes coincident with the gradual emergence of the modern environmental movement fundamentally altered both public understanding of resource issues and public strategies for addressing them. The Fishery Conservation and Management Act, a federal law enacted in 1976, apparently marked a significant discontinuity in the history of U.S. fisheries management, although many of the forces that had led to the depletion of one fishery after another over the time of California's statehood continued to operate during the years immediately following its passage.

One of the things that distinguishes human beings from other creatures is their capacity for culture – their ability to comprehend their relationship with the world around them and to manipulate that relationship to conscious purpose. It is what makes people people: By enabling human communities to adapt their social and economic behavior to the changing environments in which they find themselves, the capacity for culture has played a key role in the emergence and subsequent history of the species. If it expects to endure, a community must exercise this talent so as to sustain both itself and the environment on which it depends over the long run.[38] That, however, is precisely what the farmers in Garrett Hardin's tragedy are unable to do.

Likewise, if a people's sense of justice has a role to play in their social evolution, it is to monitor the progress of community life and to demand changes in unnecessarily destructive patterns of social behavior.[39] Resource depletion, economic waste, and inequity, so sadly characteristic of the history of California's fisheries, are thus interrelated phenomena. By the same token, justice, the standard by which people assess the functioning of their social order, may not only be a motive for effective resource management but a necessary precondition for it as well. Injustice may be preferable to total ruin, as Hardin put it, but it may also bring it about.

I

The miner's canary

2

Aboriginal fishery management

Everything in the world talks, just as we are now – the
trees, rocks, everything. But we cannot understand
them, just as the white people do not understand
Indians.   – Nomlaki informant[1]

Before the European and Asian in-migrations of the nineteenth century,
some 310,000 American Indians lived in what is now the State of California
(Figure 2.1).[2] So fertile were the habitats from which they hunted, gathered,
and fished their subsistence that human beings populated the earth more
densely here than anywhere on the continent north of central Mexico. Urban
populations in aboriginal Mesoamerica grew as dense as they did by developing intensive agriculture and by taxing the resources of outlying, subju-
gated peoples, but in California each Indian community depended primarily
on the particular combination of wild plants and animals available within its
own locality. California's extreme ecological diversity thus encouraged the
development of one of the most culturally variegated human populations the
world has ever seen. Some of the most populous, materially wealthy, and culturally elaborate California Indian communities were those that harvested
fisheries that supported commercial enterprise at a later time.

The history of the California fisheries thus began some 4,000 years before
the Spanish friars arrived. Aboriginal groups faced the problem of environment no less squarely than their technologically more advanced successors
did. Despite their relatively small numbers and simple techniques, Indian
hunting and gathering economies apparently could strain their resources
enough to damage them. There is archaeological evidence that aboriginal
hunters drove the sea otter out of the Aleutian Archipelago, for example,
drastically altering the ecology of those waters as they did so. Similar evidence exists that some California Indian communities died out because they
overharvested their supplies of shellfish, while others tailored their exploitation to conserve their resources and their livelihoods.[3] Indian weirs completely blocked the path of migrating salmon in some northwestern California
rivers and would have prevented the fish from spawning had the natives not
torn them down or let the rivers carry them away when they were through

19

Figure 2.1. California Indian tribal areas. Map drawn by Ann Bartz and C. M. Martin.
Source: *Handbook of North American Indians, v. 8: California.*

fishing. Being an Indian gave one no special advantage in confronting the problem, and different communities met it with varying degrees of success. In this, Indian fishers differed little from those who followed them.

Aboriginal fishers also shared with their successors their vulnerability to environmentally induced fluctuations in their harvests and the threat to economic stability that they posed. Many salmon-fishing groups worked at the southernmost limit of their prey's habitat, where slight changes in climate can drastically alter the magnitude of salmon runs from year to year. In southern coastal California, moreover, environmental change forced some Indian villages to change their fishing strategies and others to abandon fishing altogether, just as the sardine industry abandoned Cannery Row during the 1950s.[4] Prehistoric fishing economies had to adapt in their own ways to problems that have plagued modern industries exploiting the same resources at the same localities.

They did so by deliberately managing their use of the fisheries on which they depended. That we do not know the history of how the Indians learned to do so is no reason to presume that it was not a historical process, costly, time consuming, and probably marked by expensive failure. We can infer, however, from what record of their activities we do have how Indian communities eventually learned to balance their harvest of fish with their environment's capacity to yield them. Over time, fishing Indians carefully adjusted their use of resources so as to ensure the stability and longevity both of their stocks and of their economies. In some cases, they limited their production so that fish contributed a small but reliable share of a highly varied seasonal diet. In others, where fish were more critical to their economy, the Indians carefully circumscribed their harvests with complex systems of legal rights and religious observances. In general, the apparent antiquity and stability of California Indian societies at the time of contact with Westerners powerfully suggests the effectiveness of their strategies.[5]

Before commerce in the fishery resources of California could begin, Westerners had first to dismantle aboriginal systems of exploitation and management. This by no means peaceful process itself disturbed the ecology of the fisheries and thereby influenced profoundly the subsequent history of the fisheries and their regulation. In northwestern California, where it was at first difficult to dislodge the Indian economy, the effort to sunder the bonds between traditional Indian society and its environment continued well into the late twentieth century. Native cultures incorporated a great deal of information about fisheries ecology, some of which modern resource agencies began much later to retrieve in their effort to protect endangered resources. Much of it, however, vanished forever when commercial society drove its caretakers to extinction in the late nineteenth century.

A brief geography

In aboriginal California, fish generally formed part of a broadly based hunting and gathering economy. Indians consumed them wherever they could capture them easily with the help of simple tools. Where abundant fisheries coincided with scarcities of other wild foods, as they did along the Southern California Bight and in the lower reaches of the Klamath–Trinity river system in northwestern California, the original inhabitants depended on them more critically and developed a more advanced fishing technology accordingly.

Anadromous varieties, especially chinook salmon, were by far the most important of the finfish. California Indians also took lamprey, sucker, and other river fish where they could, but these were neither as common, as abundant, nor as suitable for large-scale harvest and storage as were salmon. Chinook salmon spawned in nearly every coastal stream from Monterey Bay to the Arctic. In California they were especially prolific in the Sacramento–San Joaquin and Klamath–Trinity systems, respectively the second and third largest streams on the coast below Puget Sound. The Smith, the Eel, and the Russian Rivers, all of which drain the coastal mountains north of the Golden Gate, also supported significant populations of salmon and of fishing Indians.

Two species of Pacific salmon frequent California rivers – the chinook and the coho – although the chinook variety is larger and more numerous. During their annual or semiannual runs to their spawning beds upstream, these species offered themselves for harvest in tremendous quantities at small expense of time, skill, and energy. They were therefore an ideal staple for the rainy winter season, when growing foods were in short supply. Indians usually fished them with harpoons, small hand nets, or simple weirs, although the specialized salmon-fishing tribes of the lower Klamath River Basin used distinctive A-frame scoop nets and more substantial weirs, some of which required many days and many hands to build.[6]

There is no reliable way to estimate how much salmon Indians harvested from California rivers in the years before 1850. For groups inhabiting the lower Klamath–Trinity Basin, for example, the Bureau of Indian Affairs conservatively placed aboriginal consumption at about 36,000 chinooks, or some half-million pounds, each winter; other estimates for the same groups range as high as 2 million pounds annually. One anthropologist, relying on estimates of Central Valley populations that were nearly doubled by later researchers, placed annual consumption in that region at nearly 9 million pounds. Such estimates are primarily guesswork. They do, however, approximate the highest yields from commercial salmon fisheries in the same regions. On the Klamath, "the greatest run of salmon known to white men" produced only 1.4 million pounds of salmon, in 1912, while yields from the Sacramento peaked at roughly 10 million pounds per annum between 1880 and 1883.[7] There is evidence, then, that Indian harvests were at least comparable to those of the commercial fishers who followed them, and thus that Indian fishing probably did exert significant pressure on the resource. What is most important is that, unlike modern fishers, the Indians sustained whatever yields they did take for centuries.

In addition to salmon, most coastal groups took smelt and other surf fish by hook and line and with handheld scoop nets. Few groups had the technical ability to fish extensively on the open ocean; those on the relatively sheltered southern coast ventured out short distances in flimsy reed boats to gather mackerel, sardine, and other nearshore species. Costanoan people fished San Francisco and Monterey Bays in similar craft as well. Specialized exceptions occurred, again, where other foodstuffs were in short supply. To compensate for an arid hinterland, coastal Chumash and Gabrielino people in southern California developed seaworthy plank canoes and carved shell fishhooks unique in aboriginal North America to take bonito, yellowtail, albacore, and other deep-sea fishes. Yurok, Tolowa, and Wiyot fishers from the northwestern redwood belt built dugout canoes to troll for salmon on the open sea and ventured as far as several miles out to hunt shellfish and marine mammals on the rocks off their coasts. No California group seems to have affected the abundance of the pelagic fishes or mammals it harvested, although fluctuations in the supply due to climatic conditions could be of great economic importance to them.[8]

Shellfish were easy to take and were an important source of protein for those groups with access to them. They were especially abundant in sheltered waters such as Humboldt, San Francisco, and Monterey Bays and along the Southern California Bight. From Monterey south to Point Conception, high cliffs and rough seas denied access to any fishery resources whatever to the generally poor groups that lived along that section of the coast. Large sea mussels of the genus *Mytilus* were the most common shellfish species all along the coast. Next in importance were abalone, which thrived in the warmer waters of the southern coast but which thinned out north of Pomo territory in what is now Mendocino County, just north of the Golden Gate. The Indians also gathered other species of clam, oyster, and scallop where they could.[9]

Like those of the salmon, aboriginal harvests of intertidal mollusks probably compared in scale with modern ones because the mollusks will bear only slight harvesting pressure. They reproduce slowly in the best of conditions and even more slowly at lower densities.[10] For this reason, the Indians who gathered them generally cooked and ate them on the spot, although the animals are easy to preserve and were an article of trade for groups on the northwestern coast. Some inland communities made annual visits to the coast to gather shellfish during the historical period, but this was probably evidence of the recent disruption of their traditional economies. Littoral groups apparently tempered their reliance on shellfish in order to sustain their harvest.[11] Huge shell middens accumulated where mollusks were especially important to native economies and today furnish archaeological records of prehistoric subsistence patterns, technology, and climate.

Only those fishing groups with seaworthy canoes could hunt marine mammals on the open ocean, and then only at some risk. The maritime Chumash and Gabrielino along the southern coast and littoral groups in the northwest took sea lions, otters, and seals with harpoons, either from canoes or from offshore rocks. If the hunters could get close enough to an animal, they would club it to death. By far the most important of the pinnipeds was the sea lion, which yielded large quantities of meat, oil, and hide. Sea otters were smaller and of less interest. The otters competed with the Indians, however, for abalone and other tidal mollusks. Unlike whales or seals, otters have no blubber to keep them warm. They compensate by growing the luxuriant pelt that made them so valuable during the nineteenth century and also by eating a great deal. Even in captivity, where they are relatively inactive, otters consume from one-fourth to one-third their body weight every day. Both Indians and otters, despite their uncertain demand for shellfish, had key roles in the ecology of Pacific nearshore and intertidal waters before 1800. By keeping the population of mollusks down, they maintained the supply of kelp, a unicellular plankter during one-half of its life cycle; in that form, it is an important food source for the herbivorous mollusks. Kelp, in turn, provides shelter and nursery, as well as food, for a great many nearshore finfishes.[12] The simultaneous near-extinction of both Indians and otters would figure largely in the subsequent history of the region's waters.

Of the Cetacea, the natives of the southern coast could hunt only the smaller porpoises, while no record whatever survives of Indians hunting whales and porpoises in the northwest. With respect to the California gray and other whales that plied the northeastern Pacific, the Indians were scavengers rather than predators; both northern and southern coastal groups highly prized the occasional dead whale that stranded or washed up dead on their beaches, but hunting them systematically was neither practical nor necessary. Unlike those in the Aleutian Archipelago, California Indians did not take enough marine mammals to make them vulnerable to depletion; nonetheless, the animals were certainly scarce resources. As such, the Indians, especially those on the northwestern coast, regulated their allocation carefully.[13]

Thus relatively simple techniques yielded a great deal of wealth to the Indian fishers of the rivers and coastal waters of California. Aboriginal society, moreover, was wealthiest and most elaborate culturally where fishery resources were most abundant. The leading California anthropologist of the first half of the twentieth century, Alfred L. Kroeber, divided California

groups into three broad ethnic or cultural categories: one in southern California, another in the central part of the state, and a third in the northwestern
region. He also identified what he called "climaxes" or "hearths" of culture
in places in which he believed the Indians were particularly innovative
culturally or were responsible for promulgating customs throughout their
respective areas. Kroeber consistently located these among fishing groups.

South of Point Conception and the Tehachapi Mountains lay the Southern
California culture area, where Kroeber identified two "hearths" of culture.
The first lay among the maritime Chumash and Gabrielino tribes of the
Southern California Bight, while another lay among those of the Gabrielino,
who pursued a land-based economy. The Chumash apparently had the more
elaborate material culture, as Kroeber ranked such things, and the most
elaborate political system in aboriginal California. The Datura or Toloache
cult, whose influence spread far to the north and east of these people, had
its origin among the fishing Gabrielino of Santa Catalina Island.[14] Hierar-
chical and taxonomic distributions of Indian cultures of the sort that Kroeber
and Harold E. Driver, his student, developed provide little information as
to why native societies took the forms that they did, although Kroeber
inferred that shared elements of culture evidenced historical relationships
between different groups.[15] The near-universal penchant of anthropologists
and other early observers for ranking Indian cultures is important here only
to indicate that those groups with access to fertile fisheries seem to have
had more disposable wealth and energy to devote to cultural pursuits than
did others and thus impressed researchers who observed them.

The people of the Central California culture area shared less in common
with tribes outside their region than did those in the Southern and Northwestern California areas. Their distinctive society arose from a hunting and
gathering economy whose degree of complexity was without parallel on the
continent. Here again, Kroeber found two foci of culture, one among the
Pomo of Clear Lake and Russian River and the other among the Maidu and
Patwin of the lower Sacramento Valley. The Kuksu religion, which was
characteristic of the entire area, had its center among the Patwin. Both areas
had abundant supplies of fish, especially salmon. Finally, in extreme northwestern California, a highly localized variant of the Pacific Northwest culture
had its center among the Yurok, Hupa, and Karok of the lower Klamath–
Trinity watershed. These last groups were at once the wealthiest of all
California Indians in terms of disposable resources and the most specialized
economically. Their main staple was the chinook salmon, which also formed
the basis of the world-renewal cult system that had its greatest flowering
among these groups.[16]

Environment, as it influenced the choices people made among the technological and cultural alternatives available to them, was vitally important
to Indian society. Before contact with Westerners disrupted their lives,

California Indians generally lived and died within ten to fifteen miles of their birthplaces, never speaking to more than perhaps 100 other people. Although trade was common between groups and particular goods might travel over great distances, individual tribes rarely trucked with any but their closest neighbors and apparently never allowed exchange to dominate their strategies for subsistence. Indian economies were first and foremost products of local resources.[17]

The extreme wealth of the fishery resources in each of Kroeber's "climax" areas without doubt contributed to their ability to support such relatively high densities of population and such prolific cultures. Ecologically, a salmon run constitutes a massive transfer of energy and materials collected over a wide expanse of ocean to a focused area, much in the same way, for example, that an empire contributes resources to its metropolis. Similarly, upwelling currents enhanced the productivity of the fisheries off the southern coast with which the maritime peoples of that area supplemented their economies. Those native groups that were able to harness such natural forces to their own purposes were more prosperous and more active culturally than those that subsisted in more tightly circumscribed energy economies.

California Indians knew how important their fisheries and other resources were to their livelihoods; they took steps to protect themselves both from overexploiting them and from seasonal variations in their productivity. California Indians closely adjusted their populations, hence their demand for food, to the capacity of their environment to yield resources to the tools they used. Tribes in the Central and Southern culture areas limited their fishing indirectly by spreading their demand for food over a number of resources. In the Lower Klamath culture area, finally, where the Indian economy rested more squarely on salmon, native societies elaborated more complex legal and ritual controls over their production of fish. This elaboration distinguishes them from other fishing groups in native California; the evidence suggests, moreover, that the great wealth and peculiar culture of the three "climax" groups in this area contributed to their significantly greater success in coping with the disaster that befell all California Indians at the hands of invading people in the nineteenth century.

California hunter-gatherers as resource managers

Indian society in California was distinctive in its high density of population, its insularity, and the remarkable complexity of its hunting and gathering economy. While groups in the northwestern and southern coastal regions shared many ethnographic traits with tribes to the north and east of them, respectively, in general the mountains, desert, and ocean that isolated California from the rest of the world physically also insulated its aboriginal cultures from outside influence, enabling them to flourish in their own ways. At the heart of these people's adaptation to their peculiar environment, which contained an extremely variegated, if thinly spread, supply of edible plants and animals, was an economy based on painstaking, seasonal, and broadly diffused effort rather than on special skills or concentration on any particular resource. Aboriginal society in California was sedentary, technologically unsophisticated, relatively free from conflict either with nature or with neighbors, and, to a degree remarkable among North American Indians, free from privation.[18]

The most critical resources were those the Indians processed and stored for use during the lean months of the winter and early spring (viz., acorns, large game, and fish). Because the addition of easily caught salmon did nothing to diminish their access to other staples, it is no surprise that the most populous tribes in central California were those along the Sacramento and San Joaquin Rivers. The Wintuan-speaking Patwin, Nomlaki, and Wintu groups living along the Sacramento from the delta to its headwaters together made up the largest coherent linguistic group in northern California and, according to Kroeber, were "[among] the most important in the development and diffusion of customs."[19] At the southern limit of the salmon, a line between Monterey Bay and the bend in the San Joaquin River, the Plains Miwok, Yokuts, and Monache people of the San Joaquin Valley also took great quantities of the fish.[20]

The Southern California Bight, between Point Conception and San Pedro Bay, and the islands offshore supported the only maritime cultures in aboriginal California, those of the Chumash and the Gabrielino. Here the coast faces to the south, protected from the prevailing winds that bring fog and high surf to more northerly areas. The rocks and cliffs that divide land from sea to the north and south here give way to sandy, gently sloping beaches. The water is calm and visibility high; the large, verdant Channel Islands loom just offshore. Their geographical situation, combined with the exceptional fertility of the Santa Barbara Channel, drew these people out onto the ocean. Here, too, adequate timber and natural petroleum seeps, not available either to the north or the south, provided planks and caulking for seaworthy canoes. These facilitated trade with the islands and fisheries for sea mammals and for many of the finfish that became commercially important after 1850. An arid hinterland inhibited food production away from the coast and further encouraged the maritime adaptation, which was unique to the area.[21]

The ability to draw on the productivity of the Channel waters, as well as a fertile coastal strip and abundant shellfish resources, permitted human populations to bloom along this part of the coast. The Chumash aggregated into villages of as many as a thousand people each along their stretch of the coast. Wealth and concentrated numbers led in turn to a flowering of culture. The Spanish reckoned the Chumash superior to all other California tribes with which they had contact. With their neighbors, the Gabrielino, the Chumash share the recognition of modern anthropologists as "the wealthiest, most populous, and most powerful ethnic nationality in aboriginal southern California."[22]

Like all hunter-gatherers, California Indians were intimately familiar with the ecology of their food resources and actively manipulated their environment in order to enhance its stability and productivity.[23] Fishery use was qualitatively different among the Yurok and other Lower Klamath culture area peoples and so merits individual treatment. Throughout the region, many groups used artificial fires, for example, with considerable skill to encourage the growth of plants upon which they and the birds and mammals they hunted depended for forage. According to Henry T. Lewis, there were probably few areas in California with any appreciable Indian population whose physical aspect was unaffected by it. In general, the nearly universal use of fire by preagricultural peoples to manipulate their environments by itself calls into question the widely assumed ecological passivity of such peoples.[24]

The Indians seem to have harvested as much from their environment as it could predictably yield. Comparing Sherburne Cook's estimates of the population of central California tribes with his own indices of the productivity of acorns, game stocks, and fisheries in each of their territories, Martin A. Baumhoff found that a linear function of resource productivity accurately predicted the populations of groups in both fertile and barren areas. He concluded that each group's population was in equilibrium with the carrying capacity of its local environment.[25] All groups traded food with each other, to some extent, and were apparently accustomed to supplying emergency rations to neighboring villages in temporary need. There was some, but not much, ability to secure a surplus beyond the community's needs in a moderately severe winter.

Carrying capacity is a function not only of the inherent productivity of a habitat but also of a people's strategies for production. It is a social measure as well as a strictly biological one.[26] That hunting and gathering economies such as those in aboriginal California operated at relatively low population densities did not relieve them of their need to husband their resources if they were to sustain their ways of life. One way in which the California Indians did so was to spread their productive effort over a wide range of resources, each in its season. If a particular crop failed or if salmon or game were scarce in any season, there were usually other foods to fall back on.[27] Central California Indians developed their fishing technology and devoted their time to fishing only to the point at which salmon provided a predictable share of their subsistence in conjunction with the other foodstuffs available to them. The overall fertility of the California environment meant that hunting and gathering could support large numbers of people; meanwhile, the Indians' broad subsistence base contributed to the great stability of their economies.

Although they also took more overt measures to limit their demand for food, one effect of this diffusion was to limit the Indians' use of fish or any other single resource to within prudent bounds.[28] Avoiding the risk of crop failure was thus the standard by which the Indians limited their harvest and kept it safely below the long-term maximum yield that any particular resource could sustain. For southern coastal groups, this was the reason for limiting their shellfish collecting to a small part of their seasonal round. Despite their advanced fishing methods, they continued to rely chiefly on a diversified economy, with acorns the main staple. One study concluded that the maritime capability was itself a response to the overuse of the shellfish upon which the Chumash and Gabrielino relied more heavily and from an earlier time. It made their basically diffuse economies more efficient and more secure but did not supplant them.[29] To have intensified their fishing or any other of their harvests, say, by developing an agricultural specialization, would have at once increased the Indians' exposure to risk and diverted labor away from other pursuits, thereby bringing an initial drop in overall productivity. The Indians, who were secure but who had stretched their economy to its limit, had no incentive to do this.[30]

Of prime importance to the California Indians was the practical concern of maintaining the security of life as they knew it. A more specialized economy held no inherent attraction for them as long as their own methods continued to support them in good style, just as it does not for hunter-gatherers surviving in the late twentieth century.[31] But their complex economic strategy did not emerge and did not endure simply as a matter of chance. They developed it, over time and no doubt at some cost, and maintained it deliberately. Because they used all the resources their habitats would yield safely to their productive system, California hunter-gatherers faced the fundamentally political problems of regulating the harvest and distributing natural resources no less than later Californians with different kinds of economies. For them, as for their successors, resource management was a function of social and political institutions.

Perhaps most basic among the social tools with which California Indians limited their demand for food was population control. The Indians' lack of technological sophistication does not fully explain their apparent ability to live within their ecological means because they could always have tried to feed more people with the same economy. Yet, they did not. Malthusian "positive" checks on population – war, famine, and the like – do not seem to have been significant to the lives of aboriginal Californians. Infanticide, abortion, taboos on intercourse during lactation, meaningful social roles for celibates, and other deliberate controls on human fertility, however, do. The Pomo apparently resorted to a number of tactics, from contraception to geronticide, to protect their relatively dense population from exposure to the risk of famine. Scattered evidence survives of systematic removal of twins, defective infants, or infants of deceased mothers among other California groups, particularly those with fertile habitats and dense populations such as the Yurok and the coastal Chumash. Deliberate, socially sanctioned regulation of their numbers, in response to perceived conditions in individual families, in the community, and in the environment, was crucial to the Indians' ability to balance their demand for food with the capacity of their habitats to produce it.[32]

More directly, California Indian communities limited access to their resources by assigning rights to them. Individual communities claimed exclusive use of all important food-producing resources and denied them to outsiders except under carefully controlled conditions.[33] In general, the more concentrated or critical a resource, the more explicitly the Indians articulated rights to it. Individual "ownership" was far more common in the Klamath River area, where salmon was of overwhelming importance, than anywhere else in California. Northwestern coastal groups lay claim to specific stretches of beach adjoining their villages and defended them against trespass. In central and southern California, where staples were more varied and dispersed, native groups commonly vested their ownership in the community at large. Individuals and households might claim sole use of a particular oak tree or fishing spot for a season, but for the most part important hunting, fishing, and gathering locations belonged in common to the whole community. Well-defined rights to resources not only limited their use but permitted tribes to monitor the effect of their harvesting at specific sites over time and to adjust their use accordingly.[34]

Although individuals sometimes held property of a sort, it was certainly not absolute and resembled a form of trusteeship rather than property in fee simple under Anglo-American common law. Individuals had no right to alienate resources that were crucial to their community's well-being.[35] Nor was shared property left to suffer "the tragedy of the commons." Tribes and villages administered the harvest of communally owned resources according to carefully prescribed and closely supervised procedures, usually in a ceremonial or ritual context. The world-renewal religion of northwestern California was the most complex such ritual system. In central California, the Kuksu religion of the Patwin, Maidu, and Pomo also contained strong elements of world renewal. In both areas, secular and administrative functions entwined with spiritual ones. Shamans, whose social role was to mediate between the community and the spiritual forces that infused the natural world, organized the harvest of key resources, supervised their distribution, and appeased their spirits so as to ensure the continued prosperity and well-being of the group.[36]

Central California communities could harvest neither acorns, fish, nor game until the local shaman performed the appropriate first-fruit rites, which might take several days. Acorn harvests were crucial to central and southern California Indian economies and were most carefully hedged about with ritual. Salmon also received the ceremonial protection of the Kuksu religion, although these rites were perfunctory as compared with those in the northwest. In southern California, civil authorities directed the harvest, storage, and distribution of acorns and presumably shellfish as well, although again not without the assistance of shamans who observed first-fruit rites for them. Individual tribes always invited their neighbors to attend their ceremonies and used the occasion to trade with them and exchange gifts. Trade and reciprocity, integrated within a ceremonial context, relieved competition for scarce resources and helped maintain good relations between neighboring groups.[37]

The ritual organization of production and exchange articulated and reaffirmed to the Indians their interdependence with each other and with the natural world.[38] According to Harold Driver, a belief in active, watchful, and potentially vengeful animal spirits was "probably universal" among North American Indians.[39] The Indians had to use them carefully and propitiate them for their sacrifice if they were to rely on their continued abundance. Animism was the way in which the Indians, like most hunter-gatherers, expressed their awareness of the fact that their lives and those of their food resources were ecologically intertwined. It was the job of the shamans to mediate between the two camps: to interpret for their communities the will of the natural world and to ensure that the former used its resources in prudent ways. This is no more or less than what modern scientific resource agencies with their staffs of ecologists do, although they do so from the standpoint of a profoundly different world view.

There is no reason to suppose that the communion between Indian society and the world around it was perfect. As one Sacramento Valley native put it, "Everything in the world talks, just as we are now, the trees, the rocks, everything. But we cannot understand them, just as the white people do not understand Indians."[40] There is also no reason to suppose that the Indians did not have to learn how to get along with their resources, that the balance they maintained among environment, production, and ideology at the time of contact with Westerners was not something that developed over a long period of time and with occasional mistakes. We have indirect evidence of some of the mistakes, but the history of the process is lost. It does seem clear, however, that the balance they eventually struck was an enduring and prosperous one. California Indians managed their fisheries and other resources by strategically gearing their productive effort to the ecological realities of the world as they understood them, so as at once to lead comfortable lives, to distribute wealth equitably, and to sustain their resources and their economies over the long run.

Salmon fisheries in the Lower Klamath culture area

Fisheries were far more important to the economies and cultures of Indians living in the far northwestern corner of California than they were to those elsewhere in the state. Here, from the Smith River south to Cape Mendocino, abundant salmon runs and the relative scarcity of other food resources forced the Indians to base their economies more squarely on fisheries. Consequently, while central and southern California tribes husbanded their fisheries primarily by keeping them to a limited share of a carefully adjusted seasonal round, Lower Klamath culture area groups took more direct steps to regulate their harvests. The social and religious systems controlling their fishery use wove through their entire culture. They had much to do, also, with the relative success of these groups in weathering the onslaught of the late nineteenth century.

Ethnographically, these tribes represented an extension of aboriginal Pacific Northwest culture, although unlike their northern neighbors they augmented their fisheries with other typically Californian wild foods. Unlike those to the south, however, Indian groups in this area were firmly committed to fishing. They relied much less than other California Indians on artificial fires, for example, to enhance the productivity of land-based resources. Baumhoff could predict their estimated populations with a function of their territories' fishery productivity alone, whereas indices of acorn and game resources correlated only randomly with population. Significantly, Baumhoff found that the relationship between resources and population was not proportional here as it was in the rest of California. Those groups with less productive fisheries, to be sure, made more use of other foods. Those living along the most productive salmon streams were not as populous as the abundance of their resources would suggest. In other words, those groups that could have made more use of their fisheries did not. Baumhoff concluded that overt social regulation, rather than the indirect effects of a diffused economy, limited these groups' use of salmon so that they lived far below the carrying capacity of their environment.[41]

Lower Klamath area culture was most highly elaborated among the Yurok, Hupa, and Karok who lived on the lower stretches of the Klamath River and its main tributary, the Trinity. Relatively few archaeological data exist for these groups, although two Yurok sites dated back to the fourteenth and seventeenth centuries reveal "approximately the same way of life as described by early historical travelers and traditional Yuroks," in the words of the anthropologist most familiar with these people.[42] Continuous occupation of the area probably dates from the tenth century A.D.; thus, the culture is not much older than the largest of the redwoods which survive in the area.[43] Despite their radically different linguistic backgrounds – the Yurok speak an Algonquian (or Algic) language, the Hupa Athapaskan, and the Karok Hokan – the three groups are practically indistinguishable socially and economically. Their distinctive culture and great affluence impressed all who observed them. A German visitor in 1851 described the coastal Yurok as "the finest looking... of all the Indians in California," whereas in 1871 Stephen Powers praised the Karok as "probably the finest tribe in California." "This civilization," Kroeber wrote, "attains on the whole to a higher level ... than any other that flourished in what is now the state of California."[44]

The geographic center of this peculiar cultural universe was the confluence of the Klamath and Trinity Rivers, at the Yurok village of Weitchpec. Away from the core area, environmental constraints were less limiting and the human inhabitants correspondingly less specialized economically. Shastan people along the Klamath above the modern town of Happy Camp lived to the east of the dense coastal forest and thus had better forage resources as well as poorer supplies of salmon. Tolowa and Wiyot people who lived at the mouths of the Smith and Eel Rivers, respectively, pursued a more diversified economy, based on the coastal resources at their disposal, than did the tribes in the core area. To the south, the Chilula and Whilkut, on Redwood Creek, and the Athapaskan-speaking groups in the upper reaches of the Eel River watershed betrayed the gradually increasing influence of the Central California culture type. The Sinkyone of Shelter Cove, just south of Cape Mendocino, occupied the southern boundary of the Lower Klamath culture area. All these groups, however, were similar enough culturally that Kroeber identified them as a coherent group, tied together by their dependence on the salmon.[45]

Indian society in the region was a loose aggregation of individuals and nuclear families clustered together in small villages along the rivers and coast. These tribes shared with coastal groups to the north a great emphasis on individualism and material wealth, although ownership and control of resources was more completely atomized here than among Pacific Northwest societies. The Yurok, the Hupa, and the Karok carefully defined private rights to all kinds of tangible and intangible property, and all such rights had monetary values. Many goods had fixed values over the entire region. Individual men claimed exclusive use of fishing sites, improved game yards, or gathering sites for themselves and their families. Good fishing spots, such

Figure 2.2. Little Ike, a Karok Indian, shown here fishing with an A-frame scoop net, ca. 1890. Photo courtesy of the Smithsonian Institution.

as that in Figure 2.2, were the property of individuals or partners and were transferable. Others could not fish at or immediately below a private spot, although a few good pools or rapids were open to common access.[46]

Resources gradually lost their private character away from the center of the area and back from the rivers and coast, where land was of less economic value, although the "high country" overlooking the Klamath River canyon was of immense spiritual significance to the Yurok.[47] The coastal Wiyot and Tolowa generally confined privatism to prestige rights to certain parts of sea mammals taken or scavenged by cooperating groups. Even here, however, individuals and households generally harvested, processed, and stored their own food. Important exceptions to this privatism occurred when people of one village or several together cooperated in building seagoing boats or salmon weirs. Here, a local notable would serve as entrepreneur, providing direction and rations to the workers and supervising the division of spoils. Leadership here, however, was utterly expedient and stemmed from no formally recognized authority. Kroeber noted that among the Yurok there was "no offense against the community, no duty owing to it, no right or power of any sort inhering in it." "No formal authority as such," he wrote, existed to restrain people's behavior. Another anthropologist described northwestern California society as "approximating ideal anarchy."[48]

Especially in the center of the region, Lower Klamath area Indians were competitive, avaricious, suspicious of strangers, and litigious in the extreme. The federal commissioner sent to treat with these people in 1851 found them "a bold, fearless, independent race; [having] had but little intercourse with whites, and no idea whatever of having any *superiors*."[49] Baumhoff found their society, significantly, "in many ways similar to that of modern America."[50] Yet relations within groups and between different tribes were on the whole peaceful and just, cemented by economic ties, ceremonial cooperation, and intermarriage. The Indians confined the avarice for which they were notorious to prestige goods such as dentalium shell, which they used as money, or woodpecker scalps. Food was neither an item of wealth nor of exchange. Reciprocal gift giving, in which the wealthy gave more than they received in return, was common on ceremonial occasions. Aged people seem to have been exempt from some of the legal and ritual controls on resource use.[51]

A kind of common law existed among the Yurok and their neighbors, its precedents transmitted orally from wealthy aristocrats to their novices. Conflicts between individuals or families over personal injuries or access to resources might be bitter and might occasionally escalate into armed confrontation, but there were few casualties. Serious disputes went for arbitration to informal panels of aristocrats or to individual go-betweens, chosen by the principals involved to represent their interests. All damages were strictly compensated and then forgotten, even between litigants of different tribes. Winners, indeed, sometimes bore heavier reparations than losers. In a remarkable way, the Indians of the Lower Klamath culture area developed an entirely informal legal system that bound them together peacefully and ensured an equitable distribution of resources among them.[52]

Woven through this peculiar social order, underwriting its legitimacy and sustaining its immediacy to its members, was a world-renewal religion that had its center among the three "climax" tribes and was the region's most distinctive cultural characteristic. Key to the cult was the life cycle of the Klamath River salmon. The Yurok and their neighbors lived in a universe dominated by the Klamath. Their cardinal directions were upriver and downriver, high country and low. Their world's center lay at Weitchpec, where the steep canyons of the Klamath and the Trinity joined a third, which led to the ocean. Through this universe, each year at the same time, rushed hordes of salmon that appeared from somewhere out in the ocean and madly forced their way into the mountains, dissipating their great strength and destroying their bodies as they made their determined way upstream. Upon these heroic animals the Indians' lives depended. Their religion, therefore, served to propitiate the salmon and to guarantee their return from season to season.[53]

Although chinook salmon entered the Klamath system in two runs, one in spring and one in fall, the latter was most important because low water in the river made it easier to harvest the fish and because fall-run fish made up most of the Indians' winter food supply. The fall harvest was thus intensely ritualized. Just after the run got under way, a formulist performed a first-salmon rite at Welkwau, near the mouth of the Klamath. He prayed "on behalf of the whole world, asking that everywhere there be money, fish and berries and food, and no sickness." When the first fish appeared, he acknowledged the salmon's paramount right to complete its life cycle by feigning a harpoon thrust at it and letting it pass. He speared the next fish he saw, killed and ate it according to prescription, and thanked it for its sacrifice:

> I am glad I caught you. You will bring many salmon into the river.
> Rich people and poor people will be happy. And you will bring it
> about that on the land there will be everything growing that there
> is to eat.

Until this was done, salmon at the mouth of the river were taboo.[54]

The key observance of the cult system took place at the peak of the fall run, some time after word of the Welkwau rite's completion made its way upriver. This was the construction of a huge weir near the Yurok village of Kepel, about 35 miles up from Welkwau and a few miles below the Klamath–Trinity confluence. Kepel was probably the best place from which to harvest large quantities of salmon. It had a good shallow stretch of river with a gravel bottom on which to build the weir, and there were only a few riffles, or rapids, below it. At this point the fish, having already had a week or so in which to burn off excess water in their flesh but not yet having expended much of their muscle and fat in struggling upstream, were in good condition for drying and eating.[55]

Kroeber and Barrett called the Kepel weir "the most elaborate undertaking of any kind among the tribes of the northwestern California region"; it may have been, as Erikson described it, "the most advanced accomplishment of California Indian cultures."[56] The entire round of ceremonies and dances that attended the construction took as much as fifty or sixty days to complete. The observance offered the region's people a chance to arbitrate conflicts with each other, to display wealth and status, and to share in the harvest. The construction itself required ten days and the cooperative effort of three communities to build. During the ten days in which the weir stood, local residents gathered a good share of the winter's supply of food. Thereafter, they dismantled it so that upstream tribes could take their shares of the run. The entire procedure took place under the strict supervision of a formulist, whose mumbled recitation was his secret personal property. Neighboring communities were dutifully informed when the construction was about to begin, and in its final stages the ceremony drew participants from many widely scattered Yurok, Hupa, Karok, and Tolowa villages.[57]

The myths that informed such ceremonies give some clue to their history and function. The Indians believed that they owed their life to a primeval race of people, the *woge*, who taught them the ways of the world before surrendering it to them, transforming themselves into the mountains, trees, and animals of the Klamath River Basin.[58] The Kepel ceremony, for example, had its origin when the *woge* of that vicinity destroyed the weir at Turip, another village just downstream, because it blocked their access to salmon. When they came to Kepel to retaliate, the downstreamers agreed with Kepel's people to let them keep their dam as long as all were informed of its construction each year and all were invited to take part in the harvest. For their part, the Kepel people would begin a dance for the weir, as the story went,

> because everything will come out well for that. But it will not be well if they omit it, even one year only: for there will be much sickness if they do not make this dam as long as there are people in the world. For we [the *woge*] are about to leave. . . .[59]

The Turip villagers then transformed themselves into the gaunt redwoods that still stand watch, some of them more than a thousand years old, at the edge of the forest below Kepel. The Kepel weir represented the Indians' most dramatic interference with the world around them. Its construction was, in consequence, an event of the utmost spiritual significance.[60]

Like the mythical *woge*, upstream neighbors would have come down the river to tear down the Kepel weir had the locals not done it themselves.[61] George Gibbs, who traveled with the treaty-making expedition of 1851, noted that salmon weirs, large and small, "form[ed] a frequent cause of quarrel among the bands inhabiting different parts of the rivers. Some understanding, however, seems to exist as to opening portions of them at times, to allow the passage of fish for the supply of those above."[62] The distinguished Army General George Crook, who early in his career was assigned to establish Fort Terwar at the mouth of the Klamath, told of breaking up such a dispute at the village of Sa-aitl, a few miles upstream from his post, during the late 1850s:

> A lot of excited Indians from up the river . . . were clamoring for the lives of its inhabitants, declaring that they were witches, etc., that

they had bewitched the salmon, and made them run through the
mountains instead of up the river where they could catch them. . . .
Their whole life seemed to be made up on such small affairs.[63]

A balance of power existed, then, between competitors who mistrusted
each other profoundly but who were nonetheless bound together by their
common dependence on the salmon of the Klamath River. Legitimized
through myth – in much the same way that the myth of the Social Contract
underwrote that which succeeded it – and sustained through the ceremonial
observances of the world-renewal religion, the Indian social order ensured
an equitable distribution of fish over the entire watershed.[64] As each community along the rivers observed the restraint demanded by the cult and
by watchful neighbors, enough salmon escaped capture to spawn in the
tributaries that fed into the river's main stem along the way. Indians and
salmon thus cooperated to ensure their mutual survival over the centuries.

World renewal permeated every aspect of the economic and social lives
of the Lower Klamath culture area, integrating the production and distribution of their key resource with the ecological needs of the resource itself.
It reaffirmed to all the ideological foundation on which their society rested.
All the life forms with which the Indians shared the world had active and
watchful spirits upon whose goodwill the continued stability and prosperity
of the world depended. That goodwill, in turn, hinged on the Indians' rev-
erent treatment of the salmon from which they drew their livelihood. This
meant allowing enough of them to pass to sustain upriver peoples and,
whether the Indians understood the mechanics of the process or not, allowing
enough to reach their spawning grounds so that the stocks perpetuated
themselves. Such protection extended to other of the Indians' prey species,
as well: A hunter prospered only by maintaining the favor of his game "by
respectful treatment."[65] Although Indian society in the Klamath basin bore
some remarkable similarities to the one that supplanted it, the natives'
radically different view of the world and their place in it compelled them
to behave in such a way as to save them from the environmental problems
that so sorely beset their heirs.

Conclusion: Indian fisheries and the wilderness myth

Native Californian hunter-gatherers had the capacity to alter or degrade
their environment significantly and took pains to control their use of resources so as to sustain their way of life. Their fisheries, in particular, were
very important to their livelihoods and confronted them with the same
challenges of environmental uncertainty and vulnerability to depletion that

continue to plague more modern resource managers. Nevertheless, it appears that the Indians managed their fisheries successfully over the long run, and at sustained levels of harvest that might well incite the envy of twentieth-century fishers and lawmakers. As the subsequent history of the region would show, modern economies use their waterways in more complex ways than did the Indians. Still, the Indians' ability to integrate fishery production into an intricate food economy, to tailor their exploitation to ecological necessity, and to enlist the cooperation of many different groups in accomplishing the task remains a remarkable achievement.[66]

Nineteenth- and twentieth-century policymakers proceeded under the interrelated assumptions, however, that the Indians lacked the technical sophistication either to deplete or to manage their resources and that the destruction of once-abundant "virgin" resources was a necessary complement to "civilized" habitation. A primeval, basically static, and unsullied wilderness, so they thought, greeted people of European stock as they moved westward across the continent, making what they would of its previously "untouched" natural wealth.[67] "In the beginning all the World was *America*," went John Locke's myth of Creation; "wild woods and uncultivated wast[e] . . . left to Nature, without any improvement, tillage, or husbandry," its inhabitants "needy and wretched."[68] The historian Walter Prescott Webb described the North American frontier as "a vast and vacant land without culture."[69] To Webb's mind, and in Frederick Jackson Turner's estimation as well, Indians entered the picture only as savages, noble or otherwise, living off the land but making no impact on it and whose annihilation had no significant impact on its subsequent history. Such assumptions did much to influence policymakers' understanding of the problems before them and their strategies for action in the years following California's admission to the Union in 1850.

Indian society was not so thinly spread over the California environment that Europeans could simply move it aside to make way for Western-style commerce. Removing the Indians from the region's aquatic food webs disturbed the ecology of the fisheries, just as would the extermination of any other important predator. Two biologists suggested that the Columbia River salmon fishery may have been as productive as it was when commercial fishing began there during the 1870s because the suspension of Indian harvesting several decades before had given the salmon time to multiply their numbers unimpeded. Likewise, contemporary observers noted that salmon increased notably in the Sacramento River after the malaria epidemic of 1833 decimated Indian fishing communities in the Central Valley. To the south, the simultaneous obliteration of sea otter and coastal Indian tribes by 1840 permitted populations of shellfish along the Southern California Bight to bloom magnificently.[70] The myth of the abundant frontier was thus the obverse of the view that such writers as Locke and Malthus took of the

Indians as people living in an impoverished, depraved state of nature.[71] Significantly, public concern with fishery conservation in California first emerged between 1870 and 1890, just as Indian populations reached their historical minima. The ecological effects of extirpating Indian society from its environment would play a significant role in poststatehood conflicts over fishery use, although late nineteenth-century observers would not recognize their real causes.

The ways in which California native groups adapted economically and culturally to their particular habitats, finally, had much to do with their different responses to contact with Europeans. In southern and central California, the natives had exploited each local habitat at or near its sustainable limit, that is, to feed the greatest number of people that could survive a winter of moderate shortage with some help from neighboring villages. While stable and secure under normal conditions, native economies in those regions collapsed utterly when European disease and competition for resources disrupted them. In the northwestern region, however, while the Indians may have maximized their harvest over the Klamath–Trinity watershed as a whole, those groups in the lower reaches of the system could have taken many more fish than they actually did while Indian society still functioned. This unused potential harvest, together with the cultural edifice that the Indians developed in their superabundant but narrowly based environment, was crucial to their much greater success in coping with the ecological catastrophe that befell the original inhabitants of California when people of a different culture came to take the earth away from them.

3

The Indian fisheries commercialized

Like the miner's canary, the Indian marks the shifts from
fresh air to poison gas in our political atmosphere.
                                        – Felix S. Cohen (1953)[1]

The presence of the Indians . . . as far as it implies the
absence of the whites, is the great protection of the supply of the Sacramento salmon.
                                        – Livingston Stone (1872)[2]

The obliteration of Indian subsistence economies in California followed the
arrival of Europeans with apocalyptic ferocity. During the sixty-five years
after the Spanish opened their first mission in 1769, Indian population in
the coastal strip between San Diego and Sonoma declined by 75 percent.
Epidemic disease and military action under Mexican rule cut further into
Indian numbers during the 1830s and 1840s; by the time Alta California fell
to the United States, only 150,000 of the original inhabitants remained where
more than twice as many had lived just eighty years before.

The scourge intensified under U.S. dominion as miners and farmers
pushed into the most remote parts of the state to seek new livelihoods in
"virgin" territory. Between 1845 and 1855 alone, two-thirds of the remaining
natives lost their lives. By the time the worst of the gold fever had passed,
only 50,000 still lived. The Indians were "burst into the air," wrote Stephen
Powers in 1871:

> Never before in history has a people been swept away with such
> terrible swiftness, or appalled into utter and unwhispering silence
> forever, as were the California Indians . . . let a tribe complain that
> the miners muddied their salmon streams, or steal a few packmules,
> and in twenty days there might not be a soul of them living.[3]

The slaughter abated after 1880. Indian population remained at a low of
about 20,000, or about 5 to 6 percent of its aboriginal strength, for another
generation before it began to inch its way upward again. "It was one of the
last human hunts of civilization," wrote Hubert Howe Bancroft, "and the
basest and most brutal of them all."[4]

The brutality of the process was a function of the rapacity with which the

41

new arrivals tore at the region's natural resources. Most California Indians simply could not get out of the way. Because they had spread their economies so broadly over their habitats and adjusted their harvesting so closely to capacity, the sudden interruption of their seasonal round at any number of points brought privation. This at once lowered their resistance to disease and compelled them to the stockraiding that was infamous for inviting reprisals against them. Fishing people were especially vulnerable. Because they tended to be densely settled along watercourses, they suffered the earliest and most extensive exposure to infection and were more likely than back-country people to hold lands that the invaders coveted. By the 1880s, the last of the fishing groups in the Central and Southern culture areas had surrendered their trusteeship of California's fisheries to the none-too-safe keeping of the commercial economy.

In the lower reaches of the Klamath–Trinity watershed, however, native society maintained its hold on its fisheries, at first withstanding and later accommodating the onslaught to a degree unmatched in the rest of the state. The sheer inhospitality of the region discouraged commercial development until well into the twentieth century, while protecting the Indians who had learned to prosper in it. The distinctive social and cultural tools with which the Indians of the area organized their fishery economy, moreover, left them better equipped to deal with Anglo-American society than were Indians elsewhere. Although much of the world-renewal religion through which the Yurok, Hupa, and Karok people had articulated their management of Klamath River salmon died out after the turn of the century, they remained in possession of the fishery. Their effort to affirm their rights to it in court after World War II brought the relationship between Indian society and its natural resources back once again to the center of management policy for one of California's most important fisheries.

The arrest of native food production

Ultimately, the conflict between natives and newcomers was over the right to make use of the environment in particular ways and to particular ends. Because native economies generally made full use, given their technology, of all the resources available to them, any competing use of any resource was likely to disrupt them. When the resources were as important to commerce as were waterways, the conflict was likely to be total. Indian fishing economies fell victim to the invaders in several ways. In most cases, fishing people perished outright from disease or violence at the hands of soldiers and settlers. In others, missionaries, private landowners, and U.S. Indian Reservations forcibly diverted Indian labor from customary channels. As large numbers of settlers moved into the area, finally, the ecological damage wrought by their economic activities fell hard upon Indian fisheries. The fortunes of fishing Indians reached their nadir in the 1880s, just as the commercial fishing industry of California achieved the peak of its short-lived nineteenth-century prosperity.

Most Indian fishers died, quite simply, of European diseases to which they had no immunity. Even before permanent settlement began in 1769, the depopulation of the Chumash coast about Point Conception and the eastern shore of San Francisco Bay was already far advanced. The sweeping epidemics began in 1802. Malaria wiped out half of the densely settled Wintuan-speaking peoples along the Sacramento River at a single stroke in 1833. One traveler passed through a crowded and busy valley on his way north in 1832 and returned a year later to find it utterly empty, save for piles of Indian corpses and noticeably increased numbers of salmon in the river. Smallpox shattered the economy of the other Central Californian "climax" group, the Pomo, in 1837. Under U.S. occupation the epidemics subsided, but the ravages of diseases now endemic to the Indians and the much more thorough mixing of the two groups multiplied losses three- or fourfold.[5]

Death also visited at the hands of settlers. The two most infamous mass murders in California history claimed fishing Indians as their victims. In 1850, in reprisal for the deaths of two settlers known for mistreating their Indian laborers, the army slaughtered 150 to 200 Clear Lake Pomo on what became known as Bloody Island. A secret league of prominent Humboldt County citizens ten years later attacked a sleeping encampment of Wiyot people on Gunther Island near Eureka, killing about 300. The Indians were primarily fishers and their families, apparently gathered there for an annual ceremony. Fishing communities were especially vulnerable to this sort of thing because they tended to be sedentary and to settle along waterways, where they were highly visible and very likely to be in the way. People dependent on salmon had to remain near their streams for several weeks at a time during spawning runs or lose their winter supply of food. As one army commander reported from Trinity River in 1855,

> this river . . . is rated as the best in the country for salmon fish, which constitutes almost the whole subsistence of the Indians. The whites took the whole river and crowded the Indians into the sterile mountains, and when they came back for fish they were usually shot.[6]

Miners and soldiers finally starved the Wintu people of the upper Trinity into submission during the hard winter of 1858–9 by driving them back into the hills, where they were unable to gather food.[7]

Spaniards, Mexicans, and Anglo-Americans also intervened by forcing native workers into new pursuits. At first, the Spanish had had to rely on the Indian economy for food. Pedro Font reported in 1776 that the Chumash were "displeased with the Spanish because of [the latter's] taking away their fish and their food to provision themselves."[8] Thereafter, to convert the Indians to Christianity and to make the agricultural economy of the missions work, the friars gradually removed the natives from their accustomed environment, set them to work on mission farms, and then resettled them on agricultural plots in the mission environs. Mission policy rigidly opposed the hunting and gathering of traditional foods, although under the dietary regimen the friars imposed upon them, according to Cook, "the Indians as a whole lived on the verge of clinical deficiency."[9] This without doubt contributed to the high incidence of disease in the missions.

Diversion of Indian labor from traditional to European methods of food production continued after the Mexican Governor of California, Figueroa, expropriated the missions in 1834. As land-grant *ranchos* gathered their labor supply from the surrounding countryside, slaving raids and other ostensibly punitive expeditions against the Indians of the Central Valley and northern coastal mountains increased in frequency, scale, and brutality. Native society among the maritime people of the Santa Barbara Channel coast gave up its last breath during this period. The abduction of Indians for use as concubines or as day laborers had begun long before secularization of the missions, but by the time of statehood it had developed into a major industry.[10]

After 1850 both the *hacienda* system and the practice of kidnapping its labor supply flourished with the legislated approval of the new State of California.[11] In some cases Indians worked for settlers more or less voluntarily, as they did for miners during a brief period early in the Gold Rush. In general, they had little choice. Anglo-Americans enthusiastically adopted the Spanish tactic of attacking Indian villages during critical food-preparing times and putting stockpiled fish and other foods to the torch. Cook estimated that every native settlement in the Klamath Basin was "sacked, if not burned, at least once."[12] Participation in the settlers' labor market helped convert the Indians from native to Western foods, either because their employers paid them in kind or because they used what cash they made to purchase staples at commercial stores.[13]

Hardly less destructive than the missions or the *ranchos* were U.S. Indian reservations, which, like the missions of the colonial days, tried to teach the Indians to make their living by farming rather than by hunting, gathering, and fishing. Inconsistent policy compounded by corruption and the persistent avarice of the settlers, however, hamstrung the effort from the start. According to Cook, "not until the middle sixties was any consistent scheme put into operation to ensure an adequate year-round food supply" to Indians on government reservations.[14] In the interim, the government denied the

Indians access to traditional means of subsistence while failing to provide them with anything in their stead.

The federal government sent Redick McKee to treat with the California Indians in 1851. Within a year he had drawn up eighteen agreements that divested the Indians of their claims to most of the state and removed them to reservations located so as to provide both traditional subsistence and the resources to begin a "civilized" economy. At the behest of its members from California, however, the Senate rejected the treaties out of hand. Congress did act in 1855 to give the President authority to establish reservations for the California Indians by executive order, and under this law the state Superintendent of Indian Affairs, Thomas J. Henley, established reservations in Colusa and Lake counties, at Noyo River on the Mendocino Coast, and at the mouth of the Klamath River. After floods destroyed the Klamath River reservation in the winter of 1861–2, another was set up in the Smith River valley to replace it.[15]

Henley's strategy for acculturating the Indians was to contract their education out to private entrepreneurs, who moved onto the reservations to develop their resources with inexpensive Indian labor. He leased a fishing station at the mouth of the Noyo River to one John H. Ray in 1856 and allowed him the use of Indian fishers from Mendocino reservation, whom he had supplied with boats and nets of U.S. manufacture. Outraged by his corruption and incompetence, Congress obtained Henley's dismissal in 1859 and took revenge on the Indians as well by cutting appropriations for the California reservations drastically.[16]

Congress acted "to provide for the better organization of Indian affairs in California" in 1864.[17] It was under this law that the four reservations extant today came into being, in southern California for the Mission Indians, at Tule River, at Round Valley in Lake County, and at Hoopa Valley on the Trinity River. Other reservations, along with whatever progress the Indians had made toward making new lives on them, were thrown to the wind. The government relinquished Mendocino Reservation in 1866 and ordered the Indians there to Round Valley, although many refused to go. "They like the place," one agent reported, "and do not like to leave their native salt air and fish of the sea-shore for the dry air and unaccustomed haunts of the interior."[18] The legal status of the reservation at the mouth of the Klamath River remained unclear because, although the Army had abandoned it after the flood of 1861–2, the government apparently regarded the land as a kind of annex to the Hoopa Valley Reservation upstream.[19] This ambiguity would confound policymaking for California salmon more than a century later.

In 1887 Congress, again frustrated by incompetence and corruption in the reservation system, passed the Dawes General Allotment Act and acculturated the Indians by fiat. The Dawes law authorized the President to allot eighty-acre homesteads to each reservation Indian family. Thereafter, the remainder of the land was to be opened for public entry.[20] The reservation experiment had been a dismal failure. The Commissioner of Indian Affairs reported in 1900 that of the 16,000 to 17,000 California Indians left alive, only 5,497 had ever received government aid of any kind.[21] Whatever gains the government made by "forcing distasteful lessons in agriculture upon a handful," wrote Hubert Howe Bancroft, had been "fully counterbalanced by the demoralizing influence of soldiers, servants, and settlers upon bands, which if left to their own wild haunts, would have long remained purer and happier."[22] Although Bancroft was certainly no admirer of the California Indians, who in his opinion had "sunk almost to the darkness of the brute" before meeting the friars, he recognized that in the end the reservation system had done little more than to make it impossible for them to survive either in the traditional or in the Western fashion.[23]

Where pestilence, mayhem, and abduction did not prevent native Californians from pursuing a normal livelihood, the Indians had to compete with the invaders for the use of resources. Nor was the competition peaceful. Although historians have paid little attention to it, heroic if generally ineffectual resistance to colonization has been the rule, not the exception, for native hunter-gatherers the world over. Mounted on Mexican horses and subsisting on stolen Mexican livestock, the formerly peaceful tribes of the Central Valley had by the early 1840s managed to push the usurpers back to the sea's edge. "The basic point," according to Cook, was "that the Indian, faced with the clear prospect of starvation, attacked the race responsible for his condition. . . . The Indian wars and difficulties up to 1865 had as their basic cause the dislocation and depletion of the aboriginal food supply."[24] The most successful such resistance among California Indians was that of the Klamath Basin tribes, who won reservations in their own territories after several years of fighting during the 1850s and 1860s.

The only fishery to assume any commercial importance before statehood had been that for the sea otter. The Chumash and Gabrielino, who had much better sources of meat and only a limited demand for prestige goods, did not prize the otter highly. To the Russian, Yankee, or Spanish trader who could collect them and ship them to fabulously wealthy customers in China, however, otter pelts were very valuable indeed. The Russians had easy access to native Aleut hunters who were skilled in taking sea otters, but to avoid losing the trade and possibly the entire coast to their competitors, the Spanish reluctantly trained and equipped mission neophytes for the hunt. Unconverted Indians got into the business in a small way as well. Others suddenly found their waters and shores infested with otter hunters as the fight for pelts turned the northeastern Pacific into what the historian of the trade called an "inferno" after 1820.[25] Kodiak and Aleut hunters in the employ of the Russians made forays to the Channel Islands on their own behalf and in one such raid reportedly killed every Gabrielino on San Nicolas Island save two or three. According to the nineteenth-century "Indianologist" Alexander S. Taylor, the Indians "had such bloody wars among themselves, for the fishing grounds of each island . . . that the priests had them all brought over to the mainland and placed in the missions."[26] By the mid-1830s the trade had helped bring the maritime cultures of southern California to the last stages of extinction, as well as the otters themselves. Abalone and other mollusks, their predators exterminated, bloomed thereafter so that Chinese fishers would find abundant supplies of them three or four decades later.

With the discovery of gold in 1848 the nature of the contest changed altogether. People from all over the world came in a rush to put the land and waters of California to uses that usually precluded coexistence with the Indians. Salmon streams became so clogged with mining debris as to be useless for fishing. Fences with armed farmers behind them blocked the natives' access to wild foods when their seasons arrived. Farmers cut down the oak groves that had been the mainstay of most tribes' economies or left them to provide forage for livestock. Not even enough acorns remained to ensure the survival of the oak species, much less that of the Indians who gathered them for food.[27]

Indian fishing suffered, especially, from the alternative uses to which the new tenants put the rivers of California. Salmon reproduce by burying their eggs in beds of coarse gravel washed by cold, swift, highly oxygenated streams. Chinook salmon eggs incubate in fifty to sixty days, and the fry move to the ocean within a few months of hatching. Spring-run salmon require deep, cold pools in which to rest for several months before moving onto their gravels to spawn in the autumn. During the entire time they live in fresh water, salmon are extremely sensitive to changes in the temperature and oxygen content of their water. Siltation, diminished flows of water, obstruction of adults' access to suitable gravels, and removal of shading vegetation from stream banks can all cut into recruitment to the fishery or cause a year class to fail altogether. Smaller proportions of young survive to breeding age at lower absolute levels of population.[28]

Placer mining in the Sierra Nevada foothills and in the upper reaches of the Klamath–Trinity river system did great damage to the salmon potential of these areas. Nineteenth-century observers referred repeatedly to the injury done by miners to salmon fishing as a cause of conflict with the Indians. This was so especially in the Northwest, where the argonauts encountered fully operative Indian economies. After the initial excitement played out, hydraulic mining in the Sacramento–San Joaquin system raised the destruction of fishery habitat to still higher levels. In the Northwest, where hydraulicking was less practical at first, the miners built wingdams to lay bare large stretches of river bottom and impaired productivity in that way.[29]

The mining of timber also damaged native fisheries, especially on the Sonoma–Mendocino coast north of San Francisco. Henry Meiggs built the first sawmill on the north coast in 1852, at the mouth of the Noyo River. By 1874 nearly every stream on that stretch of the coast had become a thoroughfare for redwood logs rather than for salmon. Timber and slash blocked the way to ascending fish, while deforested hillsides exposed their spawning beds and made them vulnerable to drought and to catastrophic flooding. By 1886, disastrous floods had become so frequent in that part of the state that the California surveyor-general recommended to the governor that all state timber lands be withdrawn from sale in order to prevent further damage to public watersheds.[30]

The destruction of salmon fisheries continued well into the twentieth century, as economic development brought railroad construction, overfishing, and the diversion of water for irrigation and power production. In all but a few areas, however, the Indians had already lost the battle. Cook wrote that by the turn of the century the California Indian population had become "fairly well established under the new conditions," its trusteeship over the river fisheries of the state utterly revoked.[31] The tribes of the lower Klamath basin had managed to hang on. In the Sacramento–San Joaquin watershed, mining had by the 1870s rendered the American and Feather tributaries all but useless for salmon production, the Indians driven away by gold rushers. Only the Little Sacramento and McCloud Rivers survived as functioning spawning habitats. On the McCloud remained what was probably the last surviving Indian fishery in the basin.

The Wintu Indians were the northernmost of the Wintuan-speaking peoples of the Sacramento Valley. They were close linguistic cousins of the Patwin, who built up one of central California's most vital cultures in the lower valley. Wintu territory straddled the headwaters of the Trinity, Salmon, and Sacramento Rivers, although settlement was most dense along the McCloud. Somehow, a number of McCloud River Wintu had managed to survive the plagues of malaria in 1833 and miners in the 1850s and were peacefully operating a subsistence fishery on the river when a U.S. Fish Commission biologist found them in August 1872.

Livingston Stone had recently arrived in California to set up a station for collecting salmon eggs for the Fish Commission, itself organized just the year before during the first flurry of concern over the conservation of U.S. fisheries. Directed by a settler, Stone made his way to a spot two miles above the confluence of the McCloud and Pit Rivers, where the Wintu had built a weir and were drying salmon by the hundreds along the riverbank. According to Stone, the Wintu were none too friendly: They were "not slow to say to the white stranger, 'These are my lands,' and 'These are my salmon.' " "The stern consequences of conflict with the whites," however, had "taught them to abstain from any violent vindication of their rights."

Figure 3.1. McCloud River Wintu, shown here drying salmon near the U.S. Fish Commission hatchery, ca. 1879. Source: George Brown Goode and Joseph W. Collins, *The Fishermen of the United States*, in *The Fisheries and Fishery Industries of the United States*, ed. George Brown Goode, sec. IV, p. 46.

Nonetheless, Stone reported, they had until that point managed to keep settlers away from their river, "with the exception of a Mr. Crooks, whom they murdered a week before I arrived." Undeterred, Stone put together his egg-collecting station and after some time reached an agreement with the extremely suspicious local authority whereby Stone took the eggs and gave the Wintu the rest of the salmon for food. Eventually Stone hired twenty or thirty of the Indians to do the actual work of collecting the fish and stripping them of their roe and milt (see Figure 3.1).[32]

The biologist, the Indians, and the fish got on quite well. Indeed, intuitively grasping a point that the U.S. Supreme Court would make a century later, Stone came to believe that the cooperation of all three was essential to the continued survival of the salmon fishery on the river below. "The supply of the Sacramento salmon has a singular natural protection," he reported, "arising from the fact that the McCloud River, containing the great spawning grounds of these fish, is held entirely by Indians":

the appearance of the white men, on the American and Feather Rivers, two great forks of the Sacramento, has been followed by the *total destruction* of the spawning beds of these once prolific streams, and the spoiling of the water, so that not a single salmon ever enters these rivers now where once they used to swarm by the millions. ... It would be an inhuman outrage to drive this superior and inoffensive race from the river, and I believe that the best policy to use with them is to let them be where they are, and if necessary, *to protect them from the encroachments of the white men.*[33]

President Grant reserved 280 acres at the hatchery site for government use, and in 1877 a garrison of soldiers joined the community as well to prevent friction between the Wintu and the settlers who were by then arriving in increasing numbers.[34]

Through the seventies and early eighties, the hatchery on the McCloud supplied salmon fry to rivers on the East Coast and abroad as well as to the the Sacramento. Although Stone's arrangement protected the heart of the system, however, progress on the river below soon caught up with him. On August 7, 1883, after the fall run of that year began as usual, there were suddenly no more fish in the river. Stone and his Indian partners stood helplessly by the still water where once they counted from 6,000 to 8,000 fish jumping every hour. They later discovered that at the mouth of the Pit River, some distance below the station, the Central Pacific Railroad had begun blasting to clear a bed for its line to Oregon. Stone was convinced that the blasting had driven the run back, although some of the workers had been blowing charges in the river itself and collecting the dead fish to sell to their comrades. At any rate, there were no more fish to be had for the rest of the season. The hatchery did not reopen until five years later.[35]

When it did reopen, the Indian fishery was dead. According to their ethnographer, the McCloud River Wintu held their last communal fish drive at Baird, where the hatchery was located, "about 1886."[36] This was when the first of the 1883 year-class fish should have returned to spawn, although the bulk of them would have been due in 1887 and 1888. The 1881 and 1882 year classes, which should have made up the remainder of the 1886 run, had been born during the two most heavily fished spawning runs in the history of the Sacramento River. Fishers on the river below reportedly had the stream completely blocked with gill nets. Stone, in fact, had noted in 1882 that breeding salmon had been "extremely scarce" at the Baird station.[37] Cannery output had fallen steadily since that year. Production in 1886 was less than one-half that of the previous season, despite the fact that the number of canneries operating had risen from six to nine. Output dropped still further in 1887, when about half of the spawning fish should have been from the 1883 year class. The runs recovered slightly in 1888–89, but the fishery was never the same again. Hatchery operations resumed at Baird in 1888, later supplemented by other installations elsewhere in the watershed. After reaching a peak in 1905, however, hatchery production in the whole system rapidly fell off.[38] Since the early 1940s, the site of the McCloud River hatchery has been at the bottom of Shasta Lake.

Successful defense in the
Klamath–Trinity watershed

By the time California achieved statehood, only one-third as many Indians were living within its boundaries as had lived there before the Spanish arrived. Of the maritime people of the Southern California Bight, hardly a trace remained. Of the salmon fishing groups of the Sacramento–San Joaquin watershed, only scattered pockets such as that on the McCloud River survived. In 1850, however, the specialized fishing groups of the northwestern coastal area remained virtually intact (see Figure 3.2). A few Yankee otter traders had visited the area shortly after the turn of the nineteenth century but had found the coast difficult of access and the natives something less than cordial. Thus, when the Southwest fell to United States dominion, the length of coast between Cape Mendocino and the Smith River remained a "wilderness," the Indians as yet unmolested.[39]

Major P. B. Redding, who had become familiar with the region on a trapping expedition a few years before, discovered gold on the upper Trinity River in 1848. Settlement of the Humboldt–Del Norte coast began in 1850, in an attempt to capture the packing trade to the mines on the upper Klamath and at Weaverville. The disintegration of Indian society followed with terrible swiftness as the impatient settlers collided head-on with people whose lives had not yet been touched by Europeans. Vigilantism, kidnapping, and rape fell harder upon the Indians in the Lower Klamath culture area than anywhere else in California. Cook estimated, for example, that in some areas fully half the Indian women of childbearing age bore children to white males. "Such a wholesale prostitution of a race," he wrote, "has seldom been seen on this continent."[40] By 1900 Indian population had declined no further in northwestern California than it had elsewhere but had done so in little more than a generation.

As Table 3.1 shows, however, the three "climax" groups that inhabited the lower reaches of the Klamath basin fared much better than did their immediate neighbors to the east, north, and south.[41] Losses among the Karok, according to Kroeber, were "relatively mild," possibly not exceeding one-half. Survival rates among the Hupa and the Yurok were also among the highest in California. "The modern Yurok," wrote Erik Erikson in 1943, were "a picture of relative historical and economic health."[42] During the

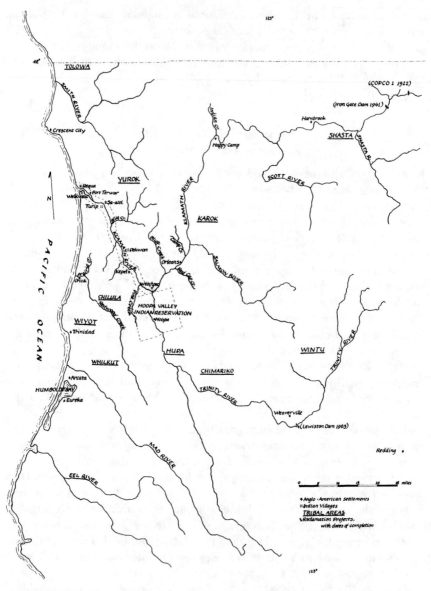

Figure 3.2. Klamath–Trinity River Basin. Map drawn by Ann Bartz and C. M. Martin.

Table 3.1. *Population of northwestern California Indians.*

Ethnic group	Precontact	1880–1910	% Residual
State total	310,000	16,350	5
Shasta	5,955	100	2
Tolowa	2,400	150	6
Yurok	3,100	700	22
Hupa	2,000	500	25
Karok	2,700	800	30
Wiyot	3,300	100	3
Athapaskan[a]	15,450	400	3

[a]Includes Chilula, Whilkut, Mattole, Kato, Wailaki, Nongatl, Lassik, and Sinkyone. *Source:* Cook, "Aboriginal Population of the North Coast," *passim*; Kroeber, *Handbook of the Indians of California*, p. 833.

1960s and 1970s, the Hoopa Valley Indian Reservation, which follows traditional Yurok and Hupa territory from the lower Trinity to the ocean, was the largest and most populous reservation, in the state. Although unemployment remained very high on the reservation, per-capita income among Humboldt County Indians, enhanced by their timber resources, was a remarkable 90 percent of that of the county as a whole.[43]

The striking difference between the demographic responses of these people to the catastrophe of the late nineteenth century was attributable to the ecology of the lower Klamath basin and to the singular adaptation that these three groups had made to it in the centuries before 1850. Although the Yurok, Hupa, and Karok were the wealthiest of all aboriginal Californians, Anglo-Americans were for many years unable to tap the resources they had learned to exploit so profitably. Conversely, the success with which the native economy had limited its use of the river fishery in normal times, both in order to share with upstream groups and to lower its risk of harvest failure, left it a natural reserve on which to draw during hard times. Nature banking, so-called, had been a fundamental aspect of the native economy; it now enabled the three core groups to remain self-sufficient during the invasion and thus weather it better than could communities that had pressed their habitats to capacity.[44] The peculiar culture of these people, finally, enabled them to deal with the invaders on their own terms far more successfully than was the case elsewhere in California. When the storm passed, the Indians of the lower Klamath–Trinity watershed remained in possession of their traditional lands and economies, while all around them their neighbors had ceased to exist in functioning communities.

For the same reason that the elaborate specialization developed by the

Yurok, Hupa, and Karok was increasingly dilute with distance from the Klamath–Trinity confluence, peripheral areas were more accessible to commerce. Shasta territory, at the headwaters of the Klamath and to the east of the densely timbered coastal strip, was auriferous and possessed good agricultural land. It was promptly and thoroughly overrun with miners: Thousands were at work within months of the gold discovery there in the spring of 1851, and in October of that year the McKee treaty-making expedition found the Shasta starving because sickness had left them too weak to hunt or fish.[45] Wintu people on the upper Trinity near Weaverville relinquished their lands to miners and soldiers during the "Wintoon War" of 1858–9. The Chimariko, a small group living in the richly auriferous Trinity River canyon, fought the miners through the early sixties but ultimately learned, as Powers put it, "that they must not presume to discuss with American miners the question of the proper color for the water in the Trinity River." By 1871, the Chimariko were utterly scattered; by the turn of the century, they were extinct.[46]

Elsewhere in northwestern California, Indian people either lived along the coast, where they were exposed to infection and attack, or in areas suitable for agriculture, where settlers soon sought them out. Newcomers first invaded Tolowa country when a group of them founded Crescent City in 1852 and others began farming the Smith River valley a year later. Although remnants of the Tolowa economy still functioned in 1880, the Indians lost great numbers to measles and cholera. Chilula and Whilkut people, just west of the Hupa, possessed rich pastures and lay in the path of pack trains to the Trinity mines. In 1856 these people rose, only to lose a destructive conflict with the intruders; those who survived scattered.[47]

The Wiyot tribe about Humboldt Bay, the largest natural harbor on the coast north of San Francisco, was by far the hardest hit of any northwestern native group. Several towns sprouted next to the bay to service the freight business to the mines before 1850 was out. The McKee party found the Wiyot already suffering serious losses to disease in 1851. Nine lumber mills ringed the bay in 1854. Sporadic violence took a mounting toll of Indian lives until the Gunther Island massacre in 1860, after which the Army moved many of the Wiyot to Fort Humboldt on the bay and thence to a reservation at Smith River for their protection. Within the next decade, most of the Wiyot villages along the coast were deserted, as were most of those formerly inhabited by Coast Yurok people north to the mouth of the Klamath River.[48]

Relatively unknown to settlers before 1854, the Eel and Mattole Rivers marked the southernmost boundary of the Lower Klamath culture area. Wiyot and southern Athapaskan communities there collapsed as their fertile valley became an important agricultural producer between 1854 and 1857. The Eel supported a substantial fall run of salmon, and H. H. Dungan of

Eureka began fishing it in 1853. By the close of the decade there were seven packing plants on the river supplying cured fish to the miners and townspeople of northwestern California as well as for export. The Eel became the second most important salmon producer in California, but the canning industry crippled it along with the Sacramento during the 1880s. Some forty of the local natives who had managed to hang on bought a parcel of land on a small island in the mouth of the river in 1869 and did day work for the packers. They were not hired to fish, however, but rather as divers for the dangerous work of clearing the riverbed for the new people's nets. They did some subsistence fishing out of season, as well, at least until 1888.[49] By that time, Anglo-Americans had largely erased Indian society from the coast and put the land to other use, except in the rugged canyons of the Klamath River.

"Nature seems to have done her best to fashion a perfect paradise for these Indians," wrote Special Agent Paris H. Folsom to the Commissioner of Indian Affairs in 1885, "and to repel the approach of the white men."[50] In the early days the only access to the region's interior from the west was by pack train. Mines in the Weaverville area were more naturally tributary to the Sacramento Valley than to Humboldt Bay. As late as 1890 the only access to Hoopa Valley was on foot or muleback over forty miles of rough country from Arcata. Yurok country on the lower Klamath was the most isolated spot in a remote region. Steep canyon walls held out roads and rails, while a sand bar at the mouth of the river denied entry to all but the lightest boats. The first road pushed through to Requa, at the river's mouth, in 1894. Not until the 1960s was there a good two-lane road from there up the river to Weitchpec.[51]

With the exception of Karok territory above Orleans Bar, the area was practically useless for placer mining; in all but a few places the gold particles were too fine and too widely scattered to repay digging. Later, the high cost of freighting equipment and supplies into the area held back more capital-intensive mining and logging as well. Although some of the upriver Karok were sick in the fall of 1851, the McKee expedition found the Yurok and Hupa in good shape. Downriver Yurok were difficult to gather for McKee's parleys: The expedition's secretary noted in his journal that these "peremptorily refused to have anything to do with the whites, as a party of whites had prevented their building a fish-dam last summer." A few Hupa came down to Weitchpec to talk but were "very impatient to be gone, saying that many of their people at home were sick; that this is the fishing time, and fish must be caught for food in the winter."[52]

George Gibbs predicted in 1851 that should the supply of placer gold give out, the Karok's land "would soon be abandoned to its former possessors."[53] He was right. After a brief exile, the Karok gradually drifted back to their homes. The California Geological Survey visited the northern edge of Karok country in 1863 and found it practically deserted, save for the Indians. Powers found the Karok getting on well in 1871–2; he found the Hupa prospering at the same time. Powers attributed their well-being to the fact that the miners had bypassed the lower Trinity, leaving the waters unmuddied and the Indians in peace.[54]

The farmers who usually succeeded miners in building western communities found no arable land of any extent in the entire basin below Shasta country. Under the reservation system, Indians in Hoopa Valley grew some crops, and the Yurok below Weitchpec had small patches of potatoes wherever there was any level ground, but in general the river was, as one government agent put it, "utterly useless for white settlement."[55] Most continued subsisting largely on fish from the river as they always had. Under the laws of the 1850s the government had established a reservation on the lowermost twenty miles of the Klamath, and some government-sponsored farming had taken place there. During the winter of 1861–2, however, a severe flood washed away topsoil and equipment, and the government abandoned the site as worthless. The Yurok knew otherwise: As the federal agents moved to a new reservation on Smith River, most of their charges simply took to the hills to wait out the flood, returning to the river and its salmon in the spring.[56]

The environment to which they were so well adapted thus served as a bulwark behind which the core tribes of the Klamath Basin gained time to adapt to the new order of things. Not to be discounted, however, was the natives' own active and skillful military defense, itself aided by the unexploited surplus of salmon in the river. The Yurok rose in 1855. In the peace concluded that year, they won the land one mile on each side of the Klamath from its mouth to a point twenty miles upriver as a reservation. Having defended the lower half of their territory, the Yurok remained peaceful thereafter. During the 1860s they were "the most numerous and powerful band in the northwestern part of the state."[57] The Hupa, perhaps with some Whilkut and Yurok joining them, fought the usurpers so successfully between 1860 and 1864 that they brought all commercial activity in the middle reaches of the watershed to a standstill, cut off all communications between the coast and the interior mines, and drove settlers back to the coastal towns. They, too, won recognition of their right to their lands after the fight, as the government evicted settlers from Hoopa Valley and set the area aside as a reservation in 1864.[58]

Reported the Commissioner of Indian Affairs at the end of the war,

> The great numbers of Indians inhabiting the Klamath and Humboldt countries, the dense redwood forests on the river bottoms, and the high, craggy, precipitous mountains back, would, to my mind, be

a serious warning against any effort to remove them by military force. . . . [59]

By 1865, the three tribes of the core area had secured their traditional fishing grounds – the Karok by default and perseverance and the Yurok and Hupa through armed resistance. Because the Klamath–Trinity system's spawning areas begin at Blue Creek, just a few miles above the estuary, much of the watershed's potential for salmon production survived the first two decades of U.S. sovereignty in Indian hands.

Given a chance, the Indians found that they could deal with the newcomers in business as well as in battle. Their senses of property and the exchange value of things were, if anything, more highly developed than those of the settlers. They had only to accept dollars instead of dentalium shell as a measure, which was not difficult to do. Yurok in the Weitchpec area refused to deal with Redick McKee until he paid them for three of their villages that packers had burned that spring and for two of their people who had been shot, but were peaceful and tractable once McKee compensated them. "They peremptorily refuse to render the slightest service without something . . . received beforehand," wrote McKee's secretary.[60] Gibbs relayed the story of Red Cap, an Orleans-area Karok who, to compensate a miner for the theft of his rifle, levied a tax of fifty cents in U.S. silver on every salmon sold by an Indian to a miner until the debt was paid off.[61] Here, the Indians' customary method of arbitrating disputes over property meshed well with U.S. legal practice and the affair did not lead to bloodshed as it would have elsewhere. Erikson, however fanciful some of his other observations, could not miss the key element of intergroup relations on the Klamath: "Yurok and the white man," he wrote, "each understand too well what the other wants, namely, possessions."[62] Here there was at least some commonality of understanding and behavior; elsewhere in the New World the utter lack of common cultural ground did much to seal the Indians' fate.[63]

U.S. currency and political connections in the U.S. government simply became additional resources for Indian use. The Indian Agent at Hoopa Valley noted that the Hupa were disinclined to work on communal projects at the reservation, "but will work industriously if left to do so on their own account."[64] When Powers visited the Yurok and Karok in 1871–2, he found people of both tribes working in nearby towns and buying food and clothing from local merchants. "These Indians are enterprising," he wrote; "they push out from their native valley."[65] Austin Wiley, the Indian Agent who negotiated an end to the war with the Hupa in 1864 and for a short while was chief of the California Indian Superintendancy, reported that he had grown up with Indian leaders in the Klamath Basin and had located the Hoopa Valley reservation on the lower Trinity at their request. More than one government official who had leverage over policy for the Klamath Basin had marriage or other kinship ties with powerful Indian families in the region.[66] "It is no little to their credit," concluded Powers, that the Indians "learned all these things by imitation, having never been on a reservation."[67]

Yurok, Hupa, and Karok people appealed to the ethnocentricity of the Office of Indian Affairs in Washington as well as to that of Powers. Apparently, the government was more willing to let a fishing people continue subsisting in the customary way than one which hunted or gathered foods that did not appeal to Anglo-American taste. If the Yurok were "in general sullen and suspicious," they at least shifted for themselves and got on relatively well at little or no public expense.[68] Their preference for living in nuclear families impressed observers also. "They form a very respectable peasantry," wrote Paris H. Folsom. "While these Indians still have a sort of tribal code, they are rapidly becoming individualized and segregated in individual interests. . . . In fact, they have the model idea of an American life."[69] Indian Affairs agents repeatedly urged their superiors to leave the Yurok alone and to protect them from outsiders.[70]

The fortunes of these tribes seem to have touched bottom during the mid-1860s, as did those of the Klamath River salmon. At that time, there were 650 Indians living at Hoopa Valley and about 2,000, presumably Yurok, along the forty miles of the Klamath River below Weitchpec. In 1865, the resident surgeon at Hoopa Valley reported that the Klamath and Trinity were very muddy from mining upstream and "almost deserted" by salmon.[71] Two years later, another agent wrote that Indian fishing was almost at a standstill, so that "only now and then one of their ingenious weirs is seen."[72] Thereafter, as mining gave way to agriculture in the interior between 1865 and 1875, the fishing improved. Powers found the fishery intact on the lower forty miles of the river, even if on a scale smaller than it had been in the early days. At the same time, the Hupa were subsisting reasonably well on their traditional economy. "Though not so plentiful as in former times yet . . . they manage to have plenty," reported the agent at Hoopa Valley in 1871.[73]

Klamath River Indians began fishing commercially for salmon in 1876, on terms to which both they and the government agreed. Two Crescent City entrepreneurs contracted with the natives in that year to catch and salt salmon at the mouth of the river. The Klamath Commercial Company, of which one of the original partners was a founder, began milling lumber and packing Indian-caught salmon on the river in 1881. Five years later, with the permission of the Indian Agent at Hoopa Valley, John Bomhoff of Crescent City established a cannery at Requa, near the mouth of the river. In marked contrast to what obtained on the Eel River, Bomhoff reserved all of the fishing and most of the cannery jobs for the Indians. The only outsiders were those who tended the packing machinery. The arrangement worked well, apparently, providing a money income as well as traditional subsistence to the Yurok.[74]

The uncertain legal status of the old Klamath River Reservation brought competition for land to the river in the 1880s. The government had vacated the old reservation on the lower twenty miles of the river after the flood of 1861–2 but had never abolished it formally. Since that time, squatters had trickled onto the old reservation, as well as onto the twenty-mile "connecting strip" between the reservation and Hoopa Valley. Through the late seventies and eighties, as bills to put the old reservation up for sale appeared in Congress, the Interior Department at last rallied to the defense of the Indians and recommended that the entire length of the river below Weitchpec be reserved for the natives. In 1877, the Army evicted settlers from the old reservation and stationed a detail from Hoopa Valley at Requa "to prevent intrusion on the Indian lands, and to protect the Indians in their only industry . . . that of fishing salmon."[75]

Pressure to open the river for settlement intensified during the mid-1880s. An 1880 act of the state legislature had declared the Klamath a navigable stream from its mouth to Orleans Bar, apparently to encourage public access to the lower river and in plain contradiction to the facts of the river's geology.[76] Squatters moved again into the canyon, claiming that the government had abandoned the reservation in 1862; the Interior Department averred, however, that it still considered the lower river part of the Hoopa Valley reservation and denied their applications for patent to the land.[77] Informed of conflict brewing between squatters and natives on the connecting strip, Interior dispatched Paris H. Folsom to the area, where in 1885 the latter found what he called his "respectable peasantry" "supporting themselves without aid from the Government, by fishing, hunting, raising a little stock, cultivating patches of soil, and by day's labor at the Arcata lumber mills. . . . In short, Sir, I have never been more pleased with any Indian community."[78] Folsom described the squatters as "bummers" and "leechers" and urged his superiors to evict them, compensate them for their improvements, and establish the river formally as part of the Hoopa Valley Reservation.

The issue came to a head when the salmon entrepreneur R. D. Hume arrived from Oregon in May, 1887, and prepared to pack fish at the mouth of the Klamath without permission. As with the others, the Interior Department had denied Hume the right to purchase land along the river with a government land warrant and in 1883 had turned down his offer to pay $50,000 for a ten-year lease on the fishery. Undeterred, Hume crossed the sandbar at the river's mouth in a light steam tug, prepared to build a floating cannery in the estuary, and at gunpoint warned Captain Daugherty, the commander of the army garrison at Requa, not to interfere. Although Hume apparently arrived with his own fishing crews, he also began purchasing fish from some of the Yurok with goods he kept in a small store aboard his tug. The Yurok, Daugherty reported, had worked very hard to clear the estuary's bottom for their nets and were "much disturbed" by the intrusion. They appealed to Daugherty to intercede, much as an earlier group had appealed to George Crook to prevent others from interfering with the fishery and as they would have appealed to their own arbitrators before U.S. authorities took over during the 1850s. The Commissioner of Indian Affairs in Washington agreed with the Indians, noting that by seining so near the river's mouth Hume would obstruct the runs and "cut the Indians off from their accustomed supply." He appealed to U.S. Attorney General Garland for a judgment on the Indians' behalf, lest the latter "undertake to defend their rights by violent means."[79]

In reply, Garland noted that since the State of California had declared the Klamath navigable the Indians enjoyed no exclusive right to its fishery, but only a right to fish in common with the public at large. Whether or not the lower river was "Indian country" and whether Hume could be excluded on that ground, he wrote, were questions "clearly justiciable in the appropriate courts at the suit of the Indians themselves who are interested in them."[80] Daugherty's garrison thereafter seized Hume's tug with its store of trading goods under a law prohibiting unlicensed trading in "Indian country."[81]

The matter then came before the federal district court in San Francisco in the case of *United States* v. *Forty-Eight Pounds of Rising Star Tea, etc.* The government's prosecution was badly handled: The U.S. attorney did not appear in court to present the Interior Department's side of the issue; Daugherty, who was in the city on other business, was the government's only witness. Judge Hoffman agreed with Hume that the Klamath was by law a navigable river and that the land around it had ceased to be an Indian reservation when the army abandoned it during the winter of 1861–2, and on appeal Judge Sawyer of the Ninth Circuit Court of Appeals sustained Hoffman's decision. Hume was free to trade or to pack fish at the mouth of the Klamath as he pleased.[82]

Hume's operations on the Klamath never turned a profit for him; after several years, he sold out at a loss to Bomhoff's Klamath River Packers' Association. He had made the breach, however, and thereafter the clamor in Del Norte County for free access to the land on the Klamath's banks grew louder and more shrill by the year. Finally, to circumvent the *Rising Star Tea* decision and on the basis of Paris Folsom's report, President Harrison officially extended the boundaries of Hoopa Valley Reservation down to the ocean in 1891. The state legislature repealed the river's navigability the same year, apparently in an effort to encourage mining upstream from the reservation. In 1892, Congress approved a bill allotting plots of land on the lower reservation to the Indians under the Dawes Act and opened the rest for sale to the general public. The river's status as an Indian reservation, however, and consequently the Indians' preferential right to the salmon fishery, were secure after the conflict of the late 1880s. Commercial packing continued on and off at low levels through the nineties and into the next century.[83]

Conclusion: new competition for
Klamath River salmon

Demographic peace returned to California at some point near the turn of the century, when the Indian population of the state began to turn upward again. During the 1880s and 1890s about 500 Indians at Hoopa Valley were subsisting on reservation crops supplemented by hunting and fishing. Along the Klamath, to the west, lived anywhere from 600 to 900 Yurok, still living "to quite an extent," according to the Indian agent, off native foods.[84] Although a good number of outsiders moved onto the river during the first decades of the twentieth century, the area nonetheless remained an Indian reservation. The Interior Department and the U.S. Supreme Court affirmed this formally in 1904 and 1913, respectively, noting pointedly that the "prevailing motive for setting apart the reservation" in the first place had been "to secure the Indians the fishing privileges of the Klamath River" and to protect them from usurpers like R. D. Hume.[85]

That the Indians of the now-extended Hoopa Valley Reservation possessed some preferential rights to the Klamath River salmon fishery was clear, although the extent of those rights remained undefined and would prove increasingly controversial as the fishery declined over the course of the twentieth century. Until 1933, when California closed the river to commercial fishing, a good many Yurok made their living from the fishery. From one to three canneries at Requa provided many with cash income, either for fish or for work in the plants themselves. The Yurok, for whom the canneries reserved most of the fishing and cannery jobs, gradually adopted U.S.-style boats and gill nets for their work and became, in essence, commercial fishers. Between 1915 and 1928, an average of eighty-two boats harvested some 52,000 chinooks, or about 725,000 pounds, each year.[86]

The world-renewal religion that had underwritten the Indians' former way of life decayed gradually as the older people who could still remember the ceremonies died and more and more of their children took up jobs on the outside. The Kepel weir and dance lapsed shortly after 1910: Not enough men could get together at one time to build the dam, and there were none left who knew the ceremony in its entirety. Away from the river, the cult was apparently extinct by the 1880s. On the reservation, however, Yurok aristocrats continued to meet to organize ceremonies and perhaps to arbitrate conflicts at Requa and in the Kepel area well into the 1930s.[87] A cultural renaissance began at Hoopa Valley during the 1960s, as logging brought a measure of prosperity to the region and as a nationwide resurgence of Indian activism made its way to northwestern California.[88] Although the Klamath Basin Indians may have adapted well to their new social environment, they nonetheless retained a strong hold on their traditional culture. While salmon had become a source of cash for many, for the tribes it remained key to their sense of themselves as Indians.

The resolution of the desperate conflict of the nineteenth century only prepared the way for a new and different one later. At the root of the new struggle, as later chapters will show, was the steady depletion of the Klamath River salmon by causes over which the Indians had little control. The people of the Lower Klamath culture area had won precious time in which to adapt to life under the new regime because they were successful in defending their territory and because the commercial economy had not been able to tap the natural wealth of their fertile but forbidding country. After 1900, economic development provided outsiders with the tools to overcome the physical barriers that earlier had shielded the area and confronted both the salmon and their Indian trustees with more dangerous a threat than they had yet faced.

For the time being, however, the fight was over. Government had at last secured the Indians' rights to the land and the fish of the Klamath Basin, and for a while what remained of the native population was left in peace. Meanwhile, government biologists had discovered the importance of pristine spawning habitat to the health of the salmon fishery and had begun to press for the establishment of natural preserves for spawning fish. The federal government set aside Afognak Island in Alaska as such a preserve in 1892.[89] The next year, one U.S. Fish Commission scientist went so far as to propose setting aside an entire watershed, somewhere on the coast, as a "great national nursery" for salmon. The Klamath, he thought, was the most likely candidate: "the land extending some distance from the mouth of the Klamath River is, I believe, a Government reservation, requiring no special legislation to close the stream to outside commerce."[90] Although the nursery never came into being, this scientist, like Livingston Stone before him, had perceived the relationship between the well-being of native society and the productivity of the coast's most valuable fishery. Into the twentieth century, now in Anglo-American law as before in native religion, the future of the region's Indians and that of its salmon remained entwined.

II

Sun, wind, and sail,
1850–1910

4

Immigrant fisheries

As a rule, they take very little interest beyond their
immediate environment. . . . These men are first fishermen, second fishermen, third fishermen and Italians.
                                        – Henry A. Fisk (1905)[1]

California waters supported a motley assortment of fishing enterprises during
the first fifty years of statehood, just as they had while in the safekeeping
of the original inhabitants. David Starr Jordan, later president of Stanford
University and one of the leading ichthyologists of his day, noted in 1879
that California fishers invariably worked "within a few miles of shore by
means of small vessels or boats too frail to face the dangers of the open sea.
These are of diverse patterns, and the predominating types come from the
central seats of antipodal civilizations."[2] Chinese junks mingled with lateen-
rigged Italian boats and New England whaleboats. Nowhere else in the
United States, and possibly the world, has a fishing industry ever been so
ethnically diverse.[3]

This was partly a function of the great variety of the fishery resources that
California had to offer. As immigrants struggled to recreate familiar patterns
of life in their new home, they began fishing wherever they found resources
to which they could adapt available skills and that they could market among
people with whom they were accustomed to dealing. This was adaptation
between culture and environment of a sort, but one very different from the
kind that the Indians had worked out. Where aboriginal fishers had over
countless seasons learned to harvest their resources so that fish and fishers
alike would endure, Italians, Anglo-Saxons, Chinese, and other immigrant
fishers found niches only where the stream of commerce chanced to bring
them onto fertile patches along the rivers and coast.

Collectively, wrote Jordan, the immigrant fishers refused "nothing for
which they [were] sure of finding a market, from the whale to the abalone."[4]
San Francisco, the economic capital of nineteenth-century California, stood
unexcelled among U.S. cities for the year-round variety and abundance of
its fishery produce.[5] But there was no one fishing "industry" in California,
any more than there had been a single Indian culture. Each immigrant group

65

carried on its business in near isolation from the others, each with its own economic organization, its own methods, and its own markets.

Although by the 1880s California was one of the nation's leading fishery states, the industry never influenced the economic development of the region the way it had in seventeenth-century New England, for example, or in frontier Alaska. "Fish are not much sought after in California," wrote a visitor to the early Mexican settlement at Monterey, "in consequence of the productions of the land being so very abundant."[6] No one would have denied the fisheries' potential, but the Sacramento basin offered more profitable outlets for investment than fishing, and rough seas and uncertain winds kept offshore resources mostly out of reach until motorized boats became available after 1900. Throughout the nineteenth century, then, fishing remained primarily the calling of poor immigrants, carried on in the interstices of the economy by people who were not much inclined to change their customary ways of doing things so as to take part in the intensely commercial mainstream culture of the state. Indeed, by the end of the century, the fisheries were something of an embarrassment to public officials who wished to modernize them and increase their output. "Except for the salmon fisheries of the Sacramento and the Columbia, and the ocean fisheries in the immediate neighborhood of San Francisco," as Jordan wrote in 1880, "the fisheries of the Pacific Coast exist only as possibilities. For the most part only shore-fishing on the smallest scale is done, and no attempt is made to discover off-shore banks, or to develop them when discovered."[7]

Their economic marginality notwithstanding, the fisheries lay at the very heart of the ecological transformation that took place in late nineteenth-century California. The immigrants, indeed, settled down in no pristine wilderness but in an environment already disrupted by the decimation of fur-bearing mammals and of Indian populations in the region. After statehood, rapacious fishing contributed further to the process, seriously damaging some of the most sensitive resources. Fishers and their prey were not the only ones to make claims on the state's limited supply of water. Together, they fared badly in competition with mining, agriculture, and other industries for fishery habitat. Meanwhile, currents changed and seasons grew warmer and cooler, drier and wetter, as they always had, in no identifiable pattern. All these changes had significant effects on the fishing industry as it developed and all had much to do with shaping public policy for conserving the fisheries as it evolved at the same time (see Chapter 5).

The final quarter of the century saw one fishery after another come into hard times, some as they depleted their resources and others as they suffered the harmful environmental effects of other forms of water use. As California's waterways grew crowded, the insularity of the business and the sharply drawn ethnic boundaries between its different sectors began to dissolve. Public authorities moved gradually to bring the reluctant fishers under their control. Private and public responses to the problems of the 1880s and 1890s reorganized the industry and prepared the way for technological change that would later make fishing an important business in its own right.

Economic development

Most economic activity in nineteenth-century California took place in the Sacramento–San Joaquin watershed, which drained the central two-thirds of the state from the crest of the Sierra Nevada, through the lush marshes and grasslands of the Central Valley, and out through San Francisco Bay and the Golden Gate (see Figure 4.1). Early visitors to the Sacramento River found a beautiful waterway, teeming with life; in 1852 one took 3,500 pounds of river perch near Sacramento City in a single day.[8] The Sacramento was, moreover, second only to the Columbia as a habitat for salmon. Gold rushers who took a few minutes away from their diggings in the late forties could pitchfork fifty-pound salmon out of the Yuba and Bear Rivers in unlimited quantities. E. Gould Buffum and a companion shot thirty-five "splendid" fish out of the American River one afternoon in 1848. "There is every possibility," Buffum wrote in his journal, "that the salmon fishery will yet prove a highly lucrative business in California."[9] Nevertheless, as long as the Gold Rush was on and "the spirit of adventure and speculation remained abroad," as Bancroft put it, fish and other goods that took time to prepare and turn over were simply a bad gamble, and the "exorbitant" costs of labor, shipping, and warehousing kept the distribution of all food products in chaos until about 1852.[10]

Fishing was one of many local industries that emerged in the wake of the juggernaut of '49. Disappointed miners drifted out of the Sierra to take up more reliable occupations through the 1850s. Heavy floods in the winter of 1861–2 and the vicious droughts of the following biennium brought a final end to the Gold Rush. With imports momentarily checked by the Civil War the state was, in Bancroft's words, "thrown more upon its own resources, to the development of much neglected wealth."[11] Californians began to fish as the developing economy provided access to consumers who would buy the kinds they knew how to catch.

Shipping on the lower Sacramento and along the coast improved rapidly after the early fifties. The salmon trade began "assuming large proportions," according to the San Francisco *Alta*, when freight on the river dropped to $10 per ton in the summer of 1851.[12] Steamship service to Hawaii opened in 1861 and to China and Japan, encouraged by subsidies from the U.S. Post Office, in 1867. Subsidies from the government of Australia brought steamers laden with California salmon to that locality during the sixties, as well. Shipping to Eureka, on the northwestern coast, increased with lumber pro-

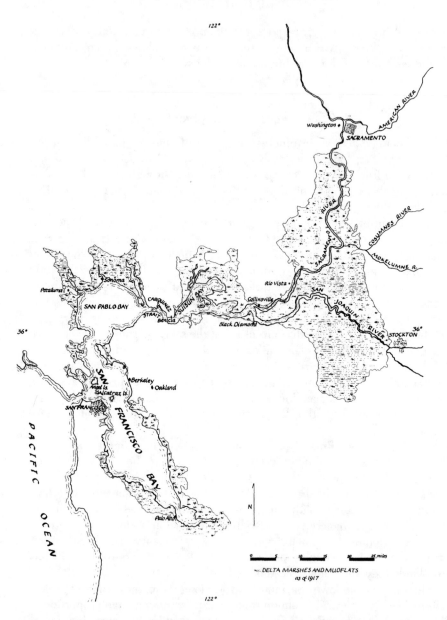

Figure 4.1. Outflow, Sacramento-San Joaquin Watershed, showing extent of marshes and mud flats in 1917. Map drawn by Ann Bartz and C. M. Martin. Source: Gilbert, *Hydraulic Mining Debris in the Sierra Nevada.*

duction during the late 1860s and early 1870s, providing transport for Eel River salmon and lumber for boatbuilding at San Francisco and southern ports.[13]

Rail construction eastward on the Central Pacific began in 1863. Thereafter, as soon as the state's rapidly expanding rail network touched a new coastal area, it lured fishing boats to it from up and down the coast. A narrow gauge railroad linked Monterey to the Southern Pacific system in 1874, stimulating agriculture and fisheries at that hitherto somnolent port. Commercial fishing began across Monterey Bay, at Santa Cruz, Soquel, and Aptos, when a line connected them with the San Francisco Bay area a short time later. Rapid settlement began in southern California during the early seventies, in anticipation of the railroad's arrival. Los Angeles was joined by rail to its harbor at San Pedro in 1869 and to the rest of the state via the Southern Pacific in 1876. San Diego, where in 1872 a frustrated local editor had wondered "Why don't some genius start a fish market in our town?," languished without rail service until 1885.[14] The most remote section of the coast, about Humboldt Bay, did not gain access to the rest of the state by rail until World War I.

One-third of the roughly 860,000 people who lived in California in 1880 were foreign born. Of the 3,000 fishers who worked there when Jordan surveyed the industry for the 1880 census, though, fully 92 percent were immigrants.[15] Fishing requires special skills as well as a tolerance for hard and dangerous work at low pay. It also has an unusual power to hold the loyalty of its workers and their children, who will to the consternation of modern economists stay in the business long after it ceases to produce incomes comparable to those in other trades. As commerce dispersed them across the state, those who took up fishing adapted skills they had brought with them to the new economic and biological environments of California. Because production required not only accessible resources but willing consumers, the immigrant fishers generally found their markets among people from cultural backgrounds similar to their own, tapping the waters of the state for a disparate collection of local and external markets. The fishing industry, then, consisted of a number of disaggregated sectors, each with its own techniques and markets and all of them transplanted to California from somewhere else.

New Englanders gave birth to the new state's most important fishery, that for Sacramento River chinook salmon. Salmon were valuable as market fish, as raw material for canning, and as quarry for the well-to-do sportfishers who first took leadership in conserving the state's wildlife. The system supported three runs of chinooks every year, the largest and most dramatic of which took place at the beginning of the fall rainy season. As the runs passed through the most densely populated part of the state, they testified to all Californians the immense natural wealth of the region. Both as a highly coveted source of wealth and as a symbol of frontier abundance, the salmon fishery more than any other shaped the development of public policy for the fishieries during the nineteenth century.

Even this most valuable fishery was slow in getting started as long as the Gold Rush kept workers wandering about in the Sierra foothills. One company organized to pack the fish in the spring of 1848, but after Marshall discovered gold at Sutter's mill in May all such efforts fell by the wayside for the time being. As late as 1858, two-thirds of the workers who had entered the fishery packed up and left for British Columbia when word reached them of a new gold strike on the Fraser River. But there were beginnings. During the fall 1849 run, three immigrants from New Haven, Connecticut, began experimenting with gill nets woven from different types of twine. After they found shoe thread heavy enough to pull twenty- to thirty-pound salmon out of the Sacramento and customers eager to pay a dollar a pound for them, several partnerships formed at once in Sacramento City. In 1852 the harvest produced 332,000 pounds of salmon at fifteen cents per pound.[16] In contrast to the generally high price of foodstuffs in California at the time, another New England native noted that fifteen cents "would be low at home."[17] The resource was abundant enough, however, to sustain a profitable fishery at that price. Shipments of cured fish began leaving San Francisco for Australia, which became one of the industry's most important markets, in 1853.[18]

Through the 1850s some sixty boats worked the Sacramento from a few miles above Sutter's Fort, at the confluence with the American River, down to its outlet into Suisun Bay. The most important landing station was at Rio Vista, which had its own steamship dock and stood just at the point where the river turned brackish and the salmon clustered for a few days before beginning their rush upstream. Although New Englanders brought the business to California, Greeks, Italians, and other Mediterranean immigrants quickly came to dominate the harvesting end of it. Their work was a model of independent, small-scale frontier enterprise. Two partners per boat, one to row and one to fish, set out their gill net just before high water and drifted down the river with the ebb tide. During the 1850s prices were apparently high enough and the fish abundant enough that one "drift" produced a satisfactory daily income; after it was over, the fishers drew in their nets, clubbed the fish to death as they came aboard, and rowed them back to market. At the height of the fall run, in September, river steamers would stop along their routes to take fish directly from the gillnetters as they worked.[19]

The fishery ran far below capacity through the fifties, held back by a still-volatile labor market and a shortage of salt for curing. Other New England immigrants, however, cleared the way for expansion by packing the fish in cans. William Hume arrived in 1852 with a gill net he had made before leaving his home on the Kennebec River in Maine, where Humes had fished

Table 4.1. *Sacramento River salmon fishery: cannery output and hatchery operations, 1872–90.*

Year	Canneries operating	Cases packed	Fish spawned at McCloud R.	Egss taken (000)
1872	—	—	12	50
1873	—	—	1,000	2,000
1874	—	2,500	—	5,752
1875	—	3,000	—	8,629
1876	2	10,000	—	7,498
1877	—	21,500	1,460	7,053
1878	6	34,017	3,600	12,246
1879	4	13,855	1,620	6,889
1880	9	62,000	2,164	7,396
1881	20	181,200	1,729	7,270
1882	19	200,000	999	3,991
1883	21	123,000	287	1,034
1884	—	81,450	0	0
1885	6	90,000	0	0
1886	9	39,300	0	0
1887	—	36,500	0	0
1888	6	68,075	—	—
1889	3	57,300	—	—
1890	—	25,065	—	—

Sources: Cobb, "Pacific Salmon Fisheries," p. 572; USFC, *Reports.*

salmon since the American Revolution. In 1864, by then joined by several of his brothers, Hume persuaded an old schoolmate who had a lobster-canning business in New Brunswick, to come to California. Aboard a scow moored at Washington (now Broderick), across the river from Sacramento City, Hume, Hapgood, and Company packed salmon for three seasons. They did not do as well as they would have liked: After all, San Francisco consumers could buy fresh salmon, and half of the 4,000 cases they packed during their first season spoiled. Just when the partners were on the verge of disbanding, a San Francisco merchant found a ready market for canned salmon in Australia and rekindled their interest. In 1867 the company moved to the Columbia River, where the runs were bigger. There, in the words of R. D. Hume's biographer, they laid "the foundation of the nineteenth-century American salmon canning business."[20]

The salmon industry grew rapidly on the Columbia. Two canneries reappeared on the Sacramento in 1874 and, four years later when a rise in prices coincided with heavy runs of fish, the industry took off.[21] Table 4.1 lists the output of canneries on the river, along with activity at Livingston Stone's hatchery on the McCloud River as a rough index of the number of fish that escaped to spawn in the river's headwaters. Harvests of raw fish averaged nearly 10 million pounds per year between 1880 and 1883. By 1884 there were twenty-one canneries on the river and more than 1,500 boats to service them. Money flowed at Rio Vista as it had in Mother Lode towns thirty years earlier. But at that point, the fishery collapsed. The fall run of 1884, according to the state Fish Commissioners, was "the lightest that was ever known in the memory of the oldest fisherman."[22] By 1886 the pack had declined to fewer than 40,000 cases. Yields from the river fishery continued to decline, with minor interruptions, until the last cannery closed its doors in 1919.

Here was the fisherman's problem in laboratory form. Access to salmon was free to anyone who could put a gill net into the water or who had capital to build a cannery. The industry's gauntlet simply permitted too few fish to escape upstream to spawn new ones for future runs. Any fisher or any canner who might have left a salmon in the water so as to conserve the resource would simply have given that fish to competitors. As the fishery collapsed, the industry moved northward more or less bodily, workers and capitalists together, to exploit as-yet-undamaged runs in the Pacific Northwest and Alaska. Enough stayed behind, however, making just enough money from the crippled fishery to stay in business, to ensure that the stock did not recover on its own.

Key to the salmon fishery's self-destruction was the fact that, to the market, a fish was a commodity with a price set by the specifically human, short-term functions of supply and demand. In economic terms, the industry paid no rent to its resource: The value of a fish's foregone contribution to sustaining the supply did not add to its price on the unregulated market. As if they were gold nuggets, the industry ripped fish out of their environment with no thought to the long-term consequences of its actions. A fish, however, is more than a gold nugget. It is part of a species – a coherent, self-perpetuating entity that *works*: It accumulates nutrients from its environment according to a genetic code adapted to its particular environment. Unfortunately for this particular species, its genetic program included instructions for collecting that accumulated food into a form, a salmon run, which happened to be convenient for the human economy to tap for its own purposes. Likewise, the fishery was more than a disaggregated collection of workers and capital. The ecological function of gill-netters and canners was to serve as this tap, or conduit, through which the useful fruits of the animals' work flowed from the ocean into the human community. The salmon's food, the species itself, fishers, canners, and consumers were all temporary repositories in a continuous stream of energy and materials, a stream from which all in their turn drew life.

Just as the salmon worked according to a common genetic program, participants in the industry worked according to shared instructions of their own – cultural rather than genetic ones they received from the market and from New England tradition, which taught them to value salmon, to catch them in a certain way, and to follow the signals of price in their use of it. Anglo-Saxon fishers thus had a collective ecological identity no less than the salmon did. While as individuals they may have made independent choices in pursuit of entrepreneurial gain, as a group they behaved in patterns that persisted over time and from place to place. They inaugurated the industry in California as they fled declining salmon fisheries on the Kennebec and other New England rivers. The market to which they supplied fish remained the same regardless of when and where they tapped the resource: Canned salmon from San Francisco, as from later fisheries in the Pacific Northwest and Alaska, went overwhelmingly to English-speaking communities in Great Britain, the eastern United States, Canada, Australia, and New Zealand.[23]

What took place on the Sacramento River was thus not an isolated phenomenon but part of a cyclical pattern. The fate of the Central Valley salmon was of a piece with the depletion of the New England salmon fisheries before it and of the northeastern Pacific salmon fisheries it colonized as it died out in its turn. In a sense, the industry behaved like a community of swidden, or slash-and-burn, farmers, working one patch of land until its fertility declined and then moving on to another. The difference was that, as long as their society and culture remain intact, swidden farmers regulate their demand for resources and their harvest over the long term, so that eventually they can return to old plots and use them again. Left intact, their social order adapts to its resources so as to perpetuate both, just as a biological species adapts to its environment over the long run. This was likewise the source of stability and longevity of the hunter-gatherer cultures of California Indians. Following the price mechanism, however, the commercial fishery left a trail of devastated resources in its wake, each with enough pressure left on it to ensure that it would not revive for future use. As long as the industry's collective behavior remained uncorrected, the catastrophic depletion of one fishery was no guarantee that the industry would not act in the same way in some other place at some other time.

Cultural and genetic programs for behavior persist or change over time in much the same way. Species and societies alike persist if their behavior promotes long-term survival within a particular context. If the context changes, for whatever reason, they must adapt or die out. Human culture is at once more flexible and more prolific than any genetic program because its medium is thought rather than molecular biology. Not only can it adapt quickly to a changing environment, but it can deliberately alter that environment so as to preserve itself. Western capitalism is the most flexible and prolific of all forms of social and cultural organization because it delegates to individuals a great deal of license to do this in their immediate self-interest.

This is precisely the source of capitalism's success in propagating itself, at the expense of other social forms; given "the fishermen's problem," it also explains the long trail of environmental devastation that capitalism has left in the wake of its history.[24] The Sacramento River salmon fishery provides only one relatively clear-cut example.

Whaling was another New England fishery that colonized California waters during the 1850s. By 1848, the U.S. whaling industry had pushed into the most remote corners of the Pacific Ocean, but as its resources grew scarce it had begun to decline even before it faced competition for its markets from petroleum products. Close by the California shore, though, were great numbers of gray, blue, and humpback whales, "inviting one apparently to come out and take them" as one observer put it; they testified to the fertility of the waters offshore no less than the salmon had those of the Central Valley.[25]

During the 1830s, Richard Henry Dana had found what became Los Angeles Harbor, "as well as all the other open ports upon the coast . . . filled with whales."[26] He referred to the California gray whale, a relatively primitive species which alone among the large whales bears its young in inshore bays and lagoons. A few Arctic whalers had tried hunting gray whales along the Baja California coast in the winter of 1846 but had abandoned the effort because the whales were too willing to fight back when harassed on their own calving grounds. During the Gold Rush whalers generally stayed clear of California because provisions were so costly there and because so many of their crew jumped ship and headed for the mines. They returned after 1855, lured by lower prices, fewer desertions, and preferential fees for pilotage in San Francisco Bay. By the end of the decade, "every winding and intricate estuary" on the lower coast was infested with ships.[27]

These vessels became the conduit through which California absorbed the Portuguese immigrants who became so important to its fishing and agricultural industries. New England whalers had since the 1820s touched at the Azores to take on supplies and cheap crew on their way south. Emigration gathered force in the 1850s as crop failure drove out surplus labor and gold fever drew men to the Pacific. A few Azoreans, having jumped ship in San Francisco or Honolulu, established colonies along the coast where they could use skills learned aboard the high-seas whalers on their own behalf. Two such colonies appeared at Monterey during the mid-1850s and two more at Crescent City and San Diego, at either end of the coast, shortly thereafter. Guided from shore, a handful of men would row out into the path of the migrating whales, kill them with hand weapons, and tow them back to shore for flensing and trying out.[28]

When Confederate cruisers brought high-seas whaling to a halt in the early sixties and the price of oil trebled, shore whaling began with a vengeance. The best season at Monterey was that of 1862–3, when each of the port's two companies produced 1,700 barrels of oil, the rough equivalent of sixty-eight male gray whales or forty-two average humpbacks. At the fishery's peak during the early 1870s, there were eleven stations along the coast from Crescent City to Punta Banda, just south of the Mexican border. By then, most had adopted modern bomb lances and harpoon guns because the animals had grown wary and increasingly difficult to catch. Humboldt Bay, meanwhile, supported a regular summer fishery for shark, whose liver yielded an oil comparable in quality to that of whales. Sea lions came under attack during the 1860s, also, for the mere half barrel of oil each contained.[29]

California shore whaling went into decline during the mid-1870s, in part because petroleum was a cheaper substitute for whale oil by then, but more importantly because the industry had nearly extinguished its prey. Oldtimers in the business told of counting up to 1,000 gray whales each day during the winter "down season," when the animals migrated from their summer haunts in the Arctic to their calving grounds on the lower coast. By 1874, however, the count was down to a hundred or two. Humpbacks, too, were scarce in 1875. By the end of the century only a few men at Monterey remained in the business. Some rejoined the high-seas fleet, while others took up market fishing in San Diego and Monterey.[30]

Although hardly a trace of the vital and expansive industry they established survived into the twentieth century, a third group of fishers began work in California in much the same way as did the others. The first camp of Chinese fishers, populated no doubt by would-be miners whom racial hostility had driven out of the Sierra, appeared on the eastern shore of San Francisco Peninsula by 1854. Chinese exports of dried fish and shellfish from San Francisco increased markedly in volume and frequency after 1856. When the railroad brought thousands of Chinese workers to California in the 1860s, Chinese fishing settlements sprouted along the entire length of the coast from Baja California to the Oregon border. Near Sacramento, Jordan found them "the most industrious and persistent fishermen on the river," fishing for freshwater species and buying up throwaway varieties from other fishers to cure for the provisioning trade. One very remote group appeared on Puget Sound that was, in Jordan's words, "wholly similar to those south of San Francisco."[31] At all of them, choice of target species, harvesting techniques, and processing methods were transplanted unaltered from China.

Most important among the Chinese fisheries were those for abalone out of San Diego and shrimp in San Francisco Bay. By the end of the 1860s there were two colonies on San Diego Bay, one on the city's waterfront to supply the local market trade and another across the bay, at Point Loma, which pursued the abalone fishery as far south as Cedros Island. In 1886, a dozen companies operated a total of eighteen junks out of San Diego, twelve of them in the abalone fleet. The largest of these measured more than fifty feet in the keel and boasted fifteen tons draft when the rest of the coastal fishing fleet claimed few vessels over five tons.[32] Jordan asserted that the

Chinese had been accustomed to drying abalone at home. Given the animal's slow rate of reproduction, they probably did so under some form of legal control. In California there were plenty to be had, probably because the animals' chief predators, the sea otters, had been exterminated some thirty years before. Had there been any otters in the areas in which the Chinese worked, there simply would not have been enough abalone to support commercial harvesting.[33] By 1880 annual landings surpassed four million pounds. Huge bales of dried abalone, piled up on the city's wharf, drew repeated notice from the *San Diego Union* in 1884 and 1885.[34]

Chinese people began shrimping in San Francisco Bay in 1871. A few Italian fishers had made some headway in the business, but could not compete with the Asians' ability to catch them cheaply and abandoned it.[35] Like the abalone fishery at San Diego, this was a highly visible activity. By the late 1880s hundreds of nets were staked out all over the bay, with fifty junks from two dozen widely scattered camps to tend them. By 1895, when the Chinese harvest reached 5.4 million pounds worth $163,000, shrimp was the most productive fishery in California. Only the Bay Area oyster business, which fattened transplanted East Coast oysters for sale, surpassed it in tonnage and market value. To a federal official, "the value of this apparently worthless fishery carried on by a few miserable but industrious barbarians [was] certainly surprising."[36]

At the peak of their power, these "miserable but industrious barbarians" made up one-third of the fishery workers in California. Their ecological function was similar to that of the salmon canning industry: They tapped California waters to supply familiar provisions to people of their kind all around the Pacific Rim. In fishing, however, as in anything else they did, the Chinese immigrants' iron determination to preserve their customary ways of doing things drew unfavorable notice from other Californians. "The whole air and look" of the junks on the Sacramento River, sniffed David Starr Jordan, "was decidedly foreign, and I might say oriental."[37] A settlement worker complained that "America may be for Americans, but at the present time China is levying upon us for an important food supply without patronizing American labor for food, clothing, or apparatus."[38] Exterminating the Chinese fisheries turned out to be as important a catalyst for the development of nineteenth-century public policy for the fisheries in California as was preserving the salmon fishery, which was the domain of "Americans."

Italians were among the latest to arrive of all the immigrant fishing groups in California, although they came to characterize the industry more than any other.[39] The first may have come to California as gold rushers like everyone else, but Mediterraneans faced the same hostility in the mines as other dark-skinned people and quickly gave it up. Most of the early arrivals were northern Italians, from Genoa and the Camogli district, where merchant ships had long stopped to trade and perhaps take on a few adventurous

Figure 4.2. Italian fishing boats at San Francisco, ca., 1880. Photo courtesy of Bancroft Library, University of California, Berkeley.

types as crew. During the 1850s they concentrated in the poorer areas of San Francisco, where they built communities as much like the ones they had left in Italy as they could make them. At North Beach they began to fish for retail markets, at first serving only their immediate neighborhoods and drawing customers from the outside as they grew. Others settled along the lower Sacramento River where, joined by a few Greek and Spanish immigrants, they entered the salmon fishery. Emigrants from southern Italy overwhelmed their northern compatriots after 1870, as trans-Atlantic shipping became cheaper and as prolonged agricultural depression drove farmers and fishers out of their old homes. By 1880 lateen-rigged Italian boats made up about two-thirds of the eighty-five or so fishing boats serving the city: Broad bands of bright blue and green that began to appear along the gunwales of the formerly all-white boats gave evidence of Sicilian inroads in the business.[40]

The Italian felucca, shown in Figure 4.2, served central California market fisheries essentially unchanged for fifty years. The lateen rig proved well adapted to the uncertain winds and seas of California because it worked easily into the wind and was light enough to permit the fishers to row if they needed to. The boats carried gear for many different kind of fish in season. Larger ones, perhaps as long as thirty-five feet in the keel and equipped with a covered hatchway that provided cramped but dry shelter for the crew of two or three on overnight trips, fished outside the Golden Gate in summer, while smaller boats kept to the Bay at all times of the year. Sicilians often began as employees of the northerners, but gradually went into business for themselves; Genoese fishers became brokers and creditors, worked more valuable deep-water fisheries outside the Gate, or moved southward along the coast. A few appeared at San Diego in 1870–1.[41]

Italian fishers resembled the Chinese in the tenacity with which they clung to traditional ways of doing business. One study of the San Francisco Italian community concluded that "fishermen proved that . . . a group could isolate itself almost totally from the larger society, recreating patterns of economic and social organization almost entirely from the Old World."[42] Fishers were more likely than other Italians to work at their old occupations with people from their places of birth, to marry within their communities, and to keep their sons in the family business. About two-thirds of the men at North Beach were unmarried, the vast majority unnaturalized and speaking no English. Several, at least, spent their working lives in San Francisco and returned home to Italy to die. Their resistance to economic incentive repeatedly drew frustrated comment from government officials.[43]

All these groups – Anglo-Saxons, Portuguese, Chinese, and Italians – colonized the California fisheries during the first half-century of statehood, bringing with them discrete and more or less coherent associations of markets, target species, and material cultures. Although unlike the Indian fishers they were willing participants in the market, they were not the autonomous, individual competitors of formal anthropology and economics. Their culture and their determination to preserve their corporate identities had everything to do with the ways in which they responded to the opportunities that the resources offered them. That some were more "American" than others or that some took greater part in the mainstream culture of the state did nothing to alter the essential similarity of the various groups' purposes as they brought the state's fishery resources into production.

They did not prosper long. Shore whaling and the salmon industry were only the most spectacular examples of collapse. Jordan noted a great decline in the freshwater fisheries of the Sacramento in 1879; where in 1852 a single fyke net would produce 250 pounds of fish every day, by the latter date it took twenty nets to catch seventy-five pounds in a day.[44] San Francisco Bay had been declining rapidly since 1866. In 1879, Jordan estimated, "probably the bay does not contain one-twentieth the number of fish that it did twenty years ago."[45] Monterey Bay had been declining since the early seventies. At San Diego, hotel keepers began complaining during the mid-1880s that they could not keep their guests supplied with fresh fish, while a fishing captain who worked nearshore grounds for that trade pointed out that his

4. Immigrant fisheries

yields were not nearly what they once had been.[46] By the mid-1
seemed as if the Chinese were the only fishers who were making good livings
from California waters.

Ecological stress

The ecological systems in which the immigrant fishers established places for
themselves during the second half of the nineteenth century were, in spite
of their fertility and diversity, vulnerable to disruption at several points.
Some of the most valuable fisheries faced outright extermination during the
ecological catastrophe that befell California after the gold discovery. Many
suffered indirectly, as human beings reclaimed their habitat for other uses
or poisoned it with waste products from their various industries. All were
subject, as they had been for millennia, to random environmental change.
Modern observers are only slightly more able, relative to the complexity of
the problem, to sort out the tangle of forces that may have had economic
effects on the nineteenth century than were the Indians or immigrants who
perceived them firsthand. Complaints of frustrated participants in the industry about how others were ruining their business are not entirely trust-
worthy, although patterns do emerge from them at times. Harvest levels
are often as likely to reflect price movements and technological change as
changes in resource productivity. Many of the ecological changes that affected them were readily apparent to interested observers at the time, however, whereas hints of others emerge from the historical record with the aid
of recent advances in our knowledge of how environmental systems function.

Some of the most valuable and easily harvested animals were those living
near the top of their food chains. These were fewer in number than other,
less complex life forms and tended to breed slowly and in intricate ways, all
of which made them vulnerable to overharvesting in short order. First to
disappear were the furbearing mammals: sea otters, seals, and beaver. Many
were depleted even before 1850, and by the turn of the century most were
close to extinction. Otters, most precious of all furbearers, became the object
of intense commercial rivalry between Spanish, Russian, British, and Yankee
fleets after the 1780s. Despite some effort on the part of Mexican governors
to protect the animals from foreign hunters, by 1840 only scattered pockets
of them remained, and within a few years more the population ceased any
longer to support a fishery by itself. This offered them scant protection,
however, because the price of their pelts continued to climb and ships
engaged in other hunts would take them whenever they found them. In the
early days of the hunt the principal market for otter skin was at Canton,
where during the 1830s a going price of $30 per pelt sustained huge profits
for ships in the China trade. Prices reached fantastic levels during the 1890s:

The last legally sold pelt brought $2,000 in London in 1900. After that, the animal was thought extinct, although the survival of a small group off the desolate Big Sur coast remained the closely guarded secret of local residents until 1938.[47]

Other furbearers received similar attention. Fur seals came in two varieties, one that bred on Guadalupe Island off the Baja California coast and a northern variety that ranged as far south as San Diego but that kept its rookeries in the Bering Sea, especially on the Pribilof Islands. Fisheries for these animals began soon after the otter hunt. By 1840 the Guadalupe fur seal had all but expired, while the more numerous northern fur seal supported an indiscriminate multinational fishery until they came under treaty protection in 1911. Beaver populated the Klamath River Basin and the lower reaches of the Sacramento, where they competed with salmon for habitat by damming and flooding streams where the fish would otherwise have spawned. Trapping began in California in the 1820s, by U.S. explorers and by the Hudson's Bay Company. Beaver were still numerous in the Sacramento Delta during the early 1840s, but most were gone by 1850. This, as well as the cessation of Indian fishing, may well account for the great abundance of salmon reported by central California observers during the 1850s.[48]

The salmon were not plentiful enough, however, to withstand the destructive harvests of the 1880s. Here, the salmon's complex and elegant strategy for replenishing its kind forced the entire stock to run a gauntlet of nets and made possible overfishing of the most brutal kind. Livingston Stone had observed as early as 1878 that a fisher's strike on the lower river had visibly increased the numbers of fish arriving at his hatchery on the McCloud. The runs were so large and the fishery so intensive, though, that the market could not absorb them. During one tremendous burst between September 15 and 17, 1880, fishers simply threw 9,000 dead salmon back into the river because no one would buy them. Only one-half of the 10.8 million pounds of fish harvested that year ended up in cans; the rest were dumped on the San Francisco retail market, with huge quantities going to waste. Such bountiful harvests lasted only four years, or precisely one normal salmon generation, and were no more.[49]

Oil fisheries for whales, sea lions, and elephant seals were similarly cruel. Lagoon whalers sought out their prey in their breeding sanctuaries, selectively choosing females with calves, as Captain Scammon put it, "that the parent animal might be easily struck."[50] The Azoreans' tools were primitive and not always lethal: at San Diego only about a third of the whales struck with harpoons ever reached the trying works onshore. The rest escaped, perhaps to die later, or sank, useless. Of the sixteen whales recovered at the Cojo Viejo station in 1879 only one did not bear scars from misfired bomb lances. The stock, which may have amounted to 15,000 animals early in the nineteenth century, declined to half that by the century's close.[51]

Elephant seals supported an intensive oil fishery along with the gray whale, declined at the same time, and were presumed extinct by the 1880s. Like the fur seals, these were easy marks for hunters because they bore their young on island rookeries. When a party of naturalists discovered a handful of them on Guadalupe Island in 1892, they shot all but one or two for use as laboratory specimens.[52] Sea lions were more resilient because they were more numerous to begin with and were of such low unit value that declining prices for oil closed the commercial fishery for them entirely.

The systematic removal by 1900 of most of the fur- and oil-bearing mammals from California waters had a significant impact on the ecology of the region and therefore on the history of other fisheries. The decimation of the Sacramento Valley beaver population, along with the cessation of Indian fishing, may well account for the great abundance of salmon reported by observers during the 1850s. Chinese abalone hunters probably found pickings as rich as they did because they came to a coast that had been stripped of its sea otters. As modern abalone fishers would learn to their chagrin, sea otters and commercial abalone gatherers cannot live in the same place at the same time. Contemporary accusations that Chinese fishers "stripped the coast bare" of abalone in the 1870s and 1880s were probably true, then, because it is not difficult to thin down such slowly reproducing animals. It is also true, however, that the Chinese were only filling an ecological niche left vacant for them by Yankee and other otter hunters.

The Chinese, moreover, may actually have been doing a service for the other fishers who complained about their depredations. Abalone and sea urchin graze voraciously on kelp, which provides food and shelter for a great many fishes important to market and recreational fisheries alike. Where there are even a few otters to keep the grazers thinned out, the kelp grows luxuriantly. Coastal waters with abundant kelp support a greater total mass of living matter than they would otherwise, and more of that mass is concentrated in the bodies of animals high enough on the food chain to be useful to people. Where there are no otters, there are more grazers but less kelp and, on the whole, less productive waters.[53]

Prehistoric hunters in the Aleutian Islands who apparently depleted their supply of otters induced dramatic changes in the ecology of neighboring waters, triggering the replacement of one community dominated by otters, kelp, and abundant finfishes by another consisting of no otters, abundant molluscs, and fewer finfishes.[54] A similar interaction may have taken place in nineteenth-century California and may help to explain the frequent references to bad times in coastal fisheries that appeared between the mid-1870s and the mid-1890s. Because even a few sea otters will keep shellfish thin enough to limit their depressing effect on nearby stands of kelp, it may not have been until the 1860s or 1870s that the otter population was low nough to permit the grazers to bloom. At that point, the productivity of

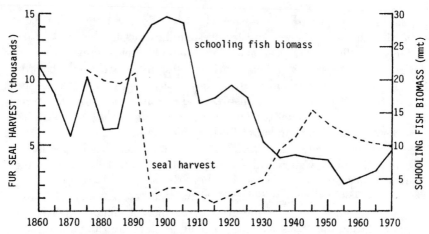

Figure 4.3. Harvest of northern fur seals at Pribilof Islands correlated with standing crops of schooling fishes in the California Current, 1860–1970. Source: FAO, *Mammals in the Seas*, v. 1, p. 242.

nearshore fisheries would begin to decline and nearshore fishers would begin to complain.

The abalone industry, then, grew rapidly as the 1870s progressed. Jordan noted that it had "stripped the whole coast [between Cedros Island and San Diego] of this shell" by 1879, and by 1888 the Chinese had thinned out intertidal areas along the Channel Islands and the nearby mainland to a perceptible degree.[55] Monterey clams and abalone were "nearly exterminated" by 1888–9.[56] Whether or not the Chinese harvested as much abalone and sea urchin as the otters had is uncertain, given the lack of reliable statistics for the fishery and the unknown size of the otter population before the hunt began, but in 1888 the kelp was so thick off Santa Barbara that steamships could not come into port without having a channel cut through the beds for them first.[57] The years after 1890, moreover, brought greatly increased catches of barracuda, bonito, groupers, sea basses, and other kelp-living fish to ports from San Diego to Monterey.[58] There is, then, a hint in the record that the Chinese activity may have had something to do with the dramatic recovery of nearshore fisheries in the 1890s.

The near extermination of the larger marine mammals by the 1890s may also have contributed to the widely noted abundance of marketable finfishes in those years. Figure 4.3 suggests such a relationship. The dashed line shows the harvest of northern fur seals at their rookeries on the Pribilof Islands in the Bering Sea. The island hunt began in the late eighteenth century, about the same time as that for sea otter; by the 1890s seals had come under some regulation, but at the same time an uncontrolled fishery for them began on the high seas. Pelagic sealing was banned by international treaty in 1911, by which time the fishery had all but expired for want of prey. The solid line shows the weight of the standing crop of coastal schooling fishes in the California Current from Appendix B. This crop reached unprecedentedly high levels at the turn of the century and then began to decline, as the seal population began to recover under effective protection. Again, the figure only hints at a relationship between the two events: "I would not even know how to test it," said the biologist who noted the correlation. Nonetheless, fur seals consume enormous amounts of such fishes; during the 1970s, biologists estimated that they took some 7 percent of the northern anchovy population each year during their time in California waters.[59] The decimation, not only of fur seals but of whales and several other mammals as well, may have contributed to such abnormally high populations of their fodder at the turn of the century. Unexploited reserves of fodder fishes, meanwhile, may have drawn larger-than-usual numbers of other predators such as salmon or albacore within reach of California fishers at the same time.

Correlations between the depletion of top predators in offshore waters and changes in ecologically related fisheries are difficult to make because such interactions are complex. Coastal fisheries were not highly developed in the nineteenth century, and only sketchy records exist for those that did come into use. Relationships between economic development and the ecology of the inshore fisheries of the Sacramento basin, however, emerge more clearly from the record. Most economic activities in the drainage made use of the system's rivers in one way or another, and the welfare of the fisheries that depended on them for life offers a clear measure of their aggregate impact on the system. The mining industry's use of water for power and for waste disposal, the dumping of municipal and industrial wastes into San Francisco Bay, and the reclamation of riparian and tide lands in the lower reaches of the drainage all had discernible effects on the fisheries and helped shape the progress both of the industry and of its political oversight.

Salmon fisheries began to suffer within a few years of the onset of mining in the Sierra foothills. Spring-run fish were the first to go; these spent as much as a year inshore before spawning. Sediment from the mines filled the pools where spring-run salmon rested; it smothered the gravel riffles where all the salmon spawned. Adult fish turned back from their courses when their gills clogged with mud. Those that completed their journey lost their progeny when sediment covered their eggs or water diversions exposed them to the air. The Sacramento had its last healthy run of spring salmon in 1852. One after another, the system's tributaries lost their salmon, the Yuba when hydraulic mining began at Nevada City in 1853 and the Mokelumne when water companies diverted the water of that stream to serve the mines of Amador County two years later. In January 1862, heavy rains carried down the accumulated debris of nine relatively dry years and sent a wave of mud washing over the Feather River bottomlands. The debris raised the bed of the Sacramento at the state capital by six or seven feet and perceptibly increased the turbidity of San Francisco Bay. The flood wiped out nearly all the oyster beds on the Marin and Alameda county bayshores; it also brought an end to what salmon remained in the Feather and American rivers.[60]

In 1872 the new State Board of Fish Commissioners concluded that "probably the most important cause for the decrease of salmon in our rivers is from mining."[61] The Humes and Hapgood attributed their bad showing at Sacramento to mining pollution, although the violent weather of the early 1860s may also have damaged the runs which they tried to harvest.[62] During the mid-1870s, however, the fishing improved. In 1875 the Commissioners reported that salmon were more plentiful than they had been at any time since the beginning of U.S. occupation. They attributed the revival to the beneficient effects of season closures and artificial propagation at Livingston Stone's hatchery on the McCloud.[63] One more likely cause, however, was the decline of gold production to unprecedented lows in 1872 and 1873. Mining output leapt forward again in 1878, but in the interim the industry had given both the salmon and the packers time to muster for the spectacular runs of the late 1870s and early 1880s.

Then, as the canners feverishly stripped the river of its salmon, hydraulic miners upstream washed entire hillsides of gravel and mud into the system to get at what gold remained in them. The streets and farms of Marysville and other valley towns were awash in debris. By 1884 the riverbed at the mouth of the Feather had risen at least twenty feet from the time mining began; in some places the bed of the Sacramento, precariously confined between fragile artificial levees, lay higher than the surrounding lands. Local residents sued in federal court to stop the mining. Judge Lorenzo Sawyer of the Ninth Circuit Court of Appeals granted the injunction in the 1884 case of *Woodruff* v. *North Bloomfield Gravel Mining Co. et al.*, noting that the devastation wrought on Central Valley agriculture and urban life far outweighed any benefit to the state's economy that the now-declining gold industry might offer.[64] But by then salmon had forsaken the San Joaquin, Tuolumne, and Stanislaus Rivers. Silt carried down into the bay, meanwhile, had smothered the last of the oyster beds on the Alameda County bayshore.[65]

Gold output reached its nineteenth-century nadir in 1889. Three years later, as the first of the 1889 generation of salmon were due to return, the Fish Commissioners hailed an "extraordinary increase" in the run and the resumption of packing by several canneries on the lower river. They were at a loss to explain the increase, except that it did "not appear to be the natural increase from the work of the Commission in hatching and depositing these fish."[66] Two years later, however, they were less reticent and took credit for the recovery.[67] By 1894, salmon were "very plentiful" in the

Mokelumne and upper San Joaquin rivers again, for the first time in decades.[68]

By the late seventies municipal and industrial pollution were apparently making inroads on the quality of estuarine waters in the state. In a report to the Fish Commission in 1879, W.N. Lockington warned that "already the fishery carried on in the Bay of San Francisco is much less productive than it was in the early days of the American occupation." The greatest injury to the Bay, he continued, was "that inflicted by the constant fouling of the waters and consequent destruction of life by the fetid outpourings of our sewers."[69] San Diego Bay fisheries were clearly in decline by 1893; local fishers attributed their losses in part to city sewage and waste disposal at the mouth of the harbor. At Port Harford, the new petroleum industry claimed its first victims between 1900 and 1904 as oil steamers that drained their ballast into the harbor utterly extinguished the fishing industry at that place.[70]

Water pollution claimed the Bay Area oyster industry during the first decade of the twentieth century. Growers moved to the southern end of San Francisco Bay to escape the heavy siltation that hydraulic mining had brought to the Marin and Alameda county bayshores but won only a short reprieve. Over the 1890s a burgeoning fruit packing industry in Santa Clara county induced radical changes in the ecology of the South Bay, fertilizing great blooms of algae with cannery effluent. By a process known as eutrophication, organic pollution gradually depletes a body of water's dissolved oxygen, thereby rendering it useless for animal life. Oysters defend themselves from oxygen-poor or otherwise inhospitable environments by closing their shells tightly and lowering their metabolism drastically. Reduced oxygen in their water, then, was probably the reason why South Bay oysters "clammed up," as it were, and ceased to feed. Oyster yields dropped by half between 1900 and 1904 and collapsed entirely after 1908.[71]

Sacramento–San Joaquin system fisheries suffered most irrevocably from the reclamation of delta and tidelands for agricultural and other uses. Artificial levees along the Sacramento protected surrounding lands from flooding so as to make them useful for human use but also short-circuited the river's natural flood-control system, thereby increasing the severity of floods that broke through the dikes in 1861–2 and afterward, reducing the river's ability to settle debris, and cutting off vast expanses of habitat for fish and wildlife. Along San Francisco Bay, the reclamation of tide and marshlands had begun immediately after U.S. occupation, as a prodigal government at Sacramento sold off thousands of acres to private owners. In a brilliant study of the effects of mining debris on the Sacramento watershed, Grove Karl Gilbert found that by 1901 15 percent of the marshland adjoining San Francisco Bay had been reclaimed. Along the eastern shore of the bay, between Newark and Berkeley, 5,000 to 6,000 acres, or one-fourth of the East Bay's inventory of marshland, had been diked off for use as salt evaporators. By 1912 San Pablo Bay had lost 42,000 acres, fully 64 percent of its original inventory of marshland. Reclamation was farthest advanced, though, in the Sacramento–San Joaquin Delta, which Gilbert estimated contained 63 percent of the entire system's fresh- and saltwater marsh.[72]

In all, San Francisco Bay lost 26 percent of its most fertile fishery habitat by the turn of the twentieth century. In addition, Gilbert concluded, tideland reclamation and the filling up of the bay with mining debris had reduced the bay's tidal volume by 4 percent. Reclamation meant lost habitat and food for fishery resources, both in the bay and outside the Golden Gate, whereas abbreviated tides meant reduced nutrients and energy for what remained of the estuary's most valuable parts. Inland, reclamation degraded freshwater fisheries more quickly and more severely than it did that for salmon, which does not feed once it enters fresh water to spawn. Federal officials reported in 1872 that "all of the fish of [the Sacramento] river except salmon are disappearing with unexampled rapidity."[73] Ironically, Chinese who fished the delta sloughs for cheap freshwater varieties and who worked the Bay for shrimp drew the blame for the decline on Sacramento watershed fisheries even though they suffered much more serious losses to pollution and reclamation than did the whites, to whom the salmon was foremost as an economic resource and as a political symbol.

Although their precise effects are impossible to trace, the blotting out of important predators and the massive ecological changes wrought by human industry had perceptible effects on the productivity of fisheries in California waters by the end of the nineteenth century. Other ecological fluctuations, having little to do with human activity, may also have influenced the business by way of their impact on the availability for harvest of commercially valuable species. Taken together, what indices of such changes are available suggest, as does the historical record, a period of hard times for most fisheries between the mid-1870s and the mid-1890s, just as public officials began to experiment with new methods for promoting and regulating the fishing industry (see Appendix A).

From a number of biological surveys undertaken by the federal government during the second half of the nineteenth century, Carl L. Hubbs of the Scripps Institution of Oceanography concluded that southern California waters were significantly warmer from at least 1850 into the 1870s than afterward. Warm-water fishes were unusually prominent in those years as far north as Monterey Bay. The phenomenon seems to have persisted as late as 1879, when Jordan surveyed the West Coast fisheries for the Tenth Census. Temperatures and fauna, according to Hubbs, remained relatively unchanged in the vicinity of San Francisco from 1850 into the 1940s, when he published his research.[74]

Because fishing remained at a relatively low level during this early period, these conditions were probably of little economic significance except insofar as warmer-than-average temperatures and below-average precipitation may have helped to depress the salmon fishery at Sacramento in the 1860s, thus inducing the Humes and Hapgood, for example, to move to Oregon. Dry season temperatures in 1864 and 1865, when the Humes packed salmon on the Sacramento, averaged two degrees above the half-century mean. After the mid-1870s, a cooler and wetter, more "marine" climate returned to California, replacing the "continental" conditions of the 1850s and 1860s. Salmon then returned in strength, along with the canners.

Hubbs found a general trend toward cooler temperatures at San Diego after 1870.[75] At Sacramento, consistently cold and wet conditions prevailed throughout the 1880s. Statewide, temperatures remained low through the 1890s and into the first decade of the new century. Salmon appeared in abundance at the southern end of their range, in the Mokelumne and San Joaquin Rivers and in Monterey Bay, where sportfishers began to take them in quantity during the mid-1890s.[76] Spawning conditions improved at the same time, as mining debris began to wash out of the Sacramento system in a huge, slow-moving wave. Its apex passed the mouth of the Yuba River in 1903. Tides began to increase at Sacramento City. Reduced from three feet to two inches by 1879, by 1913 they had increased again to eighteen inches.[77] Albacore also seems to have become plentiful in Monterey Bay, where they had seldom been seen before, and also at San Diego. Cooler temperatures probably accounted for the increase.[78] Tuna-like fishes, of which albacore was the first to be harvested, and ocean-caught salmon furnished the resources for two of the three great industrial fisheries of twentieth-century California. The third was that for sardine, which, according to the geological record, was also unusually abundant off the coast at the turn of the century.

As Appendix B shows, the total mass of coastal pelagic schooling fishes was very high from about 1835 until some time during the late 1860s. So, also, was the proportion of sardines to anchovies, suggesting good fishing for what few people were in the industry at that time. During the 1870s and 1880s, as the coastal fishing industry fell upon hard times, the mass of schooling fishes fell to about 60 percent of levels it had reached in the 1860s. The sardine-to-anchovy ratio fell dramatically, reaching its nadir just at the time when Jordan encountered so many frustrated and complaining fishers along the coast. Ecological stability and high overall productivity returned to the system about 1895, and the fishing industry began to prosper again. Swept clean of their marine mammals and drastically altered by fifty years of commercial use, the newly abundant waters of the state offered opportunities that differed greatly from those of the frontier era.

Cultural dissolution

After the shakeout of the mid-1880s, most Sacramento River salmon packers either moved northward in search of unspoiled runs or began to pack fruit instead of fish. Those few who stayed in the business consolidated in order to alleviate the destructive competition for fish that had helped ruin the salmon runs and now threatened to ruin them, as well. Following the lead of Columbia River canners, those in California formed the Sacramento River Packers' Association in 1889. In 1896 F. E. Booth, manager of the association, moved his plant to Monterey where salmon had suddenly become quite abundant. Summer sportfishers had been trolling for salmon for several years by then, and occasionally a market boat would bring in one or two, as well. When commercial trollers entered the fishery in force after 1893, Booth perceived his opportunity and moved to the coast. A substantial number of salmon crews from Black Diamond followed him a few years later.[79]

Canning was not to be the preferred use for ocean-caught salmon. Dealers of fresh fish and, after 1901, packers of mild-cure salmon, or lox, offered better prices for raw fish and readily absorbed the California harvest. By 1904 there were 175 sailing vessels in the Monterey troll fishery. The future of the industry, however, lay with the three gasoline-powered boats that had appeared by then. Over the next few decades, offshore trolling for salmon spread gradually up the coast as motorized vessels proliferated in the fishery. During World War I, output from the river fishery fell permanently behind that of the trollers.[80]

If it did not pay to can salmon at Monterey, Booth reasoned, there might be some use for the sardines that teemed in the bay. One company had already tried packing sardines, first at San Francisco and later at San Pedro, with the help of a seven-crew gasoline sloop and a purse seine. Booth began experimenting with the fish in 1902, just as the demand for lox picked up. In 1904 he bought out a Washington State salmon canner who had moved to Monterey to try his luck with sardines, and eventually made a successful go of it. Although he began by using salmon gear, it did not work on the smaller fish. After several years of experimentation, however, Booth hit on an efficient method and paying markets. The old salmon industry emerged reborn, adapted to new environmental and economic conditions, as the sardine fishery of the twentieth century.[81]

Azorean whalers had always fished for local markets during their off-seasons, and as immigration to California continued through the nineteenth century more and more new arrivals joined them in the business. Azoreans made up majorities of the non-Chinese fishers at Monterey and at San Diego, two of the most important whaling stations, during the 1880s and 1890s. After 1890, they landed increasing quantities of albacore with a multiple-hooked trawl line that, so far as the official who described it knew, was unique to those two ports in all of North America. Tuna-like fishes had long been important in the Mediterranean and near the Azores but found little market in the nineteenth-century United States because of their relatively strong flavor. The California Azoreans, however, found good markets for cured albacore among Portuguese, Italian, and Chinese field laborers in Hawaii.[82] Thus was born the third great industrial fishery of twentieth-century California, the product of Azorean immigrants who began by hunting whales but adapted to a new, suddenly abundant resource as the old one disappeared. Portuguese fishers, who still retain strong ties to their traditional culture, dominate the tuna fishery to this day. The grandson of one shore whaler became President of the American Tunaboat Association in the years after World War II.[83]

The Chinese fisheries disintegrated under the combined assault of hostile competitors and public action at many different levels of government. Congress closed off new immigration from China in 1882. At San Diego, ill feeling toward the abalone fishers increased as the railroad brought fishers of other nationalities to compete with them and as the junk operators were implicated in the smuggling of immigrants and other illegal commodities from Mexico. The abalone business concentrated into the hands of a few wealthy merchants after 1888, when an amendment to the Chinese Exclusion Act forbade the reentry of Chinese nationals who left U.S. territory to hunt abalone or for other reasons. The business finally expired in 1893, when Congress specifically acted to define "persons engaged in the taking or drying or otherwise preserving of shells or fish for home consumption or exportation" as laborers under the terms of the exclusion laws. A series of county ordinances passed shortly after the turn of the century prohibited the intertidal gathering of abalone, such as the Chinese had done, and the business passed into the hands of Japanese hard-hat divers who could continue the hunt in deeper waters.[84]

Northern California Chinese fishers met a similar fate. In 1901 the state legislature prohibited shrimping between May and September, which were the most favorable months for drying shrimp in the open air, as the Chinese had done.[85] Going further, the legislature struck the shrimp industry in its "life," as the whalers would have said, by prohibiting the export from the state of dried shrimp meat or shells.[86] A greatly attenuated shrimp industry continued at San Francisco to supply local consumers. As at San Diego, feelings toward the Chinese fishers at Monterey went from bad or indifferent to worse when larger numbers of European fishers arrived after 1895. Italians, equipped with new and more efficient gear imported for use in the sardine fishery, drove the Chinese out of the squid fishery there in 1905. In 1906 the Chinese camp at Cabrillo Point burned to the ground under mysterious circumstances and was never rebuilt.[87] The Chinese fisheries, developed to feed the immigrant community that had been so vital to the progress of California, were harassed out of business along with the community itself as an ungrateful state prepared to enter the twentieth century.

Good times for Italian market fishers ended in 1876. During that economically depressed year, a syndicate of Spanish, Greek, and Genoese fish brokers secretly imported, tested, and began operating a bottom trawl, or "paranzella" net from large vessels on the sandy stretches outside the Golden Gate. By 1892 wholesale brokers operated four such steamers in the San Francisco market, supplying demersal flatfishes in some cases at one-third to one-fifth the prices of independent boats. The market was suddenly theirs to dictate. Two paranzella firms controlled the Santa Cruz market as well by 1888. At Los Angeles wholesalers exerted similar power, although here their strength came from their position as shippers to the area's widely dispersed markets, not because they owned their own vessels.[88]

Small boat operators, more and more of whom were Sicilians, recent arrivals with fewer resources and fewer contacts outside their immediate communities, took a substantial drop in earnings and gradually lost ownership of their boats to the brokers. They began to complain about the Chinese shrimpers who, they thought, depleted the bay of fodder species and the fry of their target varieties: Jordan noted that such allegations began to appear along with the paranzella net, in 1876. They tried organizing in self-defense but were simply unable to compete with the sheer volume of the brokers' output. The result was a great deal of conflict on the San Francisco waterfront. Northern and southern Italians kept to different sides of the harbor by 1892 and to different waters – northerners offshore, southerners in the bay – after 1900. Finally, many moved to Monterey, San Diego, or some other coastal port. At San Diego they encountered the Chinese and added their voices to the rising chorus of accusations that the Asians were ruining the local market fishery.[89]

If anything, the Italians who remained in the northern California market fisheries became even more hidebound in their attachment to traditional ways. By the end of the century, public officials were greatly dismayed by the "obsolete European methods" prevailing in the business, in stark contrast to the great progress displayed in New England and Pacific Northwest ports. Fishers claimed that ice was too expensive for them to use in storing their catches, whereas newer boats were too heavy to row in the frequent calms that beset their grounds.[90] Bay Area Italians were the most intransigent of all California fishers in their resistance to government attempts to manage the fisheries during the early decades of the twentieth century.

Conclusion: the industrial fisheries born wealthy

By 1900, then, the fragmented immigrant fishing industry had lost much of its vitality. It lost some of its cultural variegation at the same time: A turn-of-the-century journalist noted that both Chinese and Italian boats at San Francisco were "gradually losing their distinctive features."[91] The commercial economy quickly devoured the most valuable and easily harvested resources, the migrating salmon and mammals that offered themselves for easy taking and the abalone that had bloomed in the absence of the still-earlier exhausted sea otter. Industrial and municipal pollution in the Sacramento drainage had crippled many of the state's freshwater fisheries at the same time. These stresses manifested themselves in friction between different participants in the industry and, as the following chapter will show, between industry and government. They also reflected an end of adolescence for the U.S. economy as a whole: In 1895 the United States became for the first time a net importer of fishery products.[92]

Here and there, there were signs that a new regime was about to begin, as loose agglomerations of workers and capital shifted from ruined fisheries to new ones that simultaneously became both plentiful and technologically accessible at the turn of the century. As the California economy industrialized, its fisheries, now pursued from vessels driven by fossil fuels rather than the wind, now processed with mechanical rather than solar power, assumed a greater relative importance to the local communities in which they took part. The new fisheries and the technology to develop them emerged from a complex interaction of market forces, environmental change, and the adaptation of traditional cultures initially scattered at random along the rivers and coast.

Ecologically, the 1890s were a good time to begin new fisheries. Salmon were plentiful in the cooling waters off northern and central California, while schooling fishes like the sardine and their predators, like the tunas, were at very high levels. By 1915, when the oceanic fisheries for salmon, sardines, and tuna began to grow explosively, the abundance of all three resources was down considerably from turn-of-the-century levels. During the 1970s, looking back on the history of the by-then defunct sardine fishery and seeking to make the point that random environmental change rather than overfishing had caused its collapse, two California fishery scientists emphasized "as a matter of perspective" that "most of man's experience in the waters off the Californias appears to be associated with low pelagic-fish productivity . . . there is yet limited appreciation of the capacity of the system."[93]

The major fisheries of the twentieth century, however, like those of the first fifty years of statehood, were born wealthy, not in barren times. F. E. Booth began experimenting with sardines in 1902. A. P. Halfhill began looking for a way to process albacore profitably in 1903. At that point pelagic fish productivity was as high as at any time since the arrival of non-Indians to California. Industry's expectations of what fishery productivity ought to be may thus have been unreasonably high, not low. Both sail-powered and mechanized fisheries opened new frontiers with plentiful and apparently "untouched" resources. But the "untapped" fisheries of both eras were as abundant as they were in part because of fortunate climatic conditions and, more important, because of ecological changes induced by previous human activity. Western commerce never encountered an empty and unused frontier in California waters. When the costs of prodigality within the industry, ecologically destructive activities in other industries, and the innate instability of California's aquatic environments began to tell on the industrial fisheries, false assumptions about the "state of nature" of the resources combined with a heritage of ambiguous lessons from past regulatory efforts to preclude effective fishery management through most of the twentieth century.

5

State power and the right to fish

Neither the fish, the public, nor the future of the business appears to have many friends. Any restrictions upon
unlimited fishing and unlimited canning, while a fish can
be found in the river, is looked upon as a personal injury,
inflicted by a meddlesome and tyrannical government.
– California Commissioners of Fisheries (1880)[1]

Despite their primitive aspect, the immigrant fisheries of nineteenth-century
California faced the same problems of depletion, "externality," and ecological
instability that troubled the larger-scale and technically more advanced industries of a century later. The motley collection of sail-powered fisheries
that lined the coast had another modern aspect to it, as well: The immigrant
fishers brought together within a single political and ecological system a
jumble of different technologies, marketing strategies, and cost–price structures, in a way the rest of the world would not become familiar with until
after 1945. Just as many different nations competed for the living resources
of the high seas after World War II, so did New England salmon canners,
Chinese shrimpers, and Italian market fishers share the Sacramento–San
Joaquin drainage in nineteenth-century California.[2] The economic Babel that
resulted complicated an already difficult set of problems for those in government who wished to manage the fisheries in the interest of all.

The law as it stood in the first few score years of California's statehood
was not of much help, conditioned as it was by nearly a century of headlong
economic expansion across an unclaimed and apparently boundless frontier.
For at least as long as the Republic had existed, lawmakers at all levels of
government had worked to encourage that expansion, adjusting the law as
they went to make it easier for individuals to bring natural resources into
production. With resources in such abundance relative to scarce supplies of
capital and labor, neither citizens nor lawmakers saw much point in tempering their use. "The thirst of a tiger for blood," wrote John Quincy Adams,
most fittingly characterized the voracity with which the U.S. economy devoured the continent's natural wealth.[3] Systematically, judges and legislators
abetted this hunger by dismantling many of the remedies individuals and

communities previously enjoyed against injuries that new forms of enterprise might inflict upon them.[4]

For some, the costs of progress were high. Farmers might find their lands flooded by downstream mill dams or expropriated by canal or railway companies, only to find the courts unwilling to assess more than minimal damages to perpetrators whose activities they deemed essential for economic progress and thus in the public interest. Urban dwellers might find their property rendered uninhabitable when neighboring factories fouled their homes and then receive no satisfaction from courts which were unwilling to let the relatively minor complaints of individual homeowners stand in the way of community development. Wageworkers whose bodies were ruined in industrial accidents, meanwhile, might be told that they had accepted the risks of working with new and dangerous machines along with their employment and would have to fend for themselves as best they could. Common-law rules of property, nuisance, or tort would formerly have protected aggrieved parties such as these, but lawmakers were unwilling to allocate such incidental costs to entrepreneurs in whose hands the future lay. Better, they reasoned, to spread them at random over society at large so that progress might in the end improve the lot of all.[5]

Fish and other forms of wildlife, particularly, were fully exposed to the destructive effects of unleashed market forces. Although they were certainly valuable, they were the private assets of no one, and in the nineteenth-century United States that was key both to the allocation of resources and to effective legal action. Following the same theory that delegated to individuals, and thus to the Invisible Hand, maximum freedom to allocate resources, legislatures and courts generally demanded that individual property interests be at stake before they would address problems of social cost.[6] Fish that swam in public waterways and game that wandered over the land belonged to no one, rendering them defenseless before the law. Whatever heritage in wildlife husbandry the United States may have received from England had been cast aside, both because wildlife seemed so abundant in the New World and because such laws had in the old country made wild game the exclusive property of the aristocracy. "He has read history to very little purpose," wrote one California judge, who did not know that game laws were a "fruitful source of the oppression of the masses of the people. . . . It was better to exterminate the game at once than to preserve it for the special benefit of a favored few."[7] Unprotected by law, U.S. wildlife stocks declined to historic lows by 1900.[8]

Fisheries, the most important kind of commercial wildlife, offered what J. Willard Hurst called "the classic example" of a commonly owned resource whose preservation required government intervention in the economy.[9] Deliberate efforts to police their harvest began shortly after the Civil War, as lawmakers in California and other states began to perceive a need to account for the mounting, if indirect, social costs of economic progress.[10] Meantime some immigrant fishers tried to fill the regulatory vacuum in which their industries floundered by regulating access to their resources on their own, on the basis of shared cultural affinities. During the 1870s, both state and federal governments established administrative agencies to oversee the fisheries, both to advance economic opportunity in the industry and to protect the productivity of the resources over the long run. The state legislatures and the courts finally searched for ways in which to police the industry and to protect it from the environmentally destructive practices of others.

By the turn of the century, California had in place a well-developed and nationally acclaimed body of fishery management law, one with which it would confront the even more difficult problems of the era to come. It developed, however, in response to the peculiar ecological and social conditions which prevailed in the fisheries during the last quarter of the nineteenth century. Just as accidents of human migration combined with accidents of nature to mold the economic character of the fishing industry, they also shaped the tactics and motives of public fishery management in California as the state entered the twentieth century.

Patterns of ethnic regulation

As long as formally constituted authorities exerted no control over the fisheries, as many regulatory efforts emerged from the industry itself as there were strategies for production. California fisheries were not peculiar in this regard: Many nineteenth-century Americans who moved into new areas before the law could establish public order fashioned their own, informal procedures for protecting their investments and ensuring the orderly development of their resources. Squatters who moved onto the public lands before federal officials had a chance to survey them established claims clubs with written constitutions in which they promised each other mutual aid in thwarting would-be claim jumpers and land engrossers. When the General Land Office got around to putting the land up for public sale, these clubs could muster an effective show of force to ensure that established settlers retained their lands and improvements at fair prices. Because the California Gold Rush took place in a legal vacuum, miners too improvised their own codes of law from bits and pieces of familiar legal tradition to protect their titles to claims, regulate the use of scarce water resources, and establish a modicum of social peace in their communities. Frequently such spontaneously generated legal forms became, in effect, predecessor law to which public authorities belatedly gave formal recognition and incorporated into subsequent statutes and case law.[11]

Fishers who migrated to California did not lack traditions from which to build such ad hoc, quasi-legal systems for ordering their working lives. Traditional ways profoundly influenced patterns of resource use and regulated the harvest of crops, timber, and wildlife in most parts of Europe until industrialization dissolved them in the nineteenth century.[12] Sudden, rapid depletion of European resources, then, was symptomatic along with the migration of farmers and fishers to the New World of the social upheaval that the Industrial Revolution brought to the Old.[13] If traditional ways of life were no longer tenable in the Old World, however, preserving them in the New assumed the force of a moral obligation for many immigrant groups. Herbert Gutman and other social historians have demonstrated how powerful old ways were in ordering immigrant life in nineteenth-century America.[14] Fishers, who lived in close proximity to one another and in near isolation from everyone else, proved more tenacious than other occupational groups in resisting the substitution of market relations for customary ones in their communities.[15]

The fishers' first task was to establish some form of tenancy over their resources, that is, to lay claim to particular fisheries and to keep others out.[16] In California this meant, first and foremost, excluding Chinese workers from fisheries in which Westerners were interested, just as gold rushers had done in the mines. One government observer noted in 1873 that the salmon business on the Sacramento river was entirely controlled by whites, "no Chinamen being allowed to participate in it." "There is no law regulating the matter," he continued, "but public opinion is so strong in relation to it . . . that any attempt, on their part, to engage in salmon-fishing would meet with a summary and probably fatal retaliation."[17] Greek fishers marked the upper ends of their "drifts" with makeshift Greek flags. From this point boats set out at fifteen- to twenty-minute intervals on their downstream courses, and Italian or other gill-netters who intruded on the ground did so at their peril.[18]

Their proprietorship over their grounds established, the fishers could then regulate the harvest as they wished. They seem, moreover, to have taken some care to do so: At a meeting of the river gill-netters in 1872, some ninety-five of the hundred or so boats then fishing salmon on the Sacramento had representatives in attendance. In 1880 the gill-netters allocated each boat a quota of forty fish per day for sale on the fresh market so as to maintain prices on what was still their most important market. Whatever surplus there was went to canners at a standard negotiated price or was salted by the fishers themselves. "Everything is governed by laws which the fishermen have made for themselves," reported David Starr Jordan.[19]

Chinese fishers fought a long and bitter struggle with Italians over rights to Bay Area shrimp and won control over it by virtue of their overwhelming ability to keep their costs of production down.[20] Without any formal authority to do so, Chinese shrimp companies recognized each other's proprietorship over certain fishing areas so as to protect the substantial investment each company made in the nets and other fixed gear that stood unattended most of the time. Each company had two or more grounds that it worked at different times of the year. Continued proprietorship did not rest on continuous use, as it did in the gold mines; indeed, a complicated set of unwritten rules kept new grounds a safe distance from old ones, thereby conserving both their productivity and social peace. The shrimpers' defense against would-be usurpers on their grounds was characteristically strenuous.[21]

Chinese shrimpers and abalone hunters arbitrated their own conflicts, as was the wont of Chinese-Americans at the time, and organized production in their own way. Capitalists squared accounts with their employees at the end of harvest season every year, after which each was free to remain with the old company or join a new one. Outsiders who expressed interest in their dealings thereby identified themselves to the Chinese as government agents, and therefore not to be trusted. David Starr Jordan, who became friendly with Chinese market fishers at San Diego while gathering specimens from them during the late 1870s, was known to them as "the Law." To Jack London, who as a teenager during the early nineties worked as a patrol deputy for the California Fish Commission, the Bay Area shrimpers were little better than pirates who kept no law but their own. Meanwhile, powerful commercial interests in the San Francisco Chinatown kept up a vigilant defense in U.S. courts against the government's assaults on the shrimp industry. So strong was this exclusively Chinese regulatory system that it still functioned as late as the 1930s, long after most of the industry had been legislated away at Sacramento.[22]

Organization along ethnic lines was most highly developed among the Italian market fishers of the Bay Area. "The Fishermen of the Bay of San Francisco" organized in 1862 to protest the impending repeal at Sacramento of a monthly license tax of Chinese fishers, "for the protection of the white fishermen, against the encroachments of the Mongolians."[23] Two years later, some 300 fishers organized the Italian Fishermen's Association to fight a city levy on Chinese fish peddlers, with whom the Italians had built up a mutually profitable relationship. Such general associations among the Italians survived in various forms well into the twentieth century, not only protecting the market fishery from interlopers but providing mutual aid and community services to the fishers as well.[24]

New arrivals learned quickly, according to one of the city's Italian newspapers, that they "should abide by the regulations of the association or they should find other places to fish."[25] "If anyone imagines that it is possible for a Chinese or member of any other nationality than an Italian to catch crabs in this bay for the market let him try it," wrote the *San Francisco Chronicle* in 1907. "If any Italian thinks it is possible to catch crabs for the market without joining the association let him try it."[26] As the Italian community divided internally after the 1870s, Sicilian organizations protected their members against the increasing power of northern Italian fish wholesalers by maintaining their own cooperative wharf and market.[27]

By the turn of the century the Bay Area market fishery was balkanized into a number of producers' associations, each specializing in a particular kind of fish, each composed of fishers from a particular locality in the old country, and each under the control of its own headman.[28] Reported a federal agent in 1888, "if the occasion calls for it, [the Italians] have the reputation of standing by each other to the bitter end, and this spirit of the trade union has, no doubt, been a most important factor in maintaining their unquestioned supremacy in the market fishery."[29] That fish marketing was as primitive as it was in San Francisco testified to the great power of these groups. In 1894, the schooner *Elwood* touched at San Francisco with the first load of iced Alaskan halibut to arrive at the city. To his dismay, the *Elwood*'s captain had to sell his fish from a stall aboard his ship even though he could offer them at one-fifth the going rate for flatfish. None of the local dealers would touch them, according to the *San Francisco Examiner*, "for fear of being boycotted by the local men."[30]

Like the salmon gill-netters, Italian market fishers controlled the harvest and distribution of their products to their best advantage. The Crab Fishermen's Protective Association limited each day's sale to specific quotas, storing whatever surplus it produced alive in cages hung from its wharf for sale the next day. The cooperative market at Fisherman's Wharf offered the catch of each member boat for sale in rotation, a box at a time. With an equitable price and an equal market share guaranteed by their association, and outsiders barred from entry, as well as sanctions against cheating swift, sure, and strenuous, individual fishers had no incentive to harvest beyond levels that provided their groups with optimal livings. Meanwhile, mutual-aid societies and insider-run boarding houses provided cheap credit and diminished thereby the incentive to convert resources into cash. Neither would-be interlopers like the *Elwood*'s captain nor law-enforcement officers could attack the fishers' hegemony in the business without encountering the kind of violent resistance that made London's *Tales of the Fish Patrol* such exciting reading. Indeed, it was not until World War II that the traditional structure of Italian society on the San Francisco waterfront began to dissolve.[31]

The Italians, Chinese, and other fishers who belonged to such ethnically based producers' coalitions were, however, more than the freebooters of London's stories or the ignorant obstacles to progress who so frustrated government observers. Whereas to outsiders their tactics may have seemed no more rational than the myths and rituals of salmon-fishing Indians, immigrant fishers no less than the Indian fishers before them tried to manage their resources so as to protect the stability and longevity of their communities. In economic terms, cultural ties between the fishers significantly lowered the cost of organizing and maintaining coalitions to regulate the harvest of fish.[32] If their retail prices were higher than what they would be on a "free" market, sustaining group power to control the fishery for the benefit of the group accounted for the premium, not necessarily the greed of a monopolist. Fishers who have no such intragroup solidarity normally find themselves trapped in "tragedies of the commons" because they lack the cash, the time, or the energy to make and enforce agreements to regulate their behavior. Coalitions of immigrant fishers tried to insulate themselves from the market forces that drive unorganized fishers collectively to ruin both their resources and their livelihoods. Of primary importance to them was not profit at the expense of competitors but the preservation of a traditional way of life, which was a moral obligation and thus had no price.

This is not to say that the immigrants' schemes for managing their fisheries were of necessity ecologically conservative. Traditional patterns of resource use may be well or poorly adapted to particular environments, and patterns of use that may be stable in one social and ecological context may not be so when transplanted to new ones. Certainly the Chinese in California worked their abalone grounds rapaciously, and the Mediterranean environment fared poorly under centuries of overgrazing. It is only to say that the immigrant fishers, where they could, tried to limit entry to their fisheries and to manage them extralegally, on the basis of shared cultural affinities. Modern studies have shown that fishers' coalitions of this type, operating in such places as Hudson's Bay in Canada and the coast of Maine, do simultaneously promote both the economic welfare of their members and the biological welfare of their resources, all without color of law.[33]

In nineteenth-century California, the immigrant fishers' resolve to maintain their traditional ways of doing things, likewise, tended in some important cases to limit access to their fisheries and to control the harvest so as to produce socially optimum yields. They were not by any means autonomous, acquisitive individuals scrambling over each other to take fish before they all disappeared; social and cultural organization held such behavior in check and bound individuals to their groups if they wished to take part in the harvest.

What is certain is that the clearly visible solidarity of these coalitions and the above-market prices for fish they charged generated insistent demands from outsiders that the law work actively to destroy them. It did so with increasing success after the turn of the century, in the process exposing the fish to the full force of market pressures and ultimately encouraging their depletion.

In the long run, traditional social structures which resisted the demands of a market society that labor and resources move as freely as possible in response to price could not survive. Ethnic diversity in the industry was one reason: In 1878–9 striking Italian and Greek salmon fishers on the Sacramento River failed to maintain their prices for raw fish because German crews continued fishing outside the Mediterraneans' territory.[34] Another reason was the overwhelming power of brokers and processors to whom the gill-netters gradually fell into debt. For example, fishers at Collinsville were at the financial mercy of the town's storekeeper, who monopolized wharfage, communications, and credit in the area.[35] As they had in the gold country, producers' cooperatives broke down in the salmon fishery when formerly independent workers fell into debt to those who provided them with essential services.

By the end of the 1880s, salmon fishers of various ethnicities on the lower Sacramento had forsaken cultural for class organization by joining the Benecia Fishermen's Association and affiliating with the San Francisco Federated Trades Council. The Fishermen's Protective Association of San Francisco likewise joined the city's trade union movement in the 1880s, as wholesale fish dealers undercut their ability to maintain prices on their own. By 1892 the ethnic fishers' coalitions were clearly under siege. "The fishermen are not organized as previously," reported a local journalist, "and much needless expense is incurred by their rivalry."[36] After the turn of the century, they faced opposition not only from competitors in the market but from the law as well.

Government science

Governments in the United States became actively concerned with fisheries after the close of the Civil War, as more and more East Coast fisheries succumbed to overuse and industrial pollution. Like other wildlife, fish had traditionally been a ready source of subsistence and cash for producers of small means and as such had a pastoral mythos about them no less powerful than the independent small-scale farms that Jefferson and his followers considered vital to the well-being of the republic. Spencer Fullerton Baird, the first U.S. Commissioner of Fisheries, wrote nostalgically of the days when "throughout the twelve months an ample supply of fish was within the reach of everyone, so that a fisherman with a small handline and an open boat was able to support his family without any difficulty."[37] As this important aspect of frontier life passed away, government agencies long preoccupied with extending the reach of the market economy bent their efforts to understanding and controlling market forces which, inexorably it seemed, doomed fish and other wildlife to destruction.

New England states were the first to act, ordaining special administrative agencies to study fisheries problems and to recommend remedial legislation.[38] By 1880, some thirty states had followed suit. One of the first was

California, which created a State Board of Fish Commissioners in 1870 "to provide for the restoration and preservation of fish in the waters of this State."[39] Congress established the U.S. Fish Commission (USFC) as part of the Smithsonian Institution the following year, as growing conflicts among fishers who worked the valuable banks off New England made clear the need for action. Baird, then Assistant Secretary of the Smithsonian, was appointed Commissioner and given a broad mandate to study the causes of decline in U.S. coastal fisheries.[40] As undertaken by cooperating state and federal fishery agencies, fishery management in California was among the most progressive such programs in the nation. The apparent successes made by the agencies, particularly of introducing exotic species of fish to California waters and of propagating important varieties artificially, established important precedents for resource management nationwide.

Establishment of the USFC may have been the first official recognition by Congress that the North American frontier was not, after all, boundless.[41] Its appearance was the more remarkable because only five years before a British Royal Commission had reaffirmed the traditional view that oceanic fisheries were inexhaustible. If certain grounds lost productivity from time to time, according to the illustrious commission's laissez-faire reasoning, declining profits would lead fishers to new grounds and give older ones time to replenish. Burdening the fisheries with laws, so the argument went, would only infringe upon the liberty of the harvesters in an arbitrary and capricious way and would "disturb in an unknown and possibly injurious manner the balance existing between the conservative and destructive agencies at work" on the stocks.[42] By undertaking an official inquiry into the dynamics of U.S. coastal fisheries, Congress proclaimed that in the future government would take some responsibility for understanding and perhaps tempering the effects of economic development on the country's natural endowment.[43]

Policing the use of fish and wildlife was not one of the powers delegated to the federal government in the Constitution and for that reason, until 1900 at least, remained a job for state governments.[44] Although it had little to do with regulating the fisheries, the USFC promoted efficiency and progress in the industry in several ways. It built an advanced laboratory for fisheries biology at Woods Hole in Massachusetts, sponsored outside research on fisheries problems, and gathered information on fishery practices in other nations through the consular corps, much as the United States Department of Agriculture (USDA) did for farmers. In 1877, when a lack of statistical information handicapped Baird in negotiations with Canadian officials, the USFC undertook a monumental study of social, economic, and biological conditions in the U.S fisheries in cooperation with the Tenth Census. David Starr Jordan and the Stanford zoologist Charles H. Gilbert surveyed the Pacific Coast fisheries as part of this effort in 1879 and 1880. Ten years later USFC sent its new research vessel, the *Albatross*, to the coast, where it discovered bountiful fishing grounds off San Diego at Cortes and Tanner Banks. Later, the *Albatross* completed a study of the physical ecology of San Francisco Bay that remained without peer until well into the twentieth century. The Commission introduced U.S. fishers to new methods and products and toward the end of the century built a prototype fishing schooner for the East Coast. Most importantly, it cooperated with state fisheries commissions in restocking damaged waterways with transplanted and artificially propagated species. The Commission's success, particularly in the last endeavor, provided important precedent for wildlife managers in the twentieth century.[45]

Baird, a skilled politician as well as one of the nation's most respected naturalists, parlayed the USFC's narrow mandate to study the problems of New English fisheries into a comprehensive effort in basic research that produced much of lasting value.[46] Baird was an early and enthusiastic follower of Darwin, who more than any other nineteenth-century scientist challenged the idea that humankind was the center and measure of the universe.[47] Yet the social and institutional contexts within which Baird worked greatly influenced both the course and the outcome of USFC's work, so that the self-perceived interests of fishery users became both the organizing principle of the USFC program and the measure of its success.

Baird had concluded by 1888 that the decline of the New England fisheries appeared "to have been the result principally of human agencies," either by way of overfishing or the degradation of inshore habitat on which commercial fisheries depended, but a federal agency had no constitutional power to control those forces.[48] Indeed, because Congressional appropriations were the lifeblood of USFC research, the agency had little incentive even to try. It thus became a promotional agency, undertaking research and development so as to expand, not restrict, the industry's access to resources. Research on the Pacific Coast, for example, was designed to "determine, for the benefit of the fishermen, the varieties of fishes distributed along the coast, and the places where they occur in the greatest abundance."[49]

Political and economic conflict within the fishing industry marked out USFC's objectives and guided its strategies. Conflict between operators of fixed gear and operators of floating gear in the New England fisheries had, after all, led to the establishment of the Fish Commission in the first place. Presented with a political problem, the agency was under pressure to find a political answer, that is, to fix blame for a problem so that Congress could eliminate the nuisance. Just as Americans placed their faith in individual enterprise as an engine of social progress, they tended also to seek fault for social problems in individuals or identifiable groups.[50] The fisher's solution to the fisher's problem, typically, is "burn every other . . . boat but mine," even though social-cost problems like fishery depletion are by definition not the fault of individuals but of many individuals together. Pressure to approach fishery problems in this way limited USFC's ability to understand and confront the problems before it in a useful way. Jordan's report on the Pacific Coast fisheries for the Tenth Census, for example, uncritically adopted the widely held view that Chinese fishers were to blame for much of the decline in fishery productivity that took place all along the coast in the 1870s and 1880s. As another observer noted, this was a libel whose "apparent bitterness . . . might rob it of force were it not reiterated from various sources," including, significantly, the U.S. Fish Commission.[51]

Jordan's protégé at Stanford, N. B. Scofield, took up the scientific attack on the Chinese fishing industry after the California State Board of Fish Commissioners, at Jordan's recommendation, retained him to study the Bay Area shrimp industry. In a series of reports laced with the virulent anti-Chinese rhetoric that was common currency in late nineteenth-century California, Scofield insisted that up to half of the shrimper's catch consisted of smelt and other small fish which were fodder and fry for other fisheries, rather than shrimp. Patrol agents of the Commission who visited the Chinese camps testified otherwise, however. The Commission's chief deputy reported in 1892 that "the drying beds of all these camps are mostly free of small fish. I do not believe that the law is violated to the extent that is complained of." "The constant claim that we do not enforce the law as regards the Chinese," he wrote, "is done for some other purpose than is apparent upon the surface."[52]

Even if some California law enforcement officers padded their incomes with payoffs from Chinese shrimpers and even if the Chinese did incidentally destroy fodder and fry of other fishers' target species, random climatic change and the massive degradation of the Sacramento watershed's ecology inflicted far more damage on those fisheries than the relatively minor impact of Chinese fishing. The nearly universal frustration with the shrimp and abalone fisheries, which manifested the Chinese community's determination to govern itself independently of the community around it and which, unlike most sectors of the industry, prospered during the 1870s and 1880s, substituted for observation and reasoned analysis of fishery problems. Scofield viewed the shrimp controversy as one between "those who would conserve the fisheries resources of San Francisco Bay and rivers, on the one hand, and the interested defenders of the Chinese, on the other." If small fish were not in evidence on the Chinese drying beds, this was only because the fishers boiled them with the shrimp "to get rid of the evidence."[53] At San Diego, shortages of fresh market fish in the late eighties led a local newspaper to demand that the state "drive the heathen from the bay."[54] The state Fish Commissioners complied after investigating the local situation by deputizing a San Diego fishing captain to arrest violators of state fishing laws.[55] Closing down the Chinese fisheries, then, became a key element of the state's fishery program at the end of the century.

Baird and others like Livingston Stone were well aware of the complexity of fisheries problems and understood that fluctuations in harvests could be products of random and human-induced environmental change as well as of overfishing. One product of this awareness was the remarkably broad ecological approach of the *Albatross* surveys after 1882.[56] They also knew that "a judicious protection of the [spawning] grounds" would help protect fish like the salmon from depletion.[57] USFC was not legally competent, however, to regulate all of the economic activities that degraded fishery habitat, and state laws which attempted to do so typically had little effect.[58] The effective premise, then, from which USFC proceeded and that it reiterated time and again in its official reports, was that the degradation of previously "unexploited" resources under the impact of commercial civilization was no less inevitable than the disappearance of Indians and buffalo from the continent. "Wherever the white man plants his foot and the so-called civilization of a country is begun," wrote Baird in 1878, "the inhabitants of the air, the land, and the water begin to disappear."[59] Laissez-faire ideology held that attempts to bring such social forces under control through the deliberate use of law were by their nature vicious: If they did not go that far, Baird and his comrades considered them pointless in any event.[60]

They did, however, have an alternative. Convinced, with John Adams, that "policy and education [could] triumph over every disadvantage" of natural endowment, Baird and others like him believed that applied science could keep pace "with the inevitable exhaustion of the native fish life . . . incident to the development of the country and the increase of population."[61] Since the opening of the Erie Canal in the 1820s, U.S. lawmakers had shown considerable ingenuity in using public policy affirmatively to unlock the economic potential of the continent's resources. In doing so, however, they paid scant attention to broadly shared or ill-defined social values, such as the longterm productivity of renewable resources, whose sacrifice made little difference in the calculations of individual market actors.[62] After 1870, as the hidden costs of such single-minded profit seeking began to mount, government agents bent their will toward sustaining the flow of resources into the market artificially.

One method of doing this was to stock depleted rivers with rapidly growing species of fish that were not native to them. Plants of shad in 1873 and of striped bass in 1879 and 1882 generated valuable commercial fisheries for those species in the Sacramento River and vindicated the practice for many years to come.[63] German carp, on the other hand, was one of the great disasters of nineteenth-century fishery science. A private landowner in Sonoma County imported the fish on his own initiative in 1872. So well did it grow that the USFC took up the cause of the carp with enthusiasm, subsidizing its introduction to waterways all over the West during the 1890s. In California it took root, drove out more valuable native species by ruining their habitat, and very quickly became what Jordan called "a positive nuisance."[64] Eastern oysters, too, transplanted in San Francisco Bay on private initiative, brought with them all sort of benign and pestiferous hitchhikers.[65] Livingston Stone introduced the brown catfish to California in 1874. Thereafter, these fish increased "beyond all belief," according to the *San Francisco Bulletin*, driving the more valuable river perch and dace out of their niches in the river. "Like the English sparrow on the land," the *Bulletin* protested, the catfish were by 1894 "beyond extermination, and are everywhere execrated."[66] In the same year, however, USFC pointed to the success of the shad and striped bass transplants as "enduring testimony to the influence of man over fish production."[67]

Artificial propagation was another attempt to replace through applied science what civilization inevitably destroyed. Here, too, California was among the most progressive states in the nation and was to those involved in the program the leading example of its efficacy. Hatcheries, primarily for salmon, consumed half of the funds appropriated for state and federal fishery agencies in the last quarter of the century. Although the hatchery program had obvious appeal to scientists and policymakers who believed that nothing could be done to control the complex forces that depleted fisheries in the first place, it proceeded without a shred of hard evidence that it was having the slightest effect on the abundance of the stocks concerned.

The hatchery movement, begun like many of the technological advances of the nineteenth century by "tinkerers and doers" in the private sector, antedated the organization of public fishery agencies.[68] "Practical fish-culturists," foremost among whom were Seth Green of New York and Livingston Stone of New Hampshire, played major roles in the hatchery programs of some of the northeastern states. In 1870, by which time the market for the private hatcheries' output was overstocked, they organized the American Fish Culturists' Association, with Stone as secretary, and dedicated themselves to "the struggle to keep ahead of man's harmful actions on rivers, streams, and lakes to the detriment of fish and fishing."[69] Two years later, with Baird's help, the Association prevailed upon Congress to authorize USFC to begin hatchery work and the federal agency soon preempted the field. At the behest of Stone and his group, Baird dispatched the former to California, where he was to gather spawn from the undamaged runs of the Sacramento River for transport to depleted waterways in the East and around the world.[70]

Stone became neighbors with the McCloud River Wintu the same year, and salmon runs in the Sacramento watersheds improved markedly thereafter. Stone and the public officials who supervised the project attributed the revival to hatchery operations: California Fish Commissioner Redding went so far as to claim that "the canneries on the [Sacramento were] dependent upon the salmon hatchery of [the McCloud] for their maintenance."[71] Artificial propagation ceased in California for a few years after the salmon fishery collapsed, and when the USFC station reopened in 1888 its entire output went to restocking the Sacramento itself. The return of good runs in 1892, more likely attributable as they had been during the 1870s to changes in climate and declines in gold production, seemed to offer conclusive proof that the hatchery program worked. By the late eighties, according to USFC, the utility of artificial propagation had "long ceased to be problematical."[72] California built several hatcheries of its own on the Sacramento and some of the northern rivers as well. By 1896 salmon were "very abundant in the Sacramento and the McCloud, and . . . on the increase," the size of the runs showing "a very marked dependence on the number of young fry hatched at the breeding stations the corresponding years."[73] By 1906 it was "an acknowledged fact that the runs of salmon in the Sacramento and San Joaquin Rivers, and their tributaries, [were] fully restored."[74]

The hatcheries promised a painless, technical solution to this particular aspect of the Gilded Age's environmental problems and were, understandably, enormously popular. "There are few enterprises undertaken by the United States Government," wrote a USFC official, "that are more popular, meet with more general and generous support, and have contributed more to the prosperity and happiness of a larger number of people than the federal fish-cultural work."[75] Noting the success of the McCloud River experiment, Columbia River salmon canners pooled their own funds and borrowed Stone from the federal commission to set up one of their own.[76]

The hatchery program so overwhelmed the USFC agenda that Congress chose a "practical fish-culturist" to succeed Baird as Fish Commissioner in 1888. Congressional representatives flooded their docket with bills to establish hatcheries in their home districts, frequently before USFC ascertained any need for them. Annual Congressional support for the program grew from a relatively modest $15,000 at the outset to $161,000 by 1887. In no region of the country was the mania so pronounced as it was on the West Coast. "While the results of salmon culture have in some places been marked," observed a USFC scientist in 1894, "this alone is not sufficient to account for the widespread advocacy of fish culture which exists among all classes and in all parts of the Pacific Coast."[77] Here was a valuable lesson for the conservationist politicians of the early twentieth century: Although Baird and others paid homage to the need to control harvesting and environmental degradation, promising to sustain the economy's supply of fish without interrupting existing patterns of use yielded far greater political rewards.

It is not clear that the hatchery program ever had any favorable impact on the fisheries with which it was concerned; indeed, the opposite is more likely true. D. F. Hobbs demonstrated in the 1930s that salmon fry survive to adulthood just as well when their parents propagate them under natural conditions as when hatcheries fertilize the ova by hand and release the fry immediately after they hatch, as was the USFC practice during the nineteenth century. Modern hatcheries raise fish to much larger sizes before releasing them into the environment, at much greater cost but with better results.[78] Not a single one of the plants of McCloud River fry in East Coast rivers proved successful, to Stone's "stupendous surprise and disappointment."[79] There was "strong suspicion" after the mid twentieth century, moreover, that egg-taking activities on the McCloud and other California rivers may actually have contributed to the fishery's decline.[80]

The failure was due primarily to the early scientists' ignorance of the life history of the salmon, especially of the importance of the young fishes' environment during the months they spend in fresh water.[81] A similar misunderstanding lay behind contemporary complaints that Chinese shrimpers injured other people's fisheries by destroying fry and fodder of their targets, as well as behind USFC's brief attempt to propagate cod artificially at Gloucester.[82] Fish, especially oceanic ones, typically produce immense numbers of viable spawn; it is only those few offspring lucky enough to find favorable environments in which to grow that survive to adulthood. Stone, moreover, did not understand that salmon breed in cycles of from four to six years. It was a mystery to him, therefore, that new runs appeared each year, before the hatchery fry of the year before had had a chance to mature.[83] Many officials did not believe that salmon died after one spawning; for his part, Jordan did not believe that the salmon migrated far from their parent streams once they entered salt water, nor did he think that the salmon homed to their natal streams to spawn.[84]

More important than a catalog of their scientific errors, however, were the reasons why nineteenth-century fishery managers persisted in their approach. Stone, for example, remained undaunted by the repeated failure of his efforts to restock East Coast rivers with California salmon. "Should the Commission make a success of a single river," he explained, "it would pay for all that has been expended in this direction."[85] He did ask his superiors repeatedly to station a trained biologist at the McCloud River hatchery, but to no avail. As long as the hatchery program yielded tangible results and increasing appropriations, USFC apparently saw no need to investigate the matter further. Indeed, after Baird died in 1884, the Commission slighted the more arcane but in the long run more important biological and ecological studies he had begun in favor of the hatchery program, which was the primary fount of its considerable and growing prestige.[86] The California Fish Commissioners justified their belief that salmon did not die after spawning once in a similar way: "If that were the case," they reasoned, "it would detract from their value."[87] That such *was* the case, however, became clear as soon as USFC sent the biologist Barton Evermann to the headwaters of the Columbia to find out in 1894 and 1895.[88]

Salmon and other fishes were first and foremost valuable commodities. USFC's primary interest was in sustaining the flow of such commodities into the market; as long as its policies seemed to work, other aspects of the resources' existence were of little import. One result of government science's narrow conception of its objects of study was an emphasis on the morphology and classification of important commercial fishes to the detriment of more important inquiries into their life histories and ecological relations, inquiries that contemporary advances in biology would have suggested were significant. In a similar way, late nineteenth-century efforts to protect fish and wildlife focused narrowly on controlling the specific interaction between harvesters and prey, when environmental changes brought on by economic development were probably more serious a threat to the well-being of both.[89]

Artificial propagation and exotic transplants offered simple, technical, intuitive solutions to the complex problems of fishery depletion. They appealed to what one economic historian called "the traditional combination of empiricism and common sense" that had up to the late nineteenth century proven more than adequate to the tasks, not only of technological innovation but of lawmaking as well.[90] More important, they seemed to fulfill the very great promise, held out by Baird and others, that applied science could revive and sustain the productivity of a ravaged environment without requiring any fundamental changes in the ways in which people used it. William A. Wilcox, a USFC agent, observed in the early years of the twentieth century that "through restrictive legislation and artificial propagation" government agencies had maintained the supply of salmon in the Sacramento basin "in the face of most unfavorable conditions."[91] That government and its scientific advisors could replace what civilization's carelessness had destroyed was an article of faith in U.S. fishery policy and one that proved very hard to discredit.

The police power and state ownership

One reason why artificial propagation and exotic transplants were so popular was they were much more easily undertaken than the enforcement of laws designed to restrain the depletion of fishery resources in the first place. It was more politic to give than to deny, to subsidize rather than police: Fishery agencies found plenty of support for scientific research and development in declining fisheries but found it rough going indeed to interfere with the economic ambitions of would-be harvesters. Equal and unlimited access to the public domain was as powerful a political canon in California, the state given birth by gold rushers, as anywhere else. For this reason the "common property" problem asserted itself in the Golden State with uncommon urgency.

Constitutionally, wildlife law was the province of state governments. These, having inherited their powers directly from the English Crown and Parliament, were less hampered by constitutional limitations than the federal government.[92] Seemingly, fisheries protection would have offered state legislatures an ideal opportunity to exercise their police power – in the words of a Massachusetts judge, the power to "establish all manner of wholesome and reasonable laws . . . as they shall judge to be for the good and welfare of the Commonwealth and [its] subjects" – so as to give weight to important social concerns too long-term, too broadly shared, or too difficult to translate into dollar values to make any impact on the economic decisions of individual resource users.[93] The U.S. Supreme Court had affirmed the power of states to regulate fishing in 1855.[94] Indeed, the legislative duty to protect citizens' rights to use public waterways for fishing and navigation formed a long-running, if slender and frayed, thread through the history of the law that proved valuable to legislatures in the last quarter of the century when they began more closely to regulate businesses they deemed "affected with a public interest."[95]

It was rough going, however. By the last quarter of the century, fish and wildlife, although clearly in need of attention from lawmakers, enjoyed few protections from democratic values, government indifference or incapacity, and above all the country's preoccupation with economic expansion. No one in California, for example, was about to call off the Gold Rush on behalf of a handful of illiterate salmon fishers.[96] A handful of fisheries statutes had passed the legislature at Sacramento during the 1850s and 1860s, and in 1870 the state's sportfishers, following the example of New Englanders, successfully pressed for the creation of a State Board of Fish Commissioners.[97] The latter spent the first decade of its career engaged in the relatively easy work of hatchery propagation and exotic transplants, at first independently and increasingly in cooperation with the federal commission.[98] During the 1880s a more rigorous approach became necessary. Like its federal sister, the state agency gained considerable prestige for its apparent successes by the turn of the century. Its victories, however, were due primarily to coincidental improvements in politically sensitive sectors of the industry rather than to any beneficial effects of management per se. The victories of the 1890s, then, would prove of little value in the state's struggle to confront the vastly magnified problems of regulating industrial fisheries in subsequent decades.

In two cases the state attempted to ensure orderly development of fisheries by consigning them to private owners. Like private property in land, exclusive rights to use a fishery delegated to the owners responsibility for keeping "free riders" out and for limiting harvests to within sustainable levels. The first oyster beds in the Bay Area, for example, had been operated as if they were mining claims. Cultivators did not own their beds outright but could file claims to use them with county officials. Poaching oysters from someone else's claim was a misdemeanor. This was not enough to encourage growers to make the considerable investment required to prepare beds for oysters, though, and in 1874 the legislature exempted privately owned tidelands and submerged lands from the claim procedure. Now able to keep poachers and claim jumpers away, two Bay Area firms stepped up their production considerably. In fact, their huge holdings along the southern bayshore were essentially long-term investments in real estate that served well as oyster farms in the short run. The Mexican government followed California's example when, alarmed by the progress of the Chinese abalone industry on the northern Baja California coast and unable to police it directly, it leased that fishery to a U.S. firm in 1889.[99]

The California legislature attempted to privatize an important part of its salmon industry in an 1859 act "to regulate salmon fisheries on Eel River."[100] This statute gave landowners on either side of the Eel exclusive rights to fish salmon from the river adjoining their property. Such landowners would still have to abide by state laws regulating seasons and allowable gear for salmon but, like the oyster growers, had the law of trespass to keep interlopers away from their grounds.[101] Indian use-rights to fishing spots had functioned in much the same way. The Pacific Coast's only effectively privatized salmon fishery was that of R. D. Hume, the transplanted New Englander who invaded the Yurok fishery on the Klamath River in the 1880s. Hume built up his own monopoly on the Rogue River, just north of the Oregon state line, by buying up all of the tidelands at the mouth of the river and all the lands suitable for landing seines for some distance upstream. Untroubled at first by competitors, Hume engineered the passage of an Oregon statute similar to the Eel River law in 1899. Defending his monopoly successfully for some three decades, Hume produced nearly a half-million cases of canned salmon between 1877 and his death in 1908. He invested his own capital to build hatcheries on the Rogue and even improved on contemporary government practice by rearing his fish until they were five or six inches long before releasing them. Significantly, the Rogue experienced no catastrophic decline in salmon harvests such as took place on the Sacramento, the Eel, and the Columbia Rivers in the 1880s.[102]

In the end, neither the Bay Area oyster business, the Eel River fishery, nor R. D. Hume were of much value as precedent. Oysters are sessile during their commercial lives and could offer no lessons for the management of swimming fishes. Eel River was a relatively small stream with no important rights of navigation attached to it and so could be privatized in a way impossible for larger rivers like the Sacramento or the Klamath. In any event, private ownership did not protect the oyster beds from poisoning after the turn of the century, nor did consignment to a relatively few users protect the Eel River salmon from suffering the same fate as those in the Sacramento in the 1880s. For his part, Hume's monopoly earned him the bitter enmity of his fellow Oregonians. That state's Supreme Court broke his monopoly in 1908 by finding the 1899 statute in violation of the privileges and immunities clause of the Oregon constitution.[103]

Hardly more successful were California's efforts to conserve the Sacramento River salmon fishery by regulating seasons and fishing gear. California's first fishing statute, passed in 1852, prohibited the erection of salmon weirs and other obstructions to the runs by all but Indians, and the next year the state placed a closed season on the salmon fishery as well. Subsequently, pressure from commercial fishers eroded closures on the San Joaquin and Eel Rivers. When canning began in earnest on the Sacramento, the legislature closed the river to fishing between August 1 and November 1. At the very next session, however, it cut the closure in half and in 1881, just as the fishery reached its most intensive stage, it shortened it still further.[104] Such ephemeral laws posed little threat to fishers. Bancroft wrote that the salmon laws were "little respected, partly owing to the frequent change of regulations."[105]

Jack London's *Tales of the Fish Patrol* offers some idea of how difficult such regulations were to enforce. As soon as the 1875 season closure became law, salmon fishers set up camps deep in the tules of the Sacramento–San Joaquin Delta and salted their catches there during the closed season. On the main river, fishers posted lookouts at either end of their drifts to signal with fire or with gunshots the approach of a suspicious-looking boat.[106] The closure was, according to fishers and Fish Commissioners alike, a "farce."[107] It deterred honest workers from their livelihoods while, in the absence of adequate enforcement, it gave lawbreakers free access to the fishery. Even if most of the fishers wished only, in the words of one, "to earn a living and obey the law," they could afford to do so only "provided that others, less honest, [were] prevented from violating it with impunity."[108] Even on the rare occasions when they did make arrests for violating the fishing laws, state agents found local juries unwilling to convict the accused.[109]

Neither was the State Board of Fish Commissioners immune to political tampering. In 1881 two men from river towns, B. H. Buckingham of Washington and A. B. Dibble of Grass Valley, took seats on the Board. Where five years before B. B. Redding and S. R. Throckmorton, well-to-do San Franciscans who had held seats on the Board since its inception, had insisted on the "absolute necessity of a patrol boat to prevent unlawful fishing," the Board now "steadfastly maintained" that fitting out a patrol vessel to combat the "desultory depredations" of salmon poachers would constitute a needless extravagance.[110] Political conflict over the Board's membership in the wake of the retirements of Redding and Throckmorton brought all work to a standstill at the critical juncture between 1886 and 1888. A steam patrol launch commissioned in 1885 was sold three years later. Enforcement im-

Figure 5.1. Chinese workers drying squid near Monterey, California, ca. 1880. Photo courtesy of Bancroft Library, University of California, Berkeley.

proved, however, when a new governor appointed San Franciscans to the Board in 1891. A new steam launch, the *Hassler*, began day and night patrols on the Sacramento River two years later, and after 1897 the gasoline-powered *Quinnat*, in the words of the Commissioners, "forcibly impressed upon the fishermen the necessity of a close observance of the regulations."[111] At the same time, the Commissioners secured passage of a law placing trials for fishing violations in superior court rather than in local magistrate's courts, which brought an instantaneous and welcome increase in convictions and guilty pleas.[112]

It was not quite so difficult to muster the political resources necessary to regulate the Chinese fisheries. These were an easy mark in the 1880s: Their methods were peculiar, their clannishness obvious to all and, worst of all, they seemed to be prospering at the expense of everybody else (see Figure 5.1). In the curious reasoning of Commissioners Buckingham, Dibble, and Sherwood in 1886, "the oft-repeated and serious complaint that fish food is becoming scarce in California furnishes a powerful reason why the Chinese exhaustion should cease, and the cause of the complaint be removed."[113] As early as 1860 a statute copied from the infamous anti-Chinese Foreign Miners' Tax levied a license fee of $4 per month on Chinese fishers in California. Sponsored by a state senator from a mining county, this "foreign fisher's tax" was clearly more an effort to make life difficult for the Chinese than one to conserve the fisheries. Revenues were never satisfactory, and although a move to repeal the tax in 1862 ran aground in the opposition of white fishers in the Bay Area, another move to repeal in 1864 was successful.[114]

The rabidly anti-Chinese Twenty-third Session of the legislature mounted a frontal attack on the Asian fishers in 1880. "An Act Related to Fishing in the Waters of the State" prohibited "all aliens incapable of becoming electors" of California [i.e., the Chinese], from fishing in the state's public waters. This was one of a number of anti-Chinese statutes, passed in a group, which failed to withstand the scrutiny of the U.S. Circuit Court. If the Chinese were universally loathed by the trade unionists who seized control of state government in the late seventies, they were nonetheless a well-knit and powerful community and had the resources to defend their rights. The fishing statute, like the others, violated Fourteenth Amendment guarantees of equal protection under the law as well as provisions of an 1868 "most-favored-nation" treaty between the United States and China.[115]

In striking down the fishing statute, Judge Sawyer had first to distinguish it from the one at issue in *McReady* v. *Virginia*, an 1877 case in which the U.S. Supreme Court had upheld a state's authority to prohibit nonresidents from taking oysters from waters which the state had power to control in the interest of its people.[116] This was the purpose of the "ineligible to become electors" provision in the statute, which California also used to discriminate against Japanese immigrants in the twentieth century. The Fourteenth Amendment guaranteed citizenship to "all persons born or naturalized in the United States," but federal law had not yet extended naturalization rights to Asians. This did not trouble Judge Sawyer greatly because the fishing statute's discriminatory purpose was so transparent: It illustrated, he wrote, "the crudities, not to say the absurdities, into which constitutional conventions and legislative bodies are liable to be betrayed by their anxiety and efforts to accomplish, by indirection and circumlocation, an unconstitutional purpose which they cannot effect by direct means."[117]

Cloaked with only a bit more conservationist legitimacy was the long series of regulations passed to control the Chinese fishers' nets and other gear on the ostensible ground that Chinese tools destroyed fry and fodder of fish which other (i.e., white) people harvested. In 1899 the Fish and Game Commission requested, and three years later received, from the legislature a closed season on shrimp between May and September, ostensibly because immature fish were then most abundant in San Francisco Bay. Conveniently, the summer months were the only ones in which the Chinese could air-dry their catches. When anti-Chinese fishing laws grew so complex as to foster the growth of protection rackets between Chinese merchants and Fish and Game patrol agents, a frustrated legislature dealt the industry a lethal blow by prohibiting the export of its produce and for good measure specifically prohibited the use of Chinese shrimp nets in 1911.[118] The anti-Chinese campaign was one of California's most consistent and energetic efforts in fisheries regulation before the turn of the century, and one whose ultimate victory added considerably to the Fish Commissioners' prestige. Sustained primarily by the political will of the (non-Chinese) fishing industry, it had almost nothing to do with actual problems in the harvest of fisheries per se.

The state's program gained in coherence and effect in the 1890s. An act of 1887 levied an annual license fee on commercial fishers, although income from this source remained light until the Legislature prescribed penalties for noncompliance with the law some years later. Legislation in 1878 had given the State Board of Fish Commissioners responsibility for protecting terrestrial game animals as well as fish, and in 1895 the Board obtained the power to hire game wardens to enforce its regulations at the county level. Laws added to the Penal Code through the 1880s prohibiting the pollution of the state's rivers and requiring operators of irrigation ditches and the like to maintain fishways, fish ladders, and fish screens took more practical effect after 1893, when the State Board of Fish Commissioners retained an attorney and began taking violators to court. In 1902, finally, a constitutional amendment allowed the legislature to divide the state into fish and game districts so as to enable it to pass regulations specifically tailored to the peculiar requirements of each.[119]

One of the lawyer's first tasks was to seek an injunction against the "particularly flagrant" pollution of the Truckee River, a Nevada County trout stream, by the sawdust of several large lumber mills. Convictions for violating the antipollution sections of the Penal Code were very hard to come by in local courts, "owing to the importance of the milling industry in the counties where the trials were obliged to be had," but in 1897 the state supreme court ruled for the Fish Commissioners in *People* v. *Truckee Lumber Company*. Even if a waterway was not navigable and even if it flowed over privately held land, the court held, "to the extent that waters are the common passageway for fish . . . they are deemed for such purposes public waters, and subject to all the laws of the state regulating the right of fishing," including, in this case, the antipollution laws.[120]

This was a significant victory. *Woodruff* v. *North Bloomfield Gravel Mining Company* in 1884 had accomplished a similarly beneficial environmental result, but only indirectly. Judge Sawyer's reasoning in that case rested on the right of the people to the untrammeled use of *navigable* waterways and, more importantly, on the fact that by 1884 mining was a declining industry in California and inflicted far more damage on agriculture and town life than it was worth. Sawyer thus did little more than to compare costs and benefits, just as state courts in the 1850s had done in allowing miners to damage what was then a still-fledgling agriculture in the Central Valley.[121] After *Truckee Lumber Company*, California could force water-using industries to account for injuries they inflicted on the fisheries, which were a minor industry to be sure but which at the same time were the most sensitive indicators of the ecological integrity of the state's waterways.

The other major legal victory of the 1890s came in the case *Ex parte Simon Maier*, decided in the state supreme court in 1894. In upholding the conviction of a Los Angeles merchant for selling venison in violation of an 1893 statute, the court gave its approval to a key change in the state's strategy for controlling the harvest of its fish and game. Instead of bringing the law to bear on individual harvesters in the field, where they were hard to catch, the 1893 law tried to eliminate the *market* for wildlife products, thus implicitly recognizing the ecological link between market behavior and the conservation of resources. Maier claimed that he had imported the venison in question from Texas, where it had been legally killed. The statute, he claimed, referred only to deer harvested in California; it did not prohibit the sale of game imported from other states, in whose wildlife California could have no conceivable interest. Because Maier had paid for the carcass, moreover, it was his property – an article of commerce like any other – and the state could not regulate his disposal of it without interfering with interstate commerce in an unconstitutional way.[122]

The California court found for the state in all particulars. Key to its decision was its finding that wild fish and game, once harvested, were not like other forms of property:

> The wild game within a state belongs to the people in their collective, sovereign capacity; it is not the subject of private ownership, except in so far as the people may elect to make it so; and they may, if they see fit, absolutely prohibit the taking of it, or any traffic or commerce in it, if deemed necessary for its protection or preservation, or the public good.[123]

The state could use its police power, then, to prohibit commercial traffic in venison, domestic or foreign, because it was "a matter of common knowledge" that the impossibility of distinguishing game poached in California from imported game once the flesh was on the market had frustrated the state's efforts to protect local populations of deer in the past. The court's denial of Maier's appeal to the federal commerce clause turned on the narrow fact that the latter had cut a pound of flesh from the deer's carcass before selling it to the arresting officer, thus breaking the original package and removing it from interstate commerce.

The state's successful assertion of title to its wild fish and game was probably the most significant advance in the law of wildlife before 1900. The U.S. Supreme Court pointed approvingly to the language in *Maier*, along with similar decisions from New York and Illinois, when it elevated the "state ownership doctrine" to constitutional status in the 1896 case of *Geer v. Connecticut*.[124] Congress gave interstate effect to the rule in the Lacey Act of 1900, which prohibited the interstate shipment of illegally harvested wildlife products and subjected all such products brought into any state to the laws of that state.[125] U.S. fish and wildlife populations had declined so precipitously through the nineteenth century because no one had been able to defend their interests, either in the market or before the law. Now armed with the *Maier* and *Geer* rulings, California intervened aggressively in the market's use of fish and fishery habitat. The state ownership rule figured centrally in the *Truckee Lumber Company* decision, which defended the people's trout against industrial pollution. It justified the prohibition against exporting shrimp, which the Chinese fishers had hitherto treated as no one's property but their own.

In 1910 the state incorporated the idea into a constitutional amendment which gave the Legislature virtually unlimited power to control fishing as it saw fit.[126] With the Chinese fisheries all but extinguished, the state then used the 1910 amendment to dismantle the other important system of informal fishery law which operated under its nose, that of the Bay Area Italians. Later on, the state ownership rule became the state's chief legal weapon in its fight to regulate the industrial fishery for sardines.

Conclusion: legal heritage of the nineteenth century

At the turn of the twentieth century, both state and federal fishery agencies thought they had good reasons to congratulate themselves. The U.S. Fish Commission, whose job it was to prospect the seas for new fishery resources and to sustain old ones artificially, had developed what a later analyst called "a well-earned reputation for scientific achievement equaled by few governmental agencies."[127] The California Board of Fish Commissioners was busy bringing polluters to court and making successful arrests on the fishing grounds. Its reward was the widespread public approval that it harvested as the long-hated Chinese fisheries dissolved and as salmon once again ran up the tributaries of the Sacramento in abundance. "By the efforts of this Board," wrote the Commissioners in 1900, "the salmon has been saved to our state."[128] One historian of state government in California took them at their word: Salmon in the first decade of the new century, he wrote, had been "made plentiful by the earlier conservation work of the California Fish Commission."[129] "It is safe to say," claimed the Commissioners, "that California has never known a Commission that has rendered such great returns for the small annual expenditure as has the California Fish Commission."[130]

Their victories, however, were more apparent than real. Salmon harvests increased during the 1890s for four reasons, none of them directly related to anything government agencies had done to improve them. Sacramento salmon survived to adulthood in greater numbers because the region's climate grew more favorable to their nursery. In *Woodruff* v. *North Bloomfield Gravel Mining Company*, Central Valley farmers and townspeople had brought the hydraulic mining industry to a halt and thus indirectly eased conditions for spawning salmon and their progeny. Coastal schooling fishes on which the salmon fed were unusually abundant during the 1890s. Finally, increasing harvests of immature adult salmon from offshore waters raised the total harvest and thus disguised stable or declining yields from the river. The recovery also disguised an important political division that would later confound fishery management in California: More salmon for everyone served the interests both of sportfishers, who dominated the California agency as they did those of other states, and the commercial fishers for whom the federal agency was chief patron. Because salmon was the political cornerstone of fishery management in California, the Golden State did not at first suffer the bitter conflict between the two groups and their respective agencies that by 1900 was already making great trouble in other states.[131]

People v. *Truckee Lumber Company* portended a new departure in fishery regulation by moving beyond the cost–benefit approach of the *Woodruff* decision to state that California had a fundamental interest in the ecological integrity of its waterways. During the twentieth century government agencies would begin haltingly to protect that interest by requiring assessment of potential damage to fish and wildlife before other economic uses of water could begin. The state ownership doctrine of *Maier* and *Geer*, on the other hand, looked backward: It was the constitutional synthesis of three decades of state efforts to halt the devastation of wildlife by market forces deliberately unchained by many more decades of progrowth legal change. As legal handiwork it was badly flawed, based on a misreading of the sources to which its authors attributed it and doomed to gradual erosion by Congress and the federal courts during the twentieth century. It nonetheless enabled state governments to insulate their fish and game somewhat from the commercial demand that was inexorably destroying them. Without it, wildlife populations would no doubt have declined even further than they did.[132]

The death of the Chinese shrimp fishery, eagerly sought by non-Asians because the Chinese were so good at it and because it symbolized their ability to keep their own law, was the state ownership rule's most tangible victory on the West Coast. Its effectiveness in that case, however, stemmed less from any vigor inherent in the rule itself than from the obsessive desire of Californians to use any means at hand to drive the Chinese out of business. If federal immigration law would not suffice, the state ownership rule would do just as well. Had the doctrine any force of its own, it might also have controlled the salmon canning industry, and to much greater ecological effect. The circumstances in either case were essentially the same: Like the Chinese, salmon canners processed vast quantities of California resources for export to consumers of their own ethnicity in other countries. Like the shrimp fishery, the salmon industry was uncontrollable because demand for its product was simply too strong.

The President of the California Academy of Sciences made this point to the Fish Commissioners in 1890. "There is no river," he said,

> however rich it may be in salmon, but must eventually become impoverished if the canner is to be allowed to pursue his vocation. . . . As his means for canning fish are unlimited, and he has the world for a market, the canner has but to increase his fishermen until the stream is so far exhausted as to be of no further value.[133]

By itself, the state ownership idea could do little to shield a resource from market pressure when harvesters could bring any political force to their demands that the harvest be kept open. Nor could it, even reinforced by the Lacey Act, protect state policy from the powerful solvent of the interstate commerce clause and gradual encroachment by federal law. As Justice Holmes would later put it, "to put the claim of the state upon title is to lean upon a slender reed."[134] Just how slender it was would become clear when the state tried to use it to fence in the sardine fishery a few decades later.

State ownership was an early and not particularly robust attempt to fit the fisherman's problem into established legal categories so that the state could deal with it. It was a legal fiction, noted the U.S. Supreme Court in a later review of the doctrine, "expressive in legal shorthand of the importance to its people that a State have power to preserve and regulate the exploitation of an important resource."[135] It was just such a legal fiction that transformed the business corporation into a kind of citizen, with civil rights to own property, make contracts, and to sue in court to protect its interests. It had been devised early in the nineteenth century because a growing economy needed such a device for concentrating the resources and talents of large numbers of individuals into a coherent whole but had a legal infrastructure that was in many ways hostile to it.[136]

Making state property out of fish and game, like granting fictive citizenship to corporations, was government's way of collecting a wide range of inter-related problems under a single relatively manipulable legal abstraction. Just as corporations were not quite like other forms of enterprise, however, fish and game were not, after all, quite like other commodities in the market-place. They were the biological manifestation of a dynamic balance between the environments that nurtured them and the forces that consumed them: They were partly what they ate, partly that which ate them. Society could no longer assume that the effects of using them were unimportant to all but their immediate individual buyers and sellers.

Nature, of course, had acted all along as if this had been the case. So had the Indians and the immigrant communities for whom fishing was as much a way of life as of making money. So too had Livingston Stone when he suggested that the future well-being of Indian society on the McCloud River was crucial to that of the salmon fishery in the river below. During the nineteenth century and far into the twentieth, however, the tendency of market forces to sunder the ecological bonds between natural resources and their environments, both cultural and natural, proved more powerful than any incipient awareness of the steadily growing social costs of allowing them to do so.

III

The industrial frontier, 1910–1950

6

Mechanized fishing

I have myself seen the carrier pigeon so that you couldn't
see the sun. There isn't a species left in the world. The
commercialism is responsible for their entire disappearance from the earth. . . . If the reduction plants are permitted to take sardines from the ocean ad lib it is only
a question of time, I do not know how long, until there
wouldn't be any left.   – F. E. Booth (1925)[1]

The sardine, Mr. Duke, some year they come lots, some
year they don't come lots. Every year they come enough
to work in the canneries.   – Peter Ferrante (1925)[2]

Elmer Higgins was ten years old in 1902, when his family moved from Iowa
to Long Beach, California. Some thirty years later, testifying to a Congressional committee in his capacity as Chief of Biological Inquiry for the U.S.
Bureau of Fisheries, Higgins recalled that as a boy he could drop a fishing
line off the end of Long Beach Pier and, with a single pull, snag as many
as two or three sardines on an unbaited hook. Shoals of the fish, one or two
feet beneath the surface and six feet thick, blackened the water of Long
Beach Harbor as far as he could see. Earl Pomeroy, an historian who grew
up in Santa Cruz during the 1920s and 1930s, likewise remembered that he
could mark schools of sardine on the horizon by the dark clouds of seabirds
feeding on them. Both men reflected that, without realizing it at the time,
they had been witness to an era in the state's ecological history that was
passing even as they watched.[3]

Los Angeles County was still primarily an agricultural region when Higgins
moved there, although the area was a hotbed of real estate speculation and
its population had grown rapidly since the 1880s. San Pedro Bay, where
Long Beach stood, harbored a number of steamships for the coastal trade
and a handful of fishing boats, some of them newly fitted out with gasoline
engines, but the area had as yet no deepwater port and only the rudiments
of an industrial economy. As generous as nature had been to California, poor
local supplies of energy had retarded the state's economic development at
the end of the nineteenth century. Its main source of fuel was coal, imported
at no small expense all the way from Australia.[4]

123

After 1900 new sources of energy changed both the economy and the environment of the state radically. During the first decade of the new century, the state became the nation's largest producer of crude oil. According to the Census of 1910, the 30 to 50 percent savings that locally refined oil offered over imported coal gave "a decided impetus to manufactures" in the Golden State.[5] Long Beach was itself the site of one of the richest oil strikes in history and boasted the world's largest oil port during the 1920s. Simultaneously, California entrepreneurs brought hydroelectric power from the Sierra Nevada to the towns and farms of the coastal and Central Valley regions. Oil and electricity were to the state's economy what canals and railroads had been to the Midwest in the nineteenth century: In the first two decades of the new century California farms became the most efficient and most thoroughly mechanized in the nation. Energy-intensive development transformed Long Beach and other California cities into major industrial centers by 1940.[6] At the same time, fossil fuels enabled Californians to tap new fisheries resources whose wealth the immigrant fishers of the late nineteenth century could scarcely have imagined.

Turn-of-the-century Californians were not unaware that their coastal waters contained resources of great value. The research vessel *Albatross* had prospected them extensively during the 1890s, and local newspaper editors had boosted their development from time to time. The Pacific, however, was rough, unpredictable, and thus largely inaccessible to the traditional gear on which the immigrant fishers steadfastly relied. Discouraged by declines in the inshore fisheries that had been important before, California capitalists invested in Alaska and the Pacific Northwest so that, while harvests increased dramatically in those areas, California's fisheries remained generally depressed until about 1910 and their share of the national harvest stagnant at about 2 percent.[7]

Thereafter, with the proliferation of motorized, seagoing fishing boats, new methods for processing fish, and the opening of new markets to California producers, three new fisheries came to life in offshore waters. First to begin was a new, open-sea troll fishery for salmon, which caught on about the turn of the century and eclipsed the traditional inshore fishery during World War I. High-seas tuna fishing began in earnest out of southern California ports during the war decade, although it quickly outgrew the capacity of local resources and moved southward into foreign waters. Most spectacular of the new industrial fisheries was that for pilchard, or sardine, which grew so rapidly during the war that it made California the premier fishing state in the country. At its peak in the 1930s, the sardine fishery was probably the most intensive in the world. It dominated the political history of California wildlife much as the salmon had earlier.

Ashore, energy-intensive agriculture transformed the California environment in ways that had profound consequences for the fisheries, both old and new. Reclamation of the swamps and floodplains of the Sacramento–San Joaquin river system proceeded very rapidly as prices for intensive crops remained strong and as the annexation of Hawaii and the opening of the Panama Canal caught the imagination of land developers. By 1920 the job was virtually complete.[8] Upstream, irrigation and hydroelectric dams closed streams in both the Sacramento–San Joaquin and the Klamath watersheds to spawning salmon one by one. A milestone of sorts in the history of California's environment came with the development of the State Water Plan in the 1930s and the completion in 1942 of its centerpiece, Shasta Dam, at the headwaters of the Sacramento. Thereafter the ecology of the Central Valley would be more artificial than natural, the fate of its salmon and other wildlife firmly in the hands of engineers. The environmental impact of California agriculture reached into offshore waters as well: Most of the sardines harvested in the 1920s and 1930s were not canned for human consumption; instead they were reduced to fishmeal, an important ingredient in commercial feeds for poultry and other livestock.

These developments were but local manifestations of a transformation that took place throughout the industrialized world beginning in the 1890s. Economic historians refer to the change as the Second Industrial Revolution, a cluster of new technological developments, particularly in electric power, internal combustion engines, and organic chemistry, which emerged simultaneously to give a new push to economic growth and generated social, political, and ecological changes no less radical than those that had attended the First Industrial Revolution a century before.[9] Deep-water fisheries on both sides of the Atlantic came under heavy assault during the 1890s. The transition did not gather momentum in the northeastern Pacific until about 1910 but proceeded very rapidly thereafter.[10] On the land, U.S. agriculture entered a new era between 1900 and 1920 as mechanization rather than new settlement became the major impetus to growth.[11] The Census Bureau may have declared the western frontier officially closed in 1890, but within a decade oil and electricity had opened an entirely new one for the conquering.

Industrial fisheries

At the turn of the century most West Coast fishers went about their business much as fishers all over the world had done for centuries, relying primarily on wind and muscle to harvest their prey. San Francisco wholesalers of halibut, sole, and other groundfish had for some years operated pairs of steam trawlers outside the Golden Gate and a few market fishers had outfitted their Italian boats with gasoline engines, but progress had been slow. Employment in the industry actually declined during the first decade of the new century. So, too, did the harvest, and California slipped from sixth to tenth place among fishing states.[12] By 1925, however, the fisheries had undergone an industrial revolution. As Tables 6.1 and 6.2 show, annual landings increased tenfold between 1899 and 1925. Although the number of fishers employed statewide remained roughly stable, many more of them now worked together on heavier, motorized vessels, and their productivity increased tremendously. The ocean-going fisheries of southern California eclipsed those of the Sacramento–San Joaquin watershed in importance, and by 1921 the Long Beach area alone harbored two-thirds of all the fishers in California. Fish packing dominated the economies of San Diego, Long Beach, and Monterey. California now led the nation in the volume and value of its fishery produce.[13]

Key to the change was the successful application of fossil fuels to fishing and the gradual modification of vessels and gear for work on the open ocean. This took place in the years before World War I, as loose aggregations of labor and capital shifted from declining stocks of fish to new ones which, for a variety of reasons, were abundant at the time. Real growth, however, awaited the opportunity to tap new and wider markets, and this did not come until the war began. Even then, only three resources – salmon, tuna, and sardines – accounted for most of the progress. The statistics disguise the transformation of the salmon industry which, although it continued to rely on a damaged and declining resource, became an essentially new enterprise as it shifted from inland to offshore waters. Other fisheries changed very little. Even as late as 1918 San Francisco's market fisheries, held in thrall by the wholesalers' "fish trust" and the determined resistance to progress of the Italian market fishers, remained more technologically backward than those of any major U.S. seaport.[14]

Sportfishers had begun trolling for salmon in Monterey Bay in the 1890s. Sensing an opportunity to break the San Francisco wholesalers' hold over the Monterey fishery, F. E. Booth of the Sacramento River Packers' Association moved in with workers from his cannery at Black Diamond (later Pittsburg), and in 1901 began curing the fish in chilled brine to make lox for export to Europe.[15] Monterey salmon were immature natives of streams in the Sacramento–San Joaquin and Klamath River watersheds, where spawning conditions had improved during the 1890s as the climate grew more favorable and as decades' worth of mining debris began to flush down toward the sea. At the turn of the century salmon were plentiful, both in the ocean and as they spawned; state authorities proclaimed it "an acknowledged fact that the runs of salmon in the Sacramento and San Joaquin rivers, and their tributaries, [were] fully restored."[16] Increased effort in the ocean fishery temporarily disguised the continued poor health of the inland fishery, and between 1901 and 1905 California once again became a net exporter of salmon.[17]

Trolling crews at first worked out of small sailing vessels, probably of the

Table 6.1. *California Fishery Production, 1889–1925 (in metric tons)*.

Year	Chinook salmon	All tunas	Sardine	All other	Total landings	% U.S. total
1899	3,323	92	1,083	14,923	19,421	2
1908	4,021	252	2,108	15,614	21,545	2
1915	3,329	9,579	1,995	25,542	40,445	3
1916	4,972	10,408	7,113	29,162	43,192	8
1917	5,027	13,889	47,320	29,162	95,398	8
1918	5,975	4,676	71,660	36,410	118,697	9
1919	5,975	16,300	69,944	28,812	121,031	10
1920	5,060	17,876	53,873	24,101	100,910	8
1921	3,632	8,945	26,969	21,975	61,521	6
1922	3,288	16,048	42,455	21,092	82,883	7
1923	3,223	17,287	71,890	22,993	115,393	10
1924	4,552	12,610	110,312	27,274	154,748	13
1925	4,330	24,305	143,315	26,914	198,865	16

Sources: USBF, *Reports*; U.S. Census Bureau, *Fisheries of the United States, 1908*; CFGC, *Biennial Reports*; Frey, *California's Living Marine Resources and Their Utilization*, pp. 136–41; Potter and Christy, *Trends in Natural Resources Commodites*, p. 302, column f.

Table 6.2. Labor, vessels, and landings per fisher, 1889–1925 (weights in metric tons).

Year	Fishers	Vessels over 5 tons	All motor and sailboats	Total landings	Landings per fisher
1899	3,243	33	1,355	19,421	6.0
1908	3,965	31	2,129	21,545	5.4
1915	4,833	73	2,598	40,445	8.4
1919	4,522	—	—	121,031	26.8
1920	5,087	—	—	100,910	19.8
1921	5,269	—	—	61,521	11.7
1922	4,467	209	1,589	82,883	18.6
1923	4,597	285	1,442	115,393	25.1
1924	4,809	337	1,645	154,748	32.2
1925	4,518	362	1,405	198,865	44.0

Sources: USBF, Reports; CFGC, Biennial Reports; California Fish and Game.

Figure 6.1. Evolution of the Italian fishing boat, ca. 1920. The photograph shows a number of boats in various stages of specialization for motorized fishing. The boat in the foreground is only slightly modified, with a lowered stern and a rudimentary wheelhouse. The one behind it is more advanced, with a more elaborate wheelhouse and a clipper bow. Note that most of the boats retain rigging for the lateen sail. Cf. Figure 4.2. Photo courtesy of the National Maritime Museum, San Francisco.

Italian type that served the Bay Area market fishery. Toward the end of the decade, Sacramento River gill-netters began using gasoline power and during their off-season moved down the coast for the summer trolling season at Monterey. Bit by bit, as Figure 6.1 shows, fishers and boatbuilders transformed the Italian boat into a new type known as the Monterey clipper, powered by single-cylinder gasoline engines designed and built in San Francisco. With raised bulwarks and a flared bow to ward off heavy seas and a lowered stern to give free play to trolling lines, the Monterey boat was adaptable to several types of fishing and able to undertake journeys of several days' duration at sea. By 1910 some 200 boats fished salmon out of Monterey, most of them still under sail and crewed by Japanese immigrants newly arrived from Hawaii. Seventy of the boats, most of which were powered, worked for the Packers' Association. Monterey landings increased steadily until 1915, by which time California's inshore and ocean salmon harvests were roughly equal.[18]

Salmon trolling, although relying on a well-used resource, was in essence a new kind of fishery and one that compounded the difficulties of public authorities in years to come. Salmon have the polite habit of feeding at sea until they are ripe and then returning to their natal streams, where they are easy for fishers to catch and biologists to study. The ocean salmon fishery, however, takes them with regard neither to their maturity nor to their stream of origin. Klamath River fish, for example, mingle with Central Valley fish as far south as Monterey, and unless they have tags on them it is impossible to tell them apart. The troll fishery thus cannot distinguish between hatchery fish and naturally propagated ones, or between fish that come from healthy stocks and those that come from endangered ones. About half of the salmon that modern trollers take are below legal size, and although fishers typically throw them back roughly half do not survive the trauma of hooking and die anyway.[19] The troll fishery for salmon is thus what one modern biologist called "an economic monstrosity," a peculiar attempt to do with gasoline what the salmon would more efficiently do by themselves, if given a chance.[20] Until 1923, moreover, by which time the industry was mature and spread along the length of the coast from Monterey to Crescent City, it operated under fewer legal constraints than any other kind of fishing save handlining from public docks.[21]

Albacore were also abundant near the turn of the century. Cool water and huge standing crops of their fodder may have encouraged them. Azorean fishers at San Diego, having abandoned whaling and inherited from the departing Chinese both the abalone camp on Point Loma and the local market fishery, began trolling for albacore as gasoline engines became safe and profitable for small boats. The annexation of Hawaii opened a market for the fish among Portuguese workers in the new territory's rapidly growing sugar industry.[22] Japanese immigrants, many having spent time in Hawaii themselves, also took up tuna fishing in the early years of the new century. One leading entrepreneur who came directly from Japan was Kondo Masaharu, a professor at the Japanese Imperial Fisheries Institute. Himself the proprietor of a substantial abalone business, Kondo came to California in 1908 to negotiate an entry into the Mexican fishery, long since abandoned by the Chinese. Finding tuna more profitable, Kondo and other Japanese newcomers introduced California to their method "chumming" the fish up with live bait and hauling them out with bamboo poles and barbless hooks. The live-bait method quickly became standard in the industry. By 1914 some 125 boats, each with three crew and fifteen- to twenty-five- horsepower engines, delivered dressed albacore to canneries at San Diego and San Pedro.[23]

Hawaiian field workers were not the ideal market for a new fishery, and in the United States, according to David Starr Jordan, albacore was "of very little value unless, as in Japan, it is eaten raw."[24] At San Pedro, though, A. P. Halfhill began experimenting early in the century with different methods of processing the fish. He eventually developed a way of baking it in steam before canning that gave the finished product the appearance and texture familiar to modern lovers of tuna salad. He put up his first substantial pack in 1911. Determined to overcome U.S. consumers' preference for canned salmon, he toured the United States by automobile to promote it personally as "chicken of the sea." Another San Pedro packer, Gilbert Van Camp, also took pains to develop the market, and in 1915 competition between tuna packers spread albacore over the country at a very low price. Thus whetted, consumer demand for it improved rapidly. Other tuna species, bluefin, yellowfin, and skipjack, occluded albacore catches from time to time but had a stronger flavor and thus drew no interest from canners at first. Albacore was a summer fish, so to keep their plants busy Halfhill, Van Camp, and the other packers usually canned sardines as well. In 1915 there were ten tuna canneries in the Long Beach area and four more at San Diego, each of them supplied by its own fleet of boats that could be equipped for sardine fishing when albacore were out of season.[25]

Both the salmon and the tuna fisheries relied primarily on sardines for bait, and no turn-of-the-century observer could have failed to note the magnificent abundance of that fish at the time. Sporadic trials had begun in several parts of the state before the nineteenth century was out, but catching sardines efficiently and most of all marketing them profitably remained obstacles to their development for several years to come. Halfhill, for example, had already established himself in the sardine business before he began experimenting with albacore at San Pedro. It was the salmon packer Booth, at Monterey, who began canning sardines experimentally in 1902 and made the business work. He began taking them with purse seines out of Sacramento River salmon boats, but under sail and with the clumsy salmon boats Booth's crews could not close on the schools quickly enough to catch them effectively. In 1905 Peter Ferrante, a fisher for Booth's Black Diamond salmon plant, solved the problem with a lampara net he had imported from Algeria. An encircling device like the purse seine, the lampara, operated from a powered Monterey clipper, was easy to set quickly and required only a few hands to haul. By 1915 it was standard gear in the sardine fishery.[26]

Before World War I, however, there was simply no market for California pilchards. There are some fifty genera of the family Clupidae, or herringlike fishes, several of which are canned and sold as sardines. Others, such as menhaden or anchovy, are of lower quality. None appealed particularly to U.S. consumers, although a substantial fishery for immature herring had grown up in Maine since the turn of the century. Foreign markets for this type of fish belonged to North Sea herring. By 1915, then, there were only two sardine canneries and twenty lampara nets at Monterey and a few more at San Pedro. Northern canneries still concentrated on salmon, southern ones on tuna, while the Monterey lampara crews derived most of their income from supplying the old Chinese market for dried squid: Like sardines, squid traveled in schools and had to be fished at night, the crews following the trails of luminescent algae that the schools left glowing in their wake.[27] Here again, a new fishery gradually took shape from the decaying remnants of an old one, as different sectors of the nineteenth-century fishing industry adapted to each other, to economic opportunity, and to the changing ecology of their resources.

Another problem that troubled packers both of sardines and of tuna was the enormous quantity of waste their canneries produced. Only one-half the raw weight of a sardine is edible muscle, and in the early days of the albacore fishery Halfhill and the others packed only the choicest, whitest part of the tuna filet and threw away the other three-quarters of the fish. At first, tons and tons of offal were barged out to sea and dumped or, worse, left to befoul local harbors as was common practice in the northern salmon fisheries. Pork processors in the early nineteenth-century Midwest had had to learn to "use everything but the squeal," as they put it, before they could make their business work on a large scale. Finding profitable uses for fishery by-products was a problem that the sardine and tuna canners would have to solve, as well.

Some Maine sardine canners processed their offal into fertilizer for sale to local farmers and a substantial fishery in the mid-Atlantic states had for decades taken menhaden for processing as well. "Reduction," as it was called, involved pressing the oil and water out of the fish and then grinding the dried residue into meal. Separated from the water in the fish, the oil was a valuable source of vitamins A and D for livestock feed or was a cheap substitute for tallow in the manufacture of soap, paint, printing ink, and the like. Fishmeal was a cheap and effective fertilizer and, if refined a bit, could be fed to livestock.[28] Never ones to waste any part of their harvest, Chinese fishers in California had all along made use of their offal. In the Bay Area and at Monterey, they sold it for fertilizer to Asian gardeners and a few enterprising orchardists, while at San Diego they fed it to chickens.[29] Poultry, in fact, became the main consumers of California sardine during the 1920s and 1930s, to the chagrin of some who thought the practice wasteful of food. Systematic manufacture of cannery by-products began first in southern California, both because tuna canneries were first to begin large-scale operations and because the region's fruit growers provided a ready market for fishmeal. At Monterey, Booth began reducing his sardine offal as early as 1910 with equipment he brought down from his salmon plant at Pittsburg.[30] Reduction became a very profitable business during World War I, when prices for fats, oil, and proteins of all kinds rose steeply, and thereafter became the focal point of controversy over management of the sardine fishery.

The wartime crucible

Great strides in the technology of fishing and processing thus set the stage for industrial growth in the business during the early years of the twentieth century. By 1915, however, California landings had only just regained their turn-of-the-century levels. The relatively primitive market fisheries of the Bay Area remained the most important money-makers in the industry state-wide, although Los Angeles was catching up quickly.[31] Mechanized, capital-intensive fisheries would not survive unless their produce found new and wider markets. In ecological terms this meant that the industry, having discovered how to tap vast new reserves of organic energy by subsidizing their harvest with fossil energy, had now to elaborate new arteries for dif-fusing them into the human economy. As before, one limiting factor was transport: The integration of logging railroads in the northern coastal region into the statewide system did much to encourage the growth of salmon trolling off that hitherto remote section of the coast. For tuna and sardines, entrepreneurs had to find markets where previously none had existed.

Individual efforts by Booth, Halfhill, and Van Camp had met with some success, but it was the powerful impetus that World War I gave to U.S. food production generally that catalyzed the latent potential of California's new industrial fisheries into headlong expansion. Demand for food was so strong that by the middle of 1917 average farm prices were more than double what they had been in 1913. Meat packers and canners of fruit, vegetables, and fish did especially well.[32] The war also opened new markets for fishery byproducts by promoting mechanization and specialization on California farms. Like most Americans, Californians began substituting higher-grade foods for grain in their diets as their real incomes rose after the turn of the century. Rapid urbanization during the war decade, encouraged by the opening of the Panama Canal, improved motor and truck transport, and electrification, added momentum to this change. At the same time, new supplies of energy and water permitted farmers to grow livestock, especially dairy cows and poultry, in intensive, factory-style operations, with hired labor, electric lights, and commercially produced, scientifically administered feeds. This in turn called for high-protein feedstocks, the best of which was fishmeal.[33]

Rapid expansion during the war set food producers up for catastrophic decline when the federal government suddenly stopped pumping money into the nation's economy at the end of 1919. The ensuing deflation brought agricultural prices down to prewar levels by 1921. Prices for fuel, mainte-nance, and manufactured goods fell less rapidly, so that farmers and fishers who had mechanized their operations during the war decade faced substantial real increases in their costs of doing business. Employment in California's fish packing business fell 55 percent between 1919 and 1921, even more than the 34 percent decline in the state's food processing sector as a whole. Growers of staple crops continued to fare poorly through the rest of the twenties and into the Great Depression. California agriculture prospered again, though, as it continued to mechanize and to increase its concentration on specialty crops. Producing mixed feeds for different kinds of livestock became an important business in its own right, with poultry growers its most important market. The state's chickens more than doubled in number to twenty-one million on the eve of the Depression. Until soybean meal became a practical substitute during the 1940s, the most important source of protein in their feed was, again, sardine meal.[34]

The industrial fisheries shared in the prosperity of the 1920s. The ocean salmon fishery reached the northernmost end of the coast, although increasingly it had to share resources with well-organized sportfishers and with those who would reclaim the fishes' spawning ground for other uses. The tuna industry expanded southward into foreign waters and thereafter became primarily a distant-water fishery, more the concern of international diplomacy than of state politics. The sardine industry dwarfed the output of all other fisheries combined. As it committed itself to the manufacture of by-products, it wove the intricate, scissile food web of the California Current into the high-octane ecology of California agribusiness. The consequences would haunt fishery managers for the rest of the century. Meanwhile, climatic fluctuations interacted with changes which people wrought in the California environment to erode the seemingly boundless productivity that had encouraged the industrial fisheries' early growth.

Salmon remained virtually untapped along the northwestern coast of California until logging railroads linked the Mendocino and Humboldt coast to truck lines in the Central Valley. Ocean-caught salmon now made their refrigerated way by rail from Eureka and Fort Bragg to markets in the Bay Area. As high prices for fresh fish during the war brought more gear out onto the ocean, the offshore catch permanently surpassed the inland harvest of Chinook salmon. The last salmon cannery on the Sacramento River closed its doors in 1919. Canning continued sporadically on the Klamath until 1933, but as the resource declined and more southerly grounds grew crowded the fishery moved northward. After 1920, trollers intercepted fully half of the Klamath River chinooks before they ever reached the mouth of their natal watershed. Meanwhile, the Redwood Highway pushed into Del Norte County and bridged the Klamath in 1926. Now motorized sportfishers came to compete with motorized trollers as well as with the Indians for Klamath River salmon. The total harvest of these fish, inshore and offshore, reached its historical peak at middecade.[35]

While harvesting pressure increased, the condition of the salmon's nursery declined precipitously. The years after 1916 brought drier winters, warmer summers, and wider ranges between summer and winter temperatures than had prevailed in the abundant salmon years at the turn of the century. Over the war decade, meanwhile, irrigated acreage in the Sacramento Valley more than doubled and the state's capacity to generate hydroelectric power more than trebled.[36] In 1917 the Anderson–Cottonwood Irrigation District built a fifteen-foot-high diversion dam across the main stem of the Sacramento near Redding, thus barring all of the basin's northern tributaries for several years until state officials forced the district to build a fishway around its facility. Runs in the San Joaquin remained healthy until 1920, when Kerkhoff Dam and Powerhouse went into operation. By then the Central Valley had lost some 80 percent of its original inventory of spawning ground. In 1928 a state investigator reported that Central Valley salmon were "threatened with extinction"; the depletion of what had once been the state's most valuable fishery "a foregone conclusion."[37]

On the Klamath, the California–Oregon Power Company built a dam near Hornbrook, in what had been Shasta territory, in 1917. In addition to cutting off many miles of spawning gravels, the utility neglected to ensure the orderly release of water through the dam into the river below. As the dam periodically stopped the flow entirely and then released torrents of water through its turbines, the Klamath's level fluctuated wildly and exposed adult fish and spawn alike to the air.[38] In 1921, finally, the Electro-Metals Company announced plans to build two dams on the lower Klamath. Thus challenged, sportfishers allied with the Fish and Game Commission in an initiative campaign to bar further reclamation on the Klamath between the mouth of the Shasta River and the ocean.[39] With their victory in the 1924 election, sportfishers emerged as a powerful political force, firmly allied with a state agency and with interests that no longer necessarily coincided with those of commercial fishers.

The war also brought expansion to the state's market fisheries, especially in Los Angeles. Very little technological change took place in the Bay Area groundfishery, which remained under the control of a handful of wholesale brokers who operated three or four pairs of trawlers, half of them powered by steam and half by gasoline. After the mid-1920s, most of the "double-draggers" converted to diesel power, but the old-fashioned paranzella net remained in the Bay Area long after other groundfisheries converted to the more efficient otter trawl.[40] Trawling is an extraordinarily "dirty" fishery: Typically three-quarters of the halibut the paranzella trawlers took, for example, were under legal size and thus killed but never landed.[41] Some observers thought the wholesalers an improvement over the small boat operators from whom they wrested control over the groundfishery because their marketing operations were more efficient and thus less "wasteful" of fish, but the only real difference between the two in this regard was that the trawlers destroyed fish at sea and thus out of public view. Enormous quantities of fish continued to spoil in Bay Area retail markets nonetheless, and controversy over their reduction to fertilizer during the war foreshadowed the conflict that later emerged over the massive quantities of sardines that went to waste, in the eyes of some, in this way.[42]

By 1920 southern California market fishers, with newer and larger boats, regularly ventured as far south as Cedros Island for fish that they returned, packed in ice, to harbor at San Diego or Long Beach. At the latter port, a new fleet of purse seiners flourished under the wartime demand for food. From small beginnings in 1915, owned and crewed mainly by immigrants from the Adriatic with a minority of Japanese, the fleet grew to number 103 by 1920. It supported an active boatbuilding industry at Long Beach for a time and dominated the harvest of bluefin tuna as well as those of such nearshore market species as barracuda, yellowtail, and sea bass. The 1920–1 deflation hit this sector of the industry harder than most, as fuel and other running costs of running the highly sophisticated boats remained high while prices for fish collapsed. By 1924 only six of the seiners remained in independent hands. The rest fell to "banks and moneyed men," in the words of the Fish and Game Commission.[43] Notable among these were the tuna canners. Beginning in 1925 the seiners entered the sardine fishery, where the real money was to be made.

When war began in Europe the albacore fishery, which produced canned food for the domestic market, was already four years into its bonanza stage. Landings that year doubled those of sardines and salmon combined. Like most bonanzas, that for tuna was neither orderly nor stable: In 1916 the *San Diego Union* found "more capital invested in canneries and boats than [could] possibly find remunerative returns."[44] The resource, moreover, was an extremely volatile one because of the albacore's spectacular migratory range and its extreme sensitivity to temperature. It seems to fish best in cool water and congregates near upwelling currents where the schooling fishes on which it feeds are abundant. The fishery had come to life during a run of relatively cool summer seasons that began during the 1890s and came to an abrupt end in 1917. The summer of 1918 was very warm, bringing shortfalls of salmon and groundfish off central California and catches of such southern denizens as barracuda far to the north of their usual haunts. Southern California landings of albacore fell to less than a quarter of what they had been just a year before. More intensive fishing helped boost landings for a few years thereafter, just as the Spanish flu had helped depress them in 1918: Environmental influences are as difficult to distinguish from social ones in catch data for this as for any other fishery. There is no doubt, however, that the albacore fishery became very erratic after 1917. It collapsed altogether between 1926 and the late 1930s, when summer temperatures were also well above those of the fishery's formative years.[45]

Caught with a heavy burden of capital and an evanescent resource base, the tuna packers began using more of each fish, packing rather than discarding the darker parts of the flesh and putting up cans of bits and flakes for salad making. They turned to the purse seine fleet to supply them with bluefin tuna after 1918. Most important, they sent their boats farther out to sea for the tropical yellowfin and skipjack varieties, which by the end of the war accounted for 77 percent of the tuna pack and remained thereafter the staples of the industry. To ensure a steady supply, the packers outfitted more boats and sold them on time to Japanese fishers even if individual crews were, in the words of *Pacific Fisherman*, "unable to make anything like reasonable catches."[46] Japanese fishers, shown at work in Figure 6.2, quickly became a highly visible part of the industry, as did their compatriots in the Central Valley who took similar advantage of credit from packers and distributors of fruit and vegetables to get started in agriculture. By 1920 they made up two-thirds of the licensed fishers in the San Pedro district; their families lived in the tuna company housing and worked in the canneries. Like the Japanese vegetable growers, Japanese tuna fishers were very good at their trade: While only half of the roughly 400 boats in the albacore fishery in 1917 had Japanese crews, they landed 80 percent of the harvest.[47]

Reconversion struck this sector as hard in 1920–1 as it did the others. By 1922, however, the packers had drawn down their inventory, reorganized their business, and begun their recovery. Van Camp emerged from the shakeout as the industry leader, with half a dozen canneries and 75 percent of the fleet at his disposal. To keep their capital working, the packers this time pushed into Mexican waters in search of new stocks of fish. Kondo Mashaharu led the way, having recruited capital and labor from Japan to begin shipping tuna in ice from his camp at Turtle Bay to San Diego. In 1924 he began using refrigerated tender ships for the job, the first such vessels to appear in southern California waters. Van Camp and the other packers lost no time in following Kondo's example.[48]

Still, transshipping the fish to southern California remained a problem, and the need to move close to shore to pick up bait brought the fleet within reach of Mexican duties on their tuna. After a few years of experimentation at San Diego, a new fleet of live-bait boats entered the fishery in 1928 and did away with both concerns. Ranging from 95 to 135 feet in the keel and powered by Diesel engines, the new boats could travel from four to five thousand miles without refueling, could stay at sea for thirty days or more at a time, and could carry up to 150 tons of tuna back to port in their refrigerated holds. Huge tanks astern, through which tons of seawater circulated, held sardine or other bait fish alive for use as needed. As before, the boats were independently owned but fished under contract to specific canneries. Van Camp was by far the largest of these, with nine of the thirty-one vessels that entered the fishery in 1928 under its command. Tuna fishing was now technologically mature, a year-round, distant-water enterprise.[49] Offspring of the nineteenth-century whaling industry, the tuna fishery behaved much as its predecessor had, pushing farther and farther outward in search of new resources until by the 1970s it had become the second truly global fishery in the nation's history.

The war gave life, finally, to the sardine fishery. When hostilities broke

Figure 6.2. Fishers aboard the seiner *Florida* hauling sardines, May 1929. Note that the crew is Japanese-American and that the seiner lacks power equipment to haul the net. Photo by D. H. Fry, Jr., courtesy of the California Department of Fish and Game.

out in Europe, F. E. Booth noted that 90 percent of his sales of mild-cure
salmon were in Germany and decided to give up that part of his business
in favor of sardine canning. These also were primarily an export commodity,
but when the war brought a halt to fishing in the North Sea Booth and his
competitors had a clear field. In 1917 California lampara boats caught 105
million pounds of sardine, or not quite half again the previous year's harvest
of all fishes, and delivered them to thirty canneries. Two years later there
were forty-four canneries in the state. California sardines made their way
to Mexico, Cuba, and South America. So cheap were they that on the western
edge of the Pacific Rim street vendors who sold California sardines by the
fish, from opened cans, competed successfully with purveyors of fresh local
fish.[50]

Rising prices also encouraged California packers to experiment with mackerel and herring during the war, but it was in the reduction sector of the
industry that the most spectacular growth took place. The federal government built a pilot plant in Santa Barbara County to reduce kelp to potash,
a fertilizer formerly imported from Germany, and iodine and acetone for
use in making explosives. By 1917 private firms in San Diego and Long
Beach joined the harvest as well, and output reached a maximum of 395,000
wet tons a year later. Shore whaling underwent a brief renaissance at Moss
Landing and Crescent City as a firm dispatched steam-powered killer vessels
from those ports. In 1919 and 1920 the Moss Landing Station took a total
of 598 whales, or about six or seven times the annual take of Monterey's
Azorean shore whalers during their heyday in the 1860s. The company
preserved the meat from the whales' flukes for export to Japan, but reduced
all the rest of the animals to by-products for domestic agriculture and industry. With reconversion, the kelp reduction industry disappeared as
quickly as it had come, and by 1921 only the government plant was still in
operation. The California Sea Products Company continued whaling from
its stations at Moss Landing and Crescent City through the mid-1920s,
although by 1922 its ships had to travel hundreds of miles in search of their
prey. In 1926 the company stationed the tanker *Lansing* and four killer boats
off San Clemente Island to operate a floating reduction factory and closed
down its shoreside plants the following year.[51]

Reduction was most important for the sardine canners. With no limit on
the number of boats and plants that could tap the fishery and no constraint
on their draft, canned sardine quickly overpowered even the international
market for it. When military demand evaporated and the North Sea fishery
revived at the end of the war, the canners found themselves awash in inventory. Production fell to prewar levels in 1921 and all but a dozen of the
state's sardine canneries closed down. Surplus gear and labor moved temporarily onto other fisheries, while those processors who survived the shakeout pared their costs of producing and marketing canned sardines. Although

the industry began to recover as quickly as the 1921–2 season, in 1922–3 the price of canned sardines fell below the cost of producing them and recovered little more than that until the 1940s.[52]

The only real profit in the business came from by-products, for which prices remained relatively firm.[53] Reduction had begun as a way of disposing profitably of viscera and spoiled or broken fish that could not be canned. Significant quantities of whole fish began moving into the fishmeal plants in 1918, when the harvest reached its wartime peak of 157 million pounds. The next spring, probably because the upwelling currents that fertilized the sardine fishery had failed during the abnormally warm summer of 1918, California canneries began receiving lots of fish that were undernourished, low in oil, and thus not good for canning. In the first half of the year some 30 million pounds of whole sardine were ground into fishmeal. State law thereafter required processors to can a certain percentage of the fish they received and allowed them to reduce the rest (see Chapter 7). A processor who had a reduction plant, then, could underbid one who did not on the canned fish. This only further eroded prices for canned fish and increased the industry's reliance on sales of fishmeal and sardine oil. After 1919 nearly every sardine cannery in the state had a reduction plant attached to it, and through the 1920s between one-quarter and one-third of the state's sardine harvest went straight into by-product manufacture.[54]

In the event, laws aimed at regulating the sardine fishery had little effect, so strong was the demand for by-products and so great the industry's capacity to provide them.[55] Reduction, wrote F. E. Booth, became "the real business of the sardine packers, and the canning... a by-product affair." "It seems to be a habit," he observed, "and hard to overcome."[56] Booth detested the reduction business because he believed that sooner or later the draft on the sardine stock would destroy it. Trapped, however, in a particularly brutish economic war of all against all and all together against the sardine, Booth had no choice but to make as much fishmeal as he could or abandon his business to his competitors.[57]

The sardine fishery matured, technologically, in 1925, when a Norwegian tuna skipper at San Pedro successfully tried out a purse seine on sardines. Worked from a diesel boat, the purse seine hauled in far greater quantities of fish, with fewer hands per ton and at greater range, than could a much smaller Monterey clipper armed with a lampara net. If more of the fish arrived at the canneries in poor condition that way, they could always be reduced to by-products. The innovation spread rapidly through southern California that season. During the next, Knut Hovden, a former Booth employee like Peter Ferrante, invited two of the Diesel seiners up to Monterey to fish for him during the lampara crews' annual strike there. Soon they were in command of the northern fishery as well.[58]

The 1925 season also saw the barge *Peralta* anchor three miles off the

Monterey coast with a reduction plant aboard. Later joined by the whale-reduction ship *Lansing*, *Peralta* was, in fact, a pirate vessel, offloading California sardines from California vessels and selling its produce on California markets, but working in international waters and thus beyond the reach of whatever legal power California authorities could muster. Thereafter shoreside packers saw little point even in making a pretense of being in business to can fish and sent their crews off to the sardine grounds without bothering to limit their contracts to their capacity to butcher and can the fish.[59]

The new industrial fisheries for salmon, tuna, and sardines came to life between 1900 and 1925 as clusters of workers, capital, and entrepreneurial talent more or less bodily abandoned resources which were in decline at the turn of the century and, adapting older tools to the use of fossil energy, found new ones. By the late 1920s, the industry had emerged in its modern form. In 1924 Congress passed an Immigration Restriction Act, thereby shutting off the influx of foreign talent that had shaped the first seventy-five years of the industry's history. During the late 1920s, where before Chinese, Italian, and other immigrant fishers had expressed little interest in their social environs, significant numbers of their successors were learning the English language and applying for U.S. citizenship.[60] Mechanization enabled them to increase their harvests, but it also drew them more closely into an increasingly interdependent, high-powered economy, thus transforming the social ecology of California's fisheries as it reshaped the nonhuman environment. By 1950, developments set in motion at the beginning of the century would produce crises in all three of the new fisheries and make clear the need for new and more modern approaches to conserving fishery resources to match the new methods of exploiting them.

An island of prosperity in a sea of depression

Depression brought only the briefest pause in the expansion of California's fishery harvest. Landings fell back in 1930 and 1931, bringing considerable hardship to owners of boats and processing plants and outright privation to crews that worked on shares and to cannery workers, whose jobs were seasonal and chancy in the best of times. But by 1934, California fishing boats were making money while few in the rest of the nation recovered even their costs of depreciation. Between 1931 and 1933, while landings of the nation's twelve leading commercial species of fish declined by 19 percent, those of tuna increased by 7 percent and those of sardines by 25 percent. California's share of the U.S. harvest, which had averaged about 20 percent during the late 1920s, began to climb in 1932 and from 1934 until the outbreak of war in the Pacific never fell below 30 percent. As had been the case during the World War I era, tuna and sardines made up almost all of the increase.

California harvests of salmon, flatfishes, and other species either declined through the thirties or remained roughly at pre-Depression levels. Sardine fishers, on the other hand, brought in a record harvest in the 1933–4 season and from then until Pearl Harbor contributed an average of just over one-fourth of the total U.S. fishery harvest. Monterey was what one official called "a local island of prosperity in a sea of depression."[61] The models for John Steinbeck's characters in *Cannery Row*, though poor, did not share the utter desperation of the field-workers he portrayed in *The Grapes of Wrath*.

As before, developments on land powerfully influenced the economics and ecology of the fisheries. Tuna, most of which were caught in Latin American waters, were largely beyond the reach of these changes, but sardines and salmon were not. Most of the gains in farm productivity that were to be had from mechanizing operations previously done by hand had been achieved during the twenties, and after 1930 agronomy and scientific animal husbandry replaced trucks and tractors as the chief engines of farm progress. For poultry growers this meant increasing reliance on commercial feeds. Cheap and abundant supplies of fishmeal were critically important to growers struggling to keep their costs under control.[62] Reclamation continued to expropriate salmon streams for California farmers. After a decade of preliminary study, California published a State Water Plan in 1930 and three years later authorized its main feature, the Central Valley Project.[63] Destined to become one of the greatest public works in history, the Project began during the 1940s to move water from place to place with little regard for the non-human creatures whose lives depended on it no less than those of farmers and city dwellers.

Recreational hunting and fishing became an industry in its own right during the interwar period. During the thirties, while California's population increased by 22 percent, sales of angling licenses increased 56 percent. Although the wildlife they harvested never went to market, hunters and sportfishers generated a great deal of income for outfitters, resort owners, guides, and the like, and under the aegis of such groups as the Izaak Walton League and the National Wildlife Federation became a very effective political force in wildlife management questions. The California Chamber of Commerce reported in 1936 that some 30,000 families vacationed that year in the Klamath–Trinity Basin, where they were served by eighteen private resorts and campgrounds and another five operated by the U.S. Forest Service. In southern California, ocean sport fishing grew steadily after 1925. Like the tuna boats, partyboats relied primarily on sardines for bait and took a small though not insignificant share of the total catch. By 1941 more than 200,000 anglers worked the Sacramento–San Joaquin watershed for striped bass, salmon, and shad. These species, which had supported commercial fisheries during the nineteenth century, now belonged to them. The annual product of commercial salmon fishers in the Sacramento Basin was a relatively paltry $356,000, compared with the $950,000 that the salmon generated as a game fish. By the 1940s sportfishing at least rivalled the commercial sector in importance to the state's economy, although its real growth did not begin until the 1950s.[64]

Sportfishers were unable to press a successful claim to the bait fishery until after World War II. Klamath River salmon, however, were an easier prize. During the late twenties, that part of the river that ran through the Hoopa Valley Indian Reservation became one of the most highly prized sportfishing streams in the country. To the Indians' dismay, hundreds of anglers jammed the Klamath estuary at the peak of every season. Commercial outfitters, campgrounds, and custom canning plants appeared to service this ostensibly non-commercial and entirely non-Indian fishery. In addition, outside brokers bought salmon from putative anglers and trucked them off the reservation "by the tons and tons," according to one Indian witness.[65] In 1933, responding to the demands of the sport lobby, the state condemned the last cannery on the river and closed the basin to commercial harvesting. The Yurok, who had had little to do with the 1924 fight to prohibit hydroelectric development on the river, now objected strenuously to the removal of an important cash resource from what was still mostly a subsistence economy. "What have we got left?" demanded one Yurok fisher of a visiting Congressional committee on the eve of the closure:

> They have taken away the last thing we ever had on the face of the earth. They lease all the land and take everything from underneath us and they get title to everything. And what have we?[66]

Whether or not the state had power to control Indian fishing on the reservation at all was constitutionally unclear, but no one stepped forward on the Indians' behalf. At any rate, Indians continued to fish salmon unmolested until the resource declined to critically low levels in the 1960s and the whole matter came to court.

Commercial landings of California salmon continued their steady decline through the depression years. Pressure on the stocks did not increase significantly. Most of the 570 trollers in the fishery in 1935 continued to use 1920s technology, although a few of them had recently installed power gurdies with which to haul in their lines.[67] Environmental conditions seem to have been responsible for most of the deterioration. Weather continued poor for salmon, although precipitation was high enough in 1938 to cause serious flooding in all parts of the state. The next year violent contrast between a very cold first six months and a very warm second six months brought the poorest salmon fishing in forty years to the state.[68] Landings touched an historical low of 2.7 million pounds in that year.

The Depression delayed further investment in reclamation. Even though the state had approved the Central Valley Project and voted a bond issue to pay for it in 1933, no lenders came forward and the project languished until Congress appropriated funds for it in 1937. Work on Shasta Dam began the following year and was finished in 1942. Shasta went up at the top of the main stem of the Sacramento and closed off about one-half of the basin's remaining nursery. Studies of what the U.S. Bureau of Fisheries infelicitously called "fish-salvage problems in relation to Shasta Dam" began only as an afterthought, after construction bids were in. As it turned out, the dam probably improved conditions for salmon in the system by mitigating the flooding that decades of unplanned diking and filling had encouraged, as the dam was designed to do, and by providing the river below with a stable flow of cool water, which was an unplanned benefit. Friant Dam, a Bureau of Reclamation facility on the San Joaquin completed the same year, did comparatively little damage to what remained of the salmon in the southern end of the valley.[69]

The sardine fishery was overwhelmingly the most dynamic sector of the business in the 1930s. Always the most volatile of California fisheries, the sardine fishery collapsed into chaos during the precipitous deflation of 1930–2. Real (1929) prices for raw fish, which had remained relatively constant at about $11 the ton through the twenties, dropped to $6 by 1932. Fishmeal dropped in real price from $74 per ton in the late 1920s to $28 by 1932. No longer able to compete on the world market, canned sardines did so poorly that profits from by-products no longer made up the loss that packers incurred on them. The thirty sardine canneries that had operated in California before the crash dwindled to twenty by 1932–3. The catch fell by half, from 325,000 tons in 1929–30 to 165,000 two seasons later. Desperate, crews who could still put to sea landed far more fish than the remaining canneries could use even for reduction, and about 2,000 tons of fish were simply thrown away during the collapse.[70]

Two things happened to set the industry back on its manic course. Table 6.3 outlines the fishery's output. As prices dropped offshore reduction became a more attractive proposition than it had been in the twenties, so in October 1932 a group of seiner owners chartered the old whale reduction ship *Lansing* and anchored it in international waters off Monterey to receive their catches. Out of fairness to the shoreside packers, then, and to relieve real want among fishers and cannery workers, the state removed its restrictions on by-product manufacture. British Columbia had allowed a reduction fishery since 1925, and in 1935 Oregon and Washington followed California's example. The sardine population now came under open assault along the entire length of its range, although California consumed by far the largest share.[73]

Fish and Game described the 1933–4 season as a "fairly prosperous one for both the fishermen and the canners," and thereafter the industry resumed its logarithmic growth.[73] Fishing effort had averaged 185 boat-months between

1925 and 1932. According to industry figures, effort nearly trebled between 1932–3 and 1936–7, from 584 to 1615 boat-months. The industry's peak season came in 1936–7, when 230 seiners delivered 726,000 tons of sardine to fifty-two processing plants in California alone. Nine of the plants were aboard factory ships, twenty-seven ashore in San Francisco and Monterey, twelve in San Pedro, and four in San Diego. To keep busy during the summer off-season, Monterey seiners went north to fish sardine in Oregon or south to take tuna or mackerel. Pacific mackerel became a major fishery and produced a maximum of 78,000 tons in 1935. By then the sardine fishery was probably the most intensive the world had ever seen. Japan's harvest of sardine-like fishes was greater at the time, but that fishery spread over a much larger expanse of water and took as many as five different species of clupeid fish, while the California industry relied on only one.[73]

Through the 1930s, about four-fifths of the total harvest went straight into reduction plants. High-grade fishmeal became available in tremendous quantities as much as 20 percent cheaper than processed meat scrap, or "tankage," its closest competitor. It consisted of two-thirds raw protein, contained all the amino acids that livestock needed, and had as well some as-yet-unidentified chemical that made animals grow faster than they would on other protein sources. A Washington State Agricultural Experiment Station found that growing chicks on a standard ration of about 5 percent fishmeal would save a farmer $4 a ton on feed. Similar savings would have amounted to 13 percent of a California poultry grower's feed budget during the Depression. Fed on fishmeal, an average Depression-era California hen produced 127 eggs in a year where as her 1920s counterpart could lay only 118. Major purchasers of the substance included the Globe and Taylor, General Mills, Quaker Oats, and Ralston–Purina companies, which were quick to convey their views to politicians whenever state or federal legislatures considered the sardine question. Significant exports to Europe began after fishmeal prices dropped in 1932.[74]

Even at its relatively low price, fishmeal yielded extraordinary profits: During the 1930s many plants recovered their entire investments in their first season. The reason was that the price of raw fish remained, as the U.S. Fish and Wildlife Service noted later, "unjustifiably low."[75] Although the real price of fishmeal roughly doubled between 1934 and 1941, so that at roughly $80 a ton in the latter year it slightly exceeded that of tankage, the price of raw fish in 1929 dollars increased only from $9.50 to $11.40 over the same period. Sardine oil, used primarily for soap, linoleum, shortening, and paint, likewise remained substantially cheaper than tallow – its cheapest substitute – until the end of the decade. Here the profits, for buyers as well as for producers, may have been even greater than they were in the case of fishmeal. One state official believed that the farmers, who were the most

Table 6.3. *Pacific Coast sardine catch (in short tons).*

Season	Pacific Northwest[a]	Northern California[b]	Offshore plants	Southern California	Total California	Baja California	Coastwide total
1924–5	1,370	67,870	0	105,150	173,020	0	174,390
1925–6	15,590	69,570	0	67,700	137,270	0	153,220
1926–7	48,500	85,380	0	66,830	152,210	0	200,710
1927–8	68,430	114,710	0	72,550	187,260	0	255,690
1928–9	80,510	133,810	0	120,670	254,480	0	334,990
1929–30	86,340	182,010	0	143,160	325,170	0	411,510
1930–1	75,070	135,590	10,960	38,570	185,120	0	260,190
1931–2	73,600	90,685	31,040	42,920	164,645	0	238,245
1932–3	44,350	108,233	58,790	83,667	250,690	0	295,040
1933–4	4,050	188,816	67,820	126,793	383,429	0	387,479
1934–5	43,000	299,331	112,040	183,683	595,054	0	638,054
1935–6	71,560	260,617	150,830	149,051	560,498	0	632,058
1936–7	65,210	347,805	235,610	142,709	726,124	0	791,334
1937–8	81,840	238,654	67,580	110,330	416,564	0	498,404
1938–9	95,270	382,194	43,890	149,203	575,287	0	670,557
1939–40	45,610	440,327	0	96,939	537,266	0	582,876
1940–1	32,740	283,790	0	176,794	460,584	0	493,324
1941–2	93,000	436,876	0	150,497	587,373	0	680,373
1942–3	68,410	300,283	0	204,378	504,661	0	573,071
1943–4	101,000	340,128	0	138,001	478,129	0	579,129
1944–5	59,140	373,844	0	181,061	554,905	0	614,045
1945–6	36,700	229,622	0	174,061	403,683	0	440,383
1946–7	14,090	34,260	0	199,542	233,802	0	247,892
1947–8	8,780	17,724	0	103,617	121,341	0	130,121
1948–9	5,370	47,974	0	135,752	183,726	0	189,096

Year							
1949–50	0	149,211	0	189,714	338,925	0	338,925
1950–1	0	46,426	0	306,662	353,088	0	353,088
1951–2	0	15,979	0	113,125	129,104	16,184	145,288
1952–3	0	49	0	5,662	5,711	9,162	14,873
1953–4	0	58	0	4,434	4,492	14,306	18,798
1954–5	0	865	0	67,609	68,465	12,440	80,905
1955–6	0	518	0	73,943	74,461	4,207	78,668
1956–7	0	63	0	33,580	33,643	13,665	47,298
1957–8	0	17	0	22,255	22,272	9,924	32,196

[a]Oregon, Washington, British Columbia.
[b]San Francisco, Monterey.
Sources: Radovich, "The Collapse of the California Sardine Fishery," pp. 110–11.

vocal defenders of the by-products industry, had been hoodwinked into joining the reduction lobby by industrial consumers of sardine oil.[76]

If the sardiners could do little to secure a self-sustaining share of the enormous stream of wealth that flowed through the fishery, the sardines could do nothing at all. Indeed, their subsistence strategy, although as elegant in its way as that of the salmon, may actually have enhanced their vulnerability to destruction by the fishery. Pilchards and their relatives school because they cannot hide from predators: Schooling minimizes their losses to attack. Schools, in turn, aggregate into school groups perhaps five miles or so in diameter. The schooling and grouping habit persists whether the total stock of fish is very large or very small, although at very low levels of population sardines, anchovy, or mackerel will take cover in schools of more abundant species. For the most part, however, as stock declines it still aggregates into large schools of fish, only fewer of them. This means that a given level of fishing effort has a far greater impact on the population when the stock is at low levels than when it is abundant. If a seiner can find fish, it will take huge catches even as it wipes out the last schools in a population.[77]

Pacific sardines also migrated great distances between their feeding and spawning grounds. There seem to have been three subpopulations, or races, of them: one that inhabited the Gulf of California, a "southern" one that rarely ventured north of the California–Mexican border, and a "northern" one. The last spawned within a hundred miles or so of the coast between Point Conception and northern Baja California and fed in the upwelled, plankton-rich waters off northern California and the Pacific Northwest. Fishers from California to British Columbia, then, harvested a common stock. During their first two years of life, while they put on most of their adult weight, sardines remained in the Southern California Bight. Two- and three-year-old fish were recruited, or entered the fishery, at San Pedro and then began to migrate northward each season, a little farther each year as they grew older and stronger. Three-year-old and older fish contributed to the winter fishery off central California. The oldest, up to ten or twelve years, could reach as far as British Columbia before returning to their spawning grounds each spring. Independently varying boundaries of fertile water to the north and suitable spawning temperatures to the south might expand or contract the fishes' migrating and spawning ranges from year to year.

Mature fish convert most of the oil they store from feeding into spawn rather than into additional body tissues. These they spread by the billions over as large an area as possible to ensure that enough larvae found patches of food to survive and thus ensure successful recruitment of a new generation. A larger population spread its breeding effort over a larger area and was thus more likely to reproduce itself safely. Breeding success could vary drastically from year to year, however, with changes in environmental conditions. An occasionally large year class would make up a sizable share of the total population through most of its life, while in other years recruitment would fail utterly. Pilchards thus hedged against breeding failures in two ways, by spawning over a large area and by living long enough that each year class had a good chance of breeding in a good year at least once before it died out. The strategy sustained the stock well, so long as the population remained large enough and long-lived enough.

By depleting the population of older fish, however, the fishery removed some of the sardine's natural insurance. Enhancing their vulnerability still further was the fact that, while in more highly developed species like cod or halibut greater percentages of young survive to recruitment when the number of spawning adults is lower, in schooling fishes the relation between adult population and recruitment is roughly linear: The percentage of sardine spawn that survive to recruitment is no higher when the parent stock is small than when it is large. This means that the sardine is much less resilient, that is, able to withstand increased predation from a fishery, than other kinds of fish. In sum, the sardine was well adapted to a volatile environment such as that of the California Current but very brittle under pressure from an intensive fishery.[78]

As Appendix B shows, standing crops of sardine began to decline from their turn-of-the-century levels even before the onset of intensive fishing. The reasons are unclear, although long-term changes in climate and the gradual recovery of marine mammal species that preyed on sardines may each have had something to do with it. The ratio of the sardine population's biomass to that of the shorter-lived anchovy, a rough indicator of stability in the California Current's ecology, remained quite high and thus favorable to sardine production through most of the interwar period. Sardines were possibly the primary consumers of food energy in the California Current system at this time. The fishery, however, began during the 1930s to draw off a significant share of the adult stock. Successful breeding between 1922 and 1926 sustained an abundant population through the onset of the Depression, but from then until 1938 there were only two good recruitments and the fishery began to eat into the stock's biological capital.[79]

How much fishing the interwar sardine population could have sustained over the long term remains a matter of considerable controversy. The first systematic study of the sardine's population dynamics, published by Garth Murphy in 1966, placed the stock's annual maximum sustainable yield between 1932 and the end of World War II at about 471,000 tons.[80] More recently, Alec MacCall placed it closer to 250,000 or 300,000 tons per year.[81] The latter figure corresponds to those put forward by Fish and Game scientists at the time. MSY for a fish like the sardine changes radically from year to year; "sustainable" in this case refers to an average figure, allowing for bad years in which the population would recruit few new adults as well as those in which abundant recruitment would make many more fish available for harvest. In any event, the fishery, which hovered about MacCall's figure through the late twenties, surpassed the more conservative estimate in the 1933–4 season and Murphy's larger one only one year later. Between 1932 and 1945 the annual take of sardine from all sections of the coast averaged 571,000 tons. As Figure 6.3 shows, the population of spawning adults began declining steeply after 1934, and in the peak season of 1936–7 the industry seined up some 40 percent of the entire population of adult fish. By that time the fish in the catch were noticeably smaller, hence younger, than they had been previously.[82]

Two very large cohorts hatched in the 1938 and 1939 spawning seasons and by themselves sustained the harvest through the early forties. At the same time, the Depression began to lift and prices for byproducts took a substantial jump. Processors continued to divert from 60 to 70 percent of the catch into reduction plants, despite the fact that the market for canned sardines was also very strong. The price of raw fish actually declined, from a peak of $14.30 in constant (1929) dollars in 1937 to $11.40 in 1941. Profits in the processing sector remained very high. The offshore reduction ships went out of business in 1938 when New Deal labor laws required them to carry separate crews for operating the ships and the reduction plants, but the sixty-nine shoreside plants which remained in 1940 easily handled all the fish the seiners could deliver. New boats and new plants continued to appear, until on the eve of the war there were more than 300 seiners in the fishery. In 1940 the Fish and Wildlife Service noted with some concern the industry's tendency to commission new seiners for what was already a seriously overcapitalized fishery.[83] The sardine was doomed, although it was left to World War II to administer the finishing coup.

Conclusion: the sardine collapse

If the Second Industrial Revolution, powered by electricity and fossil fuels, had opened a new frontier to the California economy, for the fisheries at least World War II brought that frontier to a close. In all, relatively little growth or technological development had taken place in most sectors of the industry over the preceding half-century: Three resources only – salmon, tuna, and sardines – had borne the brunt of the industry's assault as it mechanized and took to the open ocean. Emboldened by opportunity and the apparent boundlessness of the sea's wealth, fishers, processors and their customers downstream in the economy had torn at the fisheries with little thought to their capacity to sustain production either over the long term or in the face of random ecological change. Scientists and policymakers knew that such lack of foresight could have dire consequences but lacked the will or the power to slow the pace of growth (see Chapter 7). The 1940s taught

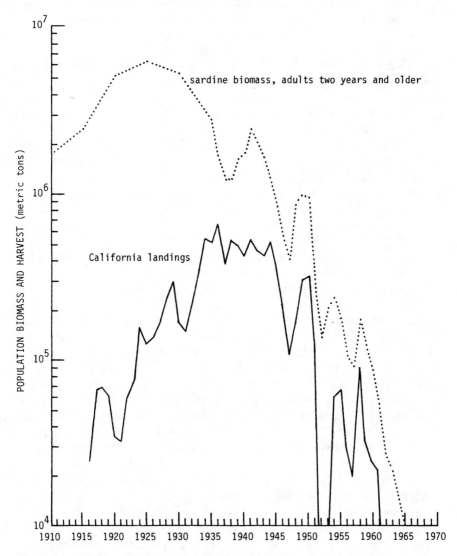

Figure 6.3. Sardine population and California harvest, 1910–65. Sources: Smith, "Biological Effects of Ocean Variability," p. 124 (1910–30); Murphy, "Population Biology of the Pacific Sardine," pp. 46–7 (1932–44); MacCall, "Population Estimates for the Waning Years of the Pacific Sardine Fishery," p. 74 (1945–65).

all concerned, harvesters as well as managers, that they would no longer enjoy that luxury. As always, the environment interacted with human events to bring the lesson home.

The war's first impact was to increase the demand for food, for labor, and for seagoing boats. The federal government commandeered most of the long-range tuna fleet for military work in the tropical Pacific. Those that remained in the fishery were forbidden to enter waters south of 10° north latitude immediately after the attack on Pearl Harbor. Thus attenuated, the industry struggled to keep up with the greatly increased demand for food and, although a great many new boats were built during the war, 1945 saw the fleet still far short of its prewar capacity.[84] The sardine fleet was reduced from more than 300 boats to about 180 by July 1942. The exclusion of enemy aliens from the fishery reduced its labor force by 17 percent, from 9,350 to 7,600, but new entries quickly made up the difference before the draft began to draw the pool down again.[85] The incarceration of Japanese Americans fell hardest on the tuna fishery where, as in agriculture, immigrants and their children saw two generations of work and savings evaporate practically overnight. Most Italian-Americans, spared internment, continued to work through the war and, as a group, finally transferred their loyalty to the United States.[86]

To everyone's surprise, salmon harvests took a remarkable jump in 1944, and commercial landings for the next three years were the largest on record. Between 1946 and 1948 every stream in the Central Valley without a barrier, including the main stem of the Sacramento, was crammed with fish. Scientists were at a loss to explain the reversal: The regular flow of cool water from Shasta dam improved spawning conditions somewhat, artificially recreating headwater conditions in the lower river where fish had not spawned in great numbers before, but this change did not begin until 1942, too late to make an impact on the fishery until 1946 or so.[87] A more likely explanation was the return of cooler and wetter weather to the coast after more than two decades of unfavorable conditions.[88] Fishing effort increased tremendously at the same time. Where in 1935 there had been 570 trollers in California waters there were more than 1,100 in 1947, and these were larger, packed their fish in ice, and made universal use of factory-made power gurdies and steel lines. A few were outfitted with radiotelephones and autopilots.[89] In any event, the surge was temporary, and by the early 1950s landings were down again. The resource was apparently enormously resilient but, as the postwar era would show, could only remain so if its environment were protected. As the Indians had known, proper management required protecting both the salmon and the harvesters from bad years, which were unpredictable but nonetheless sure to appear from time to time.

Albacore landings, after undergoing a slow rise through the late 1930s, also leapt ahead during the war years. Here, fishing probably improved with cooler weather, which made its impact earlier on the albacore fishery by bringing the fish within reach of California boats right away, while the salmon responded to improved conditions in their nursery after a typical delay of roughly four years. Off Washington and Oregon, albacore catches were the best in history and the pack exceeded even that of salmon. New long-distance vessels, meanwhile, appeared at what *Pacific Fisherman* called a "spectacular rate" through the war and the pack of tropical tuna varieties increased apace.[90] After the war, the market for canned tuna grew just as rapidly, and until the early 1950s all participants in the industry prospered. The tuna industry's problems during the 1950s were more political than biological and did as much to shape the political economy of fishing in post–World War II California as salmon and sardines had in earlier eras (see Chapter 8).

The sardine fishery collapsed at the end of the war. In May 1941, as the nation's economy began to mobilize for war, several canners approached the federal government through a contact on the U.S. Tariff Commission with a proposal to supply the military with canned sardines at cost.[91] The industry had, in fact, marketed canned sardines at or below cost through most of its history, but having a guaranteed purchaser for most of the pack freed them from competing with each other in this area and enabled them to clear their customary profits on meal and oil. Fishing became more profitable than it had been when wartime controls roughly doubled the price of raw sardines while keeping a tighter rein on byproducts. More than one-half the catch continued to go straight to reduction through the war.

To keep the fleet operating efficiently despite the military draft of men and boats, the Interior Department appointed Elton Sette, who like Elmer Higgins had begun his career in California but quickly moved up to the federal fishery agency, as Coordinator of Fisheries in San Francisco with authority to allocate harvests to individual boats and deliveries to individual canneries.[92] Sette had little trouble maintaining effort in the harvest because the fleet had been so heavily overcapitalized before the war began; his problem was to route traffic so that capital equipment was used as efficiently as possible. In addition, high profits stimulated the construction of still more boats and processing plants, just as they did in the tuna business. By 1943–4 California had 206 seiners fishing sardines and seventy-five plants processing them. New construction even gained momentum in the immediate aftermath of the war. Privately, Sette expressed misgivings about the sardines' ability to sustain the additional investment, but at the beginning of 1945 he nonetheless relayed orders from the War Food Administration to increase the catch by one-third, to about four million cases, and to consign 100 percent of the pack to military purchase.[93]

According to industry figures, fishing effort reached 1944 boat-months in 1946. This was an increase of 20 percent over the effort expended in the peak season of 1936–7 and more than double the effort of the 1932–3 season, when the fishery reached Fish and Game's estimate of its MSY. Total catches had remained steady in spite of the increased effort since the late 1930s, and until harvesting pressure began to increase again during the war the large cohorts of 1938 and 1939 kept the fishery going. Average hauls per boat-month began to decline in 1943–4. In 1944–5 the fishery took 614,000 tons out of a population which may have contained as few as 835,000 tons of adult fish in all.[94]

The Monterey fishery broke two records on September 25, 1945, one when the port received just under 9,000 tons of sardine in a single day and another when an individual boat landed 268 tons on its own. In October and November, however, landings fell off sharply. By mid-December there were no fish at all to be had off central California. Landings fell off in Oregon, Washington, and British Columbia as well. A few boats spent the remainder of the season at San Pedro, where the fishing remained good. The next season threw the industry into chaos. San Pedro Bay was jammed with seiners, including the entire central California fleet as well as boats from as far away as British Columbia and Alaska. Central California markets went haywire at the end of 1946, just as the federal government removed its ceilings on prices for raw and processed fish. One skipper who managed to land fifty tons of sardines at Monterey sold them for bait at $110 a ton, almost quadruple the price at which the season had opened. Monterey packers tried trucking fish up from San Pedro, while some even shipped them up the coast in Navy-surplus landing craft.[95] The crash was "catastrophic," in the words of the Fish and Game Commission, "to fishermen, boat owners, plant owners, and cannery workers alike."[96]

In desperation, Monterey packers began buying jack mackerel, anchovy, herring, and squid to keep their plants busy. A few moderately successful spawnings kept the southern California fishery busy for a few years, and harvests at Monterey increased somewhat in 1948–9 and 1949–50. San Pedro received a record harvest in 1946–7, although average hauls per trip declined to forty-two tons from seventy-three the previous year. By 1949 the fishery was drawing primarily on the 1946 and 1947 cohorts, the oldest of which was already depleted. This meant that the fishery, having stripped the sardine stock of older fish and thus of its ability to absorb the shock of a seasonal breeding failure, was depending on one spawning at a time. Fewer schools in the population further reduced the sardines' chances of breeding successfully by contracting the geographical range over which spawning took place. Spawning failed in 1949 and 1950, so that in 1952 the southern fishery expired in its turn.[97]

Skyrocketing prices for sardines kept the fishery going in spite of the collapse. Monterey enjoyed the most profitable season in its history in 1949–50 on the moderately successful recruitments of the 1946 and 1947 cohorts. If anything, pressure on the stock increased as boats followed the collapsing fishery southward to San Pedro. Fishmeal prices dropped somewhat during the late forties as imports rose. Demand and profits remained strong, however, because livestock production increased after the war and poultry growers still believed fishmeal an "almost essential supplement" to their feeding schedules, according to the Fish and Wildlife Service.[98]

Because the market for livestock feed remained so strong, sardine processors looked abroad for new sources of fishmeal. Just as F. E. Booth had turned to sardines when his salmon business had faltered some fifty years earlier, then, the sardine industry in turn colonized new fisheries as it disintegrated. A good number of entrepreneurial refugees built unsuccessful plants in northern Chile and one even tried his hand in Morocco in the 1950s. One San Francisco firm shipped its equipment to Chimbote, Peru, where in cooperation with a Peruvian entrepreneur it secretly began processing anchoveta for shipment to California. Large quantities of Peruvian fishmeal began appearing on the California market in the first half of 1953, just as local production dwindled to nothing. Other Peruvians got into the business quickly, relying on scientific, technical, and financial help from California firms. Such California concerns as Van Camp and Starkist were soon in Peru doing business on their own.[99] The history of the Peruvian anchoveta fishery, from foundation to boom to ultimate collapse during the early 1970s, reprised in practically every detail that of its California progenitor.

By 1950 energy-intensive food production had radically transformed the ecology of California's fisheries. The California Current remained relatively impoverished thereafter, its standing crops of schooling fishes well below historical levels. Distant-water tuna harvests continued to grow, but this sector operated in a political environment radically different from what it had been in the fishery's youth. The salmon fishery, finally, found its fate tied irrevocably to the Central Valley Project. Although the real impact of Shasta Dam on the stock was uncertain, it was clear to all concerned that whether the salmon would survive or expire would thereafter be a matter of engineering, of political choice. Public agencies charged with managing the fisheries had struggled mightily through the first half of the century to keep up with the rapid pace of change in the industry, although with indifferent results. After 1950 the failures of the interwar period, and particularly the collapse of the sardine fishery, would never be far from the minds of their successors.

7

The bureaucrat's problem

It is not enough that information may be obtained upon
which the fisheries may be managed so as to get from
them the greatest sustained yield. This information must
be used or it is effort largely wasted.
                                        – N. B. Scofield (1938)[1]

"In modern societies," wrote Justice Holmes in 1903, "every part is so
organically related to every other that what affects any portion must be felt
more or less by all the rest."[2] While he wrote in the context of economic
competition between industries, Holmes's use of biological imagery was
appropriate: For reform-minded people of the Progressive Era, the depletion
of natural resources symbolized better than any other contemporary problem
the way in which an advanced industrial economy imposed serious external
costs on society at large. Conversely, for Theodore Roosevelt, scientific
conservation was the very soul of Progressivism. Roosevelt and others who
led a remarkable wave of social reform between 1900 and 1920 believed that
only scientific planning and economic efficiency, applied to human affairs
through the deliberate use of centralized legal power, could preserve the
future of a rapidly crowding, interdependent industrial society.[3]

Late-nineteenth-century lawmakers had tried desperately to protect the
liberty and dignity of individuals by using time-honored standards of property rights and limited government to draw clear boundaries between what
belonged to private initiative exclusively and what fell within the reach of
government's power to police in the public interest. The state-ownership
rule of *Geer* v. *Connecticut* has been one not particularly elegant attempt
to do this with respect to wildlife conservation. Such Congressional statutes
as the Interstate Commerce Act of 1886, however, the Sherman Anti-Trust
Act of 1890, and the Lacey Act of 1900, evinced a growing awareness that
a more deliberate government hand would have to assist the invisible hand
of the market in sustaining both efficiency and justice in society.[4] In the
fisheries, rarely amenable to private ownership and peculiarly vulnerable to
social cost, boundaries between private and public interests, between economic and ecological processes, blurred to the point of vanishing.

"One of the oldest and most respected agencies in state government" by

156

the turn of the century, the California State Board of Fish Commissioners was well-satisfied with the accomplishments of its first thirty years.[5] After 1907, when the legislature approved an annual fee for hunting licenses, the state's wildlife agency became not only financially independent but the second wealthiest such body in the country, with an annual income in excess of a hundred thousand dollars. By 1912 the agency had taken on a small army of game wardens, a full-time attorney, and its modern name, the California Fish and Game Commission (CFGC). In 1914 it launched its own popular journal, the *California Fish and Game Quarterly*, to publicize its activities and nurture its alliance with the state's outdoorspeople. In 1927, finally, the state created for the commission a Division of Fish and Game (CDFG) in the new Department of Natural Resources to carry out its research and administrative functions.[6] The agency could well face the new era with confidence: As the *San Francisco Chronicle* noted in 1921, "with its employees in every county the commission has built up ... one of the most powerful political organizations in California."[7]

No less prestigious was the federal fishery agency, which became the U.S. Bureau of Fisheries (USBF) in the Department of Commerce and Labor in 1903. By 1910, USBF was a mature and well-established, if chronically underfunded, organization. Although it accumulated a few regulatory powers as Congress legislated federal controls over Alaska salmon in 1905 and 1924, fur seals in 1910, and black bass in 1930, its primary mission remained in research and in promoting the fishing industry. Artificial propagation continued to occupy most of its attention through the first two decades of the new century. Federal wildlife management gained impressively in coherence and vigor in 1939 and 1940, when USBF and the Agriculture Department's Bureau of Biological Survey were transferred to the Department of the Interior and then combined into the new U.S. Fish and Wildlife Service.[8] As long as the enforcement of wildlife law remained primarily the task of state government the federal fishery agency, unlike its California sister, would incur few political liabilities.

Both agencies found themselves in strange and treacherous waters, however, as mechanization revolutionized fishery production after 1910. Twentieth-century fishers pushed out to sea with much enthusiasm but little information and CFGC, hitherto a rather clubby association of biologists and aristocratic outdoors enthusiasts, had suddenly to police a highly capitalized and politically muscular industry.[9] It had simultaneously to devise controls for the new industrial fisheries and to amass biological information on which to base those controls. Inshore, it had the unenviable task of restraining the environmentally destructive activities of industries even richer and more powerful than the fisheries. State and federal agencies thus strove to gather a body of biological and technical knowledge to promote more efficient use of the fisheries and to aid in their scientific regulation. To the same ends, they endeavored to improve the traditionally chaotic marketing of fishery products as well. Government continued, finally, to strengthen its authority to control the harvest at the point of production, where fish met fisher. In all three areas, the conceptual and institutional heritages of the nineteenth century would prove ill adapted to the modern challenge.

Biology and politics

Turn-of-the-century experience with ocean fisheries, particularly in the North Atlantic, had convinced many biologists that such resources not only could be but were rapidly being exhausted.[10] Working with statistics from the North Sea plaice fishery, the Danish scientist C. G. J. Petersen developed a twofold model of overfishing in 1903. "Stock" overfishing took place when harvesters left too few adult fish uncaught to replenish the population, whereas "growth" overfishing resulted when fishers depleted the population of mature, full-size animals.[11] In such groundfisheries as those for plaice and halibut, both kinds of overfishing were readily detectable through analysis of industry data; the first from declines in catches per unit of fishing effort (CPUE) and the second from the decreasing size of individual fish in the catch.

Following the lead of Petersen and others, after 1910 biologists became increasingly interested in the dynamics of exploited fish populations.[12] First to begin work in the United States was W. F. Thompson, a Stanford-trained zoologist who studied halibut for the government of British Columbia in 1915. Thompson proved that the simple addition of more gear to a fishery could sustain increasing harvests long after the resource had begun to decline. The biologist's task, then, was to target the resource's maximum sustainable yield so that lawmakers could limit the harvest at that level. The U.S. Forest Service successfully applied the sustained-yield concept to its work during the Progressive Era. Although the theory was not worked out in its entirety for fisheries until 1957, by the 1930s it was relatively sophisticated and U.S. fisheries biologists were quite familiar with it.[13]

After 1910 California very rapidly became one of the world's leading centers of oceanic fisheries research. The Scripps Institution of Oceanography, established as a private foundation by a San Diego family in 1903, became part of the University of California in 1912 and through the interwar period remained the only academy in the country to offer advanced degrees in ocean science.[14] The state legislature levied license taxes on commercial fishers and processors to pay for Fish and Game's research and enforcement activities in 1909, 1913, and 1917.[15] In 1915, having already retained N. B. Scofield to study albacore at the behest of the industry, CFGC established a separate Department of Commercial Fisheries under his direction. Two years later Scofield induced W. F. Thompson to join him at San Pedro. Thompson's workshop became the nation's first state-operated fisheries laboratory. Its emphasis on marine biology antedated that of the USBF by some fifteen years. After 1918 the sardine commanded by far the greatest share of CFGC's scientific energy, and by the 1930s was the most thoroughly studied fishery resource in the United States.[16]

Together, Thompson and Scofield developed cooperative relationships with Stanford and the Scripps Institution and moved CFGC to the forefront of U.S. fisheries research.[17] With funds from the 1917 license tax they organized the world's first systematic program for collecting fishery statistics and set down basic strategies for marine biological research that endured for most of the century.[18] Their apprentices at the State Fisheries Laboratory, many recruited from Jordan's seminars at Stanford, included some of the leading figures in twentieth-century fisheries management. Some, including Elmer Higgins, Oscar Elton Sette, William C. Herrington, and J. O. Snyder, left California for distinguished careers in federal service. Indeed, so regular was the flow of scientists from San Pedro to Washington during the 1920s that USBF agreed to subsidize the state laboratory as a training center for its workers.[19] Other scientists, including Frances N. Clark, her younger colleague Richard S. Croker, and Scofield himself, remained with the state agency throughout the interwar period. Perhaps they had some taste for the political combat that working there necessarily entailed. Scientists not so inclined chose to avoid the messy politics of fishery regulation by moving to USBF, which in any event offered better pay and more prestige than could the state agency, in addition to a research environment less harried by political fire fighting.[20]

Thompson organized the initial sardine investigations "very specifically," he wrote in 1920, "to meet the responsibilities of the state as legal guardian" of the resources.[21] It had "become the function of government," he observed, "not only to aid in procuring the greatest possible use [of a resource], but to insure its continuance because it is the only agency uniting all factions and successive generations."[22] To this end, Thompson sought first to prevent overfishing, which he defined according to Petersen. This was a difficult task, as he had noted in his halibut work, because technological improvement, expansion of the fishing grounds, and increased quantities of gear on the fishery worked together to hide exhaustion by keeping the market price of fish low. All these compromised the Invisible Hand, loss of profit, as a natural safeguard against depletion. The CPUE measure was thus the best available index of a fishery's health.[23]

In addition, Thompson thought it vital to understand natural fluctuations in the abundance of the stock, whose economic and biological impacts were as easily hidden by the veil of price as those of simple overfishing. "The study of these natural fluctuations is linked inseparably with the study of depletion or overfishing," he wrote, "and a program of investigation can not separate these two."[24] With this very advanced perception of the nature of his task, Thompson recommended studies into meteorological and oceanographic influences on the sardine population, although Fish and Game simply lacked the resources to undertake more than a few direct measurements of the California Current's ecology. Unlike their counterparts in agriculture, for example, fishery entrepreneurs were of little help in securing additional funds for CFGC's scientific work because they thought such basic research of little practical use and, moreover, "a necessary forerunner of regulation."[25]

The sardine's biology made such considerations of profound importance. Groundfish like halibut or plaice were free swimming, distributed more or less evenly over their grounds, and grew steadily with increasing age. Data from the industry offered a relatively good sample of the target populations, while smaller fish on the dinner table generated public support for regulation of the harvest. Schooling fish like the sardine, on the other hand, achieve most of their adult size in their first two years of life. They aggregate in schools that are themselves distributed through the ocean in uneven groups. Because of their reproductive volatility, moreover, yields of such fishes can vary radically from season to season. Observed fluctuations in the sardine stock during the 1930s drew attention to the effect of environmental change on the population and lent support to the belief that any impact the fishery might have on the resource was relatively small compared to that of oceanographic conditions. As *Pacific Fisherman* insisted in 1935, "natural factors, not human use, are the essential elements in influencing the abundance of these fish."[26]

The sustained-yield theory and the CPUE measure were convenient tools for understanding and regulating groundfisheries, with which biologists had had some experience by the turn of the century. They were "objective," intuitive, and politically inoffensive. They were easy to explain because they treated each stock of fish as a single, discrete unit and simply assumed away any influence that ecology might have on productivity.[27] Risk of environmental shock and uncertainty in measurement made describing a stock of schooling fish, much less regulating it, a much more complex problem. Not least of the difficulties is the fact that assigning values to risk and uncertainty so as to compare them with the value of forgone catches, finally, is less a matter of scientific inquiry than of political choice, and one in which people with different views and objectives will necessarily weight the ill-defined factors at stake in different ways.[29]

Alarmed by scenes such as that shown in Figure 7.1, Fish and Game scientists warned repeatedly that too-rapid growth in the sardine fishery would eventually lead to its depletion. Thompson, as scientific spokesperson for the agency charged with preserving the fishery, placed a high value on the risk and uncertainty involved in managing it: "Unnecessary drain upon

Figure 7.1. Seiner *Richmond* at Terminal Island, February 1934. This famous photograph shows a seiner coming to port with a load of 43.5 tons of sardine. Note that the vessel's stern is awash from the weight of its load. Photo by D. H. Fry, Jr., courtesy of the California Department of Fish and Game.

the supply should be avoided," he wrote, "until research has shown that it is possible to detect overfishing in time."[30] By the late 1920s, the state laboratory was convinced that it had good evidence of depletion. Although the total catch was still rising, it was not doing so in proportion to the expansion in fishing effort. The average age of fish in the catch had declined from ten years to six years. Individual boats were traveling farther from port and spending more time on the water to make their catches. All were classic signs of overfishing; Scofield and Frances Clark, who by then had replaced Thompson as director of the laboratory, recommended an annual limit on the catch between 200,000 and 300,000 tons.[31]

Fishing effort, however, had only just begun to climb. Offshore reduction ships began taking significant quantities of sardine in 1930 and by 1935 were consuming one-quarter of the California harvest. Oregon and Washington initiated substantial reduction fisheries in 1935. When several bills to prohibit offshore reduction appeared in Congress in 1936, the House Committee on Merchant Marine and Fisheries and the Fisheries subcommittee of the House Committee on Commerce held joint hearings on the issue in Washington, D.C. Representatives of different agencies and different interest groups, by their lights, interpreted the ambiguous results of the California investigation in different ways.

N. B. Scofield spoke on behalf of the State Fisheries Laboratory. He cited Thompson's halibut study to explain that a fishery could produce increasing harvests from a declining resource. Though he admitted that CPUE was an ambiguous measure of a schooling population, he could point to smaller proportions of older fish in the catch, increases in the time required to find fish, and a decrease in the number of immature fish on the spawning grounds off San Diego. The last Scofield took as evidence of a decrease in the number of spawning adults. In any event, the mere fact that the sardine fishery was more intensive than any in memory was "fact enough," Scofield warned, "to make us sure that we are headed for destruction and a great loss."[32]

Speaking for USBF, Elmer Higgins pointed favorably to Scofield's testimony and agreed "that reproduction is probably not keeping pace with the present level of production: the drain on the supply is probably greater than the average long-time replacement." He went on to predict accurately, a decade in advance, that "depletion of fishery supply in northern waters probably will be evidenced by great irregularity of the catch and eventual destruction of the commercial fishery, proceeding at a progressive rate from north to south." He added, however, that there was yet "no clear-cut or convincing evidence *that will satisfy everyone* that the sardine supply is in danger of being seriously depleted," and in the name of his agency responded to this uncertainty in a way very different from that of Scofield and Thompson. "We believe very firmly," he said, "that restrictions which are unnecessary hamper or restrict legitimate business enterprise." Rather than deny the industry opportunity to use the resource, then, Higgins advocated a kind of trial-and-error approach, permitting continued growth in the catch until unambiguous evidence of depletion warranted a cutback.[34] His colleague Reginald H. Fiedler added that "to us, conservation means wise use. We do not believe in hoarding our fishery resources, but, rather, believe they should be prosecuted to a degree compatible with the abundance of the species."[34]

The Bureau of Fisheries followed Gifford Pinchot, head of the U.S. Forest Service under Theodore Roosevelt and the chief architect of Progressive-Era resource policy, in its definition of conservation. As Higgins put it,

> while we are aiming to prevent the depletion of the great resources with which our country has been blessed, it follows logically that these resources must not be permitted to lie in a state of unproductive idleness . . . the real problem of conservation, then, is plainly a problem of efficient development and wise utilization.[35]

Higgins and Fiedler recommended that Congress stay out of the offshore reduction controversy for the time being.

The federal agency thus stayed aloof from the fight, downplaying the necessary uncertainty of biological research and ignoring the necessary political ramifications of whatever it did or did not do. USBF saw itself primarily as a research agency and had throughout its history evinced neither affinity nor talent for regulating the use of resources.[36] Economic opportunity was a tangible good; to USBF its value clearly outweighed that of the risk avoidance that so preoccupied the state managers. By taking a position of "scientific" neutrality, then, USBF managed to avoid alienating the industry on account of so inchoate a contingency as some possible future disaster, or so inarticulate a constituency as "all factions and succeeding generations."

Industry representatives offered divided testimony at the 1936 hearings. The California Sardine Institute, a consortium of northern California sardine canners, condemned the offshore operators as "bootleggers." Counsel for an association of Monterey boat owners who delivered sardines to shoreside plants was "satisfied" that unless the factory ships were brought under control it would "not be an indefinite period before depletion would arrive." San Pedro boat owners favored regulating the factory ships but opposed measures that would give shoreside canners a monopoly in the harvest.[37]

The most emphatic witnesses were Lyman Henry and William Denman, who represented the offshore plants. They condemned the entire proceeding as a conspiracy among shoreside canners, Fish and Game scientists, and the sportfishing lobby to fasten monopoly on the industry and impoverish one of the Depression's few profitable enterprises. Denman "would not think of displacing a single laborer on any evidence you now have of depletion." Any observed changes in the stock, he thought, were environmentally induced. Taking the standard laissez-faire view, Denman claimed that even if the industry depressed the stock, sardines were so fecund that they would soon grow back. To ignore the testimony of the fishers themselves that the sardines were abundant, finally, was "the most brutal kind of medieval scholasticism." Denman and Henry favored transferring the sardine investigation either to

USBF or to the universities, in any case away from the "political racketeers and larger processors" who had the Fish and Game Commission in their pockets.[38]

Congress took no action on the offshore reduction problem.[39] The hearings had, however, exposed the divisions within the industry and in the scientific community over the sardine question. "Must the scientist always be on the defensive?" complained an anonymous CDFG researcher in their aftermath.[40] In 1935 a frustrated CFGC had retained Willis Rich and Frank Weymouth, respectively professors of biology and physiology at Stanford, to conduct an independent review of its evidence. While their report found no positive evidence of depletion in the data, they nonetheless concluded that *some* stable limit on the catch was imperative. They then urged all factions to support

> the conservative policy of the Fish and Game Commissioners and their desire to curb the exceedingly rapid expansion of the fishery.... Emphatically it is the duty of these state officials to be conservative.

"Any other course," they concluded, "would be a breach of trust."[41]

As Higgins had noted in his testimony at the sardine hearings, none of the state laboratory's conclusions was "of direct concern" in the issue at hand, nor were they in much dispute among scientists.[42] The real differences lay in the relative values which different interests placed on uncertainty, risk, and opportunity in acting on information that was necessarily opaque. The United States had traditionally valued opportunity above all else: Indeed, the Progressive formula for conservation, which Higgins followed, modified nineteenth-century policy's emphasis on rapid economic growth only slightly by adding "over the longest time" to "the greatest use for the greatest number." While CFGC's statutory mandate to "provide for the restoration and preservation of fish in [California] waters" was blunt and could be unwieldy in specific contests, USBF's more mathematical formula offered no room for such vague considerations as were really at stake in the sardine controversy.[43]

The one practical effect of the 1936 hearing was to change the nature of the scientific inquiry. In a private letter to Rich, Higgins expressed distaste for the political innuendo of Denman and Henry, but wondered "how much fire there may be behind all the smoke" and thought that USBF entry into the investigation might depoliticize it. To lead the federal effort he recommended Elton Sette, who had worked at the State Fisheries Laboratory before moving to USBF in 1924.[44] Rich and Weymouth agreed and offered Higgins the use of Stanford's facilities if he wished to use them.[45] The Poultry Producers' Association of Central California also urged USBF to take a hand in the study, and in October 1937 Sette arrived at Stanford to organize the South Pacific Fishery Investigations.[46]

Sette's reception in California was decidedly cool. Although his former colleagues were personally friendly, Sette found them "unwilling to admit any worthy motives on the part of the Bureau in undertaking an investigation and . . . loath to permit use of their original data."[47] California law gave USBF the right to do research in state waters, though, and after Scofield heard personally from the commissioners he promised "the feds" his cooperation.[48] The Director of Scripps Institute, Harold U. Sverdrup, mediated between the two camps and at La Jolla organized the first of an annual series of inter-agency oceanographic conferences that continue to this day. Sette arranged with Sverdrup to cooperate in the operation of SIO's research vessel.[49] Fish and Game simultaneously expanded its own program and launched the nation's first state-owned research vessel to begin sampling the California Current. With sister agencies in Oregon, Washington, and British Columbia, California began a cooperative tagging study which demonstrated that the sardine migrated the length of the coast, that is, that all four jurisdictions drew from a common pool of fish. Sette's group studied the age composition of the sardine population in cooperation with the local agencies and the Scripps Institution. By 1943 the expanded research had demonstrated that older fish were disappearing from the population and that annual mortality in the stock was very high.[50]

Formal cooperation did nothing to ease bad feelings between the State Fisheries Laboratory and USBF, which became the U.S. Fish and Wildlife Service (USFWS) in the Department of the Interior in 1940. Sette and Frances Clark continued to spar over the sharing of data.[51] In 1939, as CDFG publications increasingly displayed frustration combined with near panic, Sette wrote to Acting Commissioner of Fisheries Charles Jackson to say that any mention in USBF publications of "possible depletion" or "threatened depletion" immediately and inevitably generated letters and telegrams from industry leaders concerned, as the manger of the Sardine Products Institute put it, about "misunderstanding on [the] part of zealous conservationists and sportsmen."[52] At a 1940 meeting between state and federal researchers, N. B. Scofield's younger brother Lance insisted heatedly that Fish and Game be the sole outlet for the sardine inquiry's findings because commercial operators were using USFWS publicity on the research to thwart the former's efforts to manage the fishery. Jackson freely admitted the merit of Scofield's position but insisted nonetheless that USFWS had to inform the public of its findings and that it would continue to publish them under Interior Department auspices rather than through CDFG.[53] By 1943 the federal investigators at Stanford were careful to state what parts of their monthly reports to Washington were not for publication.[54]

After 1939, when the newly elected governor of California replaced all three members of the Fish and Game Commission with "emergency" appointees of his own, the tone of the commission's own biennial reports changed radically. Where the 1938 report had referred to "unmistakable signs of depletion in the sardine population" and the "imperative need to reduce the harvest," the 1942 report found "no reason to be concerned over the possibility of the extermination of the sardine by the fishermen," only "a possibility that if the fishery is carried on too intensively, the population will decline to a point where the success of a fishing season will depend upon the chance occurrence of an abundant year-class."[55] In fact, it already had. The 1944 report dealt in nineteenth-century fashion with statistics on the ethnicity of commercial fishers, noted that the cooperative investigations were continuing, and found the sardine population "in comparatively healthy condition."[56]

Elmer Higgins and Elton Sette knew otherwise. In May 1941 Higgins reported to the latter the sardine canners' offer to supply fish to the government, but warned that the extra production would put a strain on the supply "which may not be justified."[57] A year later, as Sette prepared to assume control over the industry for the War Production Board, he reported to Washington that very few fish had survived from the spawnings of 1940 and 1941 and that some 60–80 percent of the stock was disappearing each season, mostly due to the fishery. "If this is true," he continued,

> we have been making an abnormally high catch out of an abnormally small population and cannot expect to continue to do so during the rest of the season . . . . My guess, then, is that you would be taking a long gamble if you counted on a continuation of the present landing rate, and would be far safer to lay plans for a substantial drop in landings.[58]

The felt need to maximize production for the war effort took precedence, however, and Sette relayed orders for increased harvests until April 1945. In October of that year the sardines disappeared from the northern grounds.

Rationalizing the market

If environmental influences on the fisheries were "linked inseparably with the study of depletion," as Thompson put it, so, too, were the economic forces which drove the harvest in the first place. A fishery is an ecological system: a flow of energy and material through a network that encompasses not only environment, fish, and fishers, but also the market channels through which the nutrients stored in the fish flow after harvesting. Economics and ecology thus form a coherent whole and, as Justice Holmes said, "what affects any portion must be felt more or less by all the rest." A stable, limited fishery entails stable, limited markets.

There was some public awareness of the interplay between conservation and the marketing of fish: "As in the case of the great meat packing corporations," noted Thompson in 1919, "the public is demanding an actual regulation of the entire fishing industry, from fisherman to retail dealer."[59] What Thomspon called "economic control" was beyond his reach. "It is the Commission's concern," he continued, "to insure a supply, then to aid in its proper and efficient use, and not – at present – to exercise any legal control over the economic phases of the fisheries."[60] Thompson had to take the fishery itself as a given, something he could not manipulate but only react to as best he could. By 1928 he had narrowed his view even further: As the political firestorm over the reduction industry intensified, he became "less interested in the study of conditions in the sea which may cause fluctuations in the abundance of commercial species than . . . in what is actually happening in the fisheries themselves."[62]

Government could, however, try to improve the profitability of fishing as a business. It would not only enhance opportunity for the industry thereby, but might also decrease expansionary pressure on the harvest. Many different agencies, state and federal, thus undertook research and development to promote the more efficient use of the catch. Others tried to encourage planning and cooperation in the marketing of fishery products to the same end. Labor unions tried to exert some control over the business, claiming with some justification that their security intertwined with that of the fish, and during the New Deal the National Recovery Administration tried to bring the many interests in the business into some sort of balance. The fishing industry, however, had "more angles than the much discussed Balkan situation, and more intricacies than Russian politics," as one Progressive put it, and consistently frustrated attempts to organize it.[62]

Predictably, most of the research and development effort concentrated on the canning fisheries. Soon after large-scale sardine canning began on the East Coast, the USDA found a significant proportion of the Maine pack to be in violation of the recently passed Pure Food and Drug Act. In 1913 it established a laboratory at Eastport to study the problem. After West Coast canneries reported increasing problems with spoiled or "swelled" canned sardines, USDA began bacteriological studies on these in 1915. In 1925 it traced two deaths from botulism in Ohio to sardines canned at San Pedro. To complement the USDA's remedial work, USBF opened a laboratory at San Pedro to study methods of canning and preserving underused species like mackerel and herring.[63]

The Commissioner of Fisheries suggested in 1914 that the federal government help fishers find new and more efficient ways of plying their trade in the same way that the USDA had long assisted the nation's farmers.[64]

Although the U.S. Fish Commission had developed a prototype fishing schooner for East Coast use in the nineteenth century, not much was done along these lines for West Coast fishers during the twentieth century. The California agency did perform one important service in this vein by retaining experts from the Japanese Fisheries School, who introduced the live-bait, pole-and-line method to U.S. tuna fishers.[65]

By contrast, the reduction industry was the direct progeny of government demonstration. Alarmed by U.S. dependence on foreign supplies of potash and nitrogenous fertilizer as World War I broke out in Europe, Congress commissioned a study of the nation's fertilizer inventory in which Pacific Coast kelp was a much-discussed potential source of additional supply. The USDA published a study on kelp by-products in 1915 and two years later opened its pilot reduction plant in Santa Barbara County. Private operations followed quickly. The USDA Bureau of Soils began in 1913 to investigate possible agricultural uses for the tons of fish offal that salmon and tuna canners were letting go to waste. By 1919 the Bureau of Fisheries was actively encouraging the use of menhaden meal as a stock feed on the East Coast and planning to extend its promotional work to the West as well.[66] Such efforts, though well within the tradition of government promotion of business, ran directly counter to those of California authorities who were simultaneously trying to discourage the production of fishmeal because, as Elmer Higgins recalled, they feared that allowing a by-products industry to take root would "develop such a demand throughout the entire country that control of the fishery when depletion should occur would be impossible by legal means."[67]

One of the reasons that the quality of canned sardines was so poor in the 1920s was that the market for them was chronically flooded by too many processors desperately competing to cut their costs of production. If government could demonstrate a cheaper way of putting up a high-quality pack, so the logic went, canners could get a higher price for their product and thus ease the burden on the fishery as well as on their ledgers. USBF began work on new canning methods at San Pedro in 1920, but as long as reduction generated such large profits the canners used what they could of the new methods only to cut costs further and bothered little with making a better or more healthful food product. By 1927 not one of the Monterey packers had adopted the new process developed by USBF to improve the quality of the pack.[68]

Inefficiency and waste were not simply technical problems but economic ones as well. Fishers do not "waste" fish out of ignorance or perversity but because they work under such real-world constraints as interest rates, fixed charges, and imperfect mobility of skills and capital.[69] Such economic irrationalities as consumer preference for only a few kinds of fish and the fact that people bought most of their fish on Friday also worked against economic efficiency in the industry. As a CFGC investigator noted in 1925, "it is a fact not generally appreciated that all marine fisheries are extremely wasteful and can not be carried on under present market conditions without being so."[70] Public concern about the problem arose first in San Francisco, where market fisheries controlled by the wholesalers' "fish trust" and a collection of smaller coalitions, similarly Italian, remained visibly and odorously primitive through the end of the World War I decade.

Consumer outrage over the high price and low quality, not only of fish but of fresh fruits and vegetables, grew steadily more vocal until the 1915 California legislature approved an act to organize public markets for fresh food products.[71] The same session also passed a bill to give CFGC control over the distribution, marketing, and pricing of fresh fish, but Governor Hiram Johnson withheld his approval and turned the problem over instead to his newly appointed State Market Director, Harris Weinstock.[72] To the consternation of organized consumers and their friends at Sacramento, Weinstock stood his enabling legislation on its head and used it, not to set up public commission markets for produce, but to organize the state's growers into cooperative marketing associations such as had already proven successful among citrus and raisin producers. In 1916 Weinstock organized just such a cooperative among the five major fish wholesalers in the Bay Area. The State Fish Exchange, as he called it, fixed and advertised prices for Bay Area market fish to stimulate demand and direct it toward kinds that were plentiful. This, Weinstock thought, would at once lower prices, increase production and profits, and minimize waste. Weinstock concentrated his organizational efforts on the five wholesale firms that operated steam trawlers. When the leading broker, Achille Paladini, refused to go along with the plan, Weinstock went to the legislature and secured statutory authority to compel participation in the Fish Exchange.[73]

Fish and Game initially objected to the idea of giving Weinstock legal power over marketing; it felt that the Exchange lacked sufficient biological information with which to wield that powerful an influence over the production of fish. It also noted that a state agency had no authority to control fish caught in international waters, where the "double-draggers" took most of their flatfish. The "fish trust" thus retained independent control over most of its business. CFGC was relieved, then, when the U.S. Food Administration took temporary control over the entire business as a temporary war measure.[74]

Although one of the problems that had led to the creation of the State Fish Exchange had been the waste of surplus fish on the market, warm summers in 1917 and 1918 and enhanced demand during the war led to market *shortages* at the critical point when the federal government took control. CFGC's relief turned to horror when Food Administrator Ralph Merritt suspended many state and local fishing regulations, including those on the Sacramento River salmon fishery, and offered incentives to fishers who installed new and more efficient gear on their boats. Thus encouraged, the river fishers began pushing the legislature for increased access to the salmon, already pressed by drought and the offshore harvest.[75] "It is a period of danger," warned the commissioners in 1918. "Already there have been numerous attempts by commercial interests to shelve protective laws, and if food conditions become still more serious, it will be increasingly difficult to prevent serious inroads being made on our fish and game."[76]

Weinstock returned to work late in 1918. In 1919 he began efforts to bring not only the Los Angeles retail market under his control, but that for cannery fish as well. Weinstock's help was a great boon to the Bay Area brokers, who used it to increase their share of the market from 20 percent just before the war to 40 percent in 1918.[77] He managed to alienate just about everyone else, including consumers, fishers, the Bay Area press, and the Fish and Game Commission. The Italian fishers' coalitions fought him at every step, as did the salmon fishers in IWW-affiliated Fisherman's Protective Union of Pittsburg. In 1919 market fishers, with sardiners going out in sympathy, staged the first statewide strike in the industry's history to force Weinstock's ouster and the removal of price controls.[78]

Charging that Weinstock was in the pay of the "fish trust," consumer advocates again mounted an effort to give CFGC control over the marketing of fish. CFGC again asked to be left out of that business, and a compromise bill simply to abolish the Fish Exchange passed both houses of the legislature by overwhelming margins.[79] Weinstock's only friends were the growers, the canners, the "fish trust," and Governor William D. Stephens, who pocket-vetoed the bill. In 1920, professing ill health, Weinstock retired from his position two weeks before the state Attorney General sued to dissolve five of his agricultural cooperatives for profiteering. The Fish Exchange thereafter limited its efforts to advertising, public exhibits, and distribution of a seafood cookbook to promote demand for fish.[81]

Private rather than public cooperation came into vogue while its chief advocate, Herbert Hoover, was Secretary of Commerce during the 1920s.[81] After Weinstock's departure, the Bay Area brokers organized the California Wholesale Fish Dealers' Association to allocate access to fishing grounds, set harvest quotas, and fix prices for flatfish. Small boat fishers, meanwhile, managed the production of crabs, bait, salmon, and rockfish through the strongest of the minor coalitions, the Crab Fisherman's Protective Association. Fresh fish markets remained unorganized in the southern part of the state. As overproduction of canned sardines grew "rather desperate" in 1927–8, processors organized an export cartel under the Webb–Pomerene Act, which exempted such groups from prosecution under federal antitrust law. They also established and financed their own system for inspecting the quality of canned sardines under the supervision of the State Board of Health.[82]

Such private organizations were very difficult to sustain in the fishing industry, and few of the ones that did appear had much influence.[83] The National Recovery Administration (NRA), whose industrial code authorities combined Progressive-Era centralization and planning with Hooverian industrial self-government, did not survive long enough to make any lasting impact on the business. The effort to draw up a Sardine Code did facilitate the organization of the California Sardine Products Institute, which by 1939 had drawn up fair-trade rules for the industry. The Institute quickly became an association of northern California packers only, however. The sardine industry was simply too fragmented, both functionally and geographically, to organize. Functionally, it contained firms that both canned and reduced sardines, shoreside firms that manufactured only by-products, and those that operated reduction ships offshore. Geographically, it was divided between northern California firms that produced only sardines and southern California firms that processed both sardines and tuna. As long as many different avenues existed for tapping the sardine fishery, competition remained too powerful a solvent for private agreements to contain within prudent bounds.[84]

Each faction, as the 1936 sardine hearing made abundantly clear, had a different view of the industry's problems and a different strategy for addressing them. Compounding the industry's organizational schizophrenia was the legendary individualism of its participants, "every one" of whom, according to a Van Camp executive, "would make a fine president, but none of them . . . satisfactory privates in the ranks."[85] Political balkanization also guaranteed that the industry would fare poorly in Washington when it came time to press its views on such issues as tariff protection.[86] As a body, the industry could accomplish little save to ensure that nothing was done, either to organize its business affairs or, as N. B. Scofield discovered once again when he presented his case for conservation to the NRA in Washington, to care for the future of its resource base.[87]

The New Deal's main effort was to encourage the growth of "countervailing power" among farmers, workers, and others whose inability to defend their interests had contributed to imbalance in the economy of the twenties and thus to the Depression.[88] Hugh Hammond Bennett, leader of the USDA Soil Conservation Service and as charismatic a visionary as Pinchot had been in his day, saw economic and political self-determination for farmers and conservation of the soil as inseparable goals.[89] Soil depletion, conversely, was less a cause of poverty and powerlessness than its symptom. As another USDA official put it,

> erosion is one of the symptoms of some deep maladjustments between the soil and its farming system. Rarely can we achieve control by simple direct means, rather we must get back of the immediate symptoms and find the cause. Frequently we find weak plant cover

and declining soil fertility resulting from unstable economic conditions, bad tenure relationships, overcrowded land, poverty, disease, and wars. . . . [90]

Such a comprehensive approach to environmental problems was difficult to fit into the established institutional framework of agricultural policy, and Bennett's vision failed to overcome the strenuous opposition of agribusiness interests entrenched in the USDA's research and regulatory apparatus. [91]

Although unions got a voice in drawing up codes for the fishing industry under the NIRA, a similar approach to fishery problems failed even of coherent articulation during the New Deal. [92] Collective bargaining, however, did enable sardiners to close somewhat the gap between the prices they received for fish and those which the processors received for by-products. The main achievement of New Deal labor law was to close down the offshore factories in 1938, though this came too late to prevent the vast increase in fishing effort and shoreside reduction that the "floaters" had generated earlier in the decade.

By nurturing the union movement, in addition, the New Deal helped to bring to near completion a long struggle to dissolve the ethnically based producers' coalitions that had dominated the fisheries at the turn of the century. California took the first steps as it began to assert its power to license, tax, and police the Bay Area market fisheries. At first, state authorities and the immigrant fishers were near-equal bargainers: Corruption was the inevitable result, and several deputies were caught in a protection racket with Chinese shrimp merchants. In response, a special committee of the 1911 state legislature demanded "a thorough reorganization of the entire system of management, control, and supervision of the deputies." Fish and Game patrol officers occasionally found themselves in lethal gun battles with Indians in Lassen County and Italian crabbers in the Bay Area between 1910 and 1915. Law enforcement in those cases amounted to a bitter struggle between near-equal bargainers for control over the fisheries in question. [93]

As public power gradually overwhelmed the immigrant coalitions, state courts affirmed CFGC's authority to license fishers and compel them to submit records of their harvests between 1914 and 1920. [94] The first such decision, in the *Matter of Application of Parra*, upheld the conviction of a salmon gill-netter caught working Carquinez Strait without a fishing license and asserted that while the state constitution continued to speak of the public's "right" to fish, the amendment of 1910 had in essence redefined fishing in public waters as a privilege subject to regulation or revocation at the state's pleasure. [95] The commission allied with Harris Weinstock in his fight with Achille Paladini in the 1918 case of *Paladini* v. *Superior Court*, which affirmed the state's right to collect fees and statistics from fish dealers. [96] It established a separate Department of Patrol under centralized direction and uniformed its deputies during the mid-1920s as it modernized its operations so as to "function as a big business concern . . . [with] advanced business methods."[97]

The state broke the most intransigent of the Italian coalitions, the Crab Fisherman's Protective Association, in the 1916 case *Ex parte Cencinino*. *Cencinino* formally dealt with a 1912 Humboldt Country ordinance prohibiting the export of crabs from Humboldt Bay. The Fish and Game Commission opposed the ordinance because it stifled the development of a potentially valuable fishery. In overturning it the court found that Article IV, section 25½ of the state constitution, as amended in 1902, gave the legislature sole right to enact fish and game regulations for local areas, even though it had not actually passed a districting law until 1911.[98] One contemporary observer thought the decision a bad one because the constitution also allowed counties to enact supplementary ordinances if they wished to enforce stricter standards of conservation than those required by state statute.[99] In any event, what may have been the real purpose behind the prosecution was achieved as crabs from Eureka rushed onto the San Francisco market. Bay Area crabbers, whose high running costs had left them with a narrow margin of profit even when they controlled their market, became so desperate as to appeal to Harris Weinstock for help in 1917.[100]

The first union made up solely of sardiners appeared at Monterey in 1920, in the midst of the deflation that had cut their dockside prices from $12 to as little as $5 per ton of fish. By 1923 enough lampara crews had left Monterey that those who remained were able to establish their union as exclusive marketing agent for sardines and to force the price back up to $10. They failed to achieve their key objective in the 1923 strike, which was to close entry to the fishery by requiring processors to buy fish only from unionized crews. By the midtwenties lampara strikes had become what *Pacific Fisherman* called "an established annual institution" at Monterey. Union busting, then, was Knut Hovden's chief motive for inviting two San Pedro purse seiners to Monterey during the 1926 strike. A sudden inrush of seiners during the 1929 strike brought the reign of the lampara crews to a quick end.[101] Through the 1930s and 1940s, disputes between AFL and CIO-affiliated unions as well as different patterns of organization among fishers, boat owners, cannery workers, and reduction workers at each of the state's four sardine ports rendered labor even less capable of organizing than capital.[102]

Boat owners at Monterey originally belonged to the same union as their crews, divided their income by shares, and with them bargained collectively against the packers. Their peculiar legal position, however, – property owners on the one hand, workers for the canneries on the other – split the alliance in 1940. At that time, Monterey skippers belonged to an association which cooperated with the Seine and Line Fisherman's Union to control distribution of fish to canneries. Traditional violence and intimidation kept nonmembers out and thus reduced the potential pressure on the fishery by limiting access to it. One frustrated interloper, however, won triple damages from the owners when a federal court ruled that an association of boat owners could not bargain collectively as a labor union and that, because their boats moved in and out of the territorial sea, exclusion of outsiders constituted interference with foreign commerce under the Sherman Anti-Trust Act.[103] At nearly every turn, state power worked to dissolve informal attempts by fishers to stabilize the industry but left nothing in their place save the Hobbesian competition for fish that was inexorably driving the sardine business to ruin.

The sardine fishery came under centralized federal control in the summer of 1943. Fish and Game had tried to cooperate informally with the War Production Board the preceding season, allocating catch quotas to individual boats and distributing boats among the different ports to maximize efficiency, but Monterey packers successfully challenged its power to do so in court.[104] The Interior Department then created an Office of the Coordinator of Fisheries, staffed it with Fish and Wildlife Service personnel, and installed Elton Sette as Fishery Coordinator in San Francisco.[105] State authorities only reluctantly yielded to Sette, who repeatedly expressed his frustration over their continued lack of cooperation.[106] Although federal officials tried to discourage it in favor of canning, production of meal and oil remained quite high through the war. Federal price controls did nearly double the real price of raw sardines while holding that for by-products steady at prewar levels. They thus improved the profitability of fishing itself in a way that the unions had been unable to do. So long as no agency could limit entry to the fishery, however, increased profits only stimulated construction of new boats and new plants, despite the fact that the industry had been seriously overcapitalized before the war and there was no need for new capacity.[107] No sooner did peace return than the industry's years of overdrawing its resource, which wartime controls did nothing to correct, brought their inevitable due.

Dollar economy, fish economy, and the police power

In essence, both scientists who wished to see their research put to good use and those who wished to prevent the waste of fish after harvest fell prey to a failure of accounting in the policymaking process not unlike the more strictly economic failure that leads to "the tragedy of the commons."[108] In the "tragedy of the commons" individual resource users cannot afford to limit their use of shared resources because individual profits from overexploiting them are always greater in the short run than individual shares of the social cost. In the political version of the problem, unions, trade associations, or government agencies typically cannot afford the political cost of defending values for which they share responsibility with any number of other bodies. In 1935, for example, every one of the ten executive agencies in the federal government bore some responsibility for conserving wildlife. No one of these could rationally sacrifice its primary missions on behalf of fish and game. In some states separate agencies for game and commercial fisheries competed for jurisdiction over the same stocks of animals. Although commercial interests never succeeded in establishing their own agency in California, they successfully pursued their policy goals through the legislature while the sportfishers worked through CFGC.[109]

Indeed, even though it was precisely the job of public agencies to account for social costs beyond the vision of private parties, government institutions in the early twentieth century were organized in such a way as to thwart that function. State and federal constitutions divided responsibility and power among competing agencies deliberately, and for good reason: As Justice Brandeis noted, "separation of powers was adopted . . . not to promote efficiency but . . . to save the people from autocracy."[110] In addition, public institutions took the form they did because they were creatures of history. Like the living products of biological evolution, the framework within which policymaking took place was the residual agglomeration of past confrontations with a changing environment, each part brought into being when government faced a new problem for which old institutions would not suffice.[111] Having developed in an earlier time when the promotion of economic progress was the key function of government and modified only slightly by Progressive-Era reformers who believed that contemporary obstacles to continued growth would fall before the deliberate application of scientific expertise, government institutions in the twentieth-century were ill-prepared constitutionally to pay careful attention to the ancillary costs of growth.

California entered the twentieth century with three constitutional tools for conserving fisheries, all of them apparently proven in the closing decades of the nineteenth. To protect the environment which produced fish it had the rule in *People* v. *Truckee Lumber Company* that "to the extent that waters are the common passageway for fish . . . they are deemed for such purposes public waters and subject to all laws of the state regulating the right of fishery."[112] To shield the resources from market pressure which might otherwise overwhelm them, it had the state-ownership rule of *Ex parte Maier*. To protect the resources at the point of production, finally, the constitutional amendments of 1902 and 1910 guaranteed the legislature power to pass specific regulations for specific fisheries. Of the three, only the *Truckee Lumber Company* approach had much vitality during the first half of the twentieth century. Thus, while state and federal agencies made some progress toward protecting fishery habitat inland during the interwar period, their efforts to stave off the destruction of the sardine fishery proved utterly feckless.

Building on its success in the *Truckee Lumber Company* decision, which explicitly recognized that California rivers performed important ecological as well as industrial functions, the Fish and Game Commission devoted much energy in the first two decades of the new century, in its words, to "pollution, drainage, and power dams."[113] It established a separate Bureau of Hydraulics to carry out the work, which "brought it in contact with practically all lines of industry" in the state.[114] The most serious offender was the new petroleum industry: Oil tankers at Port Hartford, for example, wiped out fisheries there between 1900 and 1904 by dumping their ballast directly into the local harbor. Though formal prosecution was sometimes necessary to force industrial polluters to install sawdust burners, proper fittings for pipes and hoses, settling basins, and the like, informal conferences usually did the job. Price inflation during World War I encouraged refiners to recover waste oil on their own, so that pollution became noticeably less bothersome for a time.[115]

Fish and Game relied on different sections of the state penal code to keep Sacramento Basin waterways free for running salmon. Individual statutes gave the commission authority to inspect irrigation and power dams and to order their operators to build fishways or entire hatcheries, at state expense, if their obstructions were completely impassable. A 1915 law required dam operators to guarantee fish an adequate flow of water through their facilities.[116] The Hydraulics Bureau also spent much time badgering farmers to screen their irrigation ditches to keep fish out of them, but in 1933 the state legislature required the commission to pay half the cost of screening and the work stopped temporarily. The commission protested to no avail that farmers and others who used the state's water for free ought to pay something to protect the fish in them.[117] During the New Deal the Civilian Conservation Corps supplied free labor and materials for screening, as well as to remove a number of obsolete water diversions. Together with the violent floods of the 1937–8 winter, the CCC removal work probably contributed to the resurgence of salmon runs in the early forties.[118]

The commission's reactive, case-by-case approach required a great deal of hard effort, in its words, "due to the fact that the operating companies consider the fish of little or no value."[119] Moderate success with "gentlemen's agreements" and the occasional lawsuit, then, did not prepare CFGC to deal with the wholesale expropriation of fishery habitat by irrigation districts and power companies after 1915. Farmers were lackadaisical in maintaining their fish screens. Convictions for violating penal code provisions controlling water use were extremely difficult to secure from local juries until a 1937 statute gave them an incentive by allocating half of the guilty parties' fines to county wildlife preservation funds.[120] CFGC appealed time and again to the Water Rights Division of the state Public Works Department to guarantee minimal flows of water through Central Valley dams, but in vain.[121] In 1922 the commission secured an agreement from the Anderson–Cottonwood Irrigation District to build a fishway around its dam, which for five years had blocked the main stem of the Sacramento near Redding, but only after taking the extraordinary step of seeking an injunction to stop them from operating the dam.[122]

CFGC's attempts to work through regular channels failed to stop the Electro-Metals Company from damming the Klamath in the early twenties. The company mounted a very powerful cost–benefit argument in its behalf. The dam, it said, would generate far more income for the local economy than would the salmon fishery, which a local editor called a "small enterprise of only local importance" and which in any event produced only one-sixth of the Pacific Coast commercial salmon pack.[123] A local newspaper denounced the Fish and Game Commission as the tool of the "idle rich" and "dangerously near to becoming a menace to the industrial expansion of the state."[124] By contrast, CFGC claimed that comparing the costs and benefits of destroying the largest remaining free-flowing river on the Pacific Coast were simply immaterial.[125] In this case even *Pacific Fisherman*, which spoke for commercial salmon fishers, agreed.[126] The Federal Power Commission had originally denied a construction permit to the dam but reversed itself when the State Division of Water Rights approved it, claiming that it did not want to get involved in a conflict between two branches of the same state government. Fish and Game then took its case directly to the people by way of an initiative measure that succeeded through the assiduous campaigning of CFGC employees in all parts of the state. This was truly an extraordinary measure, and Fish and Game never tried it again.[127]

Only regular procedures for weighing environmental and commercial values before projects were built could prevent the inshore fishery habitat from being gradually degraded while Fish and Game dissipated its resources on numberless conflicts with local developers and other government agencies. A state law of 1919 required advance approval from CFGC before construction on water projects could proceed, but this was soon repealed.[128] Here the initiative came at the federal level during the New Deal. The Tennessee Valley Authority (TVA) was a model for interagency cooperation to promote a wide range of social and economic values. Like the Soil Conservation Service, TVA also planned development on a regional environmental basis rather than through existing political jurisdictions.[129]

The federal Fish and Wildlife Coordination Act of 1934 required the Bureau of Reclamation, the Army Corps of Engineers, and other agencies concerned with water development to consult with USBF and to give "due and adequate consideration" to protecting fisheries, although initially it made little difference in government practice.[130] The California State Water Resources Act of 1945 similarly required agencies to consider all beneficial uses of watersheds and to cooperate with state and federal wildlife agencies in the planning of developments.[131] Shasta Dam was California's first real experience with such interagency planning, although little attention was paid to CDFG and USFWS salmon studies and what favorable effects the dam had on the fishery were unintended.[132] Although effective interagency cooperation and planning did not begin until after World War II, New Deal initiatives marked an important new beginning in public wildlife policy and carried forward the premise of *Truckee Lumber Company*, that is, that the public had a wide range of interests at stake in watershed use.[133]

Less useful as a shield for wildlife was the rule in *Ex parte Maier* and *Geer v. Connecticut*, which held that the state retained a substantial interest in wildlife even after they entered the stream of commerce. The state-ownership fiction was an explicit recognition that fish and game were not like other commodities – that what happened to them after they were killed and sold bore heavily on the security of living animals in the wild. Nevertheless, it did not protect the animals from the increasingly powerful solvent of commerce in an interdependent industrial economy.

The state ownership rule began to dissolve almost immediately as Congress strengthened its power to control interstate commerce after 1900. The Lacey Act of 1900 was one of Congress's first initiatives in this area, along with similar initiatives to control interstate traffic in such ticklish commodities as lottery tickets, prostitutes, and liquor.[134] Congress preempted state control over birds which migrated across state lines in 1918.[135] The Supreme Court narrowed the scope of the *Geer* rule by prohibiting its use for purposes that were strictly economic and provincial in 1928. *Foster-Fountain Packing Company* v. *Haydel* overturned a Louisiana statue that required all shrimp taken from state waters to be processed within the state. Directly contradicting *Geer*, the Court stated that the act of harvesting the shrimp "put an end to the trust upon which the state is deemed to own or control the shrimp for the benefit of the people."[136]

In 1948 the Court struck down a similarly self-serving attempt by California to use the *Geer* rule in denying a Japanese fisher's application for a license because he was an "alien ineligible for citizenship." In *Takahashi* v. *Fish and Game Commission* it found the purported intent of the California law too thin to justify overriding Takahashi's right to equal protection of the laws and made explicit reference to Judge Lorenzo Sawyer's refusal to condone similar actions against Chinese fishers some sixty years before.[137] In a companion case to *Takahashi*, *Toomer* v. *Witsell*, the Court stripped away most of the legal obfuscation that supported the state ownership theory, noting that "the whole ownership theory, in fact, is now generally regarded as but a fiction expressive in legal shorthand of the importance to its people that a state have power to preserve and regulate the exploitation of an important resource."[138] If a state wished to manage the use of its wildlife, it would have to do so directly, by policing the harvest itself in a just and reasonable manner.

California tried to use the market-limiting strategy of *Maier* and *Geer* to keep the sardine harvest down to a safe level. CFGC's fear of the reduction industry, as a later commentator put it, stemmed from

> the perhaps not unjustified fear that the State of California, under the present management arrangements, cannot effectively control, on a scientific basis, the harvest of the large-scale fisheries necessary for this sort of industry. The problem here would seem to be institutional rather than biological, but it is important and real.[139]

The fear expressed itself in a number of ways, most frequently in the objection that reduction "wasted" fish. "It seems repugnant to every right-thinking citizen," wrote CFGC's attorney in 1927, "to see fresh food fish used for any purpose other than human consumption."[140] Preserving the sardines for the "highest use," that is, food for people, had motivated both the Fish Conservation Act of 1919 and contemporary efforts to establish state-operated fish markets.[141] Proponents of reduction considered such arguments irrational. "There is no halo around a sardine because it happens to be in a can," claimed one San Pedro fisher at the 1936 sardine hearing.[142] The defendant in one famous reduction case insisted that a fish was, after all, a fish, and "the poultry raiser is as much entitled to feed for his chicks, as the Mongolian is entitled to his can of sardines."[143]

There was nothing theoretically wrong with proscribing a specific use of a resource as a way of keeping its exploitation down to a safe level. "Reasonable, beneficial use" was a time-honored standard in California water law, for example. The goal was to avoid depleting the resource, and if the state did not have the hard information to pinpoint a safe yield regulating in terms of permissible use was flexible, easy to explain and administer, and above all greatly reduced the risk of destroying the resource that uncertainty about its behavior entailed.[144] With respect to the sardine, the key problem was that the decision to reduce a fish or put it in a can came after the harvester sold it to the processor, when the legal presumption was that it was just another article of commerce whose owner could dispose of it at will.

Nonetheless, prompted by its "duty to be conservative" and the certain knowledge that once capital was invested in a reduction fishery it would be impossible to remove, and with the help of sardine canners who feared the competition for fish as well as for the future of the resource, CFGC secured passage of the California Fish Conservation Act of 1919. Section 4 of the law prohibited "the preventable deterioration or waste" of fish taken from public waters, specifically the diversion of whole fish to reduction plants without written permission of CFGC. When the original law proved vague and gave

CFGC agents at different ports too much discretion to make different rules, the Commission's attorney wrote an amendment in 1921 that allowed canners, again with permission, to make by-products out of no more than 25 percent of the weight of sardines they could can each month. [145]

CFGC's efforts to control the "downstream" use of wildlife found consistent support in the courts. State ownership figured prominently in *Paladini* v. *Superior Court*, which affirmed Harris Weinstock's authority to regulate the marketing of fresh fish. [146] The California Supreme Court used it twice to reaffirm the reduction law, in the 1925 case of *People* v. *Stafford Packing Company* and in the more widely noted *People* v. *Monterey Fish Products Company* a year later. [147] Stafford was a San Pedro-area canning firm which reduced 88.6 percent of the 681,000 pounds of sardines it offloaded in January, 1923. It claimed that "the supply of fish in the Pacific Ocean [was] inexhaustible," and that reduction did not therefore constitute a nuisance that the state could sue to enjoin. "Experience has proven," the court found to the contrary, "that the available supply of food fish . . . may be seriously depleted, if not practically exhausted, within a period of a few years, by unrestricted fishing." This was enough, in its view, for the court to sustain an injunction to prevent a "threatened injury to the property rights of the people which are held in trust by the state."[148]

The court went further against the Monterey Fish Products Company, a firm that produced fishmeal for shipment to poultry growers in Sonoma County but canned no fish at all. Here, the defendant alleged that the reduction law was unconstitutional because it allowed canners to reduce sardines but prohibited others from doing so. The court, however, found for the state in all particulars. Within broad constitutional bounds, the determination of standards for conservation and the means of enforcing them were left entirely to the legislature, which could, moreover, "confer upon an administrative board a large measure of discretion" in carrying out the task. Whether the state could actually prove a danger to the resource from reduction per se was simply immaterial, although such a finding was "not unsupported by the evidence." If California determined, by whatever means, that reduction ran counter to public policy, then reduction was a nuisance per se and could be enjoined at the people's pleasure. Federal rulings in 1929 and 1935 seconded the *Monterey Fish Products* decision and distinguished it from the potentially damaging *Foster–Fountain* precedent because the California law was a legitimate conservation measure, whereas the Louisiana shrimp law had been a transparent subterfuge. [149] The second of these, *Bayside Fish Flour Co.* v. *Gentry et al.*, became a leading precedent for state efforts to control landings of fish caught outside their territorial waters in the post–World War II period. [150]

While obtaining judicial sanction for the reduction control program was one thing, actually carrying it out was quite another. Most processors simply flouted the law and had to be dragged into court, one by one.[151] The most critical problem, however, was that reduction quotas were fixed by statute, in the legislature, where they were vulnerable to erosion by well-organized processors and their allies in agribusiness. Rather than lose its control over the fishery entirely, CFGC yielded ground, step by step.[152] Peace seems nearly to have come to the fishery when canners, reducers, and regulators agreed to a compromise in 1929. Harvests were still near a sustainable level at that point. Two years later, however, offshore operations began in force and the game began anew.[153]

Fish and Game thus made its own contribution to political instability in the fishery, which was itself an incentive for processors to build up their capacity as fast as they could.[154] It drafted the 1921 law giving the canners a 25 percent reduction quota to help them weather the post–World War I depression, at the same time permitting them to put up a very cheap, low-quality pack "in order that they might make something on the fish meal and oil."[155] It liberalized its policy again in 1932 and 1933, both to relieve real want among the workers and because denying shore-side processors the opportunity to reduce fish when the factory ships did so with impunity did not seem fair.[156] Economic collapse placed a high discount on safety, and CFGC simply lacked the power to keep the sardines from paying the price of transforming Monterey into an "island of prosperity in a sea of depression." Every increase in reduction quotas only stimulated further expansion of canning capacity, further cuts in prices for canned fish, and further declines in the quality of the pack.[157] Making political alliance with F. E. Booth and a few of the older shore-side packers compromised CFGC's political position and left it open to charges of conspiracy such as Denman and Henry leveled at it in the 1936 sardine hearings.

Fish and Game made one last effort to control the reduction fishery after 1936, when it began issuing reduction permits only to plants that had operated the year before. As it turned out, during the late thirties and early forties few firms that had permits could actually gather enough fish to fill their quotas. In 1946 even this most slender of "slender reeds" broke when the state attorney general ruled that "grandfathering" reduction permits was discriminatory and unconstitutional. Ignoring the section of the *Monterey Fish Products* decision that linked economic efficiency in the industry with conservation of the fishery and thus with the public interest, he stated that if Fish and Game were to limit reduction it would have to do so on strictly construed conservationist grounds, as he put it, "in terms of fish economy, as opposed to dollar economy."[158] In addition to being unwieldy and politically vulnerable, the management strategy which followed from *Maier*, *Geer*, and *Monterey Fish Products* could not withstand the momentum in both state and federal law toward treating harvested fish as commodities like any other. In effect, the fish were legally divorced from their ecological context, from the forces that determined their productivity before harvest and those on the other side that threatened to destroy them. The only remaining alternative was to control the fishery directly at the point of production, by limiting the harvest in some way.[159] Here too the institutional structure within which policymaking took place militated against effective action. CFGC's rulemaking powers were actually quite weak, given the agency's seniority and prestige. Primarily, it recommended action to the state legislature, which more often than not followed its own lights in promulgating new regulations with or without scientific justification. In 1917, when CFGC first asked the legislature for the power to impose rules at its own initiative, both the State Horticultural Board and the State Board of Public Health had such power.[160] Pennsylvania and Oregon granted their wildlife agencies similar authority over the interwar period, but CFGC's political base was too narrow and too weak to secure it "plenary powers" over the opposition of the commercial operators and their friends in agribusiness.[161] The state lacked even a unified fish and game code until as late as 1933.[162] CFGC finally become a constitutionally endowed body, to which the legislature could grant plenary powers if it wished, when a model fish and game commission law, already enacted in twenty states, passed by initiative in 1940. Five years later, the legislature granted CFGC discretionary authority over the sportfisheries, but reserved to itself the power to make rules for the commercial fisheries as it always had.[163]

Regional and sectoral divisions within California were compounded by federalism, which had throughout the nation's history encouraged a kind of competition in regulatory flaccidity between states vying with each other for business investment.[164] The same situation, in which state governments took the place of the farmers in Hardin's model "tragedy of the commons," prevailed among Pacific Coast states that shared access to migrating sardines and salmon. A 1927 Fish and Game move to ban the offshore salmon fishery failed when commercial fishers pointed out that both Oregon and Washington permitted trolling and that if California prevented them from working boats from other states would get "their" fish. Thereafter California maintained contacts with other coastal states and with the federal government to develop a workable plan to control the fishery, although formal organization did not come until after World War II.[165]

Washington and Oregon removed their prohibitions on sardine reduction during the mid-1930s to prevent California operators from enjoying the bonanza by themselves.[166] Because the reduction ships anchored in international waters, Elmer Higgins thought the high-seas sardine fishery "a clearcut case where Federal control alone [would] be effective."[167] USBF had interests of its own at stake, however. In Washington to monitor the progress of bills to control the high-seas fishery in 1936, Lance Scofield discovered the USBF would just as soon have let California do the job but wanted eventually to obtain control over the extremely rich high-seas banks off the

New England coast and was thus unwilling to permit establishment of a precedent for state regulation beyond the territorial sea. Although Scofield found the congressional committee conservation minded, government conservation agencies were so hopelessly divided on the issue that the "floaters," who had collected a substantial warchest for lobbying and retained a well-known publicist to represent their interests, won the day.[168]

International politics affected California fisheries only indirectly during the interwar period and did not add yet another layer of jurisdictional conflict to an already tangled situation. N. B. Scofield early stressed the need for international cooperation to manage the sardine, tuna, and other fisheries that migrated across the Mexican border, but the U.S. Senate repudiated a draft convention to that effect in 1926.[169] North Pacific fisheries did come under a number of important international agreements, however. First and most successful of these was the Fur Seal Treaty of 1911, in which the United States, Great Britain, Russia, and Japan agreed to forswear sealing on the high seas and to share the proceeds of a controlled harvest on the animals' island breeding grounds. Subsequent recovery of the fur seal population may have contributed to the decline of the sardine stock from its turn-of-the-century high. The United States and Canada established bilateral conventions for research and regulation in the North Pacific halibut and salmon fisheries during the 1930s. The former had aroused concern as early as 1910 and had occasioned W. F. Thompson's study for the British Columbian provincial government. Japanese intrusion on the latter during the mid-1930s generated the first calls for the extension of federal power over the high seas, although the Japanese quickly withdrew rather than arouse U.S. antagonism and the matter lay dormant for a time.[170] International waters in the northeast Pacific remained relatively uncrowded until after 1950 and California, which had enough sectorial and interjurisdictional problems with which to contend already, had no need to get involved in international diplomacy as well.

Conclusion: effort largely wasted

California state waters were very crowded indeed, with fishers scrambling to take as many fish as they could as fast as they could and with public agencies unable to do much about it, either because they lacked the necessary leverage or because they were disinclined to expend the political capital necessary to impose controls on the harvest. Even though it was the job of the government to place itself between the fisheries and the market failures that drove industry to consume them, government was itself riddled with the same contradictions – interjurisdictional competition, inability to focus diffused or ill-defined social values, and the need to expend its own resources where they would have the most effect – which prevented the industry from conserving its future. Although California had built up the foremost marine research apparatus in the United States, political and economic disorder guaranteed that none of its information would have effect. The result was the sardine failure, one of the most egregious disasters in the history of U.S. wildlife management. As Lance Scofield had predicted it would, laissez-faire permitted the sardine to "adjust itself at an economic level . . . [just as] the buffalo did."[171]

One after another of the strategies on which the state had relied during the nineteenth century failed and had to be abandoned during the interwar period. In 1932 N. B. Scofield admitted that "the theory that the sardine catch would be limited by the amount of canned sardines that the market would absorb did not work."[172] By 1940 he had become impatient with restricting seasons and permissible gear as well: "If the volume of annual catch is held to the proper limit," he wrote, "it will make little difference how the proper amount is harvested." Indeed, he continued, anticipating the thinking of postwar economists, "sound economics would call for the limited harvest being gathered by the cheapest and most efficient fishing gear possible."[173] With respect to salmon, CDFG "conceded" in 1945 "that artificial propagation of anadromous fish has not proven more efficient than natural propagation, nor has it been found economically justifiable. . . . The only factor that can be affected is the rate of predation by man."[174]

The rate of human predation was, however, by no means an easily manipulated quantity. It was bound ecologically, inseparably, on the one side by economic forces that drove the harvest and on the other by a changing environment that produced, relative to the harvest, plenty of fish in some years and dangerously few in others. The very fact that the political economy assumed the fundamental autonomy of the first and the irrelevance to human affairs of the latter itself guaranteed the depletion of the sardine population.

IV

Enclosure of the ocean,
1950–1980

8

Gridlock

The canneries themselves fought the war by getting the
limit taken off fish and catching them all. It was done
for patriotic reasons but that didn't bring the fish back.
. . . It was the same noble impulse that stripped the forests of the West and right now is pumping water out of
California's earth faster than it can rain back in. When
the desert comes people will be sad; just as Cannery Row
was sad when all the pilchards were caught and canned
and eaten.

        – John Steinbeck, *Sweet Thursday* (1954)[1]

If electric power, internal combustion, and organic chemistry opened a new
economic frontier at the turn of the twentieth century, the end of World
War II signaled its impending close. Expansion continued during the postwar
era, to be sure. Frontier ideology and frontier imagery continued to color
people's thinking about the nature and future of American society. But there
were signs at the end of the war that even the modern industrial world had
finite limits, and the ensuing quarter-century seemed to bear them out.

    The atomic bomb not only gave people the power to eradicate civilization
as they knew it but, as radioactive fallout began making its way through the
environment into commercial dairy products during the early 1960s, gave
tangible proof of the ecological links among people, other living things, and
the environment. Synthetic pesticides and antibiotics, likewise, promised
at first to exterminate "enemy" insects and bacteria but, as those organisms
grew resistant to the changing chemistry of their environment, once again
taught people that nature was a living thing in which their lives were embedded and not merely the passive object of technological manipulation.

    Agriculture continued to consume massive and growing amounts of fossil
energy, increasingly in the form of pesticides and fertilizers manufactured
from petroleum rather than motor fuel per se. Returns from these energy
subsidies to food production were clearly diminishing by the 1960s, however,
and the mounting social costs of pollution and soil erosion that energy-
intensive agriculture brought with it provided yet another lesson in nature's
limited tolerance for frontal, technological assault. These changes, together

with the growing environmental concerns of an increasingly affluent population, gave birth to a new conservation movement that was, if anything, more powerful and more broadly based than its Progressive-Era counterpart.[2]

Nowhere did postwar progress and the environmental awareness that emerged with it develop more rapidly than in California. The state's economy, already mature by 1940, received a tremendous boost from the war. Population grew from 6.9 million in 1940 to 24.8 million in 1980, more than three times as fast as that of the nation as a whole. One Fish and Game scientist observed that of the millions of people who moved to California after the war equipped with fishing rods and hunting rifles, not one brought a drop of new water into the state.[3] Not only the state's rapidly growing cities, but by the mid-1970s three-quarters of its farmland as well, depended upon artificial sources of water.[4] Water, always in short supply in California, thus became both the key to the state's growth and the focus of its emergent environmentalism. The Sierra Club, which John Muir had founded during the 1890s but which over the interwar period had degenerated into little more than a social club for wealthy California outdoorspeople, moved immediately to the forefront of the new environmental movement on the strength of its victories against hydroelectric projects in the West.

Scientists assumed a much more active role in public life than they had before the war, as technology came to play an increasingly important role both in defense and in economic production.[5] Some worked in government and industry to further technological progress, while others worked on the outside to warn the public of its attendant dangers. Most famous of the latter was Rachel Carson, a zoologist who became familiar with DDT while working with the U.S. Fish and Wildlife Service during the war and whose book, *Silent Spring*, galvanized public opposition to the indiscriminate use of pesticides after it appeared in 1962. Californians made vital contributions to the ocean sciences, in the Pacific Theater during the war and afterward to the development of policy for marine resources at the state, federal, and even international levels.

Most influential of these was Wilbert McLeod Chapman, a biologist who had grown up in the Columbia Basin salmon fishery and who spent part of the war prospecting the tropical Pacific for fisheries to supply U.S. troops. On his return he worked briefly for the California Academy of Sciences and as director of the University of Washington's College of Fisheries in Seattle. Chapman served as the first advisor to the U.S. State Department on fisheries matters between 1948 and 1951. From then until his death in 1970, Chapman advised the fishing industry from his base in San Diego, first as director of research for the American Tunaboat Association and later in the employ of the Van Camp Sea Food Company. Figure 8.1 shows him at work in his San Diego office. Chapman sat on innumerable public councils at all levels

Figure 8.1. Wilbert McLeod Chapman (1910–70). Chapman is shown here in his office at San Diego. Photo courtesy of CalCOFI and Scripps Institution of Oceanography Archives.

of government and left an indelible stamp on public policy for marine resources.[6]

Chapman was no less thoroughly imbued with the ideology of the frontier than Theodore Roosevelt, Gifford Pinchot, or Spencer Fullerton Baird had been. He firmly believed that the ocean had vast, untouched reserves of food and that U.S. entrepreneurs had a mission to develop those resources for the benefit of humankind. "Fish are sufficiently abundant in the ocean," he wrote in 1964, "to provide *all* the animal protein required by the present human population of the world, and for an increase in that population at least of several fold."[7] The ocean's potential was "practically speaking, unlimited."[8] Overfishing did not greatly concern him: "When the fishing effort has increased beyond the point of maximum sustainable yield," he wrote in 1966, "the fishing can ordinarily be permitted to expand without serious damage to the resource."[9]

Chapman compared the challenge of harvesting the ocean with that of settling the Great Plains and the Southwest in the nineteenth century. The latter adventure had required extensive government help in the form of railroad land grants, the USDA, public irrigation works, and the land grant colleges. Similarly, developing the new oceanic frontier would require new tools, new ideas and, most of all, new government initiatives.[10] He saw his chance in 1946, when he met Montgomery Phister, a vice-president in the Van Camp Sea Food Company.[11] The two became lifelong friends, and for the rest of his career Chapman acted preeminently as prospector, advocate, and spokesperson for the tuna industry, both inside and outside government.

Even in the face of the country's rapid postwar growth, most sectors of the U.S. fishing industry declined throughout the period. World harvests tripled between 1950 and 1973, spurred by such technical developments as onboard freezing, Diesel engines, synthetic fibers for netting and ropes, hydraulic power, and acoustical fish finders. U.S. landings remained stagnant, however, at about 2.5 million pounds per year. Direct consumption of fish remained static at about ten or eleven pounds per person per year, although consumption of fishmeal by the livestock industry increased total use of fish products from 5 billion pounds in 1948 to 12 billion by 1964, well over twice the growth rate of the U.S. population. Imports, however, and not domestic production, made up the increase. Cheap imports and improved productivity in the livestock industry, the latter due in part to imported fishmeal, depressed prices for domestic fish and so stymied economic progress in the industry. In California, the 250 purse seiners fishing in 1947 dwindled to twenty-nine by 1969. Although family and ethnic ties remained important to the industry's character, they decayed as young people left for more lucrative callings and the industry increasingly belonged to aging men working in aging boats.[12] Cannery Row at Monterey and Fisherman's Wharf at San Francisco lost their industrial character and became tourist attractions instead, trading on their history rather than on their productive potential.

Policymaking for the industry remained mired in the bitter conflict that had led to the sardine catastrophe and which the disaster, in turn, had only exacerbated. Ironically, extended economic and political stagnation permitted new approaches to management to develop over the postwar period by driving California's local fisheries to near exhaustion. All sectors of the industry declined through the 1950s while scientists and policymakers studied their problems but squabbled incessantly over what to do about them. New pressures for growth emerged after 1960, although few sectors of the industry could respond to them as long as political and institutional barriers continued to thwart effective policymaking for the fisheries. Consequently, the 1960s brought a great deal of ferment to policymaking at both state and federal levels (see Chapter 9). It was not until after 1970 that new initiatives in fisheries management could begin in earnest. When they did begin, however, they did so in a way far different from what Chapman had envisioned.

The Pacific fisheries frontier

The war's end brought both crisis and opportunity to the West Coast fishing industry. First came the collapse of the sardine fishery, throwing both the industry and its public overseers into confusion. None could agree whether the precipitous decline in yields after 1946 was a temporary one, brought on by fluctuations in the marine environment, or a more serious result of many years of intense fishing. The tangled politics of the industry, meanwhile, continued to forestall any coherent response to the crisis whatever, either within the industry itself or in government at the state or federal level.[13] Yields of salmon had been exceptionally good between 1944 and 1947, but progress on the Central Valley Project and especially the tremendous influx of people to California from other states nonetheless alarmed the biologists working for the California Division of Fish and Game. Richard Croker, who returned from military service to become Chief of Marine Resources at Fish and Game, recalled later that "the salmon, it appeared to some of us, particularly in California, had no chance." "The salmon were doomed," he thought, by "the effects of all the water projects, pollution, too much fishing, and the rest of it."[14]

Opportunity lay westward, in the tropical Pacific, where the United States had taken possession of island trust territories enclosing vast areas of ocean containing unknown but potentially fabulous stocks of fish, especially tuna. Chapman had sampled some of these during his exploratory cruises for the Board of Economic Warfare.[15] To the industry's trade journal, the Pacific was "America's last frontier," an area of untold wealth and vital strategic importance that West Coast fishers were ready to develop "in the interest," as one biologist close to the industry put it, "of economy, security, and world diplomacy." The journal warned, however, that Japan and the Soviet Union, with financial help from the U.S. government, were prospecting those waters and outfitting modern fleets to fish them.[16]

Improved knowledge of the oceans, improved techniques for recovering their wealth, and the emerging aspirations of third world countries set off a scramble to lay claim to high-seas resources in the postwar period. The journal *Science* described the trend as "a global enclosure movement . . . in which about 35 per cent of the planet is currently passing to national control."[17] Peru and Ecuador, for example, had built tuna fleets of their own during the war and stood ready to compete with U.S. vessels in the eastern tropical Pacific, waters which the latter had had to themselves since the 1920s.[18]

The United States in fact, set off the scramble within a few weeks of V-J day, when President Truman issued proclamations unilaterally asserting U.S. rights to the resources of the continental shelf adjacent to its coast and U.S. authority to conserve the fisheries in waters overlying them.[19] The proclamations reflected a peculiar balance of concerns, including one for developing offshore oil resources and the memory of Japan's incursion on Alaskan salmon grounds immediately before the war. They ran counter to a long-standing U.S. tradition of support for free access to international waters. They also contradicted simultaneous U.S. efforts to promote internationalism through the United Nations, the General Agreement on Tariffs and Trade, and the World Bank.[20] In the event, although the U.S. Supreme Court upheld federal ownership and jurisdiction over seabed resources inside the three-mile territorial limit, Congress ceded those lands back to the states in the Submerged Lands Act of 1953. Washington did little to follow up on the fisheries proclamation although, under the terms of its peace with the Allies, Japan agreed, in the International Convention for the High Seas Fisheries of the North Pacific Ocean of 1952, to abstain from harvesting salmon and other resources that were already fully exploited and regulated by the United States and Canada.[21]

The tuna fishery had a vital interest in maintaining free acess to international waters and viewed Truman's unilateral action with trepidation. Its fears were borne out almost immediately, as first Mexico and then Panama and Costa Rica responded with similar claims of their own to jurisdiction over offshore fisheries. Even worse, in 1947 Chile and Peru made unilateral claims to jurisdiction over waters out to 200 miles from their coasts. Ecuador quickly joined them, and in 1952 the three nations met at Santiago, Chile, to reaffirm and coordinate enforcement of their claims. By 1954 Latin American nations had seized some twenty U.S. tunaboats for fishing within their proclaimed territorial waters.[22] Chapman and others saw this coming as soon as Mexico made its move: "We are getting into a competitive oceanwide game," Chapman warned in 1946, "with large resources of the Pacific at stake."[23] Scientists and industry representatives agreed that the United States would have to move quickly into the "Pacific fisheries frontier," as the trade journal called it, before it lost its chance to develop it.[24]

Chapman was living in Palo Alto in 1945, as were Elton Sette and Milner

B. Schaefer, Sette's chief lieutenant at the Stanford laboratory. Sensing an opportunity to further ocean science in the fluidity of the Pacific situation, the three seized upon a bill, recently submitted to Congress by the Hawaiian delegate, J. D. Farrington, to establish a fisheries research center at Honolulu. Ideally suited to Chapman's purposes, the bill called for coordinated oceanographic, biological, and technical research of unprecedented breadth and scale at a time when USFWS's budget for tuna research was, in Chapman's thinking, "so small in relation to the work to be done as to be ridiculous."[25] It also promised to establish a U.S. claim to the tuna of the western tropical Pacific while "the international law regarding the regulation of high seas fishery [was] in a state of flux."[26]

The three rewrote the bill, secured the reluctant support of the U.S. tuna industry, and lobbied successfully for its passage in 1946.[27] Sette moved to Honolulu to take charge of what became the Pacific Oceanic Fisheries Investigations (POFI) for the Fish and Wildlife Service. POFI's organization set a precedent for large-scale government support in ocean science, both in its scale and in the breadth of its view of fisheries problems. It also established Chapman's reputation as a political entrepreneur. In 1948, then, when the State Department established the office of Special Assistant to the Under Secretary for Fisheries and Wildlife, Chapman was the logical choice to fill it. He remained at State until 1951, when he returned to California to work for the American Tunaboat Association.[28]

Having seen to POFI's successful inauguration, Chapman then moved to capitalize on public concern over the collapse of the sardine fishery in an effort to establish a similar program for research in California coastal waters. Working closely with Phister at Van Camp and with Carl Leavitt Hubbs at the Scripps Institution, in January 1947 Chapman arranged a meeting in San Francisco between representatives of USFWS, the industry, the State Fisheries Laboratory, and the Scripps Institution. Under the elaborate plan hatched at the meeting, the state legislature and the University of California agreed to augment SIO's annual budget by $300,000. Most of the money was to go toward the purchase of "at least four" surplus Navy boats, in addition to the one research schooner that SIO already had, to undertake direct measurements of the California Current's ecology. The industry submitted to an additional tax of fifty cents per ton of sardines landed, later increased to a dollar and broadened to include other coastal schooling species as well, to support cooperative research by SIO, USFWS, Fish and Game, and the Academy of Sciences. The industry also agreed to support efforts already underway in Congress to increase support for USFWS research in Pacific waters. The entire project, which eventually became known as the California Cooperative Oceanic Fisheries Investigations (CalCOFI), was to be overseen by a Marine Research Committee (MRC), five of whose nine members were to be drawn from the fishing industry.[29]

The plan was brilliantly conceived and sailed through political channels in the University and the state legislature with little trouble. Julian Burnette of the Sardine Products Institute became chair of the new MRC and remained in that position until 1967. Regular sampling of the current began in 1949, on a rectangular grid extending from the Oregon Border south to Cabo San Lucas and out to 200 to 300 miles offshore. Designed to "conduct large-scale oceanography fishery research in order to place the entire fishing [industry] on a more secure basis," the sardine project undertook, for the first time, comprehensive, multidisciplinary research into the problems of an extractive industry.[30] Phister and the other industry representatives supported the program primarily to short-circuit pressure for restrictions on the sardine harvest or, as Chapman put it, for the "negative [purpose] of simply building a fire break to let the fire burn out." MRC was, nonetheless, critical to Chapman's plan to demonstrate the feasibility of a new style of oceanography.[31] It did ultimately make possible meaningful controls over the fishery and perhaps the sardine's eventual recovery as well, although the fishery itself nearly died out in the process.

Chapman was especially pleased by what he had done for the scientific community. "Do you realize," he wrote to Carl Hubbs as POFI and MRC got under way,

> that we have got the whole program through that I was working on and that looked like a complete pipe dream less than two years ago, and that by so doing we have injected better than $2,000,000 into fisheries research in the Pacific? More important than that, we have got a list of most important industry men all along the coast working for us, for the first time in fisheries history.[32]

MRC was the linchpin of his entire plan. "The success, or failure, of this sardine project will have profound effects upon other needed projects," he wrote to Don Saxby of the California Packing Corporation (Del Monte), "and all of us should keep this in mind."[33] Reporting to Washington on the results of an initial meeting to plan the investigation, Elton Sette could already perceive "a trend in the direction of a lively demand for funds – when the whole show gets under way this is going to be plenty of fun."[34]

While Chapman was busy trying to build bridges between state and federal fishery agencies, both levels of government began looking to their own houses. In 1951 California elevated the Division of Fish and Game to department status in the state's executive branch, thereby relieving the Fish and Game Commission of all administrative duties and confining it to rule-making and policy-formulating functions only.[35] DFG's marine apparatus decayed steadily through the 1950s in spite of the reorganization, however, as the landings taxes from which it drew its income shrivelled.[36] For its part, the Fish and Wildlife Service suffered such severe cuts in its budget in 1949 that it had to curtail sharply its plans for the sardine investigation, although in 1954 the Saltonstall–Kennedy Act provided it with new funds for research.[37] The Fish and Wildlife Act of 1956, much of it Chapman's personal handiwork, split the federal agency's commercial and sportfishing functions and created a separate Bureau of Commercial Fisheries (USBCF) in the Interior Department with a clear mandate to promote the special interests of the commercial sector.[38]

Fish and game agencies in many states became alarmed by federal initiatives in marine resources management during the 1940s. Fearful of losing control over their resources, at the end of the war California, Oregon, and Washington banded together to form the Pacific Marine Fisheries Commission (PMFC), modeled on a similar compact established earlier among East Coast states. PMFC was essentially an investigative body, with power to undertake research on fisheries of common interest but none to control the industry in any way beyond recommending legislation to the appropriate state governments. It was able to coordinate state regulation of the offshore salmon fishery between Alaska and California. Trolling effort, however, remained uncontrolled: The 1,100 boats in the California fishery at war's end grew to 1,638 by 1956. About this, PMFC could do nothing. Because it had been organized with the industry's cooperation and included voting members from the industry, PMFC was unable even to recommend restrictions on the sardine harvest and quickly abandoned the attempt. It concentrated instead on salmon and other coastal fisheries that operated under less strenuous political pressure.[39]

The early 1950s provided an unusually stable climatic context for human events in the California fisheries. Uniformly cool sea temperatures and roughly normal levels of rainfall sustained good harvests of salmon through most of the decade, although not at the level of the mid–1940s. With the exception of the sardine, which remained under heavy pressure from the fishery, coastal schooling species began to recover from the breeding failures which all had suffered between 1949 and 1951. In the winter of 1956–7 El Niño, a periodic warm-water event usually confined to the equatorial Pacific, increased ocean temperatures along the length of the eastern Pacific boundary from Peru to Alaska and visibly altered the distribution of California fishes in a way similar to what had taken place in 1918.[40] The anomaly persisted until 1959. Anchovy, which had built up its population in the Southern California Bight by middecade, extended its range northward into central California waters and began to increase there as well. Sardines from the Baja California subpopulation moved within reach of the California fishery and sustained a temporary resurgence in the harvest. Salmon landings, on the other hand, dropped by two-thirds to 3.6 million pounds between 1956 and 1958. The fall run of chinooks in the Central Valley decreased to fewer than 200,000 individual fish, or about 40 percent of the peak harvests of the 1880s.[41] Scientists working on the sardine project became very excited by the contrasting data they began to collect, while those who concerned themselves with salmon grew alarmed at the way in which the developing Central Valley Project had apparently increased the fragility of that resource.

Reclamation and salmon preservation

The challenge that the state's remarkable postwar growth posed to the salmon was immediate and strenuous. The federal Bureau of Reclamation (BuRec) had completed the main features of the Central Valley Project, Shasta Dam on the Sacramento and Friant Dam on the San Joaquin, by war's end. Although both facilities significantly reduced the valley's inventory of spawning grounds, Shasta Dam had compensated for the loss by improving spawning conditions in the main stem of the river below. What remained of the runs in the San Joaquin River appeared willing enough to spawn in water below Friant Dam.[42] The project began actually to move water from place to place in 1951. The Friant–Kern Canal transferred water that would normally have flowed into the San Joaquin to the eastern side of the valley. Sacramento water was drawn out of the Delta by a huge pumping plant at Tracy and deposited into the Delta–Mendota Canal, where it flowed southward for use in other parts of the San Joaquin Valley. Land between Friant Dam and the southern terminus of the Delta–Mendota Canal, left without water, began suddenly to dry up.[43]

California water politics have a long and tangled history, marked by intense conflict between state and federal agencies, between big and small farmers, and between northern and southern California.[44] Most of the scholarly literature on the subject deals with conflict over the little-enforced provision in federal reclamation law that limits access to project water to farms of 160 acres or less. Less attention has gone to contention between those who wished to consume water for agricultural and urban use and those who required a natural flow of water to sustain their crops or fish and wildlife. Although the federal Fish and Wildlife Coordination Acts of 1934 and 1946 required agencies that built dams to consult with wildlife agencies and to make provision for conserving wildlife in their operation and led to considerable improvement in practice, these laws cast the problem in the essentially negative terms of preventing undue damage to wildlife insofar as was possible given the presumption of moving ahead with the project. When consumptive use and natural flow were incompatible, the laws worked poorly to protect wildlife from the highly focused interests of the agencies that built the projects and their beneficiaries. Not until the late 1960s did those who wished to leave the state's rivers altogether unreclaimed find an effective political voice.[45]

Friant Dam exposed the weakness in the laws as they existed in 1951. BuRec had consulted with USFWS and with California's wildlife agency over the project but had rejected their requests for remedial measures, claiming that maintaining enough flow in the river below the dam to sustain salmon in the river and waterfowl in the adjoining grasslands would have required more than 25 percent of the dam's capacity.[46] Duck hunters, commercial fishers, and landowners below the dam began suing BuRec to ensure continued flows below Friant Dam in 1947 but lost their fight in the 1950 case of *Rank* v. *Krug*. The court recognized that the landowners had suffered an injury from the loss of water, but refused to enjoin the diversion in part because the power of Congress, and thus of BuRec, over navigable waterways was supreme.[47] Salmon fishers and other private parties had no legal right to sue a government agency on behalf of wildlife, and the State of California refused to intervene in the case.[48] Moreover, in 1951 the California Attorney General ruled that fishery interests had no legal claim to water designated for "higher use" by the California Water Code.[49]

The law thus left no recourse to the many people each of whom had minor interests in protecting fish and wildlife from the social costs of watershed reclamation. They had no chance to bargain with agribusiness in the market for rights to water and, until the 1970s, they had no right to sue government reclamation agencies in charge of building and maintaining the projects. Before the end of the war Fish and Game had lacked the resources to bargain with other agencies in the state and federal governments, and in any event could not quantify the damage which it thought such projects would do. Given this uncertainty and the weak bargaining position of wildlife managers, such values seemed inconsequential in comparison to the high costs that protecting them would have imposed on the projects. In 1960, for example, the Pacific Gas and Electric Company estimated that releasing water through its dams to protect fish life in California cost it roughly $1 million per year in forgone sales of electric power.[50]

Backed by an increasingly powerful sportfishing lobby, however, DFG began during the 1950s to bring some influence to bear on the design and operation of water projects. After the war it actively began to review every application to other agencies for water withdrawals. After the Friant Dam episode it took more strenuous opposition to projects that seriously threatened fish and wildlife. Fishing interests and local farmers managed to beat back an Army Corps of Engineers plan to build a high dam either at Table Mountain or Iron Canyon, on the Sacramento near Red Bluff. A dam at either location would seriously have damaged the salmon fishery because the spawning areas on which the fish now relied lay primarily between Shasta Dam and the proposed sites.[51] Initial plans for California's own State Water Project, published in 1955, included for the first time plans for enhancing, not merely maintaining, fisheries in the Feather River basin. The state created a unified Department of Water Resources in 1956 and, in the Davis–Dolwig Act of 1961, allocated to it clear responsibility for preserving and enhancing wildlife in reclamation projects with scientific and technical help from DFG.[52]

Fish hatcheries and other such measures, however, amounted to little more than expensive public subsidies to the hunting and sportfishing lobbies that had always been DFG's main source of political and financial support. Artificially raising a supply of fish to meet the recreational demand was almost, but not quite, the same thing as "natural" resource management.[53] DFG, then, functioned best when it acted on behalf of a special interest group just as BuRec did, and its opponents did not hesitate to point this out. This weakened the agency's position considerably in its struggle to manage the commercial fisheries in coastal waters. By the end of the 1950s the legislature's long-running investigation of the agency had thoroughly exposed its narrow, specialized constituency and its lack of clearly defined public objectives. Subsequent studies during the 1960s concentrated on the closely linked problems of defining the agency's purposes and implementing them in a coherent way.[54]

In the Klamath–Trinity watershed, demand for housing and recreation brought a new burst of commercial activity to that still-somnolent region. Postwar logging in the basin was as rapacious as any in the nation's history. The lower stretch of the river became choked with logs floating down to a sawmill at the town of Klamath and contaminated with bark and debris. Sportfishers in powerboats contended with line fishers on the river's bank for what little space remained in the river. Sawmills brought jobs and millions of dollars in cutting fees to the people of the Hoopa Valley Indian Reservation, finally dissolving the geographic and economic barriers that until then had insulated them from the rest of the world. By the mid-1950s outsiders outnumbered Indians in Hoopa Valley. The salmon fishery suffered greatly, however: By 1979, logjams and timber slash blocked as much as 50 to 80 percent of the reservation's available gravels to spawning salmon.[55] Congress, meanwhile, reversed the New Deal policy of promoting Indian self-government by placing reservation Indians in California and several other states under the jurisdiction of state law in 1953.[56] In 1957 California made the Yurok Indians on the lower river subject to the provisions of its fish and game code that controlled the use of salmon gill nets and the commercial sale of fish, although it also affirmed their right to fish for subsistence with traditional tools.[57] State officials apparently did not try to enforce such laws against the Indians at first, but they did so after 1960 and the Indians went to court to affirm their rights to the fishery.

The California Cooperative Oceanic Fisheries Investigations

If the ecological regime of the early 1950s relieved some of the pressure on the salmon resource, it did not do so for the sardine. California landings, which had climbed to 353,000 tons in the 1950–1 season on the strength of the moderately successful cohorts born between 1946 and 1948, dropped to less than 14,000 tons two seasons later, when adults from the failed seasons of 1949–51 should have become available for harvest. Northward migrating fish from the Baja California population contributed to a slight resurgence in 1958–9, but as the climate stabilized the catch dropped again, to less than 7,000 tons by 1962. By then the fleet was taking most of its fish in the first few nights of each season and few if any thereafter.[58] California poultry and swine producers, who remained so strongly loyal to fishmeal that its price remained firm even while the cost of competing foodstuffs declined, now imported most of their supplies from Peru.[59]

Some of those who established the Peruvian anchoveta fishery were veterans of the California sardine industry who, in the words of a Peruvian scientist, "came down to our area searching for new raw materials which they could use."[60] Although it was primarily local entrepreneurs who developed the fishery, they drew a good deal of scientific and technical help from California, as well as purchasing seiners and whole reduction plants at heavy discounts from California firms. Capital continued to flee the sardine fishery through the fifties, so that by the summer of 1962 only one cannery remained open at Monterey. Enough pressure remained on the crippled stock, nonetheless, that during the late fifties and early sixties the fishery took between one-third and one-half of all the adult sardines in the northern population each season.[61]

The decline took place under the watchful eye of MRC, although differences of opinion as to its cause and its significance persisted until the mid-1960s. The primary function of MRC was to promote research into the ecology of the California Current, and it did so with great success. The program's overall design closely followed that undertaken by SIO, USFWS, and the State Fisheries Laboratory after 1937, although on a much grander scale. MRC used the nearly $800,000 that it collected from landings taxes between the program's outset and 1955 as seed money to help the participating agencies pursue research along lines in which they were already established: 30 percent went to SIO's Marine Life Research Program (MLRP) to collect basic ecological data at sea, 49 percent to USFWS to survey concentrations of eggs and larvae along the coast, 7.5 percent to the Academy of Sciences to study the behavior of sardines in the laboratory, and 3 percent to Stanford's Hopkins Marine Station to study conditions in Monterey Bay. DFG, which had begun sardine studies thirty years earlier and whose responsibility the sardine's conservation was, received a relatively paltry 7.5 percent to continue its investigation into the dynamics of the fishery. The most fortunate beneficiary was SIO, which quintupled its budget between fiscal years 1946 and 1950. While MRC's own funds amounted to an average of $130,000 a year through the 1950s, contributions to CalCOFI work from the participating agencies boosted total expenditures to about $1 million annually.[62]

Under CalCOFI's aegis, the California Current became the best-studied oceanic ecosystem on the planet. As a demonstration project it served Chapman's purposes admirably and drew nationwide attention, as Chapman knew it would.[63] Workers at the State Fisheries Laboratory discovered extensive beds of shrimp off northern California and Oregon in 1950 and 1951 and generated a valuable fishery that DFG was able to manage successfully because it had discovered it. CalCOFI cruises described changes in the ocean floor off southern California, noting the effects of flood control projects inshore on life on the seafloor and pointing to the effect on the kelp beds of sea urchins, which thrived near the region's sewage outfalls. SIO developed new techniques and instrumentation for oceanographic research as part of the Marine Life Research Program. One of CalCOFI's most important contributions was to continue the series of annual conferences begun by Sverdrup in 1938: These gradually became the occasion for a great many scientists from all around the Pacific rim to share data and ideas. Particularly important in this regard was the 1958 conference, which led to important new conclusions about the interaction between atmospheric and oceanic conditions, as well as about the variability of marine climate.[64]

What CalCOFI could not do was to generate a scientific consensus on the sardine riddle, and attempts to address the question remained a major source of strain in the organization until the mid-1960s. In general, scientists from SIO and USFWS, who collected and analyzed basic ecological data from the ocean, fell into one camp. They emphasized the environmental forces at work on the population and sought to explain the fishery's demise in those terms. By contrast, scientists from the State Fisheries Laboratory pointed to the effects of harvesting pressure and repeatedly urged the state legislature to restrict the catch so as to conserve what was left of the stock. Conflict between the two camps were never far beneath the surface of anything CalCOFI did.

Asked to prepare an article on the sardine project for a popular magazine in 1950, Carl Hubbs of SIO passed the job along to two USFWS scientists. Frances Clark, then director of the State Fisheries Laboratory, was irritated because she believed that the extensive publicity that SIO and USFWS generated for what she called "the new and spectacular" ecological studies drew public attention away from the effects of the harvest on the resource and thus made her job more difficult.[65] After securing Clark's approval for their manuscript, the authors appended to it a paragraph which asserted, to Clark's great embarrassment, that "the Pacific sardine [was] not disappearing," that the recent decline had been due to environmental changes, and that "a substantial recovery [was then] taking place."[66]

For their part, Richard Croker and the other DFG scientists did not hestitate to publish *their* conclusions that the sardine had been overfished and was not likely to recover soon. Especially inflammatory was an article by Croker which appeared in 1954 under the title, "Loss of California's Sardine Fishery May Become Permanent." The answers to the sardine myster, Croker stated at the outset, were "complex but we have them. . . . The causes of scarcity can be summarized as too much fishing and not enough reproduction." Croker's article particularly annoyed John C. Marr, who had replaced Elton Sette as head of the USFWS laboratory at Stanford. Marr could "see little point in continuing our work if it [was] to be so easily ignored by our colleagues."[67]

CalCOFI published the first results from the sardine project in its 1955 report. Under the joint authorship of Clark and Marr, the paper reached both conclusions: Marr contended that environmental change would have brought on the sardine collapse even had there been no fishery, while Clark concluded that the same data pointed to the significant contribution of over-fishing to the stock's decline.[68] Because the landings tax that underwrote MRC was then before the state legislature for renewal and MRC was under pressure to show some results from its eight years of work, the Committee decided to publish the joint report anyway, so as to "present all aspects of the problem."[69]

Although they remained personally cordial, scientists from each agency guarded their territory jealously and used MRC funds primarily to pursue lines of research in which they were already established. Integrating and coordinating the sardine program, then, was from the beginning a major problem. "We should act as a unit," wrote Richard Croker in 1951, "if we expect the program to succeed and to accomplish any worthwhile results."[70] California urged MRC to appoint a coordinator to give direction and coherence to the program, but Burnette maintained that MRC could not afford one.[71] Roger Revelle, who became SIO director in 1951 and was no less skilled an entrepreneur than Chapman himself, assiduously cultivated informal relations with USFWS because the latter offered training and employment to SIO graduate students but bluntly informed MRC that the university would not tolerate formal direction of its affairs by an outside coordinator.[72] John Marr was especially frustrated by the program's incoherence, but his efforts to organize discussions of its goals and strategies drew little support. The convener of the 1953 sardine conference resisted Marr's efforts to hold a formal discussion of the "objectives of a fishery research program and what information we need to obtain such objectives" because he did not want to draw attention to "organization[al] aspects of the present program which amplify shortcomings and cause embarrassment."[73] Chapman had also wished to see a coordinator appointed. As it stood in the 1950s, he wrote, CalCOFI was "a good body without a head"; the "central purpose" of answering the sardine riddle "like the great Sphinx in the sands of the desert an idol to be venerated but for reasons not quite remembered."[74]

Industry leaders abetted this fragmentation through the 1950s because it forestalled public regulation of their activities. Phister and other southern California processors, for example, resisted expansion of the USFWS role in the program so long as sardines remained abundant in their region. Divisions between southern and northern sectors of the industry served well enough to stymie moves in the state government to regulate the fishery, and the southern processors did not wish to see "the feds" "taking over" the program "lest we would thereby lose control over their activities."[75] The industry did not, however, wish to see USFWS abandon the investigation to the state scientists. It prepared to do so in 1953, tired of participating in a "half-way" study and of its interminable conflict with the State Fisheries Laboratory. Don Saxby of Del Monte, however, told Marr's superior in Washington that the industry considered USFWS participation vital to the program. "I got the impression," the latter wrote to Marr, "that it would be extremely difficult and impolitic for us to withdraw."[76]

The industry, of course, had good reason to keep the investigation unfocused and did not hesitate to intervene in university politics so as to keep its attention on the details of an ever-broadening inquiry into the sardine's environment rather than on the impact of the fishery. At the outset of the project, when the university's president expressed outrage at Harald Sverdrup's negotiating SIO participation without university approval, a delegation of leading packers quickly visited him at Berkeley, soothed his feelings, and secured his cooperation.[77] Phister became very alarmed when Sverdrup announced his intention to resign as SIO director in 1947 because, he wrote, his support of the initial plan had rested on his personal confidence in the latter. He hoped that whoever succeeded Sverdrup would be similarly "qualified by some understanding of the relationship of his work to our research problem."[78] He found such a man in Roger Revelle. At least one scientist was passed over for a high-level position in the Marine Life Research Project because he entertained what Revelle called "the conventional conservativist's view of fishery depletion."[79]

Through the first decade of its existence, then, the MRC–CalCOFI project perpetuated a finely tuned stalemate between government agencies competing for funds and influence, while the industry that oversaw it squeezed out what life remained in the sardine fishery. Only the state agency had any real stake in preserving the resource, and it had to choose between accepting a powerless position in the MRC apparatus and losing its power to manage the resource altogether. The others, not unlike the farmers in Hardin's tragedy, valued the opportunity to pursue established lines of research with funds generated from the sardine crisis more than they did the chance to resolve the controversy. There was simply no incentive to manage the fishery, among scientists no less than among entrepreneurs. Although the investigation produced much of lasting value, it did so at the cost of tolerating further depletion of the fishery.

The university of the sea

By the late 1950s, only northern California processors took much interest in the MRC–CalCOFI program: Southern processors, for whom sardines had always been secondary to their interest in tuna, gradually abandoned their stake in California waters.[80] It was, in fact, in distant-water tuna that Chapman and his allies in the industry had placed their hopes for the "Pacific fisheries frontier." For Chapman, the sardine investigation was in essence a pilot project to demonstrate the feasibility of the kind of research he hoped would eventually put the tuna industry on a "good footing." He had not included tuna in his initial plans for California, he told one industry leader in 1947, because of the enormous expense such a program would entail and because the sardine crisis and the central Pacific investigations had an urgency about them that would more readily galvanize the state legislature and Congress, respectively, into action. Success in the first two projects, however, would prepare the way for further efforts on behalf of the tuna industry.[81]

That fishery was in serious trouble. The tuna fleet had expanded mightily at the end of the war, as new vessels were commissioned and as the Navy returned conscripted ones to their former owners. Temporarily relieved of Japanese competition, the market for canned tuna expanded still more rapidly with the tremendous burst in consumer demand that came with the peace and so kept all comers prosperous for a time. By 1950, however, Japan had regained its prewar capacity with U.S. aid and emerged as an aggressive competitor for the world tuna market. Japanese firms dumped a million and a half cases of canned fish, roughly one-fifth of the domestic tuna pack for 1949, on the U.S. market in the second half of 1950 alone. Within a year, even as California shipyards continued to launch new tunaboats, the canneries began to close down. Although the processors recovered by buying their raw material from the Japanese rather than from local boats, the competition bankrupted the American Tunaboat Association by the end of the decade. On the industry's traditional grounds in the eastern tropical Pacific, meanwhile, Latin American nations began accusing U.S. vessels of overfishing tuna and bait species off their coasts. After declaring their sovereignty over waters out to 200 miles offshore, they began seizing U.S. tunaboats caught fishing within those areas.[82] In this they did no more than to follow the example that the United States had set with President Truman's 1945 proclamations on continental shelf resources, but the tuna industry had a vital stake in maintaining access to what had hitherto been international waters.

In the Fisherman's Protective Act of 1954, Congress agreed to reimburse owners of U.S. vessels seized for fishing in what the United States considered international waters. If the oceanic commons were to become private property, then, the U.S. government would pay the rent.[83] Representing the American Tunaboat Association, Chapman persuaded the Peruvian government to license U.S. boats to catch bait in Peruvian-claimed waters without forcing them to admit the legitimacy of that country's claim to a 200-mile territorial sea.[84] But there was a more subtle approach. In 1949, while Chapman was at the State Department, he and Phister negotiated a treaty with Costa Rica to set up an Inter-American Tropical Tuna Commission (IATTC) for multilateral research and management of tuna in the eastern tropical Pacific. Milner B. Schaefer of the USFWS laboratory at Stanford became the IATTC's first director. Panama, Ecuador, and Colombia joined the commission within a few years.[85]

As Chapman later recalled to Julian Burnette, "during approximately the same period of years we tuna people had almost exactly the same sort of political-conservation problem that you sardine people had."[86] He and Phister reasoned that establishing a multilateral research commission under U.S. leadership would short-circuit pressure from the Latin American states to regulate fisheries in their waters unilaterally. Their agreement was to undertake cooperative investigation into the fishery but not to impose regulations on it until it evinced signs of overfishing. Here again, Chapman struck a workable bargain: Yellowfin tuna did not come under serious harvesting pressure until the early 1960s, and in the meantime both the fishery and the scientific effort could proceed without interference from the now-palliated coastal states.[86] Under Schaefer's able management, IATTC produced valuable research on tuna, bait species, and the oceanic environment. Schaefer's own work on the yellowfin made important contributions to the theoretical understanding of relationships between yields and harvesting effort.[87]

Because the Tuna Commission was an international body, however, it was not well-equipped to serve the California tuna industry per se. This was one of Chapman's primary motives in the creation of a separate U.S. Bureau of Commercial Fisheries in 1956, although in his words "it began to look as if we would have to take the Department of the Interior building apart brick by brick and build it up again before we got what we wanted."[88] That agency did prove responsive to the tuna fishery's interests and in 1957 subsidized a special program in tuna oceanography at the Scripps Institution.[89] At the state level, Chapman worked through the state legislature and the university, as he had done in establishing MRC.

With Revelle, Chapman began to press for the establishment of a college of fisheries within the University of California, a goal that had from the start of his public life been central to his plans.[90] The Marine Life Research Project at SIO was a key component of the sardine investigation, but was having trouble hiring and retaining top-level scientists because it was nominally a temporary program and the University could not offer tenure to its academic workers. In 1951 Chapman addressed the State Assembly Fish and Game Committee on the tuna industry's economic problems, pointed to the university's vital contribution to California agriculture, and urged them to establish a fisheries college in the university to undertake similar research and development on behalf of the fishing industry. Meanwhile, Revelle successfully lobbied within the university for his proposed Institute of Marine Resources (IMR), which was to be a permanent body headquartered at SIO but made up of faculty members in engineering, food technology, and other departments throughout the University of California system. With strenuous support from the tuna industry and after repeated warnings from University of California President Sproul to Revelle to obey the university's regulations governing relations between faculty, state officials, and the public, IMR came to life in 1954.[91]

Revelle's plans for IMR were particularly grand: While the project was in the planning stages he predicted that IMR would absorb the Marine Life Research Program and eventually grow to be larger than the Scripps Institution itself.[92] This did not happen, and IMR remained relatively small through the 1950s. It did sponsor an economic study of the California tuna industry and mapped the ocean floor for seamounts and other geological features which attract tuna. Although financial support from outside the university did not materialize to the extent that Revelle had planned, IMR did receive funds from the American Petroleum Institute to study the geology of the Gulf of Mexico, from a kelp processing firm to study kelp communities in the Southern California Bight, and form the State Water Pollution Control Board to study the toxicity to fish of various chemicals. It also undertook studies of offshore waste disposal, beach erosion, and deep-sea mining of manganese nodules.[93] It was far less, however, than the "university of the sea" which Chapman envisioned and which he, Revelle, and others sought so assiduously.

Conclusion: reorganizing the inquiry

The 1950s saw a great deal of institution building on the part of a small number of visionaries in the industry, government, and the University of California, while the state's fisheries, the industries that worked them, and its own fishery management agency declined steadily. The state legislature's investigation of the workings of the Fish and Game apparatus drew nationwide attention. The state's initial plans for reclaiming the Feather River watershed, especially, became a model for other states and for federal agencies in incorporating recreational use of wildlife into water projects. The Inter-American Tropical Tuna Commission improved relations with Latin American states, sponsored valuable work in fishery oceanography, and secured the declining tuna industry continued access to its traditional grounds.

In 1957, finally, as legislative pressure on MRC to come up with answers to the sardine problem intensified, as climatic changes rekindled interest in the CalCOFI effort, and as declining income from its tax on the harvest strained the MRC budget, an internal review of CalCOFI found "the lack of formal coordination" to be the program's chief shortcoming. It recommended the establishment of a permanent, four-member CalCOFI Committee to oversee the program under the direction of a full-time coordinator.[94] Garth Murphy became CalCOFI coordinator in 1959 and led several years of searching inquiry into the nature, objectives, and accomplishments of the sardine project. Under his guidance, CalCOFI disciplined its budgeting and brought its objectives into clearer focus, broadened considerably from its original emphasis on the sardine alone but with a definite eye to making the work promote the efficient use of resources.[95] Reorganization of the scientific inquiry, in CalCOFI as in the tuna and salmon fisheries, set the stage for real achievements in scientific management. Still, it would require corresponding changes in government and the industry to realize their potential.

9

Something of a vacuum

Perhaps it is necessary as an additional step in the in-
itiation of major fishery regulations of a conservation nature not only simply to [be] correct and understand what
you are doing, but for most of the industry people [to go
broke] first so that they also understand what you are doing.
. . . [C]ertainly there was [in the past] no disposition to regulate until people went broke on a large scale. It is a horrifying thought but it may be a social factor that requires to be
taken into account.
— Wilbert McLeod Chapman (1968)[1]

California's domestic fisheries continued to decline through most of the
1960s. " 'Cannery Row' is no more," announced the CalCOFI report for
1963.[2] Through the 1950s, the fishery for Pacific mackerel had absorbed
much of the effort displaced by the sardine failure; after 1963 this resource
failed to reproduce successfully for several years in a row and by 1965, as
fishing continued, it, too, collapsed in its turn.[3] With both the sardine and
the mackerel now gone, CalCOFI reported, the California "wetfish" fleet
became "extremely depressed."[4] Inland ports in the Sacramento area landed
their last commercial salmon harvests in 1959. Although coastal salmon ports
continued to do well through the 1960s, they did so largely on the strength
of increased harvests of coho salmon, which migrate into central California
waters but do not spawn in the Central Valley watershed. Yields of the more
valuable chinook variety fell back to the low levels of the 1930s. This time,
pollution and the accumulated loss of spawning habitat played a relatively
larger role with respect to climate in depressing the fishery than they had
in the earlier period.[5]

New life came to the tuna industry in 1959, when a fisher combined a
purse seine made of synthetic fiber with a powered hoisting block to develop
a new and more efficient way of catching the fish, without bait. Now able
to catch tuna as cheaply as the Japanese and freed from dependence on
foreign waters for bait, U.S. tunaboats quickly recovered world leadership
in the industry. A new generation of seiners like the one pictured in Figure
9.1 came into being, among the largest and most modern in the U.S. fishing
fleet. As Chapman saw it, the fishery was "rapidly becoming world-wide

Figure 9.1. Tuna seiner *Rosa Olivia* at San Diego, 1979. Built in 1971, *Rosa Olivia* is one of the larger vessels in the U.S. tuna fleet. She is 194½ feet long, 36 feet in the beam, and has a fish hold capacity of 1,100 tons. Photo by Rod Barr.

and it look[ed] increasingly upon the world ocean and the world market as single entities."[6] Most of the action, however, took place away from California. The state's two largest fish packing firms, Van Camp and Starkist, built canneries in Puerto Rico, American Samoa, South America, and even in Africa to process their catches. Where some twenty canneries had operated in California ports during the late 1950s, only about six remained a decade later.[7]

Such firms also invested in the Peruvian anchoveta fishery, which began to boom when nylon seines came into use in 1956. There were three California companies in the industry when the boom began, Starkist, Westgate, and the Wilbur–Ellis firm of San Francisco, the last of which had secretly built the first anchovy reduction plant, at Chimbote, in 1950. Van Camp entered during the early 1960s by buying out Wilbur–Ellis and two Peruvian firms and by 1962 was one of the largest producers in the industry. Van Camp now did its largest volume in fishmeal, although tuna continued to generate most of the company's income. Several very large companies entered in 1963 and 1964, among them the Ralston–Purina conglomerate, which took over Van Camp, and H. J. Heinz, which purchased Starkist. Wilbert Chapman, who for several years after the American Tunaboat Association went bankrupt had worked as a one-person charitable foundation for the Van Camp family, became director of marine resources for Ralston–Purina and spent the rest of his life both prospecting for new fisheries around the world and pursuing the political negotiations required to gain access to them.[8]

By 1969 about one-third of the Peruvian fishery was in foreign hands. Harvests reached 8 million metric tons (mmt) in 1964 and more than 12 million, or about 20 percent of the *global* harvest of all kinds of fish, by 1970. As had been the case with California sardine meal, Peruvian fishmeal went primarily to feed poultry in the United States and in Western Europe.[9] California drew most of its supply from this source. The profits, similarly, were spectacular: Chapman noted in 1965 that Van Camp could produce anchoveta meal for $50 per ton and sell it at the plant for nearly $200. The appetite for it seemed to be insatiable. Temporary excesses on the world market, such as occurred in 1960, depressed the price temporarily but only brought into the market new users who, once introduced to fishmeal, were then willing to tolerate subsequent increases. Three years after the 1960 glut, for example, global consumption of fishmeal had increased 1.7 times, even though the price had more than doubled. With Peruvian fishmeal at once cheap, abundant, and profitable, there was little incentive to develop new reduction fisheries in California waters.[10] As Chapman put it, overseas expansion by California firms and their new corporate parents left "something of a vacuum . . . in attention to problems of resource utilization in the California Current area and even in the nearby Eastern Pacific."[11]

Even if the fisheries themselves declined, public attention to ocean resources generally increased markedly after 1960. Other nations, at least, had begun taking an interest in fishery resources long the exclusive province of the United States and its immediate neighbors. Soviet factory ships appeared off the New England coast in the summer of 1960 and off Point Conception in California four summers later. U.S. fishers began to demand protection from the Soviet and other foreign fleets and more government attention to their economic problems. Gathering momentum among third-world nations for an extension of the territorial sea only added force to their demands.[12] Cold war and the nation's new commitment to space exploration underscored the strategic importance of ocean science at the same time.

Competition for high-seas resources led to increased interest in the economic and legal problems involved in developing them. H. Scott Gordon's article, "The Economic Theory of a Common Property Resource: The Fishery," was the first to appear, in 1954.[13] Resources for the Future, a nonprofit research foundation organized in 1952, published two important studies of fisheries problems, *The Common Wealth in Ocean Fisheries* by Christy and Scott in 1965 and *The Pacific Salmon Fisheries: A Study in Irrational Conservation* by Crutchfield and Pontecorvo four years later.[14] The latter boldly asserted at its outset that there was "little hope for change" in the poor condition of U.S. fisheries "unless dramatically new institutions and new forms of management can be developed and adopted."[15] With the publication of R. H. Coase's famous article, "The Problem of Social Cost," in 1960, this academic interest in the fisherman's problem broadened to encompass the effect of property rights and other legal institutions on economic activity generally, thereby bringing a new sophistication in economics to the study of public policy.[16]

Both state and federal governments began to apply economic analysis and cost–benefit budgeting to their internal affairs. In California Governor Edmund G. Brown, Sr., began a comprehensive study of the structure and function of the state's government in 1963.[17] In 1966 a Resources for the Future study applied this kind of analysis to state and federal reclamation projects in California and found them, in economic terms, to be either "all bad," "too large," or "very premature."[18] First and foremost, most of the projects were too heavily geared to irrigation and urban consumption as opposed to other uses, especially those like fisheries that required regular stream flows.[19] One official in Governor Brown's planning effort noted in 1967 that "had we used the cost-effectiveness system . . . in the agricultural areas historically, we would not have what we term in California now, agribusiness instead of agriculture."[20]

CalCOFI was in a more ambivalent situation. On the one hand it had produced a great deal of useful information during its first decade of work, but on the other it had not even come close to solving the problem for which it had been organized in the first place, that of the sardine failure. In 1963 one member of the state Assembly wondered publicly about the cost effectiveness of the landings tax that supported MRC: "All these fishermen," he said, "the laborers, the canneries [were] jumping over each other giving away the five cents per 100 pounds out of their pockets. Now why? They must be getting something out of it, but I'll swear I don't know what it is."[21] With foreign fleets ready to harvest California fisheries and with highly focussed scrutiny coming to bear on the workings of government generally, the 1960s brought a great deal of pressure on fishery managers to do business in a new and more effective way. They began to do so at middecade, but only after the extended stalemate over managing the coastal fisheries had driven both the antagonists and the resources over which they fought to near exhaustion.

The State Water Project

By the early 1960s, DFG was in many cases exerting considerable influence over planning for new facilities in California water projects, and Richard Croker and his colleagues at Fish and Game had a sense that adequate procedures were in place to protect salmon habitat in the Sacramento–San Joaquin watershed.[22] California voters approved a huge bond issue to build the state's own water system, alongside but separate from BuRec's Central Valley Project, in November 1960. The key feature of the State Water Project was to be Oroville Dam on the Feather River, plans for which had since 1955 included careful provision for enhancing fish and game for recreational use. The project was a landmark for its attempt to make a realistic assessment of the monetary value of wildlife-based recreation and, although it cost $3 million to build a fish hatchery adjacent to the new dam, water users paid for it as part of the facility's general cost.[23] Under the Davis–Dolwig Act of 1961, the California Resources Agency issued general orders for wildlife coordination in 1963. Differences arising between competing agencies concerned with water developments were to be resolved personally by the resources administrator. Centralizing responsibility for decision-making in this way improved interagency cooperation significantly.[24]

The inability of wildlife advocates to confront more powerful water users directly, either in the marketplace or in the courts, forced them to work in the labyrinths of interagency and electoral politics. That they were able to do this successfully was largely attributable to changing attitudes toward the environment in the public at large. Highly publicized contaminations of milk by radioactive fallout and fish by pesticides during the late 1950s and early 1960s, as well as books such as Carson's *Silent Spring* and Aldo Leopold's *A Sand County Almanac*, popularized the emergent science of ecology in a way that CalCOFI, for example, could not. Bit by bit, the public began to think of nature, not as a competitive struggle for individual survival in the Social Darwinist sense, but rather as a living, interdependent whole in which all parts had important roles to play.[25] Nature lobbies, most prominent of

which were the Sierra Club and the Wilderness Society, successfully opposed
BuRec's plan to build a dam at Echo Park in Dinosaur National Monument,
Colorado, in 1955. Building on their victory, they then went on the offensive
and secured enactment of the Wilderness Act of 1964 and the Wild and
Scenic Rivers Act of 1968.[26] In essence, outdoorspeople had by the 1960s
successfully pressed their claim to a share of the nation's resources, and
further development would not proceed without at least serious bargaining
in regular channels between them and project developers.

This was not the case in the Klamath–Trinity watershed, where rights to
natural resources had remained untested since the nineteenth century primarily because the technology with which to develop the basin had remained
unavailable. Much of the basin was public land under the jurisdiction of the
U.S. Forest Service. In the basin's lower reaches lay the Hoopa Valley Indian
Reservation, which had three parts (see Figure 3.2, p. 52). The largest was
"the Square," a twelve-mile by twelve-mile section of land straddling the
Trinity River above its confluence with the Klamath at Weitchpec. Created
pursuant to congressional statute in 1864, the Square was inhabited by Hupa
Indians, who elected a tribal government when timber revenues began
coming to them after World War II.

On the Klamath below Weitchpec lay "the Tail," a strip of land one mile
on either side of the river down to the ocean. The Tail, in turn, consisted
of two parts: "the Lower 20" encompassing the original Klamath River Reservation, which had been established on the lower twenty miles of the river
in 1855 but abandoned by the Army in the winter of 1861–2, and "the
Connecting Strip" between the old reservation and Hoopa Valley. President
Harrison had formally consolidated all three sections into the Hoopa Valley
Reservation in 1891. Much of the land on the Lower 20 had passed into
private hands during the 1890s under the Dawes General Allotment Act,
but the area nonetheless remained heavily populated by Yurok Indians,
organized as they had been before 1850 into tightly cohesive family groups
without any formal, tribal government. Rivalry between families and between tribes remained as intense as it had always been: A bitter dispute
between Yuroks and Hupas over allotment of timber revenues raged through
the 1960s and prevented the organization of a unified Indian government
for the reservation.[27]

Traditional Indian culture remained alive and well among both Yurok and
Hupa people on the reservation: In the words of a USFWS report, the
presence of the reservation, the region's isolation, and "the basin character
of the people" had enabled the Indians "to preserve a still identifiable cultural
entity."[28] In particular, the report noted, "it would appear that salmon have
remained important" to the people of the reservation.[29] Some drew all or
part of their livings from salmon fishing, either on the reservation itself or
in the offshore troll fishery. One Yurok family, at least, took an active part

in the offshore fishery's trade association.[30] Private rights to fishing sites on the reservation apparently remained an important source of status within the tribes.[31]

Even to those who did not fish, salmon remained a key to their traditional culture and an economic hedge. The USFWS report described the attitude as one of "using nature as a bank:" "use of land, of animals, and of fish 'when needed' – and protection of opportunity for use when not needed. It is likely fundamental to the resource approach of native peoples, including those of the Hupa tribes."[32] The Indians' legal rights to the fishery, however, had remained altogether untested since the time Harrison extended the reservation so as to circumvent the decision in the *Rising Star Tea* case.

Upstream from the Trinity confluence, the Klamath River's flow had remained intermittent and unstable since the California–Oregon Power Company had built its two hydroelectric dams during the World War I era. In 1959, after years of protracted struggle, DFG concluded an agreement with the Pacific Power and Light Company, which now owned the dams, by which the company built a reregulating dam at Iron Gate, just below the old ones, guaranteed a regular flow of water in the river below, and built a new fish hatchery. The project was complete in 1961.[33] BuRec precipitated a crisis in the basin's salmon fishery just two years later, however, when it completed Lewiston Dam on the Trinity River, above the reservation. The facility was designed to pump water over the mountains into the Central Valley to irrigate crops, to improve deteriorating water quality in the Sacramento Delta, and to provide power for other BuRec pumping plants. It also reduced the flow of water below the dam, where lay the highest concentration of spawning salmon in the basin, by some 80 percent. Already depleted by logging and roadbuilding in the basin and by fishing offshore, Trinity River runs of chinook salmon declined steadily from 75,000 fish in 1963 to about 15,000 by the end of the decade. By way of contrast, sportfishers had taken some 22,500 salmon, mostly chinooks, from Trinity River alone in 1955. During the mid–1960s they harvested about 28,000 chinooks each year from the basin as a whole, while the Indian harvest amounted to between 3,500 and 4,500 chinooks.[34]

Indian hunting and fishing rights constitute one of the most poorly organized areas in U.S. law. Historically, their development has reflected much less any doctrinal coherence or consistency than the changing whims of public policy toward Indians in general: The U.S. legal system has never been able to decide whether Indians were sovereign nations with rights to self-governance or dependent peoples ultimately destined for full assimilation into society at large.[35] With the resurgence of Indian tribal nationalism that took place nationwide during the 1960s, however, a great many litigants came to court to contest rights to harvest and police Indian resources.[36] A great many cases concerned the rights of salmon-fishing tribes in the Pacific

Northwest. These had concluded treaties with the federal government during the 1850s, by which the United States guaranteed them exclusive rights to fish on their reservations as well as "the right of taking fish at all usual and accustomed grounds and stations . . . in common with all citizens of the Territory."[37] The core of the problem, then, was that while states traditionally have the power to police the harvest of wildlife within their borders, the U.S. Constitution defines Indian treaties as "the supreme law of the land" and thus above state law. All the federal courts could do by the end of the 1960s was to offer the vague opinion that states could regulate fishing by treaty Indians off the reservation "in the interest of conservation, provided the regulation meets appropriate standards and does not discriminate against the Indians."[38]

The Yurok were in an ambiguous position because they had no treaty rights to the salmon. The Hoopa Valley reservation existed by dint of President Harrison's executive order rather than by treaty, and although the legal record showed that the reservation had been placed where it was to afford the Indians access to the salmon fishery, nowhere was there an affirmative delineation of their rights to it. The Yurok, who had complained but not mustered strenuous opposition when the state had moved to regulate the fishery in 1933, went to court during the 1960s to defend what they thought was still, first and foremost, their fishery.

In 1964, the year after Lewiston Dam cut off most of the flow in Trinity River, Fish and Game agents caught two Yurok fishers on the Connecting Strip using gillnets that were illegal under state law. In the case of *Elser* v. *Gill Net Number One*, a state court of appeals ruled that California had no power to regulate Indian fishing gear on the reservation, in spite of the fact that Congress had placed the Indians under state criminal jurisdiction in 1954 and in spite of the fact that the Yurok had no explicit treaty rights to fish.[39] Taking a different tack, the state tried again in 1969 when it confiscated the nets of one Raymond Mattz, a Yurok who had been fishing on the Lower 20. This time, the state claimed that the Lower 20 had ceased to be "Indian country" when the federal government opened it for settlement by outsiders under the Dawes Act. The state supreme court agreed.[40]

In the 1972 case of *Mattz* v. *Arnett*, however, the U.S. Supreme Court reviewed the history of the reservation and concluded that the Lower 20 did, indeed, constitute "Indian country." It overturned the state ruling and remanded the case back to the state courts to determine the extent of Mattz's rights to fish on the reservation. The latter could not help but find for Mattz. Indians had been gill-netting salmon on the Klamath for more than a century, and the state had given no evidence that they and not sportfishers, for example, were to blame for the marked decline in the salmon runs over the past three or four decades. Mattz had simply been an easier mark than either the sportfishers, the ocean trollers, or BuRec.

The courts would not let the state "make inroads into subsistence fishing by Indians on their own reservation [until] all other conservation methods should be exhausted."[41] If the Yurok lacked a tribal government through which to control their own fishing, this was not necessarily their problem, either: As the *Elser* court had pointedly observed, "the absence of such organization is most probably the result of the frequent recognized reversals of federal policy regarding the assimilation of Indians and the encouragement of tribal independence and self-government."[42] After state authority dissolved in the Klamath Basin, the Hoopa Valley reservation became the weakest link in government management of salmon along the length of the Pacific Coast.

CalCOFI's great experiment

Even as the Pacific mackerel fishery expired and the last of the California sardine canneries closed down during the early 1960s, events were in motion to generate renewed interest in a local reduction fishery. The bonanza stage in the Peruvian anchoveta fishery came to an end, as the Peruvian government began to attempt to control it in 1960 and as El Niño brought short catches and severe stress to what was already a seriously overcapitalized fishery in 1965.[43] In 1961 Governor Brown appointed Wilbert Chapman to a seat on the Marine Research Committee; through the 1950s Chapman and the big tuna firms had been well served by the IATTC and had chosen to "stay aloof from [MRC's] problems and activities," but had lately come "to believe that such aloofness [was] no longer either good business nor in the public interest."[44]

CalCOFI studies had suggested that the California Current contained many more fish, particularly anchovy, than anyone had previously thought. Chapman later recalled another MRC member's asking the scientists to translate their data on eggs and larvae in the current "into terms of live adult fish weight available, and the considerable astonishment of all of us at the figures that resulted."[45] The Fish and Game Commission had hitherto routinely rejected industry requests for permits to reduce anchovy, but in 1962 its denial raised an unprecedented furor. One industry representative spoke of his frustration over the emergence of a political climate "which could make it impossible to harvest marine resources."[46]

While serving as CalCOFI Coordinator, Garth Murphy was also a doctoral student at the Scripps Institution, using CalCOFI data to complete his dissertation on the population dynamics of the Pacific sardine. Murphy worked under a great deal of pressure because his teachers at SIO were all CalCOFI scientists with a considerable stake in the outcome; by the time he published the work in 1966, his proof was solid enough effectively to settle the decades-old sardine controversy.[47] "The decline of the sardine," he reported to MRC in 1964, "was apparently the result of an intensive fishery together with a series of years in which the environmental regime was unfavorable to the sardine."[48] His published dissertation found it "improbable that the population would have declined in the absence of fishing, whereas the fishing rates applied to the population lowered reproduction to an extent that a decline was inevitable."[49] This, of course, had been Fish and Game's position all along. The implications, however, were now inescapable. As Chapman wrote to Julian Burnette in 1962,

> I think we would be unwise to artificially downgrade the effect of the fishery from 1937 to 1947 on what happened to the sardine population after 1947. . . . [A] reasoned scientific estimate of this factor's effect would mitigate its exaggeration by others. . . . The case is beginning to look too sound to me for us to either hide from the public or to escape the conclusions of.[50]

In 1963 even John Hawk, an MRC member and representative of the Seafarers' International Union, told a state assembly committee that his group would now tolerate a firm limit on the sardine catch, although "of course we don't agree that the fishing effort depleted the sardine."[51]

Murphy had also documented a steep rise in the anchovy population, coincident with the sardine's decline through the 1950s. Figure 9.2 shows the relationship. Because the two fish are ecologically similar, Murphy concluded that the anchovy had grown to fill the niche left empty by the sardine and that its continued abundance in the current kept a "lid" on the sardine's potential recovery. This suggested, as Murphy and other CalCOFI scientists informed MRC in 1964, "that there is a real chance that simultaneously reducing the pressure on sardines and imposing pressure on achovies will reverse the present equilibrium and assist in bringing back the more valuable sardine."[52] Murphy and the others thus proposed what became known as "the great experiment": A sardine fishery limited to 10,000 tons coupled with a 200,000-ton anchovy fishery, undertaken under close scientific observation, might make possible the sardine's recovery.[53]

CalCOFI's idea got nowhere. Governor Brown, for example, observed that "some very real and very complex legal and sociological problems would have to be resolved before a program of this type could become a practical reality."[54] Environmental and sportfishing groups would have nothing to do with it until there was "an iron-clad lock that the fisheries should progress slowly."[55] Chapman, true to form, had panicked the latter by stating at an MRC meeting that he thought 200,000 tons too conservative a limit on the fishery, that the anchovy could easily support a million-ton fishery. One scientist noted on his copy of the meeting's minutes, "Here's where Chapman got the S. Fishermen riled again! Irreparable damage!"[56] For their part, the

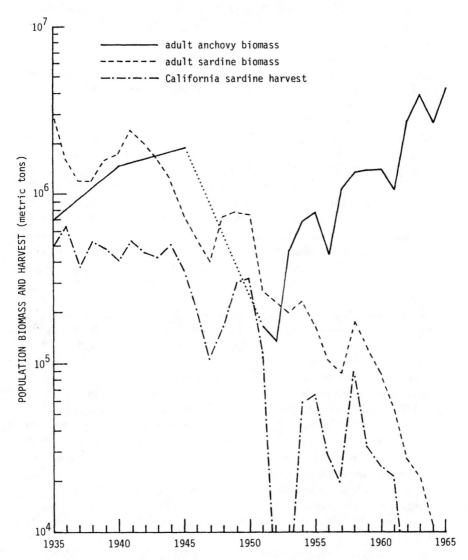

Figure 9.2. Sardine and anchovy populations, 1940–65. Sources: Murphy, "Population Biology of the Pacific Sardine," p. 47; MacCall, "Population Estimates for the Waning Years of the Pacific Sardine Fishery," p. 74; MacCall and Radovich, "A Management Model for the Central Stock of the Northern Anchovy," p. 84.

commercial firms were simply not interested because they saw little chance that the proposal would go through, because they doubted that they would make money on an anchovy fishery, and most of all because they did not want to get involved in an expensive fight with the sportfishers.[57]

So matters stood for a few months, until MRC and Governor Brown received lessons in the economics of fishmeal from Ralston–Purina and the state's producers of poultry and cotton. California poultry growers, whose chickens got their protein from a mixture of fishmeal and cottonseed meal, competed with those in the Midwest who fed their chickens soybean meal plus a synthetic form of the amino acid methionine. During the 1960s, cotton was California's premier cash crop; although California cottonseed meal was very high in quality, it lacked the amino acid lysine, which only fishmeal could replace. If the price for fishmeal went too high, prices for California eggs and broilers rose very easily to the point where it became more profitable for food distributors to import Midwestern poultry products than to buy local ones, so that both poultry and cotton growers suffered. The 1965 El Niño, in addition to labor troubles both in Peru and in California, temporarily shut off the supply of Peruvian fishmeal and suddenly everyone was in trouble. California's Secretary of Agriculture and the manager of Ralston–Purina's formula division in St. Louis made it clear, as the latter put it, that "the current supply situation in California [was] quite critical. . . . The need for a reasonably priced local [sic] produced whole fish meal in California is essential."[58]

Now things began to move. The Fishermen's Cooperative Association had drafted legislation to initiate a two-year limited-entry reduction fishery for 100,000 tons of anchovy per year. The bill passed both houses of the state legislature handily after the Agriculture Secretary informed them of what was at stake, but Governor Brown vetoed the bill on the grounds that its limited-entry provision was of dubious constitutionality and he wished to avoid the litigation that would inevitably follow its enactment into law.[59] Privately, he told Chapman that he had received more mail on the anchovy subject in 1964 than on any other.[60] Brown also had a word with the Fish and Game Commission. Now faced with the very real possibility that further obstruction would not only encourage passage of a much more liberal bill but would also lead the legislature to follow Chapman's suggestion and create a separate agency to regulate the commercial fisheries, the commission unanimously approved an experimental harvest of 75,000 tons at its November 1965 meeting.[61]

Sportfishers immediately organized an initiative campaign to wipe out the anchovy fishery and put the entire industry under DFG control, but during the following summer they failed to gather enough signatures to put the measure on the ballot. MRC, which had been surprised by the cotton growers' interest in its affairs, was even more surprised by how shallow support for the sportfishers was now that the Russian factory ships were offshore and the State Department of Agriculture had entered the controversy.[62] The political gridlock that the sardine catastrophe had cemented into place now began to dissolve as all parties suddenly became more willing to cooperate with each other.

The fishers, unfortunately, were not interested, and took only about 10,000 tons of anchovy in 1966. One problem was that the few seiners left over from the sardine fishery had been making their livings by catching mackerel and bluefin tuna, which are bigger fish than anchovy. None had a net with fine enough mesh to take anchovy; one fisher who needed a new mackerel net anyway bought a suitable one and alone took nearly half the harvest during the first season under the new quota. Neither fishers nor the lenders who might have provided them with the $10,000 to $12,000 a new seine cost thought the anchovy fishery a good gamble, given their experience with the industry's mercurial politics. Lampara boats, which fished bait, had nets that were fine enough but could not take part because the fishery was limited to waters beyond three miles offshore, out of their reach.[63]

Fishers showed somewhat more interest when the quota fishery began its second season in 1966–7. A few old sardine vessels were brought out of retirement, bringing the number of seiners in the fleet to 58 in all, and some eight to ten new nets were prepared.[64] Peruvian production revived after the temporary setback of 1965, however, and depressed the world price of fishmeal below the point at which processors could pay Californians to land anchovies and still make a profit. In 1967 the going rate for California anchovies was between $14 and $15 per ton. The next year it rose to about $17, but Chapman did not believe that fishers would make any money on the harvest below $20. Meanwhile, with anchovies available in Peru for $10 to $12, it did not pay the processors to make fishmeal in California with local anchovies any higher than $15.[65] Although California landed 37,000 tons of anchovy during the 1966–7 season, the next year's harvest fell below 7,000 tons.

Even as the Peruvian fishery kept its California sister drugged into torpor, it was beginning to show signs of strain. Acting on the advice of the Instituto del Mar del Peru (IMARPE), the Peruvian government imposed a three-month closure on the anchovy fishery in 1966 and indicated that it would try to hold catches below their 1964 level of 8 million metric tons. In 1966, however, the industry had the capacity to process twice that many fish in a season and, as long as Peruvian authorities were unable or unwilling to impose quotas on individual firms, entrepreneurs responded to the season closure simply by building bigger boats to catch more fish faster. The industry's capacity nearly doubled again by 1970.[66]

Efforts to put strict limits on the harvest had begun as early as 1960, when IMARPE was organized with help from the United Nations, but the industry had successfully resisted them. Government attempts to raise the price of fish in 1963 and 1965 had only thrown the industry into chaos.[67] Meanwhile, the fishmeal industry shared the anchovies with the seabirds of the Peru Current. These, which had numbered 25 million in 1955 but dropped to 6 million after the 1957 El Niño depressed the anchovy population, had none-theless recovered quickly to 18 million by 1963. After the 1965 El Niño, the bird population dropped as low as 4 million and by 1972 had only built itself back up to 6.5 million.[68] The anchoveta, on which the birds relied, was beginning to lose its resilience to environmental shock.

California landings of coastal schooling fishes declined to just over 50,000 tons in 1968; aside from the year the Pacific mackerel fishery collapsed, this was the industry's poorest year since the demise of the sardine. Statewide, the once-mighty sardine fleet had declined to 34 seiners and 21 lampara boats, the newest of them built more than twenty years before.[69] One member of the San Pedro fishers' union told MRC that in twenty-one years in the business he had never seen his comrades more demoralized than they were then.[70] MRC did not appear to be of much help. By 1968 it had been in business for twenty years itself, yet it had never, as one fisher put it, "gotten down to the real issue of going out and finding a way to catch fish."[71] The indifferent reception to which CalCOFI had proposed its "great experiment" only underscored this failing.

Indeed, the Pacific mackerel fishery had collapsed while CalCOFI watched. As the CalCOFI committee put it, "despite scientific evidence attesting to the [mackerel's] decline, presented over many years, no action has been taken . . . this prima facie evidence substantiates allegations that the State cannot manage its resources on a scientific basis."[72] Fishers began to point out as early as 1964 that one of the reasons it did not pay to fish anchovy was that every ton they landed carried $2 in taxes, one for DFG and one for MRC. MRC was now beginning to look like an impediment to the industry's progress, and by 1968 a movement was afoot in the state government to abolish it entirely.[73] As the state legislative analyst pointedly informed the 1969 CalCOFI conference, "if research and monitoring efforts do not lead to resource management decisions, then these efforts are point-less, and I am not certain of the need for much additional research and study."[74]

Institutional initiatives

CalCOFI's failure to get its experimental fishery started exposed what one DFG official called the "muddled situation . . . in which biology, sociology, economics, politics, and law have met head on." The fishing industry was thus caught in a "stalemate," a "vacuum in fisheries utilization which will nonetheless be filled ultimately by someone more anxious than we to make full use of what the ocean has to offer."[75] As a DFG scientist put it in 1968, "the decline of sardines and Pacific mackerel [were] so imprinted in the minds of conservationists that scientific management of other resources becomes difficult."[76] If scientists and entrepreneurs alike were now to move forward, they would have to reform the political and institutional frameworks in which they worked rather than simply manipulating them to their immediate advantage.

Increased competition for oceanic fisheries, continued stalemate in the California industry, and several years of intense study in both the economics and biology of fisheries use thus converged during the 1960s to produce a great deal of institutional ferment at all levels of government. International developments, which were of primary importance to the tuna industry, lay at the heart of the movement. U.N. conferences on the Law of the Sea in 1958 and 1960 failed to agree on the precise nature of coastal states' rights to regulate high-seas fisheries adjacent to their territorial waters. Opposition from Latin American states prevented passage of a joint U.S.–Canadian proposal for a limited extension of the territorial sea to six miles, with an additional six-mile zone reserved for exclusive fisheries use.[77] Chapman, who served on the U.S. delegations to all three conferences, was much chastened by the "horrendous" difficulties of keeping international action on the territorial sea "under reasonable control" when the United States was but one of many parties taking part in such discussions.[78] Momentum was clearly building for unilateral extensions of the territorial sea. To make matters worse, coastal South American nations began again to seize U.S. tunaboats caught fishing in waters they claimed.[79]

During the early 1960s, shortly after the "purse seine revolution" took place, the IATTC concluded that yellowfin tuna in the eastern tropical Pacific were probably overfished. The Tuna Commission began regulating the yellowfin harvest in 1966, but only to the extent of establishing an annual quota within its regulatory area. It could neither limit capital invested in the harvest nor allocate catches among nations fishing in the area. The predictable result was an international race to catch more and more fish as quickly as possible.[80] Although the tuna fishery remained the United States' most expansive fishery during the early 1970s, an already risky business was becoming increasingly dicey. As Chapman said, "no tuna fisherman, in the 30 years that I have been acquainted with the business, has ever been happy economically. He's been going broke on a higher scale all the time."[81]

The first response of U.S. domestic fisheries to the muddled international situation was to demand Congressional extension of the nation's own jurisdiction over offshore fisheries. This took place in the Bartlett Act of 1966, which created a nine-mile exclusive fisheries zone adjacent to U.S. territorial waters and prohibited foreign fishing within it.[82] Chapman and other spokespersons for U.S. distant-water fisheries resisted the extension, but well-organized support from other sectors of the industry, especially on the

West Coast, overwhelmed them.[83] As it turned out, the federal government did little to manage fisheries within the zone created by the Bartlett Act except to exclude foreign fleets from it.[84] Chapman, who much preferred negotiating bilaterally from a position of strength to provocative unilateral action, was more interested in other measures that appeared in Congress in 1965 and 1966.

Most notable of these was the Marine Resources and Engineering Act of 1966, which created two bodies for coordinating ocean affairs in the federal government. It created a National Council on Marine Resources and Engineering Development to advise the president on marine policy and a Commission on Marine Science, Engineering and Resources to study and prepare a report on national policy for marine resources.[85] The latter's report, published in 1969, recommended a comprehensive state and federal effort to manage resources both on coastal lands and in the adjacent territorial waters. Ultimately the report led to passage of the federal Coastal Zone Management Act of 1972.[86] Chapman also looked favorably on another 1966 statute to create a Sea Grant College Program similar to that which had provided assistance to U.S. farmers through the land-grant colleges since the nineteenth century.[87] A third measure, the Marine and Atmospheric Coordination Act of 1965, failed to secure passage, but in 1970 President Nixon accomplished its purpose by establishing the National Oceanic and Atmospheric Administration. NOAA consolidated the Bureau of Commercial Fisheries with such other agencies as the Weather Bureau and the Coast and Geodetic Survey under supervision of the Secretary of Commerce.[88]

In California, Governor Brown convened a special conference on "California and the Use of the Ocean" at Los Angeles early in 1964. Chapman, Revelle, and Schaefer all addressed the conference, Chapman rather pointedly to the effect that "antiquated State regulations" prevented the industry from making use of the scientific knowledge that CalCOFI had generated with industry support.[89] So enthusiastic was public response to the conference that Brown appointed a Governor's Advisory Commission on Ocean Resources (GACOR), which met several times in 1965 and 1966 and again in 1967 after reappointment by Brown's successor, Ronald Reagan. The primary recommendation set forth by GACOR was the establishment of an Interagency Council on Ocean Resources (ICOR) to prepare an inventory of natural resources in the California Coastal Zone, and Governor Reagan appointed such a body in 1967. The state legislature began its own study of marine policy in 1965, and two years later passed the California Marine Resources Conservation and Development Act "to develop . . . a comprehensive, coordinated state plan for the orderly, long-range conservation and development of marine and coastal resources." The act established a California Advisory Commission on Marine and Coastal Resources (CMC) and directed the Governor to prepare a Comprehensive Ocean Area Plan under

CMC supervision. Wilbert Chapman served on both GACOR and ICOR and as Chair of CMC.[90]

Milner B. Schaefer became Director of the University of California's Institute of Marine Resources in 1962. No less gifted an entrepreneur than Chapman or Revelle, Schaefer drew enough outside money into IMR to triple its budget by 1965. Although he noted that "the word 'resources' implies economic and social considerations," Schaefer remained frustrated by his inability to generate much interest in them.[91] He did secure a contract from the State Office of Planning, however, for a study of California's marine resources and their importance to the state's future development. IMR published its study in 1965, roughly at the same time that DFG published one of its own. The two reports contained similar suggestions for overhauling the state's fisheries management apparatus. The critical difference between them was that while DFG recommended placing the regulation of commercial fisheries in its hands the IMR study recommended giving such responsibility to a separate arm of the state government, much as Chapman had done at the federal level in 1956. Although Chapman refused to discuss the differences between the two reports in public for political reasons, he, the industry, and GACOR all favored the IMR approach.[92]

Here once again was the old stalemate between sportfishers and commercial fishers. By the end of the 1960s, then, very little had happened to break the state out of it. Even the California Ocean Area Plan, developed by ICOR and CMC and finally published in 1972, amounted to little more than what one later study called "not really a comprehensive coastal plan, but . . . an excellent statement of the need for a plan."[93] California's problems drew a great deal of national attention at the end of the decade. DFG's observer at a 1968 conference on the future of the nation's fishing industry reported that the decline of California's fisheries and the state's inability to prevent the sardine and mackerel collapses drew repeated mention, from participants of all regions. What California needed, he thought, was

> an efficient system for transforming scientific, economic, and sociological data into a management program to the satisfaction of the public. Although numerous solutions have been suggested, and many have been tried at various places in the world, a solution to this problem does not appear to be readily available at this time.[94]

Intensive study of the fisheries management bureaucracy had yielded no more fruit than CalCOFI's work on the resources themselves had.

Conclusion: science, politics, and frontier ideology

Wilbert Chapman died in 1970, hopeful as always that his political efforts had begun to dissolve "the web of inhibiting law" holding back the industry's development, but frustrated nonetheless by its continued decline while un-used and well-studied resources lay close at hand.[95] One source of Chapman's frustration had been his faith in the rationality of the political process. As he put it,

> these sociological and competitive problems that lie at the root of most of the legal problems that you are going to run into derive essentially from ignorance, and [. . .] as you perfect the biological and oceanographic knowledge which you can bring to bear upon the legal questions quite a number of these weaken or even disappear.[96]

By 1969 he could only blame unnamed, individual malefactors in the DFG and the Fish and Game Commission, who he thought perpetuated the con-troversy between sportfishers and commercial fishers "as a means of keeping their personal positions secure," for the continuing stalemate that prevented the state from "getting ahead with proper conservation and use of these marine resources for the good of the State as a whole."[97] Unable to recognize that the political and ideological issues at stake were as important as the scientific ones, Chapman could only perceive obstruction by other interests which did not share his expansive view of the ocean's potential productivity as naive, amateurish, or self-serving.

Chapman was no political innocent himself, however. He had built his career on an alliance between scientists, who used the industry's political support to garner more funds for their research, and industry leaders, who found the scientists useful for their purposes, either by way of exploring for new resources or of smothering political debate over fisheries management under mountains of ambiguous ecological data. He had no more sanguine a view of the industry's rationality than did the sportfishers: "The men in the West Coast fishing industry," he wrote in 1947, "have about as much vision in regard to the future of their supply as a near-sighted bat."[98] The depletion of individual fisheries, however, was simply not as important to Chapman as it was to some other scientists because he believed that there were always more to be had, with scientific help. Meanwhile, the political alliance with the industry had been a lucrative one, both for the industry and for most of Chapman's scientific colleagues.

Richard Croker remembered confronting Chapman on this subject on one of the many occasions when the latter, as Croker recalled, "spoke in lofty terms of five hundred, a thousand million tons, and how the world is full of fish, and people have got to eat, and we in California were so parochial":

> Then I said to him, "Wib, remember as you stream around the world writing your wonderful long letters and flying on exotic air-lines, you're in the jet set, and here I am, stuck in California. . . .

I have to take care of the salmon and the shrimp and the crab and the sport fishermen and all the nitty gritty. . . . " I never could swallow his idea that the total supply of all kinds of fish in the world was inexhaustible, and we could expand world fisheries *ad infinitum*. There we had to disagree.[99]

The caution of DFG scientists notwithstanding, Chapman's phenomenal success as a scientist-politician had rested on the basic harmony between his expansive view and that of the nation as a whole through most of its history: that resources were there to be used profitably, that the role of science and policy was to keep profits flowing, and that there was always more to be had. That view was clearly out of date by the end of the 1960s, although the sardine collapse had given fair warning of its demise two decades earlier.

Chapman was right when he observed in 1969 that "the responsible representatives of both the recreational ocean fishermen and the commercial industry have long been sick to death of this fight" and that the political positions of both sides had begun to collapse in the aftermath of the CalCOFI proposal for an experimental anchovy fishery.[100] Murphy's study had clearly demonstrated the industry's role in the sardine disaster; indeed, one had to admit that fishing effort could depress a population of fish in order to propose fishing down the anchovy so that the sardine might recover. By 1966 Chapman and a few other industry representatives were even willing to support a moratorium on the sardine fishery if that would make it easier for them to harvest anchovy.[101] For their part, the sportfishers found themselves in the unusual position of resisting scientific counsel that a limited anchovy fishery would be safe after having told the commercial operators for years to heed the advice of scientists in the State Fisheries Laboratory.[102]

A great many of the contradictions that had stymied progress in fisheries management began to collapse in the wake of Murphy's dissertation on the sardine and the CalCOFI anchovy proposal. Schaefer wrote in 1964 that "both the effects of the fishery and the effects of fishery independent environmental factors must be studied simultaneously if one is to properly understand the entire ecological regime."[103] To him, at least, the distinction between "environmental" and "economic" forces that had divided parties to the sardine debate and that underlay the very structure of the CalCOFI investigation during the 1950s had lost its meaning. So, too, did the distinction between commercial and recreational harvesting. Sportfishers had long accused commercial operators of "wasting" fish, but in 1969 one of their representatives publicly admitted that his constituents simply threw away about half of their sizable catch of ocean fish because "a lot of archaic ideas" prohibited the sale of recreationally caught fish for food.[104] Ironically, by the mid-1960s the chief drain on what was left on the sardine stock was not the commercial fishery at all but rather the sportfishing sector, to which sardines brought between $400 and $500 per ton wholesale – as much as a dollar per fish retail – on the Sacramento Delta bait market.[105]

As practical and ideological differences between camps collapsed, so, too, did corresponding differences between public agencies. Both the DFG plan for reorganizing fisheries management in the state and the alternative plan drafted by IMR and supported by GACOR and ICOR agreed that priority should go to the recreational use of California's fisheries. Commercial operators would be encouraged to harvest what surplus remained.[106] Long wedded to the sportfishing sector for many reasons, DFG received explicit instructions from the state legislature in 1968 to cooperate with the commercial sector in analyzing the latter's problems and to reorient its activities to address those problems in a systematic way.[107] The state established a San Pedro Wetfish Operational Pool in 1969–70, to which MRC contributed some $43,000 for research on new technology to improve the industry's profitability.[108]

CalCOFI, finally, learned that good science alone would not lead automatically to progress. Accordingly, in 1967 it devoted its annual conference to an unprecedented discussion of the state's marine resources and "the legal, economic, sociological, and technological problems impeding their best use." Scientists, public officials, and representatives of both sport and commercial sectors took part in the first attempt by CalCOFI to improve its communication and rapport with the general public. Philip Roedel of DFG opened the discussion by stating outright that the "basic belief of Americans" in "a philosophy of plenty so far as natural resources are concerned" had in the very recent past become obsolete. "In our society of the 1960s," he said, "there is general acceptance (grudging though it may be in some circles) . . . that the resources of the sea are not boundless, that man must exercise some restraints upon himself if he is to reap maximum benefit from what there is."[109]

The era that began when California fishers took to the open ocean in motorized boats came to an end that year, when Governor Reagan approved an emergency two-year moratorium on sardine fishing.[110] Primary opposition to the measure came, ironically, from people who packed sardines for use as bait in the sportfisheries.[111] With the sardine moratorium, the industry finally abandoned the struggle for access to the fishery which had both depleted the resource and stymied efforts to manage it since the 1930s. As it turned out, managing the fisheries meaningfully required the exhaustion both of the fisheries themselves and of the political conflict over their use. Both the harvest and the effort to reform management moved forward again after 1970, although under a very different set of attitudes than had prevailed earlier toward the ocean environment and the role of human activity in it.

10

Leaving fish in the ocean

The conclusion which arises from these ecological considerations is that benefit to the nation occurs by leaving
fish in the ocean.
        – NOAA, *Anchovy Management Plan* (1978)[1]

The modern environmental movement came of age during the early 1970s.
As had been the case with its Progressive-Era counterpart, the new movement sprung from deep roots in social and economic changes that had been
decades in the making. Rising standards of living since World War II had
led many more people than before to value outdoor recreation in "natural"
settings. Antibiotics and other changes in medical technology had all but
conquered infectious disease and left in its place environmental pollution
and what came to be known as "lifestyle" disorders as the chief threats to
public health. An era of cheap and abundant energy came to an abrupt end
with the sudden rise in oil prices in 1973–4 and the simultaneous public
awareness that nuclear power was a far more dangerous and expensive alternative than had originally been thought.[2]

Like its predecessor, the "new" conservation movement owed its remarkable power to the way in which contemporary environmental issues
symbolized a broad range of social problems. Rachel Carson's *Silent Spring*,
for example, demonstrated that chemical pollution was not an isolated problem but symptomatic of a systemic one, the result not of a technical but of
a much more serious social maladjustment: the logical outgrowth of the
society's historically imperial, manipulative approach to nature. Like turn-
of-the-century conservationists, postwar environmentalists harbored a good
deal of antimodernism in their mistrust of new technology and corporate
giantism. But they also drew from the new science of ecology, much as the
Progressives had popularized ideas of economic efficiency, to sketch the
outlines of a more intelligent and less self-destructive way of life. When such
latter-day muckrakers as Carson used ecology to show that conservation was
not only a matter of aesthetics and spiritual improvement but one of public
health and economy, moreover, environmental politics became a much more
immediate and personal, hence politically powerful, concern than it had
been in the days of the Progressives.[3]

227

A deep and thoroughgoing change in the popular culture, then, energized new approaches to the management of fisheries and other natural resources for which scientists and policymakers had prepared the way earlier. In 1982 Richard Croker, now retired, pointed to the recent change in "the public's appreciation . . . of the overall environment" as "the biggest thing that has happened" in wildlife management since he began his career a half-century before.[4] As he put it in 1972, suddenly "management got public opinion on its side. You should see the crews on the sport fishing boats insisting that their passengers keep only legal-size kelp bass."[5] Law must have the willing, automatic support of the vast majority of the people it affects if it is to have any real effect on social behavior. When environmentalism became fashionable during the 1970s, meaningful resource management became a much easier proposition. One DFG official noted in 1975 that although his agency still had to "walk in the shadow of the sardine fishery," public distrust and "the considerable agitation that prevailed in the 1960s" over the anchovy reduction issue had since given way to "less emotional reaction and agitation . . . and more belief that the State intends to safeguard the resource."[6]

Modern environmentalism emerged in the context of a burst of reform legislation that rivaled those of the Progressive Era and the New Deal in intensity. In the same way that conservation had been the heart of turn-of-the-century Progressivism, environmental law was an integral part of what David Vogel called "the new social regulation" of the late 1960s and early 1970s.[7] In some cases the new laws set strict limits on what business and government could do to the environment, firmly placing noneconomic considerations such as public health and species preservation above those of profitability or even technological feasibility.[8] In others they vastly enhanced the ability of courts and of public interest groups to intervene in the regulatory process.[9] They also reallocated the burden of environmental uncertainty and risk, requiring would-be developers to prove that protective measures were *unnecessary* before they could proceed.[10] The unprecedented political conflict that accompanied the enactment and early administration of these laws offered powerful evidence of the pervasiveness, both in the economy and in government, of the "social cost" problems they were designed to address.[11]

Such laws as the Clean Air Act of 1970 and the National Environmental Policy Act (NEPA) of 1969 were what one legal writer called "tectonic" statutes, requiring many years and much litigation before their full meaning would become apparent.[12] While some government agencies required prodding by the courts, most accepted their new responsibilities as part of a new way of doing business. Indeed, as the presidential administration of Ronald Reagan found after 1980, public support for the new laws made the initiatives of the preceding decade difficult to undo, in spite of a broad sentiment for decreasing the interference of government in private life. In many as-yet unforeseen ways, the nation was committed to abandoning the ideology of the frontier and would now have to learn to live within fundamental ecological constraints rather than trying to evade or simply ignore them as it had in the past.

Of particular importance to the fishing industry were NEPA, the Marine Mammals Protection Act of 1972, the Endangered Species Act of 1973, and the Fishery Conservation and Management Act of 1976.[13] The last, enacted near the end of the new wave of regulatory reform, declared federal jurisdiction over fisheries between 3 and 200 miles offshore and established new procedures for managing them. Although the primary motive for enacting it was an economic one; that is, to protect U.S. fisheries from foreign incursion, environmentalists played a significant role in its passage. To the industry's chagrin, environmental concerns consequently gained a significant voice in the act's implementation. The fisheries, too, would now have to work within new constraints.[14]

California fishery managers undertook initiatives of their own during the 1970s. By then intimately familiar with the importance of social, economic, and ecological factors in fisheries use, they attempted to balance the needs of the industry with those of other groups and even those of other animals, all within the context of the region's complex and volatile ecology. In some cases, the state moved in advance of the federal government; in others the two levels of government complemented and reinforced each other. The key change was that management began, in a number of ways, to knit itself into the ecology of the resources rather than acting independently of it or even in opposition to it. Some of the innovations, at both levels of government, were significant and apparently successful, although it was clear that many long-standing obstacles continued to complicate the task.

Valuing risk and uncertainty

After two decades of decline and stagnation, the California wetfish industry began to grow when the Peruvian anchoveta fishery collapsed in 1972. IMARPE surveys, advised by CalCOFI scientists and modeled after CalCOFI's example, had shown a steep and persistent decline in the annual production of anchoveta eggs between 1965 and 1971. Thus, even though the Peruvian government tried with some success to limit the harvest to between 8 and 10 million metric tons (mmt) per year, it was clear even before the 1972 El Niño set in that the stock was failing to recruit enough new individuals to sustain itself. In March 1972 IMARPE noted the onset of a severe El Niño event and announced that there would be little reproduction that year. It recommended that the government keep the fishery closed to conserve the stock of spawning adults. The government, however, did not act until June.

By that time El Niño had warmed the ocean off the Peruvian coast, the anchoveta moved in close to shore in search of cooler water, and the industry, which by then had twice as much capacity as it needed to harvest what IMARPE considered a safe yield, polished them off in short order. "It seems," reported one scientist, "that the adult stock was simply fished out."[15]

The anchoveta disaster was an event of global significance in that it signaled the end of the post–World War II expansion in the world's fisheries. These had grown at a rate of 5 percent per year, from about 20 mmt at the end of the war to a peak of just under 71 mmt by 1971. After 1971 catches stabilized at about 70 mmt, although they rose to a record 76.8 mmt in 1982. Still, the rate of growth through the 1970s was only 1 percent per year.[16] A U.N. study compared the 1945–70 period with the bonanza phase in the history of an individual fishery and pointed out that as the harvest neared the sustainable limit of the oceans' aggregate productivity – typically estimated at about 100 mmt – the rate of increase would necessarily decline to zero.[17] It became clear that the oceans were not the cornucopia they were thought to be during the 1960s; scientists now more frequently described them as "biological deserts" spotted with fertile patches, few of which remained uncropped. A great many problems, not least of which was the cost of fossil fuel, stood in the way of any significant increase in the world's harvest of fish. "Food from the sea" was apparently no answer to the problem of feeding the world's hungry; in the future management of existing fisheries for sustained yield and redistribution of their harvests would take precedence over the development of new resources.[18]

In 1970 California anchovy was the largest unexploited stock of fish left in North America, and as the Peruvian fishery failed its harvest rose dramatically. When the anchoveta harvest fell off slightly during the moderate El Niño year of 1969 California anchovy meal began a steady rise, from $147 per ton in 1969 to $175 two years later. Landings in 1972 were not as high as they might have been because that year's El Niño was strong enough to warm California waters and an abundance of bonito and bluefin tuna distracted the attention of California fishers away from the less valuable anchovy. The next year, however, anchovy meal shot as high as $600 per ton. Raw anchovies reached a record high of $57.50 and the 1973–4 harvest climbed to 120,000 tons.[19]

Even though the USDA urged poultry growers to switch from fishmeal to soybean meal, the latter remained an imperfect substitute because it lacked fishmeal's still-unidentified "growth factor."[20] Still, the U.S. price of soybeans more than tripled when the Peruvian fishery collapsed. The retail price of chicken also climbed, from 41 to 58 cents per pound. Mexico, which had begun fishing the anchovy stock to serve its developing poultry industry in 1966, quadrupled its harvest to about 100,000 tons between 1973 and 1976. At least two Peruvian seiners had moved onto the California Current by 1975; MRC learned in March of that year that there was surplus reduction equipment for sale in Peru and that one U.S. company was thinking about setting up shop in Baja California, where the Mexican government allowed the fishery to run without restriction.[21]

By contrast, the California fishery operated under rigorous control. The Fish and Game Commission had set annual quotas on the harvest since experimental fishing began in 1965. It reserved the right to close the fishery on forty-eight hours' notice and to prohibit nearshore harvesting for reduction as opposed to bait. In 1970, for example, it closed the area within twelve miles of the southern California coast to reduction fishing when the sport-fishing and live bait sectors grew alarmed at the rise in the harvest, thus effectively shutting down the reduction fishery for several months.[22] The 1973–4 season was the first in which the anchovy fishery reached its quota. The Fish and Game Commission closed the harvest down in February, although it allowed a small additional take beyond the twelve-mile limit later in the season. That the industry generally submitted quietly to such rules, the likes of which had generated intense litigation during the 1920s and 1930s, illustrated just how much the political situation had changed.[23]

Still, setting limits on the reduction harvest from year to year and adjusting the boundaries of the permitted fishing area as conflict between user groups arose was regulation of the old style. It flowed from no coherent, long-range, scientifically informed policy. It was essentially arbitrary: CalCOFI's estimate that 200,000 tons of anchovies could be taken "safely" in a year was little more than a guess. The primary motive behind the Commission's strategy was to avoid conflict between the reduction and bait sectors by separating them geographically while keeping total harvests low enough to conserve the stock.[24] During the early 1970s, however, CalCOFI research and an altered political climate allowed a new strategy to emerge. Improved knowledge of the resources and a new approach to the problems of risk and uncertainty made the change possible.

During the mid-1960s, USBCF, which became the National Marine Fisheries Service (NMFS) in the early years of the Nixon Administration, hired William Lenarz to work at its new laboratory adjacent to the SIO campus at La Jolla. Lenarz was the agency's first population dynamicist of the modern kind, trained in sampling theory and random-variable analysis. Using Murphy's data on the sardine, Lenarz developed a model fishery in a computer simulation of the stock's behavior under different regulatory regimes. The model incorporated varying degrees of error in biological measurements of the population's size and random variations from year to year in its reproductive success. The key to the model's strategy was varying the intensity of fishing according to the condition of the stock. If the spawning biomass of the population dropped below a given level, no fishing whatever took place. Changing assumptions about the accuracy of the population estimates, the level of fishing effort, and the threshold above which fishing could begin led to different yields from the fishery and differences in the frequency of seasons in which the model fishery could not operate at all.[25]

Lenarz's model treated the harvest itself as a biological variable. During the 1920s and 1930s, Fish and Game scientists had been unable to do this; they could only take the level of fishing effort as a given, try to infer some safe yield from statistics of the harvest, and then hope that the legislature would restrain the catch. Even though their guesses turned out to have been remarkably accurate, at the time they lacked the political leverage to withstand the concentrated pressure of a well-established industry. When Lenarz presented his model to the 1969 CalCOFI conference, he noted in passing that "changes in the structure of the industry and government regulations [would be] needed" before fishery managers could exercise such finely tuned control over the harvest.[26]

One of the scientific prerequisites for managing the fishery in such a way was a reliable estimate of the population's size within any given year. CalCOFI could sample the concentration of eggs and larvae in the current, but had no way of correlating their data to the actual size of the stocks until 1972. Then Paul E. Smith, another NMFS biologist, derived estimates of the populations of sardine and anchovy by correlating the CalCOFI egg-and-larvae data with earlier estimates of the sardine population that Garth Murphy had developed from statistics of the harvest.[27] Although a later study by Alec MacCall of DFG revised Smith's calibration somewhat, his research, like Murphy's had been a decade earlier, was solid enough to support a new approach to regulating the coastal schooling fisheries.[28] MacCall and John Radovich then developed a model for the anchovy fishery that did not rely on harvest statistics even indirectly, as Smith's had, and which estimated that the stock could sustain a maximum harvest of 450,000 tons as long as the spawning population remained above 2 million tons, or roughly its current level.[29]

Smith and Lenarz presented their conclusions to MRC and CalCOFI in 1971. The northern population of sardines, they thought, was probably no higher than 5,000 tons in all and might be as low as 2,000 tons. They also concluded that the anchovy population had been much higher during the 1930s than CalCOFI had previously assumed; both species had declined during the late 1940s and early 1950s, and whereas the unfished anchovy had recovered to its earlier levels, the sardine, which had remained under pressure (see Figure 9.2) had not. This suggested that CalCOFI's idea that fishing down the anchovy would automatically promote the sardine's recovery was wrong. Indeed, even as light a fishery on the sardine as the law then allowed – 250 tons for bait plus an allowance of 15 percent sardines in mixed-species catches – might ensure "that the northern sardine stock will not recover, and may even cause it to disappear completely."[30]

Applying Lenarz's computer simulation to the sardine population as they now thought it stood, they then offered a range of probabilities that the stock would recover to different levels in different lengths of time under different levels of fishing pressure. In any case a recovery to precollapse levels would take decades: "A recovery to about 1.0 million tons (the 1944–5 level) has only an even chance (0.54) of happening within 25 years starting at 2 thousand tons and assuming no fishing all along."[31] If all fishing were stopped immediately, the stock had an 84 percent chance of recovering to 10,000 tons within a decade. With even a 250-ton fishery, the probability decreased to 66 percent.[32]

MRC unanimously approved a resolution proposed by Smith, Lenarz, and Murphy urging the state legislature to impose a complete moratorium on sardine fishing. Some industry representatives objected at first, claiming that if the bait fishery were stopped Mexican boats would simply take up the slack and California boats would lose all interest in the resource. They agreed to go along with the proposal, however, provided that MRC also urged the legislature to prohibit the import of sardines from Mexico.[33] The more rigorous moratorium became law in 1973, with a provision for beginning a managed fishery once the spawning population of sardines reached 20,000 tons. So convincing was the Smith–Lenarz–Murphy argument, indeed, that without scientific justification for doing so the legislature reenacted the moratorium on Pacific mackerel along similar lines, with provision for a managed fishery once that stock recovered to 10,000 tons.[34]

Again, a changed public perspective on environmental problems underlay the ease with which the proposals passed through political channels. Smith attributed the success of the new approach to increased public familiarity with the methods that underlay it. Probability theory and random sampling had come into general currency during the 1960s with the increased use of public opinion polls and the proliferation of studies that estimated the effects of one or another hazardous chemical on public health. Smith also thought that presenting the proposal in terms of probabilities made it more palatable than the "deterministic" cause-and-effect approach that Fish and Game had used during the 1920s and 1930s and that CalCOFI had taken in offering its anchovy experiment.[35] In a sense, the scientists got better results when they self-consciously offered their conclusions as hypothetical ones leading to a number of policy alternatives from which to choose rather than as "scientific" truths with only one "correct" response in terms of policy.

In 1978 Fish and Game inaugurated a new plan for managing the anchovy. It incorporated a minimum stock size, one million tons, below which no harvesting could take place. Above that level, the law worked on a sliding-scale quota system, allowing the harvest of one-third the estimated adult population in excess of a million tons. In no case was the catch to exceed MacCall's and Radovich's limit of 450,000 tons.[36] This was a very different approach, more in line with the plans already implemented for sardine and Pacific mackerel than with pre-1970 strategies. The plan succeeded in buffering the stock against breeding failure and keying the annual harvest to direct measurements of the stock's abundance. As Lenarz had put it in 1969, "almost all populations of fish undergo considerable fluctuations, [and] we should strive to develop better ways of living with them."[37] The new policy was an attempt to do that.

By the end of the decade, the moratoria on mackerel and sardine were beginning to show results. Landings of Pacific mackerel remained very low for several years as fishers limited their take to fish mixed in with schools of the lower-priced jack mackerel. In 1975, however, fishers reported increasing numbers of Pacific mackerel mixed in with their catches of other species, and the next year the incidental catch was so high that the legislature raised the mixed-load tolerance to 40 percent. Successful spawnings between 1976 and 1978 enabled the legislature to institute a "sliding-scale" quota on the harvest in the latter year, allowing fishers to take 20 percent of the stock's total biomass in excess of 20,000 tons. Landings reached 30,000 tons in 1980–1, higher than they had been since before World War II. The stock had apparently recovered, although a DFG scientist warned that it was in need of another strong spawning and that the revival might be short lived.[38] In 1977 CalCOFI reported that the sardine "continued to remain in a very depressed state," but in 1979 sardine began to appear mixed in with schools of mackerel.[39] In 1982 southern California live-bait fishers encountered "pure" schools of sardine for the first time in many years. Two years later, after a decade under the total moratorium, DFG biologists expected that the stock would surpass the 20,000-ton threshold and that a legal fishery might soon begin again.[40]

The plans for anchovy, sardine, and Pacific mackerel represented a significant milestone in the history of fisheries management. Perhaps the most fundamental departure they entailed, at root, was a different perception of the role of management in the operation of a fishery. Rather than taking the fishery itself as an autonomous variable and the stock of fish as a static mathematical model, the new approach viewed both as parts of an interdependent system operating in a dynamic environment. Management provided intelligence to the system, monitoring the resource directly and adapting fishing effort to changes in the environment. That the intelligence itself was imperfect was less a problem than had existed previously because biological measurements of the stocks were now incorporated into the law, whereas before they could only serve as evidence in the political discussion of proposed regulations. Scientific observation, in other words, was now embedded in the interaction between society and environment rather than set off to view it from an "objective" distance.

The scientific advances of Smith, Lenarz, and others were only one reason for the change. Just as important was the fact that, politically, the anchovy plan and the moratoria on sardines and mackerel were easy to produce. Fisheries for the latter two had died out, and no one had much stake in harvesting them any more. Anchovy ranges no farther north than Monterey Bay; interregional and interstate conflicts thus played a lesser role in its management than they had in the case of the sardine. Although both Mexican and California fishers worked the anchovy stock and the international factor remained to thwart efforts to manage it, Mexican interests had no role in developing the anchovy plan itself. Within California, economic pressure on the anchovy was at a minimum because only a small fragment of the wetfish industry remained alive by the 1970s and it was no match for the sportfishing interests. There were thus few dollars to be made in the short run to compare with dollars to be saved in the future by restraining the harvest. In the end, scientists and policymakers could apply the most modern methods to their work because they operated in a political near vacuum. Those who had tried to conserve the sardine fishery had not had that luxury.

Endangered species, endangered cultures

One of the most important features of the plans for managing coastal pelagic schooling fisheries that emerged during the 1970s was the "floor," or minimum stock level below which no harvesting could take place, which they all incorporated. Leaving a safe minimum stock of fish unharvested to ensure that the populations could recover quickly from adverse changes in their environment was only one reason for it: By the 1970s, lawmakers were willing to admit that other living things had claims to the fish as valid as those of human industry and that management was responsible for leaving enough fish in the water for their use. As Radovich and MacCall noted in their article detailing a model for managing the anchovy harvest, the lower limit "recognizes the importance of the anchovy as a major trophic link in the food web. Although there is undoubtedly room for harvest of anchovies from the ecosystem, it would be unwise to place the importance of that harvest above the maintenance of the ecosystem that produced it (as well as a wealth of higher predators)."[41] If realistic assessment of risk and uncertainty was one important change in California fishery management that took place in the 1970s, giving other consumers an equal or prior right to the fish was another.

One of the first animals to merit such a claim was the brown pelican, which maintains rookeries on Anacapa Island, off Santa Barbara, and on Isla Coronado de Norte, in Mexican waters, during the winter spawning season for anchovy. Pelicans had suffered greatly during the 1960s from DDT contamination, which made its way to them from a chemical plant in Los Angeles by way of the anchovies in the Southern California Bight. Their troubles, indeed, were instrumental in leading the federal government to ban most domestic uses of the pesticide in 1972.[42] They were among the first animals protected under the Endangered Species Act of 1973, which not only outlawed killing them but also prohibited serious injury to their habitat, including their food supply. How much impact a concern for the pelicans might have on the anchovy fishery was unclear. The effect of the Peruvian fishery on the birds of that region had been dramatic, however, and California researchers could correlate high populations of anchovy with improved reproduction among the pelicans in their neighborhood. The birds did not consume a great deal of fish, to be sure, but they did require that the anchovy spawn densely enough near their rookeries to make their foraging efficient.[43] Anchovy spawning declined between 1975 and 1978, for example, and as the estimated size of the stock dropped from 3.6 to 1.3 million tons the fledging of new pelicans declined significantly. Biologists pointed to the scarcity of anchovy as the likely cause.[44]

Some scientists suggested that the million-ton threshold in the state and federal anchovy plans was too low to ensure that the pelicans got an adequate share of fish; they also suggested closing the area around Anacapa Island to commercial fishing because it was "critical habitat" for the birds under the terms of the Endangered Species Act. Such a reserve would take up between 10 and 20 percent of the anchovy grounds in the Southern California Bight. One NMFS official expressed frustration at the idea: "If we start making special arrangements for the pelicans," he wondered, "where will it stop? What about the whales, what about the sea lions?"[45] Here again, improved knowledge of biology and the strict requirements of an environmental statute posed a new kind of challenge to fishery managers.

The pelicans had something to offer in return, however. Biologists who studied their feeding habits discovered that what the pelicans ate seemed to provide as sensitive a monitor of the anchovy population as the scientists themselves could get by sampling eggs and larvae in the water. One study found a close correlation between the age distribution of anchovies taken from the pelicans' stomachs and that derived from the more complicated direct sampling method. It concluded that the technique, which did not harm the pelicans, "has potential as a practical alternate means of sampling the northern anchovy population" to the more expensive CalCOFI-type surveys.[46] "Seabirds," concluded another study, "represent a potential tool to fishery managers besides being valuable resources in themselves."[47] Such an approach to the animals, viewing them less as competitors for fish than as full partners not only in the harvest but in regulating the stock, would have been unthinkable before 1970. Thereafter, giving the pelicans and other living things an equal stake in managing ocean resources seemed more and more like the way of the future.

A number of marine mammals also began during the 1970s to emerge as significant factors in the commercial fisheries. The gray whale, the Guadalupe fur seal, the northern elephant seal, and the California sea otter, all of which had been believed extinct or nearly so at the turn of the century, were clearly recovering. The gray whale had increased from as few as 250 animals at the close of World War II to some 11,000 by the early 1970s under the protection of the usually feckless International Whaling Commission. It was the gray's good fortune to limit its migration to coastal waters and to breed in a small number of lagoons on the Baja California coast. Mexico established a sanctuary for the animals at Scammon's Lagoon in 1972 and unofficially let it be known, according to Richard Croker, "that if the whalers of any nation start taking gray whales on the high seas, Mexico would permit the complete extermination of them in the bays, and that would be the end of that."[48] Standing the fisherman's problem on its head, Mexico held the whales hostage to it. As a result, the gray was the only species of great whale in good condition by 1980.[49]

Other marine mammals came under the protection of the Endangered Species Act and the Marine Mammals Protection Act (MMPA) during the early 1970s. Although knowledge of their biology was not well developed enough to determine the effect of their recovery on the commercial fisheries, many of these mammals consumed significant quantities of anchovy and other commercial targets. Just as the combined suppression of a great many mammals at the end of the nineteenth century coincided with a remarkable increase in the standing crops of coastal schooling species, recovery in those populations might infringe substantially on the availability of anchovies and other fishes for commercial harvest. Maintaining a balance of different predators in California waters might entail seriously reduced commercial use of the fodder fishes on which all would have to depend.[50]

In the case of the sea otter, the interaction between a recovering species and its human competitors was abundantly clear. The otter had been thought extinct until 1938, when two people from the Monterey area who were trying out a new pair of binoculars at Point Sur discovered a herd of unusual-looking animals floating in the kelp offshore. A scientist from Stanford's Hopkins Marine Station identified the animals as otters and estimated their population at about 300. By 1958 about 650 of them were distributed along the rough coast between Point Conception and Carmel Bay. By 1980 there were some 2,000. The population seemed to be in equilibrium with its habitat along the central coast and a few pioneers had begun to make their way north and south, into areas frequented by abalone fishers.[51]

In 1959 the state Assembly Fish and Game Committee described the abalone industry as being "as stable as any California fishery and very productive."[52] Most of the commercial harvest came from Morro Bay, just north of Point Conception, and from the islands off the southern California coast. Meanwhile, a thriving sportfishery for the shellfish operated on the mainland shore of the Southern California Bight and along the coast north of Monterey. Little harvesting took place on the rocky and inaccessible Big Sur coast between Monterey and Morro Bay, where the otters had taken refuge. In 1963, several Morro Bay abalone divers became concerned about the otters that had recently invaded their territory, but a group of DFG biologists who toured the bay at their request did not think that the mammals had seriously depleted the area's abalone beds during the five years since they had first appeared.[53] By 1967, however, the otters had become a serious problem. Philip Roedel reported that "the interaction of sea otters on abalones in the last year or so has put sportsmen, commercial men and nature lovers at loggerheads."[54] "Unless the sea otter is eventually contained," one DFG biologist concluded, "the State's pismo clam, sea urchin, abalone, certain crabs, and possibly lobster fisheries will be precluded."[55]

Like the pelicans, however, the otters, too, had something to offer in return for preferential access to resources. Oil spills off the Santa Barbara coast, which had had much to do with the passage of NEPA in 1969, also prompted thorough study of the effects of pollution on marine life in the Southern California Bight. The oil spills, biologists discovered, had had much less serious an effect on the ecology of southern California waters than had systemic pollution: Between 1956 and 1970 the number of different species of algae in the tidal zone had declined by 63 percent. Meanwhile, sea urchins had proliferated near the sewage outfalls of southern coastal cities and, together with the direct effects of pollution, had caused the loss of huge areas of kelp forest below the tide line. The latter threatened in turn to damage more than one hundred different species of nearshore fishes which relied on the "living reef" of the kelp forests for food and shelter. By thinning the urchins which grazed on the kelp, the otters might improve the total mass, the diversity, and the stability of marine life wherever they could establish themselves.[56] At Monterey, for example, kelp beds became visibly more luxuriant as the otters moved in over the course of the 1970s. Like the pelicans, then, the otters promised on balance to promote rather than hinder human interests in the California Current, although they would require a substantial allocation of commercially valuable resources in order to do so.

The tuna fishery also ran afoul of legislated protection for marine mammals. Tuna seiners harvest yellowfin tuna by setting their nets around schools of porpoise, which the tuna tend to follow. Through the 1960s the process killed a great many porpoises, either because the animals became entangled in the tuna nets and drowned, succumbed to trauma, or refused to leave other animals trapped in the nets. NMFS estimated that more than 600,000 porpoises died in tuna-seining operations between 1970 and 1972.[57] In response, the Marine Mammals Protection Act of 1972 required the fishery to reduce its toll "to insignificant levels." Yellowfin tuna (Figure 10.1) accounted for one-third to one-half the U.S. tuna catch, so to allow the industry

Figure 10.1. Yellowfin tuna. The photo shows the fish trapped in a purse seine, before hauling. The seine's float line can be seen faintly at right and left center, and a panel seam can be seen at left just below center. Yellowfin tuna inhabit the tropical Pacific Ocean, where they support an intensive multinational fishery under the supervision of the Inter-American Tropical Tuna Commission. Average adults range between four and five feet in length and weigh between 40 and 50 pounds, although some as large as 450 pounds have been landed. Photo courtesy of National Marine Fisheries Service, Southwest Fisheries Center, La Jolla, California.

time to develop methods of protecting the animals, the act granted it a two-year exemption from the moratorium. Thereafter, the industry could apply for permits to take a small number of porpoises during the course of its work.[58]

In 1974 and 1975 NMFS granted the American Tunaboat Association permits to take unlimited numbers of porpoise, claiming that MMPA required it to balance protection of the mammals with "its responsibility not to shut down or significantly curtail the activities of the tuna fleet."[59] Environmental groups immediately sued the agency, and in 1976 a federal court found that "maintenance of a healthy tuna industry" was *not* one of NMFS's responsibilities under the act. "The interest of the marine mammals come first," the court said, "and the interests of the industry, as important as they are, must be served only after protection of the animals is assured."[60] As it turned out, the seiners were able to reduce their kill substantially in 1977 by a combination of modified gear, maneuvering the net, and helping the animals out bodily.[61] In this case it proved possible for the fishers to cooperate with the other mammals. The controversy was significant, however, in that during the 1970s porpoises, like pelicans and sea otters, acquired rights under the law that could not be balanced against the profitability or even the survival of human industry. The tuna fishery's most serious problems, in any event, stemmed from the inexorable increase in the international fleet's capacity. This, however, could only be addressed at the international level.

Indian rights to salmon were yet another area in which legal developments in the 1970s presaged new kinds of limits on the commercial use of fisheries. A 1969 decision by the federal district court for Oregon, *Sohappy* v. *Smith*, did little to clarify the muddle in which Indian fishing rights stood except to affirm that the Indians had rights to a "fair share" of the harvest along with commercial and recreational fishers.[62] The district court for western Washington took a much more aggressive stance in the case of *United States* v. *Washington*, in 1974. The court found that treaties guaranteeing the Indians' right to fish "in all usual and accustomed places in common with" U.S. citizens reserved to them up to 50 percent of all the salmon left available for commercial harvesting after deducting shares, not only for spawning but for subsistence and ceremonial Indian fishing both on and off the reservation. Tribes that demonstrated their ability to police their own fishing, moreover, were completely exempt from state regulation.[63]

The same court went further in *United States* v. *Washington (Phase II)*, in 1980, when it declared that the tribes' rights to fish included a right "to have the fishery habitat protected from man-made despoliation" inshore by timber companies, hydroelectric development, irrigation, and the like.[64] The implications of *Phase II* for land use all over the Pacific Northwest were staggering: Conceivably, any industry that damaged the spawning productivity of the salmon, whose natal streams reached into the most remote corners of three states, could come to account for violating federal treaty law. What this meant for the Indians of the Klamath Basin was, again, not immediately clear because those tribes did not hold their reservations by treaty. Another court observed that it made "little practical difference that Congress granted [the Hoopa Valley Reservation] by statute rather than by treaty. In determining the scope of these rights, therefore, the rules of Indian treaty construction should apply."[65] A subsequent decision used the *Phase II* ruling to stop the Forest Service from completing a logging road in the "high country" above Blue Creek, in part because that tributary held a significant share of the Klamath's spawning area and the project threatened to lower water quality in the river below.[66]

An older line of case law, dealing with reservation water rights, held similar implications for the Klamath Basin. In the 1908 case of *Winters* v. *United States*, the U.S. Supreme Court had enjoined the use of water from a Montana river for irrigation because the diversion lay upstream from an Indian reservation and the Indians had a right to enough water to sustain their economy.[67] In *Arizona* v. *California*, a 1963 decision, the Court ruled that the *Winters* doctrine applied to all Indian reservations, whether established by treaty or not.[68] Although the Hupa tried to use *Arizona* v. *California* in a suit to force BuRec to guarantee the release of enough water into Trinity River to safeguard their salmon fishery during the drought of 1976–7, their efforts proved unsuccessful.[69] A later decision, however, explicitly linked *Winters* to the reservation fishery in turning back efforts of offshore salmon fishers to force NMFS to regulate Yurok gill-netters on the reservation.[70] The doctrine, as old as it was, remained a tool of potentially great power for the protection of Indian lands and Indian fisheries.[71]

The Indians occupied a position that was ecologically not unlike that of the pelicans on Anacapa Island. They lived at a critical point in the range of a valuable resource, their legal rights to it probably imposed limits on the extent to which other users could exploit it, and their own use of the resource was of potential value as a tool for monitoring the health of the fishery as a whole. In 1978, for example, the California Secretary for Resources proposed that Klamath River salmon might once again be fished from Indian weirs. Because all the fish in the stock passed through the reservation, he noted, a traditional Indian harvest would permit accurate monitoring and regulation of the fishery as well as conserving fishing effort, the fish themselves, and social peace in the industry.[72] Once again, as it had been before 1850, the well-being of Indian society in the Klamath Basin lay entwined with that of the salmon.

None of these issues, whether they involved pelicans, marine mammals, or Indian reservations, were clearly settled by 1980. They nonetheless portended departures from earlier approaches to fisheries management in that both endangered species and the endangered cultures of the Indians began to impose strict limits on the exploitation of some very valuable fisheries. A more subtle change involved the goals and procedures of management. If commercial harvesting could not go so far as to jeopardize the well-being of communities that relied on the stability and productivity of their environments, then those communities' well-being itself became a guide to management. Increasingly, as the law granted preferential rights to noncommercial users of resources, scientists and policymakers would have to bend their efforts toward sustaining diversity in the environment rather than maximizing the production of valuable commodities from it. Endangered species and endangered cultures became miner's canaries: legal indices of the health of the system as a whole. An injury to one warned of impending injury to all.

The Fishery Conservation and Management Act

Congress extended the new social regulation to the fisheries in the Fishery Conservation and Management Act of 1976 (FCMA).[73] FCMA was to the twentieth century what the creation of the U.S. Fish Commission had been to the nineteenth: It recognized formally that circumstances had changed. The year before it passed a federal advisory council had announced, "the major new challenge is *fisheries management* . . . which stresses the conservation and rational allocation of these resources."[74] Where before federal policy had aimed primarily at expanding the industry's resource base through research, exploration, and development, the new law brought the national government broadly and squarely into the business of policing fisheries use for the first time. The Congressional Office of Technological Assessment described it as "potentially the most significant institutional change in the history of U.S. fisheries management."[75]

First and foremost, FCMA fulfilled the promise which President Truman's proclamation had made in 1945 by unilaterally extending U.S. jurisdiction over coastal fisheries out to 200 miles offshore. The rest of the law, however, was thoroughly in keeping with the Clean Air Act, NEPA, and the other environmental statutes of the 1970s. It established eight regional councils, made up of a mixture of state, federal, and private representatives, and charged them with drawing up fishery management plans for important species in their parts of the country in cooperation with NMFS, the National Oceanic and Atmospheric Administration (NMFS's parent agency), and the Secretary of Commerce. In general, the fisheries were to be managed so as to produce "optimum yield," which the act defined as "maximum sustainable yield . . . as modified by any relevant economic, social, or ecological factor."[76] Such language virtually guaranteed a great deal of litigation over what the law really meant. The NEPA requirement that federal agencies publish environmental impact statements detailing the reasoning behind their regulations, moreover, ensured that the industry and the public at large would have plenty to say about what "optimum yield" really meant. Like the broad scope of the act's objectives, however, this provision for public debate over the details of regulations was of a piece with the "new social regulation" of the 1970s. As NMFS itself put it, "management for optimum yield . . . is a continuing process of establishing and reevaluating goals through consideration of all aspects of the national interest and the use of the best available techniques to achieve these goals."[77]

By 1981 some dozen management plans had come into force, and many more were in preparation.[78] The Pacific Fishery Management Council (PFMC), representing Washington, Oregon, and California, had three to its credit: one for salmon, one for northern anchovy, and a third for groundfish. FCMA classified tuna as a "highly migratory species," exempt from its provisions, in a deliberate move to shield the tuna industry from possible foreign retaliation.[79] Billfish such as marlin and swordfish, which are close relatives of the tunas, were the subject of a plan drafted in 1981. Although a good deal of competition for these species existed between U.S. and foreign vessels and between commercial and recreational fishers, PFMC declined to implement its plan because so much of those species' range lay outside the 200-mile zone. Within three miles of shore, California retained control over their harvest.[80]

Advocates of FCMA presented it to Congress as an interim measure, designed to prevent the depletion of U.S. resources so long as international discussions on developing a Law of the Sea Treaty were still in progress. Although the bill's chief sponsor was a West Coast senator, Warren Magnuson of Washington, California interests played a smaller role in its passage than they had in extending federal jurisdiction to twelve miles offshore in 1966. The most serious foreign incursions had taken place off the New England coast, and it was thus New Englanders who were most vocal in supporting Magnuson's bill. California fishers benefitted from the law nonetheless. Foreign trawlers working the Pacific Coast declined from 134 vessels in 1976 to fewer than 60 just one year later. Their harvest of groundfish off the West Coast had quadrupled between 1963 and 1973, while the U.S. catch had remained steady at low levels. Some species, notably the ocean perch, had been seriously depleted by the foreign effort. After 1977 the U.S. effort began to grow as new, larger, and more technically advanced domestic trawlers entered the now-protected fishery. Foreign trawlers were limited to species, such as Alaskan pollock, in which domestic harvesters had little interest.[81]

The passage of FCMA also encouraged efforts at the state level to manage the fisheries in new ways. As long as the federal government had upheld "freedom of the seas" as national policy, controlling the access of domestic harvesters to the fisheries had been that much more difficult.[82] Limited entry, for example, had been unthinkable during the 1960s. It had provided Governor Brown with a convenient excuse for vetoing the wetfish industry's bill to liberalize restrictions on the anchovy harvest in 1965. By 1982, however, California had imposed one form of limited entry or another on several of its fisheries, first on that for herring in San Francisco Bay and later for abalone and lobster.[83] All three Pacific Coast states adopted programs to limit entry to the salmon fishery after PFMC called for such action. In California this took the form of a moratorium on new licenses to fish salmon, enacted in 1979.[84] While limiting entry to the salmon fishery did not necessarily mean that pressure on the resource would ease – those who had licenses could always fish harder – an NMFS economist observed that the measure had encouraged California salmon trollers to perceive themselves as a closed group with a collective interest in sustaining their livelihoods over the long run. One such group in Alaska established their own salmon hatchery when entry limitation relieved them of free riders some years before.[85]

Although ambiguous, the "optimum yield" provision of the FCMA greatly broadened the view of public officials toward the goals of fisheries management. Milner B. Schaefer, as director of the University of California's Institute of Marine Resources during the early 1960s, had been greatly frustrated by his inability to generate new research on the economic, political, and sociological aspects of fisheries problems. FCMA made such consideration a legal requirement, and economists played important roles in the development of fishery management plans for salmon, anchovy, and groundfish in PFMC's area.[86] Environmental change and the requirements of other predators also received consideration under the optimum yield requirement. Indeed, the plan for northern anchovy abandoned the concept of "maximum sustained yield" per se: "In the anchovy fishery, the concepts of 'maximum' and 'sustainability' tend to be mutually exclusive due to large natural fluctuations. The determination of MSY requires a probabilitistic answer." Rather than asking, in the Progressive-Era fashion, "what is the largest harvest we could take such that the population size in the following year would remain unchanged, on the average?," the anchovy plan asked "what harvesting policy will give the largest yield while minimizing the variation in annual catches, and while minimizing the risk of extremely low levels of biomass?"[87] The new strategy thus combined a concern for economic stability in the industry with a fundamental aversion to the risk of biological collapse, in a way in which the older approach could not.

There were, however, several critical problems that FCMA left unresolved. "Optimum yield" was not only an ambiguous term but one left to regional councils made up of local representatives to define. It thus left the councils plenty of room to overvalue fish caught in the near term with respect to maintaining the resource over the long term.[88] Conservation aspects of the formula might still get less consideration than the law intended. One analysis of the act's enforcement in the New England groundfishery, for example, concluded the even under FCMA management officials "moved toward immediate exploitation, in spite of danger signals from available biological assessments."[89] In 1977 the state of Maine sued the Carter Administration for allowing foreign vessels to harvest herring on Georges Bank even though scientists thought the stock might be in danger of collapse. The federal court that heard the case on appeal, however, deferred to the Administration's judgment, noting in passing that "nothing in [FCMA] declared that all foreign fishing was to be disallowed whenever stocks were incapable of sustaining the maximum sustainable yield."[90]

In California, salmon trollers sued to have PFMC's 1980 plan for managing their fishery set aside, alleging in part that the council had not adequately considered the economic hardship that it would impose on them. Although the court recognized that "much of the 1980 salmon season has been rendered useless by the Secretary's decision" to approve the plan, it nonetheless sustained the regulations after finding that both PFMC and the Secretary of Commerce had made good-faith efforts to balance what they could learn about the industry's economic needs with the needs of the resource.[91] In 1982, however, the Commerce Secretary in a new administration refused the PMFC salmon plan and rewrote the regulations himself so as to allot the trollers a larger catch.[92] Here again, the pressure of well-organized, articulate interest groups with tangible interests at stake outweighed less easily defined values of long-term conservation and stability of the resource.

In a way, FCMA'S complicated policymaking apparatus did little more than to incorporate all existing conflicts over fisheries management into one rather unwieldy system. In particular, it could do nothing to erase jurisdictional boundaries that were beyond Congress's power to invade. State governments retained authority to regulate fishing within three miles of shore, although FCMA did leave room for state control of fishing beyond three miles under such schemes as California's limitation on entry to the salmon fishery.[93] California law, moreover, gave the Director of Fish and Game authority to bring state regulations into line with federal ones without recourse to the legislature.[94] The chief weakness in the plans for managing the anchovy fishery was that 30 percent of the stock inhabited Mexican waters. The anchovy spawned poorly in 1974 and 1975, and by 1978 the California reduction fishery was in a state of "virtual collapse," according to CalCOFI.[95] The shortage aroused considerable rancor among the industry, sportfishers, DFG, and NMFS; a situation with which veterans in the industry were all too familiar.[96] Although it was not clear that the combined U.S. and Mexican fisheries, amounting together to about 200,000 tons, influenced the decline in recruitment, unimpeded Mexican access to the resource meant that the anchovy fishery still ran essentially unregulated in spite of whatever state and federal officials might do to control their part of it.[97]

The most ticklish jurisdictional problems that PFMC faced concerned the Indian salmon fishery on the Klamath River. Federal and state court decisions immunizing the Indians from government regulation confounded policymaking for the Klamath fishery and, because Klamath River fish mingle indistinguishably in the ocean with stocks from other rivers, consequently that for the entire coast as well. Indian fishing expanded greatly in the wake of these decisions. Between 1978 and 1981, Indian gill-netters took an average of 23,000 chinooks, or 34 percent of the inshore run, each year. Sportfishers took only 4 percent of the runs, while the rest escaped to spawn. Some 4,000 salmon trollers, however, took 100,000 to 160,000 Klamath River chinooks from the ocean each year, before they reached the mouth of the river. Of the total stock available between 1976 and 1984, then, Indians took 8 percent, sportfishers 2 percent, and the trollers 67 percent.[98] The danger to the stock became acute in 1976 and 1977 when drought, exacerbated by the poor condition of spawning areas upstream, brought the number of spawning fish to critically low levels. Although subsequent wet years brought larger runs, as the Indians had known in aboriginal times it was in bad years that controls on the harvest were most important.

Between 1977 and 1979, the Interior Department, which supervised the inshore fishery through the Fish and Wildlife Service, issued a series of emergency regulations to cut back the Indian harvest, most significantly by limiting and then banning outright the commercial sale of fish caught on the reservation.[99] When USFWS agents tried to enforce the new rules, fighting broke out on the river. A special Court of Indian Offenses, set up to try Indians caught violating the rules, failed to function because the Indians refused to recognize its authority and would neither give testimony nor serve as jurors. Only about 100 Yurok were responsible for the inshore fishing and, although most of the Indians on the reservation professed willingness to cooperate with federal agencies in managing the fishery, they steadfastly refused to delegate power to police it to non-Indian authorities.[100] The Hupa tribal government maintained that PFMC's failure to regulate the offshore harvest in any meaningful way invaded its people's rights to the salmon.[101]

For their part, local officials and resort owners urged Congress simply to abolish the reservation on the lower river, "as proposed many years ago."[102]

The law seemed to be on the side of the Indians. One Yurok, arrested by state agents for selling Klamath River salmon, predictably won a decision in the state supreme court holding that federal law immunized him from the state ban on the sale of such fish.[103] The U.S. District Court reached the same result with respect to the Interior Department regulations in 1985: The reservation, it said, carried with it "those rights necessary for the Indians to maintain on the land ceded to them their way of life, which included hunting and fishing." The right to fish included "not only the right to catch fish for individual consumption, but also the right to engage in commercial taking." Finally, noting that the offshore fishery, "which harvested the vast majority of Klamath and Trinity salmon, remained substantially unregulated," the court held that the Interior Department's regulations "improperly deprived [the Indians] of their federally protected tribal right to take fish from the Klamath River."[104]

"This is a very complicated situation," noted PFMC in its 1982 plan for managing the offshore fishery.[105] Although the minority of Yurok who fished indiscriminately did so against the wishes of most of their tribe, the legal right they asserted was of supreme importance to all. Other Yurok, moreover, were active in the offshore fishery and contributed from that direction to what PFMC called the "tremendous pressure from some ocean salmon fishermen not to use the Klamath River for ocean management purposes."[106]

Until this jurisdictional tangle was resolved the Klamath River salmon, probably the weakest stock along the entire coast, lay in extreme danger. At the heart of the controversy, the elaborate institutional structure set up under

FCMA notwithstanding, lay the old problem of the Indians' rights to use their traditional resources and to order their communities in their own way.

Conclusion: a constitutional change

FCMA was less a solution to the traditional fisherman's problem than a framework for developing new approaches to it: The 200-mile limit aside, it was constitutional rather than remedial legislation. Its great strength was that it incorporated the concern for endangered species and other nonmarket values that became widespread during the 1960s and 1970s and gave the regional councils some flexibility to respond to new kinds of interests such as these as they emerged. Implicitly the new law, like the other environmental statutes of the 1970s, reflected a new awareness that natural resource problems were not strictly technical ones but rather social ones as well. Policymakers would have to account not only for the scientific nature of the resources and the technological aspects of developing them but also for the social, political, and economic forces that generated fisheries problems in the first place.[107]

Earlier approaches to fisheries problems had been unable to do this: One of FCMA's first impacts in California was to make the Marine Research Committee obsolete and the state legislature abolished it in 1978.[108] A much attenuated CalCOFI continued to function through individual contributions from participating agencies. Although the new regime functioned far from perfectly and would require time to develop meaning and effect, by providing a framework in which such intangibles as the rights of endangered species and the social cohesion of user groups could gain consideration in policymaking it offered the potential for erasing the distinction between "environmental," "economic," and "social" concerns that lay at the root of the fisherman's problem.

In 1969 Alan Longhurst, who directed the USBCF laboratory at La Jolla, thought he could see in the California situation as it was unfolding "a glimpse of the future of world fisheries." "If others later face the kinds of problems we face now," he said, "then what we do here becomes a model for latecomers and may be very important indeed in the future development of world fisheries."[109] California's frontier had come to a close at the end of World War II, several decades before policymakers at the federal level had had to confront the problems of managing resources in an uncertain, volatile, and interdependent environment. By the 1960s, indeed, these problems had together brought the state's fishing industry to a near standstill. By the time the politics of resource management at the federal level began to change during the 1970s, California's knowledge of them was well developed enough that its experience could serve as such a guide as Longhurst envisioned.

Conclusion

11

An ecological community

Highest good is like water. Because water excels in ben-
efiting the myriad creatures without contending with
them and settles where none would like to be, it is like
the way. . . . It is because it does not contend that it is
never at fault.
— Lao-tzu (551–479 B.C.), *Tao Te Ching*[1]

Nearly two centuries elasped between the first commercial slaughter of sea
otters in the California Current and the development of plans for managing
the system's resources under the Fishery Conservation and Management
Act of 1976 (see Fig. 11.1). Over those two centuries, the commercial harvest
left in its wake a trail of devastation: By their end, both the quantity and
the diversity of life in the current had fallen to unprecedentedly low levels.
The destruction was both cyclical and cumulative, the different sectors of
the industry depleting their resources, colonizing new ones, and depleting
them in turn without altering significantly their essential characteristics or
patterns of behavior. Only during the 1970s, by which time California's
domestic fisheries had nearly destroyed themselves, was there any indication
that the cycle of depletion and colonization might at last be broken.

Despite changes in the style of government efforts to conserve the fisheries, the century of such efforts that preceded FCMA was continuous in
character as well. Ideally, the function of government was to account the
social costs of resource use and then to compel harvesters to behave in
ecologically conservative ways so as to save them from the self-destruction
to which a more narrowly construed market rationality might lead them.
What all public efforts to do so before the 1970s had in common, however,
was that they made the industry's search for profit the object and measure,
both of their understanding of the issues at stake and their responses to
them. Economic distress was the goad to public action and economic gain
the gauge of its effect. The resources themselves were passive objects of
technological and political manipulation, while the harvesters' freedom to
use the fisheries as they saw fit was an article of faith. The real causes of
depletion – social costs transmitted to the fisheries ecologically and the social

Figure 11.1. Sea otters. Adult males of this species typically reach a length of 4.5 feet and weigh between 70 and 80 pounds. Photo courtesy of National Marine Fisheries Service, Southwest Fisheries Center, La Jolla, California.

forces that sustained the Hobbesian struggle of all against all in which the fishers were trapped – went entirely unaccounted.

At the root of the problem lay a particular ideological conception of the relationship among individuals, communities, and the environment, conditioned and apparently proven by many years of expansion across a lightly defended frontier. Key to this conception was the idea that human life had no ecological nature at all: The earth was a store of resources to be used for the satisfaction of human wants, a passive stage for the unfolding of human progress. The historian Lynn White, Jr., traced this view to the Judeo-Christian myth of creation, in which God gave humankind absolute dominion over nature: "Man and nature are two things, and man is master. . . . [N]o item in the physical creation had any purpose save to serve man's purposes."[2] Other writers have found more recent origins for the dichotomy in early modern Europe, when the "scientific revolution" of the seventeenth century emerged hand in hand with the economic theory of capitalism to suggest that all of nature was reducible to its component parts – the links between them immaterial, in every sense of the word – and could with impunity be manipulated and rearranged in the service of human progress.[3] In either case, the radical alienation of humankind from nonhuman nature reaches very deeply into the history of Western culture. It is no less fundamental to the ideology of modern socialist states, with their equally destructive patterns of resource use, than it is to that of the capitalist ones.

In U.S. history the society–environment dichotomy manifested itself in the interlocking myths of the wilderness and the frontier, both of which until very recently were integral to public comprehension of fisheries problems. Before the advent of Western commerce, in this scheme, California was a wilderness: unproductive, unsullied, occupied only by Indians whose "primitive" economies rested only superficially on the land and its resources. Once imposed on the land, the laws of the market were progressive, immutable, and as independent of social and ecological context as the laws of motion. Efforts of Indians, immigrants, or even some public officials to interpose judgments of value, tradition, or equity between market forces and the fisheries were necessarily backward and irrational, if not positively vicious. If civilization inevitably degraded "virgin" resources, there were always new ones to be found and developed. Those already worked over might be restored through applied science or enhanced with new forms of energy. In any event, nature was thoroughly plastic, its capacity to sustain an ever-increasing flow of commodities into the market limited only by the technical facility and political will of human beings.

Linked to the dichotomy between humankind and nature in Western ideology is that between individuals and the societies in which they live.[4] The farmers in Garrett Hardin's "tragedy of the commons" are fundamentally autonomous, self-serving, irresponsible creatures, as radically alienated from each other as they are from the grass on which they feed their cows. The law might theoretically provide what Hardin called the "mutual coercion mutually agreed upon" necessary to force grazers or fishers to conserve their resources, assuming that it had the capacity to articulate and defend community values separate from those of individual market actors.[5] In practice, however, the law and the market do not stand in opposition to one another but rather work in tandem: They are, in J. Willard Hurst's term, "different modes of bargaining among interests."[6] Throughout most of its history, U.S. law worked in service to the private economy to dissolve whatever barriers either the ecology of the resources themselves or the efforts of some fishers to stabilize their relations with the fish might place in the way of sustained expansion. The fundamental autonomy and irresponsibility of market actors, which lay at the core of the fisherman's problem, was an article of constitutional faith, the perceived foundation of liberty and opportunity for harvesters. When they did attempt to curtail fishery use, lawmakers had to depend on the political favor of the industry for whatever power they had to influence the course of events. The fisherman's problem thus reproduced itself in the very structure of policy processes which were supposed to correct it.

Understood within ecological and historical context, the history of California's fisheries˙ has been far more than one of autonomous individuals scrambling over each other to extract wealth from a passive environment. A dynamic, mercurial nature, the behavior of the industry, and the legal processes through which society perceived, analyzed, and intervened in the interaction between fishers and fished evolved together over time, each changing in constant reflection of changes in the other two. The ecology of the fisheries at any point was to a significant extent the product of present and past human impacts on it. Fishers, whether conscious of it or not, worked as members of coherent groups that had ecological characteristics as groups and that evolved over time as groups no less than their resources had evolved over time as species. The law embodied at any point in its history a dynamic tension between the residual memory of past confrontations with resource problems and new problems as they arose. Insofar as society, through its use of legal process as a kind of corporate intelligence and will, conceived of itself as a collection of autonomous individuals engaged in an economic war of all against all and all together against nature, it created both itself and its environment in its own image. Its experience with any particular fishery was necessarily, therefore, nasty, brutish, and short.

How much a break with the past the developments of the 1970s represented was not immediately clear. Part of the change was a function of increased knowledge. Post–World War II biologists, armed with more funds and a more sophisticated understanding of ecology, could demonstrate convincingly that interactions between harvesting and environment were real and significant; social scientists showed that policy decisions had both sources in and consequences for economic behavior. Flexible schemes for tailoring harvesting to random changes in resource productivity entailed the realization that both production and management were embedded in a volatile environment, only imperfectly knowable, rather than standing apart from it to view it from an "objective" distance. A new way of approaching the fisherman's problem dissolved the contradictions that for a century or more had made it seem an insoluble one.

From the 1930s until as late as the 1960s, for example, debate over the sardine fishery centered around the binary question of whether fluctuations in the harvest and the fishery's ultimate collapse had been due to overharvesting or to "environmental" causes. By the 1970s the distinction between the two had collapsed: it was the *interaction* between harvesting and environmental change, not either of the two alone, that explained the fishery's behavior. Some Fish and Game scientists had tried to suggest that this was the case, but they were simply not heard because the terms of public debate on the issue posited a stark dichotomy between the two forces. Successful management, as it turned out, required eliminating that dichotomy: cooperating with each stock's own strategies for survival in its environment rather than assuming its infinite plasticity. Other living things, too, were part of that environment, and their demands on the fisheries became as important as those of the industry in policymaking. As the federal plan for managing the anchovy fishery put it, "the conclusion which arises from these ecological considerations is that benefit to the nation occurs by leaving fish in the ocean."[7] To the utilitarian managers of the 1930s, who believed that "resources must not be permitted to lie in a state of unproductive idleness," such a notion would have seemed absurd.[8]

As important to the changes of the 1970s as better science was the incorporation into law of tectonic changes in public attitudes toward natural resources and the environment – attitudes more frequently expressed in normative rather than technical language. Such expressions had not been absent from fisheries controversies earlier. Livingston Stone had written in terms of value, for example, when he decried as "an inhuman outrage" the impending dispossession of salmon-fishing Indians from the McCloud River. Part of Stone's concern had been the relationship between the Indians and their environment: He knew their removal would expose the Sacramento's last pristine spawning stream to development and thus hasten the decline of the fishery on the river below.[9] Similarly, Fish and Game's lawyer in the 1920s thought it "repugnant to every right-thinking citizen" to see sardines reduced to fishmeal for livestock feed. While the lawyer spoke in normative terms, his chief concern had been not that feeding sardines to livestock was in and of itself unethical, but rather his certainty that the practically unlimited demand for by-products would sooner or later overwhelm state power to preserve the fishery.[10] Alan Longhurst made precisely the same point in 1967 when he described the indiscriminate reduction of Peruvian anchoveta for sale to poultry growers in the industrialized countries as "economically sensible but morally indefensible."[11] Such expressions had real substance to them. They were simply not heard because they did not conform to established categories of debate over natural resource policy, which postulated fundamental distinctions between biological, economic, and social concerns.

The 1970s saw what one legal scholar, in another context, called "a change in social concern, a fundamental alteration in the type of conduct and conditions regarded as 'intolerable' and, consequently, in both the types of social action called for and the chief social institutions called upon."[12] Increased knowledge, to be sure, clarified the issues at stake and helped make the new awareness possible. But ideological changes interacted with scholarship by influencing the ways in which scientists addressed the problems before them and, most importantly, in the effects that science had on the policymaking process. A new understanding of the interplay between social, economic, and ecological processes took two forms in the law, both of them tied to a normative sense of justice or fair play for harvesters and resources alike.

The shift had a procedural as well as a substantive component. FCMA's procedures for determining "optimum yield" from the fisheries included regular participation by many different interest groups, most importantly the harvesters themselves. Environmental impact statements, a new kind of legal instrument, and judicially mandated changes in the scope of public review of administrative decisions enhanced this constitutional change in policymaking for the fisheries. Progressive-Era conservation policy had called for the application of planning and expertise to resource management through the use of centralized legal power. Its implications were profoundly antidemocratic, as Samuel P. Hays has shown.[13] This, and not ignorance and avarice, may have been the reason why turn-of-the-century immigrant fishers resisted so strenuously the encroachment of state power into their own schemes for managing their fisheries. It may also be why Klamath Basin Indians fought, in a manner not unlike the traditional one, for the right to police their salmon fishery in their own way.[14]

Regular multilateral bargaining over policy, certainly in keeping with the New Deal tradition but not brought systematically to the fisheries until FCMA, evinced an awareness that how resources were allocated was as important to their conservation as the substance of the allocations themselves. As an NMFS economist put it,

> I don't think decisionmakers are much influenced by efficiency issues in general, and for good reason. . . . what they have to do is keep the various groups in society off each other's necks, keep people feeling that there is some fairness in the system so that they don't become obstructionists.[15]

A Canadian official likewise found scientific fishery management a much easier task when "government personnel approach fishermen with a philosophy that the latter care for their resource" and "present data in a format understandable to the layman . . . 'come clean' and admit a lack of knowledge where appropriate."[16] To his own experience he added that of California as proof, noting that scientists and policymakers there had begun to do all those things during the 1970s, and with much better results than they had previously enjoyed.

Social concern for fair play had a substantive aspect as well, which surfaced in the hesitant recognition in law that endangered species and endangered cultures had rights to self-preservation that entailed preferential access to some fisheries, market costs and benefits notwithstanding. U.S. law has traditionally conceived of "rights" in terms of alienation between people: The function of property rights, especially, has been to draw "zones of privacy" around individuals, to maximize their individual freedom to use resources to their own advantage, and to limit the reach of community power in their lives.[17] As long as the continent's resources remained abundant – as John Locke put it, "at least where there is enough, and as good left in common for others" – privatism in resource use promoted both the dignity of individuals and the progress of society.[18] But as development drew taut the ecological, economic, and social links between individuals, it began to prove destructive of both.

It is also possible to see in the recognition of legal rights a sense of interdependence; an awareness that the well-being of the rights-holder is important to the welfare of the community as a whole. It is an expression of what Roberto Mangabeira Unger called "solidarity": "our feeling of responsibility for those whose lives touch in some way upon our own and our greater or lesser willingness to share their fate."[19] Native peoples thus "bargained" with their salmon because they knew that their communities' well-being depended on their treating their resources with respect and forbearance. U.S. citizens recognized rights in pelicans and marine mammals, likewise, because they realized that something had been terribly wrong with their traditional exposure of living resources to unrestrained manipulation in the service of economic and political profit. Justice for endangered species was entwined with justice for resource users: The fisherman's problem consists as much of people stealing from each other as it does of people stealing collectively from nature.

The history of California's fisheries, a laboratory example of the fisherman's problem in all its complexity, suggests that the interdependence between ecological, economic, and social processes – between environment and society – is inexorable. "The destinies of the two," as Justice Harlan wrote with regard to black and white people, "are indissolubly linked together."[20] Forsaking domination over nature for solidarity with it need not entail the exchange by humanity of reason for animism or industrialism for a hunting-gathering economy. It only means learning to care for other living things, which is at once the special talent and the special responsibility of the species.

Appendixes

APPENDIX A

Record of climate, Sacramento and San Diego, 1853–1980

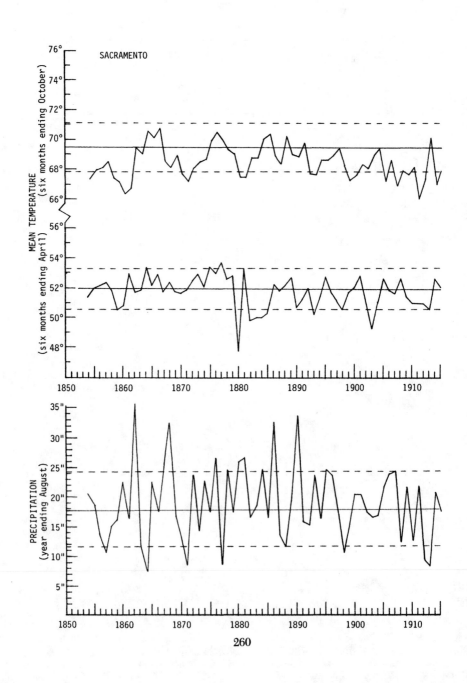

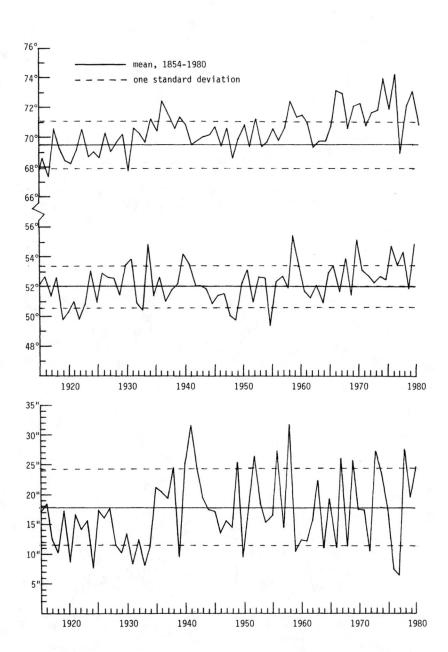

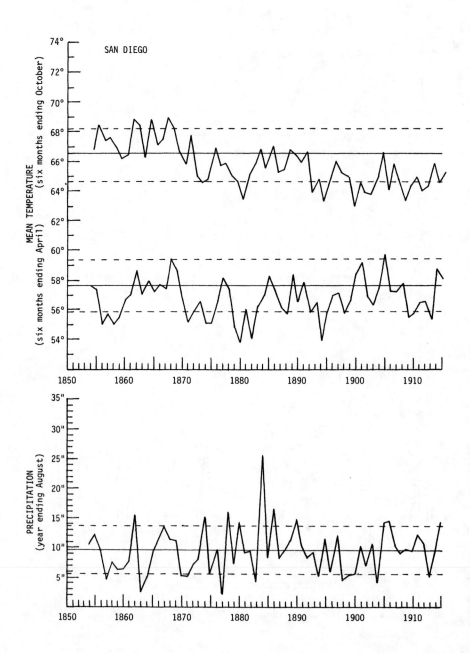

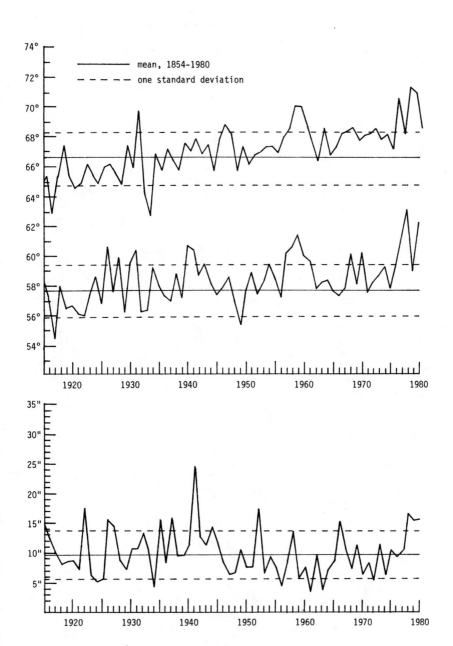

APPENDIX B

Standing crops of coastal schooling fishes, 1800–1970

Year	Pacific sardine	Northern anchovy	Ratio[a]	Pacific mackerel	Total[b]
1800	326	3,598	0.09	96	14,319
1805	326	3,034	0.10	96	12,280
1810	326	5,068	0.06	24	11,389
1815	2,054	4,909	0.41	24	15,238
1820	2,151	5,666	0.37	24	15,328
1825	3,082	5,197	0.59	24	12,672
1830	1,704	7,574	0.22	24	12,829
1835	3,975	8,993	0.44	60	21,980
1840	2,823	7,471	0.37	60	18,547
1845	3,264	5,406	0.60	24	17,039
1850	5,798	5,234	1.10	24	19,282
1855	3,944	4,742	0.83	42	15,806
1860	11,093	4,119	2.69	24	23,994
1865	6,502	4,213	1.54	24	17,731
1870	1,464	3,426	0.42	24	11,439
1875	909	8,428	0.10	60	20,829
1880	500	7,714	0.06	24	12,563
1885	1,148	7,205	0.15	33	12,686
1890	1,850	6,668	0.27	24	24,268
1895	6,504	5,873	1.10	51	28,483
1900	9,177	5,475	1.67	33	29,485
1905	3,882	5,044	0.77	33	28,817
1910	1,738	2,770	0.63	42	16,275
1915	2,444	2,598	0.94	60	17,177
1920	5,055	3,690	1.36	24	19,084
1925	6,226	4,378	1.42	60	17,029
1930	5,300	1,803	2.94	150	10,935
1935	2,900	705	4.11	132	8,113
1940	2,532	1,477	1.71	105	8,748
1945	679	1,862	0.36	114	8,107
1950	765	1,208	0.63	51	7,234
1955	732	986	0.74	69	4,587
1960	326	2,168	0.15	33	5,202
1965	553	4,755	0.12	24	6,349
1970	326	2,797	0.12	24	9,207
Mean	2,736	4,466	0.61	50	15,003

Note: Crops are given in thousands of metric tons.
[a] Sardine : anchovy.
[b] Includes Pacific saury and Pacific hake.
Source: Smith, "Biological Effects of Ocean Variability," p. 124.

Notes

In addition to giving the inclusive page range for a given article, the specific page on which a quotation appears is included (e.g., 295–394, p. 307).

Chapter 1

1. Frederick Engels, "The Part Played by Labor in the Transition from Ape to Man," in *The Origin of the Family, Private Property, and the State*, ed. Eleanor Burke Leacock (New York: International Publishers, 1972), p. 261.

2. On the ecology of California nearshore waters, see George A. Rounsefell, *Ecology, Utilization, and Management of Marine Fisheries* (St. Louis: C. V. Mosby., 1975), pp. 32–9; and K. H. Mann, *Ecology of Coastal Waters: A Systems Approach*, Studies in Ecology 8 (Berkeley and Los Angeles: University of California Press, 1982). A standard text for ecological science is Eugene P. Odum, *Fundamentals of Ecology*, 3rd ed. (Philadelphia: W. B. Saunders, 1971); perhaps more useful for the lay reader is Odum, *Ecology: The Link Between the Natural and the Social Sciences*, 2nd ed. Modern Biology Series (New York: Holt, Rinehart, and Winston, 1975). Another useful survey that focuses on current environmental problems is Paul R. Ehrlich and Anne H. Ehrlich, *Ecoscience: Population, Resources, and Environment* (San Francisco: W. H. Freeman, 1977). An indispensable guide to the economic theory of conservation is S. V. Ciriacy-Wantrup, *Resource Conservation: Economics and Policies*, 3rd ed. (Berkeley: University of California Division of Agricultural Sciences, Agricultural Experiment Station, 1968); see also Arnold M. Schultz, "The Ecosystem as a Conceptual Tool in the Management of Natural Resources," in *Natural Resources: Quality and Quantity: Papers Presented Before a Faculty Seminar at the University of California, Berkeley, 1961–1965* (Berkeley: University of California Press, 1967).

3. Useful guides to California ecology generally include Elna Bakker, *An Island Called California: An Ecological Introduction to Its Natural Communities* (Berkeley and Los Angeles: University of California Press, 1971); and William Kahrl, ed., *The California Water Atlas* (Sacramento: California State Government, 1978). On estuaries and tidelands, see Edward F. Ricketts and Jack Calvin, *Between Pacific Tides*, 4th ed., rev. Joel W. Hedgpeth (Stanford: Stanford University Press, 1968); Thomas

266 — Notes to pp. 5–7

Carefoot, *Pacific Seashores: A Guide to Intertidal Ecology* (Seattle: University of Washington Press, 1977); John Teal and Mildred Teal, *Life and Death of the Salt Marsh* (Boston: Little, Brown, 1969); Michael Josselyn, ed., *Wetland Restoration and Enhancement in California*, California Sea Grant College Program Report No. T-CSGCP–007 (La Jolla: California Sea Grant College Program, 1982); and H. Thomas Harvey, "Some Ecological Aspects of San Francisco Bay," San Francisco Bay Conservation and Development Commission, *Miscellaneous Papers*, 3 (1966).

4   J. C. Fremont, *Report of the Exploring Expedition to the Rocky Mountains in the Year 1842, and to Oregon and North California in the Years 1843–1844* (1845; repr. Readex Microprint, 1966), pp. 242–9.

5   A basic text for fisheries problems is Francis T. Christy, Jr., and Anthony Scott, *The Common Wealth in Ocean Fisheries: Some Problems of Growth and Economic Allocation*, Resources for the Future (Baltimore: John Hopkins University Press, 1965). See also William F. Royce, *Introduction to the Fishery Sciences* (New York: Academic Press, 1972), pp. 332–6; J. A. Gulland, *The Management of Marine Fisheries* (Seattle: University of Washington Press, 1974); S. V. Ciriacy-Wantrup, *Resource Conservation*, pp. 141–2; John Radovich, "Managing Pelagic Schooling Prey Species," in *Predator–Prey Systems in Fisheries Management*, ed. Henry Clepper (Washington: Sport Fishing Institute, 1979), pp. 366–9.

6   Christy and Scott, *Common Wealth in Ocean Fisheries*, pp. 79–86; Royce, *Introduction to the Fishery Sciences*, pp. 242–52, 322–7. On the sustained-yield theory, see Milner B. Schaefer, "Some Aspects of the Dynamics of Populations Important to the Management of the Commercial Marine Fisheries," IATTC, *Bulletin*, 1 (1954): 26–56; P. A. Larkin, "An Epitaph for the Concept of Maximum Sustained Yield," American Fisheries Society, *Transactions*, 106 (1977): 1–11; Hugh M. Raup, "Some Problems in Ecological Theory and Their Relation to Conservation," *Journal of Ecology*, 52 (Supp., 1964): 19–28. Overviews of the development of fishery management theory may be found in Larry A. Nielsen, "The Evolution of Fisheries Management Philosophy," *Marine Fisheries Review*, 38 (December 1976): 15–23; J. L. McHugh, "Trends in Fishery Research," in *A Century of Fisheries in North America*, ed. Norman G. Benson, American Fisheries Society Special Publication 7 (Washington: American Fisheries Society, 1970), pp. 25–56; D. H. Cushing, "A Link Between Science and Management in Fisheries," NMFS, *Fishery Bulletin*, 72 (1974): 859–64; Cushing, *Fisheries Resources of the Sea and Their Management* (Oxford: Oxford University Press, 1975); and Arthur F. McEvoy "Scientific Research and the Twentieth-Century Fishing Industry," *CalCOFI Reports*, 22 (1982): 48–55. See also Larkin, "Fisheries Management – An Essay for Ecologists," *Annual Review of Ecology and Systematics*, 9 (1978): 57–73.

7   Christy and Scott, *Common Wealth in Ocean Fisheries*, pp. 154–6; Nielsen, "Evolution of Fisheries Management Philosophy," pp. 15–7; H. Gary Knight, *Managing the Sea's Living Resources: Legal and Political Aspects of High Seas Fisheries*, Studies in Marine Affairs (Lexington, MA: D. C. Heath, 1977), ch. 3.

8   One of the best introductions to the intellectual theory of laissez-faire is Sidney Fine, *Laissez-Faire and the General-Welfare State: A Study of Conflict in American Thought, 1865–1901* (Ann Arbor: University of Michigan Press, 1956). Carolyn Merchant offers an excellent analysis of the presumed passivity of nature in modern Western thought in *The Death of Nature: Women, Ecology, and Scientific Revolution* (San Francisco: Harper & Row, 1980).

9   On "critical zones" and "safe minimum standards of conservation," see Ciriacy-Wantrup, *Resource Conservation*, pp. 38–40, 251–70. With respect to coastal pelagic schooling fishes, see Paul E. Smith, "Biological Effects of Ocean Variability: Time

and Space Scales of Biological Response," *Rapports et Proces-Verbaux des Réunions, Conseil International pour l'Exploration de la Mer (Denmark)*, 173 (1978): 117–27.

10 Smith, "Year-Class Strength and Survival of O-Group Clupeoids," *Canadian Journal of Fisheries and Aquatic Sciences*, 42 (1985): 69–82.

11 Henry R. Wagner, "Spanish Voyages to the Northwest Coast in the Sixteenth Century, Chapter XI – Father Antonio de la Ascencion's Account of Vizcaino's Voyage," *California Historical Society Quarterly*, 7 (1928): 295–394, p. 307; *Sacramento Union*, 6 June 1858.

12 Daniel R. Cayan, "Regimes and Events in Recent Climatic Variables," *CalCOFI Reports*, 21 (1980): 90–101, p. 94; Mark A. Cane, "Oceanographic Events During El Niño," *Science*, 222 (16 December 1983): 1,189–95; Eugene M. Rasmusson and John M. Wallace, "Meteorological Aspects of the El Niño/Southern Oscillation," *Science*, 222 (16 December 1983): 1,193–202; Richard T. Barber and Francisco P. Chavez, "Biological Consequences of El Niño," *Science*, 222 (16 December 1983): 1203–10. See also Sargun A. Tont and Damon A. Delistraty, "The Effects of Climate on Terrestrial and Marine Populations," *CalCOFI Reports*, 21 (1980): 85–9.

13 Carl L. Hubbs, "Changes in Fish Fauna of Western North America Correlated with Changes in Ocean Temperature," *Journal of Marine Research*, 7 (1948): 459–82, 468–9. On the historiography of climate, see Robert I. Rotberg and Theodore K. Rabb, eds., *Climate and History*, Studies in Interdisciplinary History (Princeton: Princeton University Press, 1981); and Emmanuel LeRoy Ladurie, *Times of Feast, Times of Famine: A History of Climate Since the Year 1000*, trans. Barbara Bray (Garden City, NY: Doubleday, 1971).

14 Smith, "Biological Effects of Ocean Variability," *passim.*; Andrew Soutar and John D. Isaacs, "History of Fish Populations Inferred from Fish Scales in Anaerobic Sediments off California, *CalCOFI Reports*, 13 (1969): 63–70; Soutar and Isaacs, "Abundance of Pelagic Fish During the 19th and 20th Centuries as Recorded in Anaerobic Sediment off the Californias," NMFS, *Fishery Bulletin*, 72 (1974): 257–73.

15 Smith, "Biological Effects of Ocean Variability," p. 126.

16 R. H. Coase, "The Problem of Social Cost," *Journal of Law and Economics*, 3 (1960): 1–44. See also Steven N. S. Cheung, "The Structure of a Contract and the Theory of a Non-Exclusive Resource," *Journal of Law and Economics*, 13 (1970); Ronald W. Johnson and Gary W. Libecap, "Contracting Problems and Regulation: The Case of the Fishery," *American Economic Review*, 72 (1982): 1,005–22; and Richard A. Posner, *The Economics of Justice* (Cambridge, MA: Harvard University Press, 1983), pp. 4–5.

17 A. C. Pigou, *The Economics of Welfare*, 4th ed. (London: Macmillan, 1934), pp. 29–30; Richard A. Musgrave, *The Theory of Public Finance: A Study in Public Economy* (New York: McGraw-Hill, 1959), pp. 6–9; Robert B. Haveman, "Efficiency and Equity in Natural Resource and Environmental Policy," *American Journal of Agricultural Economics*, 55 (1973): 868–78.

18 H. Scott Gordon, "The Economic Theory of a Common-Property Resource: The Fishery," *Journal of Political Economy*, 62 (1954): 124–42, p. 136.

19 Ibid., pp. 128–32. On the economics of fisheries management, especially with regard to so-called limited-entry regimes, see Anthony Scott, "The Fishery: The Objectives of Sole Ownership," *Journal of Political Economy*, 63 (1955): 116–24; Ralph Turvey, "Optimization and Suboptimization in Fishery Regulation," *American Economic Review*, 54 (1964): 64–76; Vernon L. Smith, "On Models of Commercial Fishing," *Journal of Political Economy*, 77 (1969): 181–98; James A. Crutchfield and Giulio Pontecorvo, *The Pacific Salmon Fisheries: A Study of Irrational Conservation*,

Resources for the Future (Baltimore: Johns Hopkins University Press, 1969); Ciriacy-Wantrup, "The Economics of Environmental Policy," *Land Economics*, 47 (1971): 37–45.
20   Gordon, "Economic Theory of a Common Property Resource," p. 135.
21   Ibid., p. 124.
22   Garrett Hardin, "The Tragedy of the Commons," *Science*, 162 (13 December 1968): 1,243–8; cf. Ciriacy-Wantrup, "Economics of Environmental Policy," pp. 42–5.
23   Hardin, "Tragedy of the Commons," p. 1,247; see Hardin, "Living on a Life-boat," *BioScience*, 24 (1974): 561–8. For a critique of Hardin's formulation of the population problem, see Barry Commoner, *The Closing Circle: Nature, Man & Technology* (New York: Alfred A. Knopf, 1971), pp. 295–6. cf. Harold Demsetz, "Toward a Theory of Property Rights," *American Economic Review*, 57 (Papers and Proceedings, 1967): 347–57.
24   Gordon, "Economic Theory of a Common-Property Resource," p. 136.
25   J. R. Gould, "Extinction of A Fishery by Commercial Exploitation: A Note," *Journal of Political Economy*, 80 (1972): 1,031–9; Frank T. Bachmura, "The Economics of Vanishing Species," *Natural Resources Journal*, 11 (1971): 674–92; Colin W. Clark, "Profit Maximization and the Extinction of Animal Species," *Journal of Political Economy*, 81 (1973): 950–61; Clark, "The Economics of Overexploitation," *Science*, 181 (17 August 1973): 630–4. The joke is Joel Mokyr's.
26   Ciriacy-Wantrup, "Soil Conservation in European Farm Management," *Journal of Farm Economics*, 20 (1938): 86–106; Ciriacy-Wantrup, "Economics of Environmental Policy," pp. 43–4; Ciriacy-Wantrup and Richard C. Bishop, " 'Common Property' as a Concept in Natural Resources Policy," *Natural Resources Journal*, 15 (1975): 713–28; Julian C. Juergensmeyer and James B. Wadley, "The Common Lands Concept: A 'Commons' Solution to a Common Environmental Problem," *Natural Resources Journal*, 14 (1974): 361–81. Cf. Joseph L. Sax, "The Public Trust Doctrine in Natural Resource Law: Effective Judicial Intervention," *Michigan Law Review*, 68 (1970): 471–566.
27   Mildred Dickeman, "Demographic Consequences of Infanticide in Man," *Annual Review of Ecology and Systematics*, 6 (1975): 107–37, p. 133. For a review of the literature on hunter-gatherer societies, see Eugene S. Hunn and Nancy Williams, "Introduction," in *Resource Managers: North American and Australian Hunter-Gatherers*, eds. Nancy M. Williams and Eugene S. Hunn, AAAS Selected Symposium 67 (Boulder, CO: Westview Press, 1982), pp. 1–16.
28   Ciriacy-Wantrup, "Economics of Environmental Policy," pp. 40–1.
29   Hurst's work has been of inestimable importance in influencing not only this book but an entire generation of studies on the role of law in the economy. See his *Law and Markets in United States History: Different Modes of Bargaining Among Interests* (Madison: University of Wisconsin Press, 1982); *Law and Social Order in the United States* (Ithaca, NY: Cornell University Press, 1977); *Law and the Conditions of Freedom in the Nineteenth Century United States* (Madison: University of Wisconsin Press, 1956); and *Law and Economic Growth: The Legal History of the Lumber Industry in Wisconsin, 1836–1915* (Cambridge, MA: Harvard University Press, Belknap Press, 1964). Useful reviews of Hurst's work may be found in Robert W. Gordon, "Introduction: J. Willard Hurst and the Common Law Tradition in American Legal Historiography," *Law and Society Review*, 10 (1975): 9–56; Harry N. Scheiber, "At the Borderland of Law and Economic History: The Contributions of Willard Hurst," *American Historical Review*, 75 (1970): 744–56; and Scheiber, "Public Economic Policy and the American Legal System: Historical Perspectives,"

Wisconsin Law Review (1980): 1,159–90. A basic text for U.S. legal history is Lawrence M. Friedman, *A History of American Law*, 2nd ed. (New York: Simon & Schuster, 1985).

30 Clifford Geertz, *The Interpretation of Cultures: Selected Essays* (New York: Basic Books, 1973), p. 35.

31 Ibid., p. 363. See generally Geertz, "The Impact of the Concept of Culture on the Concept of Man," in ibid., pp. 33–54.

32 William Cronon discusses the role of legal ideology in transforming the ecology of a particular region in his excellent study, *Changes in the Land: Indians, Colonists, and the Ecology of New England* (New York: Hill & Wang, 1983), pp. 58–79. See also Karl Polanyi, *The Great Transformation: The Political and Economic Origins of Our Time* (Boston: Beacon Press, 1944); and Laurence H. Tribe, "Ways Not to Think About Plastic Trees: New Foundations for Environmental Law," *Yale Law Journal*, 83 (1974): 1,315–48. On the intellectual history of nature, see Merchant, *The Death of Nature*, supra, note 8; Roderick Nash, *Wilderness and the American Mind*, rev. ed. (New Haven: Yale University Press, 1973); Donald Worster, *Nature's Economy: The Roots of Ecology* (San Francisco: Sierra Club Books, 1977); Keith Thomas, *Man and the Natural World: A History of the Modern Sensibility* (New York: Pantheon, 1983); and Clarence J. Glacken, *Traces on the Rhodian Shore: Nature and Culture in Western Thought from Ancient Times to the End of the Eighteenth Century* (Berkeley and Los Angeles: University of California Press, 1967).

33 Hurst, "Legal Elements in United States History," *Perspectives in American History*, 5 (1971): 3–92, p. 5.

34 Max Weber, *Economy and Society: An Outline of Interpretive Sociology*, eds. Guenther Roth and Claus Wittich (Berkeley and Los Angeles: University of California Press, 1978), v. I, pp. 212–16. Legal scholars have recently begun to analyze the forms and processes of law in terms of the ideologies and world views underlying them. The so-called critical legal studies movement undertakes the theoretical study of law as doctrine, in an effort to analyze the hegemonic function of legal language, symbolism, and process, that is, the ways in which law both reflects and reinforces particular ways of understanding life in the world and the relationships between those patterns of understanding and particular modes of social organization. Useful introductions to this method of legal study may be found in David Kairys, ed., *The Politics of Law: A Progressive Critique* (New York: Pantheon, 1982); a good theoretical introduction is that of Roberto Mangabeira Unger, "The Critical Legal Studies Movement," *Harvard Law Review*, 96 (1983): 563–675. See also Mark Tushnet, "Post-Realist Legal Scholarship," *Wisconsin Law Review* (1980 vol.): 1,383–402; Alan Hunt, "The Ideology of the Law: Advances and Problems in Recent Applications of the Concept of Ideology to the Analysis of Law," *Law and Society Review*, 19 (1985): 11–38; Robert W. Gordon, "Historicism in Legal Scholarship," *Yale Law Journal*, 90 (1981): 1,017–56; and Geertz, "Ideology as a Cultural System," in *The Interpretation of Cultures*, pp. 193–233.

35 See Calvin Woodard, "Reality and Social Reform: The Transition from Laissez-Faire to the Welfare State," *Yale Law Journal*, 72 (1962): 286–328.

36 Larkin, "Fisheries Management – An Essay for Ecologists," p. 57; Richard A. Walker, "Wetland Preservation and Management on Chesapeake Bay: The Role of Science in Natural Resource Policy," *Coastal Zone Management Journal*, 1 (1973): 75–101, pp. 92–9. See also Richard Walker and Michael Storper, "Erosion of the Clean Air Act of 1970: A Study in the Failure of Government Regulation and Planning," *Boston College Environmental Affairs Law Review*, 7 (1978): 189–275, pp. 252–5.

37 Crutchfield, "Economic and Political Objectives in Fishery Management," *American Fisheries Society, Transactions,* 102 (1973): 481–91, p. 481.
38 See William H. Durham, "The Adaptive Significance of Cultural Behavior," *Human Ecology,* 4 (1976): 89–121; F. T. Cloak, Jr., "Is A Cultural Ethology Possible?" *Human Ecology,* 3 (1975): 161–82; Ramon Margalef, *Perspectives in Ecological Theory* (Chicago: University of Chicago Press, 1968); Richard N. Adams, *Paradoxical Harvest: Energy and Explanation in British History, 1870–1914,* Arnold and Caroline Rose Monograph Series of the American Sociological Association (Cambridge: Cambridge University Press, 1982), pp. 1, 115–26. E. L. Jones offered a fascinating account of the interaction between European culture and environment in *The European Miracle: Environments, Economies, and Geopolitics in the History of Europe and Asia* (Cambridge: Cambridge University Press, 1981).
39 Woodard, "Reality and Social Reform," pp. 286–7.

Chapter 2

1 Walter R. Goldschmidt, "Nomlaki Ethnography," *UC-PAAE,* 42 (1951): 303–443, p. 348.
2 The population of California Indians before contact with Westerners has been a matter of some controversy. The estimates of Sherburne F. Cook are generally accepted as definitive. Cook, *The Population of the California Indians, 1768–1970* (Berkeley and Los Angeles: University of California Press, 1976). Cook reviewed the methods and findings of earlier demographers in "Historical Demography," in *Handbook of North Amercian Indians,* v. 8: *California,* ed. Robert F. Heizer (Washington, DC: Smithsonian Institution, 1978), pp. 91–8. On the cultural diversity of the region see William F. Shipley, "Native Languages in California," ibid., pp. 80–90, and Joseph G. Jorgensen, *Western Indians: Comparative Environments, Languages, and Cultures of 172 Western American Indian Tribes* (San Francisco: W. H. Freeman, 1980), pp. 360–1. A standard, but dated, reference to California Indians is Alfred L. Kroeber, *Handbook of the Indians of California,* Smithsonian Institution Bureau of American Ethnology, Bulletin 78 (Washington, DC: GPO, 1925; repr. New York: Dover Publications, 1976). See also Harold E. Driver, *Indians of North America,* 2nd ed., rev. (Chicago: University of Chicago Press, 1969).
3 Charles A. Simenstad, James A. Estes, and Karl W. Kenyon, "Aleuts, Sea Otters, and Alternate Stable-State Communities," *Science,* 200 (28 April 1978): 403–11; Clement W. Meighan, "The Little Harbor Site, Catalina Island: An Example of Ecological Interpretation in Archaeology," *American Antiquity,* 24 (1959): 383–405, pp. 402–3; Louis James Tartaglia, "Prehistoric Maritime Adaptations in Southern California" (Ph.D. diss., University of California at Los Angeles, 1976), pp. 123–8.
4 Frederick Noble Hicks, "Ecological Aspects of Aboriginal Culture in the Western Yuman Area" (Ph.D. diss., University of California at Los Angeles, 1963), pp. 42, 143–6.
5 Anthropologists are divided on the question of relationships between American Indian culture and ecology. So-called "formalist" scholars posit a preeminently rational, "economic" human nature independent of time, place, and culture. Limitations in demand and technology, then, must account for observed instances of restraint among such people. A corollary view is that the forms that Indian cultures took in particular places had little to do with organizing their husbandry of resources, that is, that culture does not carry ecological information. In general, such scholars posit dichotomies between the economic behavior, cultural traits, and resource endowments of different groups. See, for example, Joseph G. Jorgensen, *Western Indians*:

Comparative Environments, Languages and Cultures of 172 Western American Indian Tribes (San Francisco: W. H. Freeman, 1980), pp. 98–100, 130. "Substantivist" anthropologists, on the other hand, maintain that economic behavior is embedded in and controlled by a society's culture. Cultural behavior, then, facilitated a people's successful or unsuccessful adaptation to particular habitats. See, for example, Lowell John Bean and Harry Lawton, "Some Explanations for the Rise of Cultural Complexity in Native California with Comments on Proto-Agriculture and Agriculture," in *Native Californians: A Theoretical Perspective*, eds. Lowell John Bean and Thomas C. Blackburn (Ramona, CA: Ballena Press, 1976), pp. 19–48. Jonathan Friedman criticized some of the more outlandish claims of substantivist studies in "Marxism, Structuralism, and Vulgar Materialism," *Man*, 9 (1974): 444–69. For an economist's analysis of Indian groups' disinclination to behave in "normal," utility-maximizing ways, see E. E. Rich, "Trade Habits and Economic Motivation Among the Indians of North America," *Canadian Journal of Economics and Political Science*, 26 (1960): 35–53. An outstanding example of historical research on Indians from a substantivist perspective is Richard White, *The Roots of Dependency: Subsistence, Environment, and Social Change among the Choctaws, Pawnees, and Navajos* (Lincoln: University of Nebraska Press, 1983). A modern study of Cree Indians who fish with traditional tools on James Bay in northern Canada found that those people had a measurable ecological impact on their environment, and that they avoided depleting their fisheries by maintaining a "high degree of order" in their work: "social practices regulating the fishing intensity, locations, and minimum mesh sizes control against the overfishing of stocks." [Fikret Berkes, "Fishery Resource Use in a Sub-Arctic Indian Community," *Human Ecology*, 5 (1977): 289–307, pp. 305–6.]

6 A. L. Kroeber and Samual A. Barrett, "Fishing Among the Indians of Northwestern California," *UCAR*, 21 (1960): 1–210, pp. 8, 10, 26; Thomas T. Waterman and Kroeber, "The Kepel Fish Dam," *UC-PAAE*, 35 (1938): 49–80; Martin A. Baumhoff, "Ecological Determinants of Aboriginal California Populations," *UC-PAAE*, 49 (1963): 155–236, p. 170.

7 USFWS, "Final Environmental Impact Statement on the Management of River Flows to Mitigate the Loss of the Anadromous Fishery of the Trinity River, California," INT/FES 80–52 (Sacramento: USFWS, 1980), p. C7–2; USDI, BIA, "Environmental Impact Statement for a Proposal to Modify the Indian Fishing Regulations to Authorize Commercial Harvesting of Anadromous Fish," DES 85–21 (Hoopa Valley Indian Reservation, California: BIA, 1985), p. 2, citing D. R. Hoptoit, "Klamath-Trinity Salmon Restoration Project – Final Report" (Sacramento: California Resources Agency, 1980), p. 13; Gordon W. Hewes, "Aboriginal Use of Fishery Resources in Northwestern North America" (Ph.D. diss., University of California at Berkeley, 1947), p. 228. For modern harvests, see John O. Snyder, "Salmon of the Klamath River, California," CDFG, *Fish Bulletin No. 34* (1931), p. 87; and John N. Cobb, "Pacific Salmon Fisheries," USBF Document No. 1092, USBF *Report* (1930): 570–2.

8 Kroeber, *Handbook of the Indians of California*, pp. 899–900; Hewes, "Aboriginal Use of Fishery Resources, pp. 53–4; Kroeber and Barrett, "Fishing Among the Indians of Northwestern California," pp. 7, 89, 116; Tartaglia, "Prehistoric Maritime Adaptations in Southern California," p. 143.

9 Kroeber and Barrett, "Fishing Among the Indians of Northwestern California," p. 111; Robert E. Greengo, "Shellfish Foods of the California Indians," *Kroeber Anthropological Society Papers*, 7 (1952): 63–114, pp. 64–5.

10 Tartaglia, "Prehistoric Maritime Adaptations in Southern California," p. 133; Willis G. Hewatt, "Ecological Succession in the *Mytilus californianus* Habitat, as

Observed in Monterey Bay, California," *Ecology*, 16 (1935): 244–51, p. 250; Edward F. Ricketts and Jack Calvin, *Between Pacific Tides*, 4th ed., rev. Joel W. Hedgpeth (Stanford: Stanford University Press, 1968), pp. 391–8; Wolfgang Berger, "Seasonality of Mollusk Collecting at a N. W. Baja California Midden Site Determined by O–18 Measurements," photocopied (La Jolla: Scripps Institution of Oceanography, n.d.).

11   Baumhoff, "Environmental Background," in *Handbook of North American Indians*, v. 8: *California*, pp. 16–24, pp. 16–17; Tartaglia, "Prehistoric Maritime Adaptations in Southern California," pp. 180–1.

12   Kroeber and Barrett, "Fishing Among the Indians of Northwestern California," pp. 115–16; Hewes, "Aboriginal Use of Fishery Resources," p. 70. On the role of sea otters in nearshore marine ecology, see Ricketts and Calvin, *Between Pacific Tides*, pp. 89–90; Herbert W. Frey, ed., *California's Living Marine Resources and Their Utilization* (Sacramento: CDFG, 1971), pp. 6, 114–16; Simenstad, Estes, and Kenyon, "Aleuts, Sea Otters, and Alternate Stable-State Communities," pp. 403–4; Estes and John F. Palmisano, "Sea Otters: Their Role in Structuring Nearshore Communities," *Science*, 185 (20 September 1974); 1,058–60.

13   Campbell Grant, "Eastern Coastal Chumash," in *Handbook of North American Indians*, v. 8: *California*, pp. 509–19, p. 517; Kroeber and Barrett, "Fishing Among the Indians of Northwestern California," pp. 123–5.

14   Kroeber, *Handbook of the Indians of California*, p. 913; Kroeber, "Culture Element Distributions, III: Area and Climax," *UC-PAAE*, 37 (1936): 101–16, pp. 106, 110–11.

15   Jorgensen, *Western Indians*, p. 87.

16   Kroeber, *Handbook of the Indians of California*, pp. 1–8, 364, 903–13; Kroeber, "Culture Element Distributions, III," pp. 105, 110. See generally Kroeber and Edward L. Gifford, "World-Renewal: A Cult System of Native Northwest California," *UCAR*, 13 (1949): 1–156.

17   Robert F. Heizer, "Natural Forces and Native World View," in *Handbook of North American Indians*, v. 8: *California*, pp. 649–53, p. 649; Heizer, "Trade and Trails," ibid., pp. 690–4, p. 690–1; Richard A. Gould, "To Have and Have Not: The Ecology of Sharing Among Hunter-Gatherers," in *Resource Managers: North American and Australian Hunter-Gatherers*, eds. Nancy M. Williams and Eugene S. Hunn, AAAS Symposium No. 67 (Boulder, CO: Westview Press, 1982), pp. 69–92, p. 75; Cora A. DuBois, "The Wealth Concept as an Integrative Factor in Tolowa-Tututni Culture," in *Essays in Anthropology*, ed. R. H. Lowie (Berkeley: University of California Press, 1936), pp. 49–65, pp. 50–1. On the role of environment in culture, see *supra*, ch. 2, note 5. R. A. Gould relied on what he called the "principle of negative determinism," a conservative enough stance that will suffice here: " . . . certain key ecological requirements must be met by every cultural system. Failure to meet these basic requirements will lead to failure or change in the cultural system. The ecological requirements in question do not necessarily determine the specific characteristics of the cultural response . . . but they do limit the options open to people in any given habitat and they do mean that prolonged lack of cultural conformity to these requirements will not occur." (Gould, "Ecology and Adaptive Response Among the Tolowa Indians of Northwestern California," in *Native Californians: A Theoretical Perspective*, pp. 49–78, p. 53.)

18   Jorgensen, *Western Indians*, pp. 60–1, 92–3; Kroeber, *Handbook of the Indians of California*, pp. 41, 915–17; Kroeber, "Culture Element Distributions, III," p. 105; Baumhoff, "Environmental Background," pp. 20–1.

19   Cook, *Population of California Indians*, p. 8; Kroeber, *Handbook of the Indians of California*, p. 351.
20   Hewes, "Indian Fisheries Productivity," pp. 137–8; Hewes, "Aboriginal Use of Fishery Resources, pp. 214–24.
21   Kroeber, *Handbook of the Indians of California*, p. 550; Hewes, "Aboriginal Use of Fishery Resources," p. 70.
22   Lowell J. Bean and Charles R. Smith, "Gabrielino," in *Handbook of North American Indians*, v. 8: *California*, pp. 538–49, p. 538.
23   Bean and Lawton, "Some Explanations for the Rise of Cultural Complexity in Native California," pp. 29–35. See generally Eugene S. Hunn and Nancy Williams, "Introduction," in *Resource Managers*, eds. Hunn and Williams, pp. 1–14.
24   Henry Lewis, "Fire Technology and Resource Development in Aboriginal North America," in *Resource Managers*, eds. Hunn and Williams pp. 45–68, pp. 46, 55–8; Lewis, "Patterns of Burning in California: Ecology and Ethnohistory," *Ballena Press Anthropological Papers*, 1 (Ramona, CA: Ballena Press, 1973).
25   Baumhoff, "Ecological Determinants of Aboriginal California Populations," pp. 221–4.
26   Eugene S. Hunn, "Mobility as a Factor Limiting Resource Use in the Columbia Plateau of North America, in *Resource Managers*, eds. Hunn and Williams, pp. 17–44, pp. 18–20.
27   Gould, "To Have and Have Not," p. 74.
28   Hunn, "Mobility as a Factor in Limiting Resource Use," *passim.*
29   Grant, "Eastern Coastal Chumash," p. 517; Tartaglia, "Prehistoric Maritime Adaptations in Southern California," pp. 123, 180.
30   Bean and Lawton, "Some Explanations for the Rise of Cultural Complexity," pp. 45–8; Heizer, "Prehistoric Central California: A Problem in Historical-Developmental Classification," *UC-ASR*, 41 (1958): 19–26, pp. 20–1. Ester Boserup reasoned that a shift to more intensive agricultural production is more likely to raise labor costs with respect to output than it is to lower them. Technological progress in food production comes about when increasing population demands higher gross output and provides the added labor to produce it under a new technological regime. Other changes associated with increased population density, such as lowered information costs or division of labor, can bring about increases in labor productivity, but intensifying food production per se will decrease it. Ester Boserup, *The Conditions of Agricultural Growth: The Economics of Agrarian Change under Population Pressure* (Chicago: Aldine Press, 1965), pp. 117–18. Boserup makes the point that people typically have a large repertoire of tools from which to choose, and will adopt those best suited to their needs. They will, moreover, resist qualitative changes in their productive methods until events force them to adopt new methods. Note that for Boserup, however, increasing population is *deus ex machina*: She does not acknowledge the fact of deliberate fertility control among hunter-gatherer and peasant peoples the world over. See also Michael J. Harner, "Population Pressure and the Social Evolution of Agriculturalists," *Southern Journal of Anthropology*, 26 (1970): 67–86; and Mildred Dickeman, "Demographic Consequences of Infanticide in Man," *Annual Review of Ecology and Systematics*, 6 (1975): 107–37.
31   Daniel R. Gross and others found that hunter-gatherers in twentieth-century Brazil resist participation in the market economy until constriction of their territory makes it impossible for them to pursue their traditional economies. Gross et al., "Ecology and Acculturation Among Native Peoples of Central Brazil," *Science*, 206 (30 November 1979): 1,043–50. Historical evidence, likewise, abounds to the effect

274   *Notes to pp. 29–33*

that North American Indian groups steadfastly resisted the allure of Western goods and Western trade until their own economies and the cultures in which they were embedded had been destroyed. Calvin Martin, *Keepers of the Game: Indian–Animal Relationships and the Fur Trade* (Berkeley and Los Angeles: University of California Press, 1978), pp. 55–9; Rich, "Trade Habits and Economic Motivation," *passim;* White, *The Roots of Dependency*, pp. 34–7.

32 Hunn, "Mobility as a Factor Limiting Resource Use," p. 35; Bean and Dorothea Theophrastus, "Western Pomo and Northeastern Pomo," in *Handbook of North American Indians*, v. 8: *California*, pp. 289–305, p. 295; Burt W. Aginsky, "Population Control in the Shanel (Pomo) Tribe," *American Sociological Review*, 10 (1939): 209–16, pp. 210, 214; Arnold R. Pilling, "Yurok," in *Handbook of North American Indians*, v. 8: *California*, pp. 137–54, p. 142; Grant, "Eastern Coastal Chumash," p. 511. Baumhoff stated that "nearly all tribes practiced infanticide," but the incidence was "presumably not great" (Baumhoff, "Ecological Determinants of Aboriginal California Populations," p. 157). He offers no evidence for his presumption, however, and gives no attention to other potential means of population control such as abortion, contraception, intercourse taboos during lactation, and meaningful social roles for celibates. Dickeman, on the other hand, pointed to the natural reluctance on the part both of anthropologists and their subjects to discuss the issue and suggested that this was a reason for our generally poor knowledge of such practices. She estimated that systematic infanticide took place at rates of between 5 and 50 percent of all live births in hunter-gatherer, horticultural, and stratified agrarian societies. Dickemann, "Demographic Consequences of Infanticide," p. 130. See also Don F. Dumond, "The Limitation of Human Population: A Natural History," *Science*, 187 (28 February 1975): 713–21.

33 Jorgensen, *Western Indians*, pp. 136, 141.

34 Ibid., pp. 136–8; Gould, "To Have and Have Not," p. 43.

35 Jorgensen, *Western Indians*, p. 138.

36 Bean and Sylvia Brakke Vane, "Cults and Their Transformations," in *Handbook of North American Indians*, v. 8: *California*, pp. 662–72, p. 665; Edwin M. Loeb, "The Western Kuksu Cult," *UC-PAAE*, 33 (1932): 1–137; Loeb, "The Eastern Kuksu Cult," *UC-PAAE*, 33 (1933): 139–232. See also Roy A. Rappaport, "The Sacred in Human Evolution," *Annual Review of Ecology and Systematics*, 2 (1971): 23–44; Rappaport, "Ritual, Sanctity, and Cybernetics," *American Anthropologist*, 73 (1971): 59–76; Clifford Geertz, "Religion as a Cultural System," in *The Interpretation of Cultures*, ed. Geertz (New York: Basic Books, 1973), pp. 87–125.

37 Kroeber, *Handbook of the Indians of California*, pp. 383–4, 437; Bean and Vane, "Cults and Their Transformations," p. 665; Sean Sweezey, "The Energetics of Subsistence-Assurance Ritual in Native California," *Contributions of the University of California Archaeological Research Facility*, 23 (1975): 1–46, pp. 14–16.

38 Hunn and Williams, "Introduction," p. 13.

39 Driver, *Indians of North America*, p. 98.

40 Goldschmidt, "Nomlaki Ethnography," p. 348.

41 Kroeber, *Handbook of the Indians of California*, p. 1; Jorgensen, *Western Indians*, p. 262; Lewis, "Fire Technology and Resource Management," p 57; Baumhoff, "Ecological Determinants of Aboriginal California Populations," p. 57. See also Joseph L. Chartkoff and Kerry K. Chartkoff, "Late Period Settlement of the Middle Klamath River of Northwest California," *American Antiquity*, 40 (1975): 172–9.

42 Pilling, "Yurok," p. 138.

43 Albert B. Elsasser, "Development of Regional Prehistoric Cultures," in *Handbook of North American Indians*, v. 8: *California*, pp. 37–57, pp. 50–2.

44 Carl Meyer, *Nach dem Sacramento: Reisebilder eines Heimgekehrten* (1855), in *The Four Ages of Tsurai: A Documentary History of the Indian Village on Trinidad Bay*, ed. Robert F. Heizer (Berkeley and Los Angeles: University of California Press, 1952), pp. 119–34, p. 122; Stephen Powers, *Tribes of California*, U.S. Geographical and Geological Survey of the Rocky Mountain Region, Contributions to North American Ethnology, 3 (1877; repr. Berkeley and Los Angeles: University of California Press, 1976), p. 49.

45 Kroeber, *Handbook of the Indians of California*, pp. 5, 97, 191–3; Jorgensen, *Western Indians*, p. 263; Kroeber and Barrett, "Fishing Among the Indians of Northwestern California," pp. 1, 12; Albert B. Elsasser, "Mattole, Nongatl, Sinkyone, Lassik, and Wailaki," in *Handbook of the Indians of North America*, v. 8: *California*, pp. 190–204; Gould, "To Have and Have Not," p. 128.

46 Kroeber, *Handbook of the Indians of California*, pp. 20–1; Jorgensen, *Western Indians*, pp. 138, 143–4. On Yurok law, see Kroeber, "Law of the Yurok Indians," *Proceedings of the Twenty-Second International Congress of Americanists* (1926), v. II: 511–16. On Pacific Northwest economic systems, see Andrew P. Vayda, "A Re-Examination of Northwest Coast Economic Systems," *Transactions of the New York Academy of Sciences*, 2d, 23 (1961): 618–24; Stuart Piddocke, "The Potlach System of the Southern Kwakiutl: A New Perspective," *Southwestern Journal of Anthropology*, 21 (1965): 244–64.

47 On the continuing importance of the "high country" to Indians of the region, see USDA, Forest Service, "Draft Environmental Statement: Gasquet-Orleans Road, Chimney Rock Section, Six Rivers National Forest, California Region," USDA-FS-R5–DES (Adm)-78-02 (San Francisco: U.S. Forest Service, 1977), Appendices K–T, pp. 217–485; also *Northwest Indian Cemetery Protective Association et al. v. Peterson et al.*, 565 F. Supp. 586, 591, 594 (N.D. Cal. 1983), *modified on appeal*, 764 F.2d 581 (9th Cir. 1985).

48 Kroeber, *Handbook of the Indians of California*, pp. 3, 13, 20, 33–4, 54, 127, 176, 184; Kroeber and Barrett, "Fishing Among the Indians of Northwestern California," p. 12; Gould, "To Have and Have Not," pp. 75, 83; William Bright, "Karok," in *Handbook of North American Indians*, v. 8: *California*, pp. 180–9, p. 184; Baumhoff, "Environmental Background," p. 19.

49 Redick McKee to Charles E. Mix, 3 October 1851, "Report of the Secretary of the Interior, Communicating . . . Correspondence between the Department of the Interior and the Indian Agents and Commissioners in California," U.S. Congress, Senate, 33rd Cong., special sess. (1853), *Senate Executive Document* 4, pp. 191–2. Emphasis in original.

50 Baumhoff, "Ecological Determinants of Aboriginal California Populations," p. 177.

51 DuBois, "The Wealth Concept as an Integrative Factor," pp. 50–1; Jorgensen, *Western Indians*, pp. 144–6.

52 Pilling, "Yurok," pp. 142–3; Kroeber, *Handbook of the Indians of California*, pp. 49, 264; Kroeber, "Law of the Yurok Indians," pp. 511–16; Shirley Silver, "Shastan Peoples," in *Handbook of North American Indians*, v. 8: *California*, pp. 211–24, pp. 216–17; Thomas McCorkle, "Intergroup Conflict," ibid., pp. 694–700, p. 700.

53 On the biology of chinook salmon, see Frey, *California's Living Marine Resources*, pp. 43–6. On the world-renewal religion, see Kroeber and Gifford, "World Renewal," p. 105; Erik H. Erikson, "Observations on the Yurok: Childhood and Self-Image," *UC- PAAE*, 35 (1943): 257–302, pp. 277–8, 300–1. Like Kroeber, Erikson observed a great many things about the Yurok and recorded them. Some of his observations, such as the relationship between Yurok religion and the salmon life cycle, retain some value for modern researchers. Others, such as his inferences from salmon biology to Indian sexual mores, are more fantastic but detract little from the usefulness of his basic observations.

54   Robert Spott and Kroeber, "Yurok Narratives," *UC- PAAE*, 35 (1942): 143–256, pp. 171–9; Waterman and Kroeber, "The Kepel Fish Dam," p. 52; Swezey, "Energetics of Subsistence-Assurance Ritual," pp. 23–5.

55   Peter Matthiessen offers a description of the Yurok environment and what it means to them today in his *Indian Country* (New York: Viking Press, 1984), pp. 165–200.

56   Kroeber and Barrett, "Fishing Among the Indians of Northwestern California," p. 12; Erikson, "Observations on the Yurok," p. 300.

57   Waterman and Kroeber, "The Kepel Fish Dam," pp. 50–61, 78.

58   Heizer, "Natural Forces and Native World View," p. 649.

59   Kroeber, *Yurok Myths* (Berkeley and Los Angeles: University of California Press, 1976), pp. 393–7.

60   Erikson, "Observations on the Yurok," p. 279.

61   Waterman and Kroeber, "The Kepel Fish Dam," p. 50.

62   George Gibbs, *George Gibbs's Journal of Redick McKee's Expedition Through Northwest California in 1851*, ed. R. F. Heizer (Berkeley: University of California Department of Anthropology, 1972), p. 146.

63   George Crook, *General George Crook: His Autobiography*, ed. Martin F. Schmitt (Norman, Ok.: University of Oklahoma Press, 1946), p. 77.

64   The anthropologist Clifford Geertz described "religion" as "(1) a system of symbols which acts to (2) establish powerful, pervasive, and long-lasting moods and motivations in men by (3) formulating conceptions of a general order of existence and (4) clothing these conceptions with such an aura of factuality that (5) the moods and motivations seem uniquely realistic." [Geertz, *The Interpretation of Cultures: Selected Essays* (New York: Basic Books, 1973), p. 90.] The Social Contract, which such political theorists as Locke and Rousseau described as taking place when people living in a state of nature contracted to society their right to enforce the law in return for society's protection of their fundamental liberties, is no less a symbolic or mythical articulation of the metaphysical nature of social life for citizens of capitalist democracies than the myths of the *woge* were for the pre-1850 Yurok. See Geertz, "Ideology as a Cultural System," in *The Interpretation of Cultures*, pp. 193–233.

65   Kroeber, *Handbook of the Indians of California*, pp. 68–9.

66   See Martin, *Keepers of the Game*, pp. 157–8; and Thomas W. Overholt, "American Indians as 'Natural Ecologists,' " *American Indian Journal*, 5 (September 1979): 9–16. Martin's book aroused a great deal of controversy for its explication of the relationship between Indian culture and resource ecology. See Shepard Krech III, ed., *Indians, Animals, and the Fur Trade: A Critique of Keepers of the Game* (Athens, GA: University of Georgia Press, 1981). Martin asserted that the Indians of what is now eastern Canada maintained a spiritually articulated contractual relationship with the beaver and other animals they harvested, in which the Indians used the animals conservatively so that the animal spirits would sustain the well-being of Indian society. Indians became active abusers of the beaver when Europeans arrived, Martin claimed, not because Western trade held any special attraction for them but because they perceived their losses to European disease as evidence that the spirits had abrogated their contract. They apostasized from their religion, then, and took vengeance on their former allies, the game. It is the apostasy that has raised most of the opposition to Martin's book. Martin, however, need not have gone so far to explain the change in the Indians' behavior or to buttress his most important point,

that is, that Indian society was fundamentally nondestructive of nature and that the spiritual contract with the animals kept it that way. That Martin's subjects wantonly depleted their game is evidence neither of apostasy nor of any inherent human tendency to pursue profit at the expense of community and environment, but only of the historical disintegration of the social and cultural controls which formerly would have organized their behavior. See Dickeman, "Demographic Consequences of Infanticide in Man," p. 133.

67   A good discussion of this idea and its implications for resource management may be found in Hugh M. Raup, "Some Problems in Ecological Theory and Their Relation to Conservation," *Journal of Ecology*, 52 (Supp. 1964): 19–28, pp. 20–1. See generally Roderick Nash, *Wilderness and the American Mind*, rev. ed. (New Haven: Yale University Press, 1973).

68   John Locke, *Two Treatises of Government* (New York: New American Library, 1960), II: ch. 5, §§ 37, 49.

69   Walter Prescott Webb, *The Great Frontier* (Boston: Houghton-Mifflin, 1952), p. 8.

70   Joseph A. Craig and Robert L. Hacker, "History and Development of the Fisheries of the Columbia River," USBF, *Bulletin*, 32 (1947): 132–216, p. 150; Sherburne F. Cook, "The Conflict Between the California Indian and White Civilization, II: The Physical and Demographic Reaction of the Nonmission Indians in Colonial and Provincial California," *Ibero-Americana*, 22 (1943; repr. Berkeley and Los Angeles: University of California Press, 1976): 1–55, p. 16.

71   See Annette Hamilton, "The Unity of Hunting-Gathering Societies," in *Resource Managers*, eds. Hunn and Williams, pp. 229–48, p. 239. See also Neal Wood, *John Locke and Agrarian Capitalism* (Berkeley and Los Angeles: University of California Press, 1984), pp. 49–71.

Chapter 3

1   Felix S. Cohen, *Felix S. Cohen's Handbook of Federal Indian Law*, 1982 ed. (Charlottesville, VA: Michie Bobbs-Merrill, 1982), p. v.

2   USFC, *Report* (1872–3): 179.

3   Stephen Powers, *Tribes of California*, U.S. Geographical and Geological Survey of the Rocky Mountain Region, Contributions to North American Ethnology, 3 (1877; repr. Berkeley and Los Angeles: University of California Press, 1976), pp. 404–5.

4   Hubert Howe Bancroft, *The History of California* (San Francisco: The History Company, 1888), v. 7, p. 474. The residual of about 5 percent is typical for North American Indians. See Sherburne F. Cook, "Historical Demography," in *Handbook of North American Indians*, v. 8: *California*, ed. Robert F. Heizer (Washington, DC: Smithsonian Institution, 1978), pp. 91–8, p. 93; Alfred W. Crosby, Jr., *The Columbian Exchange: Biological and Cultural Consequences of 1492* (Westport, CT: Greenwood, 1972), p. 39.

5   Cook, "The Conflict Between the California Indian and White Civilization, I: The Indian Versus the Spanish Mission," *Ibero-Americana*, 21 (1943): 1–194, p. 8; Cook, "The Conflict Between the California Indian and White Civilization, II: The Physical and Demographic Reaction of the Non-Mission Indians in Colonial and Provincial California," ibid., 22 (1943): 1–53, pp. 16–18; Cook, "The Conflict Between the California Indian and White Civilization, III: The American Invasion, 1848–1870," ibid., 23 (1943): 1–111, p. 25. Cook's "Conflict" series is collected and reprinted in *The Conflict Between the California Indian and White Civilization* (Berkeley and Los Angeles: University of California Press, 1976).

6 General G. F. Beale, cited in Cook, "The American Invasion," p. 27, note 20.
7 Sally McLendon and Michael J. Lowy, "Eastern Pomo and Southeastern Pomo,"
in *Handbook of North American Indians*, v. 8: *California*, pp. 306–23, p. 319; Albert
B. Elsasser, "Wiyot," in ibid., pp. 155–63, p. 159; A. J. Bledsoe, *Indian Wars of
the Northwest: A California Sketch* (1885; repr. Oakland: Biobooks, 1956), pp. 150,
169–72; Cook, "The American Invasion," p. 27, note 29. For firsthand accounts of
the incidents, see Robert F. Heizer, ed., *The Destruction of California Indians*,
(Santa Barbara: Peregrine Press, 1974), pp. 244–7, 253–65.
8 Pedro Font, *Anza's California Expeditions*, ed. and trans. Herbert E. Bolton
(New York: Russell and Russell, 1966), v. 4, *Font's Complete Diary of the Second
Anza Expedition*, p. 256.
9 Cook, "The Indian Versus the Spanish Mission," p. 55; see also Gary Coombs
and Fred Plog, "The Conversion of the Chumash Indians: An Ecological Interpretation," *Human Ecology*, 5 (1977): 309–28, pp. 327–8.
10 Cook, "The Reaction of the Non-Mission Indians, pp. 27–8; Edward D. Castillo,
"The Impact of Euro-American Exploration and Settlement," in *Handbook of North
American Indians*, v. 8: *California*, pp. 99–127, p. 105.
11 Robert F. Heizer and Alan F. Almquist, *The Other Californians: Prejudice and
Discrimination Under Spain, Mexico, and the United States to 1920* (Berkeley and
Los Angeles: University of California Press, 1971), pp. 39–58.
12 Cook, "The American Invasion," pp. 32–3, 66–7.
13 Cook, "The Mechanism and Extent of Dietary Adaptation Among Certain
Groups of California and Nevada Indians," *Ibero-Americana*, 19 (1941): 1–59, pp. 7–
10.
14 Cook, "The American Invasion," p. 31.
15 10 *Statutes at Large* 686, 699 (1855); Edward E. Hill, *The Office of Indian
Affairs, 1824–1880: Historical Sketches* (New York: Clearwater, 1974), p. 23.
16 Bancroft, *History of California*, v. 7, p. 491; U.S. Congress, Senate, Joint Special Committee, "Condition of the Indian Tribes: Report of the Joint Special Committee Appointed Under Joint Resolution of March 3, 1865," 39th Congr., 2nd sess.
(1866–7), *Senate Report 156*, pp. 510–12; Alexander Smith Taylor, "The Indianology
of California. . . . " Published in The California Farmer from 1860 to 1863, comp.
Bancroft Library, p. 22; Castillo, "The Impact of Euro-American Exploration and
Settlement," p. 111.
17 13 *Statutes at Large* 39 (1864).
18 Robert Stevens, 1 January 1867, in U.S. Office of Indian Affairs, Reports of the
California Superintendency, 1861–1871, comp. Bancroft Library.
19 For a legal history of the Klamath River and Hoopa Valley Indian Reservations,
see *Jessie Short et al.* v. *United States*, 202 Ct. Cl. 870, 873–940 (1973). See also
William H. Ellison, "The Federal Indian Policy in California, 1846–1860," *Mississippi
Valley Historical Review*, 9 (1922): 37–67.
20 24 *Statutes at Large* 388 (1887), amended, 26 *Statutes at Large* 794 (1891).
21 *AR-CIA* (1900): 638.
22 Bancroft, *History of California*, v. 7, p. 492, note 24.
23 Bancroft, *The Native Races of the Pacific States* (San Francisco: A. L. Bancroft
& Co., 1883), v. 1, p. 324.
24 Annette Hamilton, "The Unity of Hunting-Gathering Societies: Reflections on
Economic Forms and Resource Management," in *Resource Managers: North American and Australian Hunter-Gatherers*, ed. Nancy M. Williams and Eugene S. Hunn,
AAAS Selected Symposium 67 (Boulder, CO: Westview Press, 1982), pp. 229–48,

pp. 239–40; Cook, "The Reaction of the Non-Mission Indians," p. 24; Cook, "The American Invasion," pp. 1, 37.
25 Alfred L. Kroeber and S. A. Barrett, "Fishing Among the Indians of North-western California," *UC-AR*, 21 (1960): 1–210, p. 116; Adele Ogden, *The California Sea Otter Trade*, 1784–1848 (1941; repr. Berkeley and Los Angeles: University of California Press, 1975), pp. 16–24, 43.
26 Taylor, "The Indianology of California," p. 9. Taylor may have erred on his dates here. Ogden states that the Russians limited their hunting to the coast north of Bodega Head, north of the Golden Gate, from 1814–15 until after 1823 (Ogden, *The California Sea Otter Trade*, p. 63). Such things could certainly have happened after 1820, however. By "among themselves" Taylor probably referred to conflicts between local Indians and the Aleut employees of the Russians.
27 Cook, "The Indian Versus the Spanish Mission," pp. 34–5; Peter Steinhart, "California's Oaks: Soon You Won't See the Forest – or the Trees," *Los Angeles Times* (5 March 1978):
28 Herbert F. Frey, ed., *California's Living Marine Resources and Their Utilization* (Sacramento: CDFG, 1971), pp. 44–5; P. A. Larkin, "Maybe You Can't Get There from Here: A Foreshortened History of Research in Relation to Management of Pacific Salmon," *Journal of the Fisheries Research Board of Canada*, 36 (1979): 98–106, p. 102.
29 Powers, *Tribes of California*, pp. 93–4; Bledsoe, *Indian Wars of the Northwest*, pp. 75–7. On the technology of gold mining, see Rodman W. Paul, *California Gold: The Beginning of Mining in the Far West* (Cambridge, MA: Harvard University Press, 1947); Robert L. Kelley, *Gold vs. Grain: The Hydraulic Mining Controversy in California's Sacramento Valley: A Chapter in the Decline of the Concept of Laissez-Faire* (Glendale, CA: Arthur H. Clark, 1959); Eileen M. Glaholt, "Office Report: History of the Klamath River Region" (Sacramento: California Resources Agency, 1975), p. 38.
30 Thomas R. Cox, *Mills and Markets: A History of the Pacific Coast Lumber Industry to 1900* (Seattle: University of Washington Press, 1974), pp. 67–8; Charles Nordhoff, *Northern California, Oregon, and the Sandwich Islands* (New York: Harper & Brothers, 1874), p. 36; California Surveyor-General, *Report* (1 August 1884–1 August 1886): 8.
31 Cook, *The Population of California Indians* (Berkeley and Los Angeles: University of California Press, 1976), p. 61.
32 USFC, *Report* (1872–3): 168–9, 177–8; ibid. (1879): 699. See also Cora DuBois, "Wintu Ethnography," *UC-PAAE*, 36 (1935): 1–148, p. 1; Kroeber, *Handbook of the Indians of California*, Smithsonian Institution Bureau of American Ethnology, Bulletin 78 (Washington: GPO, 1925; repr. New York: Dover Publications, 1976), pp. 351–2; Powers, *Tribes of California*, pp. 233–4; Joel W. Hedgpeth, "Livingston Stone and Fish Culture in California," *California Fish and Game*, 27 (1941): 126–48.
33 USFC, *Report* (1872–3): 193–4, emphasis in original.
34 Ibid. (1879): 700.
35 Stone reported that two six-horse wagonloads of black powder went into a single charge at the blasting site and that this was kept up day and night as rapidly as the workers could charge and fire the explosions, ibid. (1883): 989–90. See also ibid. (1884): 169; G. H. Clark, "Sacramento–San Joaquin Salmon (*Oncorhynchus tschawytscha*) Fishery of California," CDFG, *Fish Bulletin No. 17* (1929), p. 13.
36 DuBois, "Wintu Ethnography," p. 15.

37   CCF, *Biennial Report* (1883–4): 5; USFC, *Report* (1882): 840.
38   Clark, "Sacramento–San Joaquin Salmon Fishery," pp. 14–16.
39   Bledsoe, *Indian Wars of the Northwest*, p. 73; Odgen, *California Sea Otter Trade*, p. 3; William Dane Phelps, "Solid Men of Boston in the Northwest," in *The Four Ages of Tsurai: A Documentary History of the Indian Village on Trinidad Bay*, ed. Heizer (Berkeley and Los Angeles: University of California Press, 1952), pp. 82–3; Owen C. Coy, *The Humboldt Bay Region, 1850–1875: A Study in the Amerian Colonization of California* (Los Angeles: California State Historical Association, 1929), pp. 27–8, 36.
40   Coy, *Humboldt Bay Region*, p. 37; Bancroft, *History of California*, v. 6, p. 364; Cook, *Population of California Indians*, p. 160.
41   The chart uses Cook's estimates for aboriginal population but relies on U.S. Census data, as reported by Kroeber, for the 1880–1910 period. The latter figures are likely to be low and disproportionately more so for tribes outside the core region, who would have been more dispersed and therefore harder to count. The difference is striking, however, and is corroborated by secondary evidence. See Cook, *Population of California Indians*, p. 71.
42   Kroeber, *Handbook of the Indians of California*, pp. 102, 130; Erikson, "Observations on the Yurok: Childhood and World Image," *UC-PAAE*, 35 (1943): 257–302, pp. 257–8.
43   California Department of Industrial Relations, Division of Fair Employment Practices, *American Indians in California: Population Employment, Income, Education* (San Francisco: California Department of Industrial Relations, 1965), p. 8; California State Advisory Commission on Indian Affairs (Senate Bill No. 1007), *Progress Report to the Governor and the Legislature on Indians in Rural and Reservation Areas* (Sacramento, State Printing Office, 1966), p. 24. USFWS, "Final Environmental Impact Statement on the Management of River Flows to Mitigate the Loss of the Anadromous Fishery of the Trinity River, California" INT/FES 80–52 (1980), p. C7-5.
44   USFWS, "Final Environmental Impact Statement on the Management of River Flows," p. C7-8. See also Hamilton, "The Unity of Hunting-Gathering Societies," p. 240.
45   "Minutes kept by John McKee, Secretary, on the Expedition from Sonoma, through Northern California," in "Report of the Secretary of the Interior, Communicating . . . Correspondence between the Department of the Interior and the Indian Agents and Commissioners in California," U.S. Congress, Senate, 33rd Cong., special sess. (1853), *Senate Executive Document 4*, pp. 134–78, pp. 165–7; Redick McKee to Charles E. Mix, 15 November 1851, ibid., pp. 219–24.
46   Powers, *Tribes to California*, p. 94; Gibbs, *George Gibb's Journal*, pp. 159–62; Glaholt, "History of the Klamath River Region," pp. 12, 38, 44–6; Bledsoe, *Indian Wars of the Northwest*, p. 150.
47   Bledsoe, *Indian Wars of the Northwest*, pp. 67–70; Bledsoe, *History of Del Norte County, California, with a Business Directory and Traveler's Guide* (Eureka, CA, 1881; repr. Crescent City, CA: Wendy's Books, 1971), pp. 103–7; Richard A. Gould, "Tolowa," in *Handbook of North American Indians*, v. 8: *California*, pp. 128–36, p. 130; Coy, *Humboldt Bay Region*, p. 14; Gibbs, *George Gibbs's Journal*, p. 133.
48   Bledsoe, *Indian Wars of the Northwest*, pp. 63–4, 92, 111; Coy, *Humboldt Bay Region*, pp. 118, 173–4; Gibbs, *George Gibbs's Journal*, p. 128; Elsasser, "Wiyot," p. 162.
49   Bledsoe, *Indian Wars of the Northwest*, pp. 92, 111; Coy, *Humboldt Bay Region*, p. 136; John N. Cobb, "Pacific Salmon Fisheries," USBF Document No. 1092,

USBF, *Report* (1930): 555–7; (Eureka) *Humboldt Times*, 29 October 1859, 4 July 1869, 27 September 1888.

50   *AR-CIA* (1885): 490.

51   USDI, Census Office, *Eleventh Census (1890): Report on Indians Taxed and Indians Not Taxed in the United States (except Alaska)*, p. 245; Glaholt, "History of the Klamath River Region," p. 63; Titus Fey Cronise, *The Natural Wealth of California* (San Francisco: H. H. Bancroft, 1868), p. 200.

52   Redick McKee to Charles E. Mix, 7 October 1851, in "Report of the Secretary of the Interior, Communicating . . . Correspondence between the Department of the Interior and California," pp. 194–5; "Minutes Kept by John McKee," ibid., pp. 158, 160.

53   Gibbs, *George Gibbs's Journal*, pp. 138, 172.

54   Cronise, *Natural Wealth of California*, pp. 202–4; California Surveyor-General, *Report* (1859): 27; ibid. (1 November 1865–1 November 1867): 121; William H. Brewer, *Up and Down California in 1860–1864: The Journal of William H. Brewer*, ed. Francis P. Farquhar (Berkeley and Los Angeles: University of California Press, 1966), pp. 477–83; Powers, *Tribes of California*, pp. 73, 188–9.

55   *AR-CIA* (1871): 374.

56   Cook, "The American Invasion," p. 43; *AR-CIA* (1864): 122.

57   US Congress, Senate, Joint Special Committee, "Condition of the Indian Tribes," p. 498; Bledsoe, *Indian Wars of the Northwest*, p. 91.

58   Brewer, *Up and Down California*, pp. 493–4; Coy, *Humboldt Bay Region*, pp. 191–4, 197–8; California Surveyor-General, *Report* (1862): 90, 113; ibid. (1863): 121.

59   *AR-CIA* (1864): 122; USFWS, "Final Report: Hoopa Valley Indian Reservation . . . Review of the History and Status of Anadromous Fishery Resources of the Klamath River Basin," photocopied (Arcata, Ca.: USFWS, Arcata Field Station, 15 March 1979), pp. 16, 62.

60   Redick McKee to Charles E. Mix, 3 October 1851, in "Report of the Secretary of the Interior, Communicating . . . Correspondence between the Department of the Interior and California," pp. 191–2; "Minutes Kept by John McKee," ibid., p. 157.

61   Gibbs, *George Gibbs's Journal*, p. 149.

62   Erikson, "Observations on the Yurok," p. 258.

63   Tzvetan Todorov, *The Conquest of America: The Question of the Other*, tr. Richard Howard (New York: Harper & Row, 1982), is a fascinating discussion of the discovery and conquest of Mesoamerica in terms of the confrontation between cultures all but lacking commonality of experience and understanding.

64   *AR-CIA* (1872): 454.

65   Powers, *Tribes of California*, p. 46.

66   Arnold R. Pilling, "Yurok," in *Handbook of North American Indians*, v. 8: *California*, pp. 137–54, p. 141; Pilling, personal correspondence, 22 May 1983.

67   Powers, *Tribes of California*, p. 46.

68   *AR-CIA* (1884): 55.

69   Ibid. (1885): 490–2.

70   Ibid. (1871): 374; *AR-DOI* (1864): 266.

71   *AR-CIA* (1865): 111; ibid. (1866): 94; *AR-DOI* (1864): 261; Powers, *Tribes of California*, p. 59.

72   *AR-CIA* (1867): 129.

73   Ibid. (1871): 157; Powers, *Tribes of California*, pp. 48–9.

74   *AR-CIA* (1888): 10; U.S. Congress, Senate, Committee on Indian Affairs, *Survey of Conditions of the Indians of the United States: Hearings Before a Subcommittee*

of the Committee on Indian Affairs, 72nd Cong., 1st sess. (1934), *Pt.* 29: *California*, p. 15653; *Humboldt Times*, 19 May 1887.

75 *AR-CIA* (1886): 261; Frances Turner McBeth, *Lower Klamath Country* (Berkeley: Anchor Press,.1950), pp. 46–7; see also *Short* v. *United States*, 202 Ct. Cl. at 875–907.

76 1880 *California Statutes* 136; U.S. Congress, Senate, "Report Relative to the Survey and Sale of the Klamath Indian Reservation," 50th Cong., 2nd sess. (1888), *Senate Executive Document 140*, p. 15.

77 *Re John McCarthy*, 2 L.D. 460 (1883).

78 *AR-CIA* (1885): 490–2.

79 Glaholt, "History of the Klamath River Region," p. 72; *Short* v. *United States*, 202 Ct. Cl. at 912–13; Gordon B. Dodds, *The Salmon King of Oregon: R. D. Hume and the Pacific Fisheries* (Chapel Hill, NC: University of North Carolina Press, 1959), pp. 174–7; U.S. Congress, Senate, "Report Relative to the Survey and Sale of the Klamath Indian Reservation," p. 13.

80 19 *Opinions, US Attorney General* 35, 56 (1887).

81 *AR-CIA* (1887–8): 91; ibid (1888): 10; *Humboldt Times*, 9 June 1887; 10 *Opinions, US Attorney General* 35–7, 56–7 (1887).

82 *U.S.* v. *Forty-Eight Pounds of Rising Star Tea, etc.*, 35 F. 403 (N.D. Cal. 1888), *affirmed*, 38 F. 400 (C.C.D. Cal. 1889); U.S. Congress, Senate, "Report Relative to the Survey and Sale of the Klamath Indian Reservation," p. 23.

83 Dodds, *Salmon King of Oregon*, pp.178–9; U.S. Congress, House, "The Klamath River Indian Reservation: Report to Accompany H. R. 3454, 46th Congress, 2nd sess. (1880), *House Report 1354*; Bledsoe, *History of Del Norte County*, pp. 148–61; Executive Order dated 16 October 1891, C. Kappler, *Indian Affairs: Laws and Treaties*, 1 (1904): 815; 1891 *California Statutes* 10; Glaholt, "History of the Klamath River Region," p. 39; 27 *Statutes at Large* 52 (1892); *Short* v. *United States*, 202 Ct. Cl. at 883, 902–3.

84 *AR-CIA* (1892): 230; Cook, *Population of California Indians*, p. 73.

85 *Crichton* v. *Shelton*, 33 L.D. 205 (1906); *Donnelly* v. *United States*, 228 U.S. 243, 259 (1913).

86 U.S. Congress, Senate, Committee on Indian Affairs, *Survey of the Condition of the Indians*, pt. 29: *California*, pp. 15572, 15653; U.S. Congress, House, Committee on Merchant Marine and Fisheries, "Klamath River Fishing Rights Oversight," Hearings before the Subcommittee on Fisheries and Wildlife Conservation and Environment, 96th Congress, 1st sess. (1979), *House Serial 96–11*, pp. 240, 305; *AR-CIA* (1892): 230; USDI, Bureau of Indian Affairs, "Environmental Impact Statement for a Proposal to Modify the Indian Fishing Regulations to Authorize Commercial Harvesting of Anadromous Fish" DES 85–21 (1985), p. 17.

87 Kroeber, *Handbook of the Indians of California*, p. 60; Thomas T. Waterman and Kroeber, "The Kepel Fish Dam," *UC-PAAE*, 35 (1938): 49–80, p. 70; Kroeber and E. W. Gifford, "World-Renewal: A Cult System of Native Northwestern California," *UC-AR*, 13 (1952): 1–156, p. 82; Pilling, "Yurok," p. 143.

88 John H. Bushnell, "From American Indian to Indian American: The Changing Identity of the Hupa," *American Anthropologist*, 70 (1968): 1,108–16. See also U.S. Congress, House, Committee on Merchant Marine and Fisheries, "Klamath River Fishing Rights Oversight," pp. 124–5; *Northwest Indian Cemetery Protective Association et al.* v. *Peterson et al.*, 565 F. Supp. 586 (N.D. Cal. 1983).

89 Hedgepeth, "Livingston Stone and Fish Culture in California," p. 139.

90 J. J. Bryce, "Establishment of Stations for the Propagation of Salmon on the Pacific Coast," USFC, *Report* (1893): 391.

Chapter 4

1   Henry A. Fisk, "The Fishermen of San Francisco Bay," *Proceedings of the National Conference of Charities and Correction at the Thirty-Second Annual Session*, ed. Alexander Johnson (Portland, July 15–21, 1905), pp. 383–92, pp. 390–2.

2   David Starr Jordan, "The Fisheries of the Pacific Coast," in *The Fisheries and Fishery Industries of the United States*, ed. George Brown Goode, U.S. Congress, Senate, 47th Cong., 1st sess. (1887th, *Senate Miscellaneous Document 124*, Sec. II (pt. 16), p. 592.

3   J. W. Collins, "Report on the Fisheries of the Pacific Coast of the United States," USFC, *Report* (1888): 21, 69.

4   Jordan, "Fisheries of the Pacific Coast," p. 593.

5   Hugh M. Smith, "Notes on a Reconnaissance of the Fisheries of the Pacific Coast of the United States in 1894," USFC, *Bulletin*, 14 (1894): 282.

6   Captain F. N. Beechey, R.N., *Narrative of a Voyage to the Pacific and Beering's Strait, to Cooperate with the Polar Expeditions Performed in His Majesty's Ship Blossom in the Years 1825, 26, 27, 28* (London: Henry Colburn and Richard Bentley, 1831), v. II, p. 83. A classic history of fishery-led economic development is Harold A. Innis, *The Cod Fisheries: The History of an International Economy* rev. (1954; repr. Toronto: University of Toronto Press, 1978).

7   Jordan, "The Sea-Fishing Grounds of the Pacific Coast of the United States, from the Straits of Fuca to Lower California," in *The Fisheries and Fishery Industries of the United States*, Sec. III, p. 79; Collins, "Report on the Fisheries of the Pacific Coast," USFC, *Report* (1888): 137–9; Jordan, "The Fisheries of California," *Overland Monthly* 2d, 20 (1892): 469–78, p. 476; Philip Weaver, Jr., "Salt Water Fisheries of the Pacific Coast," *Overland Monthly* 2d, 20 (1892): 149–63, p. 156; Wilcox, "Notes on the Fisheries of the Pacific Coast in 1895," USFC, *Report* (1896): 632.

8   *Sacramento Bee*, 31 December 1885.

9   E. Gould Buffum, *Six Months in the Gold Mines, from a Journal of Three Years Observance in Upper and Lower California, 1847–8–9* (Philadelphia: Lea & Blanchard, 1850), pp. 55–6; Joseph A. McGowan, *History of the Sacramento Valley* (New York: Lewis Historical Publishing Co., 1961), v. 1, p. 353.

10   McGowan, "San Francisco–Sacramento Shipping" (M.A. thesis, University of California, Berkeley, 1939), pp. 19–20; Hubert Howe Bancroft, *History of California* (San Francisco: The History Company, 1884–1890), v. 7, p. 105; Joan Margo, "The Food Supply Problem of the California Gold Mines" (M.A. thesis, University of California, Berkeley, 1947), pp. 28–31.

11   Bancroft, *History of California*, v. 7, p. 115.

12   *San Francisco Alta*, 4 April 1851.

13   Bancroft, *History of California*, v. 7, p. 117, note 22, p. 129; *San Francisco Alta*, 11 June 1853; John Haskell Kemble, *The Panama Route, 1848–1869*, University of California Publications in History, 29 (1943), p. 101; Owen C. Coy, *The Humboldt Bay Region, 1850–1875: A Study in the American Colonization of California* (Los Angeles: California State Historical Association, 1929), pp. 259, 263; Collins, "Report on the Fisheries of the Pacific Coast," USFC, *Report* (1888): 129; Henry Hall, "Shipbuilding Industry in the United States," in USDI, Census Office, *Tenth Census* (1880), v. 8, p. 131.

14   *San Diego World*, 13 August 1872; Bancroft, *History of California*, v. 7, p. 82; Carey McWilliams, *Southern California: An Island on the Land* (1946; repr. Santa Barbara: Peregrine Press, 1973), pp. 116–17; Franklyn Hoyt, "The Los Angeles and San Pedro: First Railroad South of the Tehachapis," *California Historical Society*

Quarterly, 32 (1948): 327–48, p. 332; W. L. Scofield, "California Fishing Ports," CDFG, *Fish Bulletin No. 96* (1954), p. 130.

15   U.S. Census Office, *Twelfth Census of the United States* (1900), *Census Reports*, v. 1: *Population*, pt. 1, p. 495; USDI, Census Office, *Statistics of the Population of the United States at the Tenth Census* (1880), p. 811.

16   *San Francisco Californian*, 19 April 1848; Bancroft, *History of California*, v. 7, pp. 81–2; *Sacramento Union*, 1 January 1859; *Sacramento Bee*, 31 December 1885.

17   Justin Turner, ed., "The Sacramento Flood in the 1850s," *Pacific Historian*, 8 (1964): 129–33, p. 129.

18   Bancroft, *History of California*, v. 7, p. 117, note 22; *San Francisco Alta*, 11 June 1853.

19   *Sacramento Union*, 5 May 1858; Marguerite Hunt and Harry Lawrence Hunt, *History of Solano County and History of Contra Costa County from their Earliest Settlement to the Present Time* (Chicago: S. S. Clark Publishing Co., 1926), v. 1, p. 229; McGowan, *History of the Sacramento Valley*, v. 1, p. 335; anon., *History of Solano County* (San Francisco: Wood, Alley, 1879), pp. 272–3; CCF, *Biennial Report* (1883–4): 4; *Sacramento Union*, 1 January 1859.

20   Gordon B. Dodds, *The Salmon King of Oregon: R. D. Hume and the Pacific Fisheries* (Chapel Hill, NC: University of North Carolina Press, 1959), pp. 4–5; Dodds, ed., *A Pygmy Monopolist: The Life and Doings of R. D. Hume Written by Himself and Dedicated to His Neighbors* (Madison, WI: State Historical Society of Wisconsin, 1961), pp. 30–1. See generally Vernon Carstensen, "The Fisherman's Frontier on the Pacific Coast: The Rise of the Salmon Canning Industry," in *The Frontier Challenge: Responses to the Trans-Mississippi West*, ed. John G. Clark (Lawrence, KS: University Press of Kansas, 1971), pp. 57–80.

21   Daniel B. DeLoach, *The Salmon Canning Industry*, Oregon State Monographs: Economic Studies No. 1 (Corvallis, OR "Oregon State College, 1939), p. 12.

22   CCF, *Report* (1881–2): 3 ibid. (1883–4): 4–5, 32; John N. Cobb, "Pacific Salmon Fisheries," USBF Document No. 1092, USBF, *Report* (1930): 572; Herbert W. Frey, ed., *California's Living Marine Resources and Their Utilization* (Sacramento: DFG, 1971), p. 43.

23   Anthony Netboy, *The Salmon: Their Fight for Survival* (Boston: Houghton-Mifflin, 1974), pp. 177, 82; William H. Dall, "Notes on the Pacific Coast Trade in Shells, Shrimp, Cod, and Salmon," USFC *Bulletin*, 6 (1888): 399.

24   See, for example, Tzvetan Todorov, *The Conquest of America*, tr. Richard Howard (New York: Harper & Row, 1984), esp. 116–19; and E. L. Jones, *The European Miracle: Environments, Economies, and Geopolitics in the History of Europe and Asia* (Cambridge: Cambridge University Press, 1981).

25   James E. Scarff, "The International Management of Whales, Dolphins, and Porpoises: An Interdisciplinary Assessment," *Ecology Law Quarterly*, 6 (1977): 323–427, pp. 343–5; Weaver, "Salt Water Fisheries of the Pacific Coast," p. 155.

26   Richard Henry Dana, Jr. *Two Years Before the Mast* (1841; repr. New York: New American Library, 1964), p. 129–30.

27   Ivan T. Sanderson, *Follow the Whale* (Boston: Little, Brown, 1956), pp. 258–9; Charles M. Scammon, *The Marine Mammals of the Northwestern Coast of North America, Together with an Account of the Amercan Whale-Fishery* (1874; repr. New York: Dover, 1968), pp. 268–70; A. Howard Clark, "The Whale Fishery, I: History and Present Condition of the Fishery," in *The Fisheries and Fishery Industries of the United States*, Sec. V, pt. 15, pp. 23–4; Karl Brandt, *Whale Oil: An Economic Analysis*, Stanford University Food Research Institute Fats and Oils Study No. 7 (Stanford: Stanford University Press, 1940), p. 53; Frank Soule, John G. Gihon, and

James Nisbet, *The Annals of San Francisco* (New York: D. Appleton, 1855), p. 164; *San Francisco Bulletin*, 3 September 1856; 1856 *California Senate Journal* 30; Theodore Hittell, *History of California* (San Francisco: N. J. Stone, 1897), v. 4, pp. 168–9; Ira B. Cross, *A History of the Labor Movement in California* (Berkeley: University of California Press, 1935), pp. 10–11.

28 Scammon wrote that the first colony at Monterey was established in 1851, but the weight of the evidence indicates 1854 as the more likely date. The first station was established by a Captain Davenport, a naturalized Azorean who Anglicized his name as did many others of his kind and who had settled in Santa Cruz to ship timber and lime during the early 1840s. See Scammon, *Marine Mammals of the Northwestern Coast*, p. 247; Edwin C. Starks, "A History of California Shore Whaling," CFGC, *Fish Bulletin No. 6* (1922), pp. 8, 17; *Sacramento Union*, 14 March 1855; *San Francisco Bulletin*, 5 September 1856; W. L. Scofield, "California Fishing Ports," pp. 87–8; *Humboldt Times*, 20 January 1855, 23 June 1855; 7 July 1855, 21 July 1855, 28 July 1855; W. E. Smythe, *History of San Diego, 1542–1907: An Account of the Rise and Progress of the Pioneer Settlement on the Pacific Coast of the United States* (San Diego: The History Company, 1908), p. 110; *San Francisco Bulletin*, 17 January 1858; *San Francisco Alta*, 13 November 1857. I am indebted to F. Ross Holland, Jr., of the U.S. National Parks Service for a copy of his paper, "Shore Whaling on the California Coast with Special Reference to San Diego" (paper delivered to Cabrillo Festival Historical Seminar: San Diego Maritime History, 27 September 1979). On the Azorean immigrants, see Carlos Almeida, "San Leandro and the Portuguese," *Pacific Historian*, 6 (1972): 36–46; George Brown Goode and Joseph W. Collins, "The Fishermen of the United States," in *The Fisheries and Fishery Industries of the United States*, Sec. IV, p. 21; Frederick G. Bohme, "The Portuguese of California," *California Historical Society Quarterly*, 35 (1956): 233–52; U.S. Congress, House, "Consular Reports: Labor in Europe," 48th Cong., 2nd sess. (1884–5), *House Executive Document 54*, p. 1,651; Josef Berger [Jeremiah Digges], *In Great Waters: The Story of the Portuguese Fishermen* (New York: Macmillan, 1941).

29 Earl H. Rosenberg, "A History of the Fishing and Canning Industries in Monterey, California," (M.A. thesis, University of Nevada, Reno, 1961), p. 27; Scammon, *Marine Mammals of the Northwestern Coast*, pp. 21, 40; Coy, *Humboldt Bay Region*, p. 135; Jordan, "The Fisheries of the Pacific Coast," p. 623; Hittell, *The Resources of California, Comprising the Society, Climate, Salubrity, Scenery, Commerce, and Industry of the State* (San Francisco: A Roman, 1874), pp. 197–8; Paul Bonnot, "Report on the Seals and Sea Lions of California," CDFG, *Fish Bulletin No. 14* (1928), p. 10; Henry W. Elliot, "The Sea Lion Hunt," in *The Fisheries and Fishery Industries of the United States*, Sec. 5, v. 2, p. 473.

30 Scammon, *Marine Mammals of the Northwestern Coast*, p. 259; Clark, "History and Present Condition of the Whale Fishery, p. 56; *San Francisco Bulletin*, 5 September 1856.

31 Jordan, "Fisheries of the Pacific Coast," p. 626: Jordan and Charles H. Gilbert, "The Salmon Fishing and Canning Interests of the Pacific Coast," in *The Fisheries and Fishery Industries of the United States*, Sec. V, pt. 13, v. 1, p. 738; *Sacramento Union*, 1 January 1859. Good introductions to the history of Chinese immigrants in California are Gunther Barth, *Bitter Strength: A History of the Chinese in the United States, 1850–1970* (Cambridge, MA: Harvard University Press, 1964); Alexander Saxton, *The Indispensable Enemy: Labor and the Anti-Chinese Movement in California* (Berkeley and Los Angeles: University of Calfornia Press, 1971); and Thomas W. Chinn, ed., *A History of the Chinese in California: A Syllabus* (San Francisco: Chinese Historical Society of America, 1969). On the beginning of the Chinese fisheries, see Robert Alan Nash, "The Chinese Shrimp Fishery in California" (Ph.D. diss., University of California, Los Angeles, 1973), p. 18; Robert F. G. Spier, "Food Habits of Nineteenth-Century California Chinese," *California Historical Society Quarterly*, 37 (1958): 79–84, 129–36, p. 135; *San Francisco Prices Current and Shipping List*, 31 December, 1853; *San Francisco Bulletin*, 31 December 1858, Supp., p. 2; Langdon Sully, *No Tears for the General: The Life of Alfred Sully, 1821–1879* (Palo Alto: American West Publishing Co., 1974), pp. 89, 95; Arthur F. McEvoy, "In Places Men Reject: The Chinese Fishermen at San Diego, 1870–1893," *Journal of San Diego History*, 22 (Fall 1977): 12–24.

32   On the San Diego settlements, see Chinn, *History of the Chinese in California*, p. 37; "Statements of Property of Chinese," Misc. box file no. 1, SDHS, p. 13; John Davidson, *Place Names of San Diego County, No. 259: Chinatown*, SDHS; Goode and Collins, "The Fishermen of the United States," pp. 37, 40; Don M. Stewart, *Frontier Port: A Chapter in San Diego's History* (Los Angeles: The Ward Ritchie Press, 1965), pp. 15–17. A very rare example of a personal diary, written in English, by a California Chinese merchant peripherally involved in the fishing business is Ah Quin, *The Diary of Ah Quin*, for access to which I am grateful to Dr. Thomas Q. Kong of Ventura, California, and Ms. Sylvia Arden of the San Diego Historical Society Library. Descriptions of the abalone junks may be found in George Johnson to Spencer F. Baird, March 1886, Record Group 36, series 143, NARS-LA; Johnson to the Secretary of the Treasury, 12 January 1886, ibid.; Johnson to the Commissioner of Navigation, 25 November 1885; U.S. Bureau of Customs, San Diego Office, Tonnage Admeasurements, 1889–1917, Record Group 36, series 158, NARS-LA; Collins, "The Fishing Vessels of the Pacific Coast," in USFC, *Bulletin*, 10 (1890): 40, 46; John R. Berry to the Secretary of the Treasury, 12 September 1891, Record Group 36, series 143, NARS-LA.

33   See Daniel J. Miller, "The Sea Otter in California," *CalCOFI Reports*, 21 (1980): 79–81.

34   Keith W. Cox, "California Abalones, Family Haliotidae," CDFG, *Fish Bulletin No. 18* (1962), p. 76; *San Diego Union*, 23 May 1884, 7 June 1884, 23 August 1884, 24 January 1885.

35   N. B. Scofield, "Shrimp Fisheries of California," *California Fish and Game*, 5 (1919): 1–12, p. 2.

36   W. H. Dall, "Notes on Fishery Products Exported from San Francisco, California, During the Year 1883," USFC, *Bulletin*, 4 (1884): 125; Wilcox, "Notes on the Fisheries of the Pacific Coast in 1895," USFC, *Report* (1896): 659; Wilcox, "The Fisheries of the Pacific Coast," USFC, *Report* (1893): 199, 206–7.

37   Collins, "Report on the Fisheries of the Pacific Coast," USFC, *Report* (1888): 22; Wilcox, "Fisheries of the Pacific Coast," ibid. (1893): 153; Jordan and Gilbert, "The Salmon Fishing and Canning Interests of the Pacific Coast," p. 738.

38   Fisk, "The Fishermen of San Francisco Bay," p. 386. It was an effective system, however. Chinese workers on the railroads and in the mining camps were apparently better fed and healthier than their comrades of other nationalities. See Speier, "Food Habits of Nineteenth-Century California Chinese," pp. 131, 135.

39   A good study of Italian immigrants in California is Dino Cinel, *From Italy to San Francisco: The Immigrant Experience* (Stanford: Stanford University Press, 1982).

40   Ibid., pp. 103, 213, 259, 140–2; Bancroft, *History of California*, v. 7, pp. 28–9; Fisk, "The Fishermen of San Francisco Bay," p. 385; Cross, *History of the Labor Movement in California*, p. 17; Demitra Georgas, "Greek Settlement in the San Francisco Bay Area" (M.A. thesis, University of California, Berkeley, 1951), p. 10;

Goode and Collins, "The Fishermen of the United States, pp. 34–5; Deanna Paoli Gumina, *The Italians of San Francisco/Gli Italiani di San Francisco* (New York: Center for Migration Studies, 1978), p. 81; U.S. Congress, House, "United States Consular Reports: Labor in Europe," p. 1537; Howard I. Chappelle, "Comments by Chappelle Regarding the Frisco Felucca," in pamphlet file, "Felucca – San Francisco Bay," National Maritime Museum, San Francisco; Hall, "Shipbuilding Industry of the United States," p. 131; Jordan, "The Fisheries of the Pacific Coast." p. 608.

41   Cinel, *From Italy to San Francisco*, pp. 147–50; Weaver, "Salt Water Fisheries of the Pacific Coast," p. 151; Gumina, *The Italians of San Francisco*, pp. 79, 81; Andrew F. Rolle, *The Immigrant Upraised: Italian Adventurers and Colonists in an Expanding America* (Norman, OK: University of Oklahoma Press, 1968), p. 265; *San Diego Weekly*, 30 November 1871; *San Diego Union*, 14 June 1872.

42   Cinel, *From Italy to San Francisco*, p. 221.

43   Ibid., pp. 113, 130–50, 175; Goode and Collins, "The Fishermen of the United States," p. 42; Ernest Peixotto, "Italy in California," *Scribner's Magazine*, 48 (1910): 75–84, p. 84; Weaver, "Salt Water Fisheries of the Pacific Coast," p. 156; Wilcox, "Notes on the Fisheries of the Pacific Coast in 1895," USFC, *Report* (1896): 632.

44   Jordan and Gilbert, "The Salmon Fishing and Canning Interests of the Pacific Coast," p. 738.

45   Ibid., p. 731; Jordan, "Fisheries of the Pacific Coast," p. 609.

46   McEvoy, "In Places Men Reject," pp. 17–20; *San Diego Union*, 23 May 1884, 7 June 1884, 6 February 1885, 1 September 1887, 25 April 1888, 10 November 1888.

47   Frey, *California's Living Marine Resources and Their Utilization*, pp. 115, 118; Collins, "Report on the Fisheries of the Pacific Coast," USFC, *Report* (1888): 21, 28, 37, 72; Wilcox, "Notes on the Fisheries of the Pacific Coast in 1899," USFC, *Report* (1901): 505, 550; Ogden, *The California Sea Otter Trade*, pp. 1–3, 146; Wilcox, "The Fisheries of the Pacific Coast," USFC, *Report* (1893): 201; Peter Mattheissen, *Wildlife in America* (New York: Viking Press, 1959), p. 105. On seal fisheries generally, see Briton Cooper Busch, *The War Against the Seals: A History of the North American Seal Fishery* (Kingston and Montreal: McGill-Queens University Press, 1985).

48   Lionel A. Walford, *Living Resources of the Sea: Opportunities for Research and Expansion* (New York: Ronald Press, 1958), pp. 267–9; Mattheissen, *Wildlife in America*, pp. 100–9; U.N. Food and Agriculture Organization, Advisory Committee on Marine Resources Research, Working Party on Marine Mammals, *Mammals in the Seas*, FAO Fisheries Series No. 5 (Rome: Food and Agriculture Organization, 1979), v. 2, pp. 19–25; Joseph Grinnell, Joseph S. Dixon, and Jean M. Linsdale, *Fur-Bearing Mammals of California: Their Natural History, Systematic Status, and Relations to Man*, contributions from the Museum of Vertebrate Zoology, University of California (Berkeley: University of California Press, 1937), pp. 7–10, 687–8.

49   CCF, *Report* (1880): 6–7; ibid. (1878–9): 5.

50   Scammon, *Marine Mammals of the Northwestern Coast*, p. 259.

51   Hammond, "Shore Whaling on the California Coast," pp. 3–5; FAO, *Mammals in the Seas*, v. 1 (1978), p. 57.

52   Ibid., pp. 110–13; Busch, *The War Against the Seals*, p. 187.

53   James A. Estes and John F. Palmisano, "Sea Otters: Their Role in Structuring Nearshore Communities," *Science*, 185 (20 September 1974): 1058–60.

54   Charles A. Simenstad, James A. Estes, and Karl W. Kenyon, "Aleuts, Sea Otters, and Alternate Stable-State Communities," *Science*, 200 (28 April 1978): 403–10.

55   Collins, "Report on the Fisheries of the Pacific Coast," USFC, *Report* (1–88): 45.

56 Ibid., p. 58.

57 Ibid., pp. 37, 43.

58 Richard Rathbun, "Summary of Fishery Investigations Conducted in the North Pacific Ocean and Bering Sea from July 1, 1888, to July 1, 1892, by the U.S. Fish Commission Steamer *Albatross*," USFC, *Bulletin*, 12 (1892): 194; Smith, "Notes on a Reconnaissance of the Fisheries of the Pacific Coast," pp. 230–1; *San Diego Union*, 16 December 1895, 20 December 1895, 12 August 1903.

59 FAO, *Mammals in the Seas*, v. 1, p. 243; Paul E. Smith, "Biological Consequences of Ocean Variability: Time and Space Scales of Biological Response," *Rapports et Proces-Verbaux des Réunions, Conseil International pour l'Exploration de la Mer (Denmark)*,173 (1978): 117–27, p. 125; NOAA, "Implementation of Northern Anchovy Fishery Management Plan: Solicitation of Public Comments," 43 *Federal Register* (21 July 1978): 31,651–879, p. 31,688; W. Nigel Bonner, *Seals and Man: A Study of Interactions*, Washington Sea Grant Publication (Seattle: University of Washington Press, 1982), pp. 46–53; personal interview, Paul E. Smith, 16 December 1982.

60 C. A. Kirkpatrick, "Salmon-Fishing on the Sacramento River,"*Hutching's California Magazine*, 4 (1860): 529–34, p. 530; U.S. Congress, House, "Report in Relation to the Mining Debris in the Sacramento River," 46th cong., 2nd sess. (1881), *House Executive Document 69;* Buffum, *Six Months in the Gold Mines*, p. 72; *Sacramento Union*, 1 January 1859; CCF, *Report* (1876–7): 5; Henry L. Abbot, "Report of Lieut. Henry L. Abbot, Corps of Topographical Engineers, Upon Explorations for a Railroad Route from the Sacramento Valley to the Columbia River," in U.S. Congress, Senate, "Reports of Explorations and Surveys to Ascertain the Most Practical and Economical Route for a Railroad from the Mississippi River to the Pacific Ocean, Made Under the Direction of the Secretary of War in 1853–1856," 33rd Cong., 2nd sess (1855), *Senate Executive Document 78*, v. VI, pt. 1, p. 57; Phil. E. Drescher, Sutter County, 15 September 1885, in Bancroft Library Pamphlets on Mining, v. 5, no. 11; testimony of B. B. Redding, "Testimony Taken by the Committee on Mining Debris as Reported to the Assembly, 22nd Sess., 1877–1878," Bancroft Library Pamphlets on Mining, v. 5, no. 12, pp. 23, 98, 128; William H. Brewer, *Up and Down California in 1860–1864: The Journal of William H. Brewer*, ed. Francis P. Farquhar (Berkeley and Los Angeles: University of California Press, 1966), p. 295; Elinore M. Barrett, "The California Oyster Industry," CDFG, *Fish Bulletin No. 123*(1963), p. 25; CCF, *Report* (1880): 5.

61 CCF, *Report* (1871–2): 8.

62 Dodds, *The Salmon King of Oregon*, p.5.

63 CCF, *Report* (1874–5): 9.

64 CCF, *Report* (1876–7): 10; William B. Clark, "Gold Districts of California," California Divison of Mines and Geology, *Bulletin No. 193* (1970), p. 4. See generally Robert L. Kelley, *Gold vs. Grain: The Hydraulic Mining Controversy in California's Sacramento Valley: A Chapter in the Decline of Laissez Faire* (Glendale, CA: Arthur H. Clark, 1959). Sawyer's injuction against the mining came down in *Woodruff* v. *North Bloomfield Gravel Mining Co. et al.*, 18 F. 753 (C.C.D. Cal. 1884). The decision itself offers a remarkable history of the mining industry and its environmental effects.

65 CCF, *Report* (1885–6): 15, 20; Charles H. Townsend, "Report of Observations Respecting the Oyster Resources and the Oyster Fishery of the Pacific Coast," USFC, *Report* (1889–91): 354.

66 CSFC, *Biennial Report* (1891–2): 8–9.

67 Ibid. (1893–4): 12.

68 Ibid. (1893–4): 53.

69 CCF, *Report* (1878–9): 19.
70 Wilcox, "The Fisheries of the Pacific Coast," USFC, *Report* (1893): 189; Stewart, *Frontier Port,* p. 120; Wilcox, "Commercial Fisheries of the Pacific Coast States in 1904," USBF, *Report* (1905): 54.
71 Barrett, "The California Oyster Industry," pp. 1920; Wilcox, "The Commercial Fisheries of the Pacific Coast States in 1904," USBF, *Report* (1905): 17; U.S. Department of Commerce and Labor, Bureau of the Census, *Special Reports: Fisheries of the United States, 1908* (Washington: GPO, 1911), p. 88; Erman A. Pearson, *'Reduced Area' Investigation of San Francisco Bay* (Lafayette, CA: California State Water Pollution Control Board, 1958), pp. 206–8.
72 See generally Grove Karl Gilbert, "Hydraulic-Mining Debris in the Sierra Nevada," USDI, Geological Survey, *Professional Paper No. 105* (1917). On the history of San Francisco Bay tidelands, see Mel Scott, *The Future of San Francisco Bay,* University of California Institute of Government Studies (Berkeley: University of California Press, 1963), pp. 1–12; also Gary Feess, "Comment: The Tidelands Trust: Economic Currents in a Traditional Legal Doctrine," *UCLA Law Review,* 21 (1974): 826–91, pp. 832–6. On solar salt production, see William E. VerPlank, "Salt in California," California Department of Natural Resources, Division of Mines, *Bulletin No. 175* (1958).
73 USFC, *Report* (1873): 384. On the reduction in the Bay's tidal prism, see Gilbert, "Hydraulic-Mining Debris," p. 88.
74 Carl L. Hubbs, "Changes in the Fish Fauna of Western North America Correlated with Changes in Ocean Temperature," *Journal of Marine Research,* 7 (1948): 459–82, pp. 464–5.
75 Ibid., p. 473.
76 W. L. Scofield, "Trolling Gear in California," CDFG, *Fish Bulletin No. 103* (1956), p. 11.
77 Gilbert, "Hydraulic-Mining Debris," pp. 29–31.
78 Wilcox, "Notes on the Fisheries of the Pacific Coast in 1895," USFC, *Report* (1896): 642.
79 Collins, "Report on the Fisheries of the Pacific Coast," USFC, *Report* (1888): 168; Julius Wangenheim, "Julius Wangenheim – An Autobiography," *California Historical Society Quarterly,* 35 (1956): 111–44, 253–74, 345–66, p. 123; "Italy by the Golden Gate," *San Francisco Chronicle* (spec. supp., 12 October 1954); Collins, "Report on the Fisheries of the Pacific Coast," USFC, *Report* (1888): 168; DeLoach, *The Salmon Canning Industry,* p. 16; CSFC, *Biennial Report* (1895–6): 15.
80 CSFC, *Biennial Report* (1895–6): 15; Scofield, "Trolling Gear in California," p. 11.
81 W. L. Scofield, "Purse Seines and Other Round-Haul Gear in California," CDFG, *Fish Bulletin No. 81* (1951), pp. 26–9; Smith, "Notes on a Reconnaissance of the Pacific Coast Fisheries in 1894," USFC, *Bulletin,* 14 (1894): 228–9; *Monterey Peninsula Herald* (25 March 1938), pp. 5–6.
82 Collins, "Report on the Fisheries of the Pacific Coast," USFC, *Report* (1888): 28; Wilcox, "The Fisheries of the Pacific Coast," ibid. (1893): 195; Wilcox, "Notes on the Fisheries of the Pacific Coast in 1895," ibid. (1896): 642–3; Dwight T. Reed, "The Fisheries of Spain in 1879," ibid. (1893): 1,195–6; L. DuPont Syle, "The Fisheries of Madeira in 1882," ibid. (1893): 1,196; Bohme, "The Portuguese of California," pp. 239–40; *San Diego Union,* 1 October 1891, 7 April 1892.
83 Vern Griffin, "Tuna Fleet Here a World Leader," *San Diego Union* (27 August 1979), p. B-1.
84 McEvoy, "In Places Men Reject," pp. 18–20.

290   Notes to pp. 89–94

85   1901 *California Statutes* 54.
86   1905 *California Statutes* 196.
87   W. Gordon Fields, "The Structure, Development, Food Relations, Reproduction, and Life History of the Squid *Loligo opalescens* Berry," CDFG, *Fish Bulletin No. 131* (1965), p. 16; Rosenberg, "History of the Fishing and Canning Industries in Monterey," p. 39; Helen Spangenberg, "The Long Road Began in China," [Monterey] *Game & Gossip*, 17 (15 September 1972), pp. 11, 38.
88   Collins, "Report on the Fisheries of the Pacific Coast," USFC, *Report* (1888): 63, 65–6; Wilcox, "Fisheries of the Pacific Coast," ibid (1893): 189; Weaver, "Salt Water Fisheries of the Pacific Coast," p. 152; CSFC, *Biennial Report* (1893–4): 43; Rathbun, "Summary of Fishery Investigations," USFC, *Bulletin*, 12 (1892): 175.
89   Collins, "Report on the Fisheries of the Pacific Coast," USFC, *Report* (1888): 33, 128; Jordan, "Fisheries of the Pacific Coast," pp. 609–10; Goode and Collins, "The Fishermen of the United States," p. 39; Weaver, "Salt Water Fisheries of the Pacific Coast," p. 155; CSFC, *Biennial Report* (1893–4): 43; Cinel, *From Italy to San Francisco*, pp. 131, 219; Richard F. Pourade, *The History of San Diego* (San Diego: Union-Tribune, 1964), v. 4, p. 229.
90   Collins, "Report on the Fisheries of the Pacific Coast," USFC, *Report* (1888): 39, 134, 137–9; Wilcox, "Notes on the Fisheries of the Pacific Coast in 1895," ibid. (1896): 632; Jordan, "The Fisheries of California," p. 476.
91   William Brooks, "Fishing Boats of San Francisco," *The Rudder*, 11 (1900): 237–9, p. 237.
92   U.S. Department of Commerce and Labor, Bureau of the Census, *Special Reports: Fisheries of the United States*, 1908, p. 288.
93   Andrew Soutar and John D. Isaacs, "Abundance of Pelagic Fish During the 19th and 20th Centuries as Recorded in Anaerobic Sediments off the Californias," NMFS, *Fishery Bulletin*, 72 (1974): 257–73, pp. 270–2.

Chapter 5

1   CCF, *Report* (1880): 5.
2   Cf. Francis T. Christy, Jr., and Anthony Scott, *The Common Wealth in Ocean Fisheries: Some Problems of Growth and Economic Allocation*, Resources for the Future (Baltimore: Johns Hopkins University Press, 1965), pp. 26–7.
3   Cited in J. Willard Hurst, *Law and the Conditions of Freedom in the Nineteeth-Century United States* (Madison: University of Wisconsin Press, 1956), p. 68.
4   See S. V. Ciriacy-Wantrup, *Resource Conservation: Economics and Policies*, 3rd (Berkeley: University of California Division of Agricultural Sciences, Agricultural Experiment Station, 1968), p. 226. The deliberate manipulation of common-law rules so as to promote what Hurst called "the release of entrepreneurial energy" is a major theme in nineteenth-century American law. See, for example Hurst, *Law and the Conditions of Freedom*, pp. 3–32; Harry N. Scheiber, "Public Economic Policy and the American Legal System: Historical Perspectives," *Wisconsin Law Review* (1980): 1,159–90, pp. 1,161–72; Scheiber, "Property Law, Expropriation, and Resource Allocation by Government, 1789–1910," in *American Law and the Constitutional Order: Historical Perspectives*, eds. Lawrence M. Friedman and Harry N. Scheiber (Cambridge, MA: Harvard University Press, 1978), pp. 132–41; Morton J. Horwitz, *The Transformation of American Law, 1780–1860* (Cambridge, MA: Harvard University Press, 1977), pp. 1–30; Hurst, *Law and Economic Growth: The Legal History of the Lumber Industry in Wisconsin, 1836–1915* (Cambridge, MA: Harvard University Press, Belknap Press, 1964), pp. 48, 114–15. For California, see Charles W.

McCurdy, "Stephen J. Field and Public Land Law Development in California, 1850–1866: A Case Study of Judicial Resource Allocation in Nineteenth-Century America," *Law and Society Review*, 10 (1976): 235–66; and Scheiber and McCurdy, "Eminent Domain Law and Western Agriculture, 1849–1900," *Agricultural History*, 49 (1975): 112–30.

5 Lawrence M. Friedman and Jack Ladinsky, "Social Change and the Law of Industrial Accidents," *Columbia Law Review*, 67 (1967): 50–82, pp. 53–8; Joel Franklin Brenner, "Nuisance Law and the Industrial Revolution," *Journal of Legal Studies*, 3 (1974): 403–33; Hurst, *Law and the Conditions of Freedom*, pp. 6–7; Scheiber, "Property Law, Expropriation, and Resource Allocation," *passim.*

6 Hurst, *Law and Markets in United States History: Different Modes of Bargaining Among Interests* (Madison: University of Wisconsin Press, 1982), p. 127; Hurst, *Law and Economic Growth*, p. 162, note 37, p. 542, note 31; Ciriacy-Wantrup, *Resource Conservation,*pp. 139–49.

7 *Ex parte Kenneke*, 136 Cal. 527, 530–1 (1902) (Van Dyke, J., dissenting). On the oppression to which Van Dyke made reference see E. P. Thompson, *Whigs and Hunters: The Origin of the Black Act* (New York: Random House, 1975); and Douglas Hay, "Poaching and the Game Laws on Cannock Chase," in Hay et al., *Albion's Fatal Tree: Crime and Society in Eighteenth-Century England* (New York: Random House, 1975), pp. 189–254.

8 Robert H. Connery, *Governmental Problems in Wild Life Conservation*, Studies in History, Economics, and Public Law No. 411 (New York: Columbia University Press, 1935), p. 31; Thomas A. Lund, *American Wildlife Law* (Berkeley and Los Angeles: University of California Press, 1980), p. 78.

9 Hurst, *Law and Economic Growth*, p. 440; Lund, *American Wildlife Law*, p. 73.

10 Ciriacy-Wantrup, *Resource Conservation*, pp. 54–5, 252–9; Hurst, *Law and the Conditions of Freedom*, pp. 98–100; Hurst, *Law and Markets in United States History*, p. 136; K. William Kapp, *The Social Costs of Private Enterprise* (New York: Schocken Books, 1971), pp. 228–31; Christopher D. Stone, "Should Trees Have Standing? Toward Legal Rights for Natural Objects," *Southern California Law Review*, 45 (1972): 450–80, pp. 459–63, 474–9.

11 Hurst, *Law and the Conditions of Freedom*, pp. 3–5: Gerald D. Nash, *State Government and Economic Development: A History of Administrative Policies in California, 1849–1933*, Institute of Governmental Studies (Berkeley: University of California Printing Department, 1964), pp. 34, 76–7; McCurdy, "Stephen J. Field and Public Land Law," pp. 236–7, 239–46; Paul W. Gates, *The Farmer's Age: Agriculture, 1815–1860*, The Economic History of the United States, v. III (New York: Holt, Rinehart, and Winston, 1960), p. 67.

12 Ciriacy-Wantrup, *Resource Conservation*, p. 13, See also Dino Cinel, *From Italy to San Francisco: The Immigrant Experience* (Stanford: Stanford University Press, 1982),pp. 115–16; William S. Cooter, "Ecological Dimensions of Medieval Agrarian Systems," *Agricultural History*, 52 (1978): 458–77; Ciriacy-Wantrup, "Soil Conservation in European Farm Management," *Journal of Farm Economics*, 20 (1938): 86–101; E. Estyn Evans, "The Ecology of Peasant Life in Western Europe," in *Mans Role in Changing The Face of the Earth*, eds. William L. Thomas et al. (Chicago: University of Chicago Press, 1956), pp. 217–39.

13 Ciriacy-Wantrup, *Resource Conservation*, pp. 109–10. It is important to understand industrialization as a worldwide social change, spreading gradually out from its center in England to transform society, politics, and environment in other parts of the world, including, eventually, California. See Brinley Thomas, *Migration and*

Notes to pp. 95–8

Economic Growth: A Study of Great Britain and the Atlantic Economy, 2nd ed. (Cambridge: Cambridge University Press, 1973), pp. 30–1; Philip Taylor, *The Distant Magnet: European Migration to the U.S.A.* (New York: Harper & Row, Torchbook edition, 1971), pp. 1, 25; and generally Karl Polanyi, *The Great Transformation: The Political and Économic Origins of Our Time* (1944; repr. Boston: Beacon Press, 1957), esp. ch. 15.

14 Herbert G. Gutman, "Work, Culture, and Society in Industrializing America, 1815–1919," in *Work, Culture, and Society in Industrializing America*, ed. Gutman (Oxford: Basil Blackwell, 1977), pp. 3–78, p. 41.

15 Cinel, *From Italy to San Francisco*, pp. 197–8, 220.

16 On tenancy, see Ciriacy-Wantrup, *Resource Conservation*, pp. 150–2.

17 USFC, *Report* (1873–4): 382.

18 Henry A. Fisk, "The Fishermen of San Francisco Bay," in *Proceedings of the National Conference of Charities and Corrections at the Thirty-Second Annual Session*, ed. Alexander Johnson (Portland, July 15–21, 1905), pp. 383–92, p. 382.

19 David Starr Jordan and Charles H. Gilbert, "The Salmon Fishing and Canning Interests of the Pacific Coast," in *The Fisheries and Fishery Industries of the United States*, ed. George Brown Goode, U.S. Congress, Senate, 47th Cong., 1st sess. (1887), *Senate Miscellaneous Document 124*, Sec. V, v. 1, pt. 13, pp. 732–3.

20 *San Francisco Chronicle* (8 September 1907), p. 40.

21 Robert Alan Nash, "The Chinese Shrimp Industry in California" (Ph.D. diss., University of California, Los Angeles, 1973), p. 159; Paul Bonnot, "The California Shrimp Industry," CDFG, *Fish Bulletin No. 38* (1932), pp. 5–7.

22 Jordan, "The Fisheries of California," *Overland Monthly* 2d, 20 (1892): 469–78, p. 473; CSFC, *Biennial Report* (1899–1900): 17. See Jack London, *Tales of the Fish Patrol* (New York: Macmillan, 1905); Joan London, *Jack London and His Times: An Unconventional Biography* (New York: Doubleday, 1939), pp. 40–6; Jerold S. Auerbach, *Justice Without Law? Resolving Disputes without Lawyers* (Oxford: Oxford University Press, 1983), pp. 73–6.

23 Fishermen of the Bay of San Francisco, "Resolution, January 12, 1862," Bancroft Library.

24 Ira B. Cross, *A History of the Labor Movement in California* (Berkeley: University of California Press, 1935), p. 36; Deanna Paoli Gumina, *The Italians of San Francisco/Gli Italiani di San Francisco* (New York: Center for Migration Studies, 1978), pp. 87–9; Jordan, "The Fisheries of the Pacific Coast," in *The Fisheries and Fishery Industries of the United States*, Sec. II, pt. 16, pp. 608–9.

25 Cited in Cinel, *From Italy to San Francisco*, p. 220.

26 *San Francisco Chronicle* (8 September 1907), p. 40.

27 Cross, *History of the Labor Movement in California*, p. 134, p. 135, note 12; Gumina, *The Italians of San Francisco*, p. 89; J. W. Collins, "Report on the Fisheries of the Pacific Coast," USFC, *Report* (1888): 127.

28 *San Francisco Call*, 20 April 1913.

29 Collins, "Report on the Fisheries of the Pacific Coast," USFC, *Report* (1888): 127–8.

30 *San Francisco Examiner*, 10 June 1894.

31 Gumina, *The Italians of San Francisco*, p. 87; Gumina, "The Fishermen of San Francisco Bay: The Men of 'Italy Harbor,'" *Pacific Historian*, 20 (1976): 8–21, p. 13; Jordan, "The Fisheries of the Pacific Coast," pp. 608–9; Cinel, *From Italy to San Francisco*, p. 196; Andrew F. Rolle, *The Immigrant Upraised: Italian Adventurers and Colonists in an Expanding America* (Norman, OK: University of Oklahoma Press, 1968), p. 265.

32 P. S. Dasgupta and G. M. Heal, *Economic Theory and Exhaustible Resources* (Cambridge: Cambridge University Press, 1979), pp. 13–17, 58–9.

33 Ciriacy-Wantrup, *Resource Conservation*, pp. 127–8. See also Fikret Berkes, "Fishery Resource Use in a Subarctic Indian Community," *Human Ecology*, 5 (1977): 289–307; James M. Acheson, "The Lobster Fiefs: Economic and Ecological Effects of Territoriality in the Maine Lobster Industry," *Human Ecology*, 3 (1975): 183–207.

34 CCF, *Report* (1878–9): 5.

35 Ibid. (1878–9): 6; cf. Hurst, *Law and Economic Growth*, p. 431.

36 Cross, *History of the Labor Movement in California*, pp. 134, 198; Collins, "Report on the Fisheries of the Pacific Coast," USFC, *Report* (1888): 127; Philip Weaver, Jr., "Salt Water Fisheries of the Pacific Coast," *Overland Monthly* 2d, 20 (1892): 149–63, p. 155.

37 USFC, *Report* (1878): xlix.

38 Raymond McFarland, *A History of the New England Fisheries* (New York: D. Appleton, 1911), pp. 218–19; Dean Conrad Allard, *Spencer Fullerton Baird and the U. S. Fish Commission* (New York: Arno Press, 1978), pp. 117, 121.

39 1869–70 *California Statutes* 663.

40 George Brown Goode, "The First Decade of the United States Fish Commission," USFC, *Report* (1880): 60; Livingston Stone, "The Artificial Propagation of Salmon on the Pacific Coast of the United States, with Notes on the Natural History of the Quinnat Salmon," USFC, *Bulletin*, 16 (1896): 205–6; Allard, *Spencer Fullerton Baird*, pp. 69–86.

41 Connery, *Governmental Problems in Wild Life Conservation*, pp. 115–16; A. Hunter Dupree, *Science in the Federal Government: A History of Policies and Activities to 1940* (Cambridge, MA: Harvard University Press, Belknap Press, 1957), p. 232.

42 Larry A. Nielsen, "The Evolution of Fisheries Management Philosophy," *Marine Fisheries Review*, 38 (December 1976): 15–23, pp. 15–16.

43 Hurst, *Law and the Conditions of Freedom*, pp. 99–100.

44 Lund, *American Wildlife Law*, pp. 46–7; James A. Tober, *Who Owns the Wildlife? The Political Economy of Conservation in Nineteenth-Century America*, Contributions in Economics and Economic History, No. 37 (Westport, CT : Greenwood Press, 1981), p. 226; Connery, *Governmental Problems in Wild Life Conservation*, p. 178.

45 USFC, *Report* (1881): xxix; Hugh M. Smith, "The United States Bureau of Fisheries: Its Establishment, Functions, Organization, Resources, Operations, and Achievements," USBF, *Bulletin*, 27 (1908): pt. 2, p. 1411; USFC, *Report* (1888): xi, xlviii–xliv; Richard Rathbun, "Summary of Fishery Investigations Conducted in the North Pacific Ocean and Bering Sea from July 1, 1888, to July 1, 1892, by the U. S. Fish Commission Steamer *Albatross*," USFC, *Bulletin*, 12 (1892): 190; Francis B. Sumner et al., "A Report upon the Physical Conditions of San Francisco Bay, Based upon the Operations of the United States Fisheries Steamer 'Albatross' During the Years 1912 and 1913," *University of California Publications in Zoology*, 14 (1914); Tober, *Who Owns the Wildlife?*, p. 227.

46 Allard, *Spencer Fullerton Baird*, p. 110; Dupree, *Science in the Federal Government*, pp. 64, 237.

47 See Calvin Woodard, "Reality and Social Reform: The Transition from Laissez-Faire to the Welfare State," *Yale Law Journal*, 72 (1962): 286–328, pp. 292–6, 324.

48 USFC, *Report* (1888): xliv.

49 Ibid. (1888): xlviii.

50 Woodard, "Reality and Social Reform," pp. 291–300; Hurst, *Law and Social*

Order in the United States (Ithaca, NY: Cornell University Press, 1977), p. 214; Jan G. Laitos, "Continuities from the Past Affecting Resource Use and Conservation Patterns," *Oklahoma Law Review*, 28 (1975): 60–96, p. 77.

51   Collins, "Report on the Fisheries of the Pacific Coast," USFC, *Report* (1888): 150; Jordan, "Fisheries of the Pacific Coast," pp. 595, 697; Jordan and Gilbert, "The Salmon Fishing and Canning Interests on the Pacific Coast," p. 738; Robert F. Walsh, "Chinese and the Fisheries in California," *The Californian Illustrated Magazine*, 4 (1893): 833–9.

52   Thomas Tunstead, "Report of Deputy Thomas Tunstead, July 13, 1892," CSFC, Biennial Report (1891–2): 15; CSFC, Biennial Report (1897–8): 18.

53   N. B. Scofield, "Shrimp Fisheries of California," *California Fish and Game*, 5 (1919): 1–12, pp. 2–3.

54   *San Diego Union*, 6 October 1887.

55   Ibid., 12 October 1887, 27 October 1887, 28 October 1887; see also Arthur F. McEvoy, "In Places Men Reject: The Chinese Fishermen at San Diego, 1870–1893," *Journal of San Diego History*, 23 (Fall 1977): 12–24, pp. 17–18.

56   J. L. McHugh, "Trends in Fishery Research," in *A Century of Fisheries in North America*, ed. Norman G. Benson, American Fisheries Society Special Publication No. 7 (Washington: American Fisheries Society, 1970), pp. 25–56, p. 27; David S. Favre, "Wildlife Rights: The Ever-Widening Circle," *Environmental Law*, 9 (1979): 241–81, p. 260; Connery, *Governmental Problems in Wild Life Conservation*, p. 119; USFC, *Report* (1888): xi–xv.

57   USFC, *Report* (1888): xliv.

58   Connery, *Governmental Problems in Wild Life Conservation*, pp. 214–15.

59   USFC, *Report* (1878): xlv.

60   Woodard, "Reality and Social Reform," pp. 292–6.

61   Smith, "The United States Bureau of Fisheries," USBF, *Bulletin*, 27 (1908): 1371. Adams quoted in Clarence J. Glacken, *Traces on the Rhodian Shore: Nature and Culture in Western Thought from Ancient Times to the End of the Eighteenth Century* (Berkeley and Los Angeles: University of California Press, 1967), p. 685.

62   Hurst, *Law and Markets in United States History*, pp. 57–81; Hurst, *Law and Economic Growth*, p. 50; Hurst, *Law and the Conditions of Freedom*, pp. 67–70, 96–100.

63   Weaver, "Salt Water Fisheries of the Pacific Coast," p. 254; Lund, *American Wildlife Law*, p. 68.

64   Jordan, "The Fisheries of California," p. 476.

65   Edward F. Ricketts and Jack Calvin, *Between Pacific Tides*, 4th ed., rev. Joel W. Hedgpeth (Stanford: Stanford University Press, 1968), p. 378.

66   *San Francisco Bulletin*, 29 May 1894; Hugh M. Smith, "A Review of the History and Results of Attempts to Acclimatize Fish and Other Water Animals in the Pacific States," USFC, *Bulletin*, 15 (1895): 396. On the ecology of exotic species, see C. S. Elton, *The Ecology of Invasions by Animals and Plants* (London: Methuen, 1958).

67   Smith, "Notes on a Reconnaissance of the Fisheries of the Pacific Coast of the United States in 1894," USFC, *Bulletin*, 14 (1894): 226.

68   Hurst, *Law and Social Order in the United States*, pp. 157–64; Nathan Rosenberg, *Technology and American Economic Growth* (New York: Harper Torchbooks, 1974), pp. 120, 125; David S. Landes, *The Unbound Prometheus: Technological Change and Industrial Development in Western Europe from 1750 to the Present* (Cambridge: Cambridge University Press, 1972), p. 324.

69   Paul E. Thompson, "The First Fifty Years – the Exciting Ones," in *A Century of Fisheries in North America*, pp. 1–12, p. 3.

70   Smith, "The United States Bureau of Fisheries," USBF, *Bulletin*, 27, pt. 2 (1908): 1371; Allard, *Spencer Fullerton Baird*, pp. 111–31; USFC, *Report* (1878): lv–lvi; Connery, *Governmental Problems in Wild Life Conservation*, pp. 119–21. Livingston Stone is one of the most interesting figures in the history of nineteenth-century conservation. Born in Cambridge, Massachusetts, in 1836, Stone was educated at Harvard and became a Unitarian preacher before poor health led him to take up aquaculture. This enabled him to spend much of his time outdoors and eventually led him to California, where he founded the USFC's fish hatchery program on the McCloud River. A well-loved man, Stone was offered the post of Commissioner of Fisheries when Baird died in 1884, but refused. Stone was a leading advocate of artificial propagation of salmon, but was at the same time very aware of the importance of habitat in the preservation of the resource. His descriptions of the McCloud River Wintu are first-rate ethnographic sources for the period; they are rare for his time in their empathy for California Indian culture and their appreciation of the bonds between Indian culture and the environment. A brief biography may be found in Joel W. Hedgpeth, "Livingston Stone and Fish Culture in California," *California Fish and Game*, 27 (1941): 126–48.

71   Livingston Stone, "The Artificial Propagation of Salmon on the Pacific Coast of the United States," USFC, *Bulletin*, 16 (1896): 219.

72   USFC, *Report* (1888): xliv.

73   Stone, "Artificial Propagation of Salmon," USFC, *Bulletin*, 16 (1896): 218–19, 233.

74   CSFC, *Biennial Report* (1905–6): 25.

75   Smith, "The United States Bureau of Fisheries," USBF, *Bulletin*, 27, pt. 2 (1908): 1382; Allard, *Spencer Fullerton Baird*, pp. 157–63.

76   USFC, *Report* (1877): 31.

77   Smith, "Notes on a Reconnaissance of the Fisheries of the Pacific Coast in 1894," USFC, *Bulletin*, 14 (1894): 226; Connery, *Governmental Problems in Wild Life Conservation*, pp. 119–21.

78   See Hedgpeth, "Livingston Stone and Fish Culture in California," p. 144; also P. A. Larkin, "Maybe You Can't Get There from Here: A Foreshortened History of Research in Relation to Management of Pacific Salmon," *Journal of the Fisheries Research Board of Canada*, 36 (1979): 98–106, p. 101.

79   Stone, "Artificial Propagation of Salmon," USFC, *Bulletin*, 16 (1896): 219.

80   W. E. Ricker, "Heredity and Environmental Factors Affecting Certain Salmonid Populations," in *The Stock Concept in Pacific Salmon*, ed. Raymond C. Simon and Peter A. Larkin, H. R. Macmillan Lectures in Fisheries (Vancouver: University of British Columbia, 1972), pp. 19–160, p. 33.

81   John E. Bardach, John H. Rhyther, and William V. McLarney, *Aquaculture: The Farming and Husbanding of Freshwater and Marine Organisms* (New York: Wiley, 1972), p. 470.

82   USFC, *Report* (1878): lvi.

83   Stone, "Artificial Propagation of Salmon," USFC, *Bulletin*, 16 (1896): 235.

84   CSFC, Biennial Report (1893–4): 131, 135.

85   CCF, *Report* (1974–5): 18.

86   Clarence P. Idyll, "Fisheries and Aquatic Resources: Coastal and Marine Waters," in *Origins of American Conservation*, ed. Henry Clepper (New York: Ronald Press, 1966), pp. 74–89, p. 78; cf. Gerald D. Nash, "The Conflict Between Pure and Applied Science in Nineteenth-Century Public Policy: The California Geological Survey, 1860–1874," in *Science in America Since 1820*, ed. Nathan Reingold (New York: Science History Publications, 1976), pp. 174–85.

87   CCF, *Report* (1876–7): 7.

88   Barton C. Evermann, "A Report upon Salmon Investigations in Headwaters of the Columbia River, in the State of Idaho, in 1895, Together with Notes upon the Fishes Observed in that State in 1894 and 1895," USFC, *Bulletin*, 16 (1896): 10–11.

89   Lund, *American Wildlife Law*, pp. 58–9; Tober, *Who Owns the Wildlife?*, pp. 57, 85–8; Carl L. Hubbs, "History of Icthyology in the United States after 1850," *Copeia*, 1964: 42–60. George Perkins Marsh was one mid-nineteenth century naturalist who had a clear view of the impact of human use on the environment. See his *Man and Nature: Or, Physical Geography as Modified by Human Action* (1864; repr. Cambridge, Ma.: Harvard University Press, Belknap Press, 1965).

90   Landes, *The Unbound Prometheus*, p. 324; Hurst, *Law and Social Order in the United States*, pp. 163–4; Laitos, "Continuities from the Past," p. 90.

91   Wilcox, "The Commercial Fisheries of the Pacific Coast States in 1904," USBF, *Report* (1905): 10–11.

92   *Martin v. Waddell*, 41 U.S. (16 Pet.) 234, 263 (1842); Hurst, *Law and Social Order in the United States*, pp. 88, 97; Hurst, *Law and Markets in United States History*, p. 119.

93   *Commonwealth v. Alger*, 61 Mass. (7 Cush.) 53, 84–5 (1851); Hurst, *Law and Economic Growth*, pp. 172, 440; Hurst, *Law and Markets in United States History*, pp. 54–66.

94   *Smith v. Maryland*, 59 U.S. (18 How.) 71 (1855).

95   See Scheiber, "The Road to *Munn*: Eminent Domain and the Concept of Public Purpose in the State Courts," *Perspectives in American History*, 5 (1971): 329–404, esp. 384–5.

96   Ibid., pp. 337–8; Hurst, *Law and Economic Growth*, p. 50; McCurdy, "Stephen J. Field and Public Land Law," pp. 246–8.

97   1869–70 *California Statutes* 663.

98   Nash, *State Government and Economic Development*, p. 204.

99   1851 *California Statutes* 432; 1866 *California Statutes* 848; cf. *Darbee and Immel Oyster and Land Company v. Pacific Oyster Company*, 150 Cal. 392, 88 P. 1090 (1907); 1873–4 *California Statutes* 940; Barrett, "The California Oyster Industry," p. 34; Erman A. Pearson, *'Reduced Area' Investigation of San Francisco Bay* (Lafayette, CA: California State Water Pollution Control Board, 1958), p. 204. On the Baja California abalone fishery, see *San Diego Union*, 5 June 1889, 9 August 1889, 12 July 1897.

100   1859 *California Statutes* 298.

101   See, for example, *Heckman v. Swett et al.*, 99 Cal. 303, 33 P. 1099 (1893).

102   1899 *Oregon Laws* 72. See Gordon B. Dodds, ed., *A Pygmy Monopolist: The Life and Doings of R. D. Hume Written By Himself and Dedicated to His Neighbors* (Madison: State Historical Society of Wisconsin, 1961), pp. 46–9, 50–3; 77; Dodds, "Rogue River Monopoly," *Pacific Historical Review*, 27 (1958): 263–80; Dodds, "Artificial Propagation of Salmon in Oregon, 1875–1910: A Chapter in American Conservation," *Pacific Northwest Quarterly*, 50 (1959): 125–32; Dodds, "The Fight to Close the Rogue," *Oregon Historical Quarterly*, 40 (1959): 461–74.

103   *Hume v. Rogue River Packing Co.*, 51 Or. 237, 92 P. 1065 (1908). See Dodds, "Rogue River Monopoly," p. 280; Dodds, ed., *A Pygmy Monopolist*, pp. 82–3.

104   1852 *California Statutes* 135; 1853 *California Statutes* 54; 1854 *California Statutes* 122; 1855 *California Statutes* 220; 1855 *California Senate Journal* 678, 682; 1859 *California Statutes* 298; 1875–6 *California Amendments to the Codes* 114; 1877–8 *California Amendments to the Codes* 120; 1881 *California Statutes* 13.

105   Hubert Howe Bancroft, *History of California* (San Francisco: The History

Company, 1884–90), v. 7, p. 82; cf. Ciriacy-Wantrup, *Resource Conservation*, pp. 111–28.

106 CCF, *Report* (1876–7): 18; Jordan and Gilbert, "The Salmon Fishing and Canning Interests of the Pacific Coast," p. 734;; CSFC, *Biennial Report* (1893–4): 50.

107 "Petition to the Legislature by the Fishermen of San Francisco and Vicinity, Asking the Abolishment of the Close Season on Salmon Fishing," 1880 *California Senate and Assembly Journal, Appendix*, v. 5, app. 14.

108 CCF, *Report* (1876–7): 20.

109 CCF, *Report* (1880): 7.

110 CCF, *Report* (1876–7): 21; ibid. (1881–2): 4.

111 CSFC, *Biennial Report* (1886–8): 3–4; ibid. (1891–2): 4; W. L. Scofield, "Marine Fisheries Dates," photocopied (Sacramento: DFG, 1957), p. 9.

112 CSFC, *Biennial Report* (1897–8): 7; cf. Connery, *Governmental Problems in Wild Life Conservation*, p. 215.

113 CCF, *Report* (1885–6): 12–13.

114 Fishermen of the Bay of San Francisco, "Resolution, January 12, 1862," Bancroft Library; *Sacramento Union*, 16 January 1862; 1863–4 *California Statutes* 492.

115 1880 *California Statutes* 123; *In re Ah Chong, In re Wong Hoy, In re Ah You, In re Foo Hoy, In re Foo Hee, In re Ah Mee*, 6 C.C.D.C. (Sawyer) 451 (1880). See also *In re Tiburcio Parrot*, 6 C.C.D.C. (Sawyer) 349 (1880).

116 *McReady v. Virginia*, 94 U.S. 395 (1877).

117 *In re Ah Chong et al.*, 6 C.C.D.C. at 458.

118 CSFC, *Biennial Report* (1897–8): 18–20; 1901 *California Statutes* 54; 1905 *California Statutes* 186; Nash, "The Chinese Shrimp Industry in California," p. 138.

119 1887 *California Statutes* 232; CSFC, *Biennial Report* (1886–8): 6; Scofield, "Marine Fisheries Dates," pp. 28, 33; Joseph A. McGowan, *History of the Sacramento Valley* (New York: Lewis Historical Publishing Co., 1961), v. 1, p. 369; 1880 *California Statutes* 121; 1889 *California Statutes* 61; 1901 *California Statutes* 55; *California Constitution*, Art IV, §25½, approved 4 November 1902, amended 5 November 1940, replaced by Art IV, §20(a), 8 November 1966.

120 CSFC, *Biennial Report* (1893–4): 37; *People v. Truckee Lumber Company*, 116 Cal. 397, 48 P. 374 (1897).

121 *Woodruff v. North Bloomfield Gravel Mining Co., et al.*, 18 F. 753 (C.C.D. Cal. 1884). See McCurdy, "Stephen J. Field and Public Land Law," pp. 262–3.

122 *Ex parte Simon Maier*, 103 Cal. 476, 37 P. 402 (1894).

123 Ibid. at 483.

124 *Geer v. Connecticut*, 161 U.S. 519, 529 (1896).

125 31 *Statutes at Large* 187 (1900); Tober, *Who Owns the Wildlife?*, p. 148; Lund, *American Wildlife Law*, p. 49; Connery, *Governmental Problems in Wild Life Conservation*, pp. 65–7.

126 *California Constitution*, Art. I, §25, approved 8 November 1910; California Constitution Revision Commission, "Background Study: Article I: Declaration of Rights," photocopy (Sacramento: California Constitution Revision Commission, 1969), pp. 58–9.

127 Connery, *Governmental Problems in Wild Life Conservation*, p. 142.

128 CSFC, Biennial Report (1899–1900): 4.

129 Nash, *State Government and Economic Development*, p. 292.

130 CSFC, *Biennial Report* (1899–1900): 4.

131 Oregon Milton Dennis, "Some Reasons for the Failure 'of Fish Protective Legislation and Some Suggested Remedies," USBF, *Bulletin*, 28, v. 1 (1908): 187–98.

132 Tober, *Who Owns the Wildlife?*, pp. 163–4; Connery, *Governmental Problems* *in Wild Life Conservation,* pp. 54–64. On the subsequent history of the *Geer* ruling, see George Cameron Coggins, "Wildlife and the Constitution: The Walls Come Tumbling Down," *Washington Law Review,* 55 (1980): 285–358, pp. 304–8, 313–21.

133   CSFC, *Biennial Report* (1888–90): 67.

134   *Missouri* v. *Holland,* 252 U.S. 416, 434 (1920).

135   *Toomer* v. *Witsell,* 334 U.S. 385, 402 (1948).

136   See Hurst, *Law and the Conditions of Freedom,* pp. 15–18. See also Hurst, *The Legitimacy of the Business Corporation in the Law of the United States* (Charlottesville, VA: University Press of Virginia, 1970); Louis Hartz, *Economic Policy and Democratic Thought: Pennsylvania 1776–1860* (Cambridge, MA: Harvard University Press, 1948), esp. ch. 7; Christopher D. Stone, *Where the Law Ends: The Social Control of Corporate Behavior* (New York: Harper & Row, 1975), esp. pp. 3–25.

Chapter 6

1   *People* v. *Monterey Fish Products Co.,* 195 Cal. 548, 234 P. 398 (1925), reporter's transcript (California State Archives file #22221), p. 18.

2   Ibid., p. 94.

3   U.S. Congress, House, Committee on Merchant Marine and Fisheries and Committee on Commerce, Subcommittee on Fisheries, *Sardine Fisheries,* 74th Cong., 2nd sess (10–11 March 1936), pp. 101–2; Earl Pomeroy, personal correspondence, 16 July 1984.

4   Thomas P. Hughes, *Networks of Power: Electrification in Western Society, 1880–1930* (Baltimore: Johns Hopkins University Press, 1983), p. 266. A useful introduction to the history of southern California is Carey McWilliams, *Southern California: An Island on the Land* (1946; repr. Santa Barbara: Peregrine Press, 1973).

5   U.S. Department of Commerce and Labor, Bureau of the Census, *Thirteenth Census of the United States* (1910), v. IX: *Manufactures, 1909: Reports by States,* p. 69.

6   Hughes, *Networks of Power,* pp. 262–5; C. D. Kinsman, "An Appraisal of Power Used on Farms in the United States," USDA, *Department Bulletin No. 1348* (July 1925), pp. 53–6; Earle D. Ross, "Retardation in Farm Technology Before the Power Age," *Agricultural History,* 30 (1956): 11–18; William L. Calvert, "The Technological Revolution in Agriculture, 1910–1955," ibid., pp. 18–27; California Crop and Livestock Reporting Service, "California Livestock and Poultry," (Sacramento: California Department of Agriculture, ca. 1942), p. 12.

7   USBF, *Reports, passim;* U.S. Department of Commerce, Bureau of the Census, *Special Reports: Fisheries of the United States, 1908* (Washington: GPO, 1911); Neal Potter and Francis T. Christy, Jr., *Trends in Natural Resource Commodities: Statistics of Prices, Output, Consumption, Foreign Trade, and Employment in the United States, 1870–1957,* Resources for the Future (Baltimore: Johns Hopkins University Press, 1962), p. 302, column F.

8   John Thompson and Edward A. Dutra, *The Tule Breakers: The Story of the California Dredge* (Stockton: Stockton Corral of Westerners, University of the Pacific, 1983), pp. 151–9, 232, 284.

9   David S. Landes, *The Unbound Prometheus: Technological Change and Industrial Development in Western Europe from 1750 to the Present* (Cambridge: Cambridge University Press, 1972), p. 235; Nathan Rosenberg, *Technology and American Economic Growth* (New York: Harper Torchbooks, 1972), ch. 5 *passim;* James Willard Hurst, *Law and Markets in United States History: Different Modes*

of *Bargaining Among Interests* (Madison: University of Wisconsin Press, 1982), pp. 187–213.

10 William F. Thompson and Norman C. Freeman, *History of the Pacific Halibut Fishery*, International Fisheries Commission Report No. 5 (Vancouver: Wrigley Printing Co., 1930), p. 11; Vernon Carstensen, "The Fisherman's Frontier on the Pacific Coast: The Rise of the Salmon Canning Industry," in *The Frontier Challenge: Responses to the Trans-Mississippi West*, ed. John G. Clark (Lawrence, KS : University Press of Kansas, 1971), pp. 57–80, p. 65, note 125.

11 John C. Ellickson and John M. Brewster, "Technological Advance and the Structure of American Agriculture," *Journal of Farm Economics*, 29 (1947): 827–47, pp. 827–30; R. Burnell Held and Marion Clawson, *Soil Conservation in Perspective*, Resources for the Future (Baltimore: Johns Hopkins University Press, 1965), pp. 92–5; John H. Perkins, *Insects, Experts, and the Insecticide Crisis: The Quest for New Pest Management Strategies* (New York: Plenum, 1982), pp. 223–4; John S. Steinhart and Carol Steinhart, "Energy Use in the U.S. Food System," *Science*, 184 (19 April 1974): 307–16, pp. 310–12.

12 William A. Wilcox, "Notes on the Fisheries of the Pacific Coast in 1899," USFC, *Report* (1901): 505; Wilcox, "The Commercial Fisheries of the Pacific Coast States in 1904," USBF, *Report* (1905): 5, 11, 26, 55; U.S. Department of Commerce, Bureau of the Census, *Special Reports: Fisheries of the United States, 1908* (Washington, DC: GPO, 1911), pp. 25, 86.

13 Oscar E. Sette, "Fishery Industries of the United States 1924," USBF, *Report* (1925): 279, 313; CFGC, *Biennial Report* (1920–2): 12.

14 Robert J. Browning, *Fisheries of the North Pacific: History, Species, Gear & Processes* (Anchorage: Alaska Northwest Publishing Co., 1974), p. 276; *San Francisco Chronicle* (8 September 1907), p. 40; ibid. (12 September 1907), p. 5.

15 John N. Cobb, "The Salmon Fisheries of the Pacific Coast," USBF Document No. 1,092, USBF, *Report* (1930): 60–2. A good technical review of the mild-curing process for salmon can be found in W. L. Scofield, "Mild Curing of Salmon in California," USBF, *Report* (1925): 1–14; *Monterey Peninsula Herald* (25 March 1938), p. 6.

16 CSFC, *Biennial Report* (1905–6): 25.

17 Ibid., p. 26.

18 Donald H. Fry, Jr., and Eldon P. Hughes, "The California Salmon Troll Fishery," PMFC, *Bulletin No. 2* (1951), p. 10; W. L. Scofield, "Sardine Fishing Methods at Monterey, California," CDFG, *Fish Bulletin No. 19* (1929), pp. 19–20; Hans Buckwalter, "San Pedro Felucca Outlasted San Francisco Bay Brethren," in Felucca – San Francisco Bay, pamphlet file, National Maritime Museum, San Francisco, n.d.; Howard I. Chappelle, "Comments by Chappelle Regarding the Frisco Felucca," ibid., n.d.; Earl H. Rosenberg, "A History of the Fishing and Canning Industries of Monterey, California" (M.A. thesis, University of Nevada, Reno, 1961), pp. 59–60; *Monterey Peninsula Herald* (10 January 1938), p. 1.

19 Gary L. Rankel, "Depleted Chinook Salmon Runs in the Klamath River Basin: Causes, Consequences and Constraints on Management," photocopied (Arcata, CA: USFWS, 1980), p. 14.

20 P. A. Larkin, "An Epitaph for the Concept of Maximum Sustained Yield," American Fisheries Society, *Transactions*, 106 (1977): 1–11. See generally Larkin, "Maybe You Can't Get There From Here: A Foreshortened History of Research in Relation to Management of Pacific Salmon," *Journal of the Fisheries Research Board of Canada*, 36 (1979): 98–106; also James A. Crutchfield and Giulio Pontecorvo, *Pacific Salmon Fisheries: A Study of Irrational Conservation*, Resources for the Future (Baltimore: Johns Hopkins University Press, 1969).

21   Rosenberg, "History of the Fishing and Canning Industries in Monterey," p. 61; CFGC, *Biennial Report* (1922–4): 51; W. L. Scofield, "Trolling Gear in California," CDFG, *Fish Bulletin No. 103* (1956), p.16.

22   Gerald D. Nash, *State Government and Economic Development: A History of Administrative Policies in California, 1849–1933*, University of California Institute of Governmental Studies (Berkeley: University of California Printing Department, 1964), p. 296: CFGC, *Biennial Report* (1914–16): 80. On Japanese immigration to Hawaii and California, see Hilary Controy, *The Japanese Frontier in Hawaii, 1868–1898*, University of California Publications in History, v. 46 (Berkeley: University of California Press, 1953); and Ronald Takaki, *Pau Hana: Plantation Life and Labor in Hawaii, 1835–1920* (Honolulu: University of Hawaii Press, 1983).

23   Scofield, "Trolling Gear in California," p. 14; N. B. Scofield, "The Tuna Canning Industry of Southern California," in CFGC, *Biennial Report* (1912–14): 111–20; Don Estes, "Kondo Masaharu and the Best of All Fishermen," *Journal of San Diego History*, 23 (Summer 1977): 1–19.

24   (Seattle) *Pacific Fisherman Yearbook* (1915), p. 76; CFGC, *Biennial Report* (1914–16): 84; Lewis Radcliffe, "Fishery Industries of the United States: Report of the Division of Statistics and Methods of the Fisheries for 1918," USBF, *Report* (1918): 130.

25   Milner B. Schaefer, Oscar E. Sette, and John C. Marr, "Growth of the Pacific Coast Pilchard Fishery to 1942," USFWS *Research Report 29* (1951), pp. 3–4; Pacific Fisherman Yearbook (1915), pp. 76–7; Scofield, "The Tuna Canning Industry," CFGC, *Biennial Report* (1914–6): 122.

26   *Monterey Peninsula Herald* (25 March 1938), pp. 5–6; W. L. Scofield, "Purse Seines and Other Round Haul Gear of California," CDFG, *Fish Bulletin No. 81*, p. 28; W. F. Thompson, "The California Sardine and the Study of the Available Supply," CFGC, *Fish Bulletin No. 11* (1926), p. 32; Browning, *Fisheries of the North Pacific*, p. 12; Rosenberg, "History of the Fishing and Canning Industries in Monterey," p. 81.

27   *Pacific Fisherman Yearbook* (1916), p. 75; Rosenberg, "History of the Fishing and Canning Industries in Monterey," p. 80; W. Gordon Fields, "The Structure, Development, Food Relations, Reproduction, and Life History of the Squid *Loligo opalescens* Berry," DFG, *Fish Bulletin No. 131* (1965), p. 17; Schaefer, Sette, and Marr, "Growth of the Pacific Coast Pilchard Fishery," p. 3.

28   H. R. Halloran, "Marine Products in Poultry Feeds," *Nulaid News*, 27:8 (December 1949): 10–12; George H. Hart et al., "Wealth Pyramiding in the Production of Livestock," in *California Agriculture: By Members of the Faculty of Agriculture of the University of California*, ed. Claude B. Hutchison (Berkeley and Los Angeles: University of California Press, 1946), pp. 56–104, pp. 60–1.

29   Charles W. Smiley, "The Extent of the Use of Fish Guano as a Fertilizer," USFC, *Report* (1881): 663–6, 694–5.

30   *Pacific Fisherman* (May 1922), p. 10; Rosenberg, "History of the Fishing and Canning Industries in Monterey," pp. 79–80.

31   Radcliffe, "Fishery Industries of the United States, 1918," USBF, *Report* (1918): 183–4.

32   George Soule, *Prosperity Decade: From War to Depression, 1917–1929*, Economic History of the United States, v. 8 (New York: Rinehart & Co., 1947), pp. 20–2.

33   M. R. Benedict, "The Economic and Social Structure of California Agriculture," in *California Agriculture*, ed. Hutchison, pp. 397–433, pp. 408–10. See Louise Page and Berta Friend, "The Changing United States Diet," *BioScience*, 28 (1978): 192–8.

34 Soule, *Prosperity Decade*, pp. 96, 124, 240; US Department of Commerce, Bureau of the Census, *Biennial Census of Manufactures* (1921), p. 48; Ralph D. Jennings, "Consumption of Feed by Livestock, 1909–47," USDA, *Circular No. 836* (December 1949), pp. 8–9; Hart, "Wealth Pyramiding in the Production of Livestock" pp. 56–77.

35 John O. Snyder, "Salmon of the Klamath River, California," CDFG, *Fish Bulletin No. 34* (1931), pp. 84, 99; (Crescent City) *Del Norte Triplicate* (10 March 1924), p. 3; ibid. (3 May 1924), p. 3; N.B. Scofield, "The Status of Salmon in California," *California Fish and Game*, 15 (1929): 13–18.

36 U.S. Department of Commerce, Bureau of the Census, *Fourteenth Census* (1920), v. VII: *Irrigation and Drainage*, pp. 127, 132; U.S. Department of Commerce, Bureau of the Census, *Census of Electrical Industries, 1917: Central Electric Light and Power Stations, with Summary of the Electrical Industries* (Washington, DC: GPO, 1920), p. 149.

37 CFGC, *Biennial Report* (1918–20): 20, 86; ibid. (1920–2): 85; G. H. Clark, "Sacramento-San Joaquin (*Onchorhynchus tschawytscha*) Salmon Fishery of California," CDFG, *Fish Bulletin No. 17* (1929), pp. 23, 31, 35; Charles M. Coleman, *P. G. and E. of California: The Centennial Story of Pacific Gas and Electric Company, 1852–1952* (New York: McGraw-Hill, 1952), p. 199.

38 Eileen M. Glaholt, "Office Report: History of the Klamath River Region," photocopied (Sacramento: California Resources Agency, 1975), pp. 75–6; California Legislature, Assembly, "Report of the Interim Committee on Klamath River," 56th sess. (1935), p. 12.

39 CFGC, *Biennial Report* (1920–2): 34, 85; 1925 *California Statutes* xclii; Snyder, "Indian Methods of Fishing on Trinity River, and Some Notes on the King Salmon of That Stream," *California Fish and Game*, 10 (1924): 163–8, p. 162; Glaholt, "Office Report: History of the Klamath River Region," p. 74.

40 G. H. Clark, "San Francisco Trawl Fishery," *California Fish and Game*, 21 (1935): 22–37, pp. 22–3.

41 CFGC, *Biennial Report* (1914–16): 90.

42 Philip Weaver, Jr., "Salt Water Fisheries of the Pacific Coast," *Overland Monthly* 2d, 20 (1892): 149–63, p. 153; California State Market Commission, *Annual Report* (1919): 103.

43 CFGC, *Biennial Report* (1922–4): 68. See also ibid. (1918–20): 73; ibid. (1920–2): 78; Tage Skogsberg, "Preliminary Investigation of the Purse Seine Industry of Southern California," CDFG, *Fish Bulletin No. 9* (1925).

44 *San Diego Union*, 1 January 1947.

45 California State Market Commission, *Annual Report* (1918): 97, 103; Herbert W. Frey, ed., *California's Living Marine Resources and Their Utilization* (Sacramento: CDFG, 1971), pp. 83–4. See also R. Michael Laurs, "The North Pacific Albacore – An Important Visitor to California Current Waters," *CalCOFI Reports*, 24 (1983): 99–106, pp. 104–6.

46 *Pacific Fisherman Yearbook* (1917), p. 85; Milner B. Schaefer, "Management of the American Pacific Tuna Fishery," in *A Century of Fisheries in North America*, ed. Norman G. Benson, American Fisheries Society Special Publication No. 7 (Washington: American Fisheries Society, 1970), pp. 237–48, p. 237.

47 N. B. Scofield, "Commercial Fishery Notes," *California Fish and Game*, 3 (1917): 34–5. On Japanese immigrants in Central Valley agriculture, see California State Board of Control, *California and the Oriental* (Sacramento: State Printing Office, 1920), p. 52.

48 *Pacific Fisherman Yearbook* (1925), p. 124; Estes, "Kondo Masaharu and the Best of All Fishermen," pp. 3, 7–11; *Pacific Fisherman Yearbook* (1924), p. 84.

49 *Pacific Fisherman Statistical Number* (25 January 1929), pp. 170–3; *Pacific Fisherman Yearbook* (1923), p. 84; CFGC, *Biennial Report* (1922–4): 65; Sette, "Fishery Industries of the United States, 1923" USBF, *Report* (1924): 151, 186.
50 Rosenberg, "History of the Fishing and Canning Industries in Monterey," p. 88; Scofield, "Sardine Fishing Methods at Monterey," p. 10; R. H. Fiedler, "Review of the Fisheries of California," USBF, *Report* (1930): 229; Harry R. Beard, "Preparation of Fish for Canning as Sardines," USBF, *Report* (1927): 71.
51 C. W. Lang and R. S. Fellers, "Commercial Packing of California Mackerel: Preliminary Reports," *University of California Publications in Public Health*, 1 (1929), p. 295; (Seattle) *Coast Seamen's Journal*, 4 October 1916; CFGC, *Biennial Report* (1914–16): 51; W. L Scofield, "Marine Fisheries Dates," photocopied (Sacramento: DFG, 1957), p. 26; CFGC, *Biennial Report* (1918–20): 71; *Pacific Fisherman Yearbook* (1925), p. 158; ibid. (1926), p. 166; ibid. (1927), p. 210; ibid. (1928), p. 210. See generally Edwin C. Starks, "A History of California Shore Whaling," CFGC, *Fish Bulletin No. 6* (1922).
52 *Pacific Fisherman Yearbook* (1923), p. 86; ibid. (1924), p. 85; ibid. (1925), p. 106; Scofield, "Sardine Fishing Methods at Monterey," p. 15; Sette, "Fishery Industries of the United States, 1924" USBF, *Report* (1925): 229; Fiedler, "Review of the Fisheries of California," ibid. (1930): 351; *People v. Monterey Fish Products Co.*, 195 Cal. 548, reporter's transcript, pp. 14–5.
53 *Pacific Fisherman* (February 1921), p. 54.
54 *Pacific Fisherman* (September 1919), p. 62; *Pacific Fisherman Yearbook* (1925), p. 106; CFGC, *Biennial Report* (1918–20): 72; Schaefer, Sette, and Marr, "Growth of the Pacific Coast Pilchard Fishery," p. 18; Elbert H. Ahlstrom and John Radovich, "Management of the Pacific Sardine," in *A Century of Fisheries in North America*, ed. Benson, pp. 183–93, p. 186.
55 Schaefer, Sette, and Marr, "Growth of the Pacific Coast Pilchard Fishery," pp. 6–12.
56 *Pacific Fisherman Yearbook* (1926), p. 110.
57 *People v. Monterey Fish Products Co.*, 195 Cal. 548, reporter's transcript, p. 18.
58 Scofield, "Sardine Fishing Methods at Monterey," p. 26; Scofield, "Purse Seines and Other Round Haul Gear of California," p. 30; J. C. Phillips, "Success of the Purse Seine Boat in the Sardine Fishery at Monterey, California," CDFG, *Fish Bulletin No. 23* (1930); CDFG, *Biennial Report* (1928–30): 113–14; *Monterey Peninsula Herald* (25 March 1938), pp. 3–4; *Pacific Fisherman Yearbook* (1927), p. 167; ibid. (1929), p. 178.
59 Schaefer, Sette, and Marr, "Growth of the Pacific Coast Pilchard Fishery," p. 24; Rosenberg, "History of the Fishing and Canning Industries in Monterey," p. 131.
60 Scofield, "Sardine Fishing Methods at Monterey," p. 17.
61 W. L. Scofield, "Sardine Oil in Our Troubled Waters," *California Fish and Game*, 24 (1938): 210–23, p. 215; John R. Arnold, *Evidence Study No. 13 of the Fishery Industry* (Washington: National Recovery Administration, Division of Review, 1936), p. 7; Scofield, "Marine Fisheries Dates," p. 30; Arthur T. Sutherland, "Earnings and Hours in Pacific Coast Fish Canneries," U.S. Department of Labor, Women's Bureau, *Bulletin No. 186* (1941), pp. 13, 25.
62 Jennings, "Consumption of Feed by Livestock," p. 23; Ellickson, "Technological Advance and the Structure of American Agriculture," pp. 827, 830; Hart, "Wealth Pyramiding in the Production of Livestock," p. 61; Perkins, *Insects, Experts, and the Insecticide Crisis*, pp. 231–2.

63 California State Department of Public Works, Division of Water Resources, "Report to the Legislature of 1931 on State Water Plan," *Bulletin* No. 25 (1930); 1933 *California Statutes*, ch. 1042, §15.
64 Stephen Fox, *John Muir and His Legacy: The American Conservation Movement* (Boston: Little, Brown, 1981), pp. 163, 188, 198; California State Chamber of Commerce, Conservation Department, "Report of the Klamath–Trinity River Fact Finding Committee," mimeographed (Sacramento: California State Chamber of Commerce, 1936), p. 20; CDFG, *Biennial Report* (1936–8): 57; ibid. (1946–8): 43; Richard Van Cleve, "A Preliminary Report on the Fishery Resources of California in Relation to the Central Valley Project," *California Fish and Game*, 31 (1945): 35–52, pp. 37–41; Roy Archibald, "Fish and Game Conservation and Preservation," mimeographed (Berkeley: University of California Bureau of Public Administration, 1947), pp. 36–8.
65 U.S. Congress, Senate, Committee on Indian Affairs, *Survey of Conditions of Indians of the United States: Hearings Before a Subcommittee of the Committee on Indian Affairs*, pt. 29: *California*, 72nd Cong., 1st sess. (1934), p. 15653; Glaholt, "Office Report: History of the Klamath River Region," p. 67; Snyder, "Salmon of the Klamath River," p. 43.
66 U.S. Congress, Senate, Committee on Indian Affairs, *Survey of Conditions of Indians*, pt. 29: *California*, p. 15571. See also ibid., pp. 15,571–3, 15,653–4; 1933 *California Statutes* 394, at 411; 1933 *California Statutes* 1697.
67 Fry and Hughes, "The California Salmon Troll Fishery," pp. 10–11.
68 Clark, "Sacramento–San Joaquin Salmon Fishery," p. 53; "Report on the 1952 Sardine Conference, 29–31 July," CLHP, "CalCOFI–Sardine Conference, 1952."
69 See S. Ross Hatton, "Progress Report on the Central Valley Fisheries Investigations," *California Fish and Game*, 26 (1940): 334–70; Van Cleve, "Preliminary Report on the Fishery Resources of California in Relation to the Central Valley Project," pp. 35–52; J. W. Moffet, "The First Four Years of King Salmon Maintenance Below Shasta Dam," *California Fish and Game*, 35 (1949): 77–102, pp. 100–2; Donald Arthur Duerr, "Conflicts Between Water Development Projects and Fish and Wildlife Conservation in the Central Valley Basin, California" (M.A. thesis, University of California, Berkeley, 1955), pp. 221–6.
70 *Pacific Fisherman* (November 1932), p. 18; ibid. (August 1935), p. 78; U.S. Congress, House, Committee on Merchant Marine and Fisheries, *Sardine Fisheries*, p. 99; CDFG, *Biennial Report* (1930–2): 68; ibid. (1936–8): 104–5. Prices for by-products and competing commodities are taken from USDA, *Agricultural Statistics*, published annually.
71 Schaefer, Sette, and Marr, "Growth of the Pacific Coast Pilchard Fishery," pp. 15–17; CDFG, *Biennial Report* (1930–2): 70.
72 CDFG, *Biennial Report* (1932–4): 50; Archibald, "Fish and Game Conservation and Preservation," pp. 39–40.
73 Garth I. Murphy, "Population Biology of the Pacific Sardine (*Sardinops caerulea*)," California Academy of Sciences, *Proceedings*, 4th (1966), p. 15; *Pacific Fisherman Yearbook* (1948): 209; U.S. Congress, House, Committee on Merchant Marine and Fisheries, *Sardine Fisheries*, p. 66; CDFG, *Biennial Report* (1936–8: 104–5; *Monterey Peninsula Herald* (25 March 1938), p. 12; Hiroshi Kasahara, *Fisheries Resources of the North Pacific Ocean: A Series of Lectures Presented at the University of British Columbia, January and February, 1960*, H. F. Macmillan Lectures in Fisheries, pt. 1 (New York: Macmillan, 1961), p. 124.
74 *Pacific Fisherman* (August 1935), pp. 66, 78; California Crop and Livestock Reporting Service, "California Livestock and Poultry," pp. 112–13; N. B. Scofield

to Henry O'Malley, 11 May 1923, USBF Division of Scientific Inquiry, General Correspondence, Box 1, Record Group 22, series 121, NARS-DC; O'Malley to Scofield, 2 May 1923, ibid. See also R. B. Easson, *California Poultry Production* (San Francisco: Pacific Rural Press, 1923), p. 65; C. R. Grau, F. H. Kratzer, and W. E. Newlon, "Feed for Chickens," University of California, Agricultural Extension Service, *Circular No. 149* (December 1949), pp. 17–29; Joseph Havlicek, Jr., and Faustino Ccama, "U. S. Demand for Fish Meal" (Contributed Paper, American Agricultural Economics Association Meetings, San Diego, July 31–August 3, 1977), photocopied (copy on file, Giannini Foundation of Agricultural Economics Library, University of California, Berkeley), p. 1.

75 USFWS, "Commercial Fisheries Outlook," *Fishery Leaflet 336* (April 1949), p. 5.

76 Scofield, "Sardine Oil in Our Troubled Waters," p. 213; U.S. Congress, House, Committee on Merchant Marine and Fisheries, *Sardine Fisheries*, p. 65; *Pacific Fisherman* (July 1933), p. 47; personal interview, Frances N. Clark, 11 September 1982.

77 John Radovich, "Managing Pelagic Schooling Prey Species," in *Predator–Prey Systems in Fisheries Management*, ed. Henry Clepper, International Symposium on Predator–Prey Systems in Fish Communities and Their Role in Fisheries Management, Atlanta, July 24–27, 1978 (Washington, DC: Sport Fishing Institute, 1979), pp. 365–75, p. 369; Paul E. Smith, "Biologic Effects of Ocean Variability: Time and Space Scales of Biological Response," *Rapports et Proces-Verbaux des Réunions, Conseil International pour l'Exploration de la Mer* (Denmark), 173 (1978): 117–27, pp. 119–24.

78 Frances N. Clark, "A Summary of the Life-History of the California Sardine and Its Influence on the Fishery," *California Fish and Game*, 21 (1935): 1–9; Radovich, "Managing Pelagic Schooling Prey Species," *passim*; Smith and Reuben Lasker, "Position of Larval Fish in an Ecosystem,"*Rapports et Proces-Verbaux des Réunions, Conseil International pour l'Exploration de la Mer* (Denmark), 173 (1978): 77–84.

79 Clark, "Summary of the Life-History of the California Sardine," p. 6; Murphy, "Population Biology of the Pacific Sardine," pp. 76–7.

80 Murphy, "Population Biology of the Pacific Sardine," p. 77.

81 Alec D. MacCall, "Population Estimates for the Waning Years of the Pacific Sardine Fishery," *CalCOFI Reports*, 20 (1979); 72–82.

82 Murphy, "Population Biology of the Pacific Sardine," pp. 44–6; U.S. Congress, House, Committee on Merchant Marine and Fisheries, *Sardine Fisheries*, p. 32.

83 *Pacific Fisherman* (October 1939), p. 32, ibid. (August 1940), p. 14; *Monterey Peninsula Herald* (10 January 1938), p. 1; CDFG, *Biennial Report* (1938–40): 40; ibid. (1940–2): 47; California State Chamber of Commerce, Research Department, "The California Sardine Industry: Prepared at the Request of the Subcommittee on the Sardine Industry of the Statewide Natural Resources Committee," mimeographed (San Francisco: California Chamber of Commerce, 1946), p. 6.

84 CDFG, *Biennial Report* (1940–2): 49; *Pacific Fisherman* (December 1940), p. 21; *Pacific Fisherman Yearbook* (1945), pp. 67– 73, 205–13; Lester Ballinger to Leonard R. Linsenmayer, 8 November 1957, CLHP, Fisheries: Tuna.

85 CDFG, *Biennial Report* (1940–2): 47; ibid. (1942–4): 34.

86 Dino Cinel, *From Italy to San Francisco: The Immigrant Experience* (Stanford: Stanford University Press, 1982), p. 254. On the internment of the Japanese-Americans, see Roger Daniels, *Concentration Camps, North America: Japanese in the United States and Canada During World War II* (Malabar, FL: Robert E. Krieger

Publishing Co., 1981); Audrey Girdner and Annie Loftis, *The Great Betrayal* (New York: Macmillan, 1969).

87 CDFG, *Biennial Report* (1946–8): 32; *Pacific Fisherman* (October 1948), p. 29; Moffet, "The First Four Years of King Salmon Maintenance Below Shasta Dam," p. 102.

88 Fry and Hughes, "The California Salmon Troll Fishery," p. 16; Duerr, "Conflicts Between Water Development Projects and Fish and Wildlife Conservation," pp. 105–6.

89 Fry and Hughes, "The California Salmon Troll Fishery," pp. 10–12.

90 *Pacific Fisherman Yearbook* (1945), p. 70; Ballinger to Linsenmayer, 8 November 1957, CLHP, Fisheries: Tuna.

91 Elmer Higgins to Elton Sette, 9 May 1941, USBCF General Classified Correspondence, Record Group 22, Series 121, Box 479, file 825.1, NARS-DC.

92 Sette to Higgins, 18 November 1942, ibid.; CDFG, *Biennial Report* (1942–4): 36.

93 Sette to L. T. Hopkinson, 23 October 1942, USBCF General Classified Correspondence, Box 479, file 825.1; Sette, "Pacific Coast Pilchard" (mimeographed, 2 July 1946), USBCF General Classified Correspondence, Record Group 22, Series 121, Box 480, file 825.1; *Pacific Fisherman Yearbook* (1945), pp. 71, 207; CDFG, *Biennial Report* (1942–4): 71, 100–1; *Pacific Fisherman* (February 1945), p. 33; ibid. (April 1945), p. 36.

94 Murphy, "Population Biology of the Pacific Sardine," p. 46; *Pacific Fisherman Yearbook* (1948): p. 109.

95 *Pacific Fisherman* (November 1945), p. 29; ibid. (December 1946), p. 21; *San Diego Union*, 7 October 1947.

96 CDFG, *Biennial Report* (1946–8): 23.

97 Murphy, "Population Biology of the Pacific Sardine," p. 76; *Pacific Fisherman* (January 1948), p. 42; "Pilchard and Sardine Conference, 1949," CLHP, CalCOFI Sardine Conference 1949.

98 USFWS, *Fishery Leaflet 336b* (October 1949), pp. 15, 20; USFWS, *Fishery Leaflet 336f* (October 1950), pp. 22; USFWS, *Fishery Leaflet 336k* (January–March 1952) p. 28; USFWS, *Fishery Leaflet 336q* (July 1953), p. 34; *Monterey Peninsula Herald* (26 August 1949), p. 1; ibid. "Fifteenth Annual Sardine Edition" (28 February 1950), p. 1.

99 Manuel Elguerra, "A Policy for Marine Resources: Peru's Experience," in *California and the World Ocean*, Governor's Conference on California and the World Ocean, 31 January–1 February 1964 (California: State Government, special publication, 1964), pp. 53–5; USFWS, *Fishery Leaflet 336q* (July 1953), p. 36; personal interview, Richard Croker, 3 September 1982; Michael Roemer, *Fishing for Growth: Export-Led Development in Peru, 1950–67* (Cambridge: MA: Harvard University Press, 1970), pp. 82–3. Erik Eckholm offers a brief history of the Peruvian fishery in his *Losing Ground: Environmental Stress and World Food Prospects*, Worldwatch Institute (New York: Norton, 1976), pp. 157–60. See also Georg Borgstrom, "Ecological Aspects of Protein Feeding – The Case of Peru," in *The Careless Technology: Ecology and International Development*, eds. M. Taghi Farvar and John P. Milton (Garden City, NY: Natural History Press, 1972), pp. 753–4.

Chapter 7

1 CDFG, *Biennial Report* (1936–8): 60.

2 *Diamond Glue Co.* v.*United States Glue Co.*, 187 U.S. 611, 616 (1903).

3 Samuel P. Hays, *Conservation and the Gospel of Efficiency: The Progressive*

Conservation Movement, 1890–1920 (1959; repr. New York: Atheneum, 1980), esp. ch. 12.

4   See J. Willard Hurst, *Law and the Conditions of Freedom in the Nineteenth Century United States* (Madison: University of Wisconsin Press, 1956), pp. 99–103.

5   Gerald D. Nash, *State Government and Economic Development: A History of Administrative Policies in California, 1849–1933*, University of California Institute of Governmental Studies (Berkeley: University of California, 1964), p. 293.

6   1907 *California Statutes* 247; CSFC, *Biennial Report* (1908–10): 7; CFGC, *Biennial Report* (1920–2): 8; 1927 *California Statutes* 239.

7   *San Francisco Chronicle* (23 March 1921), p. 3; cf. Grant McConnell, *The Decline of Agrarian Democracy* (1953; repr.; New York: Atheneum, 1969).

8   Roy Archibald, "Fish and Game Conservation and Preservation," photocopied (Berkeley: University of California Bureau of Public Administration, 1947), pp. 15–19; Robert H. Connery, *Governmental Problems in Wild Life Conservation*, Studies in History, Economics, and Public Law No. 411 (New York: Columbia University Press, 1935), pp. 123–5; Richard A. Cooley, *Politics and Conservation: The Decline of the Alaska Salmon* (New York: Harper & Row, 1963), pp. 77–8, 86.

9   N. B. Scofield, "Problems of a Fishery Administrator," n.d. (1923?), USBF Division of Scientific Inquiry, General Correspondence, Record Group 22, Series 121, Box 1, NARS-DC, p. 1.

10   Larry A. Nielsen, "The Evolution of Fisheries Management Philosophy," *Marine Fisheries Review*, 38 (December 1976): 15–23, p. 17.

11   C. G. J. Petersen, "What is Over-fishing?" *Journal of the Marine Biological Association* (U.K.), 6 (1903–6): 587–95.

12   J. L. McHugh, "Trends in Fishery Research," in *A Century of Fisheries in North America*, ed. Norman G. Benson, American Fisheries Society Special Publication No. 7 (Washington, DC: American Fisheries Society, 1970), pp. 25–56, pp. 38–9; W. F. Thompson and Norman C. Freeman, *History of the Pacific Halibut Fishery*, Report of the International Fisheries Commission No. 5 (Vancouver: Wrigley Printing, 1930): see also Thompson, "The Fisheries of California and Their Care," *California Fish and Game*, 8 (1922): 170–5, pp. 170–1.

13   Nielsen, "Evolution of Fisheries Management Philosophy," p. 18; P. A. Larkin, "An Epitaph for the Concept of Maximum Sustained Yield," American Fisheries Society, *Transactions*, 106 (1977): 1–11, pp. 1–3; McHugh, "Trends in Fishery Research," p. 34.

14   Elizabeth Noble Shor, *Scripps Institution of Oceanography: Probing the Oceans, 1936–1976* (San Diego: Tofua Press, 1978), pp. 3, 24.

15   1909 *California Statutes* 302; 1913 *California Statutes* 985; 1917 *California Statutes* 1673; CFGC, *Biennial Report* (1912–14): 53; ibid (1916–18): 54.

16   Scofield, "Problems of a Fishery Administrator," pp. 3–4; CFGC, *Biennial Report* (1914–16): 80; Nash, *State Government and Economic Development*, p. 296; Thompson, "The Scientific Investigation of Marine Fisheries as Related to the Work of the Fish and Game Commission in Southern California," CFGC, *Fish Bulletin No. 2* (1919), p. 1; W. L. Scofield, "Marine Fisheries Dates," photocopied (Sacramento: CDFG, 1957), pp. 27, 49; McHugh, "Trends in Fishery Research," p. 27; U.S. Congress, House, Committee on Merchant Marine and Fisheries and Committee on Commerce, Subcommittee on Fisheries, *Sardine Fisheries*, 74th Cong., 2nd sess. (10–11 March 1936), p. 103.

17   CFGC, *Biennial Report* (1910–12): 13.

18   Ibid. (1918–20): 56; "The Marine Research Committee: 1947–55," CalCOFI, *Progress Report* (1 July 1953–31 March 1955), pp. 7–9; personal interview, Richard

Croker, 3 September 1982; personal interview, Frances N. Clark, 11 September 1982.

19 "Editorial," *California Fish and Game*, 10 (1924): 28; *California Fish and Game*, 12 (1926): 146; Frances N. Clark, "California Marine Fisheries Investigations, 1914–1939," *CalCOFI Reports*, 23 (1982): pp. 25–28, p. 26.

20 Personal interview, Richard Croker, 3 September 1982. CFGC was likewise a useful training camp for lawyers. Robert Duke, who helped write the first statutes to control sardine reduction and who represented the state in *People* v. *Stafford Packing Co.*, its first proceeding against a sardine canner in 1923, resigned the next year to represent the defendant company in the famous case of *People* v. *Monterey Fish Products Co.* (10 *California Fish and Game*, 10 [1924]: 122, 190). His successor, D. B. Marx Greene, successfully opposed Duke in the *Monterey Fish Products* case and supervised the reorganization of the Commission's bureaucracy as its first executive director. Greene then left the agency in 1927 to organize the sardine packers' export cartel until the Webb–Pomerene Act. In 1929 he represented the Van Camp company in federal proceedings against the state over the reduction issue (CFGC, *Biennial Report* [1924–6]: 9–13; ibid. [1926–8]: 25). Greene's successor, in turn, was Ralph W. Scott, who as Deputy Attorney General for California twenty years later administered the coup de grace to CFGC's effort to control the reduction industry. Attorneys and scientists alike apparently found it difficult to sustain the energy and commitment required to work for as beleaguered an agency as CFGC became during the interwar period.

21 Thompson, "Notes from the State Fisheries Laboratory," *California Fish and Game*, 6 (1920): 177–80, p. 177.

22 Thompson, "The Scientific Investigation of Marine Fisheries," p. 2.

23 Ibid., p. 12; Thompson, "The Fisheries of California and Their Care," pp. 170–1.

24 Thompson, "The Scientific Investigation of Marine Fisheries," p. 6.

25 W. M. Chapman to Vern Knudsen, 22 October 1947, cited in Arthur F. McEvoy and Harry N. Scheiber, "Scientists, Entrepreneurs, and the Policy Process: A Study of the Post-1945 California Sardine Depletion," *Journal of Economic History*, 44 (1984): 393–406, at note 24; Thompson, "The Fisheries of California and Their Care," pp. 172–5.

26 (Seattle) *Pacific Fisherman* (August 1935), p. 60; John Radovich, "The Collapse of the Sardine Fishery: What Have We Learned?" in *Resource Management and Environmental Uncertainty: Lessons from Coastal Upwelling Fisheries*, eds. Michael H. Glantz and J. Dana Thompson (New York: Wiley, 1981), pp. 107–36, p. 117. See also Paul E. Smith, "Year-Class Strength and Survival of O-Group Clupeoids," *Canadian Journal of Fisheries and Aquatic Sciences*, 42 (1985): 69–82.

27 Nielsen, "The Evolution of Fisheries Management Philosophy," pp. 19–20.

28 Personal interview, Paul E. Smith, 16 September 1982. See Smith, "Biological Effects of Ocean Variability: Time and Space Scales of Biological Response," *Rapports et Proces-Verbaux des Réunions, Conseil International pour l'Exploration de la Mer (Denmark)*, 173 (1978): 117–27; Larkin, "Fisheries Management – An Essay for Ecologists," *Annual Review of Ecology and Systematics*, 9 (1978): 57–73, pp. 61–2; William H. Lenarz, "Modeling the Resource Base," *CalCOFI Reports*, 15 (1971): 28–32.

29 The problem of valuing risk and uncertainty is a significant one in modern environmental law. See Paolo F. Ricci and Lawrence S. Molton, "Risk and Benefit in Environmental Law," *Science*, 214 (4 December 1981): 1,096–100; Sheila Jasanoff and Dorothy Nelkin, "Science, Technology, and the Limits of Judicial Competence,"

Science, 214 (11 December 1981): 1,211–15, p. 1212. On the economics of uncertainty, see P. S. Dasgupta and G. M. Heal, *Economic Theory and Exhaustible Resources*, Cambridge Economic Handbooks (Cambridge: Cambridge University Press, 1981), ch. 13–4. For an introduction to recent psychological studies which suggest that people do not value uncertainty "rationally," as economists and probability theorists assume that they do, see Daniel Kahneman, Paul Slovic, and Amos Tversky, eds., *Judgment Under Uncertainty: Heuristics and Biases* (Cambridge: Cambridge University Press, 1982).

30   CDFG, *Biennial Report* (1922–4): 64.

31   Ibid. (1928–30): 108; W. L. Scofield, "Sardine Oil in Our Troubled Waters," *California Fish and Game*, 24 (1938): 210–33, pp. 217–19; Clark, "Can the Supply of Sardines Be Maintained in California Waters?" ibid., 25 (1939): 172–6, pp. 173–4; U.S. Congress, House, Committee on Merchant Marine and Fisheries, *Sardine Fisheries*, p. 25.

32   U.S. Congress, House, Committee on Merchant Marine and Fisheries, *Sardine Fisheries*, pp. 32–4.

33   Ibid., pp. 101–9, emphasis added.

34   Ibid, p. 97.

35   Elmer Higgins, "Memorandum to Mr. Kerlin," 22 June 1936, USBCF General Files, Record Group 22, Series 121, Box 486, file 825.9, NARS-DC.

36   In Alaska, where USBF did have such responsibility, its desire for political chastity worked to the advantage of absentee salmon packers in Washington state and California and to the disadvantage both of the salmon and of local interest groups who wished to see the resource developed in an orderly way to local benefit. As late as 1949, USFWS followed the fishing industry in claiming that the long-term decline in Alaska salmon productivity had been due primarily to little-understood "environmental" causes and not to overfishing, thus protecting itself from responsibility for taking the regulatory initiative (Cooley, *Politics and Conservation*, pp. 178, 186, 203).

37   U.S. Congress, House, Committee on Merchant Marine and Fisheries, *Sardine Fisheries*, pp. 7, 35, 57, 73.

38   Ibid., pp. 46–7, 92, 140–59.

39   Higgins to Willis H. Rich, 22 April 1936, USBCF General Files, Box 486, file 825.9.

40   Anon., "Must the Scientist Always Be on the Defensive?" *California Fish and Game*, 24 (1938): 290–3.

41   Willis H. Rich and Frank W. Weymouth, "A Review of the Evidence of Depletion of the California Sardine," mimeographed (Palo Alto: CDFG, 1936), p. 1.

42   U.S. Congress, House, Committee on Merchant Marine and Fisheries, *Sardine Fisheries*, pp. 102–3.

43   See S. V. Ciriacy-Wantrup, *Resource Conservation: Economics and Policies*, 3rd ed. (Berkeley: University of California Division of Agricultural Sciences, Agricultural Experiment Station, 1968), pp. 49, 83–9.

44   Higgins to Rich, 22 April 1936, USBCF General Files, Box 486, file 825.9.

45   Rich to Higgins, 30 April 1936, ibid.

46   John Lawler to USBF, 8 January 1937, ibid., Box 486, file 825.9; Lawler to Commissioner of Fisheries, 23 January 1937, ibid.; "Monthly Report: South Pacific Fishery Investigations" (November 1937), ibid., Box 485A, file 825.2, p. 1.

47   Ibid., p. 2.

48   Ibid., p. 1; Elton Sette to Clark, 7 September 1939, ibid., Box 486, file 825.5; Clark to Sette, 8 September 1939, ibid.; 1933 *California Statutes*, ch. 73, §34.

49 "Monthly Report: South Pacific Fishery Investigations" (May 1938), ibid., Box 485A, file 825.2.

50 Ibid. (January 1938), p. 5; ibid. (September 1938), p. 5; ibid. (December 1938), p. 1; *Pacific Fisherman* (June 1939), p. 26; McHugh and Elbert H. Ahlstrom, "Is the Pacific Sardine Disappearing?" *Scientific Monthly*, 72 (1951): 377–81, pp. 378–9; personal interview, Frances N. Clark, 11 September 1982; "Monthly Report: South Pacific Fishery Investigations" (November 1943), USBCF General Files, Box 485A, file 825.2, pp. 2–3.

51 Clark to Sette, 24 August 1940, ibid., Box 486, file 825.5.

52 Higgins to Charles Jackson, 24 November 1939, ibid., Box 486, file 825.9; H. J. Anderson to Jackson, 17 November 1939, ibid.; Jackson to Anderson, 18 November 1939, ibid.; Anderson to Jackson, 25 November 1939, ibid.; Higgins to Sette, 30 November 1939, ibid.

53 "Memorandum of meeting held between the staffs of the South Pacific Investigations, United States Fish and Wildlife Service, and the California Division of Fish and Game at the Ferry Building, San Francisco, California, September 13, 1940," ibid., Box 486, file 825.5.

54 "Monthly Reports South Pacific Fishery Investigations" (November, 1943), ibid., Box 485A, file 825.2, pp. 2–3.

55 *Pacific Fisherman* (February 1939), p. 18; CDFG, *Biennial Report* (1936–8): 57; ibid. (1940–2): 49.

56 Ibid. (1942–4): 37.

57 Higgins to Sette, 9 May 1941, USBCF General Classified Correspondence, Record Group 22, Series 121, Box 479, file 825.1, NARS-DC.

58 Sette to L. T. Hopkinson, 23 October 1942, ibid.

59 Thompson, "The Scientific Investigation of Marine Fisheries," p. 6; cf. *Pacific Fisherman* (January 1917), p. 24.

60 Thompson, "The Scientific Investigation of Marine Fisheries," p. 6.

61 CDFG, *Biennial Report* (1926–8): 105.

62 California State Market Commission, *Annual Report* (1918): 96.

63 F. C. Weber, H. W. Houghton, and J. B. Wilson, "The Maine Sardine Industry," USDA, *Department Bulletin No. 908* (18 January 1921), pp. 6, 20; Wilfrid Sadler, "The Bacteriology of Swelled Canned Sardines," *American Journal of Public Health*, 8 (1918): 216–20; Harry W. Redfield, "Food and Drugs: Botulism from Canned Sardines," ibid., 15 (1925): 927; CDFG, *Biennial Report* (1920–2): 82.

64 Hugh M. Smith "Pacific Policy on Bureau of Fisheries," *Pacific Fisherman* (July 1914), p. 13.

65 Don Estes, "Kondo Masaharu and the Best of All Fishermen," *Journal of San Diego History*, 23 (Summer 1977): 1–19, p. 7; Scofield, "Marine Fisheries Dates," p. 15.

66 U. S. Congress, Senate, "Fertilizer Resources of the United States," 62nd Cong., 2nd sess. (1911), *Senate Document 190*, pp. 5–6; Scofield, "Marine Fisheries Dates," p. 26; J. W. Turrentine, "Utilization of the Fish Waste of the Pacific Coast for the Manufacture of Fertilizer," USDA, *Department Bulletin No. 150* (23 January 1915), pp. 1, 16–17; Turrentine, "The Fish-Scrap Fertilizer Industry of the Atlantic Coast," *USDA Bulletin No. 2* (27 December 1913), p. 15; F. C. Weber, "Fish Meal: Its Use as a Stock and Poultry Food," USDA, *Department Bulletin No. 378* (22 August 1916), p. 18; Herbert S. Bailey and B. E. Reuter, "The Production and Conservation of Fats and Oils in the United States," USDA, *Department Bulletin 769* (10 February 1919), pp. 39–44; *Pacific Fisherman* (September 1919), p. 62.

67   U.S. Congress, House, Committee on Merchant Marine and Fisheries, *Sardine Fisheries*, p. 106; *Pacific Fisherman* (June 1923), p. 8.
68   Harry R. Beard, "Preparation of Fish for Canning as Sardines," USBF, *Report* (1927): 68, 90; CFGC, *Biennial Report* (1922–4): 49; W. L. Scofield, "Sardine Fishing Methods at Monterey, California," CFGC, *Fish Bulletin No. 19* (1919), p. 10.
69   Ciriacy-Wantrup, *Resource Conservation*, pp. 102, 109–10.
70   Thompson, "The Scientific Investigation of Marine Fisheries," p. 14.
71   Mansel G. Blackford, *The Politics of Business in California, 1890–1920* (Columbus, OH: Ohio State University Press, 1977), p. 30; Carl C. Plehn, "The State Market Commission of California: Its Beginnings, 1915–1917," *American Economic Review*, 8 (1918): 1–27, p. 9; Grace Larsen, "A Progressive in Agriculture: Harris Weinstock," *Agricultural History*, 32 (1958): 187–93, p. 191; 1915 *California Statutes* 1390.
72   CSFC, *Biennial Report* (1908–10): 11; *Pacific Fisherman* (June 1915), p. 12; ibid. (July 1915), p. 20; *Pacific Fisherman Yearbook* (1917), p. 64; California State Market Commission, *Annual Report* (1917): 46.
73   A contemporary economist observed that "a commission market [was] just as different from a market commission as a chestnut horse is from a horse chestnut" (Plehn, "The State Market Commission of California," p. 10). See also Blackford, *Politics of Business in California*, p. 31; O. B. Jesness, "Cooperative Purchasing and Marketing Organizations Among Farmers in the United States," USDA, *Department Bulletin No. 547* (19 September 1917), p. 59; California State Market Commission, *Annual Report* (1916): 46–52; ibid. (1917): 5; 1917 *California Statutes* 1673; *San Francisco Examiner*, 18 August 1916, 24 November 1916; *San Francisco Call*, 17 August 1916; *San Francisco Bulletin*, 3 October 1916, 22 March 1917; *San Francisco Retail Grocers' Advocate*, 6 October 1916.
74   *Oakland Tribune*, 27 February 1918; *Oakland Enquirer*, 28 February 1918).
75   *San Francisco Chronicle*, 1 August 1918, 3 August 1918; CFGC, *Biennial Report* (1920–2): 64–5.
76   CFGC, *Biennial Report* 1916–18): 7.
77   California State Market Commission, *Annual Report* (1918): 121; *San Pedro News*, 21 July 1919.
78   California State Market Commission, *Annual Report* (1917): 8; ibid. (1918) 112–13; ibid (1919); 106: Blackford, *Politics of Business in California*, p. 37; *San Francisco Chronicle*, 24 February 1917; *Broderick Independent* 23 February 1917; *Oakland Enquirer*, 28 February 1918, 7 March 1918; *Pacific Fisherman* (May 1919), pp. 80–2.
79   California State Market Commission, *Annual Report* (1918): 149–50; *San Francisco Bulletin*, 27 February 1919; *San Francisco Daily News*, 28 May 1919.
80   *Pacific Fisherman* (August 1919), p. 68; *Sacramento Bee*, 16 January 1920; *Berkeley Times*, 16 January 1920; *San Francisco Bulletin*, 6 February 1920; R. H. Fiedler, "Review of the Fisheries of California," USBF, *Report* (1930): 364; *Pacific Fisherman Yearbook* (1929), p. 133.
81   See Ellis Hawley, "Three Facets of Hooverian Associationalism: Lumber, Aviation, and the Movies, 1921–1930," in *Regulation in Perspective: Historical Essays*, ed. Thomas K. McCraw (Cambridge, MA: Harvard University Press, 1981), pp. 56–94.
82   *San Francisco Examiner*, 8 September 1920; Fiedler, "Review of the Fisheries of California," USBF, *Report* (1930): 362–4; CDFG, *Biennial Report* (1926–8): 106–7. See also George Soule, *Prosperity Decade: From War to Depression, 1917–1929*, Economic History of the United States, v. 8 (New York: Rinehart, 1947), p. 145.
83   *Pacific Fisherman* (February 1934), p. 16; John R. Arnold, *Evidence Study No.*

16 of the Fishery Industry (Washington, DC: National Recovery Administration, Division of Review, 1936), pp. 29–30.

84 Ibid., pp. 1, 32–3; *Pacific Fisherman* (July 1933), p. 12; ibid. (September 1933), p. 23; ibid. (November 1933), p. 9; ibid. (August 1939), pp. 15–16.

85 Montgomery Phister to W. M. Chapman, 29 December 1950, cited in McEvoy and Scheiber, "Scientists, Entrepreneurs, and the Policy Process," p. 402, note 36.

86 *Pacific Fisherman* (July 1929), p. 29; ibid. (November 1932), p. 18; ibid. (January 1934), p. 10; ibid. (August 1935), p. 78.

87 Ibid. (June 1934), pp. 22–3; U.S. Congress, House, Committee on Merchant Marine and Fisheries, "Sardine Fisheries," pp. 144–6.

88 A useful history of the politics of New Deal regulation is Ellis W. Hawley, *The New Deal and the Problem of Monopoly: A Study in Economic Ambivalence* (Princeton, NJ: Princeton University Press, 1966).

89 H. H. Bennet, "Development of Natural Resources: The Coming Technological Revolution on the Land," *Science*, 105 (3 January 1947): 1–4, p. 3. See also Donald Worster's treatment of Bennet and the Soil Conservation Service in his *Dust Bowl: The Southern Plains in the 1930s* (Oxford: Oxford University Press, 1979), pp. 201–15. On the fate of the SCS, see McConnell, *The Decline of Agrarian Democracy*, pp. 128–32.

90 Cited in Charles M. Hardin, *The Politics of Agriculture: Soil Conservation and the Struggle for Power in Rural America* (Glencoe, IL: The Free Press, 1952), p. 239.

91 R. Burnell Held and Marion Clawson, *Soil Conservation in Perspective*, Resources for the Future, (Baltimore: Johns Hopkins University Press, 1965), pp. 43–4, 76–7.

92 Cooley, *Politics and Conservation*, pp. 136–9.

93 CSFC, *Biennial Report* (1905–6): 53; CFGC, *Biennial Report* (1912–14): 52; ibid (1914–16): 116; California Legislature, Assembly, Special Committee on the Investigation of the California Fish and Game Commission, "Report of the Special Committee . . . " (Sacramento: California State Printing Office, 1911), pp. 6–8; *San Francisco Chronicle* (2 April 1913), p. 26; *Oakland Enquirer*, 29 September 1917.

94 *Matter of Application of Parra*, 24 Cal. App. 339, 141 P. 393 (1914; *Ex parte Cencinino*, 31 Cal. App. 238, 160 P. 167 (1916); *Paladini* v. *Superior Court*, 138 Cal. 369, 173 P. 588 (1918); *In re Marincovich*, 48 Cal. App. 474, 192 P. 156 (1920); *Ex parte Makings*, 200 Cal. 474, 253 P. 918 (1927).

95 *Matter of Application of Parra*, 24 Cal. App. at 342.

96 *Paladini* v. *Superior Court*, 138 Cal. 369; CFGC, *Biennial Report* (1914–16): 115; California State Market Commission, *Annual Report* (1918): 114–17.

97 CFGC, *Biennial Report* (1924–6): 10–11; Archibald, "Fish and Conservation and Preservation," p. 11.

98 *Ex parte Cencinino*, 31 Cal. App. 238; CFGC, *Biennial Report* (1914–16): 91; 1911 *California Statutes* 425, amended 1913 *California Statutes* 988; cf. *Matter of Application of Mascolo*, 25 Cal. App. 92, 142 P. 903; CSFC, *Biennial Report* (1905–6): 7–8.

99 *Ex parte Cencinino*, 31 Cal. App. at 170. Such stricter legislation, the commentator thought, should have been allowed under the concurrent powers clause of the state constitution [*California Constitution*, Art. XI, § 11; J. L. Knowles, "Comment on Recent Cases: Constitutional Law: Construction of Fish and Game Act," *California Law Review*, 5 (1917): 162–3].

100 California State Market Commission, State Fish Exchange, *Annual Report* (1918): 33.

101 Earl H. Rosenberg, "A History of the Fishing and Canning Industries in Monterey, California" (M. A. thesis, University of Nevada, Reno, 1961), p. 119; J. C. Phillips, "Success of the Purse Seine Boat in the Sardine Fishery at Monterey, California," CDFG, *Fish Bulletin No. 23* (1930); W. L. Scofield, "Purse Seines and Other Round Haul Gear of California," CDFG, *Fish Bulletin No. 81* (1951), p. 30; W. L. Scofield, "Sardine Fishing Methods at Monterey, California," CDFG, *Fish Bulletin No. 19* (1919), pp. 17–19; *Pacific Fisherman Yearbook* (1924), p. 87; ibid. (1928), p. 143; ibid. (1929), p. 178; *Monterey Peninsula Herald* (25 March 1938), pp. 3–4.

102 *Pacific Fisherman Yearbook* (October 1939), pp. 32–3; *Monterey Peninsula Herald* (22 August 1938), pp. 1–2; ibid. (28 September 1938), pp. 7, 9.

103 *Manaka* v. *Monterey Sardine Industries*, 41 F. Supp. 531 (N.D. Cal. 1941).

104 CDFG, *Biennial Report* (1946–8): 36.

105 USDI, Office of Fishery Coordination, "Miscellaneous Publications," mimeographed (San Francisco: U.S. Office of the Fishery Coordinator, 1943).

106 Sette to Higgins, 18 November 1942, USBCF General Classified Correspondence, Box 479, file 825.1; *Pacific Fisherman* (January 1945), p. 35.

107 *Pacific Fisherman Yearbook* (March 1945), p. 48.

108 Ciriacy-Wantrup, *Resource Conservation*, pp. 236–45. On the similarity between political and market processes, see Hurst, *Law and Markets in United States History*, ch. 3, *passim;* also Richard Walker and Michael Storper, "Erosion of the Clean Air Act of 1970: A Study in the Failure of Government Regulation and Planning," *Boston College Environmental Affairs Law Review*, 7 (1978): 189–257, pp. 191, 252–4.

109 Connery, *Governmental Problems in Wild Life Conservation*, pp. 144, 179–80.

110 *Myers* v. *United States*, 272 U.S. 52, 293 (1926) (Brandeis, J. dissenting).

111 Ciriacy-Wantrup, *Resource Conservation*, pp. 140, 226; Richard N. Adams, *Paradoxical Harvest: Energy and Explanation in British History, 1870–1914*, Arnold and Caroline Rose Monograph Series of the American Sociological Association (Cambridge: Cambridge University Press, 1982), pp. 16–8, 123–4.

112 *People* v. *Truckee Lumber Company*, 116 Cal. 397, 401, 48 P. 374 (1897).

113 CFGC, *Biennial Report* (1922–4): 22.

114 CDFG, *Biennial Report* (1926–8): 73.

115 CFGC, *Biennial Report* (1910–12): 12; ibib. (1914–16): 114–16; ibid. (1916–18): 43; ibid. (1918–20): 88.

116 1903 *California Statutes* 23; 1915 *California Statutes* 820; 1917 *California Statutes* 155.

117 CDFG, *Biennial Report* (1932–4): 16.

118 Ibid. (1936–8): 72–3.

119 CFGC, *Biennial Report* (1920–2): 84.

120 Ibid.; CDFG, *Biennial Report* (1936–8): 46.

121 CFGC, *Biennial Report* (1922–4): 47.

122 Ibid. (1920–2): 85.

123 (Crescent City) *Del Norte Triplicate*, 3 May 1924, 31 May 1924; CFGC, *Biennial Report* (1920–2): 85.

124 *Del Norte Triplicate*, (10 May 1924), p. 10; ibid. (18 October 1924), p. 3.

125 (Yreka) *Siskiyou News* (25 September 1924), p. 2; ibid. (30 October 1924), p. 3.

126 *Pacific Fisherman* (April 1924), p. 16; ibid. (June 1924), p. 8.

127 1925 *California Statutes* xclii; *Del Norte Triplicate* (26 July 1924), p. 6; ibid. (9 August 1924), p. 6; ibid. (16 August 1924), p. 17; John O. Snyder, "Indian Methods

of Fishing in Trinity River and Some Notes on the King Salmon of That Stream," *California Fish and Game*, 10 (1924): 163–8, p. 163; CFGC, *Biennial Report* (1920–2): 34, 85.
128 1919 *California Statutes* 779; 1925 *California Statutes* 926.
129 See Philip Selznick, *TVA and the Grass Roots: A Study in the Sociology of Formal Organizations* (1949, repr. New York: Harper & Row, 1966).
130 48 *Statutes at Large* 401 (1934). See Donald Arthur Duerr, "Conflicts Between Water Development Projects and Fish and Wildlife Preservation in the Central Valley Basin, California (M.A. thesis, University of California, Berkeley, 1955), pp. 49–61.
131 Duerr, "Conflicts Between Water Development Projects and Fish and Wildlife Conservation," pp. 114–18.
132 Ibid., pp. 129–54, 161.
133 Ibid., pp. 3–7; Connery, *Governmental Problems in Wild Life Conservation*, p. 15.
134 31 *Statutes at Large* 187 (1900). On the so-called commerce-police power, see *Champion v. Ames*, 188 U.S. 321 (1903). At the same time he permitted states to regulate fishing in public waters in 1842, Justice Taney had warned that state power to regulate "the public common of piscary" remained subject to superior federal powers that he did not care to define at the time [*Martin v. Waddell*, 41 U.S. (16 Peters) 234, 263–4 (1842)].
135 Migratory Bird Treaty Act of 1918, 40 *Statutes at Large* 755 (1918), *upheld, Missouri v. Holland*, 252 U.S. 416 (1920).
136 *Foster-Fountain Packing Co. v. Haydel*, 278 U.S. 1, 13 (1928). The Supreme Court finally overturned *Geer* in *Hughes v. Oklahoma*, 441 U.S. 322 (1979). See George Cameron Coggins, "Wildlife and the Constitution: The Walls Come Tumbling Down," *Washington Law Review*, 55 (1980): 295–358.
137 *Takahashi v. Fish and Game Commission*, 334 U.S. 410 (1948). Although California got away with using the state ownership rule to ban the export of shrimp so as to harass the Chinese, twenty years before that Judge Sawyer used precisely the same reasoning as did the *Takahashi* court in overturning anti-Chinese fishing laws enacted in the 1880s (see *supra*, ch. 5, p. 113). The U.S. Supreme Court did uphold a Louisiana statute placing a severance tax on fur-bearing mammals as a legitimate police exercise in *La Coste v. Department of Conservation*, 263 U.S. 545 (1924).
138 *Toomer v. Witsell*, 334 U.S. 385, 402 (1948).
139 Milner B. Schaefer, "Problems of Quality and Quantity in the Management of the Living Resources of the Sea," in *Natural Resources: Quality and Quantity: Papers Presented Before a Faculty Seminar at the University of California, Berkeley, 1961–1965*, eds. S. V. Ciriacy-Wantrup and James J. Parsons (Berkeley: University of California Press, 1967), pp. 87–101, p. 99.
140 B. D. Marx Greene, "An Historical Review of the Legal Aspects of the Use of Food Fish for Reduction Purposes," *California Fish and Game*, 13 (1927): 1–17, p. 1.
141 *Pacific Fisherman* (January 1917), p. 24.
142 U.S. Congress, House, Committee on Merchant Marine and Fisheries, *Sardine Fisheries*, p. 57.
143 *People v. Monterey Fish Products Co.*, 195 Cal. 548, 234 P. 398 (1925), respondent's brief (California State Archives File #22221), p. 15.
144 See Ciriacy-Wantrup, *Resource Conservation*, pp. 250–9, 268, 287–90.
145 1919 *California Statutes* 1203, amended, 1921 *California Statutes* 459. See also *Pacific Fisherman* (June 1924), pp. 7–8; N. B. Scofield to Henry O'Malley, 11

May 1923, USBF Division of Scientific Inquiry, General Correspondence, Box 1; Scofield, "The Problems of a Fishery Administrator," ibid., p. 9.

146 *Paladini* v. *Superior Court,* 138 Cal. 369.

147 *People* v. *Stafford Packing Co.*, 193 Cal. 719, 227 P. 485 (1924); *People* v. *Monterey Fish Products Co.*, 195 Cal. 548.

148 *People* v. *Stafford Packing Co.*, 193 Cal. at 487–9.

149 *People* v. *Monterey Fish Products Co.*, 195 Cal. at 400–5; *Van Camp Sea Food Co. et al.* v. *Department of Natural Resources of the State of California*, 30 F.2d 111 (1929); *Bayside Fish Flour Co.* v. *Gentry et al.*, 297 U.S. 422 (1935). Following the *Monterey Fish Products* decision, southern California processors banded together to challenge CDFG's authority to hold hearings to determine their capacity to can fish but were turned away on this score, as well. See *Globe Cotton Mills* v. *Zellerbach,* 200 Cal. 121, 252 P. 1038 (1927); *People* v. *Globe Grain and Milling Co.*, 211 Cal. 121, 294 P. 3 (1930). See also *Van Camp Sea Food Co.* v. *State Fish and Game Commission,* Cal. App. 764, 243 P. 702 (1925); and *Van Camp Sea Vood Co.* v. *Newbert,* 76 Cal. App. 445, 244 P. 946 (1926).

150 "Note: The Fishery Conservation and Management Act of 1976: State Regulation of Fishing Beyond the Territorial Sea," *Maine Law Review,* 31 (1979–80): 303–32, pp. 306–9.

151 CFGC, *Biennial Report* (1920–2): 86. During the late 1920s superior courts in southern California regularly came up with different findings from those that northern California courts would reach on similar facts. Fish and Game would then have to take each issue to the appellate level and even into federal court to secure a stable rule [CDFG, *Biennial Report* (1926–8): 109–10; ibid. (1928–30): 111].

152 1925 *California Statutes* 595, 597; CFGC, *Biennial Report* (1924–6): 65–6; *Pacific Fisherman* (June 1923), pp. 7–8; Scofield to O'Malley, 11 May 1923, USBF Division of Scientific Inquiry, General Correspondence, Box 1; O'Malley to Scofield, 2 May 1923, ibid.; San Xavier Fish Firm to O'Malley, 30 April 1923, ibid. For a review of the reduction laws, see Milner B. Schaefer, Oscar E. Sette, and John C. Marr, "Growth of the Pacific Coast Pilchard Fishery to 1942," USFWS *Research Report 29* (1951), pp. 17–29.

153 CDFG, *Biennial Report* (1928–30): 109–12; (San Pedro) *West Coast Fisheries* (September 1929), p. 16. Bills to control the factory ships made varying degrees of progress through the state legislature in the early 1930s, but all eventually fell before the power of the reductionists and their customers. See *Pacific Fisherman, Thirtieth Annual Statistical Number* (1932), p. 235; *Pacific Fisherman* (May 1933), p. 17; ibid. (April 1935), p. 37. W. L. Scofield believed that farmers had been hoodwinked into supporting the reduction interests by purchasers of sardine oil, who made the largest profits and were therefore, in his eyes, the real villains (Scofield, "Sardine Oil in Our Troubled Waters," p. 213). Only rarely, however, does the record yield evidence of oil purchasers' involvement in the controversy. See, for example, U.S. Congress, House, Committee on Merchant Marine and Fisheries, *Sardine Fisheries*, pp. 59–73.

154 Political instability, in economic terms, increases the cost of uncertainty for fishery users. See Ciriacy-Wantrup, *Resource Conservation*, p. 146.

155 CFGC, *Biennial Report* (1922–4): 49; Scofield to O'Malley, *supra*, note 145.

156 CDFG, *Biennial Report* (1932–4): 41, 50–1; *Pacific Fisherman* (August 1933), p. 46.

157 CFGC, *Biennial Report* (1922–4): 50.

158 7 *Opinions, California Attorney General* 298 (1946); *People* v. *Monterey Fish*

Products Co., 195 Cal. at 401; California State Chamber of Commerce Research Department, "The California Sardine Industry, Prepared at the Request of the Subcommittee on the Sardine Industry of the Statewide Natural Resources Committee," mimeographed (San Francisco: California State Chamber of Commerce, 1946), p. 21; cf. *Railway Express Agency* v. *New York*, 336 U.S. 106 (1949).

159 *Monterey Peninsula Herald, Thirteenth Annual Sardine Edition* (2 April 1948), pp. 1, 3.

160 *Pacific Fisherman* (February 1917), p. 12; *California Fish and Game*, 4 (1918): 80–1; Harold C. Bryant, "Discretionary Power and Game Conservation," ibid., pp. 129–37, pp. 129–32.

161 *Monterey Peninsula Herald* (10 January 1938), p. 1; *West Coast Fisheries* (December 1929), pp. 8–9, 21; ibid. (December 1931), p. 7.

162 1933 *California Statutes* 595.

163 *Monterey Peninsula Herald* (6 April 1949), p. 2; *California Constitution*, Art. IV, §25½, amendment adopted 5 November 1940, replaced by Art. IV, §20(a), 8 November 1966; 1945 *California Statutes* 1302; California Department of State, *Proposed Amendments to the Constitution, Propositions, and Proposed Laws ... General Election ... November 5, 1940* (Sacramento: California Department of State, 1940). See also Steven I. Baser, "'Fast-Fish and Loose Fish': Extended Fisheries Jurisdiction and the Need for an Improved California Fisheries Management System," *Southern California Law Review*, 49 (1976): 569–96, pp. 574–7.

164 See Harry N. Scheiber, "Federalism and Legal Process: Historical and Contemporary Analysis of the American System," *Law and Society Review*, 14 (1980): 663–722, p. 688.

165 CDFG, *Biennial Report* (1928–30): 13–14.

166 M. T. Hoyt, "Report on the Pilchard Fishery of Oregon," (Salem: Oregon Fish Commission, 1938), p. 5 (copy on file, California State Fisheries Laboratory Library, Long Beach): 1935 *Washington Laws* 403; 1935 *Oregon Laws* 678. The Washington and Oregon statutes were signed within a day of each other in March 1935.

167 Elmer Higgins to Willis H. Rich, 8 May 1936, USBCF General Files, Box 486, file 825.9.

168 W. L. Scofield to Carl Hubbs, 3 April 1938, CLHP, file W. C. 8: Legislature.

169 N. B. Scofield, "Problems of a Fishery Administrator," USBF Division of Scientific Inquiry, General Correspondence, Box 1, p. 10; John Walker Sundstrom, "Problems in Administration of Pacific Coast Fisheries" (M.A. thesis, University of California, Berkeley, 1941), p. 45.

170 Francis T. Christy, Jr., and Anthony Scott, *The Common Wealth in Ocean Fisheries: Some Problems of Growth and Economic Allocation*, Resources for the Future (Baltimore: Johns Hopkins University Press, 1965), pp. 158–61; Ann L. Hollick, *U. S. Foreign Policy and the Law of the Sea* (Princeton, NJ: Princeton University Press, 1981), pp. 19–20. On international conflicts of the 1930s, see generally Homer E. Gregory and Kathleen Barnes, *North Pacific Fisheries: With Special Reference to Alaska Salmon*, American Council, Institute of Pacific Relations, Studies of the Pacific No. 3 (New York: American Council, Institute of Pacific Relations, 1939, repr. New York: Kraus Reprint, 1976).

171 Scofield, "Sardine Oil in Our Troubled Waters," p. 217.

172 CDFG, *Biennial Report* (1930–2): 67.

173 *Pacific Fisherman* (February 1940), p. 25.

174 Richard Van Cleve, "Program of the Bureau of Marine Fisheries," *California Fish and Game*, 31 (1945): 81–5, p. 83.

Chapter 8

1 John Steinbeck, *Sweet Thursday* (New York: Viking, 1954), p. 1. J. R. T. Hughes inspired the title to this chapter. See his "The Great Strike at Nushagak Station, 1951: Institutional Gridlock," *Journal of Economic History*, 42 (1982): 1–20.

2 On the social and ideological origins of modern environmentalism, see Samuel P. Hays, "From Conservation to Environment: Environmental Politics in the United States Since World War Two," *Environmental Review*, 6 (Fall 1982): 14–41; Donald Fleming, "Roots of the New Conservation Movement," *Perspectives in American History*, 6 (1971): 7–91; Stephen Fox, *John Muir and His Legacy: The American Conservation Movement* (Boston: Little, Brown, 1981), ch. 8; Donald Worster, *Nature's Economy: The Roots of Ecology* (San Francisco: Sierra Club, 1977), epilogue.

3 Personal interview, Richard Croker, 3 September 1982. On post-World War II development in California, see Walton E. Bean, *California: An Interpretive History*, 2nd ed. (New York: McGraw-Hill, 1973), ch. 34–43; Carey McWilliams, *California: The Great Exception* (1949; repr. Santa Barbara: Peregrine-Smith, 1976); and Raymond F. Dasmann, *The Destruction of California* (New York: Macmillan, 1976).

4 O. P. Blaich, "Feed Supply and Consumption in California," paper presented to the Animal Industry Conference, Fresno, 17 October 1961, photocopy (copy on file at Giannini Foundation of Agricultural Economics Library, University of California, Berkeley), p. 1; Robert C. Fellmeth, *The Politics of Land: Ralph Nader's Study Group Report on Land Use in California* (New York: Grossman, 1973), p. 84.

5 See J. Willard Hurst, *Law and Social Order in the United States* (Ithaca, NY: Cornell University Press, 1977), pp. 196–213; Nathan Rosenberg, *Technology and American Economic Growth* (New York: Harper Torchbooks, 1972), pp. 176–86.

6 See Harry N. Scheiber, "Science, Public Policy, and Natural Resources: Wilbert Chapman and the Pacific Fisheries, 1935–70," paper presented to annual meeting, Pacific Coast Branch, American Historical Association, Seattle, Washington, 16–18 August 1984. Chapman sketched his own life in a letter to Charles Jackson, 24 August 1965, WMCP (71/8).

7 Chapman to Gilbert Van Camp, 28 June 1964, WMCP (70/15), p. 2.

8 Chapman to H. G. Ploger, 7 September 1965, WMCP (71/9), p. 2.

9 Quoted in Carleton Ray, "Ecology, Law, and the 'Marine Revolution,'" in *Oceanography: Contemporary Readings in Ocean Sciences*, 2nd ed., ed. R. Gordon Pirie (New York: Oxford University Press, 1977), pp. 359–72, p. 363.

10 Chapman to John Mehos, 23 August 1965, WMCP (71/8), pp. 1–2. See also Arthur F. McEvoy and Harry Scheiber, "Scientists, Entrepreneurs, and the Policy Process: A Study of the Post-1945 California Sardine Depletion," *Journal of Economic History*, 44 (1984): 393–406.

11 Chapman to Jackson, 24 August 1965, WMCP (71–8), p. 2.

12 Gruen Gruen and Associates, *A Socio-economic Analysis of California's Sport and Commercial Fishing Industries*, Report to the State of California Resources Agency (San Francisco: Gruen Gruen and Associates, 1972), pp. 25–6; Chapman, "World Fisheries," *CalCOFI Reports*, 14 (1970): 43–56, pp. 43, 53; Chapman to H. L. Wilkie, 8 September 1965, WMCP (71/9), p. 11.

13 See McEvoy and Scheiber, "Scientists, Entrepreneurs, and the Policy Process," p. 398; *Pacific Fisherman* (January 1947), p. 37; see also Carl Hubbs's notes to the 1949 Sardine Conference, in CLHP, CalCOFI Sardine Conference 1949.

14 Richard S. Croker, "50 Years of Pacific Fisheries, 1947–1997," PMFC, *Annual Report* (1972): 4–8, p. 4.

15 Chapman to R. C. Miller, 4 April 1945, CLHP, Fisheries: Tuna.

16 *Pacific Fisherman* (August 1947), pp. 58–9.

17 David A. Ross, "The Importance of Marine Affairs," *Science*, 201 (28 July 1978): 305.

18 W. G. Clark, "The Lessons of the Peruvian Anchoveta Fishery," *CalCOFI Reports*, 19 (1977): 57–63, p. 57.

19 Presidential Proclamation No. 2667, Concerning the Policy of the United States with Respect to the Natural Resources of the Subsoil and Sea-Bed of the Continental Shelf of 28 September 1945, 59 *Statutes at Large* 884 (1945); Presidential Proclamation No. 2668, Concerning the Policy of the United States with Respect to Coastal Fisheries in Certain Areas of the High Seas of 28 September 1945, 59 *Statutes at Large* 885 (1945). See also Ann L. Hollick, *U. S. Foreign Policy and the Law of the Sea* (Princeton, NJ: Princeton University Press, 1981), pp. 18–61; also Donald Cameron Watt, "First Step in the Enclosure of the Oceans: The Origins of Truman's Proclamation on the Resources of the Continental Shelf, 28 September 1945," *Marine Policy*, 3 (1979): 211–24.

20 Hollick, *U. S. Foreign Policy and the Law of the Sea*, p. 61.

21 Ibid., pp. 98–99.

22 Ibid., pp. 67–95; H. Gary Knight, *Managing the Sea's Living Resources: Legal and Political Aspects of High Seas Fisheries*, Studies in Marine Affairs (Lexington, MA: D.C. Heath, 1977), pp. 50–1.

23 Chapman to Nick Bez, 2 December 1946, CLHP, Fisheries: Tuna.

24 See "Proceedings of the Pacific Fisheries Conference, Los Angeles, Jan. 11, 1946," *Pacific Fisherman* (February 1946), pp. 33–40; "Who Will Harvest the Pacific? An Outline for Venture – by Fisherman and Business – On the Oceanic Frontier," ibid. (August 1947), pp. 49–63; "A Policy for Fisheries: A Policy for Peace," ibid. (October 1947), pp. 35–6.

25 Chapman to J. Hardin Petersen, 14 December 1945, CLHP, Fisheries: Tuna, p. 2.

26 Chapman to Guy Gordon, 21 February 1947, CLHP, Fisheries: Tuna, p. 4.

27 Chapman to Arthur J. Heighway, 14 May 1962, WMCP (69/17), p. 2.

28 Hollick, *U. S. Foreign Policy and the Law of the Sea*, pp. 66–7; Scheiber, "Science, Public Policy and Natural Resources," pp. 11–16. On Chapman's career at the State Department, see ibid., pp. 21–31.

29 Chapman to Julian C. Burnette, 5 February 1966, WMCP (100/2), pp. 1–2. See also McEvoy and Scheiber, "Scientists, Entrepreneurs, and the Policy Process," pp. 400–1.

30 Notes on Meeting in San Francisco on January 24, 1947, SIO Subject Files, SIO Archives, Sardine Program, MLRP 1947, p. 1.

31 Chapman to Herbert C. Davis, 10 July 1962, WMCP (70/3), p. 1.

32 Chapman to Hubbs, 13 August 1947, SIO Subject Files, Marine Life Research: General, Correspondence, p. 1.

33 Chapman to Don Saxby, 18 March 1947, SIO Subject Files, Marine Life Research: General, Correspondence.

34 O. E. Sette to L. A. Walford, 7 November 1947, USBCF General Classified Files, Record Group 22, Box 480, file 825.11, NARS-DC, p. 2.

35 1951 *California Statutes*, ch. 715; California Legislative Auditor's Office, "Administrative Survey of the California Department of Fish and Game," mimeographed (Sacramento: California Legislative Auditor, 1956), p. 14.

36 Ibid., p. 11; Chapman to Richard Croker, 10 May 1962, WMCP (69/17); Chapman to Ray Arnett, 15 March 1969, WMCP (99/4), p. 1.

37 MRC, Minutes of Meeting (18 November 1954), Records of the Marine Research Committee (81–8), SIO Archives, p. 6 (hereafter referred to as MRC Minutes).
38 Margaret A. Dewar, *Industry in Trouble: The Federal Government and the New England Fisheries* (Philadelphia: Temple University Press, 1983), pp. 67–8, 79; Harold F. Cary, "The Point of View of Industry: The Processor," *CalCOFI Reports*, 13 (1969): 103–7, p. 104; PL 94- 1024, 70 *Statutes at Large* 1,119 (1956).
39 "Pilchard and Sardine Conference, 1949" (notes of Carl L. Hubbs), CLHP, CalCOFI Sardine Conference 1949; "History and Development of the Commission," PMFC, *Annual Report* (1948): 5–11, pp. 5–6; "Coordinated Plans for Management of the Fisheries of the Pacific Coast," ibid.: 12–63, pp. 12–13; W. Markham Morton, "Fishery Events Leading to Establishment of Pacific Marine Fisheries Commission and Progress and Changes, 1948–1967," ibid. (1972): 11–21, pp. 14–15; California Legislature, Assembly, Interim Committee on Fish and Game, "Final Report," *Assembly Interim Committee Reports*, v. 5, no. 6 (1957–9), pp. 20–1.
40 Carl L. Hubbs, "Changes in the Fish Fauna of Western North America Correlated with Changes in Ocean Temperature," *Journal of Marine Research*, 7 (1948): 459–82. On El Niño, see *supra*, p. 7.
41 California Legislature, Assembly, Interim Committee on Fish and Game, "Final Report," pp. 20–1; Oscar E. Sette, "The Long Term Historical Record of Meterological, Oceanographic and Biological Data," *CalCOFI Reports*, 7 (1960): 181–94, p. 192; Sette and John Dove Isaacs, "Editors' Summary of the Symposium," ibid.: 211–17, pp. 211–13.
42 California Legislature, Joint Legislative Interim Committee on Fish and Game, "Report," (January 1945), p. 10; Donald Arthur Duerr, "Conflicts Between Water Development Projects and Fish and Wildlife Conservation in the Central Valley Basin, California" (M.A. thesis, University of California, Berkeley, 1955), p. 228.
43 Duerr, "Conflicts Between Water Development Projects and Fish and Wildlife Conservation," pp. 183–4, 320.
44 See, for example, Paul S. Taylor, "California Water Project: Law and Politics," *Ecology Law Quarterly*, 5 (1975): 1–52; Clayton R. Koppes, "Public Water, Private Land: Origins of the Acreage Limitation Controversy, 1933–1953," *Pacific Historical Review*, 47 (1978): 607–36; Erwin Cooper, *Aqueduct Empire: A Guide to Water in California, Its Turbulent History and Its Management Today* (Glendale, CA: Arthur H. Clark, 1968); Joe S. Bain, Richard E. Caves, and Julius Margolis, *Northern California's Water Industry: The Comparative Efficiency of Public Enterprise in Developing a Scarce Natural Resource*, Resources for the Future (Baltimore: Johns Hopkins University Press, 1966). Two earlier works on the Central Valley Project are Robert deRoos, *The Thirsty Land: The Story of the Central Valley Project* (Stanford: Stanford University Press, 1948); and Sheridan Downey, *They Would Rule the Valley* (San Francisco: Sheridan Downey, 1947).
45 Duerr, "Conflicts Between Water Development Projects and Fish and Wildlife Conservation," pp. 76–9, 326–7; Bain, Caves, and Margolis, *Northern California's Water Industry*, p. 511; William L. Kahrl, ed., *The California Water Atlas* (Sacramento: State of California, 1979), p. 92.
46 Bain, Caves, and Margolis, *Northern California's Water Industry*, p. 512, note 25.
47 *Rank* v. *Krug*, 90 Fed. supp. 773, 789 (S.D. Cal., 1950).
48 Ibid. at 801.
49 California Attorney General, *Opinions*, No. 50–89 (23 July 1951).
50 Bain, Caves, and Margolis, *Northern California's Water Industry*, p. 511, 513–14, 518.

51   Duerr, "Conflicts Between Water Development Projects and Fish and Game Conservation," pp. 162–9, 181.

52   1961 *California Statutes*, ch. 867; California Legislature, Assembly, Interim Committee on Fish and Game, "Reservation of Water for Fish and Wildlife," Transcript of Hearing, San Francisco, 30–1 January 1964, pp. 80, 103–5; Bain, Caves, and Margolis, *Northern California's Water Industry*, pp. 99; Kahrl, *The California Water Atlas*, pp. 90–1.

53   California Legislature, Assembly Interim Committee on Fish and Game, "Final Report," *Assembly Interim Committee Reports*, v. 5, no. 9 (January 1965) pp. 12–13.

54   Ibid., p. 11.

55   Dasmann, *The Destruction of California*, p. 83; California Legislature, Assembly Interim Committee on Fish and Game, "Report to the Legislature, 1957 Session," *Assembly Interim Committee Reports*, v. 5, no. 3 (1955–7), pp. 23–4; John H. Bushnell, "From American Indian to Indian American: The Changing Identity of the Hupa," *American Anthropologist*, 70 (1968): 1,108–16, pp. 1,112–13; USFWS, "Final Report: Hoopa Valley Indian Reservation: Inventory of Reservation Waters, Fish Rearing Feasibility Study, and a Review of the History and Status of Anadromous Fishery Resources of the Klamath River Basin," photocopied (Arcata, CA: USFWS, Arcata Field Station, 1979), p. 39.

56   57 *Statutes at Large* 588 (1953), codified at 18 U.S.C.A. § 1,162.

57   1957 *California Statutes*, ch. 456, § 7,155, § 12,300.

58   MRC Minutes (24 October 1961), p. 2.

59   USFWS, *Fishery Leaflet* 336q (July 1953): 34.

60   Z. Popovici, "Remarks on the Peruvian Anchovy Fishery," Document VIII, MRC Minutes (6 March 1964), p. 4.

61   E. V. K. FitzGerald, *The Political Economy of Peru, 1956–78: Economic Development and the Restructuring of Capital* (Cambridge: Cambridge University Press, 1979), pp. 113–15; Rosemary Thorp and Geoffrey Bertram, *Peru, 1890–1877: Growth and Policy in an Open Economy* (New York: Columbia University Press, 1978), pp. 244–5. See Alec D. MacCall, "Population Estimates for the Waning Years of the Pacific Sardine Fishery," *CalCOFI Reports*, 20 (1979): 72–82, pp. 73–4.

62   "The Marine Research Committee, 1947–55," CalCOFI, *Progress Report* 4 (1 July 1953–31 March 1955): 7–9; University of California Budget and Planning Office, *University of California Budget* (1946–7), p. 277; ibid. (1949–50), p. 369; MRC Minutes (1 December 1959), p. 4. I am grateful to Roger P. Hewitt for a copy of his paper, "California Cooperative Oceanic Fisheries Investigations: A Historical Review," photocopied (La Jolla: NMFS, n.d.), which helped greatly at the outset of this research.

63   Columbus Iselin to Roger Revelle, 5 October 1949, SIO Subject Files, "MLRP, June–December 1949;" see also McEvoy and Scheiber, "Scientists, Entrepreneurs, and the Policy Process," p. 402.

64   See W. B. White and T. P. Barnett, "A Possible Explanation of Anomalous Events Observed in the Ocean/Atmosphere System of the North Pacific, 1955–1960," *CalCOFI Reports*. 17 (1974): 39–47, p. 39; also J. D. Isaacs and O. E. Sette, "Editor's Summary of the Symposium," *CalCOFI Reports*, 7 (1960): 211–17.

65   Gladys Keener to Carl Hubbs, 10 May 1950, SIO Subject Files, MLRP: News and Publicity; Frances Clark to Hubbs, 23 May 1950, ibid; Hubbs to Clark, 31 May 1950, ibid.; Clark to Hubbs, 1 June 1950, ibid.; Clark to Hubbs, 7 August 1950, ibid.; J.L. McHugh to Clark, 27 August 1951, ibid.

66   J. L. McHugh and Elbert H. Ahlstrom, "Is the Pacific Sardine Disappearing?"

Scientific Monthly, 72 (1951): 377–81, p. 381; John C. Marr to E. H. Dahlgren, 3 January 1951, USBCF General Classified Files, Box 483, file 825.11; Marr to Dahlgren, 15 January 1951, ibid.; Dahlgren to Marr, 24 January 1951, ibid.; Marr to Dahlgren, 12 June 1951, ibid.; Richard Croker to Robert Miller, 22 August 1951, ibid.

67   Marr to Croker, 4 January 1955, SIO Subject Files, MLRP, 1955, 1958, 1960; Croker, "Loss of California's Sardine Fishery May Become Permanent," *Outdoor California*, 15:1 (January 1954): 1–8, p. 1. Personal interview, Richard Croker, 3 September 1982.

68   Frances N. Clark and John C. Marr, "Population Dynamics of the Pacific Sardine," CalCOFI, *Progress Report*, 4 (1 July 1953–31 March 1955): 12–48.

69   MRC Minutes (15 July 1955), p. 4.

70   Croker R. C. Miller, 22 August 1951, CLHP, CalCOFI–Marine Research Committee.

71   MRC Minutes (14 November 1954), pp. 1–2.

72   Ibid.; M. C. James to John Marr, 11 October 1951, USBCF General Classified Files, Box 483, file 825.11; Roger Revelle to L. A. Walford, 12 April 1954, ibid. See also Marr to Dahlgren, 27 September 1951, ibid.; Revelle to Marr, 18 September 1951, ibid.; and Marr to Revelle, 28 September 1951, ibid.

73   Marr to Paul Horrer, 16 March 1953, CLHP, CalCOFI–Sardine Conference 1953; Horrer to Marr, 1 May 1953, ibid.

74   Chapman to Burnette, n.d. (1961 or 1962), WMCP (100/1), p. 1.

75   Walford to Revelle, 13 April 1949, SIO Subject Files, MLRP 1949; McEvoy and Schieber, "Scientists, Entrepreneurs, and the Policy Process," p. 404.

76   Walford to J. Kask, 3 March 1953, USBCF General Classified Files, Box 482, file 825.11; Walford to Kask, 8 January 1953, ibid.; Walford to Kask, 2 March 1953, ibid.

77   Robert G. Sproul to Harald U. Sverdrup, 14 March 1947, SIO Subject Files, Sardine Program; Sproul to Sverdrup, 17 April 1947, ibid.

78   Phister to Sverdrup, 24 June 1947, ibid.

79   Revelle to Carl H. Eckart, n.d. (1948), ibid.

80   Chapman to Burnette, 6 April 1966, WMCP (100/2), p. 7; Chapman to Burnette, n.d. (1961 or 1962), WMCP (100/1), p. 3.

81   Chapman to W. A. Wallace, 18 March 1947, SIO Subject Files, Marine Life Research: General, Correspondence.

82   Chapman, "Industry and the Economy of the Sea," *California and the World Ocean*, Governor's Conference on California and the World Ocean, Los Angeles, 31 January–1 February 1964 (Sacramento: California State Government Special Publication, 1964), pp. 63–76, p. 71; *Pacific Fisherman* (August 1947), p. 49; Chapman to Jackson, 24 August 1965, WMCP (71/8), p. 10; Chapman to Burnette, n.d. (1961 or 1962), WMCP (100/1), pp. 1–2; Knight, *Managing the Sea's Living Resources*, pp. 50–1; Hollick, *U. S. Foreign Policy and the Law of the Sea*, pp. 67–95.

83   NMFS, "Fisheries Management Under Extended Jurisdiction: A Study of the Principles and Policies," Staff Report to the Associate Administrator for Marine Resources, NOAA (Washington, DC: NOAA, n.d.), p. 35; Knight, *Managing the Sea's Living Resources*, pp. 50–1, 75.

84   Bobbie B. Smetherman and Robert M. Smetherman, *Territorial Seas and Inter-American Relations: With Case Studies of the Peruvian and U. S. Fishing Industries* (New York: Praeger, 1974), p. 24.

85   Francis T. Christy, Jr., and Anthony Scott, *The Common Wealth in Ocean*

Fisheries: Some Problems of Growth and Economic Allocation, Resources for the Future (Baltimore: Johns Hopkins University Press, 1965), p. 199.

86 Chapman to Burnette, n.d. (1961 or 1962), WMCP (100/1), pp. 1–2.

87 Christy and Scott, *The Common Wealth in Ocean Fisheries*, p. 199.

88 Chapman, "Tuna Ocean Research and the Industry," talk delivered at meeting of the Shrimp Association of the Americas, Mexico City, 20 June 1959, CLHP, Fisheries: Tuna/American Tunaboat Association, pp. 4, 7.

89 Elizabeth Noble Shor, *Scripps Institution of Oceanography: Probing the Oceans, 1936–1976* (San Diego: Tofua Press, 1978), p. 136.

90 Chapman to Warren Wooster, 16 July 1962, WMCP (70/3), p. 2.

91 Marr to Burnette, 7 June 1951, CLHP, Institute of Marine Resources; Miller to Burnette, 28 May 1951, CLHP, CalCOFI–Marine Research Committee; Chapman, "Statement Made to the Assembly Committee on Fish and Game" (San Diego, 1 October 1951), CLHP, Fisheries: Tuna; Milner B. Schaefer, "On the Policies and Program of the Institute of Marine Resources," n.d. (1961?), CLHP, Institute of Marine Resources; Revelle to James H. Corley, 10 December 1951, ibid.; Revelle, "Prospectus of the Proposed Institute of Marine Resources," n.d. (1951), ibid.; Revelle to Baldwin D. Woods, 1 December 1951, ibid.; Sproul to Revelle, 4 January 1952 Records of the University of California Institute of Marine Resources, Box 1, IMR: 1952, SIO Archives; James H. Corley to Vincent Thomas, 7 January 1952, ibid.; Sproul to Chapman, 8 January 1952, ibid.; "Max Gorby to Sproul, 21 May 1953, ibid., Box 6, file 376; James B. Lane to Sproul, 29 October 1953, ibid., file 377; Sproul to Vice Presidents and Chief Campus Administrative Officers, 19 October 1953, ibid., file 377.

92 Chapman, "Industry and the Economy of the Sea," *California and the World Ocean*, p. 23; Shor, *Scripps Institution of Oceanography*, p. 120.

93 Schaefer, "On the Policies and Program of the Institute of Marine Resources," CLHP, Institute of Marine Resources, pp. 5–6; "Annual Reports, Institute of Marine Resources," 1955–60 *passim*, CLHP, Institute of Marine Resources.

94 MRC Minutes (25 September 1957), pp. 7–9; ibid. (19 December 1957), pp. 2–4; Garth I. Murphy, "Operational Analysis of CalCOFI Research," Exhibit 1, ibid. (4 October 1960), pp. 3–4; Chapman to Burnette, 6 April 1966, WMCP (100/3), p. 4.

95 MRC Minutes (4 October 1960), p. 4; John L. Baxter, "The Role of the Marine Research Committee and CalCOFI," *CalCOFI Reports*, 23 (1982): 35–8, p. 37.

Chapter 9

1 W. M. Chapman to John Gulland, 29 January 1968, WMCP (102/14), p. 3.

2 "Review of the Pelagic Wet Fisheries During the 1961–62 and 1962–63 Seasons," *CalCOFI Reports*, 10 (1965): 8–9, p. 8.

3 Richard H. Parrish and C. E. Blunt, Jr., "The Pacific Mackerel Fishery: A Summary of Biological Knowledge and the Current Status of the Resource," Appendix III, MRC, Minutes of Meeting (13 March 1968); Records of the Marine Research Committee (81–8), SIO Archives, p. 8 (hereafter referred to as MRC Minutes).

4 Richard A. Klingbeil, "Pacific Mackerel: A Resurgent Resource and Fishery of the California Current," *CalCOFI Reports*, 24 (1983): 35–45, p. 36.

5 Herbert W. Frey, ed., *California's Living Marine Resources and Their Utilization* (Sacramento: CDFG, 1972), pp. 44–5; California Legislature, Assembly, Legislative Interim Committee on Fish and Game, "Study of Salmon," hearing (Los Angeles, 12 December 1963), pp. 25–6.

6 Chapman to John Dohm, 17 July 1962, WMCP (70/3), p. 8.

7 Chapman to Milton G. Johnson, 22 March 1966, WMCP (71/15), p. 1; Bobbie B. Smetherman and Robert M. Smetherman, *Territorial Seas and Inter-American Relations: With Case Studies of the Peruvian and U.S. Fishing Industries* (New York: Praeger, 1974), pp. 94–5.

8 Michael Roemer, *Fishing for Growth: Export-Led Development in Peru, 1950–1967* (Cambridge, MA: Harvard University Press, 1970), pp. 82–3; Chapman to J. Steele Culbertson, 20 August 1962, WMCP (70/7); Rosemary Throp and Geoffrey Bertram, *Peru, 1890–1977: Growth and Policy in an Open Economy* (New York: Columbia University Press, 1978), pp. 243, 249–50; Chapman to H. L. Wilkie, 8 September 1965, WMCP (71/9), p. 12; Chapman to Donald L. McKernan, 15 January 1965, WMCP (70/15), pp. 3–4; Chapman to John Tasso, 6 April 1966, WMCP (71/16), pp. 7–8.

9 D. D. Huppert, "An Analysis of the United States Demand for Fish Meal," NMFS *Fishery Bulletin*, 78 (1980): 267–76, p. 267; Philip M. Roedel, "A Consideration of Living Marine Resources off California and the Factors Affecting Their Use," *CalCOFI Reports*, 13 (1969): 19–23, p. 20.

10 Chapman to Wilkie, 8 September 1965, WMCP (71/9), p. 14; Huppert, "Analysis of the United States Demand for Fish Meal," p. 267; Gordon C. Broadhead, "Development of a Fishery Resource," *CalCOFI Reports*, 13 (1969): 120–1, p. 121.

11 Chapman to John L. Kask, 14 December 1962, WMCP (70/11), p. 6.

12 Margaret A. Dewar, *Industry in Trouble: The Federal Government and the New England Fisheries* (Philadelphia: Temple University Press, 1983), pp. 107–11; MRC Minutes (19 January 1965), p. 9.

13 H. Scott Gordon, "The Economic Theory of a Common-Property Resource: The Fishery," *Journal of Political Economy*, 62 (1954): 124–42; see *supra*, pp. 10–11.

14 Francis T. Christy, Jr., and Anthony Scott, *The Common Wealth in Ocean Fisheries: Some Problems of Growth and Economic Allocation*, Resources for the Future (Baltimore: Johns Hopkins University Press, 1965); James A. Crutchfield and Giulio Pontecorvo, *The Pacific Salmon Fisheries: A Study of Irrational Conservation*, Resources for the Future (Baltimore: Johns Hopkins University Press, 1969).

15 Crutchfield and Pontecorvo, *The Pacific Salmon Fisheries*, p. v.

16 R. H. Coase, "The Problem of Social Cost," *Journal of Law and Economics*, 3 (1960): 1–44; see also Richard A. Posner, *The Economics of Justice*, (Cambridge, MA: Harvard University Press, 1983), p. 4.

17 Chapman to Julian G. Burnette, 5 February 1966, WMCP (100/2), p. 10.

18 Joe S. Bain, Richard E. Caves, and Julius Margolis, *Northern California's Water Industry: The Comparative Efficiency of Public Enterprise in Developing a Scarce Natural Resource*, Resources for the Future (Baltimore: Johns Hopkins University Press, 1966), p. 575; see also Colin Clark, *The Economics of Irrigation*, 2nd ed. (Oxford: Pergamon, 1970).

19 Bain, Caves, and Margolis, *Northern California's Water Industry*, pp. 574–5.

20 T. R. Gillenwaters, "The State's Involvement in Maritime and Ocean Resources Development," *CalCOFI Reports*, 13 (1969): 88–90, p. 88.

21 California Legislature, Assembly, Interim Committee on Fish and Game, "Study of Marine Research," hearing (San Diego, 12 November 1963), p. 31. See also MRC Minutes (11 May 1965), p. 13.

22 Bain, Caves, and Margolis, *Northern California's Water Industry*, pp. 514–18; personal interview, Richard Croker, 3 September 1982.

23 California Legislature, Assembly, Interim Committee on Fish and Game, "Final Report," *Assembly Interim Committee Reports*, v. 5, no. 6 (1957–9), p. 20. See

also California State Water Resources Board, *The California Water Plan*, Bulletin No. 3 (Sacramento: California State Water Resources Board, 1957).

24 1961 *California Statutes*, ch. 867.

25 Stephen Fox, *John Muir and His Legacy: The American Conservation Movement* (Boston: Little, Brown, 1981), p. 263.

26 Ibid., pp. 281–9.

27 See *Jessie Short et al.* v. *United States*, 202 Ct. CL. 820 (1973).

28 USFWS, "Final Environmental Impact Statement on the Management of River Flows to Mitigate the Loss of the Anadromous Fishery of the Trinity River, California" INT/FES 80–52 (1980), p. C7–3. As one anthropologist who studied the Hupa in the 1960s wrote: "For those who have grown up on the reservation, it can probably be fairly said that nearly everyone from the least to the most acculturated gives credence . . . to the power of native prayer, to the presence of Indian spirits, . . . [and] to the inevitability with which retribution will follow violation of a religious proscription. . . . This persisting substratum of belief in the continuing sanctity of Indian paraphernalia . . . can be seen as one of the more significant forces serving to perpetuate an enduring core of Indian identity in the midst of a twentieth-century America." (John H. Bushnell, "From American Indian to Indian American: The Changing Identity of the Hupa," *American Anthropologist*, 70 [1968]; 1,108–16, p. 1,115). On the persistence of traditional culture among the Yurok, see U.S. Congress, House, Committee on Merchant Marine and Fisheries, "Klamath River Fishing Rights Oversight," Hearings before the Subcommittee on Fisheries and Wildlife Conservation and Environment, 96th Cong. 1st sess. (1979), *House Serial 96–11*, pp. 124–5; USDA, Forest Service, "Draft Environmental Statement: Six Rivers National Forest: Gasquet-Orleans Road, Chimney Rock Section," USDA-FS-R5-DES (Adm)–78–02 (1977), appendices K-T, pp. 217–485; and *Northwest Indian Cemetery Protective Association et al.* v. *Petersen et al.*, 565 F. Supp. 586 (N.D. Cal. 1983).

29 USFWS, "Final Environmental Impact Statement on the Management of River Flows, Trinity River," p. C7–5.

30 Arnold Pilling, personal correspondence, 22 May 1983.

31 USFWS, "Final Environmental Impact Statement on the Management of River Flows, Trinity River," pp. D28–9.

32 Ibid., p. C7–8.

33 California Legislature, Senate, Fact Finding Committee on Natural Resources, "Iron Gate Dam – Its Effect on the Klamath River Fisheries," hearings (Yreka, 31 August 1961), pp. 3–12.

34 Bain, Caves, and Margolis, *Northern California's Water Industry*, p. 409; Gary L. Rankel, "Depleted Chinook Salmon Runs in the Klamath River Basin: Causes, Consequences and Constraints on Management," photocopied (Arcata, CA: USFWS Fisheries Assistance Office, 1980), pp. 5–7; USFWS, "Final Report: Hoopa Valley Indian Reservation: Inventory of Reservation Waters, Fish Rearing Feasibility Study, and a Review of the History and Status of Anadromous Fishery Resources of the Klamath River Basin," photocopied (Arcata, CA: USFWS Arcata Field Station, 1979), pp. 8, 36.

35 Charles A. Hobbs, "Indian Hunting and Fishing Rights," *George Washington Law Review*, 32 (1963–4): 504–32; Hobbs, "Indian Hunting and Fishing Rights, II," ibid., 37 (1969): 1,251–73; Robert Ericson and D. Rebecca Snow, "Comment: The Indian Battle for Self-Determination," *California Law Review*, 58 (1970): 445–90, pp. 445–6. On Indian law generally see Russel Lawrence Barsh and James Youngblood Henderson, *The Road: Indian Tribes and Political Liberty* (Berkeley and Los Angeles: University of California Press, 1980). On treaty fishing rights in the Pacific

Northwest, see Barsh, *The Washington Fishing Rights Controversy: An Economic Critique*, rev. ed. (Seattle: University of Washington Graduate School of Business Administration, 1979).

36 Daniel H. Israel, "The Resurgence of Tribal Nationalism and Its Impact on Reservation Resource Development," *University of Colorado Law Review*, 47 (1975–6): 617–52, p. 617.

37 Jack L. Landau, "Empty Victories: Indian Treaty Fishing Rights in the Pacific Northwest," *Environmental Law*, 10 (1980): 413–56, pp. 417–18.

38 *Puyallup Tribe* v. *Department of Game of Washington*, 391 U.S. 392, 398 (1968).

39 *Elser* v. *Gill Net Number One*, 246 Cal. App. 2d 30, 54 Cal. Rptr. 568 (1966).

40 *Arnett* v. *5 Gill Nets, etc.*, 20 Cal. App. 3d 729, 97 Cal. Rptr. 894 (1971).

41 *Mattz* v. *Arnett, Director, Department of Fish and Game*, 412 U.S. 481 (1973); *Arnett* v. *5 Gill Nets et al.*, 48 Cal. App. 3d 454, 464, 121 Cal. Rptr. 906 (1975), *cert. denied*, 425 U.S. 907 (1976).

42 *Elser* v. *Gill Net Number One*, 246 Cal. App. 2d at 38.

43 E. V. K. Fitzgerald, *The Political Economy of Peru, 1956–78: Economic Development and the Restructuring of Capital* (Cambridge: Cambridge University Press, 1979), pp. 113–14.

44 Chapman to Julian G. Burnette, n.d. (1961 or 1962), WMCP (100/1), p. 3; Chapman to Charles Jackson, 24 August 1965, WMCP (71/8), p. 12.

45 Chapman to Charles R. Carry, 9 April 1967, WMCP (100/3), p. 3.

46 MRC Minutes (12 June 1962), p. 7.

47 Chapman to Carry, 9 April 1967, WMCP (100/3), p. 13.

48 G. I. Murphy, J. D. Isaacs, J. L. Baxter, and E. H. Ahlstrom, "Requirements for Understanding the Impact of a New Fishery in the California Current System," Document XII, MRC Minutes (6 March 1964), p. 1.

49 Garth I. Murphy, "Population Biology of the Pacific Sardine (*Sardinops caerulea*)," *Proceedings of the California Academy of Sciences*, 4th series, 34: 1 (26 July 1966), p. 76.

50 Chapman to Burnette, 13 December 1962, WMCP (100/1), p. 2.

51 California Legislature, Assembly, Interim Committee on Fish and Game, "Study of Marine Research," hearing (San Diego, 12 November 1963), pp. 55, 58.

52 Murphy, Isaacs, Baxter, and Ahlstrom, "Requirements for Understanding the Impact of a New Fishery," p. 1.

53 Ibid., p. 2.

54 Edmund G. Brown, Sr., to Burnette, 4 August 1964, appended to MRC Minutes (21 May 1964).

55 R. A. Izor, "The Point of View of the Partyboat and Live Bait Industries," *CalCOFI Reports*, 13 (1969): 113–16, p. 113.

56 The notes appear on the SIO Archives copy of MRC Minutes (21 May 1964), p. 4. The handwriting is that of John Dove Isaacs.

57 Chapman to Charles Carry, 9 April 1967, WMCP (100/3), p. 3.

58 J. R. Snyder to Chapman, 19 August 1965, Appendix II, MRC Minutes (26 August 1965). Snyder apparently wrote the letter to Chapman at Chapman's request (Chapman to Wilkie, 8 September 1965, WMCP [71/9], pp. 1–2.

59 Chapman to David S. Potter, 22 September 1965, WMCP (98/22), pp. 4–6.

60 Chapman to Donald L. McKernan, 10 December 1965, WMCP (71/10), p. 2.

61 Robert G. Kaneen, "A Look at the Anchovy Reduction Permits," Appendix II, MRC Minutes (14 February 1966), pp. 1–2; MRC Minutes (8 June 1966), p. 7;

Chapman to Potter, 22 September 1965, WMCP (98/22), pp. 4–6; Chapman to Wilkie, 8 September 1965, WMCP (71/9) pp. 2–3.

62 Chapman to Charles R. Carry, 9 April 1967, WMCP (100/3), pp. 6–8.

63 Chapman, "Statement of W. M. Chapman Before the California Fish and Game Commission Respecting the Anchovy Fishery, Anchovy Population Size, Biological Research, Impact of Fishery on Environment and Sport Fishery, and its Regulation for Maximum Use and Conservation of the Resource, San Francisco, California – August 26, 1966," Appendix II, MRC, Minutes (8 August 1967), pp. 9–10; Chapman to John Tasso, 6 April 1966, WMCP (71/16), p. 6.

64 James E. Hardwick, "Review of the Pelagic Wet Fisheries During the 1966–67 Season," *CalCOFI Reports*, 12 (1968): 22–3, p. 22.

65 Robson A. Collins, "Review of the Pelagic Wet Fisheries During the 1967–68 Season," *CalCOFI Reports*, 13 (1969): 11; Chapman, "Statement of W. M. Chapman," Appendix II, MRC Minutes (8 August 1967), p. 9.

66 W. G. Clark, "The Lessons of the Peruvian Anchoveta Fishery," *CalCOFI Reports*, 19 (1977): 57–63, p. 60; Thorp and Bertram, *Peru, 1890- 1977*, p. 246.

67 Thorp and Bertram, *Peru, 1890–1977*, p. 246.

68 Clark, "The Lessons of the Peruvian Anchoveta Fishery," 59; see also G. J. Paulik, "Anchovies, Birds, and Fishermen in the Peru Current," in *Environment: Resources, Pollution, and Society*, ed. W. W. Murdock (Stamford, CT: Sinaur, 1971), pp. 156–85.

69 W. F. Perrin, "Economic Condition of the San Pedro Wetfish Boat Fleet," Appendix III, MRC Minutes (9 April 1969), pp. 1–2; David Ganssle, "Review of the Pelagic Wet Fisheries for 1968 and 1969," *CalCOFI Reports*, 14 (1970): 14–15, p. 14; Stephen J. Crooke, "Review of the Pelagic Wet Fisheries for 1970 and 1971," *CalCOFI Reports*, 16 (1972): 15–16, p. 15.

70 MRC Minutes (21–2 September 1967), p. 23.

71 MRC Minutes (11 September 1969), p. 7.

72 J. L. Baxter, J. D. Isaacs, A. R. Longhurst, and P. M. Roedel, "Report of the CalCOFI Committee," *CalCOFI Reports*, 12 (1968): 5–9, p. 9.

73 MRC Minutes (15 January 1968), p. 11; MRC, Minutes (3 June 1968), p. 14.

74 A. Alan Post, "California and Commercial Fishery Problems," *CalCOFI Reports*, 15 (1971): 19–21, p. 21.

75 P. M. Roedel, "A Consideration of the Living Marine Resources off California and the Factors Affecting Their Use," *CalCOFI Reports*, 13 (1969): 19–23, p. 20.

76 John Radovich, "Report on the Conference on the Future of the United States Fishing Industry, Seattle, Washington, March 24–7, 1968," WMCP (85/16), p. 15.

77 Smetherman and Smetherman, *Territorial Seas and Inter-American Relations*, pp. 22–3.

78 Chapman to Paul O. Bleeker, 25 July 1965, WMCP (71/7), pp. 6–7.

79 Ann L. Hollick, *U. S. Foreign Policy and the Law of the Sea* (Princeton, NJ: Princeton University Press, 1981), pp. 153–9; James Joseph and Joseph W. Greenough, *International Management of Tuna, Porpoise, and Billfish: Biological, Legal, and Political Aspects* (Seattle: University of Washington Press, 1979), pp. 25–6; Smetherman and Smetherman, *Territorial Seas and Inter-American Relations*, p. 36, note 75.

80 Joseph and Greenough, *International Management of Tuna, Porpoise, and Billfish*, pp. 1–37; Smetherman and Smetherman, *Territorial Seas and Inter-American Relations*, p. 92.

81 "General Panel Discussion: Symposium on Population and Fisheries," *CalCOFI Reports*, 14 (1970): 67–70, p. 67.

82   P. L. 89–658, 80 *Statutes at Large* 908 (1966).

83   Kline R. Swygard, "Politics of the North Pacific Fisheries – with Special Reference to the Twelve-Mile Bill," *Washington Law Review*, 12 (1967): 269–82, pp. 273–6.

84   H. Gary Knight, "Management Procedures in the US Fishery Conservation Zone," *Marine Policy* 2 (1978): 22–9, p. 23; NMFS, "Fisheries Management Under Extended Jurisdiction: A Study of Principles and Policies: Staff Report to the Associate Administrator for Marine Resources, National Oceanic and Atmospheric Administration," Washington: NOAA, n.d., p. 10.

85   P. L. 89–454, 80 *Statutes at Large* 203 (1966); Hollick, *U. S. Foreign Policy and the Law of the Sea*, p. 191.

86   P. L. 92–583, 86 *Statutes at Large* 1,280 (1972), amended P. L. 94-370, 90 *Statutes at Large* 1,013 (1976), 16 U.S.C.A. §§ 1,451–64.

87   P. L. 89–688, 80 *Statutes at Large* 998 (1966).

88   Reorganization Plan No. 4 of 1970, 84 *Statutes at Large* 1,090; Chapman to Edmund R. Muskie, 20 July 1965, WMCP (71/5), pp. 1–2; Chapman to Charles E. Jackson, 24 July 1965, WMCP (71/7), pp. 1–2.

89   Chapman, "Industry and the Economy of the Sea," *California and the World Ocean*, Governor's Conference on California and the World Ocean, Los Angeles, 31 January–1 February 1964 (Sacramento: California State Government Special Publication, 1964), pp. 63–76, p. 76. See also Chapman, "Social and Political Factors in the Development of Fish Production by United States Flag Vessels," *The Future of the Fishing Industry of the United States*, University of Washington Publications in Fisheries – New Series, v. IV (1968), pp. 262–8, pp. 266–7.

90   1967 *California Statutes*, ch. 1,642; Chapman to Alan Cranston, 26 July 1969, WMCP (99/7), pp. 1–3; Stanley Scott, *Governing California's Coast* (Berkeley: University of California Institute of Governmental Studies, 1975), pp. 9–10; Winfield A. Shoemaker, "Use of the Pelagic Living Resources: The Legislative Point of View," *CalCOFI Reports*, 13 (1969): 97–8, p. 97.

91   Milner B. Schaefer, "On the Policies and Programs of the Institute of Marine Resources," n.d. (1961?), CLHP, "Institute of Marine Resources," pp. 7–8. See also Schaefer, "The Resources of the Sea: What Does the Ocean Offer?" *California and the World Ocean*, pp. 35–40, pp. 39–40.

92   MRC Minutes (14 February 1966), p. 3.

93   Scott, *Governing California's Coast*, p. 14.

94   Radovich, "Report on the Conference on the Future of the United States Fishing Industry," WMCP (85/16), pp. 10, 15.

95   Chapman to A. F. Rollins, 29 June 1965, WMCP (71/3), p. 5; Chapman to All Commissioners, 13 March 1969, WMCP (99/4).

96   Chapman to A. F. Rollins, 29 June 1965, WMCP (71/3), p. 9.

97   Chapman to All Commissioners, 13 March 1969, WMCP (99/4), p. 3.

98   Chapman to Montgomery Phister, 6 March 1947, WMCP (5/22).

99   Richard S. Croker, "An Iconoclast's View of California Fisheries Research, 1929–1962," *CalCOFI Reports*, 23 (1982): 29–34, p. 34.

100   Chapman to All Commissioners, 13 March 1969, WMCP (99/4), p. 3.

101   MRC Minutes (26 August 1965), p. 15; Chapman to Burnette, 6 April 1966, WMCP (100/2), p. 14.

102   MRC Minutes (2 July 1968), p. 9.

103   Milner B. Schaefer to Donald R. Johnson, 15 April 1964, WMCP (58/14), p. 7.

104 R. A. Izor, "The Point of View of the Partyboat and Live Bait Industries," *CalCOFI Reports*, 13 (1969): 113–16, p. 114.

105 California, Resources Agency, Department of Fish and Game, "Report on Pelagic Wetfish Inventory, Management and Utilization, and Interrelationship, Prepared in Response to Assembly Bill 564, 1969 Session (January 1970), p. 12; personal interview, Paul E. Smith, 16 September 1982.

106 E. C. Greenhood, "Report on the California Fish and Wildlife Plan," Appendix I, MRC Minutes (14 February 1966), p. 3.

107 A. Alan Post, "California and Commercial Fishery Problems," *CalCOFI Reports*, 15 (1971): 19–21, p. 19.

108 MRC Minutes (11 August 1970), p. 3.

109 Roedel, "A Consideration of the Living Marine Resources off California and Factors Affecting Their Use," pp. 19–20.

110 1967 *California Statutes*, ch. 278.

111 MRC Minutes (8 August 1967), p. 4.

Chapter 10

1 NOAA, "Implementation of Northern Anchovy Fishery Management Plan: Solicitation of Public Comments," 43 *Federal Register* 31,651– 879, 31,699 (21 July 1978).

2 See Samuel P. Hays, "From Conservation to Environment: Environmental Politics in the United States Since World War Two,"*Environmental Review*, 6 (Fall 1982) : 14–41; and Donald Fleming, "Roots of the New Conservation Movement," *Perspectives in American History*, (1971): 7–91.

3 Stephen Fox, *John Muir and His Legacy: The American Conservation Movement* (Boston: Little, Brown, 1981), ch. 9.

4 Personal interview, Richard Croker, 3 September 1982.

5 Croker, "50 Years of Pacific Fisheries, 1947–1997," Pacific Marine Fisheries Commission, *Annual Report* (1972): 4–10, p. 6.

6 Robert G. Kaneen, "California's View of Anchovy Management,"*CalCOFI Reports*, 19 (1 July 1975–30 June 1976): 25–7.

7 See David Vogel, "The 'New' Social Regulation in Historical and Comparative Perspective," in *Regulation in Perspective: Historical Essays*, ed. Thomas K. McCraw (Cambridge, MA.: Harvard University Press, 1981), pp. 155–86,

8 On the Clean Air Amendments of 1970, see Richard A. Walker and Michael Storper, "Erosion of the Clean Air Act of 1970: A Study in the Failure of Government Regulation and Planning," *Boston College Environmental Affairs Law Review*, 7 (1978): 189–257; Bruce M. Kramer, "Economics, Technology, and the Clean Air Amendments of 1970: The First Six Years," *Ecology Law Quarterly*, 6 (1976): 161–230; Patrick Del Duca, "The Clean Air Act; A Realistic Assessment of Cost-Effectiveness," *Harvard Environmental Law Review*, 5 (1981) : 184–203; and William F. Pedersen, Jr., "Why the Clean Air Act Works Badly," *University of Pennsylvania Law Review*, 129 (1981): 1,059–109. On the Occupational Health and Safety Act of 1970, see Paolo F. Ricci and Lawrence S. Molton, "Risk and Benefit in Environmental Law," *Science*, 214 (4 December 1981): 1,096–100. On the Consumer Product Safety Act of 1972, see Michael Pertschuk, *Revolt Against Regulation: The Rise and Pause of the Consumer Movement* (Berkeley and Los Angeles: University of California Press, 1982). On the Endangered Species Act of 1973, see *Tennessee Valley Authority v. Hill*, 437 United States 153 (1978). On the Marine Mammals Protection Act of

1972, see *Committee for Humane Legislation, Inc.* v. *Richardson et al.*, 414 F. Supp. 297 (D.C. Dist. 1976); and James Joseph and Joseph W. Greenough, *International Management of Tuna, Porpoise, and Billfish: Biological, Legal, and Political Aspects* (Seattle: University of Washington Press, 1979), pp. 144–53.

9   *John Muir and His Legacy*, pp. 304–5; *Scenic Hudson Preservation Conference* v. *Federal Power Commission (I)*, 354 F.2d 608 (2nd Cir. 1965); *Scenic Hudson Preservation Conference* v. *Federal Power Commission (II)*, 453 F.2d 463 (2nd Cir. 1971), *cert. denied*, 407 *United States* 926 (1972); *Sierra Club* v. *Morton*, 405 United States 727 (1972). See also Christopher D. Stone, "Should Trees Have Standing? – Toward Legal Rights for Natural Objects," *Southern California Law Review*, 45 (1972): 450–80, pp. 464–73.

10   *In re Consolidated Edison Company of New York, Inc., (Indian Point Station Unit No. 2)*, 6 A.E.C. 751 (25 September 1973); David M. Trubek, "Faculty Research Note: Allocating the Burden of Environmental Uncertainty: The NRC Interprets NEPA's Substantive Mandate," *Wisconsin Law Review* (1977 vol.) : 747–76; Ricci and Molton, "Risk and Benefit in Environmental Law," pp. 1,096–100.

11   Vogel, "The 'New' Social Regulation," pp. 163, 158–61; Walker and Storper, "Erosion of the Clean Air Act of 1970," pp. 243–52. See generally J. Willard Hurst, *Law and Markets in United States History: Different Modes of Bargaining Among Interests* (Madison: University of Wisconsin Press, 1982), esp. ch. 3.

12   William H. Rogers, Jr., *Environmental Law*, Hornbook Series (St. Paul: West Publishing, 1977), pp. 697–704; Walker and Storper, "Erosion of the Clean Air Act of 1970," pp. 193-4.

13   National Environmental Policy Act of 1969, P.L. 91-180, 83 *Statutes at Large* 852, 42 U.S.C.A. §§4,331–2; Marine Mammals Protection Act of 1972, P.L. 92-522, 86 *Statutes at Large* 1027, 16 U.S.C.A. §§1,361-1407; Endangered Species Act of 1973, P.L. 93-205, 87 *Statutes at Large* 884, 16 U.S.C.A. §§1,531-43, *amended*, P.L. 95-632, 92 *Statutes at Large* 3751 (1978); Fishery Conservation and Management Act of 1976, P.L. 94–265, 90 *Statutes at Large* 331, 16 U.S.C.A. §§1,801–81.

14   Margaret E. Dewar, *Industry in Trouble: The Federal Government and the New England Fisheries* (Philadelphia: Temple University Press, 1983), pp. 136–44. See also Langdon S. Warner, Barbara A. Finamore, and Michael J. Bean, "Practical Application of the Conservation Aspects of the Fishery Conservation and Management Act," *Harvard Environmental Law Review*, 5 (1981) : 30–70; and J.A. Gulland, "World Fisheries and Fish Stocks," *Marine Policy*, 1 (1977) : 179–89, pp. 186–7.

15   W. G. Clark, "The Lessons of the Peruvian Anchoveta Fishery,"*CalCOFI Reports*, 19 (1977): 57–63, p. 62.

16   Gulland, "World Fisheries and Fish Stocks," p. 180; "World Fishing Flounders," (London) *Economist* (23 June 1984), pp. 70–1.

17   John H.Rhyther, "Photosynthesis and Fish Production in the Sea," *Science*, 166 (6 October 1969): 76–81. For a discussion of Rhyther's estimates, see D.L. Alverson, A.E. Longhurst, and J.A. Gulland, "How Much Food from the Sea?" *Science*, 190 (21 November 1975): 758–9. Lester R. Brown with Erik P. Eckholm, *By Bread Alone*, Overseas Development Council (New York: Praeger 1974), p. 149; and Gulland, "World Fisheries and Fish Stocks," pp. 186–7.

18   "World Fishing Flounders," *Economist* (23 June 1984), pp. 70-1; Luther J. Carter, "Law of the Sea: Fisheries Plight Poses Dilemma for United States," *Science*, 185 (26 July 1974): 336–9, p. 337.

19   Vi Murphy, "Mexico Poises for Anchovy Bid," *San Diego Union* (1 August 1976), pp. H1, 12–13; Vickie Wine, "Review of the Pelagic Wet-Fisheries for 1973," *CalCOFI Reports*, 18 (1976): 19–20, p. 19.

20 Murphy, "Mexico Poises for Anchovy Bid," p. Hl; Joseph Havilcek, Jr., and Faustino Ccama, "U.S. Demand for Fish Meal," (Contributed Paper, American Agricultural Economics Association Meetings, San Diego, 31 July–3 August 1977), photocopied (copy on file, Giannini Foundation of Agricultural Economics Library, University of California, Berkeley), p. 9.

21 Laurel Sorenson, "Scientists Study the Climatic Effects of El Niño, A Fickle Warm-Sea Phenomenon in the Pacific," *Wall Street Journal* (24 March 1983), p. 50; Murphy, "Mexico Poises for Anchovy Bid," pp. H1, 12–13; MRC Minutes of Meeting (21–2 September 1967), Records of the Marine Research Committee (81–8), pp. 11–12 (hereafter referred to as MRC Minutes); Daniel Lluch B., "The Mexican View of the Basic Research Needs for the Management of the Anchovy Fishery,"*CalCOFI Reports*, 19 (1977): 28–32, p. 30; MRC Minutes (11 March 1975), pp. 3–4.

22 Herbert W. Frey, "Review of the Pelagic Wet-Fisheries for 1969 and 1970," *CalCOFI Reports*, 15 (1971): 13–14.

23 The Commission's authority stems from *Cal. Fish & Game Code* §8,180 (West, 1984). See *People* v. *Zankich*, 20 Cal App. 3rd 971, 98 Cal. Rptr. 387 (1971). See also Phil Lehtonen, "Review of Pelagic Wet Fisheries 1974," *CalCOFI Reports*, 18 (1976): 21–2; NOAA, Implementation of Northern Anchovy Fishery Management Plan: Solicitation of Public Comments," 43 *Federal Register* 31,651–31,879, 31,665 (1978).

24 Richard A. Klingbeil, "Review of the Pelagic Wet Fisheries for 1976 with Notes on the History of These Fisheries," *CalCOFI Reports*, 20 (1979): 6–12, p. 8; NOAA, "Implementation of Northern Anchovy Fishery Management Plan," p. 31680.

25 William H. Lenarz, "Modeling the Resource Base," *CalCOFI Reports*, 15 (1971): 28–32.

26 Ibid., p. 28

27 Paul E. Smith, "The Increase in Spawning Biomass of Northern Anchovy, *Engraulis mordax*," NMFS *Fishery Bulletin*, 70 (1972): 849–74.

28 Alec D. MacCall, "Population Estimates for the Waning Years of the Pacific Sardine Fishery," *CalCOFI Reports*, 20 (1979): 72–82, p. 77.

29 John Radovich and Alec D. MacCall, "A Management Model for the Central Stock of Northern Anchovy, *Engraulis mordax*," *CalCOFI Reports*, 20 (1979) : 83–8.

30 Alan Longhurst to Marston Sargent, 24 May 1971 (photocopy courtesy of Paul E. Smith), p. 5

31 Ibid., p. 4.

32 Ibid,; MRC Minutes (8 February 1972), pp. 9–10.

33 Minutes (8 May 1973), p. 11.

34 Personal interview, Paul E. Smith, 16 September 1982; 1972 *California Statutes*, ch. 608; 1973 *California Statutes*, ch. 638.

35 Personal interview, Paul E. Smith, 16 September 1982.

36 NOAA, "Implementation of Northern Anchovy Fishery Management Plan," p. 31664.

37 Lenarz, "Modeling the Resource Base," p. 30.

38 Richard A. Klingbeil, "Pacific Mackerel: A Resurgent Resource and Fishery of the California Current," *CalCOFI Reports*, 24 (1983): 35–45.

39 Klingbeil, "Review of the Pelagic Wet Fisheries 1977," *CalCOFI Reports*, 20, (1979) : 10–12, p. 11.

40 Timothy Larimer, "Sardines Return to Monterey Bay, but There's No One Left to Shout," *Chicago Tribune* (1 January 1985), sec. 51, p. 3.

41   Radovich and MacCall, "A Management Model for the Central Stock of Northern Anchovy," p. 87.

42   Daniel W. Anderson, Franklin Gress, Kenneth F. Mais, and Paul R. Kelly, "Brown Pelicans as Anchovy Stock Indicators and Their Relationships to Commercial Fishing," *CalCOFI Reports*, 21 (1980): 54–61, pp. 56–7; Dan Guravich and Joseph E. Brown, *The Return of the Brown Pelican* (Baton Rouge: Louisiana State University Press, 1983), pp. 84–109; Thomas R. Dunlap, *DDT: Scientists, Citizens, and Public Policy* (Princeton, N.J. Princeton University Press, 1981), pp. 221–2.

43   Endangered Species Act of 1973, § 7, 16 U.S.C.A. § 1,536; see also *Tennessee Valley Authority* v. *Hill*, 437 U.S. 153 (1978). See Anderson, Gress, Mais, and Kelly, "Brown Pelicans as Anchovy Stock Indicators," p. 54; NOAA, "Implementation of Northern Anchovy Fishery Management Plan," pp. 31,690, 31,698.

44   Robert A. Jones, "Dramatic Case of the Pelican and the Bureaucrats," *Los Angeles Times* (3 September 1979), pp. II: 1, 8; Jerry Rublow, "Pelican is Watching the Anchovy, Too," *Los Angeles Times* (29 December 1979), p. II:1; Guravich and Brown, *The Return of the Brown Pelican*, pp. 108–9; Endangered Species Act, 16 U.S.C.A. §1,536.

45   Quoted in Jones, "The Dramatic Case of the Pelican and the Bureaucrats," p. II: 1.

46   John S. Sunada, Irene S. Yamashita, Paul R. Kelly, and Franklin Gress, "The Brown Pelican as a Sampling Instrument of Age Group Structure in the Northern Anchovy Population," *CalCOFI Reports*, 22 (1981): 65–8, p. 68.

47   Anderson, Gress, Mais, and Kelly, "Brown Pelicans as Anchovy Stock Indicators," p. 60.

48   Croker, "50 Years of Pacific Fisheries," Pacific Marine Fisheries Commission, *Annual Report* (1972) : 4–10, p. 5

49   Friends of the Earth, *The Whale Manual* (San Francisco: Friends of the Earth, 1978), pp. 108–9; United Nations, Food and Agriculture Organization, *Mammals in the Seas: Report of the FAO Advisory Committee on Marine Resources Research, Working Party on Marine Mammals*, FAO Fisheries Series No. 5, v. 1 (Rome: FAO, 1978), p. 57. The last land-based whaling station in the United States remained open near San Francisco until 1971, when it was closed under the provisions of federal endangered species law (ibid., pp. 241–2).

50   George A. Antonelis, Jr., and Clifford H. Fiscus, "The Pinnipeds of the California Current," *CalCOFI Reports*, 21 (1980): 68–78, p. 76; NOAA, "Implementation of Northern Anchovy Fishery Management Plan," p. 31,688; personal interview, Paul E. Smith, 16 September 1982.

51   California Legislature, Senate, Fact Finding Committee on Natural Resources, Subcommittee on Sea Otters, "Effect of the Sea Otter on the Abalone Resource," hearing (San Luis Obispo, 19 November 1963), pp. 4–7; Daniel J. Miller, "The Sea Otter in California," *CalCOFI Reports*, 21 (1980): 79–81.

52   California Legislature, Assembly, Interim Committee on Fish and Game, "Final Report," *Assembly Interim Commitee Reports*, v. 5, no. 6 (1957–9), p. 13.

53   California Legislature, Senate, Fact Finding Committee on Natural Resources, Subcommittee on Sea Otters, "Effect of the Sea Otter on the Abalone Resource," hearing (San Luis Obispo, 19 November 1963), pp. 4–7.

54   Philip M. Roedel, "A Consideration of the Living Marine Resources Off California and the Factors Affecting Their Use," *CalCOFI Reports*, 13 (1969): 19–23, p. 22.

55   Miller, "The Sea Otter in California," p. 79.

56 James A. Estes and John F. Palmisano, "Sea Otters: Their Role in Structuring Nearshore Communities," *Science*, 185 (20 September 1974): 1058–60.

57 *Committee for Humane Legislation, Inc.*, v. *Richardson*, 414 F. Supp. at 300.

58 16 U.S.C.A. §1,371 (c) (2).

59 Cited in *Committee for Humane Legislation, Inc.*, v. *Richardson*, 414 F. Supp. at 305.

60 Cited in ibid. at 309.

61 Laurel Lee Hyde, "Comment: Dolphin Controversy in the Tuna Industry: The United States' Role in an International Problem," *San Diego Law Review*, 16 (1979): 665–704, p. 680; Joseph and Greenough, *International Management of Tuna, Porpoise, and Billfish*, pp. 152, 154–68.

62 *Sohappy* v. *Smith*, 302 F. Supp. 899, 911 (D. Or. 1969). See Jack L. Landau, "Empty Victories: Indian Treaty Fishing Rights in the Pacific Northwest," *Environmental Law*, 10 (1980): 413–56, p. 438; Peter J. Aschenbrenner, "Comments: State Power and the Indian Treaty Right to Fish," *California Law Review*, 59 (1971) : 485–524.

63 *United States* v. *Washington*, 384 F. Supp. 312 (W.D. Wash., 1974), *affirmed*, 520 F.2d 676 (9th Cir. 1975), *cert. denied*, 423 U. S. 1,086, *substantially affirmed*, *Washington* v. *Washington State Commercial Passenger Fishing Vessel Association*, 443 U. S. 658 (1979).

64 *United States* v. *Washington (Phase II)*, 506 F. Supp. 187, 203 (W.D. Wash. 1980), *modified*, 694 F. 2d 1374 (9th Cir. 1982). See Peter C. Monson, "Casenote: *United States* v. *Washington (Phase II)*: The Indian Fishing Conflict Moves Upstream," *Enbironmental Law*, 12 (1982): 468–503, p. 502.

65 *United States* v. *Wilson*, 611 F. Sup. 813, 818 (N.D. Cal. 1985). See also *Blake* v. *Arnett, et al.*, 663 F.2d 906, 909 (9th Cir. 1981).

66 *Northwest Indian Cemetery Protective Association et al.* v. *Peterson et al.*, 565 F. Supp. 586, 605 (N.D. Cal. 1983), *modified on appeal*, 764 F.2d 581 (9th Cir. 1985).

67 *Winters* v. *United States*, 207 U.S. 564 (1908). See Robert S. Pelcyger, "The *Winters* Doctrine and the Greening of the Reservations," *Journal of Contemporary Law*, 4 (1977): 19–37.

68 *Arizona* v. *California* 373 U.S. 546, 594–601 (1963).

69 *County of Trinity* v. *Andrus*, 438 F. Supp. 1368, 1385 (E.D. Cal. 1977).

70 *Pacific Coast Federation of Fishermen's Association, Inc., et al.* v. *Secretary of Commerce et al.*, 494 F. Supp. 626,632–4 (N.D. Cal. 1980).

71 Pelcyger, 'The *Winters* Doctrine and the Greening of the Reservations," pp. 35–7.

72 Huey D. Johnson to James A. Joseph, 4 August 1978 (photocopy courtesy of Paul Jensen).

73 P.L. 94–265, 16 U.S.C.A. §§ 1,801–81.

74 Quoted in United States Congress, House, Committee on Merchant Marine and Fisheries, "Report to Accompany H.R. 200, Marine Fisheries Conservation Act of 1975," 94th Con., 1st sess. (1975), *House Report 94-455*, p. 44. Emphasis in original.

75 United States Congress, Office of Technology Assessment, "Establishing a 200-Mile Fisheries Zone" (Washington, D.C.: GPO, 1977), p. 61.

76 16 U.S.C.A. § 1802(18). See H.A. Larkins, "Management Under FCMA: Development of a Fishery Management Plan," *Marine Policy*, 4 (1980): 170–82; Giulio Pontecorvo, "Fishery Management and the General Welfare: Implications of the

New Structure," *Washington Law Review*, 52 (1977): 641–56; Francis T. Christy, Jr., "The Fishery Conservation and Management Act of 1976: Management Objectives and the Distribution of Benefits and Costs," *Washington Law Review*, 52 (1977): 657–80; Oran R. Young, *Natural Resources and the State: The Political Economy of Resource Management*, Studies in International Political Economy (Berkeley and Los Angeles: University of California Press, 1981), ch. 4.

77 NMFS, "Fisheries Management Under Extended Jurisdiction," p. 7.

78 Warner, Finamore, and Bean, "Practical Application of the Conservation Aspects of the Fishery Conservation and Management Act," p. 31.

79 H. Gary Knight, "Management Procedures in the U.S. Fishery Conservation Zone," *Marine Policy*, 2 (1978): 22–9, p. 23.

80 Dennis W. Bedford and Frederick B. Hagerman, "The Billfish Fishery Resource of the California Current," *CalCOFI Reports*, 24 (1983): 70–8; Joseph and Greenough, *International Management of Tuna, Porpoise, and Billfish*, pp. 172–9.

81 Pacific Marine Fisheries Commission, *Annual Report* (1977): 5–6; Dennis Bedford et al., "Review of Some California Fisheries for 1980 and 1981," *CalCOFI Reports*, 23 (1982): 8–14, pp. 12–13; personal interview, Daniel D. Huppert, 18 September 1982.

82 NMFS, "Fisheries Management Under Extended Jurisdiction," pp. 2–3.

83 Personal interview, Daniel D. Huppert, 18 September 1982; 1973 *California Statutes*, ch. 733, §2.

84 PFMC, "Final Environmental Impact Statement and Fishery Management Plan for Commercial and Recreational Salmon Fisheries off the Coasts of Washington, Oregon, and California Commencing in 1978 " (Portland, OR: PFMC, March 1978), pp. 111–112; 1979 *California Statutes*, ch. 1,096, *superceded by* 1982 *California Statutes*, ch. 1,486.

85 Personal interview, Daniel D. Huppert, 18 September 1982. See Anon., "Legal Dimensions of Entry Fishery Management," *William and Mary Law Review*, 17 (1976): 757–79.

86 See United States Congress, Office of Technology Assessment, "Establishing a 200-Mile Fisheries Zone," pp. 61, 89; *Pacific Coast Federation of Fishermen's Association, Inc.* v. *Secretary of Commerce*, 494 F. Supp. 626.

87 NOAA, "Implementation of Northern Anchovy Fishery Management Plan," p. 31,695.

88 Pontecorvo, "Fishery Management and the General Welfare, p. 664.

89 Warner, Finamore, and Bean, "Practical Application of the Fishery Conservation and Management Act," p. 58.

90 *State of Maine et al.* v. *Kreps et al.*, 563 F.2d 1,043, 1,048 (1st Cir. 1977), *rehearing denied*, 563 F.2d 1,052 (1st Cir. 1977).

91 *Pacific Coast Federation of Fishermen's Association, Inc.* v. *Secretary of Commerce*, 494 F. Supp. at 635.

92 Personal interview, Daniel D. Huppert, 18 September 1982; 47 *Federal Register* 21,256–66 (18 May 1982) ; 47 *Federal Register* 24,134–6 (31 June 1982); 47 *Federal Register* 38,545–7 (1 September 1982).

93 16 U.S.C.A. § 1,865(a); see "Note: The Fishery Conservation and Management Act of 1976: State Regulation of Fishing Beyond the Territorial Sea," *Maine Law Review*, 31 (1979–80) : 303–22.

94 1976 *California Statutes*, ch. 1,160.

95 Richard A. Klingbeil, John S. Sunada, and Jerome D. Spratt, "Review of the Pelagic Wet Fisheries for 1978 and 1979," *CalCOFI Reports*, 21 (1980) : 8–11, p. 8.

96 Jerry Ruhlow, "Anchovy Catch Dives to a Near-Record Law," *Los Angeles*

Times (12 February 1979), pp. II: 1, 4, 10; Jerry Ruhlow, "Management of Anchovy Program Under Fire," ibid. (27 December 1979), pp. II: 1,10–11.
97 MRC Minutes (11 March 1975), p. 6
98 NOAA, PFMC, "Proposed Plan for Managing the 1982 Salmon Fisheries off the Coasts of California, Oregon, and Washington (amended)," (Portland, OR: PFMC, May 1982), pp. 11-III, 13-III; USDI, BIA, "Environmental Impact Statement for a Proposal to Modify the Indian Fishing Regulations to Authorize Commercial Harvesting of Anadromous Fish," DES 85–21 (Hoopa Valley Indian Reservation, CA: BIA, 1985), p. 29; Gary L. Rankel, "Depleted Chinook Salmon Runs in the Klamath River Basin: Causes, Consequences, and Constraints on Management," photocopied (Arcata, CA: USFWS Fisheries Assistance Office, 1980), p. 3.
99 42 *Federal Register* 40,904–5 (12 August 1977) (commercial harvest by Indians limited to five fish per day); 43 *Federal Register* 30,048 (13 July 1978) (eligible fishers allowed to fish commercially during limited season); 44 *Federal Register* 17,144–51 (20 March 1979) (all commercial fishing and sale of salmon caught on the reservation prohibited).
100 U.S. Congress, House, Committee on Merchant Marine and Fisheries, "Klamath River Fishing Rights Oversight," hearings before the Subcommittee on Fisheries and Wildlife Conservation and Management, 96th Cong., 1st sess. (1979), *House Serial 96–11*, pp. 16–23, 28, 165.
101 *Hoopa Valley Tribe* v. *Baldridge et al.*, Civil No. C-82-3145 MHP (N.D. Cal. 1982)
102 U.S. Congress, House, Committee on Merchant Marine and Fisheries "Klamath River Fishing Rights Oversight," p. 103.
103 *People* v. *McCovey*, 36 Cal. 3d 517, 205 Cal. Rptr. 643, 685 P.2d 687 (1984).
104 *United States* v. *Wilson*, 611 F. Supp. 813, 817–19 (N.D. Cal. 1985). See also *Menominee Tribe of Indians* v. *United States*, 391 U.S. 404, 406 (1968) (reservation grant includes rights to maintain way of life, including hunting and fishing).
105 PFMC, "Proposed Plan for Managing the 1982 Salmon Fisheries," p. 13-III.
106 Ibid., p. 13-IV.
107 See Richard Walker, "Wetlands Preservation and Management on Chesapeake Bay: The Role of Science in Natural Resource Policy," *Coastal Zone Management Journal*, 1 (1973): 75–101, pp. 98–9.
108 MRC Minutes (29 June 1978), pp. 5–6; 1978 *California Statutes*, ch. 691.
109 Alan R. Longhurst, "How Can the Scientific Community Best Contribute to the Resolution of These Varied Problems?" *CalCOFI Reports*, 13 (1969): 127–8, p. 127.

Chapter 11

1 Lao Tzu, *Tao Te Ching*, tr. D.C. Lau (Middlesex: Penguin, 1963), p. 64.
2 Lynn White, Jr., "The Historical Roots of Our Ecological Crisis," *Science*, 155 (10 March 1967) : 1,203–7, p. 1205.
3 Roberto Mangabeira Unger, *Knowledge and Politics* (New York: Free Press, 1975), pp. 25, 205–13; Carolyn Merchant, *The Death of Nature: Women, Ecology, and the Scientific Revolution* (San Francisco: Harper & Row, 1980), ch. 8–10; Karl Polanyi, *The Great Transformation: The Political and Economic Origins of Our Time* (Boston: Beacon Press, 1944), ch. 15; Laurence Tribe, "Ways Not to Think About Plastic Trees: New Foundations for Environmental Law," *Yale Law Journal*, 83 (1974): 1,315–48, pp. 1,332–4.
4 Unger described the relationship between such dichotomies in the modern

liberal worldview as one of style, appositeness, or logical entailment: "It cannot in fact be demonstrated that the different premises of the liberal doctrine follow from one another by a strict logical necessity, nor would such a demonstration be consistent with the discovery that these premises lead to contradictory conclusions. But it would be equally misleading to suppose that the liberal principles form no system at all."(Unger, *Knowledge and Politics*, p. 15.)

5   Garrett Hardin, "The Tragedy of the Commons," *Science*, 162 (13 December 1968): 1243–8, p. 1247.

6   J. Willard Hurst, *Law and Markets in United States History: Different Modes of Bargaining Among Interests* (Madison: University of Wisconsin Press, 1982), esp. ch. 3.

7   NOAA, "Implementation of Northern Anchovy Fishery Management Plan: Solicitation of Public Comments," 43 *Federal Register* 31,651-879, 31,699 (21 July 1978).

8   *Supra*, p. 163.

9   *Supra*, pp. 49–50.

10   *Supra*, p. 179.

11   Alan R. Longhurst, "How Can the Scientific Community Best Contribute to the Resolution of These Varied Problems?" *CalCOFI Reports*, 13 (1969): 127–8, p. 127. Indeed, a U. N. conference had pointed to the same issue twelve years earlier when it agreed that "the coastal state be regarded as having a special interest in the conservation of the living resources of the sea adjacent to its coasts" and that "the people nearest to, and dependent upon, the resources for food should be given first consideration" in their management. [Report of the International Technical Conference on the Conservation of the Living Resources of the Sea, Rome, 18 April–10 May 1955, United Nations Document A/conf. 10/5 Rev. 2, p. 16; cited in Barry B.L. Auguste, *The Continental Shelf: The Practice and Policy of the Latin American States with Special Reference to Chile, Ecuador, and Peru* (Geneva: Librairie E. Droz, 1960), pp. 210–11.] George Borgstrom concluded that the Peruvian anchoveta fishery amounted to an enormous subsidy to agriculture in the industrialized countries, and moreover one that surpassed "both in absolute and relative terms, anything done in the postwar period to alleviate the shortages of the Hungry World." It amounted, he thought, "to nothing less than a resurrected colonialism in the marine context." [Borgstrom, "Ecological Aspects of Protein Feeding–The Case of Peru," in *The Careless Technology: Ecology and International Development*, eds. M. Taghi Farvar and John P. Milton (Garden City, NY: Natural History Press, 1972), pp. 753–74, pp. 771, 769.]

12   Calvin Woodard, "Reality and Social Reform: The Transition from Laissez-Faire to the Welfare State," *Yale Law Journal*, 72 (1962): 286–328, pp. 287–8.

13   Samuel P. Hays, *Conservation and the Gospel of Efficiency: The Progressive Conservation Movement, 1890–1920* (1959; repr. New York: Atheneum, 1980), esp. ch. 13.

14   A USFWS report in 1980 noted a strong traditional element in contemporary Indian approaches to the controversy over the Klamath–Trinity salmon fishery: "the strong and sometimes violent reaction of the [Hoopa Valley Reservation Indians] to recent short-falls in Trinity River stocks, and associated attempts to cut back the catching effort . . . seems, in its more violent aspects, closely parallel to the historic raiding party dispatched to destroy a weir that was unduly inhibiting access of salmon to upstream reaches of the river." [USDI, USFWS, "Environmental Impact Statement on the Management of River Flows to Mitigate the Loss of the Anadromous Fishery of the Trinity River, California" INT/FES 80–52 (Sacramento: USFWS, 1980), p. C7–8, p. C8–12, note 51.]

15 Personal interview, Daniel D. Huppert, 17 December 1982.

16 J.D. Pringle, 'The Human Factor in Fishery Resource Management," *Canadian Journal of Fisheries and Aquatic Sciences*, 42 (1985): 389–92, p. 392.

17 Charles A. Reich, 'The New Property," in *American Law and the Constitutional Order: Historical Perspectives*, eds. Lawrence M. Friedman and Harry N. Scheiber (Cambridge, MA: Harvard University Press, 1978), pp. 377–94, p. 390. See Edward S. Corwin, "The Basic Doctrine of American Constitutional Law," *Michigan Law Review*, 12 (1914) : 247–76.

18 John Locke, *Second Treatise of Civil Government*, ed. Peter Laslett (New York: New American Library, 1963), ch. 5, §27.

19 Unger, *Law in Modern Society: Toward a Criticism of Social Theory* (New York: The Free Press, 1976), p. 206. See also Christopher D. Stone, "Should Trees Have Standing?–Toward Legal Rights for Natural Objects," *Southern California Law Review*, 45 (1972): 450–80; and Tribe, "Ways Not to Think About Plastic Trees," *passim*. For an illuminating discussion of the "ethics of justice and care" in relationship to interdependence, see Carol Gilligan, *In a Different Voice: Psychological Theory and Women's Development* (Cambridge, MA: Harvard University Press, 1982), pp. 62–3 *et passim*.

20 *Plessy* v. *Ferguson*, 163 U.S. 537, 560 (1897) (Harlan, J. dissenting).

Selected bibliography

A. Books and articles

1. History, General

Adams, Richard N. 1982. *Paradoxical Harvest: Energy and Explanation in British History*. Arnold and Caroline Rose Monograph Series of the American Sociological Association. Cambridge: Cambridge University Press.

Allard, Dean Conrad, Jr. 1967. *Spencer Fullerton Baird and the U.S. Fish Commission*. Ph. D. diss., George Washington University. (Reprinted New York: Arno Press, 1978.)

Bamford, Edwin F. 1921. "Social Aspects of the Fishing Industry in Los Angeles Harbor." Social Monograph No. 18. *Studies in Sociology*, 5 (2).

Bancroft, Hubert Howe. 1874–6. *The Native Races of the Pacific States of North America*. 5 vols. New York: D. Appleton.

1886–90. *The History of California*. 7 vols. San Francisco: The History Company.

Barth, Gunther. 1964. *Bitter Strength: A History of the Chinese in the United States, 1850–1870*. Cambridge, MA: Harvard University Press.

Bates, D. B. 1857. *Incidents on Land and Water, or Four Years on the Pacific Coast*. Boston: James French and Co.

Bean, Walton E. 1973. *California: An Interpretive History*. 2nd ed. New York: McGraw-Hill.

Beechey, Capt. F.W., R.N. 1831. *Narrative of a Voyage to the Pacific and Beering's Strait, to Cooperate with the Polar Expeditions Performed in His Majesty's Ship Blossom . . . in the Years 1825, 26, 27, 28*. 2 vols. London: Henry Colburn & Richard Bentley. (Repr. New York: Da Capo Press, 1968.)

Bitting, A. W. 1937. *Appertizing: Or the Art of Canning, Its History and Development*. San Francisco: The Trade Pressroom.

Blackford, Mansel G. 1977. *The Politics of Business in California, 1890–1920*. Columbus: Ohio State University Press.

Bledsoe, Anthony J. 1881. *History of Del Norte County, California, with a Business Directory and Traveler's Guide*. Eureka, CA: Wyman.

1885. *Indian Wars of the Northwest: A California Sketch*. (Repr. Oakland: Biobooks, 1950.)

Bohme, Frederick G. 1956. The Portuguese of California. *California Historical Society Quarterly*, 35: 233–52.

Brewer, William H. 1930. *Up and Down California in 1860–1864: The Journal of William H. Brewer*. Edited by Francis P. Farquhar. (Repr. Berkeley and Los Angeles: University of California Press, 1966.)

Browning, Robert J. 1974. *Fisheries of the North Pacific: History, Species, Gear & Processes*. Anchorage: Alaska Northwest Publishing Co.

Bryant, Edwin. 1948. *What I Saw in California: Being the Journal of a Tour . . . in the Years 1846, 1847.* New York: D. Appleton,

Busch, Briton Cooper, 1985. *The War Against the Seals: A History of the North American Seal Fishery.* Kingston and Montreal: McGill-Queens University Press.

Buffum, E. Gould. 1850. *Six Months in the Gold Mines, from a Journal of Three Years Observance in Upper and Lower California.* Philadelphia: Lea and Blanchard.

Chinn, Thomas, ed. 1969. *A History of the Chinese in California: A Syllabus.* San Francisco: Chinese Historical Society of America.

Chu, George. 1970. "Chinatowns in the Delta: The Chinese in the Sacramento-San Joaquin Delta, 1870–1960." *California Historical Society Quarterly,* 49: 21–37.

Cinel, Dino. 1982. *From Italy to San Francisco: The Immigrant Experience.* Stanford: Stanford University Press.

Clark, John G., ed. 1971. *The Frontier Challenge: Responses to the Trans-Mississippi West.* Lawrence: The University Press of Kansas.

Clepper, Henry, ed. 1966. *Origins of American Conservation.* New York: Ronald Press.

Conroy, Hilary. 1953. *The Japanese Frontier in Hawaii, 1868–1898.* University of California Publications in History, no. 46. Berkeley and Los Angeles: University of California Press.

Cooley, Richard A. 1963. *Politics and Conservation: The Decline of the Alaska Salmon.* New York: Harper & Row.

Coy, Owen C. 1929. *The Humboldt Bay Region, 1850-1875: A Study in the American Colonization of California.* Los Angeles: California State Historical Association.

Cronise, Titus Fey. 1868. *The Natural Wealth of California.* San Francisco: H.H. Bancroft.

Cronon, William. 1983. *Changes in the Land: Indians, Colonists, and the Ecology of New England.* New York: Hill and Wang.

Cross, Ira B. 1935. *A History of the Labor Movement in California.* Berkeley: University of California Press.

Dana, Julian. 1934. *Sutter of California: A Biography.* New York: The Press of the Pioneers

Dana, Richard Henry, Jr. 1841. *Two Years Before the Mast.* (Repr. New York: New American Library, 1964.)

Dewar, Margaret A. 1983. *Industry in Trouble: The Federal Government and the New England Fisheries.* Philadelphia: Temple University Press.

Dodds, Gordon B. 1958. "The Rogue River Monopoly." *Pacific Historical Review,* 27, 263–80.

    1959. "The Fight to Close the Rogue." *Oregon Historical Quarterly,* 40: 461–74.

    1959. "Artificial Propagation of Salmon in Oregon, 1875–1910: A Chapter in American Conservation." *Pacific Northwest Quarterly,* 50: 125–32.

    1959. *The Salmon King of Oregon: R.D. Hume and the Pacific Fisheries.* Chapel Hill: University of North Carolina Press.

    ed. 1961. *A Pygmy Monopolist: The Life and Doings of R.D. Hume, Written by Himself and Dedicated to His Neighbors.* Madison: State Historical Society of Wisconsin.

Dupree, A. Hunter. 1957. *Science in the Federal Government: A History of Policies and Activities to 1940.* Cambridge, MA: Belknap Press, Harvard University Press.

Estes, Don. 1977. "Kondo Masaharu and the Best of All Fishermen." *Journal of San Diego History,* 23: 1–19.

Farvar, M. Taghi, and John P. Milton, eds. 1972. *The Careless Technology: Ecology and International Development.* Record of the Conference on the Ecological Aspects of International Development Convened by the Conservation Foundation and the Center for the Biology of Natural Resources, Washington University, December 8–11, 1968. (Garden City, NY: The Natural History Press.)

Fleming, Donald. 1971. "The Roots of the New Conservation Movement." *Perspectives in American History,* 6: 7–91.

Font, Pedro. 1966. *Anza's California Expeditions.* Translated by Herbert Eugene Bolton. 4 vols. New York: Russell and Russell.

Fox, Stephen. 1981. *John Muir and His Legacy: The American Conservation Movement.* Boston: Little, Brown.

Fremont, J.C. 1845. *Report of the Exploring Expedition to the Rocky Mountains in the Year 1842, and to Oregon and North California in the Years 1843–1844.* Washington: Gales and Seaton, Readex Microprint, 1966.

Gates, Paul Wallace. 1960. *The Farmer's Age: Agriculture, 1815-1860.* Economic History of the United States, v. III. New York: Holt, Rinehart and Winston.

Gibbs, George. n. d. *George Gibbs's Journal of Redick McKee's Expedition Through Northwest California in 1851.* Edited by Robert F. Heizer. Berkeley: University of California, Berkeley, Department of Anthropology, 1972.

Gilbert, DeWitt, ed. 1968. *The Future of the Fishing Industry of the United States.* University of Washington Publications in Fisheries, New Series, v. IV. Seattle: University of Washington Press.

Greene, John C. 1981. *Science, Ideology, and World View: Essays in the History of Evolutionary Ideas.* Berkeley and Los Angeles: University of California Press.

Gregory, Homer E., and Kathleen Barnes. 1939. *North Pacific Fisheries: With Special Reference to Alaska Salmon.* Studies of the Pacific no. 3. American Council, Institute of Pacific Relations.(Rep. New York: Kraus Reprint Co., 1976.)

Guravich, Dan, and Joseph E. Brown. 1983. *The Return of the Brown Pelican.* Baton Rouge: Louisiana State University Press.

Gutman, Herbert G. 1976. *Work, Culture, and Society in Industrializing America.* Oxford: Basil Blackwell.

Hardin, Charles M. 1952. *The Politics of Agriculture: Soil Conservation and the Struggle for Power in Rural America.* Glencoe, IL: The Free Press.

Hardin, Garrett. 1968. "The Tragedy of the Commons." *Science,* 162: 1243–8.

Hawley, Ellis W. 1966. *The New Deal and the Problem of Monopoly: A Study in Economic Ambivalence.* Princeton: Princeton University Press.

Hays, Samuel P. 1959. *Conservation and the Gospel of Efficiency: The Progressive Conservation Movement, 1890–1920.* Cambridge, MA: Harvard University Press.

1982. "From Conservation to Environment: Environmental Politics in the United States Since World War Two." *Environmental Review,* 2: 14–41.

Heilbron, Carl H., ed. 1936. *History of San Diego County.* San Diego: San Diego Press Club.

Heizer, Robert F., and Alan J. Almquist. 1972. *The Other Californians: Prejudice and Discrimination under Spain, Mexico, and the United States to 1920.* Berkeley and Los Angeles: University of California Press.

ed. 1974. *The Destruction of California Indians: A Collection of Documents from the Period 1847 to 1865 in Which Are Described Some of the Things That Happened to Some of the Indians of California.* Santa Barbara: Peregrine Press.

Held, R. Burnell, and Marion Clawson, 1965. *Soil Conservation in Perspective: Resources for the Future.* Baltimore: Johns Hopkins University Press.

Hittell, John S. 1874. *The Resources of California, Comprising the Society, Climate, Salubrity, Commerce, and Industry of the State*. San Francisco: A. Roman.
Hittell, Theodore S. 1885–97. *History of California*. 4 vols. San Francisco: N. J. Stone, Pacjfic Press.
Hughes, Thomas P. 1983. *Networks of Power: Electrification in Western Society, 1880–1930*. Baltimore and London: Johns Hopkins University Press.
Hutchison, Claude B., ed. 1946. *California Agriculture: By Members of the Faculty of the College of Agriculture, University of California*. Berkeley and Los Angeles: University of California Press.
Jones, E. L. 1981. *The European Miracle: Environments, Economies, and Geopolitics in the History of Europe and Asia*. Cambridge: Cambridge University Press.
Jordan, David Starr. 1892. "The Fisheries of California." *Overland Monthly*, 20: 469–78.
Kelley, Robert L. 1959. *Gold vs. Grain: The Hydraulic Mining Controversy in California's Central Valley: A Chapter in the Decline of Laissez-Faire*. Glendale, CA: Arthur H. Clark.
Kemble, John Haskell. 1943. *The Panama Route, 1848–1869*. University of California Publications in History no. 29. Berkeley: University of California Press.
Kuhn, Thomas S. 1970. *The Structure of Scientific Revolutions*, 2nd. International Encyclopedia of Unified Science, v. 2, no. 2. Chicago: University of Chicago Press.
Landes, David S. 1972. *The Unbound Prometheus: Technological Change and Industrial Development in Western Europe from 1750 to the Present*. Cambridge: Cambridge University Press.
London, Jack. 1905. *Tales of the Fish Patrol*. New York: Macmillan.
LeRoy Ladurie, Emmanuel. 1971. *Times of Feast, Times of Famine: A History of Climate Since the Year 1000*. Translated by Barbara Bray. Garden City, NY: Doubleday.
McBeth, Frances Turner. 1950. *Lower Klamath Country*. Berkeley: Anchor Press.
McConnell, Grant. 1954. "The Conservation Movement – Past and Present." *Western Political Quarterly*, 7: 463–78.
McEvoy, Arthur F. 1977. "In Places Men Reject: The Chinese Fishermen at San Diego, 1870–1893." *Journal of San Diego History*, 23, 12–24.
McFarland, Raymond. 1911. *A History of the New England Fisheries*. New York: D. Appleton.
McGowan, Joseph A. 1961. *History of the Sacramento Valley*. 3 vols. New York: Lewis Historical Publishing Co.
McWilliams, Carey. 1946. *Southern California: An Island on the Land*. Repr. Santa Barbara: Peregrine Press, 1973.
Marsh, George Perkins. 1864. *Man and Nature: Or, Physical Geography as Modified by Human Action*. (Repr. Cambridge, MA: Belknap Press, Harvard University Press, 1965.)
Martin, Calvin. 1978. *Keepers of the Game: Indian–Animal Relationships and the Fur Trade*. Berkeley and Los Angeles: University of California Press.
Mattheissen, Peter. 1959. *Wildlife in America*. New York: Viking Press.
1984. *Indian Country*. New York: Viking Press.
Merchant, Carolyn. 1980. *The Death of Nature: Women, Ecology, and the Scientific Revolution*. San Francisco: Harper & Row.
Mitchell, Broadus. 1947. *Depression Decade: From New Era Through New Deal, 1929–1941*. Economic History of the United States, v. 9. New York: Rinehart.
Mowry, George E. 1963. *The California Progressives*. Chicago: Quadrangle.
Mullendore, William Clinton. 1941. *History of the United States Food Administra-*

tion, 1917–1919. Hoover Institution on War, Revolution, and Peace Publication no. 18. Stanford: Stanford University Press.

Nash, Roderick. 1967. *Wilderness and the American Mind.* rev. ed. New Haven: Yale University Press.

Netboy, Anthony. *The Salmon: Their Fight for Survival.* Boston: Houghton-Mifflin.

Nordhoff, Charles. 1874. *Northern California, Oregon, and the Sandwich Islands.* New York: Harper and Brothers.

1882. *California for Health, Pleasure, and Residence.* New York: Harper and Brothers.

1888. *Peninsular California: Some Account of the Climate, Soil, Productions, and Present Condition Chiefly of the Northern Half of Lower California.* New York: Harper and Brothers.

Ogden, Adele. 1941. *The California Sea Otter Trade, 1784–1848.* (Repr. Berkeley and Los Angeles: University of California Press, 1975.)

Oleson, Alexandra, and John Voss, eds. 1979. *The Organization of Knowledge in Modern America.* Baltimore and London: John Hopkins University Press.

Page, Louise, and Berta Friend. 1978. "The Changing United States Diet."*Bio-Science,* 28: 192–8.

Paul, Rodman W. 1947. *California Gold: The Beginning of Mining in the Far West.* Lincoln: University of Nebraska Press.

Perkins, John H. 1982. *Insects, Experts, and the Insecticide Crisis: The Quest for New Pest Management Strategies.* New York and London: Plenum.

Pinchot, Gifford. 1937. "How Conservation Began in the United States."*Agricultural History,* 11: 255–65.

Pomeroy, Earl. 1965. *The Pacific Slope: A History of California, Oregon, Washington, Idaho, Utah, & Nevada.* Seattle: University of Washington Press.

Pratt, Joseph A. 1980. "Letting the Grandchildren Do It: Environmental Planning During the Ascent of Oil as a Major Energy Source." *Public Historian,* 2: 28–61.

Rosenberg, Nathan. 1972. *Technology and American Economic Growth.* New York: Harper & Row, Torchbook edition.

Rotberg, Robert I., and Theodore K. Rabb. 1981. *Climate and History: Studies in Interdisciplinary History.* Princeton, NJ: Princeton University Press.

Scammon, Charles M. 1874. *The Marine Mammals of the Northwestern Coast of North America, Described and Illustrated, with an Account of the American Whale Fishery.* San Francisco: John H.Cormay.

Schmitt, Martin F., ed. 1946. *General George Crook: His Autobiography.* Norman: University of Oklahoma Press.

Scott, Mel. 1963. *The Future of San Francisco Bay.* Berkeley: University of California Institute of Governmental Studies.

Shor, Elizabeth Noble. 1978. *Scripps Institution of Oceanography: Probing the Oceans, 1936–1976.* San Diego: Tofua Press.

Smetherman, Bobbie B., and Robert M. Smetherman. 1974. *Territorial Seas and Inter-American Relations: With Case Studies of the Peruvian and U.S. Fishing Industries.* New York: Praeger.

Smythe, William E. 1908. *History of San Diego, 1542–1907: An Account of the Rise and Progress of the Pioneer Settlement on the Pacific Coast of the United States.* San Diego: The History Company.

Soule, Frank, John H. Gihon, and James Nisbet. 1855. *The Annals of San Francisco.* New York: D. Appleton.

Soule, George. 1947. *Prosperity Decade: From War to Depression, 1917–1929.* Economic History of the United States, v. 8. New York: Rinehart.

Spier, Robert F. G. 1958. "Food Habits of Nineteenth-Century California Chinese." *California Historical Society Quarterly,* 37: 79–84, 129–36.

Steinhart, John S., and Carol Steinhart. 1974. "Energy Use in the U.S. Food System." *Science,* 184: 307–16.

Steinbeck, John. 1939. *The Grapes of Wrath.* New York: Viking Press.

1945. *Cannery Row.* New York: Viking Press.

1954. *Sweet Thursday.* New York: Viking Press.

Stewart, Don M. 1965. *Frontier Port: A Chapter in San Diego's History.* Los Angeles: The Ward Ritchie Press.

Sully, Langdon. 1974. *No Tears for the General: The Life of Alfred Sully, 1821–1879.* Western Biography Series. Palo Alto, CA: American West Publishing Co.

Taylor, Philip. 1971. *The Distant Magnet: European Migration to the U.S.A.* New York: Harper & Row, Torchbook edition.

Thompson, John, and Edward A. Dutra. 1983. *The Tule Breakers: The Story of the California Dredge.* Stockton Corral of Westerners. Stockton: University of the Pacific.

Tonneson, J.N., and A.O. Johnsen. 1982. *The History of Modern Whaling.* Translated by R.I. Christophersen. Berkeley and Los Angeles: University of California Press.

Turner, Frederick Jackson. 1920. *The Frontier in American History.* New York: Henry Holt.

Turner, Justin, ed. 1964. "The Sacramento Floods in the 1850s." *Pacific Historian,* 8: 129–33.

Van Hise, Charles R. 1914. *The Conservation of Natural Resources in the United States.* New York: Macmillan.

Wagner, Henry R. 1928. "Spanish Voyages to the Northwest Coast in the Sixteenth Century, Chapter IX – Father Antonio de la Ascension's Account of Vizcaino's Voyage." *California Historical Society Quarterly,* 7: 295–394.

Wangenheim, Julius. 1956. "Julius Wangenheim – An Autobiography." *California Historical Society Quarterly,* 35: 119–44, 253–74, 345–66.

Weaver, Philip L., Jr. 1892. "Salt Water Fisheries of the Pacific Coast." *Overland Monthly,* 20: 149–63.

Webb, Walter Prescott. 1951. *The Great Frontier.* Austin: University of Texas Press.

White, Richard. 1983. *The Roots of Dependency: Subsistence, Environment, and Social Change among the Choctaws, Pawnees, and Navajos.* Lincoln: University of Nebraska Press.

Worster, Donald. 1977. *Nature's Economy: The Roots of Ecology.* San Francisco: Sierra Club Books.

1979. *Dust Bowl: The Southern Plains in the 1930s.* Oxford: Oxford University Press, 1979.

Young, Oran R. 1981. *Natural Resources and the State: The Political Economy of Resource Management.* Studies in International Political Economy. Berkeley and Los Angeles: University of California Press.

2. Legal studies

Anonymous. 1976. "Legal Dimensions of Entry Fishery Management." *William and Mary Law Review,* 17: 757–79.

Aschenbrenner, Peter J. 1971. "Comments: State Power and the Indian Treaty Right to Fish." *California Law Review*, 59: 485–524.

Barsh, Russel Lawrence, and James Youngblood Henderson. 1981. *The Road: Indian Tribes and Political Liberty*. Berkeley and Los Angeles: University of California Press.

Baser, Steven I. 1976. " 'Fast-Fish and Loose-Fish': Extended Fisheries Jurisdiction and the Need for an Improved California Fisheries Management System." *Southern California Law Review*, 49: 569–96.

Brenner, Joel Franklin. 1974. "Nuisance Law and the Industrial Revolution." *Journal of Legal Studies*, 3: 403–33.

Coggins, George Cameron. 1980. "Wildlife and the Constitution: The Walls Come Tumbling Down." *Washington Law Review*, 55: 285–358.

Coggins, George Cameron, and William Modcrin. 1979. "Native American Indians and Federal Wildlife Law." *Stanford Law Review*, 31: 375–423.

Connery, Robert H. 1935. *Governmental Problems in Wild Life Conservation*. Studies in History, Economics, and Public Law no. 411. New York: Columbia University Press.

Ericson, Robert, and D. Rebecca Snow. 1970. "Comment: The Indian Battle for Self-Determination." *California Law Review*, 58: 445–90.

Favre, David S. 1979. "Wildlife Rights: The Ever-Widening Circle." *Environmental Law*, 9: 241–81.

Feess, Gary. 1974. "Comments: The Tideland Trust: Economic Currents in a Traditional Legal Doctrine." *UCLA Law Review*, 21: 826–91.

Friedman, Lawrence M. 1985. *A History of American Law*, 2nd ed. New York: Simon & Schuster, Touchstone.

and Jack Ladinsky. 1967. "Social Change and the Law of Industrial Accidents."*Columbia Law Review*, 67: 50–82.

and Harry N. Scheiber. 1978. *American Law and the Constitutional Order: Historical Perspectives*. Cambridge, MA: Harvard University Press.

Haveman, Richard H. 1973. "Efficiency and Equity in Natural Resource and Environmental Policy." *American Journal of Agricultural Economics*, 55: 868–78.

Hobbs, Charles A. 1963–4. "Indian Hunting and Fishing Rights." *George Washington Law Review*, 32: 504–32.

1969. "Indian Hunting and Fishing Rights," II. *George Washington Law Review*, 37: 1251–73.

Hollick, Ann L. 1981. *U.S. Foreign Policy and the Law of the Sea*. Princeton, NJ: Princeton University Press.

Horwitz, Morton J. 1977. *The Transformation of American Law, 1780–1860*. Cambridge, MA: Harvard University Press.

Hurst, James Willard. 1956. *Law and the Conditions of Freedom in the Nineteenth Century United States*. Madison: University of Wisconsin Press.

1964. *Law and Economic Growth: The Legal History of the Lumber Industry in Wisconsin, 1836–1915*. Cambridge, MA: Belknap Press, Harvard University Press.

1977. *Law and Social Order in the United States*. Ithaca, NY: Cornell University Press.

1982. *Law and Markets in United States History: Different Modes of Bargaining Among Interests*. Madison: University of Wisconsin Press.

Hyde, Laurel Lee. 1979. "Comment: Dolphin Controversy in the Tuna Industry: The United States' Role in an International Problem." *San Diego Law Review*, 16: 665–704.

Israel, Daniel H. 1975–6. "The Reemergence of Tribal Nationalism and Its Impact on Reservation Resource Development." *University of Colorado Law Review*, 47: 617–52.

Jasanoff, Shiela, and Dorothy Nelkin. 1981. "Science, Technology, and the Limits of Judicial Competence." *Science*, 214: 1211–15.

Joseph, James, and Joseph W. Greenough. 1979. *International Management of Tuna, Porpoise, and Billfish: Biological, Legal, and Political Aspects*. Seattle: University of Washington Press.

Kelly, John E. 1978. "The Fishery Conservation and Management Act of 1976: Organizational Structure and Conceptual Framework." *Marine Policy*, 2: 30–6.

Knight, H. Gary. 1977. *Managing the Sea's Living Resources: Legal and Political Aspects of High Seas Fisheries*. Studies in Marine Affairs, ed. John King Gamble. Lexington, MA: D.C. Heath.

1978. "Management Procedures in the U. S. Fishery Conservation Zone." *Marine Policy*, 2: 22–9.

Knowles, J.L. 1917. "Comment on Recent Cases: Constitutional Law: Construction of Fish and Game Act." *California Law Review*, 5: 162–3.

Laitos, Jan G. 1975. "Continuities from the Past Affecting Resource Use and Conservation Pattern." *Oklahoma Law Review*, 28: 60–96.

1975. "Legal Institutions and Pollution: Some Intersections Between Law and History." *Natural Resources Journal*, 15: 423–51.

Landau, Jack L. 1980. "Empty Victories: Indian Treaty Fishing Rights in the Pacific Northwest." *Environmental Law*, 10: 413–56.

Larkins, H. A. 1980. "Management Under FCMA: Development of a Fishery Management Plan." *Marine Policy*, 4: 170–82.

Lund, Thomas A. 1980. *American Wildlife Law*, Berkeley and Los Angeles: University of California Press.

McCraw, Thomas K., ed. 1981. *Regulation in Perspective: Historical Essays*. Boston: Division of Research, Graduate School of Business Administration, Harvard University.

McCurdy, Charles W. 1976. "Stephen J. Field and Public Land Law Development in California, 1850–1866: A Case Study of Judicial Resource Allocation in Nineteenth-Century America." *Law and Society Review*, 10: 235–66.

McEvoy, Arthur F. 1982. "Scientific Research and the Twentieth-Century Fishing Industry." California Cooperative Oceanic Fisheries Investigations, *Reports*, 23: 48–55.

1983. "Law, Public Policy, and Industrialization in the California Fisheries, 1900–1925." *Business History Review*, 57: 494–521.

and Harry N. Scheiber. 1984. "Scientists, Entrepreneurs, and the Policy Process: A Study of the Post-1945 California Sardine Depletion." *Journal of Economic History*, 44: 393–406.

Monson, Peter C. 1982. "Casenote: *United States* v. *Washington (Phase II)*: The Indian Fishing Conflict Moves Upstream." *Environmental Law*, 12: 468–503.

Nash, Gerald D. 1964. *State Government and Economic Development: A History of Administrative Policies in California, 1849–1933*. University of California Institute of Governmental Studies. Berkeley: University of California.

Pelcyger, Robert S. 1977. "The *Winters* Doctrine and the Greening of the Reservations." *Journal of Contemporary Law*, 4: 19–37.

Ricci, Paolo, and Lawrence S. Molton. 1981. "Risk and Benefit in Environmental Law." *Science*, 214: 1096–100.

Scarff, James E. 1977. "The International Management of Whales, Dolphins, and Porpoises: An Interdisciplinary Assessment." *Ecology Law Quarterly*, 6: 323–427, 574–638.

Scheiber, Harry N. 1971. "The Road to *Munn*: Eminent Domain and the Concept of Public Purpose in the State Courts." *Perspectives in American History*, 5: 287–328.

1975. "Federalism and the American Economic Order, 1789-1910." *Law and Society Review*, 10: 57–118.

1980. "Federalism and Legal Process: Historical and Contemporary Analysis of the American System." *Law and Society Review*, 14: 663–722.

1980. "Public Economic Policy and the American Legal System: Historical Perspectives." *Wisconsin Law Review*, v. 1980, 1159–90.

and Charles W. McCurdy. 1975. "Eminent Domain Law and Western Agriculture, 1849–1900." *Agricultural History*, 49: 112–30.

Scott, Stanley. 1975. *Governing California's Coast*. Berkeley: University of California Institute of Governmental Studies.

Selvin, Molly. 1980. "The Public Trust Doctrine in American Law and Economic Policy, 1789–1920." *Wisconsin Law Review*, v. 1980: 1403–42.

Swygard, Kline R. 1967. "Politics of the North Pacific Fisheries – with Special Reference to the Twelve-Mile Bill." *Washington Law Review*, 12: 269–82.

Taylor, Paul S. 1975. "California Water Project: Law and Politics." *Ecology Law Quarterly*, 5: 1–52.

Tober, James A. 1981. *Who Owns the Wildlife? The Political Economy of Conservation in Nineteenth-Century America*. Contributions in Economics and Economic History no. 37. Westport, CT: Greenwood Press.

Tribe, Lawrence H. 1974. "Ways Not to Think About Plastic Trees: New Foundations for Environmental Law." *Yale Law Journal*, 83: 1315–48.

1975. "From Environmental Foundations to Constitutional Structures: Learning from Nature's Future." *Yale Law Journal*, 84: 545–56.

Unger, Roberto Mangabiera. 1984. *Knowledge and Politics*. New York: The Free Press.

Walker, Richard A. 1973. "Wetlands Preservation and Management on Chesapeake Bay: The Role of Science in Natural Resource Policy." *Coastal Zone Management Journal*, 1: 75–101.

and Michael Storper. 1978. "Erosion of the Clean Air Act of 1970: A Study in the Failure of Government Regulation and Planning." *Boston College Environmental Affairs Law Review*, 7: 189–257.

Warner, Langdon S., Barbara A. Finamore, and Michael J. Bean. 1981. "Practical Application of the Conservation Aspects of the Fishery Conservation and Management Act." *Harvard Environmental Law Review*, 5: 30–70

Watt, Donald Cameron. 1979. "First Step in the Enclosure of the Oceans: The Origins of Truman's Proclamation on the Resources of the Continental Shelf, 28 September 1945." *Marine Policy*, 3: 211–24.

Wilkinson, Charles F., and John M. Volkman. 1975. "Judicial Review of Indian Treaty Abrogation: 'As Long as Water Flows, or Grass Grows Upon the Earth' – How Long a Time Is That?" *California Law Review*, 63: 601–66.

Will, J. Kemper. 1978. "Indian Lands Environment – Who Should Protect it?" *Natural Resources Journal*, 18: 465–504

3. Economics

Bachmura, Frank T. 1974. "The Economics of Vanishing Species." *Natural Resources Journal*, 11: 675–92.

Bain, Joe S., Richard E. Caves, and Julius Margolis. 1966. *Northern California's Water Industry: The Comparative Efficiency of Public Enterprise in Developing a Scarce Economic Resource*. Resources for the Future. Baltimore: John Hopkins University Press.

Boserup, Ester. 1965. *The Conditions of Agricultural Growth: The Economics of Agrarian Change Under Population Pressure*. Chicago: Aldine.

Cheung, Steven N.S. 1970. "The Structure of a Contract and the Theory of a Non-Exclusive Resource." *Journal of Law and Economics*, 13: 49–70.

Christy, Francis T., Jr. 1977. "The Fishery Conservation and Management Act of 1976: Management Objectives and the Distribution of Benefits and Costs." *Washington Law Review*, 52: 657–80.

and Anthony Scott. 1965. *The Common Wealth in Ocean Fisheries: Some Problems of Growth and Economic Allocation*. Resources for the Future. Baltimore: Johns Hopkins University Press.

Ciriacy-Wantrup, S.V. 1968. *Resource Conservation: Economics and Policies*, 3rd ed. Berkeley: University of California Division of Agricultural Sciences, Agricultural Experiment Station.

1971. "Economics of Environmental Policy." *Land Economics*, 47: 37–45.

Clark, Colin. 1970. *The Economics of Irrigaton*, 2nd ed. Oxford: Pergamon.

1973. "The Economics of Overexploitation." *Science*, 181: 630–4.

1973. "Profit Maximization and the Extinction of Animal Species." *Journal of Political Economy*, 81: 950–61.

Coase, R.H. 1960. "The Problem of Social Cost." *Journal of Law and Economics*, 3: 1–44.

Crutchfield, James A. 1967. "Management of the North Pacific Fisheries: Economic Objectives and Issues." *Washington Law Review*, 43: 283–307.

and Giulio Pontecorvo. 1969. *The Pacific Salmon Fisheries: A Study of Irrational Conservation*. Resources for the Future. Baltimore: Johns Hopkins University Press.

Dasgupta, P. S., and G. M. Heal. 1979. *Economic Theory and Exhaustible Resources*. Cambridge Economic Handbooks. Cambridge: Cambridge University Press.

DeLoach, Daniel G. 1939. *The Salmon Canning Industry*. Oregon State Monographs, Economic Studies no. 1. Corvallis: Oregon State College.

FitzGerald, E. V. K. 1979. *The Political Economy of Peru, 1956–78: Economic Development and the Restructuring of Capital*. Cambridge: Cambridge University Press.

Gordon, H. Scott. 1954. 'The Economic Theory of a Common-Property Resource: The Fishery." *Journal of Political Economy*, 62: 124–42.

Gould, J. R. 1972. "Extinction of a Fishery by Commercial Exploitation: A Note." *Journal of Political Economy*, 80: 1031–9.

Johnson, Ronald W., and Gary D. Libecap. 1982. "Contracting Problems and Regulation: The Case of the Fishery." *American Economic Review*, 72: 1005–22.

Kahneman, Daniel, Paul Slovic, and Amos Tversky, eds. 1982. *Judgment Under Uncertainty: Heuristics and Biases* Cambridge: Cambridge University Press.

Musgrave, Richard A. 1969. *The Theory of Public Finance: A Study in Public Economy*. New York: McGraw-Hill.

Pigou, A. C. 1932. *The Economics of Welfare*, 4th ed. London: Macmillan.
Plehn, Carl C. 1918. "The State Market Commission of California: Its Beginnings, 1915–1917." *American Economic Review*, 8: 1–27.
Polanyi, Karl. 1944. *The Great Transformation: The Political and Economic Origins of Our Time*. (Repr. Boston: Beacon Press, 1957).
Pontecorvo, Giulio. 1977. "Fishery Management and the General Welfare: Implications of the New Structure." *Washington Law Review*, 52: 641–56.
Posner, Richard A. 1983. *The Economics of Justice*. Cambridge, MA: Harvard University Press.
Rich, E. E. 1960. "Trade Habits and Economic Motivation Among the Indians of North America." *Canadian Journal of Economics and Political Science*, 26: 35–53.
Roemer, Michael. 1970. *Fishing for Growth: Export-Led Development in Peru, 1950–1967*. Cambridge, MA: Harvard University Press.
Scott, Anthony. 1955. "The Fishery: The Objectives of Sole Ownership." *Journal of Political Economy*, 63: 116–24.
Smith, Vernon L. 1969. "On Models of Commercial Fishing." *Journal of Political Economy*, 77: 181–98.
Thomas, Brinley. 1973. *Migration and Economic Growth: A Study of Great Britain and the Atlantic Economy*, 2nd ed. Cambridge: Cambridge University Press.
Thorp, Rosemary, and Geoffrey Bertram. 1978. *Peru 1890–1977: Growth and Policy in an Open Economy*. New York: Columbia University Press.
Tobin, Bernard F., and Henry B. Arthur. 1964. *Dynamics of Adjustment in the Broiler Industry*. Boston: Harvard University, Division of Research, Graduate School of Business Administration.
Turvey, Ralph. 1964. "Optimization and Suboptimization in Fishery Regulation." *American Economic Review*, 54: 64–76.

4. Natural sciences (see also under Government publications)

Bakker, Elna. 1971. *An Island Called California: An Ecological Introduction to Its Natural Communities*. Berkeley and Los Angeles: University of California Press.
Barber, Richard T., and Francisco P. Chavez. 1983. "Biological Consequences of El Niño." *Science*, 222: 1203–10.
Barbour, Michael G., Robert B. Craig, Frank R. Drysdale, and Michael T. Ghiselin. 1973. *Coastal Ecology: Bodega Head*. Berkeley and Los Angeles: University of California Press.
Benson, Norman G., ed. 1970. *A Century of Fisheries in North America*. Special Publication no. 7. Washington: American Fisheries Society.
Cane, Mark A. 1983. "Oceanographic Events During El Niño." *Science*, 222: 1189–95.
Ciriacy-Wantrup, S. V., and James J. Parsons, eds. 1967. *Natural Resources, Quality and Quanity: Papers Presented Before a Faculty Seminar at the University of California, Berkeley, 1961–1965*. Berkeley: University of California Press.
Clepper, Henry, ed. 1979. *Predator–Prey Systems in Fisheries Management*. International Symposium on Predator–Prey Systems in Fish Communities and Their Role in Fisheries Management, Atlanta, Georgia, 24–27 July 1978. Washington: Sport Fishing Institute.
Croker, Richard S. 1954. "Loss of California's Sardine Fishery May Become Permanent." *Outdoor California*, 15(1), 1–8.

Cushing, David. 1975. *Fisheries Resources of the Sea and Their Management*. London: Oxford University Press.

Estes, James A., and John F. Palmisano. 1974. "Sea Otters: Their Role in Structuring Nearshore Communities." *Science*, 185: 1058–60.

Glantz, Michael H., and J. Dana Thompson. 1981. *Resource Management and Environmental Uncertainty: Lessons from Coastal Upwelling Fisheries*. New York: Wiley.

Grinnell, Joseph, Joseph S. Dixon, and Jean M. Linsdale. 1937. *Fur-Bearing Mammals of California: Their Natural History, Systematic Status, and Relations to Man*. Contributions from the Museum of Vertebrate Zoology, University of California, Berkeley. 2 vols. Berkeley: University of California Press.

Gulland, J. A. 1974. *The Management of Marine Fisheries*. Seattle: University of Washington Press.

——— 1977. "World Fisheries and Fish Stocks." *Marine Policy*, 1: 179–89.

Hedgpeth, Joel W. 1944. "The Passing of the Salmon." *Scientific Monthly*, 59: 370–8.

Hubbs, Carl L. 1948. "Changes in the Fish Fauna of Western North America Correlated with Changes in Ocean Temperature." *Journal of Marine Research*, 7: 459–82.

——— 1964. "History of Ichthyology in the United States After 1850." *Copeia*, v. 1964, 42–60.

Kasahara, Hiroshi. 1961. *Fisheries Resources of the North Pacific Ocean*. Lectures presented at the University of British Columbia, January and February 1960. H. F. Macmillan Lectures in Fisheries, pt. 1. New York: Macmillan.

Larkin, P. A. 1977. "An Epitaph for the Concept of Maximum Sustained Yield." *Transactions of the American Fisheries Society*, 106: 1–11.

——— 1978. "Fisheries Management: An Essay for Ecologists." *Annual Review of Ecology and Systematics*, 9: 57–73.

——— 1979. "Maybe You Can't Get There from Here: A Foreshortened History of Research in Relation to Management of Pacific Salmon." *Journal of the Fisheries Research Board of Canada*, 36: 98–106.

Mann, K. H. 1982. *Ecology of Coastal Waters: A Systematic Approach*. Studies in Ecology, v. 9. Berkeley and Los Angeles: University of California Press.

Margalef, Ramon. 1968. *Perspectives in Ecological Theory*. Chicago: University of Chicago Press.

Murphy, Garth I. 1966. "Population Biology of the Pacific Sardine (*Sardinops caerulea*)." *Proceedings of the California Academy of Sciences*, 4th ser. 34(1).

Nielsen, Larry A. 1976. "Evolution of Fisheries Management Philosophy." *Marine Fisheries Review*, 38: 15–23.

Odum, Eugene P. 1971. *Fundamentals of Ecology*, 3rd ed. Philadelphia: W. B. Saunders.

Packard, E. L. 1918. "A Quantitative Analysis of the Molluscan Fauna of San Francisco Bay." *University of California Publications in Zoology*, 18(13): 229–336.

Petersen, C. G. J. 1903–6. "What Is Over-fishing?" *Journal of the Marine Biological Association (UK)*, 6: 587–95.

Rasmusson, Eugene M., and John M. Wallace. 1983. "Meteorological Aspects of the El Niño/Southern Oscillation." *Science*, 222: 1195–202.

Raup, Hugh M. 1964. "Some Problems in Ecological Theory and Their Relation to Conservation." *Journal of Ecology*, 52 (supp): 19–28.

Ricketts, Edward F., and Jack Calvin. 1968. *Between Pacific Tides*, 4th ed. rev. Joel Hedgpeth. Stanford: Stanford University Press.

Rounsefell, George A. 1975. *Ecology, Utilization, and Management of Marine Fisheries*. St. Louis: C.V. Mosby.

Royce, William F. 1972. *Introduction to the Fishery Sciences*. New York: Academic Press.

Schreiber, Ralph W., and Elizabeth Anne Schreiber. 1984. "Central Pacific Seabirds and the El Niño Southern Oscillation: 1982 to 1983 Perspective." *Science*, 225: 713–16.

Simenstad, Charles A., James A. Estes, and Karl W. Kenyon. 1978. "Aleuts, Sea Otters, and Alternate Stable-State Communities." *Science*, 200: 403–11.

Simon, Raymond C., and Larkin, P. A., eds. 1972. *The Stock Concept in Pacific Salmon*. Series of Papers Presented at a Stock Identification Workshop at the Montlake Biological Laboratory, United States Bureau of Commercial Fisheries, Seattle, Washington, April 8, 1970. Vancouver: University of British Columbia.

Smith, Paul E. 1978. "Biological Effects of Ocean Variability: Time and Space Scales of Biological Response." *Rapports et Proces-Verbaux des Réunions, Conseil International pour l'Exploration de la Mer (Denmark)*, 173: 117–27.

and Reuben Lasker. 1978. "Position of Larval Fish in an Ecosystem." *Rapports et Proces-Verbaux des Réunions, Conseil International pour l'Exploration de la Mer (Denmark)*, 173: 77–84.

Steele, John H. 1974. *The Structure of Marine Ecosystems*. Cambridge, MA: Harvard University Press.

Sumner, James B., George D. Louderback, Waldo L. Schmitt, and Edward C. Johnston. 1914. "A Report upon the Physical Conditions in San Francisco Bay, Based upon the Operations of the United States Fisheries Steamer 'Albatross' During the Years 1912 and 1913." *University of California Publications in Zoology*, 14(1): 1–198.

5. Anthropology

Acheson, James M. 1975. "The Lobster Fiefs: Economic and Ecological Effects of Territoriality in the Maine Lobster Industry." *Human Ecology*, 3: 183–207.

Baumhoff, Martin A. 1963. "Ecological Determinants of Aboriginal California Populations." *University of California Publications in American Archaeology and Ethnology*, 49(2): 155–236.

Bean, Lowell J., and Thomas C. Blackburn, eds. 1976. *Native Californians: A Theoretical Perspective*. Ramona, CA: Ballena Press.

and Thomas F. King, eds. 1974. *Antap: California Native Political and Economic Organization*. Ballena Press Anthropological Papers no. 2. Ramona, CA: Ballena Press.

Berkes, Fikret. 1977. "Fishery Resource Use in a Subarctic Indian Community." *Human Ecology*, 5: 289–307.

Bushnell, John H. 1968. "From Americna Indian to Indian American: The Changing Identity of the Hupa." *American Anthropologist*, 70: 1108–16.

Caplan, Arthur L., ed. 1978. *The Sociobiology Debate: Readings on the Ethical and Scientific Issues Concerning Sociobiology*. New York: Harper & Row.

Cloak, F. T., Jr. 1975. "Is a Cultural Ethology Possible?" *Human Ecology*, 3: 161–82.

Cook, Sherburne F. 1976. *The Conflict Between the California Indian and White Civilization*. Berkeley and Los Angeles: University of California Press.

1976. *The Population of California Indians.* Berkeley and Los Angeles: University of California Press.

Coombs, Gary, and Fred Plog. 1977. "The Conversion of the Chumash Indians: An Ecological Interpretation." *Human Ecology,* 5: 309–28.

Dawkins, Richard. 1976. *The Selfish Gene.* New York: Oxford University Press.

Dickeman, Mildred. 1975. "Demographic Consequences of Infanticide in Man." *Annual Review of Ecology and Systematics,* 6: 107–37.

Driver, Harold E. 1969. *Indians of North America,* 2nd rev. ed. Chicago: University of Chicago Press.

DuBois, Cora. 1935. "Wintu Ethnography." *University of California Publications in American Archaeology and Ethnology,* 36(1): 1–148.

Durham, William H. 1976 . "The Adaptive Significance of Cultural Behavior." *Human Ecology,* 4: 89–121.

1976. "Resource Competition and Human Aggression, Part I: A Review of Primitive War." *Quarterly Review of Biology,* 51: 385–415.

Friedman, Jonathan. 1974. "Marxism, Structuralism, and Vulgar Materialism." *Man,* 9: 444–69.

Geertz, Clifford. 1973. *The Interpretation of Cultures: Selected Essays.* New York: Basic Books.

Gross, Daniel R., George Eiten, Nancy M. Flowers, Francisca M. Leoi, Madeline Lattman Ritter, and Dennis W. Werner, 1979. "Ecology and Acculturation Among Native Peoples of Central Brazil." *Science,* 206: 1043–50.

Hardesty, Donald L. 1972. "The Human Ecological Niche." *American Anthropologist,* 74: 458–66.

Hebda, Richard J., and Rolf W. Mathewes. 1984. "Holocene History of Cedar and Native Indian Cultures of the North American Pacific Coast." *Science,* 225: 711–12.

Heizer, Robert F., volume ed. 1978. *Handbook of North American Indians,* v. 8: *California.* Series ed. William F. Sturtevant. Washington, DC: Smithsonian Institution.

Jorgensen, Joseph G. 1980. *Western Indians: Comparative Environments, Languages, and Cultures of 172 Western American Indian Tribes.* San Francisco: W. H. Freeman.

Kroeber, A. L. 1925. *Handbook of the Indians of California.* Bureau of American Ethnology Bulletin no. 78. (Repr. New York: Dover Publications, 1976.)

1926. "The Law of the Yurok Indians." *Proceedings of the 22nd International Congress of Americanists,* II: 511–16.

and S. A. Barrett. 1960. "Fishing Among the Indians of Northwestern California." *University of California Anthropological Records,* 21(1): 1–210.

and E. W. Gifford. 1949. "World Renewal: A Cult System of Native Northwestern California." *University of California Anthropological Records,* 13(1): 1–156.

Orbach, Michael K. 1977. *Hunters, Seamen, and Entrepreneurs: The Tuna Seinermen of San Diego.* Berkeley and Los Angeles: University of California Press.

Powers, Stephen. 1877. *Tribes of California.* Contributions to North American Ethnology, U.S. Geographical and Geological Survey.

Rappaport, Roy A. 1971. "Ritual, Sanctity, and Cybernetics." *American Anthropologist,* 73: 59–76.

1971. "The Sacred in Human Evolution." *Annual Review of Ecology and Systematics,* 2: 23–44.

Sahlins, Marshall. 1972. *Stone Age Economics.* New York: Aldine.

Spott, Robert, and A. L. Kroeber. 1942. "Yurok Narratives." *University of California Publications in American Archaeology and Ethnology*, 35(9): 143–256.

Waterman, Thomas T. 1920. "Yurok Geography." *University of California Publications in American Archaeology and Ethnology*, 16(5): 177–314.

and A. L. Kroeber, 1938. "The Kepel Fish Dam." *University of California Publications in American Archaeology and Ethnology*. 35(6): 49–80.

Williams, Nancy M., and Eugene S. Hunn, eds. 1982. *Resource Managers: North American and Australian Hunter-Gatherers*. AAAS Selected Symposium no. 67. Boulder, CO: Westview Press.

B. Government Publications

1. United States

Bailey, Herbert S., and B. E. Reuter. 1919. "The Production and Conservation of Fats and Oils in the United States." U.S. Department of Agriculture, *Department Bulletin* 769.

Bitting, A. W. 1915. "Methods Followed in the Commercial Canning of Foods." U.S. Department of Agriculture, *Department Bulletin* 196.

Craig, Joseph A., and Robert L. Hacker. 1940."The History and Development of the Fisheries of the Columbia River." U.S. Bureau of Fisheries, *Bulletin*, 49: 133–216.

Cushing, D. H. 1974. "A Link Between Science and Management in Fisheries." *Fishery Bulletin U.S.*, 72: 859–64.

Gilbert, Grove Karl. 1917. "Hydraulic-Mining Debris in the Sierra Nevada." U.S. Geological Survey, *Professional Paper* 105.

Goode, George Brown, ed. 1887. The Fisheries and Fishery Industries of the United States, Prepared Through the Cooperation of the Commissioner of Fisheries and the Superintendent of the Tenth Census. 47th cong., lst sess. *Senate Miscellaneous Document* 124.

Hagen, William, Jr. 1953. "Pacific Salmon: Hatchery Propagation and Its Role in Fishery Management." U.S. Department of the Interior, Fish and Wildlife Service, *Circular* 24.

Huppert, D. D. 1980. "An Analysis of the United States Demand for Fish Meal." *Fishery Bulletin U.S.*, 78: 267–76.

Hutchins, Wells A. 1931. "Irrigation Districts, Their Organization, Operation, and Financing." U.S. Department of Agriculture, *Technical Bulletin* 354.

Jameison, George S. 1927. "Production and Utilization of Fats, Fatty Oils, and Waxes in the United States." U.S. Department of Agriculture, *Department Bulletin* 1475.

Jesness, O. B. 1917. "Cooperative Purchasing and Marketing Organizations Among Farmers in the United States." U.S. Department of Agriculture, *Department Bulletin* 547.

Jennings, Ralph D. 1949. "Consumption of Feed by Livestock, 1909–47." U.S. Department of Agriculture, *Circular* 836.

King, Gordon A. 1958. "The Demand and Price Structure for Byproduct Feeds." U.S. Department of Agriculture, *Technical Bulletin* 1183.

Kinsman, C. D. 1925. "An Appraisal of Power Used on Farms in the United States." U.S. Department of Agriculture, *Department Bulletin* 1348.

McAdie, Alexander G. 1903. "Climatology of California." U.S. Department of Agriculture, Weather Bureau, *Bulletin* L.

Nichols, Donald R., and Nancy A. Wright. 1971. "Preliminary Map of Historical Margins of Marshland, San Francisco Bay, California." U.S. Department of the Interior, Geological Survey, San Francisco Bay Region Environment and Resources Planning Study, *Basic Data Contribution* 9.

Rankel, Gary. 1980. "Depleted Chinook Salmon Runs in the Klamath River Basin: Causes, Consequences, and Constraints on Management." Photocopied. Arcata, CA: U.S. Department of the Interior, Fish and Wildlife Service, Arcata Fisheries Assistance Office.

Schaefer, Milner B., Oscar E. Sette, and John C. Marr. 1951. "Growth of the Pacific Coast Pilchard Fishery to 1942." U.S. Department of the Interior, Fish and Wildlife Service, *Research Report* 29.

Smith, Paul E. 1972. "The Increase in the Spawning Biomass of the Northern Anchovy, *Engraulis mordax*." *Fishery Bulletin U.S.*, 70: 849–74.

Soutar, Andrew, and John D. Isaacs. 1974. "Abundance of Pelagic Fish During the 19th and 20th Centuries as Recorded in Anaerobic Sediments off the Californias." *Fishery Bulletin U.S.*, 72: 257–73.

Turrentine, J.W. 1913. "The Fish-Scrap Fertilizer Industry of the Atlantic Coast." U.S. Department of Agriculture, *Department Bulletin* 2.

1915. "Utilization of the Fish Waste of the Pacific Coast for the Manufacture of Fertilizer." U.S. Department of Agriculture, *Department Bulletin* 150.

U.S. Bureau of Fisheries. 1908. *Bulletin.*

1903–30. *Report.*

U.S. Commissioner of Fish and Fisheries. 1883–1902. *Bulletin.*

1873–1902. *Report.*

U.S. Congress, American Indian Policy Review Commission. 1976. *Report on Federal, State, and Tribal Jurisdiction.*

U.S. Congress, House. 1881. The Klamath River Indian Reservation. 46th Cong., 2nd sess. *House Report* 1354.

1884–5. United States Consular Reports: Labor in Europe. 48th Cong., 2nd sess. *House Executive Document* 54.

1891. Report on the Climatology of the Arid Regions of the United States, with Reference to Irrigation. 51st Cong., 2nd sess. *House Executive Document* 287.

1891. Immigration Investigation. 51st Cong., 2nd sess. *House Report* 4048.

1893. Enforcement of the Geary Law. 53rd Cong., 1st sess. *House Executive Document* 10.

U.S. Congress, Committee on Indian Affairs. 1926. Indian Tribes of California: Hearing Before a Subcommittee of the Committee on Indian Affairs on H.R. 8036 and H.R. 9497. 69th Cong., 1st sess.

U.S. Congress, Committee on Merchant Marine and Fisheries. 1975. Report to Accompany H.R. 200, Marine Fisheries Conservation Act of 1975. 94th Cong., 1st sess. *House Report* 95-455.

1979. Klamath River Fishing Rights Oversight. Hearings Before Subcommittee on Fisheries and Wildlife Conservation and the Environment, 21, 26 May 1979. 96th Cong., 1st sess. *House Serial* 96-11.

and Committee on Commerce, Subcommittee on Fisheries. 1936. Sardine Fisheries. Hearings, 10-11 March 1936. 74th Cong., 2nd sess.

U.S. Congress, Office of Technology Assessment. 1977. *Establishing a 200-Mile Fisheries Zone.* Washington: Government Printing Office.

U.S. Congress, Senate. 1857. Reports of Explorations and Surveys to Ascertain the

Most Practical and Economical Route for a Railroad from the Mississippi River to the Pacific Ocean, Made Under the Direction of the Secretary of War in 1852–56. 33rd Cong., 2nd sess. *Senate Executive Document 78.*

Joint Special Committee. 1866–7. Condition of the Indian Tribes: Report of the Joint Special Committee Appointed Under Joint Resolution of March 3, 1865. 39th Cong., 2nd sess. *Senate Report 156.*

1889. Report Relative to the Survey and Sale of the Klamath River Reservation. 50th Cong., 2nd sess. *Senate Executive Document 140.*

Fertilizer Resources of the United States. 62nd Cong., 2nd sess. *Senate Document 190.*

Committee on Indian Affairs. 1934. Survey of the Condition of the Indians of the United States. Pt. 29: California. Hearings. 72nd Cong., 1st sess.

U.S. Department of Agriculture. 1942–70. *Agricultural Statistics.*

Forest Service. California Region. 1977. Draft Environmental Statement: Six Rivers National Forest: Gasquet–Orleans Road, Chimney Rock Section. USDA-FS-R5-DES (adm)78-02.

Weather Bureau. 1931. *Climatic Summary of the United States.* Washington, DC: Government Printing Office.

1931–41. *Climatological Data.*

U.S. Department of Commerce, Bureau of the Census. 1900. *Twelfth Census of the United States.*

1905. *Census of Manufactures.*

1911. *Special Reports: Fisheries of the United States, 1908.*

1910. *Thirteenth Census of the United States.*

1914. *Census of Manufactures.*

1920. *Census of Electrical Industries, 1917: Central Electric Light and Power Stations, with Summary of the Electrical Industries.*

1920. *Fourteenth Census of the United States.*

1924. *Biennial Census of Manufactures, 1921.*

1926. *Biennial Census of Manufactures, 1923.*

1928. *Biennial Census of Manufactures, 1925.*

1930. *Fifteenth Census of the United States.*

1939. *Census of Electrical Industries, 1937: Electrical Light and Power Industry, 1937.*

1960. *Historical Statistics of the United States, Colonial Times to 1957.*

U.S. Department of Commerce, Bureau of Fisheries. 1908. *Bulletin.*

1903–30. *Report of the Commissioner of Fisheries.*

U.S. Department of Commerce, National Oceanic and Atmospheric Administration, Pacific Fishery Management Council. 1978. "Implementation of Northern Anchovy Fishery Management Plan: Solicitation of Public Comments." *Federal Register*, 43(141): 31651–879.

1982. Proposed Plan for Managing the 1982 Salmon Fisheries off the Coasts of California, Oregon, and Washington.

U.S. Department of Commerce, Weather Bureau. 1942–80. *Climatological Data.*

U.S. Department of the Interior. 1860. *Eighth Census of the United States.*

1872–1897. *Annual Reports.*

Bureau of Indian Affairs. 1985. Environmental Impact Statement for a Proposal to Modify the Indian Fishing Regulations to Authorize Commercial Harvesting of Anadromous Fish. DES 85-21.

Superintendent of the Census. 1870. *Ninth Census of the United States.*

Census Office. 1880. *Tenth Census of the United States.*

1890. *Eleventh Census of the United States.*

U.S. Department of the Interior, Fish and Wildlife Service. 1980. Final Environmental Impact Statement on the Management of River Flows to Mitigate the Loss of the Anadromous Fishery of the Trinity River, California. INT/FES 80-52.

1983. Final Environmental Impact Statement: Trinity River Basin Fish and Wildlife Management Program. INT/FES 83-53.

Arcata Field Station. 1979. Final Report: Hoopa Valley Indian Reservation: Inventory of Reservation Waters, Fish Rearing Feasibility Study, and a Review of the History and Status of Anadromous Fishery Resources of the Klamath River Basin. Photocopied.

U.S. National Recovery Administration. Division of Review. 1936. *Evidence Study no. 13 of the Fishery Industry.* Prepared by John R. Arnold.

Weber, F.C. 1916. "Fish Meal: Its Use as a Stock and Poultry Food." U.S. Department of Agriculture, *Department Bulletin 378.*

H.W. Houghton, and J.B. Wilson. 1921. "The Maine Sardine Industry." U.S. Department of Agriculture, *Department Bulletin 908.*

2. California

Archibald, Roy. 1947. Fish and Game Conservation and Preservation. University of California, Bureau of Public Administration. Mimeographed.

Barrett, Elinore M. 1963. "The California Oyster Industry." Resources Agency of California. *Fish Bulletin 123.*

Bonnot, Paul. 1928. "Report on the Seals and Sea Lions of California." California Department of Natural Resources, Division of Fish and Game. *Fish Bulletin 14.*

1932. "The California Shrimp Industry. California Department of Natural Resources, Division of Fish and Game." *Fish Bulletin 38.*

California, Bureau of Labor Statistics. 1885–6. *Biennial Report.*

California, Coastal Zone Conservation Commissions. 1975. *California Coastal Plan.*

California, Commissioners of Fisheries. 1871–1886. *Biennial Reports.*

California, Constitution Review Commission. 1969. "Background Study: Article I: Declaration of Rights." *Background Study 3.*

California, Department of Agriculture. Crop and Livestock Reporting Service. 1942. California Livestock and Poultry.

1943, "California Livestock and Poultry: A Statistical Summary, 1867–1942." *Special Publications 193.*

California, Department of Industrial Relations. Divison of Fair Employment Practices. 1965. *American Indians in California: Population, Employment, Income, Education.* San Francisco.

California, Department of Natural Resources. Division of Fish and Game. 1926–1952. *Biennial Reports.*

1926. "The California Sardine." California Fish and Game Commission. *Fish Bulletin 11.*

California, Fish and Game Commission. 1910–1926. *Biennial Reports.*

California, Governor. 1964. *California and the World Ocean.* Governor's Conference on California and the World Ocean, held Los Angeles January 31–February 1, 1964.

Advisory Commission on Marine and Coastal Resources. 1969–73. *Annual Reports.*

California, Legislature. Assembly. Interim Committee on the Klamath River. 1935.

Report of the 1935 California Assembly Interim Committee on the Klamath River, Pursuant to a Resolution Adopted May 25, 1935.
Interim Committee on Fish and Game. 1945–65. *Hearings.*
1945–65. *Reports.*
Special Committee on the Investigation of the California Fish and Game Commission. 1911. *Report.*
Senate. Fact Finding Committee on Natural Resources. 1961. *Iron Gate Dam – Its Effect on the Klamath River Fisheries.* Hearings. Yreka, CA, 31 August 1961.
California, State Advisory Commission on Indian Affairs (Senate Bill no. 1007). 1966. *Progress Report to the Governor and the Legislature on Indians in Rural and Reservation Areas.*
1969. *Final Report to the Governor and the Legislature.*
California, Resources Agency. Klamath–Trinity Salmon Restoration Project. 1980. Final Report.
California, State Agricultural Society. 1864–74. *Transactions.*
California, State Board of Fish Commissioners. 1886–1910. *Biennial Reports.*
California, State Market Commission. 1916–19. *Annual Reports.*
California, Surveyor-General. 1854–86. *Annual Reports.*
California, University. 1938–1958. *Budget of the University of California.* Berkeley.
Clark, Frances N. 1935. "A Summary of the Life History of the California Sardine and Its Influence on the Fishery." *California Fish and Gsme*, 21: 1–9.
1939. "Measures of Abundance of the Sardine, *Sardinops caerulea*, in California Waters." California Department of Natural Resources, Division of Fish and Game. *Fish Bulletin 53.*
1939. "Can the Supply of Sardines Be Maintained in California Waters?" *California Fish and Game*, 25: 172–6.
Clark, G. H. 1929. "Sacramento–San Joaquin Salmon (*Onchorhynchus tschawytscha*) Fishery of California." California Department of Natural Resources, Division of Fish and Game. *Fish Bulletin 17.*
Clark, William B. 1970. "Gold Districts of California." California Division of Mines and Geology. *Bulletin 193.*
Fields, W. Gordon. 1865. "The Structure, Development, Food Relations, Reproduction, and Life History of the Squid *Loligo opalescens* Berry." California Resources Agency, Department of Fish and Game. *Fish Bulletin 131.*
Frey, Herbert W., ed. 1971. *California's Living Marine Resources and Their Utilization.* Sacramento: California Resources Agency, Department of Fish and Game.
Glaholt, Eileen M. 1975. Office Report: History of the Klamath River Region. Photocopied.
Godsil, H.C. 1938. "The High Seas Tuna Fishery of California." California Department of Natural Resources, Division of Fish and Game. *Fish Bulletin 51.*
Greene, B. D. Marx. 1927. An Historical Review of the Legal Aspects of the Use of Food Fish for Reduction Purposes. *California Fish and Game*, 13: 1–17, 42–4.
Gruen, Gruen and Associates. 1972. *A Socio-Economic Analysis of California's Sport and Commercial Fishing Industries.* Report to the State of California Resources Agency. San Francisco: Gruen, Gruen and Associates.
Hains, Arthur. 1941. Citizenship and Nativity of Commercial Fishermen in California. University of California, Berkeley, Bureau of Public Administration. Mimeographed.
Harvey, H. Thomas. 1966. "Some Ecological Aspects of San Francisco Bay." San

356   *Selected bibliography*

Francisco Bay Conservation and Development Commission. *Miscellaneous Papers* 3.

Hatton, H. Ross. 1940. "Progress Report on the Central Valley Project Fisherie Investigations." *California Fish and Game*, 26: 334–70.

Hedgpeth, Joel W. 1941. "Livingston Stone and Fish Culture in California." *fornia Fish and Game*, 27:126–48.

Kahrl, William L., ed. 1979. *The California Water Atlas*. Sacramento: State California.

Moffett, James W. 1949. "The First Four Years of King Salmon Maintenance Below Shasta Dam." *California Fish and Game*, 35: 77–102.

Pearson, Erman A. 1958. *'Reduced Area' Investigation of San Francisco Bay*. Lafayette, CA: California State Water Pollution Control Board.

Phillips, J.C. 1930. "Success of the Purse Seine Boat in the Sardine Fishery at Monterey, California." California Department of Natural Rersources, Division of Fish and Game. *Fish Bulletin* 23.

Radovich, John. 1961. "Relationships of Some Marine Organisms of the Northeast Pacific to Water Temperatures, Particularly During 1957 Through 1959." California Department of Fish and Game. *Fish Bulletin* 112.

Rich, Willis H., and Frank Weymouth. 1936. A Review of the Evidence of Depletion of the Califonia Sardine. Mimeographed.

San Francisco Bay Conservation and Development Commission. 1966. "Marshes and Mudflats of San Francisco Bay." San Francisco Bay Conservation and Development Commission. *Miscellaneous Papers* 2.

Scofield, N. B. 1919. "Shrimp Fisheries of California." *California Fish and Game*, 5: 1–12.

Scofield, W. L. 1929. "Sardine Fishing Methods at Monterey, California." California Department of Natural Resources, Division of Fish and Game. *Fish Bulletin* 19.

1938. "Sardine Oil in Our Troubled Waters." *California Fish and Game*, 24, 210–23.

1948. "Trawling Gear in California." California Department of Natural Resources, Division of Fish and Game. *Fish Bulletin* 72.

1951. "Purse Seines and Other Round Haul Nets of California." California Department of Natural Resources, Division of Fish and Game. *Fish Bulletin* 81.

1954. "California Fishing Ports." California Department of Fish and Game. *Fish Bulletin* 96.

1956. "Trolling Gear in California." California Department of Fish and Game. *Fish Bulletin* 103.

1957. Marine Fisheries Dates. Photocopied.

Skinner, John E. 1962. "An Historical Review of the Fish and Wildlife Resources of the San Francisco Bay Area." California Resources Agency, Department of Fish and Game, Water Projects Branch. *Report* 1.

Skogsnberg, Tage. 1925. "Preliminary Investigation of the Purse Seine Industry of Southern California." California Fish and Game Commission. *Fish Bulletin* 9.

Snyder, John O. 1931. "Salmon of the Klamath River, California." California Department of Natural Resources, Division of Fish and Game. *Fish Bulletin* 34.

Starks, edwin C. 1922. "A History of California Shore Whaling." California Fish and Game Commission. *Fish Bulletin* 6.

Thompson, William F. 1919."The Scientific Investigation of Marine Fisheries as Related to the Work of the Fish and Game Commission in Southern California." California Fish and Game Commission. *Fish Bulletin* 2.

1922. "The Fisheries of California and Their Care." *California Fish and Game*, 8: 170–5.

Van Cleve, Richard. 1945. "A Preliminary Report on the Fishery Resources of California in Relation to the Central Valley Project." *California Fish and Game*, 31: 35–52.

Verplank, William E. 1958. "Salt in California." California Department of Natural Resources, Division of Mines. *Bulletin 175.*

3. Other

Australia. Inquiry into Whales and Whaling. 1979. *The Whaling Question: The Inquiry by Sir Sydney Front of Australia*. San Francisco: Friends of the Earth.

Clark, Frances N., and John C. Marr. 1956."Population Dynamics of the Pacific Sardine." California Cooperative Oceanic Fisheries Investigations. *Reports*, 4: 11–48.

Klingbeil, Richard A. 1983. "Pacific Mackerel: A Resurgent Resource and Fishery of the California Current." California Cooperative Oceanic Fisheries Investigations. *Reports*, 24: 35–45.

Lenarz, William H. 1971. "Modeling the Resource Base." California Cooperative Oceanic Fisheries Investigations. *Reports*, 15: 28–32.

MacCall, Alec D. 1979. "Population Estimates for the Waning Years of the Pacific Sardine Fishery." California Cooperative Oceanic Fisheries Investigations. *Reports*, 20: 72–82.

McEvoy, Arthur F. 1982. "Scientific Research and the Twentieth-Century Fishing Industry." California Cooperative Oceanic Fisheries Investigations. *Reports*, 23: 48–55.

Pacific Marine Fisheries Commission. 1948–72. *Annual Reports*.

Soutar, Andrew, and John D. Isaacs. 1969. "History of Fish Populations Inferred from Fish Scales in Anaerobic Sediments off California." California Cooperative Oceanic Fisheries Investigations. *Reports*, 13: 63–70.

Thompson, William F., and Norman C. Freeman. 1930. "History of the Pacific Halibut Fishery." International Fisheries Commission, *Report 5*. Vancouver: Wrigley

United Nations, Food and Agriculture Organization. Advisory Committee on Marine Resources Research, Working Party on Marine Mammals. 1978. *Mammals in the Seas*. FAO Fisheries Series no. 5. 2 vols. Rome: Food and Agriculture Organization of the United Nations.

1971. *The Fish Resources of the Ocean*. Compiled and edited by John A. Gulland. Surrey, England: Fishing News, Ltd.

C. Newspapers

(Crescent City, CA.) *Del Norte Triplicate*. 1924.
Los Angeles Times.
Monterey Peninsula Herald. 1938–50.
Sacramento Bee.
Sacramento Union.
(San Diego) *Daily San Diegan*. 1881–5.
San Diego Daily World. 1872.
San Diego Union.

358   *Selected bibliography*

(San Francisco) *Alta California.* 1850–3.
San Francisco Bulletin.
(San Francisco) *Californian.* 1848.
(San Francisco) *California Star.* 1848.
San Francisco Chronicle
San Francisco Examiner.
San Francisco Prices Current and Shipping List. 1850–4.
(San Pedro, CA.) *The West Coast Fisheries.* 1930–2.
(Seattle) *Coast Seamen's Journal.* 1910–20.
(Seattle) *Pacific Fisherman.* 1915–53.
(Yrkea, CA.) *Siskiyou News.* 1924.

D. Manuscript sources

1. Bancroft Library, University of California, Berkeley

Bancroft Scraps, set w, 33: California Fisheries.
Bancroft Scraps, set w, 36: California Indians.
Fishermen of the Bay of San Francisco, Resolution, 13 January 1862.
Pamplets on Mining.
U.S. Office of Indian Affairs, California Superintendency, Reports.

2. California State Archives, Sacramento

Ex parte Simon Maier, 193 Cal. 476, 37 P. 402 (1894), docket no. 21116, file no. 10383.
Matter of Application of A. Parra, 24 Cal. App. 339 (1914), criminal docket no. 258, 3rd appellate district, file no. 25496.
Paladini v. Superior Court, 138 Cal. 369, 173 P. 588 (1918), S.F. docket no. 8697, file no. 23499.
People v. Stafford Packing Co., 193 Cal. 719, 227 P. 485 (1924), L.A. docket no. 7669, folder and volume. 2 documents.
People v. Monterey Fish Products Co., 195 Cal. 548, 234 P. 398 (1925), S.F. Docket no. 11376, file no. 22221.
In re Makings, 200 Cal. 474, 253 P. 918 (1927), criminal docket no. 2931, file no. 29584.

3. California State Historical Society, San Francisco

Schellens, Richard N. Papers.
Sutro, Adolph. Papers.

4. California State Library, Sacramento

Weinstock, Harris. Scrapbooks.

5. Humboldt Room, California State University, Humboldt, Arcata

Fountain, Susie Baker. Papers.
Wainwright, Duane L. 1965. The Fisheries of Humboldt County from 1854 to 1892. Term Paper, Fisheries 125. Photocopied.

6. National Archives and Records Service, Washington, D.C.

U.S. Department of Commerce. Bureau of Fisheries. Division of Scientific Inquiry. General Correspondence. Record Group 22, Series 121.
U.S. Department of the Interior, Fish and Wildlife Service, Bureau of Commercial Fisheries. General Classified Correspondence. Record Group 22, Series 121.
General Classified Files. Record Group 22, Series 121.
Office of the Commissioner. Legislation and Related Records. Record Group 22, Series 205.

7. National Archives and Records Service, Los Angeles Federal Records Center, Laguna Niguel

United States Department of the Interior, Bureau of the Census. 1870. Manuscript Census.
1880. Manuscript Census.
1890. Manuscript Census.
United States Department of Justice. District Court. Southern District. Central Division. Docket Books: Commissoner's Records, William M. Van Dyke, 1888–93. Record Group 21, Series 90. 6 vols.
United States Department of the Treasury. Bureau of Customs. San Diego Office. Collector of Customs Correspondence Out 1885–1908. Record Group 36, series 143. 12 vols.
Correspondence from the Secretary of the Treasury to the San Diego Collector of Customs. Record Group 36, series 144. 11 vols.
Special Agents' Correspondence 1885–95. Record Group 36, series 153. 4 boxes.
Tonnage Admeasurements 1889–1917. Record Group 36, series 158. 1 vol.

8. National Maritime Museum, San Francisco

Boatbuilders. Pamphlet file.
Felucca – San Francisco Bay. Pamphlet file.

9. San Diego Historical Society Library and Manuscripts Collection, San Diego

Hensley, Herbert C. Memoirs. Typescript.
Hume, Walter. Interview by Edgar Hastings. 28 March 1957.
Madruga, Manual. Interview by Edgar Hastings. 26 April 1957.
Quin, Ah. Diary of Ah Quin. 6 vols.
San Diego Historical Society. Statements of Property of Chinese. Miscellaneous Box File no. 1.
Chinese in San Diego. Vertical File no. 27.
Fish – Fisheries; Fishing Industries. Vertical File no. 180.
Wentworth, Lucy. Lucy Wentworth's Notes.

10. University of California, Scripps Institution of Oceanography Archives, La Jolla

California. Marine Research Committee. 1848–78. Records of the Marine Research Committee (81–8)

Hubbs, Carl Leavitt. 1927-79. Papers (81-18).
Scripps Institution of Oceanography, Office of the Director (Sverdrup, 1936–48). Records (82–56).
(Eckart). Records: 1948–54 (81-21).
SIO Subject Files (81-16).
University of California, Institute of Marine Resources. Records of the U.C. Institute of Marine Resources, Office of the Director, 1951–70, AC 3.

11. University of Washington Library, Manuscripts Division, Seattle

Chapman, Wilbert McLeod. Papers.

E. Personal interviews

Clark, Frances N. 11 September 1982. La Jolla.
Croker, Richard S. 3 September 1982. Laguna Niguel.
Huppert, Dan. 17 September 1982. La Jolla.
Smith, Paul E. 16 September 1982. La Jolla.

F. Unpublished theses and dissertations

Duerr, Donald Arthur, 1955. Conflicts Between Water Development Projects and Fish and Wildlife Conservation in the Central Valley Basin, California. M.A. thesis, University of California, Berkeley.
Georgas, Demitra. 1951. Greek Settlement in the San Francisco Bay Area. M.A. thesis, University of California, Berkeley.
Haynor, Genevive. 1941. The History of Gold Dredging in California. M.A. thesis, University of California, Berkeley.
Hewes, Gordon Winant. 1947. Aboriginal Use of Fishery Resources in Northwestern North America. Ph.D. diss., University of California, Berkeley.
Hicks, Frederick Noble. 1963. Ecological Aspects of Aboriginal Culture in the Western Yuman Area. Ph. D. diss., University of California, Los Angeles.
Kennedy, Clyde C. 1912. A Sanitary Survey of the Oyster Beds of San Francisco Bay. M.A. thesis, University of California, Berkeley.
McEvoy, Arthur F. 1979. Economy, Law, and Ecology in the California Fisheries to 1925. Ph. D. diss. University of California, San Diego.
McGowan, Joseph A. 1939. San Francisco–Sacramento Shipping. M.A. thesis, University of California, Berkeley.
Margo, Joan. 1947. The Food Supply Problem of the California Gold Mines. M.A. thesis, University of California, Berkeley.
Nash, Robert Alan. 1973. The Chinese Shrimp Industry in California. Ph. D. diss., University of California, Los Angeles.
Reed, Addison Doyle. 1951. Improving California Poultry Management. Ph. D. thesis, University of California, Berkeley.
Rosenberg, Earl H. 1961. A History of the Fishing and Canning Industries in Monterey, California. M.A. thesis, University of Nevada, Reno.
Selvin, Molly. 1978. "This Tender and Delicate Business": The Public Trust Doctrine in American Law and Economic Policy, 1789–1920. Ph.D. diss., University of California, San Diego.

Selected bibliography 361

Sundstrom, John Walker. 1941. Problems in Administration of Pacific Coast Fisheries. M.A. thesis, University of California, Berkeley.

Tartaglia, Louis James. 1976. Prehistoric Maritime Adaptations in Southern California. Ph. D. diss., University of California, Los Angeles.

Index

abalone, 23, 75–6, 81, 130, 237–8
agriculture (see also reclamation; reduction)
    and energy, 124–5, 155, 187–8
    political power, 145, 164–5, 181, 218
    poultry and livestock, 133, 145, 154–5, 190, 199, 209, 218
albacore, see tunas
American Tunaboat Association, 89, 188, 203, 239
anchovy, 7, 89, 215–20, 232–6, 242, 245
Azoreans
    emigration, 74
    in tuna fishery, 88–9
    in whale fishery, 74–5, 80–1

Baird, Spencer F., 100–2, 105–6, 189
Bancroft, Hubert Howe, 41, 46, 67
Baumhoff, Martin A., 28, 32, 35
Bayside Fish Flour Co. v. Gentry, 180
boats and boatbuilding, 65
    Chinese, 75
    Indian, 23–4, 27
    Italian, 77–8
    "Monterey clipper," 128–9
    purse seiners (sardine), 136–7, 140, 153, 190
    reduction ships, 139, 140–1
    tunaboats, 37, 203, 207
Booth, F. E., 88, 91, 123, 126, 139–40, 181
Brown, Edmund G., Sr., 210, 215–18, 222
Burnette, Julian, 194, 201, 204, 216

California Academy of Sciences, 118, 193, 199
California Cooperative Oceanic Fisheries Investigations (see Marine Research Committee)
California Current, 3, 149, 160, 194, 200
California Department of Fish and Game (see also California Fish and Game Commission)
    and FCMA, 245
    and Indian fishing, 43, 214
    and MRC–CalCOFI, 193, 199–200, 218

organization, 157, 194
    relations with federal agency, 117, 159, 165, 182–3
    and sardine fishery, 158–62, 164–6, 179–83, 199, 223, 228
    water quality, 176–8, 196–8, 211–12
California Division of Fish and Game (see California Department of Fish and Game)
California Fish and Game Commission (see also California Department of Fish and Game)
    anchovy fishery, 215, 218, 231, 233–5
    anti-Chinese campaign, 103, 112–14
    appointments to, 111–12, 165–6
    artificial propagation, 84, 109
    attorneys, 14, 187, 307n20
    law enforcement, 111–12, 157–8, 172–3, 179–80
    marketing of fish, 167–70
    organization, 156–7, 194
    regulatory powers, 101, 182
    relations with sportfishers, 157, 163–4, 175, 197–8, 224, 226
    water quality, 84–5, 114
California Governor's Advisory Commission on Ocean Resources, 222
California State Board of Fish Commissioners (see California Fish and Game Commission)
California State Water Project (see also Central Valley Project), 197, 205–6, 211–2
canning (see also reduction)
    mackerel, 139
    salmon, 50–1, 55, 58–61, 71–2, 88, 117–18, 134
    sardine, 131, 139, 144–8, 167–8
    tunas, 130–1
    waste, 132
Carson, Rachel, 188, 211, 227
Central Valley Project, 142–4, 152, 155, 178, 196–8, 211, 213–14
Channel Islands, 27, 46–7, 235–6

363

Index